BRISTOL CITY
The Post-War Years
1946-1967

HISTORIES OF BRISTOL CITY AND BRISTOL ROVERS BY DESERT ISLAND BOOKS

by David Woods   ISBN
Bristol City: The Early Years 1894-1915   978-1-905328-51-2
Bristol City: From War to War 1915-1946   978-1-905328-43-7
Bristol City: The Post-War Years 1946-1967   978-1-905328-93-2
Bristol City: The Modern Era 1967-2007   978-1-905328-27-7

by Edward Giles
Bristol Rovers: The Bert Tann Era
        A Personal Memoir   978-1-905328-37-6
Bristol City: From Atyeo to Dicks
        A Personal Memoir   978-1-905328-67-3

BRISTOL CITY

THE POST-WAR YEARS
1946-1967

Series Consultant: Leigh Edwards
Series Editor: Clive Leatherdale

David Woods

DESERT ISLAND BOOKS

First published in 2011
by
DESERT ISLAND BOOKS LIMITED
32 Lascelles Gardens, Ashingdon, Rochford, Essex SS4 3BP
United Kingdom
www.desertislandbooks.com

© 2011 David Woods

The right of David Woods to be identified as author of this work has been
asserted under The Copyright Designs and Patents Act 1988

British Library Cataloguing-in-Publication Data
A catalogue record for this book is available from the British Library

ISBN 978-1-905328-93-2

All photographs taken from the author's private collection

Printed and bound in Great Britain by
4edge Ltd, Hockley. www.4edge.co.uk

Contents

Acknowledgements

As with the other three Bristol City volumes in this series – *The Early Years*, *From War to War*, and *The Modern Era* – this undertaking would not have been possible but for the activities of the local press over the years. For this offering, the writings of journalists Herbert Gillam and Graham Russell (*Western Daily Press*), John Coe, Peter Godsiff, Edward Giles and Bill Pinnell (*Bristol Evening Post* and the *Green 'Un*), George Baker and David Foot (*Bristol Evening World* and the *Pink 'Un*) have been much read. Thanks are also due to Mervyn Baker, Andrew Crabtree, Leigh Edwards, Tom Hopegood, Mike Jay, Harley Lawer, Jonathan Morgan, Gerry Pearce, Geoff Rose, Roy Shoesmith, Matthew Stevens, Mike Swain, Tony Ticktum and Colin Timbrell, as well as Tracy Harrison for her diligent proof-reading. Finally, last but not least, the staff at the Bristol Central Library and those at the British Newspaper Library in Colindale, north London.

Note: with regard to the team line-ups, these are laid out in the standard 2-3-5 formation of the time. Hence No 9 is the centre-forward, 7 and 11 (wingers), 8 and 10 (inside-forwards), 4 and 6 (wing-halves), 5 (centre-half), 2 and 3 (full-backs) and 1 (goalkeeper).

The attendances shown are those kept by the Football League, which include season-ticket holders, and are often at variance with those in the newspapers, which tend to only record those who actually paid on the day. However, it would seem that there are likely errors in these Football League figures, as illustrated by the fact that whilst the newspapers give attendances of 10,256 v Bolton (a) on 8 January 1966 and 10,405 v Rotherham (a) on 29 January 1966, the Football League shows these as 10,405 and 10,667 respectively.

Bibliography

Bristol City: The Complete History of the Club by Peter Godsiff (Wensum Books, Norwich, 1979).

Bristol City: The Complete Record 1894-1987 by David Woods with Andrew Crabtree (Breedon Books, Derby, 1987).

Bristol Rovers: The Complete Record 1883-1987 by Mike Jay (Breedon Books, Derby, 1987).

A Mixed Bag of Peppermints (Newquay Centenary History 1889-1989) by Sandra Biggin.

The Bristol Babe: The First 100 Years of Bristol City FC by David Woods (Yore Publications, Harefield, Middlesex, 1994).

Mansfield Town: The First 100 Years by Jack Retter with Paul Taylor (Glen Publications, Norwich, 1997).

Atyeo: The Hero Next Door by Tom Hopegood and John Hudson (Redcliffe Press, Bristol, 2005).

Leyton Orient: The Untold Story Of The O's Best Ever Team by Tony McDonald (Football World, Hornchurch, 2006).

Bristol City: From Atyeo to Dicks by Edward Giles (Desert Island Books, Southend-on-Sea, 2009).

Bristol Rovers: The Bert Tann Era by Edward Giles (Desert Island Books, Southend-on-Sea, 2007).

Arthur Milton: The Last of the Double Internationals by Mike Vockins (Sports Books Ltd., Cheltenham, 2011).

Foreword

Following on from the publication of Volume One (*The Early Years*), Volume Two (*From War To War*), and Volume Four (*The Modern Era*), this third volume fills the missing gap in the recording of Bristol City FC's history in the unique and comprehensive Desert Island Books format. It is thanks to the indulgence of Clive Leatherdale that Bristol City are the first club to have such a readily accessible and complete record.

During the period under investigation the author saw his first match, although the experience was often uncomfortable, as his father used to perch him on top of a crush barrier at the Covered End at Ashton Gate. Early memories include a great performance by Cyril Williams in a friendly versus Stuttgart Kickers on 8 November 1955, as well as a trip to Swindon the previous season to see City draw 2-2.

A family story tells of your author, when very young, becoming separated from his father at Eastville and watching the game pitchside with a friendly policeman. Presumably this was a local derby, although his father used to attend regularly at both Ashton Gate and Eastville.

Weeks after leaving the Bristol Technical School of Engineering to commence his working life, the author's interest in Bristol City FC began to blossom. Seeing them beat Ipswich 1-0 on 15 March 1958 helped, but it took the local derby thriller at Eastville three weeks later to really hook him.

Whilst John Atyeo was always a great presence for Bristol City during the period covered by this book, the author's particular favourites included Bert Tindill, Wally Hinshelwood, Tommy Casey, Brian Clark, Tony Cook, Bobby Williams, Alex Tait, Jack Connor, Mike Gibson, and Johnny Quigley.

It is hoped that this volume, together with the others in the series, will serve as a suitable tribute to all those who have added much colour and excitement to the lives of City's many fans over the decades.

DEDICATION

Whilst not of this era, as no doubt he would hasten to remind us, it seems appropriate to dedicate this book to the great work done by Stephen Lansdown on behalf of Bristol City FC. Fortunately, despite standing down after almost nine years as chairman on 31 May 2011, his influence will likely continue as the power behind the throne.

Chapter One

Normal Service 1946-52

Despite the departure of Roy Bentley, transferred to Newcastle United for a record £8,500 fee, many local fans felt that Bristol City's fourteen-year exile from the Second Division would soon come to an end. Having kept going throughout seven difficult wartime seasons, City had developed an impressive side, including hot-shot centre-forward Don Clark, skilful winger Jack Hargreaves (signed from Leeds after having guested for the Robins during the war) and the brilliant Cyril Williams, and all now looked set fair for success. This certainly seemed the case when the 1946-47 season started with a 6-3 victory against Plymouth Argyle in a friendly at Home Park on 24 August. Unfortunately, not only was the dream to be delayed for a further nine seasons, but during the interim the Rovers were to take over City's mantle as the top team in Bristol.

Not yet, however, as the Rovers, who had closed down after just one solitary wartime season, had to start from scratch. With limited funds, they mainly recruited locals – a number of which were being brought through from the Colts side started up in 1944 for the purpose of unearthing local talent. Initially, City remained the dominant force, but things were to change. As the Rovers side developed they were good enough to finish higher than City for fourteen consecutive seasons from 1948-49 to 1961-62.

Such a prospect appeared remote when the Football League resumed normal service on 31 August 1946, with a fixture list identical to that for the aborted 1939-40 campaign. As had been the case pre-war, Bob Hewison was in charge of the team and George Jenkins chairman, but City failed to repeat their 1939-40 victory at Aldershot, losing 3-4. However, after three games they had three points, the same number as when League football had been curtailed seven years earlier.

For the fans, an extra three pence had to be found to pre-war prices as, bowing to the wishes of the Chancellor of the Exchequer, the imposition of an entertainment tax brought an end to the 'bob-gate'. This did little to deter the spectators, as gates boomed in the early post-war years. This period was a golden era for attendances on English football grounds and City's average home League crowd of 18,847 in 1946-47 would peak at 26,575 in 1955-56.

The Bristol soccer public was hungry for success. 'AJS', a witness to the local scene ever since City's formation in 1894, writing in the *Bristol*

Evening Post Green 'Un Football Guide for 1946-47, pondered the question: 'How best or will the best be obtained with the least possible delay?' For his part, he did not mind whose methods were best, so long as they achieved the results: 'Certainly no one hopes more genuinely than I do that the plans of campaign that Ashton and Eastville have embarked upon (which in the case of the "No Buy, No Sale" policy of Bristol Rovers was so clearly outlined by their vice-chairman John Hare) will achieve all the success their authors envisage.'

However, the City directors were soon criticised for not having their players on full-time contracts. The team quickly improved, however, and a 3-0 win over the Rovers on 28 September had the Robins up to second place in the Third Division (South) table. Although, Cardiff City were setting a hot pace at the top, City and QPR maintained a keen pursuit. Unfortunately, injuries came along – Alex Ferguson, Ivor Guy and Jack Bailey all being out of action at the same time – and these unkindly blows exposed that there were not the necessary reserves in the Ashton Gate camp.

With the advent of the heavier grounds, City's persistence with their short-passing game and over-elaboration brought about a calamitous December. A 23,109 Boxing Day crowd at Ashton Gate saw City slip to fourth as Northampton Town brought off a surprise 3-2 win in the atrocious conditions. City battled against a high wind prior to half-time. In fact, the game was briefly halted by a hail-storm midway through the second half.

Fortunately, the month ended on a high, with the Robins beating Aldershot 9-0 to register their record League win (their previous best being the 9-4 demolition of Gillingham during the 1926-27 campaign). It was also Aldershot's heaviest ever defeat in the Football League. In front of a 17,690 crowd, City goalkeeper John Eddolls was a spectator for most of this affair, whereas his opposite number, Albert Gage, had plenty of activity in retrieving the ball from his net. The home forwards and halves did not over-do their close passing, and it was pleasing to see them play more open football – producing just the right mixture of science and dash.

City scored in their very first attack and never looked back. Right-half Ernie 'Ginger' Peacock started the move and Jack Hargreaves finished it by firing into an open net after Cyril Williams had collided with the Aldershot goalkeeper. In the fifth minute Hargreaves scored again, his cross misjudged by Gage. Another error by the goalkeeper brought up the third goal in the tenth minute – Don Clark's shot straight at Gage somehow going beneath the keeper's body.

Fortunately, the goalkeeper could not be faulted for City's fourth goal, midway through the first half, when Clark headed in a free-kick, but Hargreaves was the beneficiary of an error in the 36th minute with a shot through a crowd of players. Gage reached the ball, but it went from his hands into the net. The sixth, shortly before the interval, was a header – Williams converting a Hargreaves corner.

The fans had to wait until the 70th minute for another goal, when Clark headed in from Ken Chilcott's centre. Ten minutes later wing-half Ernie Jones found the net with a long-range effort, before the scoring was concluded from the penalty-spot when Williams was brought down. There was no temptation to include Eddolls on the scoresheet. Instead Clark scored his fourth of the game to become the League's highest scorer with 22 goals.

Clark led the forward line with skill, and Alf Rowland, the Aldershot centre-half, will not readily forget his gruelling afternoon. He and left-back Hedley Sheppard worked like Trojans, but at times they were simply overwhelmed. Former City player Ernie Brinton must have been glad that he had been left out of the Aldershot team for this match.

Unfortunately for City, indifferent form soon returned and it took a 4-0 home victory over Rovers on 1 February to end a run of three League games without a win. This proved to be but a rare blot on Rovers' record for the second half of the season, which saw them recover from being bottom just before Christmas. With Harry Bamford excelling on being moved to right-back, the Rovers stormed up the table – winning ten and drawing one of the thirteen games they played up to 29 March.

With Port Vale's Hanley ground being snow-covered for City's Monday afternoon visit on 17 February, the goalposts were painted blue. Unfortunately, in a 1-2 defeat, the colour seemed to have a fatal fascination for City, as Sid Williams, Don Clark, Ken Chilcott and Sid Kearney (signed from Accrington Stanley at the turn of the year) all hit the woodwork.

With high-scoring victories over Torquay United and Reading, a massive 32,535 crowd turned up at Ashton Gate on 4 April for the clash with runaway leaders Cardiff City when a 2-1 victory gave home fans hope of a late City surge over the final nine games. A 1-1 draw at Ninian Park on 7 April was watched by a record Third Division (South) attendance of 49,310, but by then City's promotion hopes had been extinguished by a 2-3 defeat at Ipswich two days earlier. There was just one more loss, 0-1 at Loftus Road on 19 April, when, against the towering home backs, City's forward line did not contain a man over 5ft 7inches tall. The end of the campaign found City in third place, a massive fifteen points behind

Cardiff City and six in the wake of QPR. Nevertheless, it was an exciting season, with City congratulating themselves on being the division's top goalscorers and Don Clark heading the list of the Third Division (South) hot-shots.

Meanwhile, Bristol Rovers were making progress. Despite only finishing fourteenth in the Third Division table, they put on spirited display in the Gloucestershire Senior Professional Cup final with a 2-2 draw at Eastville Stadium on 26 May. Fortunately, for the City fans, goals from Sid Williams and Bill Thomas brought success in the replay in front of an 11,434 crowd on 7 June.

Nine days earlier there had been an even bigger gathering at the Gate when a German Prisoner of War XI provided the opposition. No doubt lured by free admission, some 20,000 were present as the Germans were beaten 4-0.

The attendance boom was reflected in the balance sheet, City declaring a record £5,450 2s 5d profit at the AGM held at Ashton Gate on 10 February 1948. This would have been more, but for the fact that the Number One Grandstand had been destroyed during the war. This meant that only 262 season ticket were sold, raising just £383 3s 6d.

Attempting to cash in on the attendance boom, a Fourth Division was contemplated, but this caused alarm amongst the Southern Section clubs. According to the *Bristol Evening World Pink 'Un* of 22 February 1947, the Southern Section clubs followed their Northern counterparts, who had rejected the proposal at their meeting in Manchester on 4 February. With feelings being somewhat mixed at the Southern gathering, City chairman George Jenkins proposed to defer the question for two years, which, on being amended to one, was carried by eleven votes to ten with one absentee. In the event, it was to be another ten years before a Fourth Division came into being.

Whilst it can be understood that some of the lesser lights in the bottom half of the table might have been against such a proposal, it seems incredible that any aspiring club would seek to cut down on their promotion opportunities. That Jenkins appears to have been against such a necessary change, possibly explains why City languished for so long in football's nether regions.

The two local sports papers, the *Green 'Un*, published by the *Bristol Evening Post*, and *Bristol Evening World's Pink 'Un*, which had started up again during the previous campaign on 22 September, began to look like their old selves from 14 September 1946, when coloured paper was in use once more. Throughout the season many interesting topics were raised in these Saturday night sports papers, not least being the dissatisfaction of 'many fans regarding City's part-time policy, as well the No buy, No sale' stance adopted by Bristol Rovers. For those of a nostalgic bent, the *Pink 'Un* ran a series called 'Fifty Years of Bristol Soccer'.

The thorny question of substitutes raised its head during the campaign. According to George Baker, writing in the *Pink 'Un* of 1 March 1947, the Football Association were thought to be coming round in favour of allowing substitutes for injured players. In the event, nothing happened, and it was not until 1965-66 that English football followed what had long been the case in European football.

However, the biggest bombshell to appear in the local sporting press hit the pages of the *Pink 'Un* two weeks later on 15 March. With the football schedule being much effected by the weather, George Baker reported: 'Almost everyone concerned with football management expects promotion and relegation to be scrapped for this season. The alternatives, such as playing behind closed doors or extending the season until the end of June do not seem feasible. The announcement in Parliament that football would be played on Saturdays and statutory holidays only, seems to clinch the argument.'

Fortunately, Baker's worst fears were not to be realised, as the season was extended into June and clubs such as Cardiff, who had topped the table, were deservedly promoted.

A successful first season to mark football's return to normality, but there was a blot. After thrashing Hayes 9-3 in the FA Cup, City were rewarded with another home game against non-league opposition. Gillingham were thought of as being sacrificial lambs, but they caused an upset by obtaining a well-deserved 2-1 success. Not surprisingly, the Gills went on to clinch the Southern League Championship and in 1950 regained the Football League place they had lost in 1938. While City endured a few scares against non-league opposition in subsequent years, this was to prove to be their only post-war defeat by the lesser lights.

City's retained list, revealed on 22 April 1947, contained few surprises. Although a decision was deferred in respect of Bill Dymond, who eventually went to Exeter City, Alex Ferguson, who ended up with Swindon Town, and Jack Hargreaves (Reading), the likes of Edwin Cunningham, Rogers and Gordon Spiring found themselves on the free-transfer list. Bob Allen, who had been signed from Notts County the previous November, was placed on the open to transfer list.

The *Pink 'Un*, when summing up the season, thought that City played really good football at times, especially during the run of thirteen undefeated matches early in the season. Unfortunately, injuries to Ivor Guy and Ernie Jones at Reading upset that combination, and the team never quite recaptured the form which had made them such an attractive side to watch.

Handicapped by a lack of good reserves, a look at City's record shows that whilst they scored a very satisfactory 94 goals, they – despite many excellent displays by Dennis Roberts – conceded 56, far too many for a promotion-seeking side.

Once in a while, City found themselves not too well off in defence. 42-year-old Alex Ferguson has been dependable, and at times brilliant – especially in the Cardiff games – but he was in the veteran stage, having commenced his career 21 years earlier. Roy Fox came into the side at left-back in a difficult period, and did well, in spite of the fact that his best position was probably wing-half. Ernie Jones gave some fine attacking displays and Cliff Morgan's experience had often proved invaluable. Ernie Peacock, young and strong, showed great possibilities, whilst Sid Kearney had brought skill and experience to the side.

The forward line brings us automatically to Don Clark, without a doubt the player of the season. His success was gratifying because he was a scrupulously clean and accomplished player. Put the ball on the floor in front of him, and it was likely to be a goal. Described as one of the three best centre-forwards in the country, there were not many who would dis-agree. Cyril Williams had an arduous season and displayed much skill, while no one worked harder than Bill Thomas. Arnie White proved to be an obvious find and looked set for a long career. The wing positions gave City some concerns, although Ken Chilcott had a big heart and Jack Hargreaves much artistry.

The Reserves, after playing in the Western League in 1945-46, found themselves back with the big boys in what was now called the Football Combination, instead of the old title of the London Combination. Finishing fifteenth in Section B of the League competition, they ended up fourth in Section 4 of the Cup. Meanwhile, City's third team, the Colts, also finished fifteenth in the First Division of the Western League – a competition not completed because bad weather had caused many postponements.

The end of the soccer season saw Bedminster Cricket Club, who had a long association with Bristol City Football Club, making preparations for celebrating their centenary with a festival week commencing on 5 July. No doubt many at this event would have been able to recall the time when they shared Ashton Gate with the City before departing to the sce-nic Clanage venue in 1912.

At the Football League AGM on Monday, 30 June 1947, City's Bob Hewison, who four years earlier had received a medal marking 21 years' service in club management, was presented with another long-service award to mark his 25 years as a manager.

No doubt encouraged by the club's healthy finances, and the fact that the promotion prize had been within their grasp, City's directors pushed the boat out for 1947-48. A record £5,000 secured the services of Len Townsend from Brentford, whilst Idris Hopkins and Bristolian Maurice Roberts were also signed from the Griffin Park club, as well as Hyam Dimmer coming on board from Aldershot to add to the nucleus of what most commentators thought would be a real promotion side. With young and accomplished players like Ivor Guy, Jack Bailey, Ernie Peacock (with a little less impetuosity) and Arnie White, coupled with Don Clark, Dennis Roberts and Cyril Williams, City were expected to do well.

Prior to the season getting under way came an athletics meeting at Ashton Gate. A large crowd at the Somerset County Championships on 2 August, saw CL Lawrence of Bristol Athletic Club win the 880 yards in 2 mins 4 secs from his clubmate PG Sharpe and EJ Aplin of Somerset AC. Those attending saw Ashton Gate smartened up, with a new home dressing room being built on the site of the blitzed Number One stand. No improvement for the opposition though; they had to carry on changing in the hut, which had been moved alongside.

Despite Townsend topping the Third Division (South) scoring charts with 31 goals, the promotion gamble failed, as City could only finish seventh. They posted a loss of £2,222, even though the selling of 478 season tickets had brought in £2,493.

Making things worse was the fact that QPR had built on their runners-up position of the previous campaign to take top spot with 61 points, eighteen more than City. However, all this lay in the future when City kicked off the 1947-78 season with a 6-0 demolition of Southend, in which Townsend's diving header got things rolling. Unfortunately, the euphoria generated by this victory soon evaporated as the very next game was lost 0-1 against relegated Newport at Somerton Park. A 1-3 defeat at Meadow Lane followed, before City went on the rampage, winning nine of the next ten games. No doubt 'Ashton Alf' was feeling satisfied with himself during this run as City hammered six goals past Leyton Orient and Ipswich, as well as bringing off a remarkable 7-2 success at Reading on 4 October. Sadly, it did not last and the wheels came off with only one victory being registered in eight attempts. It was not until the visit of Notts County in the New Year that City showed real improvement.

With the recent signing of England international centre-forward Tommy Lawton from Chelsea for £20,000, the Meadow Lane outfit were the glamour team of the Third Division, attracting big crowds wherever they went. It was no different at Ashton Gate, where a 35,287 crowd paid record receipts on 3 January to see one of Len Townsend's trademark diving header's secure both points for City.

After such a deserved win, the 1-6 defeat at Swansea that followed was hard to take, but the fans were consoled somewhat by a 4-0 success at Northampton, before Bournemouth gave City a taste of their own medicine with a 4-0 victory at Ashton Gate. Topsy-turvy form for the rest of the season saw City ending the campaign seventh.

Bill Pinnell ('The Traveller') writing in the *Green 'Un Football Guide* said that: 'Season 1947-48 will go down in history as one of most disappointing in the annals of the City, who after a really promising start just led their many supporters up the garden path, because it was a case of flattering to deceive.'

George Baker, in the *Pink 'Un Sports Annual*, agreed with such assessment, commenting that: 'The team most of all lacked balance. Once again they scored more goals than any other side in the section, but I think that an early-season reputation for goalscoring gave them an obsession for undue reliance on attack. At times, especially when they won 7-2 at Reading, they raised our hopes, but the flame of success burned a little too brightly to be genuine. Len Townsend, who had the distinction of being the leading scorer in the Football League, was the outstanding player. He brought a determination of purpose to his work which was lacking in some parts of the team. Whilst it may be said that he did not always fulfil his job in helping the defence, in attack he missed very few opportunities and he scored many goals by sheer strength and persistence, and his anticipation was needle sharp; a player of courage, who is very good in the air.'

In the FA Cup, Townsend added to his tally with three in City's 9-2 replay demolition of Dartford, but in the following round Crystal Palace gained revenge for the previous season's defeat thanks to Albert Robson's extra-time winner. The Rovers added to City's misery by winning the Gloucestershire Cup with a 2-1 success in front of a 15,727 crowd at Ashton Gate on 8 May.

Given the public outcry in June over the departure of Cyril Williams to Second Division WBA in exchange for Cliff Edwards and £500 in a deal valued at £7,000, and with the Rovers only having escaped applying for re-election on goal-average after winning five of their last seven games, the Bristol soccer scene did not look rosy at the start of 1948-49. For the Rovers, though, it was to be the start of their local eminence.

With wingers Idris Hopkins and Harry Osman having been released, together with the departure of goalkeeper George Marks to Reading in exchange for Vic Barney, City recruited Danny Boxshall from QPR and Gordon Eveleigh (Guildford), whilst wing-halves John Davies and Don Sheldon joined from Plymouth and Cardiff respectively.

Unfortunately, despite a forward line containing Len Townsend and Don Clark, the City found goals hard to come by. Just eight goals and two victories in the opening ten games quickly dispelled any promotion hopes. Indeed, with City down in twentieth place, minds became focused on keeping clear of the bottom. A brief revival, with six victories in their next eleven games, had City up to tenth going into the New Year, but a shocking 1-6 home defeat by Norwich on 15 January 1949 set alarm bells ringing. Don Clark's twisted knee, sustained in the 1-3 defeat at Leyton Orient, was a blow, but, despite only winning two of their last thirteen games, the season's end found City nine points clear of bottom club Crystal Palace. In contrast, Bristol Rovers lay fifth, twelve points better off than the City.

With City giving some terribly bad displays and not winning a match from 18 December until 5 March, it was hardly surprising that there were changes at the top. The fans were not satisfied and neither was City's board, which had seen the appointment of Arthur Amor, George Jones, Norman Jones and the Reverend FC Vyvyan-Jones in February. Thus was the manager Hewison's influence weakened, and no doubt that of his chairman also.

A 2-0 success at Torquay ended the ten-match winless run, but following a row with the board over team selection, Bob Hewison, whose contract had been renewed as recently as 16 December, was informed at a directors meeting on 8 March that, as they were going to appoint a new man he would have no alternative other than to hand in his resignation.

However, Hewison denied in an article in the following day's *Bristol Evening World* that he had acted on the directors' advice to resign, stating: 'I was quite willing to go, but I did not hand in my resignation. That is quite clear.' After seventeen years' service, Hewison eventually left a month later on 12 April 1949.

He was not out of work for long, however, as he signed a three-year contract as manager of Third Division (North) side Gateshead in May 1949. Unfortunately, Hewison, unwilling to move from his Bristol home, only stayed until October, citing business reasons for his departure. Seven months later, on 2 June 1950, he was appointed manager of Southern League Guildford City, where he put in a three-year stint. Hewison then scouted for Bristol Rovers until May 1957, when he took over at Bath City, whom he piloted to the Southern League Championship in 1959-60 before retiring at the conclusion of the following campaign.

A football man through and through, Hewison died in Bristol in April 1964. Born in Blackworth, Newcastle, on 25 March 1899, he had played for East Hollywell Villa and Whitley Athletic prior to joining Newcastle United as a wing-half in July 1908. During the First World War he began playing for Leeds City, and whilst recovering from a broken leg he acted as secretary through the period that the club was wound up. Returning to Newcastle, he played a few games before becoming the player-manager of Northampton. Taking over at QPR in the summer of 1925, he remained at Loftus Road until joining Bristol City seven years later.

However, despite the decision to seek a new manager, the storm clouds were gathering and on 11 March 1949 chairman Jenkins denied rumours that he had resigned, saying: 'Provided I am still alive, I shall definitely take the chair at next Tuesday's annual meeting.' Just three days after the death of former City manager Alex Raisbeck in a Liverpool hospital, Jenkins was true to his word, maintaining his record of never missing a meeting in his 27 years with the club. Perhaps, though, he would have wished to have missed the acrimonious event at the Grand Hotel, Broad Street, Bristol, which brought about his departure. 'No matter how many meetings you go to in the future, you'll never see another like this,' was the comment afterwards.

Standing for re-election, George Jenkins was voted off the board by a show of hands when it was revealed that he was the only director out of ten who refused to loan City £1,000. As the major shareholder, he then demanded a poll which was likely to have guaranteed his re-election, but a vote of no confidence was called, and in the light of the hostile attitude of the 140 shareholders present he withdrew his nomination and left the board, declining a life membership.

The fact of Roy Bentley's return to Ashton Gate on 8 January, when he scored two late goals to take Chelsea through to the fourth round of the FA Cup, did not help, as Jenkins was blamed by many shareholders for the selling of both Bentley and Cyril Williams. It was a sad end for a man who had guided the club through many difficult years. Six years later, on 3 September 1955, he died at the age of 73.

With vice-chairman ARP Bray being another casualty, a meeting of the reconstituted board on 22 March saw Harry Dolman take the helm with Arthur Sperring as his deputy. This was envisaged to last just twelve months, but with the death of Sperring, who had been scheduled to take over the following year, Dolman was to remain as chairman for 25 years until stepping down on 12 March 1974 when he became the first president of the club. He died, aged 80, on 9 November 1977, having witnessed city's return to the top flight in 1976.

One of seven children, Henry James Dolman was born on 6 August 1897 in Yatton Keynell, a village near Chippenham, Wiltshire. Becoming an engineering apprentice on leaving school at fourteen, he later served with the Wiltshire Yeomanry on the Somme and at Ypres during the First World War, before spending eighteen months at the Merchant Venturers College in Bristol. Joining the Bristol Engineering firm Brecknell, Munro & Rogers as a junior draughtsman in 1921, his talent for design quickly came to the fore; he became a director of the company six years later. Later, he took over the company in a shrewd deal that was to typify the businesslike manner in which he was to run Bristol City. With all 40 employees facing the dole because the order book were empty, Dolman, with no money of his own, took a calculated gamble when he and a partner were offered the £75,000 share capital for just £11,000. The business, which became Brecknell, Dolman & Rogers, prospered and by the time he left the workforce had grown to 1,600. A qualified referee and initially a fan of Bristol Rovers, Dolman was thinking over an offer of joining their board, but on attending two of their meetings he was perturbed by the fact that the main topic of discussion was the sale of Eastville Stadium to the greyhound company which ran races there. Allowing himself to be persuaded by Captain AJ Prince Cox (the former Rovers manager and Football League referee) that he would be better off on the other side of the river, he was elected to the Bristol City board in 1939.

As Bristol City's chairman, Dolman's first task was to look for a new manager. He approached Bill Dodgin at Southampton and Chelmsford's Arthur Rowe, but the man he most wanted was Irish International inside-forward Peter Doherty at Huddersfield. The Yorkshire club wanted £10,000, Dolman offered £4,000, and Doherty eventually became player-manager, not with City but with Doncaster.

Rumour was rife and Cradley Heath's Ted Vizard, the former Bolton player who had also managed Wolves, QPR and Swindon, felt constrained to deny that he was applying for the post. On 13 April, Dolman turned to a lesser-known candidate, 35-year-old Bob Wright, assistant to the famous Jimmy Seed at Charlton. Probably, Wright was persuaded to take the vacant position by Dolman's comment: 'You have a marvellous opportunity in Bristol – an opportunity that does not exist elsewhere in the country.' This was backed up by Jimmy Seed who said that, 'if I had to start my career all over again I would like to start it in Bristol.' Famous last words perhaps, because as fate would have it, Mr Seed himself would have a stint at Ashton Gate, but more of that later.

After attending a farewell party at Charlton that same night, Wright, who had been promised a free-hand and a salary of £850, commenced work the following day. Among those offering their congratulations was Bristol Rovers boss Bert Tann, who had made his Charlton debut at the same time as Wright – both lining up against Portsmouth at Fratton Park in 1937.

Wright, who during the war had risen to the rank of captain in the Royal Armoured Division, quickly made his presence felt by appointing Charlton's assistant trainer Eddie Nash as first-team trainer. City's long-serving Lemmo Southway was demoted to assistant, whilst the former Ireland and Chelsea half-back Billy Mitchell, who had guested for City during the war, became coach, with the club's pre-war goalkeeper George Sommerville as scout.

Coinciding with Wright's appointment was the dictat by Harry Dolman that in future all players would be required to live in Bristol. With those such Boxshall and Townsend being domiciled in London, Clack (Witney), Davies (Wrexham), Edwards (Birmingham), Eveleigh (Leamington Spa), Lewis (Brecon), Mullen (Barrow-in-Furness) and Sheldon (Barry), the club purchased five houses and committed them-selves to looking out for more.

However, despite the boardroom changes and a new manager, there was to be no quick cure for City's ills. Rovers compounded the Bristol Babe's season of turmoil by retaining their hold on the Gloucestershire Cup with a 2-0 victory in front of 15,111 spectators at Eastville in May.

A new broom sweeps clean, they say, so optimism was once more in the air during the close season of 1949, as Bob Wright returned to his old club and paid £2,000 to sign Ken Mitchelson, Don Freeman and Roy Bicknell, whilst a further £1,500 was stumped up to recruit winger Tom Rudkin from Southampton. Another new face was Dartford goalkeeper Frank Coombs, much to the disappointment of Everton, equally keen to sign this goalkeeper who, despite being at the receiving end of a 2-9 defeat, had shone in the FA Cup matches against City two years earlier.

With the departure of Len Townsend for £2,000 to Millwall, follow-ing his refusal to sign as a full-time professional, City were caught out by the fact that Don Clark broke down in the first game of the season, when Northampton were beaten 3-1 in front of a 27,463 crowd. Unfortunately, his cartilage operation was not a success. He never regained his speed and, after a valiant struggle, making five League and three FA Cup appearances in 1950-51, he was forced to retire.

September 1949 brought the signing of Welsh international George Lowrie from Newcastle for a record £10,000 fee, and the following month £5,000 was found to bring in Arnold Rodgers from Huddersfield Town.

Lowrie marked his debut with a fine goal against Bristol Rovers in front of a 34,463 crowd at Eastville Stadium on 10 September, but the best bargain turned out to be Alec Eisentrager from Trowbridge, who notched four goals in City's 6-0 victory versus Newport a week earlier on 3 September. As an amateur, this former German prisoner of war cost nothing.

The end of the 1949-50 season brought some financial assistance for Maurice Roberts who had lost his sight shortly after City signed him from Brentford three years previously. A testimonial at Ashton Gate on 3 May attracted some 4,500 fans, paying receipts of £262 13s 0d, who saw Brentford beaten 4-1. Fortunately, by this time, Roberts had regained the sight in one of his eyes. A week later many of the 8,250 crowd who turned up at Ashton Gate when Cardiff were beaten 2-0 in the James Howell Cup – a contest in aid of blind charities – were surprised to read in the following day's *Bristol Evening Post* and the *Bristol Evening World* that manager Bob Wright had handed in his resignation.

Bob Wright, who had not signed the three-year contract he had been offered in December, handed in a letter on 11 May 1950 giving two months' notice of terminating his employment. 'The reason,' Wright told a news conference, 'is a simple one. I wanted a completely free hand. They would give me one verbally, but they were not willing to put it in writing in my contract.'

In response, Mr Dolman issued a statement: 'The directors were quite willing to give Mr Wright a free hand in many respects, but we had to make reservations in the event of things going wrong. That's where we broke down. Bob wouldn't budge.'

Clause Three in the draft agreement drawn up by the board stated: The employees shall obey from time to time the board of directors or any one of them. 'That was their let-out,' said Mr Wright, revealing that he had demanded in its place a new clause giving him a free hand in three respects:

(i) Team selection.

(ii) Tactics.

(iii) General administration, discipline and control of the playing, ground and scouting staffs.

A man of such principal is rare indeed, but Wright hit the nail on the head by stating: 'In effect the policy of free-hand means nothing to the directors, even though they do not want me to go. Unfortunately, holding the convictions I do there is no alternative.' A courageous decision indeed by the popular, well-dressed and quietly-spoken Scot, who, with his wife and two daughters, had to vacate the club house in Henleaze.

Fortunately, Wright was to leave City in a far better condition than he found them. Behind the scenes, he had done much reorganising – giving the players better conditions (modern medical equipment and a recreation room), as well as instituting revolutionary training and tactics (evolving a new defensive system). Whilst this encouraged improved performances on the pitch, City again finished a disappointing fifteenth, but this time they were only three points worse off than ninth-placed Rovers.

Despite overseeing the 2-0 home win over the Rovers in the Gloucestershire Cup on 13 May, Wright did not go on City's German tour, although he was at Ashton Gate on 18 May to watch the players depart, as shown by a photograph on the front page of that evening's *Bristol Evening Post* captioned: 'Oh Dennis! – Mr Bob Wright manager of Bristol City FC, adjusts Dennis Roberts's club tie before the team left Ashton Gate today.'

On leaving City, Wright became licensee of the White Hart in Lower Maudlin Street, as well as having a year as part-time assistant to his ex-Charlton colleague Bert Tann at Bristol Rovers.

The fact that the City party, which took the night ferry from Harwich to the Hook of Holland, looked smart ambassadors for the club was down to the players, whose idea it was to have a uniform dress code, which they paid for themselves. Decked out in double-breasted navy blue blazers, with the club badge (robin) on the left chest pocket, dark grey trousers, cream shirts and club ties, the seventeen players, accompanied by nine directors (from the eleven-strong board) including chairman HJ Dolman, vice-chairman CW Crawford, AJ Amor, WG Garland, George Jones and the Reverend FC Vyvyan-Jones, were to join up with Alous (Alec) Eisentrager, who was already in Germany.

The fact that City had signed former German prisoner of war Alec Eisentrager from Trowbridge Town was the reason why the club had been invited to tour, in preference to any First Division team. Joining City on amateur forms in the close season of 1949, the stocky 5ft 2in ball-playing winger scored four goals in the 6-0 defeat of Newport on 3 September 1949. Classified as an 'alien', he had to complete his residential qualification before being able to turn professional in January 1950. Eisentrager was to remain at Ashton Gate until July 1958, when he was transferred to Merthyr Tydfil

The week-long tour started with a goalless draw at Wuppertal, where some 200 British soldiers made 'Ginger' Peacock a particular favourite of theirs. It would have been better, but for Bill Spalding having a beautiful second-half effort disallowed. Fortunately, the two German chocolate firms who had offered samples of their wares to those who scored the first and second goals, allowed the treats to be shared. At Hamborn, it was George Brewster's turn to have a goal disallowed as City tumbled to a 2-3 defeat, whilst fine football was the hallmark of City's 5-2 victory over Alemannia, before the tour concluded with a 3-1 win at Borussia Moenchengladbach. This game was refereed by company sergeant-major Martin, a former Football League official, who, when stationed at Corsham, had controlled matches at Ashton Gate during the war.

The end of the season in which a loss of £24,575 was reported saw a notable capture. Jimmy Rogers was signed after being given a free-transfer by Wolves. Meanwhile, Danny Boxshall moved to Bournemouth for £2,575.

The 1949-50 campaign had also seen the formation of the current supporters club, this being the fourth such body connected with Bristol City. The first mention of a supporters club had come around the turn of the century, whilst a second such organisation came into being on 25 April 1919. This also floundered, and a third body – the Bristol City Supporters Association – was set up following a meeting convened by Mr AH Wookey and presided over by local journalist JG Ure (the Judge), at the Ford Memorial Hall, Bedminster, on 16 October 1936.

Quite how long this Bristol City Supporters Association survived is unclear, but at their AGM at the Grosvenor Hotel, the Arcade Bedminster, on 11 August 1939 a credit balance of £4 1s 3d was declared from income of £110 17s 7d. Probably the war years brought about its demise, thus bringing about the birth of the current organisation at a meeting held at Crown & Dove Hotel, Bridwell Street, Bristol on 9 October 1949, when the original committee comprised: R Hurley (chairman), L Derrick (secretary), Les Cutmore (treasurer), W Burn and A Taylor. This organisation has performed much good work in the intervening years, raising many thousands of pounds for the club. Their help towards the building of the Grandstand in the 1951-53 period was much appreciated by the board and they were granted space in the Grandstand for their clubroom, which was opened in August 1955 and enlarged to twice the size ten years later. Having these premises at the ground, coupled with City's promotion, produced a boom in membership, which in 1957 was in excess of 5,000 who had each paid a subscription of 1s 9d. Arthur Fowler, who was much involved until being ousted in a coup on 18 December 1984, was the first clubroom steward, whilst ex-City winger Billy Pocock was chairman in 1955-56.

The first donation that the organisation made to the club was in 1950, when they handed over the £80 that had been collected by raffling an autographed soccer ball. Taking over the catering rights at Ashton Gate allowed them to generate more income. In 1958 they forked out half the £6,400 fee for Bert Tindill, and the following year took on the responsibility for paying the £12,000 cost of relaying the Ashton Gate pitch.

They started organising away trips in 1951 and opened the very first club shop in the old offices at the Park (Open) End of the ground in 1967 – then moving to the officials' car park, opposite the Grandstand in 1969 when it was named the Robbie Robin Shop. July 1967 brought the formation of the Young Robins Club, the committee comprising Mike Draper, Norman Hook and Don Tuckfield.

Whilst Harry Dolman pondered his second managerial appointment, he was active in the search for new players and personally sought out the services of Welsh international right-winger Sid Thomas, who had impressed when playing for the All-Star team against a Combined City & Rovers side on 25 April. Whilst the 21,419 crowd, who generated £1,570 for City's popular trainer, were thrilled by the skilful play of the visitors, it was a 70th-minute Sid Williams goal that won the game for the combined side.

Combined City & Rovers: Stretton (Luton); Bamford (Rovers), Bailey (City); Pitt (Rovers), Roberts (City), Peacock (City); Boxshall (City), Eisentrager (City), Rodgers (City), Lowrie (City), Sid Williams (City).

All Star XI: Kelly (Fulham & Ireland); Sherwood (Cardiff & Wales), Cummings (Villa & Scotland); Hollyman (Cardiff & Wales), Martin (Villa & Ireland), Burgess (Spurs & Wales); Thomas (Fulham & Wales), Stobbart (Luton), McGibbon (Bournemouth), Beasley (Fulham & England), Duffy (Charlton).

On Monday, 12 June, Dolman and fellow director George Jones travelled by road to Thomas's home in Machynlleth, North Wales to agree terms and the following day it was back to Bristol for Thomas and his wife to view a club house in Airport Road, right opposite that of his fellow Welsh international George Lowrie.

With all being satisfied, the transfer was completed that afternoon, with City paying Fulham £8,000 for his services. Unfortunately, after only thirteen games Thomas was taken seriously ill with tuberculosis and retired. Seeking compensation, Dolman's suggestion that Fulham give City a reserve player for nothing fell on deaf ears as the Football League washed their hands of the controversy. Fortunately, City's second transaction with the Craven Cottage club was to be far more successful.

There were over two dozen applicants for City's management vacancy, including Leslie Jones, the old Arsenal and Wales international, but after interviewing Northampton's Bob Dennison, the City directors appointed Pat Beasley on 19 July 1950. Awarded a five-year contract, the

longest ever issued by the club up to then, Beasley was engaged as player-manager for two years at £12 per week and three years as manager on
an annual salary of £1,250. It would seem that Beasley was always the
front runner, as chairman Dolman, impressed by what Peter Doherty and
Raich Carter had achieved at Doncaster and Hull respectively, was keen
on having a player-manager at Ashton Gate. Availability ruled out the
likes of Jimmy Hagan (Sheffield United), Johnny Carey (Manchester
United) and Bristolian Phil Taylor (Liverpool), but with wing-half Archie
Macauley joining Fulham from Arsenal, it left the way clear for City to try
for Beasley, who had played so attractively in Len Southway's benefit
match.

Born in Stourbridge on 16 July 1913, Beasley made his name at out-
side-left, often exploiting his penchant for cutting inside to devastating
effect. Starting with Cooksley, a Kidderminster League side, he turned
professional with Stourbridge, for whom he played less than a dozen
times, before being transferred to Arsenal for £550 in 1931. At Highbury
when the Gunners won the championship three years in a row under
manager Herbert Chapman, Beasley made 43 appearances and scored
sixteen goals to pick up two championship medals (1933-34 and 1934-35)
as Arsenal rounded up their hat-trick of titles.

Transferred to Huddersfield for £750 in 1936, he made up for missing out on two FA Cup final appearances for Arsenal by playing at
Wembley in 1938, when Andy Mutch's spot-kick in the last moments of
extra-time won the trophy for Preston. On 15 April 1939, Beasley gained
his solitary England cap. Against Scotland, Beasley's 70th-minute equaliser paved the way for England's first win at Hampden Park in twelve years.
Going on the FA tour of South Africa that summer, it is likely he would
have made many more international appearances, but for the intervention
of war.

Helping Huddersfield secure the North-East Regional Championship
in the first wartime season, Beasley guested for Arsenal and Spurs before
joining Fulham in 1945. Becoming captain at Craven Cottage, Beasley,
playing at left-half, inspired them to the Second Division Championship
in 1948-49, as well as making 37 appearances during the following term
as Fulham held on to their top-flight status.

For one of his first City signings, Beasley returned to his Stourbridge
roots to snap up left-winger Jack Boxley for £2,000 and the 1950-51 season got underway with both the Southern and the Northern Sections of
the Third Division having been increased by two clubs, from 22 to 24.

This change had been agreed by an overwhelming majority (only three
dissenting votes) at the Football League AGM in London on 3 June 1950.

Fortunately, the opposition of Major H Keyes (WBA) did not attract much interest. His alternative proposal, seconded by Dr CS Baxter (Everton), was for the Third Divisions to be split into North, Midlands and South, with the three winners playing off for the two promotion places.

The clubs seeking re-election – Millwall, Newport, Halifax and York – were all successful, following which the meeting considered the question of new members. Three clubs were rejected on the basis that the League opposed stadia used for greyhound racing, whilst Bangor City withdrew their application. Following the failure of a proposed amendment to three-up and three-down, because no seconder could be found, the ballot for the new clubs took place. For the Southern Section, Gillingham topped the poll with 44 votes, followed by Colchester 28 (also elected), Worcester eleven, Chelmsford eight, Peterborough five, Yeovil one, Merthyr Tydfil one. The Northern Section proved more difficult, and three ballots proved necessary. Shrewsbury with 30 votes were elected on the first ballot, whilst Workington and Wigan both polled nineteen, Scunthorpe seventeen, Nelson eleven, Northwich Victoria one, South Liverpool one. Following a second ballot that resulted in a tie, Scunthorpe and Wigan each receiving fifteen votes, the issue was eventually resolved in Scunthorpe's favour by 30 votes to eighteen.

Peter Barnes, writing in the *Pink 'Un Sports Annual*, congratulated the City directors on performing a master coup in producing a manager without spending a penny piece. Fulham had let Beasley leave as reward for five years' faithful service, during which time he had captained the team that gained promotion to the First Division.

It is tempting to think that Pat Beasley had something to do with City changing the nondescript shirt badge that the players had worn the previous season – a robin on a ball hardly matching the class of Spurs' cockerel. The introduction of the coat of arms of the City and County of Bristol, which was to remain on shirts until the end of the 1959-60 season, was an improvement, as was the decision, which surely Beasley (or perhaps trainer Wilf Copping) did influence, for City to perform in Arsenal-style kit throughout the 1954-55 campaign.

With the terracing on the site of the blitzed grandstand being extended by a dozen steps, the City fared better in the League than most expected, given the loss of key players. They finished tenth in 1950-51, and in the FA Cup progressed to the fifth round for the first time since 1934-35. It was the Beasley spirit that was mainly responsible and if they had been stronger up front they might easily have accounted for Birmingham at St Andrews. It was a tragedy for City that, after thirteen games, in which he sparkled and dazzled on the right wing, Sid Thomas had to quit football after contracting tuberculosis. A month later George Lowrie broke his leg playing against Nottingham Forest, and City had lost £18,000 worth of football talent – a staggering blow that no Third Division club could easily take.

Despite the Gloucestershire Cup being drawn 1-1 in front of a 16,673 crowd at Eastville on 12 May 1951, no extra-time was played and, with no provision for a replay, the trophy was shared for the first time.

With 1951 being Festival of Britain Year, many Festival Fund games were played throughout the country. It was no different in Bristol, where City beat Hamborn 07 and Dinamo Zagreb, as well as venturing to Castle Cary where the homesters were dispatched 6-1 on 10 May. City then made a short tour of Cornwall, winning 2-0 at Helston before concluding the season by winning 7-1 at Truro.

However, John Coe, writing in the *Green 'Un Football Guide*, was of the opinion that 1950-51, with Rovers reaching the last eight of the FA Cup, brought Bristol football nearer to the golden age than at any time since 1926-27, when City had won the Third Division (South) Championship.

Following agreement with the War Damage Commission in respect of compensation for the Number One Stand that had been razed by German bombs in January and April 1941, the easing of building restrictions meant that work started on a replacement in the summer of 1951. It was, however, to cost the club £30,000; much more than the £16,500 (based on 1939 valuation of £7,500 plus 120 per cent) that they received. As it was, a steel shortage and lack of funds (the supporters club donating £3,000) delayed completion until 1953.

Whilst work commenced on what is now known as the Williams Stand, the most significant event at this time was the signing of Peter John Walter Atyeo. Long thought of as a Wiltshire boy, it was revealed in the brilliant book about his career, *The Hero Next Door*, by Tom Hopegood and John Hudson, published by Redcliffe Press in 2005, that he was actually born in Standerwick, Somerset on 7 February 1932. However, Dilton Marsh, near Warminster, Wiltshire was his home, where managers such as Ted Drake (Reading), Louis Page (Swindon), Dave Magnall (QPR) ventured in search of Atyeo's signature. The nineteen-year-old England Youth International and former Trowbridge High School pupil had the opportunity to sign for First Division Portsmouth, for whom he had twice played the previous season – versus Charlton (h) 3-3 on 11 November and Arsenal (h) 1-1 on Easter Monday, 26 March – but he wished to continue his apprenticeship as a quantity surveyor. According to Peter Godsiff in his book *Bristol City: The Complete History of the Club* published in October 1979 by Wensum Books, when Dolman followed the well-trodden path to Atyeo's door, he had to wait for his man. As Dolman pulled up outside Atyeo's home he spotted Bristol Rovers manager Bert Tann's Austin Seven car. Fortunately, Dolman's patience was rewarded and on 14 June 1951 Atyeo entered into a personal contract as follows:

(i) Atyeo would always be on top wages.

(ii) Atyeo would be allowed to live at home and continue his apprenticeship as a quantity surveyor, attending Ashton Gate for training on Tuesdays and Thursdays.

(iii) Atyeo would be allowed to drive a car to Bristol for training.

(iv) A donation of £100 would be given to Atyeo's amateur club Westbury United.

(v) A first-team Friendly would be played at Westbury at the end of the following season.

(vi) Atyeo would not be placed on City's transfer list without his father's consent.

This was thought to be the end of the matter, but the Football League raised questions; wanting to know why Atyeo wished to sign for a Third Division club when he was already on the books of First Division Portsmouth, and top sides Arsenal, Spurs and Fulham rumoured to be interested. There were three exchanges of letters, and it was not until 8 August that it was announced that Atyeo's registration with the City had been accepted, on condition that the clause relating to subsequent transfer was deleted. This was complied with, but the club let it be known by nods and winks that the original deal would hold good.

With Atyeo, hailed as a bright star in embryo, as well as the return of Cyril Williams for £4,500 from WBA, City's determination to improve was clearly demonstrated. Although the 1951-52 season began with a flourish, injuries again wrecked City's hopes. Jack Boxley missed almost a third of the campaign after receiving a leg injury that required two operations, whilst Ivor Guy and 'Ginger' Peacock were also sidelined for a spell. Finishing a lowly fifteenth, whilst the Rovers ended up seventh, was not what the City fans expected, so they had to take comfort in the fact that Con Sullivan emerged as one of the club's best-ever goalkeepers.

'The Traveller,' writing in the 1952-53 edition of the *Green 'Un Football Guide*, commented that: 'The forwards gave some disappointing displays and frequent changes were made with a view to infusing more thrust into the attack. Somewhat surprisingly, George Lowrie did not get a run out until late October, and four months later was transferred to one of his former clubs, Coventry City for £2,750.'

'The Traveller' added: 'The signing of Ernie Jones for £4,875 from Southampton helped, whilst Jimmy Rogers showed himself to be a rare type – a man with the devil in him who has learnt to harness his natural buoyancy so as to fully exploit opposition weakness.' Curiously, he did not appear particularly impressed in regard to Atyeo's first season at Ashton Gate, being of the opinion that, 'He did not really live up to his reputation as a goal-getter,' a statement which he qualified by adding that, 'Lack of support undoubtedly had something to do with it.'

It would seem, therefore, that the jury was still out with regard to Atyeo's merits, but such waverers were soon to be convinced as he went on to add to the five England Youth appearances he had made in 1949-50. He played for the FA XI, England Under-23s, and England B, before being awarded his first full cap, when he scored in the 4-1 victory over Spain at Wembley on 30 November 1955. Becoming only the third Bristol City player ever to turn out for England, Atyeo would make five more appearances for the national team and add a further four goals. At Dalymount Park, Dublin on 19 May 1957, Atyeo's last-gasp header that salvaged a draw with Eire and took England to the finals of the 1958 World Cup was destined to be his final act on the international stage.

Five goals in six international appearances – an impressive record that suggests Atyeo was discarded too soon. It is tempting to think that if his part-time status had not caused concern amongst the members of the selection committee, then England might well have done better in Sweden. For City, Atyeo would continue to ratchet up goals and appearances, and by the time he retired at the conclusion of the 1965-66 campaign he was the club's record holder in both departments with 395 goals in 698 appearances, including friendlies. Never sent off or indeed cautioned during his career, Atyeo, who equalled the club record set by Arnold Rodgers four years previously in netting after just nine seconds versus Bury at Ashton Gate on 16 March 1957, also made two appearances for the Football League XI (one goal), four appearances (four goals) for the FA XI, as well as one game for the Football Combination Select, when he netted twice.

However, returning to 1951-52, City's worst spell was in November and December with only one win in nine games, this a 2-0 home success over Northampton on 29 December. However, during this period they did progress in the FA Cup with an unexpected 2-1 victory over Brighton at the Goldstone Ground. Unfortunately, City were unable to survive the second round at Layer Road, where Colchester beat them 2-1.

Whilst a 2-1 success over the Rovers in the Gloucestershire Cup final at Ashton Gate on 10 May was a sop of sorts for the home supporters in the 16,214 crowd, the game was notable for the fact of bringing the curtain down on Pat Beasley's playing career.

A disappointing season then, as made clear by Peter Barnes, writing in the *Pink 'Un Sports Annual*, who said that the City side, over which there were optimistic hopes at the start of the season, turned out to be built without firm foundations. Flattery deceived us as the forward line made a firm start with three goals in the first 24 minutes of the campaign, yet they only scored another 55 goals in the remaining 45 league games.

Chapter Two

Renaissance 1952-60

City fans were unsure what to expect for 1952-53, though the appointment in June, on the recommendation of FA Secretary Stanley Rous, of Reg Mountford, who had been coaching the Denmark national team for years, suggested that chairman Harry Dolman was as ambitious as ever. Fortunately, City much improved, but it was the Rovers who took the glory, winning the Third (South) championship with 64 points. An unbeaten spell of 27 games brought a worthy reward for the Pirates. City gave them a good fight, though, and for quite a time they were the only serious challengers for the coveted prize, with the Bristol clubs filling the top two places in the table from 21 February to 4 April. Eventually, City had to be content with fifth spot, though only five points behind the Rovers.

A poor start cost City, and with just two points from the opening five games, the visit of Ipswich on 9 September attracted the lowest crowd since the war – 7,622. Fortunately, City got things moving with a 4-2 victory and they surged up the table. A 1-0 win at Brighton on 3 January took them to third, and a 3-1 success at Crystal Palace three weeks later had them hot on the heels of their Eastville rivals. Unfortunately, a 1-4 loss at Bournemouth on 6 April saw City slip to fourth, a situation that was not improved by losing the following games against Colchester and Norwich. Despite ending the season with three wins and draw, the damage had been done.

A 2-0 win at Plainmoor in a benefit game for Sammy Collins, whom City had let go to Torquay in 1948, was followed by a short Cornish tour, which brought 6-1 and 9-1 wins over Penzance and Newquay. The season concluded with goals from John Atyeo and Alec Eisentrager, bringing victory over the Rovers in the Gloucestershire Cup on 8 May.

The 1952-53 campaign was notable in that it brought floodlighting to Ashton Gate, thanks to chairman Harry Dolman, who designed the system that was used for the first time on 27 January 1953 – Wolves winning 4-2 in front of a 23,866 crowd, after fog had brought about postponement a week earlier.

Costing £3,500, Dolman's initial scheme comprised fourteen metal pylons (seven on each side of the pitch) approximately 40ft high with a cluster of three lights on top. However, it was soon found necessary to add six more pylons – three at each end of the pitch.

City's first experience of playing under artificial light had come two years earlier – losing 1-2 at Swindon on 2 April 1951, but with floodlights now in place at the Gate, City were able to cash in. Many stirring flood-lit friendlies followed, against the likes of Arsenal, Spurs and East Fife, as well as a number of continental clubs, but it was not until the 1956-57 season that League games were allowed to be played under artificial light. At Ashton Gate, this meant the clash with Notts County, which City won 3-0 on 20 February 1957.

With receipts ranging from £1,345 generated by a 9,391 crowd to see Stuttgart Kickers on 8 November 1955, to a high of £3,821 when 28,991 turned up to see Arsenal beaten 3-1 on 30 March 1954, the beneficial effect on City's finances can well be appreciated. Also adding to the pot was the fact that Bristol Rugby played five floodlit games at Ashton Gate between 1956 and 1960. These lights served City well, but in the summer of 1965 they were sold to Southern Burton Albion for £2,000.

However, City's new lights were not ready to be switched on until 28 December 1965, when Wolves were again the visitors, though this time in a Second Division encounter, which the visitors won 1-0 to inflict on City their first home defeat in twenty matches. This new system cost £27,000 and consisted of 48 lamps on each angled head atop four 160ft high pylons set in the four corners of the ground. They were destined to be a feature at Ashton Gate for 27 years, and many felt the ground lost much of its character when the pylons and the distinctive heads were removed on 8 June 1992, to find a new home at Wigan's Springfield Park. City's third set of lights, erected on the roofs of the Grandstand (named the Des Williams Stand on 4 June 1992) and the Dolman Stand, were fully in use for the first time on 5 November 1991 when Plymouth were beaten 2-0.

The work that had started to replace the bombed Grandstand in 1951 was finally completed in 1953, after a steel shortage and lack of funds had delayed progress. Coupled with the floodlighting, this meant that the facilities were good enough for Ashton Gate to be chosen for an England Under-23 International, which resulted in a goalless draw with France on 17 October 1956, the day that Britain's first Nuclear Power Station opened at Calder Hall.

The crowd of 25,817 (£4,610) saw the talented Doncaster player Alick Jeffrey break his leg in a ninth-minute tackle with Richard Tylinski, the French centre-half. After eight months with his leg in plaster, Jeffrey resumed training with Doncaster, but in February 1959 was told that he was finished as a first-class footballer. It is thought that Doherty made an attempt to be reunited with his protégé, thinking he owed it to the lad to try and get him fit enough for League football, but Doncaster and Jeffrey took the insurance payout and it appeared that this potentially great player was lost to the game. Fortunately, George Raynor, the recently appointed manager of Midland League Skegness Town (having coached Sweden to the final of the 1958 World Cup, which they lost 2-5 to Brazil), offered Jeffrey encouragement and support. Scoring three goals for Skegness in a Charity Match at Louth – his first game since the injury – Jeffrey suffered a double fracture of his other leg after scoring three more goals in a practice game.

Undismayed, Jeffrey returned to such good effect that he re-signed for Doncaster in December 1963, adding to his original record of 34 goals in 71 games with another 95 goals in 191 League games before finally bowing out at Belle Vue in January 1969 at the age of 30, when he managed another three goals in seventeen appearances for Lincoln. Twice Jeffrey helped Doncaster win the Fourth Division Championship, and in 1964-65 he topped the Football League scoring charts with 36 goals. By coincidence, one of Jeffrey's first games was back at the Gate. Luckily, he did not suffer any further injury on 7 January 1964, when City beat Doncaster 2-0 in an FA Cup replay.

In subsequent years many Under-23 and Under-21 games have taken place at the Gate, and on 21 October 1992 the Football League did battle with Italian Serie 'B'. Unfortunately, by that time the public's appetite for such contests was on the wane as only 3,360 turned out to witness the Football League's 3-1 triumph. The FA have also used the ground for minor representative games. After twice availing themselves of the sparse facilities on offer during the Second World War, an FA representative side came to Ashton Gate on 2 March 1954 for a special match to celebrate the Diamond Jubilee of the Western League. With the FA leading 4-0 in front of 5,089 spectators, heavy snow brought an end to the proceedings midway through the second half. Undeterred, the teams returned for a second attempt a year later on 22 March 1955 – a 4,278 crowd seeing the FA lads win 3-0. On 8 October 1958, 14,457 turned up, presumably enticed by the fact that John Atyeo was in the FA line-up. No doubt they were pleased to see the great man score, but, against an RAF XI, this was not enough to prevent a 1-4 defeat.

With Rovers in the Second Division for the first time in their history in 1953-54, the pressure was really on City to reclaim the status they last held in 1931-32. With economies being made, the close-season departure of coach Reg Mountford and Billy Mitchell did not auger well, but City managed to produce their best effort since 1946-47. Home form was their undoing, too many points being dropped at Ashton Gate early in the campaign. They really ought not to have lost to the champions Ipswich or runners-up Brighton. As was the case during the previous season, City certainly had their chances.

With Andy Micklewright and Len Pickard signed on free transfers from Bristol Rovers, and £1,050 found to obtain Jimmy Regan from Rotherham, City did not lose at home after conceding both points to Ipswich on 10 October. They certainly played much good football, and Atyeo's goalscoring prowess attracted a bid £20,000, plus two players, from Liverpool in November, which was turned down. The injury-plagued Ernie Jones joined Rhyl as player-manager in March, not long after goalkeeper Con Sullivan, who had lost his place through a broken thumb, moved to Arsenal for £3,500. With Tony Cook in great form between the sticks, no doubt it was thought sensible to cash in, especially as the Gunners agreed to play a floodlit friendly at the Gate, which City won 3-1 in front of a 28,991 crowd on 30 March. Unfortunately, within a week City found themselves in a dilemma when Cook was hospitalised with appendicitis, but the Rovers helped out by loaning Bob Anderson. In the event, Syd Morgan took over between the sticks and City won seven of their last nine games to finish third in the table, trailing in eight points behind champions Ipswich.

With the Gloucestershire Cup being drawn 2-2 on 3 May, the end of the season marked the retirement of centre-half Dennis Roberts, who had given City great service since before the war, whilst full-back Norman Jackson was signed from Sheffield Wednesday.

In the FA Cup, City won 3-1 at Torquay, before pulling off a 3-0 success at Rhyl to set up a home clash with Second Division Rotherham. Unfortunately, the Millers proved too good for a City side, handicapped by injuries to Jimmy Regan and Arnold Rodgers, playing in the blue and white quarters of Bristol Rovers.

With Rovers having made a big impression in the Second Division, the City fans felt it imperative that their favourites achieve promotion in 1954-55. They were not to be disappointed, but a tremendous Leyton Orient side chased them to such an extent that City equalled the 70 points record set by Nottingham Forest four years earlier, and nationwide were only headed in the goal stakes by Second Division Blackburn.

The 1954 close season brought a shock for Pat Beasley, who was on holiday when he heard that his trainer Eddie Nash had accepted a similar position with Cardiff. However, within a few days a replacement had been found, Beasley making his most important staff signing, engaging his former Arsenal colleague Wilf Copping, who had been the hard-man of the famous 1930s Highbury side and won twenty England caps.

Many were less than impressed when City started with a disappointing 1-1 draw at Gillingham, but it was not until their fourteenth game that they suffered defeat – going down 2-3 at Southend on 9 October. A 6-1 success over Aldershot followed, but a 0-2 drubbing at Northampton and an abysmal 1-2 home defeat by Southend in the FA Cup raised concerns.

Beasley learned that Tommy Burden was at loggerheads with Leeds, as the player wished to work in the time-and-motion study department of Clarks, the well-known shoe company. Beasley contacted the Elland Road club with an offer of £1,500 for his services. The offer was rejected, but eventually agreement was reached on 28 October 1954, with £1,500 down and payments of £500 a year for the following three seasons.

Quite a snip for City, as Burden was a well-respected player who had played alongside Billy Wright with Wolves during the war. After guesting for Chester, he was snapped up by Leeds in 1948. However, it was not to be the best of starts for Burden, as his first game for City was the aforementioned defeat at Northampton, where Jack Bailey broke his arm and missed the rest of the season. A week later, on 13 November, another disaster saw Cook break his arm after just four minutes against Watford. Fortunately, Ivor Guy played heroically as the emergency goalkeeper and City scraped home 1-0 thanks to Jack Boxley's late winner. With reserve keeper Syd Morgan out with a cut knee, City again looked across to Eastville and signed Bob Anderson on a permanent basis for an outlay of £500.

Gillingham's visit on 18 December was not the Christmas present the City fans were hoping for. Forfeiting their fourteen-month unbeaten home league record, City found themselves knocked off the top of the table. A quick double over Reading had City back in pole position for the visit to challengers Leyton Orient on 1 January 1965. Despite being annihilated 1-4, it was not until losing at home to Norwich a week later that City found themselves knocked off their perch again. Switching Cyril Williams to left-half, moving Tommy Burden into the attack and changing Jimmy Rogers from outside-right to centre-forward brought revenge at Carrow Road on 29 January. But it took until 26 February, when Southend were beaten 3-2 at the Gate, coupled with Orient's surprise home defeat by Watford, to allow top spot to be reclaimed.

In mid-season, with England international Arthur Milton thinking of retiring from the game to concentrate on his cricket with Gloucestershire, City were successful in securing his services from Arsenal for £4,000. Bristolian Milton, destined to be the last man capped at both football and cricket – making the first of his six test appearances against New Zealand at Headingly in 1958 – helped City to promotion. Unbeaten in their last eighteen games, City finished nine points ahead of Leyton Orient. The relief at ending 23 years of frustration brought a 27,726 crowd to Ashton Gate to see the championship shield presented by the Football League vice-president Arthur Oakley to City captain Jack White at the conclusion of a disappointing goalless encounter with lowly Newport on 23 April 1955.

With 27-year-old Milton seemingly content to retire at the end of the season, and with City having half of his transfer fee reimbursed, as agreed, it would seem that all were satisfied, but is this the real story? The mild-mannered and courteous Milton, who died in April 2007 at the age of 79, seemed to suggest otherwise with his comment many years later that he was never actually asked as to whether he wished to stay on.

Overall it was Jimmy Rogers' season, his speed, zest and determination being harnessed to produce a 25-goal haul. Meanwhile, John Atyeo, for whom Spurs proposed a transfer, continued to develop. He planted his feet firmly on the first steps of an international career with outstanding displays for the FA XI – against the RAF at Highbury on 20 October and the Army at Hillsborough two weeks later – before making his England Under-23 debut against Italy at Stamford Bridge on 19 January 1955, when he scored in a 5-1 victory.

Analysis in the local press at the end of the season serves to inform us just what a fine Bristol City side this 1954-55 team was, and in repeating such comments here we are left to reflect on the fact that it is now approaching 57 years since the club won a divisional championship.

Skipper Jack White set a fine example and nobody played with greater determination. He was one of the most consistent and lion-hearted players in the Southern Section. Another model of consistency was Ivor Guy, and it is doubtful if he ever had a better season, whilst Jack Bailey, was having one of his best campaigns until having the misfortune to break his arm.

Centre-half 'Ginger' Peacock played a full part in City's fine defensive record, whilst Mike Thresher, who came into the side as Bailey's deputy, after starting the season as an inside-forward, could be pleased with his displays. Possessing two important qualities for a full-back – courage and speed – the rest was expected to surely come. It was a shrewd piece of business when goalkeeper Bob Anderson was signed from Bristol Rovers. The lanky north-eastener played many outstanding games, showing the best form of his career. Arnold Rodgers, Jimmy Reagan and Tony Cook were valuable members of the side early in the season, whilst Jack Boxley proved himself to be an enterprising left-winger. It was a lucky day when Tommy Burden was signed, as there was not a more talented player in the

Southern Section, and the introduction of this former Leeds captain brought added class to the side, complimenting the splendid ball play and distribution of the ageless Cyril Williams.

Unfortunately, nothing stays rosy in City's garden for very long, as seen by many of the 20,097 Gloucestershire Cup crowd at Eastville who witnessed City's 1-2 defeat on 2 May. Perhaps things would have been different if Arthur Milton had played, but with his job done the man who was to become England's last double international (capped at soccer versus Austria in 1951, he won the first of his six test caps against New Zealand in 1958), had retired from football at the age of just 27.

A third Cornish tour, which brought a 1-0 success at St Blazey and a 5-1 victory over Helston Athletic, was followed by a trip to Germany. Despite two goals by Jimmy Rogers as well as strikes by Doug Regan, Jack White and Jack Boxley bringing a handsome 5-1 win over Hamborn, the goals dried up at Augsburgh, where the 2,000 spectators witnessed a 0-0 draw. City managed a goal at Linz ASK, but whilst this could not prevent a 1-2 defeat, Atyeo's strike brought victory over Stuttgart Kickers before a 3-2 success at Singen concluded the visit on 1 June.

City's first-team success was almost matched by their reserves, who in their second season back in Division One of the Football Combination, after a two-year sojourn in Division Two, finished runners-up. Six seasons of lowly finishes had seen them in Division Two in 1952-53, where they continued to disappoint by being placed fifteenth. Fortunately, the following season's third place brought a return to the reserves' top flight, where they excelled. 1955-56 would see them fifth in a one-division set-up that was to last for two more seasons, when City finished fourth and third in 1956-57 and 1957-58 respectively. 1958-59 saw them eighth in Division One, followed by fourteenth-placed finishes in both 1959-60 and 1960-61. The reserve team then resigned and took over from their Colts in the Western League, winning its championship in 1961-62 and 1962-63. It would be four seasons before they rejoined the Football Combination, finishing eighth in Division Two in 1965-66 and third the following season.

Both City and Rovers set the Second Division alight in 1955-56 and for a time Bristol was soccer's boom city. At Christmas, a *Daily Herald* poll of various soccer experts had City marked as promotion favourites: City totalled 48 votes, Sheffield Wednesday 36, Liverpool 26, Leeds 10, Swansea 9, Leicester 7, Stoke 7, Bristol Rovers 3, Port Vale 2.

Unfortunately, City were unable to live up to the expectations and they fell away to finish eleventh, whilst the Rovers missed out by just four points.

With Swansea supplying the opposition at Ashton Gate, City's return to the Second Division got off to a good start with Jimmy Rogers firing the ball into the Covered End net after thirteen minutes. With the Swans reduced to ten men following the 32nd-minute departure of their player-manager Ron Burgess with a leg injury, Cyril Williams doubled City's advantage early in the second half, prior to Cliff Jones cleverly back heeling the visitors' late reply.

A 3-1 win at Rotherham followed before City were brought down to earth by a 2-3 defeat, their first in the League since January, at Notts County. A 5-2 victory completed the double over Rotherham, but form was somewhat inconsistent until Bury were beaten 3-1 at Ashton Gate on 17 September. This sparked an unbeaten ten-match run, culminating in a thrilling 3-2 success over Sheffield Wednesday that propelled City to the top of the table on 19 November. Sadly, in the next game City lost 2-3 at Doncaster, where they squandered a 2-0 lead. The 5-1 demolition of Lincoln on 3 December kept City at the top of the pile, but the third of four consecutive losses knocked them off their perch. A 0-5 Boxing Day defeat at Home Park, where they were seeking their first ever League win, was hardly a surprise, but restitution was on hand the following day with a 6-0 success over Plymouth at Ashton Gate.

Form continued to be erratic for the rest of the season, which Jimmy Rogers later attributed to the fact that City changed the style of football that had gained them promotion. A 3-0 win over Bristol Rovers at Eastville on 3 March and a 4-1 success over a Doncaster side that, as well as boy-wonder Alick Jeffrey, also included the future comedian Charlie Williams, Harry Gregg (later Manchester United), and Bert Tindill, who was to join City two years later, kept promotion hopes alive.

With just one goal to show for some fine football over the three Easter games, a 0-2 defeat at Lincoln, with just three matches remaining, finally extinguished all such hopes on 14 April. A disappointing 0-3 loss at West Ham brought the curtain down on a season that had promised so much. City's eighth position after losing at Upton Park would eventually become eleventh as other clubs completed their fixtures. On the face of it, the City looked well out of the promotion race, but with runners-up Leeds only seven points ahead it can be appreciated how close the contest actually was. Indeed, had the Rovers won their penultimate game at Leeds, then it is likely that Bristol would have had a club in the top flight for the first time in 45 years.

Disappointment then, but a good season for all that, even though City lost out at Goodison Park in the FA Cup, where Everton achieved a flattering 3-1 victory on 7 January. City also disappointed in the semi-final of the FA Youth Cup, a competition that had commenced four years earlier. After hammering Trowbridge 8-0 (h), City accounted for St Austell (a) 3-0, Plymouth (h) 2-1, Portsmouth (h) 3-0 and Arsenal (h) 4-3 before coming a cropper against Chesterfield – losing 1-2 at Saltergate before drawing at home 1-1.

In that other important cup competition, a keen tussle for local honours saw Barrie Meyer's tenth-minute shot clinch the Gloucestershire Cup for Bristol Rovers on 30 April, before City brought their season to a close with wins at Newquay and Helston, prior to popping over the Channel to beat Nice 3-1.

Ashton Gate hosted a schoolboys' international for the second time on 12 May 1956 when a bumper crowd of 17,400 turned up to see England beat Wales 3-2. Ten years later, on 7 May 1966, a 6,068 crowd saw Wales beaten 3-1, to make it a trio of Ashton Gate defeats for the visitors, who had succumbed to a Phil Taylor goal right on the final whistle in front of 9,800 spectators on 9 April 1932.

It was certainly a good season for John Atyeo. A few weeks after playing for England 'B' versus Yugoslavia, he made his full England debut against Spain at Wembley on 30 November 1955, becoming City's first England international since Billy Wedlock played his last game for his country 41 years earlier. England won 4-1 and Atyeo opened his account after just eleven minutes. Later in the season, he played in the 4-2 win over Brazil at Wembley, where he squandered a penalty, and during the summer won his third cap in a 0-0 draw against Sweden in Stockholm.

Departures saw Andy Micklewright sold to Swindon for £1,000 and Jimmy Regan move to Coventry for £3,750 in March, whilst in the close season Arnold Rodgers went to Shrewsbury for £750, ex-Newport defender Tony Nelson to Bournemouth for £500, and Dick Steel off to York for £625, whilst Norman Jackson was given a free. Another departure was promising amateur David Burnside, who finally obtained his release and signed professionally for WBA. He would be back at Ashton Gate in 1971-72, making just one appearance before moving on to Colchester. Later, as a member of City's staff in 1999-2000 he, together with Tony Fawthrop and Leroy Rosenior, picked the team following the mid-season departure of manager Tony Pulis.

Unfortunately, 1956-57 proved to be a case of after the Lord Mayor's show. The season started disastrously with just four points being picked up in the first eight games. This seemed like a hang-over from the collapse during the second half of the previous campaign, and City relied almost exclusively on John Atyeo for goals. A draw at Sheffield United and a 5-3 success over Bristol Rovers was the cue for a temporary revival with twelve points from eight matches, but the improvement was not sustained as City got bogged down in the muddy pitches. Staring relegation in the face at Christmas, City recovered to obtain 21 points from their final seventeen matches and finish thirteenth.

Success in the FA Cup, with victories over Rotherham and Welsh League Rhyl, and a 5-1 League win over Sheffield United on 19 January heralded the start of the revival. The goals flowed throughout the rest of the season, highlighted by a 4-0 win over Doncaster and 4-2 over Leyton Orient, but the most memorable was in the grand performance City gave in their 1-2 FA Cup defeat at Villa Park, where John Atyeo scored with a 25-yard thunderbolt – a goal he always claimed as his best ever. In front of a 63,099 crowd that included 12,000 travelling supporters, City could have forced a draw had a late scoring chance not fallen to the injured 'Ginger' Peacock. The Aston Villa captain, Johnny Dixon, after winning the Cup at Wembley, said that the City game was the hardest his team had during the competition.

During the season, trainer Wilf Copping, as well as forwards Jimmy Rogers and Jack Boxley, joined Coventry. However, City made a smart move by employing to help as scout Jimmy Seed, the ex-Charlton Athletic manager.

Don Clark resigned after 21 years with the club, and was succeeded as assistant secretary by Bert Bush. Aged 42, Bush was formerly assistant at Norwich and Southampton, as well as being an ex-League referee. Sid Hawkins who, after being assistant secretary at Bristol Rovers in 1934, joined City as Bob Hewison's assistant in 1946, would remain as secretary until Bush took over in July 1963.

Early in the campaign came the sad death of one of City's promising young reserve players whilst on National Service in Cyprus. While City were beating Blackburn at Ashton Gate on 29 September, the mother of Colin Read was receiving news that her 21-year-old son had died from gunshots wounds received in a terrorist ambush.

Goals from John Atyeo and Dermot Curtis brought Gloucestershire Cup success at Eastville, before City concluded their 1956-57 activities with a five-a-side tournament at St James Park, Exeter, on 10 May. After disposing of Barnstaple and Bideford, the AS Line Cup was secured by beating Exeter 17-10 in front of a 1,773 crowd.

With bustling Curtis – the Eire international centre-forward signed for £5,5000 from Shelbourne in September 1956 – coming good with eleven goals in his last nine games, and another successful newcomer, inside-left Bobby Etheridge from Gloucester City, hopes were high at the start of the 1957-58 campaign.

Unfortunately, despite an excellent performance at home to Stoke on 3 September, mid-season form was so dreadful that nearly every Ashton Gate fan, even the super-optimists, felt that Third Division football was ominously near. It was hardly surprising, therefore, that it was 'mutually agreed' to terminate Pat Beasley's contract on 6 January 1958, although the directors acceded to his request to oversee the following evening's FA Cup replay with Accrington Stanley, which saw City wear the blue and white Bristol Rovers quarters for the second time in four seasons.

Within a few weeks Beasley got fixed up with Birmingham, initially as joint manager in tandem with Arthur Turner, for seven months, and he helped guide the St Andrew's club to the final of the Fairs Cup before resigning in May 1960. A spell as scout with Fulham followed before he took up the managerial reins again with Dover Athletic (1961-64). Following retirement, he settled in Chard, and died in Taunton Hospital on 27 February 1986.

Following Beasley's departure, trainer Les Bardsley and Harry Dolman selected City's team prior to Jimmy Seed becoming caretaker-manager. Seed was in charge for just nine days before quitting on 22 January to take over as manager of Millwall.

Whilst Cliff Britton and Ted Fenton were on City's short list, the resignation of Peter Doherty at Doncaster allowed Dolman to get the man he had sought eight years previously. Following a meeting at Nottingham prior to City's fourth round FA Cup win at Meadow Lane, Doherty – who had caught the eye when playing for the Managers XI against City on 12 November 1956, causing the *Bristol Evening Post* to note that 'Peter Pan Doherty gave City's youngsters an object lesson' – signed a three-year contract at £2,000 per annum and immediately appointed Cliff Duffin as chief scout.

Breezing into Ashton Gate with a bundle of new ideas, an infectious optimism and a new psychological approach, the shrewd and eloquent Irishman – who had been one of the greatest forwards of all-time – soon began to turn things around. What was Doncaster's loss was City's gain in more ways than one, as the key factor proved to be the signing of 31-year-old Bert Tindill on 3 February. Without this proven marksman, who had scored 130 goals in 400 games, Doncaster were relegated and destined to require 50 years to regain their second tier status. That gave them plenty of time to question the wisdom of letting Tindill go for just £6,400.

Doherty, however, did not bring instant success, as his first match, a trip back to Belle Vue, ended in a 1-2 defeat even though George Walker had given City a fifth-minute lead. Rotherham then came to the Gate and took the points with Albert Broadbent's 88th-minute goal. City then end-ing up disappointed after the FA Cup fifth round home clash with Bristol Rovers on 15 February 1958, when a record was surely created in that each round had seen a different person in charge of the City team.

Robbed some would say, as Geoff Bradford looked offside when he ran through to net the Rovers winner in front of an all-ticket crowd of 39,160 paying receipts of £5,439.

A 0-0 draw at Huddersfield was an improvement but a 2-3 defeat at West Ham meant it was five matches without a win since Doherty took over. However, all the gloom was swept away by the winds of March as City started the month with a 4-0 home success over bottom of the table Lincoln. Few among the 20,041 gathered at Ashton Gate that day would have thought it likely that Lincoln would escape from the drop, but they were to effect a revival even more dramatic than City's.

Taking heart from this victory, City returned to Meadow Lane and repeated their cup success in the league, and Tindill's 78th-minute goal at home to Ipswich brought up a hat-trick of wins. However, a 0-5 defeat at Blackburn, followed by Sheffield United's 4-1 victory at Ashton Gate brought a return of the jitters, which were only slightly calmed by a 3-2 victory at Ninian Park, which kicked-off an unbeaten five-game run. A thrilling 3-3 draw at Eastville, with all the goals scored by half-time, and home wins over Cardiff and Barnsley, pulled City well clear of relegation by the time of their visit to Fulham on 19 April. With Johnny Haynes absent on international duty for England, it all seemed so easy for a City side coasting on a 4-0 lead until Tosh Chamberlain netted for the Cottagers in the 78th minute. Two late goals by Tony Barton had City hanging on 4-3 at the close.

Mission accomplished then for City with two games left, but for oth-ers there remained much to play for. Whilst Tindill and Atyeo had goals disallowed at Sincil Bank, City's 0-4 defeat – a much-valued success for 21st-placed Lincoln, as they chased an improbable escape from relegation – raised some eyebrows. However, City's home fixture with Swansea that brought the curtain down on the season was to ferment much specula-tion. With Swansea securing the victory they needed to retain their status, rumours of match-fixing were such that local journalist David Foot in his *Bristol Evening World* match report felt compelled to comment: 'Bristol City were no better nor worse than Swansea Town. But scotch any of those ridiculous notions that these were a couple of give-away points to a club desperately keen to stay in the Second Division. The suggestion, which doesn't bear examination, though, surprisingly, I have heard it from so many, is an insult to the Welsh club.'

The story persisted, however, and it was thought that George Walker, on opening the scoring after just two minutes, was told to ease off by some of his team-mates.

Fortunately, the bitter taste of this result was erased three days later by City's 4-1 Gloucestershire Cup victory over the Rovers in front of a 10,590 Ashton Gate crowd on 29 April. A short French tour was the players' reward, starting in Nice with a 0-3 defeat on 15 May. A 2-1 success at Bordeaux followed before Peter Doherty donned City's colours to play the whole 90 minutes against Ruffec, who were beaten 4-3 on 22 May.

Prominent in City's 1957-58 salvation was Wally Hinshelwood, who stormed back to form in the second half of the season. Many of his displays had Doherty raving: 'What I like most of all about Hinshelwood is his ability – rare among present-day footballers – of taking the ball to the dead-ball line.' However, it would be the following season that Hinshelwood was seen at his very best, with superb displays against Swansea and Blackpool.

Meanwhile, needing to reduce City's 44 professionals, loyal servants Jack Bailey, Alec Eisentrager, Syd Morgan, Cyril Williams, Jack White and Terry Compton were released. Doherty, who was awarded a £500 per annum rise, paid £3,500 to Coventry to bring back Jimmy Rogers, but turned down Birmingham's £20,000 bid for John Atyeo.

However, Peter Doherty was in demand elsewhere. Following the resignation of Arsenal's manager Jack Crayston, the *Bristol Evening Post* of 21 May reported Doherty as saying: 'I have a contented staff and an ambitious set of directors and we are endeavouring to build up a promotion side. I would not be interested in moving now, even to Highbury.' Chairman Harry Dolman added his comments: 'Forget these unfounded reports, Peter Doherty will remain at Ashton Gate. He is the tops.'

Despite the excitement of City's successful fight against relegation and the Rovers finishing tenth in the Second Division, it was the Bristol Boys team that took the honours in 1957-58, winning the English Schools Trophy for the first, and only time to date. When, on 22 April, the 21,595 spectators at Ashton Gate witnessed Adrian Williams notch up Bristol Boys' fifth goal in the dying seconds (Burt 12, Williams 23, 70, Summers 50, Clark 62), few would have thought that the second leg would be little more than a formality.

Bristol: H Booth; C Smith, M Thomas; D Stone, S Poole, P Prewett; T Burt, B Clark, D Summers, A Williams, J Derrick.

Swansea: M Falvey; E Lewis, R Griffiths; S Mitchell, D Cana, R Harris; R Evans, J Watson, B Hole, Jones, Saunders.

However, in front of 10,000 at the Vetch nine days later, Bristol Boys had to conjure up much resolve to recover from being 0-3 down at the interval before securing the trophy 9-4 on aggregate.

Perhaps the Bristol Boys were over-confident, as it was Swansea who set the pace and Dowdall had the ball in the visitors' net after just three minutes, only for the effort to be disallowed. Failing to heed the warning, Bristol found themselves trailing in the ninth minute when Evans volleyed in the opener and, keeping up the pressure, Hole doubled the Swans' advantage when diverting in Watson's free-kick. Within a minute Watson, with a brilliant goal, added further to Bristol's woe.

Fortunately, the visitors were given the encouragement of goal soon after the interval – Burt netting with a fine effort. Summers then banged in a second before Brian Clark obtained the best goal of the game with a shot from 30 yards. Summers then fired Bristol 4-3 in front on the day, only for Smith to conclude this thrilling affair by diverting Mitchell's effort into his own net right on time.

Bristol: H Booth; C Smith, M Thomas; D Stone, S Poole, P Prewett; T Burt, B Clark, D Summers, A Williams, J Derrick.

Swansea: M Falvey; E Lewis, R Griffiths; S Mitchell, D Cana, R Harris; G Payne, J Watson, P Dowdall, B Hole, R Evans.

Five years later, Bristol Boys had the opportunity to win the trophy once more. This time Stoke Boys proved much too good at Eastville, where they won the first leg 3-0 in front of 18,178 spectators on 13 May 1963, and went on to secure the trophy 5-1 on aggregate.

The 1958-59 season would see City post their first financial loss since 1952-53, but with Doherty fresh from having led his Northern Ireland team to the quarter-finals of the World Cup in Sweden, there was much optimism in the air when the campaign opened with a 6-1 success over Rotherham. If this was not enough, the next fixture had the City fans in dreamland as their favourites pulled off a 7-4 win at Barnsley to create a post-war record of scoring thirteen goals in the opening two games.

Having hit six in the opening match of the season, City went one better in the second. Following one of their finest post-war displays, manager Peter Doherty was moved to comment that he had not seen any finer football during the recent World Cup in Sweden. Former England international Raich Carter, who was a spectator at this game, concurred. He thought City, on this form, would beat any team in the League. The key thrust came from the dual centre-forward plan, with John Atyeo and Bert Tindill scoring five of City's seven goals.

Yet City did not have the game all their own way. The Barnsley game ebbed and flowed, and only when Tindill made 6-4 in the 82nd minute did it look probable that City had both points. Barnsley had opened the scoring, Lol Chappell steering the ball into the net from close range, but Bobby Etheridge hooked the ball past Harry Hough for the equaliser.

Ten minutes prior to the interval came the goal of the game. Johnny Watkins took a pass from Mike Thresher, lobbed the ball over John Short and then, to use the words of the *Bristol Evening Post*, 'volleyed it home with the speed of a guided missile.'

Within a three-minute period early in the second half, Chappell levelled, Atyeo put City ahead, and Chappell restored parity yet again before Tindill fired in from 25 yards to put City 4-3 up after 67 minutes.

Not until the 80th minute did City achieve a two-goal advantage (the Atyeo-Tindill combination working an opening for Atyeo to supply the finishing touch), but Chappell's immediate reply kept Barnsley in the game. Then came City's sixth, from Tindill, before the same player put Atyeo in the clear with three minutes left. The big centre-forward rounded the advancing goalkeeper and fired into an open net to cap an extraordinarily rare 7-4 scoreline.

A 0-4 defeat at Sheffield United quickly brought City back to earth, but, undeterred, the team continued to ratchet up victories. Right-winger Derek Virgin came in for his first game of the season when Sunderland, in their first campaign outside the top division, visited on 25 October. No doubt inspired by the fact that singer Frankie Vaughan came on the pitch prior to the kick-off, Virgin turned in a sparking display in which he also grabbed a couple of goals in City's 4-1 success. Two weeks earlier, Wally Hinshelwood also put on a stylish display in the 4-0 win over Swansea.

Unfortunately, the day got much worse for two visiting fans. Walking along Coronation Road after the game, 43-year-old Richard Williams jumped over the railings thinking it was the perimeter of the park. He plunged 30ft into the river and, whilst his friend, 48-year-old Wilfred Hyde, attempted a rescue, during which he suffered a head injury, Williams was lost in the darkness.

A 2-1 success over the Rovers at Eastville followed, but that game was overshadowed by the death of Harry Bamford on 31 October, following a road accident three days earlier when riding his scooter to Clifton College to take a coaching session. All Bristol was saddened by the death of this fine Bristol Rovers full-back, who had played in every game during the FA's tour of Australia in 1951.

The table-topping clash with Fulham on 8 November 1958 was eagerly anticipated, and whilst the game did not disappoint, City were indebted to Bobby Etheridge's prowess from the spot for a share of the spoils. A hard-won point then, but it did not get much easier as next up was another top of the table encounter, this time versus Sheffield Wednesday at Hillsborough.

Even though City lay third, this game was seen as something of a formality for a Sheffield Wednesday side striving to return to the top flight at the first attempt. City had other ideas, however, and the author can recall David Coleman expressing his surprise on reading the result from BBC TV Grandstand's ticker-tape machine, as last-minute goals by Alan Williams and John Atyeo brought City an outstanding 3-2 success.

It was not just that City upset the Second Division pacesetters on their own ground, where they had won their first eight home games of the season, but the way they did it. Two goals down after seventeen minutes, City staged a magnificent fight-back and fully deserved the win that their late couple of goals brought.

The first half was a tale of two left-wingers. City's Johnny Watkins might have scored twice – one effort being saved by Ron Springett and the other hitting an upright – whereas Wednesday's Alan Finney did net twice. Finney's first goal came when he shot though a ruck of players after his initial effort had been charged down by Tony Cook. His second was a long-range header from Tom McAnearney's free-kick.

After 27 minutes City engineered an excellent reply. Bobby Etheridge started the move and Peter McCall penetrated the defence with a 25-yard grounder which found Bert Tindill running into space to thump the ball past Springett's right-hand from twenty yards. Just on the interval, McCall was unlucky with a 35-yard shot, which Springett touched onto the crossbar and over the top for a corner.

For the opening fifteen minutes of the second half, Wednesday looked likely to increase their lead, but suddenly control of the match switched. City pushed Wednesday back into their own half, although the equaliser was a long time arriving. Watkins crossed, Tindill headed down, Atyeo beat Springett to the ball, and centre-half Alan Williams was the scorer.

With seconds left to play, Wally Hinshelwood sent over a ground-level centre and Atyeo netted the winner from ten yards to consign Wednesday to what proved to be their only home defeat of the season.

With City still in third spot, the visit of promoted Scunthorpe, struggling near the foot of the table, was looked on as a formality. However, the Iron did not read the script as they left the Gate with a 2-1 success. Thus started City's slide from grace, despite winning on the road at both Lincoln and Rotherham before the end of the year. Having beaten injury-hit Doncaster in the FA Cup, City's early form returned on 24 January for the mouth-watering fourth-round Cup-tie with First Division Blackpool.

This visit of the famous Tangerines set the Bristol public agog with anticipation. A crowd of 42,594 (paying record receipts of £5,569), were rewarded, after watching the antics of Puskas (Blackpool's duck mascot) with a stirring contest. Blackpool manager Ron Suart called it the best Cup-tie he had seen since the war, whilst the England team manager, Walter Winterbottom, was reported as saying that he thought City were the better team.

Seven of the Blackpool team had won international caps during their careers, but none was more famous than legendary outside-right Stanley Matthews. However, on this occasion Matthews was overshadowed by City's right-winger, 29-year-old spiky-haired Battersea-born Wally Hinshelwood, who was in sparkling form.

The game never lacked thrills, and City, wearing Cardiff's blue shirts, contributed much of the skill. With Mike Thresher keeping Matthews quiet, City went ahead when Gordon Hopkinson, on the edge of the penalty area, drove Hinshelwood's short corner across to Bert Tindill, who swivelled and struck the ball past George Farm.

For a time, Blackpool, who played in white shirts with tangerine edgings, came back strongly, but City finished the first half in control, searching for the second goal that might well have put the game beyond the Seasiders' reach.

The equaliser came in the 54th minute, following intense Blackpool pressure. Matthews took a short corner, collected a rebound and centred for Ray Charnley to shake off the attentions of Peter McCall and Alan Williams and force the ball into the net. Enthused by this, Blackpool took charge, but City weathered the storm and for the last twenty minutes they looked likely to settle the contest. The home fans roared, but a dramatic winner failed to come.

For the replay, City took the easy route by flying to the north-west, where David Durie's 59th-minute curler brought disappointment in the fog at Bloomfield Road.

Back in the League, a 2-3 defeat at Liverpool, where Tony Cook saved Ronnie Moran's spot-kick, was followed by a home draw against Middlesbrough and defeat at Charlton. John Atyeo stopped the rot with an Ashton Gate winner against Grimsby, but form continued to be patchy for the rest of the season, which concluded with City a disappointing tenth.

Notable in this 1958-59 campaign were the exploits of goalkeeper Tony Cook, who saved six out of the nine spot-kicks he faced, whilst 21-year-old centre-half Alan Williams was unlucky to be robbed of an England Under-23 cap versus Scotland by the snowy weather in Glasgow.

Meanwhile, Atyeo brought the curtain down on his representative career by scoring twice for the Football Combination team that beat Holland in Rotterdam towards the end of the season.

The season concluded with a Combined Bristol team taking the field at Eastville in memory of the late Bristol Rovers full-back Harry Bamford. With Arsenal supplying the opposition, the 28,347 crowd on 8 May helped swell the Harry Bamford Memorial Fund by £3,709 and witnessed a thrilling encounter which the home side won 5-4. Geoff Bradford netted twice, as did John Atyeo, whilst Dai Ward made up the nap hand for the locals. For the Gunners, Vic Groves, Danny Clapton and Jackie Henderson got on the scoresheet.

Combined Bristol XI: Cook (City); Burden (City), Watling (Rovers); Sykes (Rovers), Alan Williams (City), Mabbutt (Rovers); Hinshelwood (City), Atyeo (City), Bradford (Rovers), Ward (Rovers), Hooper (Rovers).

Arsenal: Sims (Aston Villa); Wills, Evans; Everitt, Docherty, Bowen; O'Neill (Clapton 45), Groves, Charles, Bloomfield, Henderson.

Referee: David Smith (Stonehouse).

To perpetuate Bamford's memory, a trophy was offered for annual award to a local footballer who exhibited great sportsmanship. Sadly, this was allowed to lapse in 1972, when the list of recipients read as follows:

1958-59 Geoff Bradford (Bristol Rovers)
1959-60 Colin Mitchell (Clifton St Vincent's)
1960-61 Bob Anderson (Bristol City)
1961-62 Burt Britton (Avonmouth)
1962-63 Albert Allen (Parson Street Old Boys)
1963-64 John Atyeo (Bristol City)
1964-65 Ray Mabbutt (Bristol Rovers)
1965-66 Ray Bean (Soundwell)
1966-67 Jack Connor (Bristol City)
1967-68 Bert Biggs (St Philip's Marsh Adult School)
1968-69 Harold Jarman (Bristol Rovers)
1969-70 Terry Bush (Bristol City)
1970-71 John Honeyfield (St Adhelm's)
1971-72 Bobby Jones (Bristol Rovers)

The ending of veteran 'Ginger' Peacock's career at the end of 1958-59 was hardly a surprise, but the bad feeling caused by the decision to release left-winger Johnny Watkins was to have serious repercussions. Watkins himself was terribly upset, but it turned out well for him in the end. On offer at £4,000, he joined Cardiff for just £2,500.

With Northern Irish international Tommy Casey having signed for
£5,000 from Portsmouth in March, the summer addition of Barnsley's
exciting left-wing pairing of Malcolm Graham and Scottish 'B' international Johnny McCann, in exchange for £14,500 and the want-away Bert
Tindill, had City marked as one of the pre-season promotion favourites.
Unfortunately, problems in regard to Graham's left knee, which many put
down to the player's mindset, and McCann's breaking a leg in City's 4-1
Boxing Day win at Plymouth, meant that they would have a less than successful stay at Ashton Gate.

Atyeo still harboured bad memories of an incident with Doherty in
the tunnel after City had beaten Doncaster 4-1 on 7 April 1956, and it did
not take much for flames of discontent to rage through Ashton Gate.
The £2,500 signing from Doncaster of the competitive Tommy
Cavanagh, whom Doherty had been chasing for more than a year, was
probably the straw that broke the camel's back, especially as he was
appointed captain. Doherty had already been undermined when he wanted those players not in the first team to accept less money. Chairman
Harry Dolman, loyal to those who had won promotion four years earlier, over-ruled the manager following protests by Tommy Burden, John
Atyeo and Mike Thresher.

The club became polarised into two groups, variously described as a
north-south divide or a rift between protestants and catholics. However,
on a personal level, most of the players got on well with newcomers
Casey, Collinson, Hopkinson, McCann and Taylor, which suggests that
City's split camp was founded on something more complex than personality problems.

Was it partially down to parochialism and small-mindedness?
Whatever it was, it certainly had a disastrous effect on City's season and
right from the start the fact that Tommy Cavanagh felt the need to comment in the City programme that he was an Anglican suggests that reli-
gious bigotry was undermining the club.

Cavanagh, though, lived for football and always demanded 100 per
cent. A no-nonsense character, it seemed that his competitive nature did
not go down well at Ashton Gate, whilst the fact that the elegantly attired
Malcolm Graham drove an expensive Daimler caused some jealousies.
However, Graham's cause was not helped by a mysterious injury. Despite
being the fastest sprinter in training and kicking a ball powerfully, he was
not risked in action for some months. Whether he was worried about the
health of his little boy, who had serious leg problems, or being away from
South Yorkshire for the first time in his life, who knows, but throughout
his season at Ashton Gate concerns over his knee remained an issue.

Graham wrote of his time at Ashton Gate in Tony McDonald's book *Leyton Orient: The Untold Story Of The O's Greatest Ever Team*. He put the trouble down to a simple north-south divide, as well as making the point that 'Doherty had been a marvellous player and was a lovely fella, but good ex-players don't always make good managers. It was a hard time for the club'. Graham goes on to say he enjoyed playing alongside the legendary former England centre-forward John Atyeo, mentioning that it was during his time at Ashton Gate that he homed his lethal left-foot by learning to strike the ball much harder. Apparently, Atyeo had Graham, despite a knee buggered by an earlier cartilage injury, firing in long-range shots in his stockinged feet, no boots! This would seem to demonstrate that the rift between the players was not as great as most observers seemed to think, but on the other hand it does not seem the wisest thing to do given the heavy leather footballs of the time.

Following Doherty's departure from Doncaster, several of their youth players (Roger Collinson, Gordon Hopkinson, Mike Quinlan and Archie Taylor) had switched to Ashton Gate. However, in the case of Collinson, a farcical situation developed when he refused to re-sign for the south Yorkshire club, preferring to become a professional with the City. The Football League deliberated for two months before refusing to accept City's registration, whilst the FA did accept it, which meant he could play for City in all but League games.

A meeting was held in October 1958 in a Sheffield Hotel, attended by Football League President Joe Richards, Secretary Alan Hardaker, Doncaster chairman Jack Garnham, manager Jack Crayston and secretary Derek Bestall, at which Roger Collinson and his mother Eva attempted to resolve the issue. Despite Mrs Collinson's letter to Doherty at the end of the 1957-58 season, stating how keen she was for her son to continue his development under Doherty, the League was unbending. Hardaker insisted that Collinson's registration with City would never be accepted. In the meantime, Collinson played half-a-dozen reserve matches in City's colours and eventually a compensation payment of £1,000 induced Doncaster to relent.

Almost a year went by before Collinson actually made his League debut, but his mother was not there to see it. Unaware of his surprise call up at the start of what is now known as City's infamous 1959-60 season, she had gone off on holiday to Skegness with her youngest son. The news got through to her husband though, and he was at the Old Show Ground to see Roger give an outstanding display in a 1-1 draw against Scunthorpe. The following Saturday, City's home programme got under-way with Rotherham winning 3-2 to avenge their previous season's heavy defeat. It was not until the fourth game that full points were secured, thanks to a Jimmy Rogers goal in a Tuesday-night floodlit thriller against Liverpool at Ashton Gate, but form proved elusive even though Doherty confidently expected that Atyeo's taking up full-time status would soon bring out the best in his star man.

After six successive defeats, centre-half Alan Williams spearheaded City's attack at home to second-placed Middlesbrough (Brian Clough, Peter Taylor *et al*) on 26 September. Williams scored in a 2-0 success, but a 0-3 defeat at Derby a week later saw the experiment abandoned.

As victories became ever more elusive, the factions in the camp began to show themselves ever more clearly. However, Malcolm Graham's brilliant two-goal display in a 3-1 win at Stoke when making his long-delayed debut on 31 October appeared to have everyone singing from the same hymn sheet, especially as it was followed by a 2-0 home success over Portsmouth. With Doherty having put his faith in youth by giving debuts to Frank Jacobs and Phil Coggins, the introduction of new signing Ally Hill from Dundee promised much.

But Hill and the rest of the City team looked somewhat out of their depth as Aston Villa won 5-0 at Ashton Gate on 21 November, just a week after they had banged eleven goals into Charlton's net. The defeats kept piling up, including a 1-6 hammering at Huddersfield on 12 December, before a Christmas double over Plymouth raised the spirits of City fans and players alike.

It was not to last and, when City squandered a 2-0 half-time advantage to bow out of the FA Cup versus Charlton on 9 January, it was noticeable that separate groups of players congratulated goalscorers John Atyeo and Tommy Cavanagh.

Following an abysmal 1-5 defeat at Brighton on 12 March, the inevitable happened with the dismissal of Doherty three days later. He would never manage again, but took on assistant and scouting roles at Notts County, Aston Villa. Preston, Sunderland and Blackpool. Living in Fleetwood, he died on 6 April 1990.

John Atyeo demonstrated his pleasure at the manager's departure by driving into the Ashton Gate car park with his car horn blaring. 'Well, we got you in the end,' he said on seeing Doherty walking out. Despite much subsequent regret over his part in the happenings of that season, Atyeo would recount this event for the rest of his life, seemingly oblivious to the fact that it did not cast the most favourable light on his legendary loyalty to City's cause.

With long-standing City players getting their way, it was thought that escape from the drop was still possible. The first casualty was Tommy

Cavanagh, who never played for City again. Creating an unenviable relegation hat-trick – having also gone down with Huddersfield in 1955-56 and Doncaster in 1957-58, Cavanagh moved on to Carlisle and then became player-manager at Cheltenham before taking charge at Brentford. Thereafter, he continued in the game as trainer-coach at Nottingham Forest (1966-72), Hull (1972) and Manchester United (1972-81). He later assisted Arthur Cox at Newcastle before becoming assistant manager at Rosenborg (Norway) and Burnley (1984-1985), where he took over as manager for eight months following Martin Buchan's resignation. On leaving the Turf Moor club, Cavanagh worked at the FA School of Excellence at Lilleshall, as well as having a spell coaching Wigan. Thomas Henry Cavanagh, born in Liverpool on 29 June 1928, was diagnosed with Alzheimer's disease in 2002 and died in Driffield on 14 March 2007.

Team affairs were taken on by a committee comprising trainer Les Bardsley, board members Harry Dolman, Bill Kew and Reverend FC Vyvyan-Jones, as well as player Tommy Burden, who once more took on the captaincy. Certainly, form improved enough for the fans to question why the players had offered so little before. For the 1-0 home win over Lincoln on 19 March there was no place in the team for two of Doherty's signings (Casey and Cavanagh) or for Wally Hinshelwood, who was another, like Cavanagh, never to play for the club again.

A 0-2 defeat at Portsmouth dampened the mood, but Atyeo, playing one of his best games of the season, headed the winner against Sunderland, before an away reverse in front of a 33,556 crowd at Villa Park continued the one step forward, one step back pattern, to leave City still in the relegation zone. However, that 1-2 defeat against champions-elect Aston Villa was unjust as it took two disputed second-half penalties to beat them after Roger Collinson had put City in front with a wonder goal – firing the ball into the Holte End net from 35 yards out wide on the right touch-line. Despite this setback, the next five games offered City a realistic chance to escape relegation, especially as rumours abounded about behind-the-scene deals.

The Easter programme brought three games in four days, about which there was much speculation regarding attempts to bribe certain opposition players to take it easy. The fact that Huddersfield grabbed two late goals to earn victory at Ashton Gate on 16 April suggests there was nothing untoward about that Easter Saturday game. It is possible, however, that an approach was made, even though future City player Jack Connor, who scored for Huddersfield, was non-commital when questioned many years later. He merely said that if an offer had been made, then he did not know of it.

That result, though, was but the meat in the sandwich, as it was the two games against Ipswich before and after the Huddersfield affair which caused most doubts in the minds of the City supporters. A City win at Portman Road is a rare event at any time and Good Friday's 3-1 success seemed almost a miracle. Perhaps mid-table Ipswich had an off-day, but at Ashton Gate on Easter Monday the visitors were so poor it was almost untrue, and rumours were rife as City cantered to a 5-1 victory.

Even so, the best laid plans counted for little as, the following evening, companions in distress Plymouth pulled off an unexpected 1-0 win at Ninian Park, where promotion-bound Cardiff squandered a couple of penalty-kicks.

With City on the brink of the abyss, if any illicit approach was made to Leyton Orient on 23 April then it was not reflected in the result. City's 1-3 defeat confirmed relegation, leaving Harry Dolman to pledge: 'We will be back and quickly.' An understandable comment no doubt, but in the event it would take five years to regain lost ground. With two games left to play, there was, therefore, no need for City to seek redemption from Swansea for the previous season's favour. Despite this, the Swans fielded a youthful side which still proved much too good for City, who sunk to a horrific 1-6 defeat. Yet another horror display brought the League season to a close with Stoke winning 2-1 at Ashton Gate, even though they were reduced to ten men following the departure of the injured Dennis Wilson after barely eight minutes.

Thus did City ignominiously forfeit the Second Division status that they had so magnificently secured just five years earlier. With justice done, many fans put the blame firmly in the players' court, it being thought that the immature attitude of some of them served to cost the club very dear indeed.

Whilst Doherty had received much criticism at City's AGM, held in the canteen at Messrs Brecknell, Dolman & Rogers on 26 January 1960, there is little doubt that he could have taken the club far if he had not been undermined from within. Sacrificing his post as Northern Ireland manager in order to concentrate all his energies in City's cause, the end came a little over a month later. With talk of fights amongst the players in training, the shambles came to the boil with an appalling display at Brighton on 12 March. Herbert Gillam, sports editor of the *Western Daily Press*, was alarmed at the lack of discipline on show at the Goldstone Ground, where he witnessed one of City's worst ever displays, the players roundly bickering amongst themselves.

Whilst those involved have never come clean over what actually took place in City's vain attempt to avoid the drop, John Atyeo never ceased to be haunted by this insight into an aspect of football that disturbed and appalled him.

Fortunately, City restored a measure of pride in the annual tussle for the Gloucestershire Cup. Trailing to Alfie Biggs's opener in front of a 7,195 crowd at Eastville, a couple of Atyeo headers as well as a narrow-angled Rogers effort helped City to a 3-2 victory over Bristol Rovers on 2 May. Meanwhile, contrasting fortune saw City's former winger Johnny Watkins on his way to the top flight after being instrumental in Cardiff's promotion.

## Chapter Three

Paying the Price 1960-67

Back in the lower reaches, despite chairman Harry Dolman's long-held declaration of intent, where now for City? With their debts reaching a staggering £55,000, the club was helped out of a financial hole by Dolman donating 25,424 four-shilling units of shares in his company, Brecknell, Dolman & Rogers. Unfortunately, the gift came at a price as Dolman, for some unknown reason, sought (and obtained) the resignation of the Reverend Vyvyan-Jones, as well as George Jones, the proprietor of Wessex Coaches, the firm who for many years were charged with the responsibility of transporting City supporters to away matches.

Frederick Charles Vyvyan-Jones, who died at the age of 87 on 7 August 1990, was born in Swansea and moved to Bristol with his wife in 1929. Becoming rector of St Michael's on the Mount in 1935, he held the post for more than 50 years, making him Bristol's longest serving clergyman. Elected Labour councillor for Easton in 1945, he was made an alderman in 1964. Serving as the Education Committee chairman from 1963 to 1967, he was Lord Mayor in 1967. Following the reorganisation of local government, he was councillor for Hillfields from 1974 until 1979. Installed as Canon at Bristol Cathedral in 1980, he retired from St Michael's in 1981. Widely travelled, for years he ferried vanloads of parishioners around Europe. His barrister son Michael, who died in 1981, fathered illustrator Marc and cake artist Dominic. After the death of his wife, Lily, Canon Jones married Kathleen Durbin in 1986.

The remaining board members, chairman Dolman and his vice-chairman Bill Kew, grocer Arthur Amor, licensee Bill Garland, and engineer Norman Jones, were soon added to with the appointment on 21 June of farmer Lionel Smart, electrical engineer Graham Whittock, local industrialist Roy Poeton, and solicitor Stephen Kew.

City needed a new manager. The qualities of Fred Ford stood out, even though he did not number among the 60 applicants. Coach at Bristol Rovers and trainer of the England Under-23 team, Ford turned down Dolman's initial approach, but whilst on an FA course at Lilleshall Ford met up with Les Bardsley and Bill Harvey (City coach), who made it clear that the job would be his for the asking. Sensing he would be mad to turn his back on such an opportunity, Ford made contact with Dolman by telephone and was appointed on 14 July 1960 when a three-year contract was signed at a salary of £2,750 per annum.

With the club notorious for its rancorous dressing-room atmosphere that could be cut with a knife, Ford found himself needing to deal with a couple of the older professionals on his first morning's training. That Ford was to be successful at Ashton Gate is of great credit to him, as coming from City's arch-rivals he had to win over the fans as well as the players. Initially the fans were not greatly impressed in having an Eastville man at the helm, but the entertaining football that was played through most of his period in charge changed all that.

With Tommy Cavanagh sold to Carlisle for £1,000 and Hinshelwood to Millwall for £1,1000, one of Ford's first tasks was to re-sign Frank Jacobs, who was on the point of joining Bristol Rovers, and persuade Archie Taylor not to sign for York. Ford then parted with nearly £5,000 to Newcastle to secure the services of Alex Tait, a qualified schoolmaster, as well as obtaining on free transfers goalkeeper Harry Nicholson (Leyton Orient) hot-shot John Ryan (Newcastle) and Jack Boxley (Coventry). The unfortunate Graham and McCann story was closed with the summer transfer of the former to Leyton Orient for £5,250 and the latter's October move to Huddersfield. McCann went in exchange for centre-half Jack Connor, with City later parting with £3,000 to the Leeds Road club for twenty-year-old rangy half-back Gordon Low.

For all that, the 1960-61 campaign was difficult, with John Atyeo injured in an opening-day defeat at Bradford City. In the national Third Division, created in 1958-59 when the top halves of the North and South sections joined together, with the remainder making up Division Four, City's attack was always potent. They were never to score fewer than 50 home League goals in any of the five seasons that they were destined to inhabit this sphere. As a counter-balance, away form in 1960-61 threatened further relegation, but improvement from mid-January saw City rise up the table. It was not until 25 February that City obtained their first League win on their travels, when Andy Porter's 86th-minute own-goal brought a 1-0 success at Watford, but home form improved to such an extent that fourteenth place was secured by the end of the season.

Of City's League games, the visit of Torquay on 31 March stands out because of Terry Bush marking his debut with two goals in the 2-1 success. The first of these after barely 65 seconds was outstanding – lobbing the ball in from the edge of the area.

With Bristol Rovers beating Fulham 2-1 in the first ever Football League Cup-tie, by virtue of kicking-off earlier than the rest on 26 September, City, who had a first-round bye, opened their account in the competition when Jack Boxley shot in off an upright to earn a 1-1 draw at Aldershot on 10 October. Winning the replay 3-0 brought a trip to

Nottingham Forest for a Tuesday afternoon tie, which was lost 1-2 in front of just 3,690 spectators on 15 November.

However, it was in the FA Cup where the goals really flowed. It was a Guy Fawkes spectacular at Ashton Gate against luckless Sussex amateurs Chichester, who had chosen to forfeit home advantage. City took no prisoners in the first half as they romped into an 8-0 lead. To the annoyance of the home fans, they eased up after the break as they made unsuccessful attempts to set up Jantzen Derrick to score. Still, an 11-0 victory at the finish was their biggest winning margin since beating Eastleigh 14-1 on 26 January 1898.

It had been apparent from the kick-off that City were yards faster than their opponents and later in the game their superior stamina showed through as well. The score could easily have been as high as twenty if the players had not become careless with their shooting and approach work. Bobby Williams had an enjoyable time, playing some masterful football and, with his namesake, Adrian, was much too clever for the ponderous visitors, making and missing some six chances. Thrice in the space of the first eight minutes of the second half, he cut through the defence, walked round centre-half Bailey, and calmly steered open-goal opportunities wide of the target.

Fred Ford dismissed the game's spurned chances by stating: 'People expected us to win 6-0, we got eleven so there can be no complaints. It takes some doing to get eleven goals in any type of football, as it doesn't even happen in light-hearted practise games.' Individual honours naturally belonged to the forwards, John Atyeo topping the list with five goals, scoring his first three in the space of eleven minutes towards the end of the first half, when City were already three up. His best goal was also the best of the game, his second, when he lobbed Jack Connor's pass first-time into the top corner of the net. Bobby Williams netted twice, the second a deflection off Bailey's leg. Alex Tait got one and Adrian Williams, who opened the scoring after five minutes, grabbed three, but Derrick, who with Tait played wide on the flanks in accordance with instructions, did not shine as brightly as he might have done.

A replay win over Southern League King's Lynn followed, and a 1-0 victory at Second Division Plymouth set up a tie with top-flight Leicester. At Filbert Street, against the eventual Cup finalists, City lost 1-5 after the first game had been abandoned at the interval due to the waterlogged pitch.

Despite City beating the Rovers in the Gloucestershire Cup at the end of the season, it could not disguise the fact that some of their League displays had not been inspiring. However, it was thought that the future was bright, as under Fred Ford there was no suggestion of the split there had been the previous season. The new manager, though, was fortunate in having inherited Doherty's thriving youth set up, which had seen City reach the FA Youth Cup semi-final in 1959-60 when an 18,181 crowd on 5 April 1960 saw Chelsea win the first leg 3-0 at Ashton Gate. The ex-manager's Wessex Youth League brainchild was up and running in 1960-61 when the City finished runners-up to Swindon. The competition was to continue for seven seasons, with City winning the championship in 1961-62, 1964-65, 1965-66 and 1966-67, as well as finishing runners-up in 1962-63 and 1967-68.

Along with the departure to Oldham for £1,000 of Alan Williams, who had lost form after looking one of the best City discoveries for years, others who moved on were Cliff Duffin, who was replaced by ex-City player Cliff Morgan as scout, as well as Bob Anderson who finally called it a day after a fruitless two-year attempt to recover from a slipped disc. Adding to this list, the close season saw Tommy Burden's retirement, and the departure of Gordon Hopkinson, whilst Roger Collinson went off to Stockport on a free transfer.

Sturdy full-back Alec Briggs was emerging from City's reserves, as were Brian Clark and Roger Peters, who both made their debuts in the final League match, against Brentford, when the band lustily played to mark Tommy Burden's last game. Left-winger David Noake was bought from Luton for £750, and the former Bristol Rovers goalkeeper Ron Nicholls – the Gloucestershire cricket opening batsman – was signed from Cardiff.

Despite City cutting their cost by misguidedly withdrawing their reserves from the Football Combination, optimism was once more in the air as the 1961-62 campaign dawned, but the ending of the maximum wage was to threaten the stability of many clubs and bring us to the point of absurdity to which the game has descended in recent years.

The fans were not to be disappointed in 1961-62, even though promotion would remain beyond City's grasp. With the FA soon to lift their ban on pre-season friendlies, the long-standing tradition of public pre-season trial matches at Ashton Gate came to an end in front of a 1,476 crowd on 12 August 1961 when the Reds beat the Whites 3-2.

With Notts County celebrating their centenary year, City's 0-1 defeat in the season's opener at Meadow Lane was not unexpected, even though Roy Horobin's last-minute penalty winner was hard to take. Matters soon evened themselves out, though, as in the next game against Northampton John Atyeo availed himself of Jimmy Moran's 30-yard injudicious back-pass to clinch a fortunate victory. After completing the double over

Northampton a week later, there followed a visit to Peterborough, where City turned in a fine performance, winning 4-3 to deprive the Posh of their unblemished record.

That win had the effect of sending City into a tailspin, with only one point being gained from the next five games. Extra firepower was needed, with ex-Rover Barrie Meyer recruited from Newport for £800. A 3-2 success at home to Southend on 26 September sparked a revival, and with 3-0 victories at home to Grimsby and Brentford, as well as a thrilling 5-3 win over Swindon, things appeared to be on the up until a 3-7 reverse was suffered at Barnsley on 11 November. Happily, the next four games were won, among them the hammering of six goals into the Notts County net on 16 December. A thrilling 4-3 success at Halifax on 27 January was followed two weeks later by another six-goal haul, this time against Bradford Park Avenue, which served to put City in the promotion places for the first time.

It could not last, and it did not – two away defeats followed, including a 0-1 loss at Grimsby when City borrowed the Mariners' sky blue and white change kit. Second-half goals from John Atyeo and Tommy Casey stopped the rot as Watford were beaten 2-1 on 3 March, but the visit of leaders Portsmouth three days later provided a rude awakening with City being run off their feet as the visitors won 4-0.

A 4-0 success at Swindon and a 4-1 beating of Torquay restored belief before swords had to be crossed once more with Portsmouth. Again put in their place in losing 0-5 at Fratton Park, City's season petered out, and with just a couple of wins in the remaining seven games, City had to be satisfied with a finishing position of sixth.

Perhaps manager Fred Ford could be faulted for persevering with too many out of form players, but overall he had done a good job. City's outstanding player was Jack Connor, a popular personality, and there was no doubt he was the best centre-half in the Third Division. The Ashton Gate find of the season was seventeen-year-old full-back Tony Ford, who had joined winger Roger 'Lou' Peters on a week's tour of Israel with the England Youth team after winning his cap versus Germany. Notable among those who moved on was Peter McCall, later to play for England at bowls. He went off to Oldham, where he teamed up again with Alan Williams.

The 1961-62 season was notable for the fact that the *Pink 'Un* sports paper breathed its last on 27 January 1962, the same day as the *Bristol Evening World* met its demise. Fortunately, the *Bristol Evening Post* continued to publish the *Green 'Un*, although the use of green paper was discontinued from the issue of 8 December 1962.

A touch of déjà-vu at the end of 1961-62, with yet another of City's discarded players inspiring their new club to top-flight status. This time it was Malcolm Graham, whose ability at Ashton Gate had never been in doubt with eight goals in the fourteen games played. Scoring seven goals in nineteen appearances during his first season at Brisbane Road, his fitness improved to such an extent the following campaign that he made 29 League appearances and scored thirteen goals. A season in the top flight was his reward, finishing as top scorer with nine goals in 27 appearances for bottom-placed Leyton Orient.

City fans were no longer much concerned with the accomplishments of Malcolm Graham; the question for them was whether their favourites could improve further in 1962-63, when once more hostilities would be renewed with Bristol Rovers, following their relegation from the Second Division. The answer turned out to be no as, despite notching up a century of goals, a disappointing campaign ensued which saw City finish fourteenth. Happily, even this lowly position was good enough to better that of nineteenth-placed Rovers and thus bring to an end their rivals' fourteen-season reign as the best team in Bristol.

Unfortunately, it would not mark complete superiority for City, as in front of an 8,018 Eastville crowd, Rovers regained the Gloucestershire Cup with a 2-1 success on 23 May 1963.

Many City fans were sorry to see the energetic and popular David Noake among those released. Derrick Lythgoe and Ray Savino were signed from Norwich for £4,000 and £5,000 respectively, as well as £2,000 being found to capture David Pyle from Bristol Rovers.

The start of the 1962-63 season saw, for the fifth time since 1914, a Combined Bristol team assembled. Arsenal were again the visitors, as they had been three years earlier, but on this occasion, in front of a 19,962 crowd, generating £3,400 receipts in aid of the St Mary Redcliffe Church Restoration Fund, the Gunners proved much too good. A Keith Williams 70th-minute strike could not overcome John Barnwell's two first-half goals into the Covered End net at Ashton Gate on 8 August 1962.

Combined XI: Million (Rovers); Bradford (Rovers), Thresher (City); Sykes (Rovers), Connor (City), Casey (City); Savino (City) (sub Derrick (City), Atyeo (City), K Williams (Rovers), R Williams (City), R Jones (Rovers).

Arsenal: McKechnie; Magill, McCullough; Clamp, Neill, Sneddon (Brown); McLeod (Strong), Barnwell, Baker, Eastham, Skirton.

Sadly, in contrast to the previous season, 1962-63 was to prove very disappointing, except for the fact that City ratcheted up a century of league goals, despite their fourteenth position being the lowest ever for a club achieving this feat. Requiring four goals against Reading in their final game it was not until the 71st minute that Alex Tait headed in to bring up the three-figure mark.

The 5-2 success at Bradford Park Avenue on 29 September was possibly City's best display of the season, but other high-scoring encounters at Carlisle (5-2) and Halifax (5-2), as well as those at home to Southend (6-3) and Barnsley (5-2), produced much in the way of excitement.

Amazingly, Barrie Meyer notched a hat-trick in the 6-3 home win over Southend on 16 April, only to find himself dropped for the next game. Even more amazingly for the Gloucestershire wicket-keeper, who would go on to become a test match umpire, this was to be his last ever game for the City.

The season was badly disrupted by 'the big freeze'. The winter of 1962-63 was the worse since 1947, with heavy snowfall at the turn of the year and freezing conditions persisting right through until March. This brought about much delay in settling City's FA Cup encounter with Aston Villa. Originally scheduled to be played at Ashton Gate on 5 January, it was twice postponed before a 1-1 draw was played eleven days later. This then set up a sequence of nine more postponements before the tie was finally brought off at Villa Park on 7 March, where City put on a fine performance before losing 2-3.

Whilst 'the big freeze' disrupted football on the pitch, it was the betting scandal that threatened the game's very foundations. As previously mentioned in regard to certain City games in 1958-59 and 1959-60, fans had always been aware of certain matches not being played in the spirit of the game, but such suspicions hardly touched the depths of the organised betting syndicate now exposed. The whistle was blown by the Bristol Rovers manager, Bert Tann, one of the most honest and upright people you could ever wish to meet.

In April 1963, the Rovers hit the headlines following allegations by *The People* that their keeper Esmond Million had accepted a £300 inducement to allow Bradford to win a vital relegation clash on 20 April. It was alleged that Million had admitted letting in two goals which he could have saved. With Rovers having stormed into a 2-0 lead, Million's two obvious errors aroused instant suspicions. The first was a simple back-pass, which he let slip through his fingers; the second was the result of 'missing' a cross. With an accomplice in striker Keith Williams, who had a change of heart and laid on the pass for the opening goal, the pair had also tried unsuccessfully to lure full-back Gwyn Jones into the act.

Both Million and Williams were to pay a heavy price, which must have been even worse for them as, with the afflicted game being drawn, they did not receive any of the bribe money. From this exposé, the poisonous details of a well-organised betting syndicate emerged. Neither the fact of the Rovers being in desperate straits near the foot of the table, or that both players had been signed for hefty fees at the start of the season, dissuaded Tann from immediately suspending both men.

Three months later they appeared at Doncaster Magistrates Court, alongside Brian Phillips, the Mansfield defender and ex-team-mate of Million. Phillips emerged as the syndicate's 'middle man' and both he and Williams were fined £50, and Million £100. All three were suspended for life by the Football Association. Eventually, with Mansfield's Jimmy Gauld identified as the ringleader, others were caught up in the affair and ten players, including England internationals Tony Kay and Peter Swan, were called to account at Nottingham Assizes, where their eleven-day trial started on 12 January 1965. All were found guilty and Mr Justice Lawton pronounced sentences as follows: Jimmy Gauld four years imprisonment and ordered to pay costs of £5,000; Brian Phillips (Mansfield) and John Fountain (York) fifteen months; Richard Beattie (Peterborough) nine months; Sammy Chapman (Mansfield), Ron Howells (Walsall) and Ken Thomson (Hartlepools) six months; Tony Kay (Everton), David 'Bronco' Layne (Sheffield Wednesday) and Peter Swan (Sheffield Wednesday) four months. A tale of the times maybe, but it is sad to reflect that despite the ending of the maximum wage in 1961 there were still those willing to defraud the paying public in such a way.

As with the Bristol Rovers players eighteen months earlier, all received life bans from the Football Association, but they were allowed to appeal against this after seven years. With the bans being lifted in 1972, Swan returned to action with Sheffield Wednesday. After making fifteen further appearances, plus two as substitute for Wednesday in 1972-73, he saw out his Football League career with Bury the following season. Layne also returned to Sheffield Wednesday, but only turned out for their reserves before making four appearances for Hereford United.

Prior to the 1963-64 campaign getting started, City turned out in a friendly at Portsmouth on 17 August, when goals from John Atyeo and Jantzen Derrick could not prevent a 2-3 defeat. Having signed skilful midfielder Ken Waterhouse for £3,000 from Rotherham and goalkeeper Mike Gibson from Shrewsbury for £5,000 towards the end of the previous season, City's defence was much improved. Certainly in Gibson, City picked up a gem, probably their best ever goalkeeper to that point. Adding ex-Rovers hot-shot Peter Hooper to the mix after being signed in the close season for £11,250 from Cardiff, all seemed set for an interesting season ahead.

The fans did not know quite what to think when the Rovers were trounced 3-0 in a lack-lustre League opener, but a 2-1 success in City's next game at promoted Brentford made them think all was rosy. A 1-4 defeat at Port Vale then brought everyone back to earth. Despite a 2-0 home victory over Notts County on 7 September, there followed an eight-game winless sequence, before a 3-1 home success over Peterborough restored a measure of confidence. With City in fourteenth place there was surely only one way to go, and that was up. Fortunately, this proved to be the case, and with away victories at Bournemouth (1-0), Luton (4-1), Barnsley (4-2), QPR (2-0), Oldham (2-1), Millwall (1-0), as well as notable home wins over Luton (5-1), Walsall (5-1), Wrexham (4-0) and Barnsley (5-2), City climbed the table to find themselves occupying fifth spot at the season's conclusion.

A satisfactory campaign, although losing 0-4 at Eastville against the Rovers on 14 December was a blot, as was the 0-4 defeat inflicted by Mansfield on their muddy Field Mill ground on 30 March, a result that effectively torpedoed City's promotion ambitions. This very talented Mansfield side, who had played brilliantly in the first half at Ashton Gate three days earlier in winning 3-2, narrowly missed out on promotion the following season, but more on that later.

A somewhat strange transfer during the season saw John Kurila join the City from Canadian Club Hamilton Steelers for £3,000. He then made the club a quick £2,000 profit when sold to his former English club Northampton just four months later.

City's FA Cup defeat by Sunderland at Roker Park on 25 January 1964 was not without its irony for those fans who travelled by special train. Costing £1 10s, this trip started from Parson Street Station at 11.20pm on Friday evening, when, despite the bitter weather, the carriage heating was so excessive that the windows had to be opened. This proved to be unwise, as it was not long before the heating broke down, and a freezing train-load of supporters had to shiver outside Birmingham for three hours while a cow on the line was 'dealt with'. Arriving at Sunderland at 11am instead of the scheduled 8.02am, a forlorn group of supporters then witnessed a 1-6 defeat orchestrated by Johnny Crossan, whom City had signed from Coleraine in October 1958. Due to allegations that he had been paid whilst an amateur, his registration was refused. Banned from playing in England, Crossan joined Sparta Rotterdam, and later played in the European Cup with Standard Liege, before the ban was lifted. He signed for Sunderland in October 1962.

The FA Cup run had started by beating Corby away on 16 November before going to St James Park to face an Exeter side that included centre-forward Dermot Curtis. He had been a City player when playing for Eire against John Atyeo's England in two World Cup qualifiers in 1956-57. Whilst Atyeo netted twice against Exeter, it was neither of the two internationals who impressed. The star was City keeper Mike Gibson who pulled off at least eight fine saves to keep Exeter at bay. Progressing to the third round by winning 2-0, City were lucky to survive at Doncaster, where they took it too easily after dominating the first half. With City saved by Clark's scrambled equaliser, it brought Doncaster's inside-left Alick Jeffrey back to Ashton Gate, where he had suffered his horrific injury seven years earlier. Fortunately, other than City winning 2-0, his return passed without incident.

The 1963-64 season concluded with the Gloucestershire Cup being drawn 2-2 on 28 April, prior to City popping over to Ireland where victories were gained at the expense of Cork Hibs and Limerick.

Disappointment, certainly, in missing out on promotion, but City had certainly given value for money in 1963-64 as they frequently played with style and swagger. The inside trio of Clark, Atyeo and Williams linked up wonderfully, but in the end it proved not to be enough and the manager decided upon a more direct style for the following season.

The 1964-65 campaign dawned with high expectations of City gaining promotion. In this respect the fans were not to be disappointed, but it was a close-run thing. With Hull and Bristol Rovers virtually throwing their chances away, the championship was secured by unfancied Carlisle, with City second by virtue of a better goal-average than Mansfield.

City had added to their squad with the capture of Charles 'Chuck' Drury from WBA for £7,500 and Brian Thurlow from Norwich for £2,800. In the event, Thurlow never made the first team, whilst injury saw Drury make just one appearance during the first half of the season, before being one of the stars of City's late promotion push.

Losing the opening match 2-5 at relegated Scunthorpe was hardly the start City were hoping for, but as the author remarked to his friends on the drive back to Bristol from the Old Show Ground, City had lost by the same scoreline at the start of their record-breaking 1905-06 campaign. The goals then flowed, with City scoring 25 times whilst only conceding four in the process of winning five and drawing one to go top of the table on 14 September. Predictably, this form was not to be sustained and in losing their next game 2-3 at Hull, decline set in. A 3-7 loss to Oldham at Boundary Park on 28 October served to push City down to eleventh, and more inconsistent form had many fans dismissing promotion as wishful thinking, especially when a Kit Napier goal consigned City to defeat on a chilly Friday night at Workington on 15 January.

Perhaps some of the City players had imbued too much at the Gretna Green wedding of nineteen-year-old Sheffield Beauty Queen Denise Franklin and photographer Harry Pressley, which they had attended earlier in the day. With John Atyeo being dropped for the first time since fully establishing himself, it was hardly surprising that City returned from promotion-chasers Gillingham both pointless and goalless on 5 February. Rumours of manager Fred Ford's imminent sacking began to circulate.

The following week's home game was looked upon as City's 'last chance saloon' and it really did seem all up when Joe Davis dispatched a penalty to give Bristol Rovers the lead. But goals from Brian Clark and Terry Bush produced a 2-1 win, which was to set City up for an amazing run of success – losing just one of their remaining fixtures.

Even so, it was not until a 3-0 victory at Shrewsbury in the penultimate game that City found themselves in a promotion spot, thanks to a better goal-average than that of Mansfield, who had beaten City 3-0 on their Field Mill ground on 20 March. With just one game left, the tension leading up to City's home clash with Oldham was unbearable. With Mansfield expected to win at bottom of the table Barnsley, many of the 28,248 fans who crammed into Ashton Gate on 24 April had pieces of paper with various goal-average permutations written thereupon. They certainly had need of them, because Mansfield won 3-2, but with City beating an Oldham side containing two old Ashton Gate favourites, Peter McCall and Alan Williams, the promotion prize was secured with a goal average of 1.6727 compared to Mansfield's 1.5574.

John Atyeo wept, the partisan Ashton Gate crowd cheered loudly, and manager Ford felt satisfied and fulfilled with City beating Oldham to clinch promotion.

The game itself did not reach the dizzy heights of the celebrations, there being too much at stake for City not to be nervous. With Ken Branagan having cleared off the line from Atyeo, the City supporters remained on edge until first half-time injury-time. Gerry Sharpe, deputising for the injured Ray Savino, sent over a ball which evaded everyone until finding Roger Peters, whose mis-hit shot was dribbling wide until Brian Clark nipped in to score his 22nd League goal of the season.

After the interval, Branagan effected another goal-line clearance to thwart Atyeo, but City's veteran forward was not to be denied seven minutes from the finish. Pulling down a centre from Terry Bush, Atyeo fired a low, hard shot into the Oldham net.

Pure relief, then, at the final whistle, which perhaps explains City losing 2-3 against Bristol Rovers in the Gloucestershire Cup, in front of an 8,907 Eastville crowd on 26 April.

City enjoyed a decent run in the FA Cup. Beating Fourth Division promotion chasers Brighton, who had ex-Spurs players Bobby Smith and Mel Hopkins in their side, City clinched a 3-0 victory over Bournemouth at Dean Court, just a week after having won there in the League. With the big boys in the third round, City were unfortunate not to do more than draw against First Division Sheffield United at Ashton Gate, before losing the replay 0-3 at Bramall Lane, where Bobby 'Shadow' Williams caught the eye of Rotherham boss Danny Williams, who splashed out £9,200 to obtain his signature.

Whilst there was joy on one side of Bristol and despair on the other, both sets of supporters were saddened by the final appearance of the iconic sports cartoons in the local press. Throughout this early post-war period Jim Neal ('Speed') in the *Bristol Evening World* and Bob Bennett in the *Bristol Evening Post* kept us entertained with their work, but it all came to a close for City fans on 15 March 1965 with the latter's depiction of Saturday's 1-0 win over Luton.

With City reinforced by the signing of George Showell from Wolves for £3,000, the 1965-66 season presented a mouth-watering prospect for the fans, who were excited by the prospect of Bolton, Derby, Manchester City, Preston, and Wolves coming to Ashton Gate. Unlikely as it would have seemed in August, City should have clinched a second successive promotion, but as in 1906-07 when they lost out for the League title, they were undone over Easter. On Good Friday, Southampton departed from Ashton Gate with a 1-0 success despite being outplayed, whilst at the Dell three days later a last-minute goal by Terry Paine salvaged a point for the Saints.

The difference between success and failure is very slim and in City's case it was. Those two results meant it was the Saints who claimed the promotion prize. Still, for City to finish fifth on their return to the Second Division was no mean achievement, especially as it was not until the last game of the season that they managed to score more than two goals in a home game. With John Atyeo having announced his retirement, the fixture against Ipswich on 10 May was his last game. Needing to score twice to bring his total to 350 in League and Cup, he duly complied with a 75th-minute header and a firm shot nine minutes later to clinch a 4-1 success.

Two days later the Rovers came to Ashton Gate and kept their hold on the Gloucestershire Cup with a 1-0 win in front of a 9,431 crowd.

A successful season though, this success being reflected in a profit of £22,701 declared, adding to that of £13,917 the previous campaign.

The summer of 1966 brought the demolition of the Number Two Stand at Ashton Gate, a structure which had been partially destroyed by fire on the evening of 31 August 1929. Erected by Bedminster FC when they owned the ground in the late 1890s, it was turned sideways to fit in with the revised orientation of the pitch when City moved here in 1904. A ramshackle structure it may well have been, but the look of the stadium was hardly improved by its removal, as it was to be four years before the Dolman Stand would rise in its place.

Now we turn to 1966-67, the final season of the early post-war era. The excitement of England winning the World Cup at Wembley was not readily apparent at Ashton Gate during the early part of the campaign, although a group of City fans, including your author, formed Bristol Casuals AFC to take part in the inaugural season of the Bristol & District Amateur Sunday Football League. After losing their opener 4-9 against the Showmen's Guild on Clevedon Town's Teignmouth Road ground on 4 September, the Casuals won their second match, 4-2 away to the South West Regional Hospital Board.

Clutching at straws, maybe, but at least City managed to halt their long losing run in the Football League Cup, even though they still failed to make progress in the competition. A 1-1 home draw with Swansea on 13 September brought to an end a run of six successive defeats that started at Nottingham Forest in the third round in 1960-61, and continued with exits against York (a), Rotherham (h), Gillingham (a), Carlisle (a) and Shrewsbury (a). After Dickie Down had given City a third-minute lead at the Vetch, Keith Todd levelled to force extra-time. Brian Evans then fired in a low-angled drive to win the game for the Swans.

Thankfully, City would do much better in the FA Cup. Overcoming Halifax at home after drawing at the Shay, First Division Southampton were beaten at Ashton Gate before a trip to White Hart Lane to face Tottenham Hotspur in the fifth round. Here it was a tale of two penalties, with Chris Crowe firing wide from a re-take after Tony Ford had his effort saved. It took ace goalscorer Jimmy Greaves to show them how it should be done, slotting home his last-minute spot-kick to consign City to a 0-2 defeat.

In the League, City struggled after losing their opening four games. There was talk of coaxing John Atyeo back from retirement. Whilst this came to nought, he did grace the Ashton Gate pitch once more, on the occasion of his benefit match when star-studded Leeds provided the opposition on 10 October. The Jules Rimet Trophy, which England had won at Wembley a few months earlier, was paraded around the pitch to the delight of the 17,425 spectators who turned up hoping to see Atyeo score at least one more time. They were doomed to disappointment, the big man failing to register as Leeds brought off a 4-2 success.

With Brian Clark out of form, he went to Huddersfield in exchange for the skilful John Quigley and £2,500. Clark was to rediscover his zest, especially on moving to Cardiff a year later, whilst City had the benefit of a skilful and industrious midfielder who would prove to be one of the best players they have ever had. Despite this, however, City continued to languish and it took the signing of Chris Crowe from Nottingham Forest for £15,000 and Hugh McIlmoyle, who cost a club record fee of £27,000 from Wolves, to turn things around. After losing 1-5 at Cardiff on 31 December, City's beating of Wolves at Ashton Gate on 7 January inspired the team to such an extent that they suffered only five more reverses during the rest of the season and finished fifteenth.

Given the high transfer expenditure, it occasioned little surprise that a loss of £26,890 was announced at the AGM held in the 51 Club at Ashton Gate on 13 November 1967.

The euphoria generated by this revival was such that it enticed an unusually large 17,433 crowd at Eastville for the Gloucestershire Cup clash on 9 May. Goals from Peters, Crowe, as well as Ford's 70th-minute penalty made sure of City winning the prized trophy outright for the first time since 1961-62.

Unfortunately, City were not able to wrest the Friendship Cup from Hanover's grasp. In this competition for the handsome trophy put up by the *Bristol Evening Post* in celebration of 21 years of twinning of the two cities, the Robins, having lost 2-3 in front of a 4,599 crowd at Ashton Gate on 16 November, went down 1-2 in Germany on 23 May.

With what was thought of as a settled and exciting team, the City fans were confident of a promotion bid in 1967-68 but, as we all know, matters are rarely that straightforward for the Ashton Gate club. The story of 1967 onwards is now taken up in *Bristol City: The Modern Era*.

Don Clark heads in City's opener versus Swansea Town
at Ashton Gate on 6 September 1947

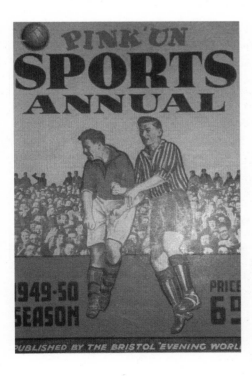

Ashton Gate action from the first round FA Cup clash
against Gloucester City on 25 November 1950

City won this second round FA Cup-tie against Wrexham
at Ashton Gate 2-1 on 9 December 1950

Bristol City's championship winning side of 1954-55. Note the smart Arsenal-style kit.
Left to right: Back row: Wilf Copping (trainer), Arthur Milton, Ivor Guy,
Bob Anderson, John Atyeo, Cyril Williams, Mike Thresher. Front row: 'Ginger'
Peacock, Jimmy Rogers, Jack White (captain), Tommy Burden, Jack Boxley

Jack Boxley, John Atyeo, Jimmy Rogers, Harry Dolman, Bob Anderson, and 'Ginger' Peacock look on as Arthur Oakley presents the Third Division (South) Championship Shield to City captain Jack White after the home draw with Newport on 23 April 1955

John Atyeo's shot finds the back of the net at Vicarage Road to clinch a 2-0 success over Watford on 2 April 1955

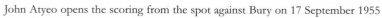

John Atyeo opens the scoring from the spot against Bury on 17 September 1955

Alec Eisentrager is unsuccessful with this effort during City's 3-1 win
against Bury on 17 September 1955

The referee makes sure he is well placed to see when City's winning goal crosses the
line against Sheffield Wednesday on 19 November 1955

This Speed cartoon of City's controversial game versus Swansea Town appeared in the
Bristol Evening World of 28 April 1958

This aerial view shows Ashton Gate in the mid to late 1950s

Johnny Haynes and John Atyeo look on as Stanley Matthews shakes hands with
Earl Mountbatten prior to an England game

John Atyeo heads in for City versus Peterborough United
at Ashton Gate on 13 January 1962

City training 1950s style outside of the Covered End turnstiles at Ashton Gate

Alex Tait celebrates during City's 2-0 home win over Lincoln City on 3 February 1962

John Atyeo challenges the Watford goalkeeper Dave Underwood
at Ashton Gate on 3 March 1962

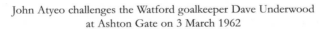

John Atyeo and Alex Tait find themselves outnumbered by the Halifax defenders at
Ashton Gate on 14 April 1962

This Bob Bennett cartoon of City's 5-2 thrashing of Barnsley appeared in the
Bristol Evening Post of 29 October 1962

Peter Hooper lurks at the far post, whilst John Atyeo (No 9) is prominent in City's
attack versus Oldham Athletic at Ashton Gate on 29 February 1964

City's iconic floodlights being
installed at Ashton Gate during
December 1965

Bristol City 1965-66. Note the all-red strip that was introduced this season.
Left to right: Back row: 'Chuck' Drury, Jack Connor, Tony Ford,
Mike Gibson, Alec Briggs, Gordon Low.
Front row: 'Lou' Peters, John Atyeo, Terry Bush, Brian Clark, Peter Hooper

A Fred Ford team-talk in 1966-67

TACTICS TALK BY FRED FORD

Manager Fred Ford briefs the forward line during a recent training session. Left to right: John Quigley, Jantzen Derrick, Terry Bush, Chris Crowe and Roger Peters.

GUIDE TO SEASONAL SUMMARIES

Col 1: Match number (for league fixtures); Round (for cup-ties).
        e.g. 4R means 'Fourth round replay.'

Col 2: Date of the fixture and whether Home (H), Away (A), or Neutral (N).

Col 3: Opposition.

Col 4: Attendances. Home gates appear in roman; Away gates in *italics*.
        Figures in **bold** indicate the largest and smallest gates, at home and away.
        Average home and away attendances appear after the final league match.

Col 5: Respective league positions of City and opponents after the game.
        City's position appears on the top line in roman.
        Their opponents' position appears on the second line in *italics*.
        For cup-ties, the division and position of opponents is provided.
        e.g. 2:12 means the opposition are twelfth in Division 2.

Col 6: The top line shows the result: W(in), D(raw), or L(ose).
        The second line shows City's cumulative points total.

Col 7: The match score, City's given first.
        Scores in **bold** show City's biggest league win and heaviest defeat.

Col 8: The half-time score, City' given first.

Col 9: The top line shows City's scorers and times of goals in roman.
        The second line shows opponents' scorers and times of goals in *italics*.
        A 'p' after the time of a goal denotes a penalty; 'og' an own-goal.
        The third line gives the name of the match referee.

Team line-ups: City's line-ups appear on top line, irrespective of whether
        they are home or away. Opposition teams are on the second line in *italics*.
        Players of either side who are sent off are marked !
        City's players making their league debuts are displayed in **bold**.

Substitutes: Names of substitutes appear only if they actually took the field.
        A player substituted is marked *

N.B.   For clarity, all information appearing in *italics* relates to opposing teams.

LEAGUE DIVISION 3 (SOUTH) Manager: Bob Hewison SEASON 1946-47

Match Results

No		Date	Opponent	Att	Pos	Res	Pt	F-A	H-T	Scorers, Times, and Referees
1	A	31/8	ALDERSHOT	6,483		L	0	3-4	0-1	Rowland 61(og), Clark 75, Thomas 90, Brooks 83 / Griffiths 38p, 55, 71, Brooks 83. Ref: G Searle
2	H	4/9	NORWICH	12,033 (£728.4.8)		W	2	2-1	0-1	Clark 55, Hargreaves 65 / Guy 37
3	H	7/9	BRIGHTON	21,316 (£1,318.12.3)	11	D	3	0-0	0-0	
4	A	11/9	NOTTS CO	17,522	6	W	5	3-0	2-0	Thomas 1, Chilcott 20, Clark 58. Ref: F Green
5	A	14/9	EXETER	13,100	3	W	7	3-1	2-1	Clark 34, 44, 50 / Wardle 1. Ref: J Wiltshire
6	A	18/9	NORWICH	11,038	4	D	8	2-2	0-1	Clark 69, 75 / Jones 17, Furness 89
7	H	21/9	PORT VALE	21,284 (£1,333.19.11)	3	W	10	3-0	2-0	Clark 10p, Williams 12, 83. Ref: F Milner
8	A	28/9	BRISTOL ROV	25,859 (£1,903.6.3)	2	W	12	3-0	3-0	Williams 2, Hargreaves 32, Clark 42. Ref: G Clark
9	A	5/10	SWINDON	25,031 (£1,909)	3	D	13	1-1	1-0	Thomas 43 / Williams 50. Ref: F Milner
10	H	12/10	BOURNEMOUTH	22,336 (£1,404.18.11)	3	W	15	1-0	1-0	Morgan 2. Ref: C Wakley (Cliff Morgan 2nd Benefit)

Line-ups (City in roman, opponents in italic)

No	1	2	3	4	5	6	7	8	9	10	11
1	Ferguson / *Reynolds*	Guy / *Rogers*	Bailey / *Sheppard*	Morgan / *Fitzgerald*	Roberts / *Rowland*	Jones / *Brown*	Dymond / *Hobbs*	Thomas / *Griffiths*	Clark / *Brooks*	Williams C / *Anderson*	Hargreaves / *Hassell*
2	Ferguson / *Hall*	Guy / *Reed*	Bailey / *Taylor*	Morgan / *Flack*	Roberts / *Robinson G*	Jones / *Robinson B*	Dymond / *Plunkett*	Thomas / *Walker*	Clark / *Guy*	Williams C / *Furness*	Hargreaves / *Church*
3	Ferguson / *Baldwin*	Guy / *Marriot*	Bailey / *Green*	Morgan / *Darling*	Roberts / *Trainor*	Jones / *Dugnall*	Dymond / *Stephens*	Thomas / *Wilson*	Clark / *Hindley*	Williams C / *Barker*	Hargreaves / *Hanlon*
4	Ferguson / *Brown*	Guy / *Corkhill*	Bailey / *Robinson*	Morgan / *Gannon*	Roberts / *Toser*	Jones / *Hubbard*	Chilcott / *Beresford*	Thomas / *Brown*	Clark / *Morral*	Williams C / *Cumner*	Hargreaves / *Parks*
5	Ferguson / *Hoyle*	Guy / *Murray*	Bailey / *Thompson*	Morgan / *Cutting*	Roberts / *Hanford*	Jones / *Walker*	Chilcott / *Wardle*	Thomas / *Hammond*	Clark / *Etdon*	Williams C / *Wright*	Hargreaves / *Regan*
6	Ferguson / *Davis*	Guy / *Flack*	Bailey / *Taylor*	Morgan / *Robinson*	Roberts / *Proctor*	Jones / *Williams*	Chilcott / *Plunkett*	Thomas / *Russell*	Clark / *Johnson*	Williams C / *Furness*	Hargreaves / *Jones*
7	Ferguson / *Heppell*	Guy / *Smith W*	Bailey / *Pursell*	Morgan / *Hallam*	Roberts / *Cheadle*	Jones / *McGarry*	Chilcott / *Byrne*	Thomas / *Allen*	Clark / *Lyman*	Williams C / *Jones W*	Hargreaves / *Bellin*
8	Ferguson / *Weare*	Guy / *Smith W*	Bailey / *Watkin*	Morgan / *Pitt*	Roberts / *Warren*	Jones / *Whitefield*	Chilcott / *Lewis*	Thomas / *Baldie*	Clark / *Lambden*	Williams C / *Curran*	Hargreaves / *Carr*
9	Ferguson / *Boulton*	Guy / *Trim*	Bailey / *Young*	Morgan / *Bingham*	Roberts / *Ithell*	Jones / *Cousins*	Chilcott / *Williams*	Thomas / *Lloyd*	Clark / *Stephens*	Williams C / *Lucas*	Hargreaves / *Jones*
10	Ferguson / *Bird*	Oram / *Marsden*	Bailey / *Sanaghan*	Morgan / *Gallacher*	Roberts / *Wilson*	Jones / *Woodward*	Chilcott / *Currie*	Thomas / *Paton*	Clark / *Kirkham*	Williams C / *Tagg*	Hargreaves / *McDonald*

Match Reports

1. The return of League Football, after a seven-year break due to the War, brings the same fixtures as the aborted 39-40 campaign. Unfortunately, for City it's not the same result as in this thriller they only have cause to be thankful that Steve Griffiths puts his 84th-minute spot-kick wide.

2. Norwich go in front against the run of play when Ferguson, thinking James Guy offside, lets the wet ball escape his grasp. Despite the visitors' goal having some amazing escapes, City fight back to win thanks to Clark's neat back-header and a well-placed free-kick by Hargreaves.

3. After City lose the toss and are set to defend the Open end, the fans are treated to a lively display, even though a lack of punch prevents a home win. Clark missed when clean through just before half-time, whilst keeper Harry Baldwin does well to save Guy's 35-yarder after the interval.

4. City find the form that had demolished Second Division Plymouth in their pre-season friendly. Notts had no answer after Chilcott had set up Thomas with his early score, before lobbing in the second himself. Following the interval, Clark's shot found the net with comparative ease.

5. City, playing in white shirts, soon recovered from the shock of going behind when George Wardle back-heeled the ball past Ferguson. They completely outshone the previously unbeaten home side and went on to take the points after Clark's fierce 20-yarder had brought them level.

6. With both the City and the officials being incorrectly informed of a 6pm kick-off instead of 5.30pm, this game started some 15 minutes after the scheduled time. Consequently the closing stages were played in semi-darkness and hardly anyone saw Billy Furness head in the equaliser.

7. City's fast and aggressive play, with Jones acting as a sixth forward, has Vale in a spin. Tom Cheadle's handball allows Clark to score easily from the spot shortly before Williams slots in number two. After the interval a carefully placed daisy-cutter sees Williams register yet again.

8. The girl band of the ATC entertained the crowd before this game, in which the Rovers battled gallantly against City's rock-like defence after the break. Following the half-volleyed opener, an offside-looking Hargreaves flicked in the second prior to Clark's header making it three.

9. A new record crowd at the County ground, including many travelling supporters and a spectator perched on the top of a telegraph pole, witness this dazzling game. A reverse pass by Hargreaves sets up Thomas to force in the opener, but Gordon Williams fires in Swindon's equaliser.

10. With Dennis Oram (the Knowle cricketer) taking the place of the injured Guy, City are given a hard fight against rivals who have often proved difficult. Fittingly, City skipper Cliff Morgan, on his second benefit, won the game when his free-kick slipped through the goalkeeper's hands.

Match Record (matches 11–21)

11 · H · MANSFIELD · 19/10
League position 2 · **W 5-2** (HT 3-2) · Opp pos 8 · Pts 17 · Att 17,357 (£1,008.9.7)
Thomas 1, Clark 15, 43, 46, *Bryant 3, Guy 38 (og)* [Williams 72]
Ref: G Appleyard

Ferguson	Guy	Bailey	Morgan	Roberts	Jones	Chilcott	Thomas	Clark	Williams C	Hargreaves
Wright	*Bramley*	*Everett*	*Smith*	*Barke*	*Chessell*	*Harper*	*Copestake*	*Bryant*	*Hogg*	*Calverley*

City's fast, constructive play, in this thrill-a-minute affair brings a well-deserved success. Both sides register with headers in a hectic opening spell, then Guy deflects in a shot from Eric Bryant after Clark had fired City back in front. A handily placed Williams taps in City's fifth.

---

12 · A · TORQUAY · 26/10
League position 2 · **W 3-2** (HT 2-0) · Opp pos 18 · Pts 19 · Att 7,682
Chilcott 3, 87, Morgan 11, *Calland 60p, Mercer 80*
Ref: J Wiltshire

Ferguson	Guy	Bailey	Morgan	Roberts	Jones	Chilcott	Thomas	Clark	Williams C	Hargreaves
Joslin	*Markham*	*Calland*	*Phillips*	*Head*	*Conley*	*Hillard*	*Pryde*	*Conley*	*Kernick*	*Mercer*

Thomas shoots the ball home for City's early lead and Morgan's fierce 20-yarder doubles the advantage. After Ferguson's collision with Joe Conley brings Torquay their spot-kick, City are shocked by Arthur Mercer's cross-shot leveller. Fortunately, Chilcott heads City's late winner.

---

13 · H · CRYSTAL PALACE · 2/11
League position 2 · **W 3-0** (HT 1-0) · Opp pos 16 · Pts 21 · Att 26,418 (£1,630.17.0)
Clark 13, 65, Williams 75

Ferguson	Guy	Bailey	Morgan	Roberts	Jones	Chilcott	Thomas	Clark	Williams C	Hargreaves
Graham	*Hudgell*	*Dawes*	*Lewis J*	*Bassett*	*Guthrie*	*Robson*	*Reece*	*Kurz*	*Lewis G*	*Girling*

Clark opens the scoring with a first-half rocket, then after the break gently slides in a ball that stops a few inches after trickling over the line. City's almost non-stop attacking after the interval brings further reward when Williams, receiving a Thomas pass, places the ball into the net.

---

14 · A · READING · 9/11
League position 2 · **W 5-2** (HT 3-1) · Opp pos 13 · Pts 23 · Att 16,208 (£1,313)
Williams 16, 90, Hargreaves 43, *McPh' 31, McK' 75* [Th' 45, Clark 50]

Ferguson	Guy	Bailey	Morgan	Roberts	Jones	Chilcott	Thomas	Clark	Williams C	Hargreaves
Churchill	*Glidden*	*Gulliver*	*Young*	*Wallbanks*	*McKenna*	*Chitty*	*Edelston M*	*McPhee*	*Layton*	*Deverall*

City, despite Magnus McPhee shooting the home side level after Williams had driven in the opener, show their promotion credentials at Elm Park. Clark's great 30-yarder and a Williams cross-drive tie up truly stunning victory after a Hargreaves header had restored City's advantage.

---

15 · H · WALSALL · 16/11
League position 3 · **L 1-2** (HT 1-0) · Opp pos 6 · Pts 23 · Att 26,424 (£1,613.17.2)
Peacock 35, *Darby 55, Skidmore 86p*
Ref: R Greenwood

Ferguson	Guy	Bailey	Morgan	Roberts	**Peacock**	Chilcott	Thomas	Clark	Williams C	Hargreaves
Lewis	*Methley*	*Skidmore*	*Newman*	*Foulkes*	*Crutchley*	*Maund*	*Talbot*	*Darby*	*Wilshaw*	*Davies*

Despite Ginger Peacock putting City ahead with a screamer from fully 35 yards that enters the net just under the bar, City's thirteen-match unbeaten run comes to an end. Doug Darby headed the Saddlers level, before being brought down by Bailey for the match-winning penalty.

---

16 · A · WATFORD · 23/11
League position 3 · **W 3-2** (HT 2-2) · Opp pos 11 · Pts 25 · Att 11,415 (£849.16.0)
Hargreaves 8, 85, Williams 21, *Evans 1, Harris 23*
Ref: J Tregallis

Ferguson	Oram	Bailey	Morgan	Roberts	Peacock	Chilcott	Thomas	Clark	Williams C	Hargreaves
Rigg	*Morgan*	*Gray*	*Ross*	*Farnen*	*Davies*	*Harper*	*Young*	*Dunderdale*	*Evans*	*Harris*

Despite the fates conspiring against them at the start when the referee fails to spot Ralph Evans handling the ball before driving in the opener, City take all the points at Vicarage Road. After Hargreaves bundled the keeper into the net for the equaliser, Williams side-foots City in front.

---

17 · A · LEYTON ORIENT · 7/12
League position 3 · **L 1-4** (HT 1-2) · Opp pos 21 · Pts 25 · Att 7,600
Williams 30, *Pullen 13, 70, 75, Morrad 40*
Ref: W Plyer

Ferguson	Guy	Bailey	Morgan	Roberts	Jones	Chilcott	Thomas	Clark	Williams C	Hargreaves
Tolliday	*Fullbrook*	*Ritson*	*Bacon*	*Bartlett*	*Ballard*	*Roberts*	*Hunt*	*Morrad*	*Pullen*	*Willshaw*

On a treacherous Osborne Road pitch, Orient's display belies their position at the foot of the table. After Walter Pullen drove in their opener, when Frank Morrad and Ferguson collided, City, despite Williams firing in a great equaliser, are unable to match the home side's enthusiasm.

---

18 · A · SOUTHEND · 21/12
League position 3 · **L 1-4** (HT 1-2) · Opp pos 4 · Pts 25 · Att 8,007
Clark 12, *Sibley 10p, Thompson 19, 60, 80*
Ref: A Devine

Eddolls	**Fox**	Bailey	Morgan	Roberts	Jones	Chilcott	Thomas	Clark	Williams C	**Cunningham**
Hankey	*Linton*	*Walton*	*Harris*	*Jackson*	*Montgomery*	*Sibley*	*Smirk*	*Thompson*	*Bennett*	*Lane*

The fog causes City a disrupted train journey to Southend and they only arrive five minutes prior to the kick-off. Against the run of play, the homesters take the lead with a harsh penalty, but Clark fires in a close-range leveller. Cyril Thompson runs clean through to claim his hat-trick.

---

19 · A · NORTHAMPTON · 25/12
League position 3 · **D 2-2** (HT 1-1) · Opp pos 15 · Pts 26 · Att 13,501
Williams, Hargreaves, *Smith, Garrett*

Eddolls	Fox	Bailey	Morgan	Roberts	Jones	Chilcott	Thomas	Clark	Williams C	Hargreaves
Jones	*Smalley*	*Barron*	*Lowery*	*Dennison*	*Blunt*	*Morrall*	*Smith*	*Garrett*	*Thompson*	*Roberts*

In this game, played on Christmas morning, City, after twice falling behind, battle well to pick up a point and halt a run of three successive defeats. Unfortunately, their lack of success this month has now left them lagging well behind Cardiff and QPR in the promotion stakes.

---

20 · H · NORTHAMPTON · 26/12
League position 4 · **L 2-3** (HT 2-1) · Opp pos 13 · Pts 26 · Att 23,109 (£1,402.9.10)
Thomas 8, Clark 30, *Smith 43, Garrett 50, Morrall 70*

Eddolls	Bailey	Fox	Morgan	Roberts	Jones	Chilcott	Thomas	Clark	Williams C	Hargreaves
Jones	*Smalley*	*Barron*	*Thompson*	*Dennison*	*McKenna*	*Roberts*	*Smith*	*Garrett*	*Morrall*	*Fowler*

Despite battling against a strong wind in the first half, City still manage to turn on the style to deservedly lead with goals from Thomas and Clark. Unfortunately, not only does the wind reverse direction after the break, but a terrific hailstorm renders the pitch an absolute quagmire.

---

21 · H · ALDERSHOT · 28/12
League position 3 · **W 9-0** (HT 6-0) · Opp pos 19 · Pts 28 · Att 17,690 (£1,060.8.9)
Hargreaves 1, 5, 36, Williams 44, [Clark 10, 25, 70, 87p, Jones 80]
Ref: G Searle

Eddolls	Morgan	Fox	Peacock	Roberts	Jones	Chilcott	Thomas	Clark	Williams C	Hargreaves
Gage	*Rogers*	*Sheppard*	*Fitzgerald*	*Rowland*	*Brown*	*Hobbs*	*White*	*Brooks*	*Griffiths*	*Hassell*

City's record League victory owes much to the Shots keeper who hardly lives up to his name. His collision with Williams allows Hargreaves to fire the opener into a vacant net, then, prior to letting Clark's drive go under his body for the third, he badly misjudges a cross for the second.

LEAGUE DIVISION 3 (SOUTH)

Manager: Bob Hewison — SEASON 1946-47

Each cell shows the City player (first) / the opponent's player (second).

No	Date		Opponent	1	2	3	4	5	6	7	8	9	10	11	Res	H-T	F-A	Att	Pos	Pt
22	4/1	A	BRIGHTON	Eddolls / Ball	Allen / Marriott	Fox / Willense	Peacock / Wilson	Roberts / Dugnolle	Jones / Darling	Chilcott / Stephens	Thomas / James	Clark / Sim	Williams C / Chapman	Hargreaves / Hanlon	D	1-0	1-1	9,527 (£994.8.9)	17	29
23	11/1	H	IPSWICH	Eddolls / Burns	Morgan / Bell	Fox / Rumbold	Peacock / Perrett	Roberts / O'Mahony	Jones / Baird	Chilcott / Day	Thomas / Pole	Clark / Parker S	Williams C / Parker T	Hargreaves / Little	L	1-2	1-2	16,894	6	29
24	18/1	H	EXETER	Cousins / Singleton	Guy / Thompson	Fox / Blood	Peacock / Cutting	Roberts / Hanford	Jones / Walker	Chilcott / Granville	Thomas / Owen	Clark / Ebdon	Williams C / Wright	Hargreaves / Regan	D	1-1	2-2	20,415 (£1,234.1.2)	10	30
25	1/2	H	BRISTOL ROV	Cousins / Weare	Guy / Bamford	Fox / Watkins	Peacock / Pitt	Roberts / Warren	Jones / McArthur	Chilcott / Wookey	Thomas / Hodges	Clark / Leamon	Williams C / Morgan J	Williams S / Carr	W	2-0	4-0	17,450 (£1,019.19.0)	20	32
26	8/2	H	SWINDON	Cousins / Boulton	Guy / Lloyd	Fox / Young	Peacock / Lovesay	Roberts / Ithell	Jones / Painter	Chilcott / Stephens W	Thomas / Lucas	Clark / Owen	Williams C / Paterson	Williams S / Emery	W	0-0	3-1	13,502 (£799.14.5)	7	34
27	15/2	A	BOURNEMOUTH	Ferguson / Bird	Guy / Marsden	Fox / Sanaghan	Peacock / Burke	Roberts / Wilson	Jones / Woodward	Chilcott / Dickie	Thomas / Gray	Clark / Currie	Williams C / Tagg	Williams S / McDonald	D	0-0	0-0	10,159	13	35
28	17/2	A	PORT VALE	Ferguson / Heppell	Heppell / Smith W	Fox / Pursell	Peacock / Todd	Roberts / Cheadle	Jones / Hallam	Chilcott / Triner	Thomas / Bryne	Clark / Painton	Williams C / Jones W	Williams S / Bellis	L	0-2	1-2	8,264	10	35
29	1/3	H	TORQUAY	Ferguson / Matier	Bailey / Keeton	Fox / Calland	Peacock / Towers	Roberts / Head	Kearney / Pryde	Chilcott / Smith C	Thomas / Shaw	Clark / Conley	Williams C / Harrower	Williams S / Mercer	W	2-0	5-0	20,596 (£1,223.8.3)	9	37
30	15/3	H	READING	Ferguson / O'Sullivan	Bailey / Clover	Fox / Gulliver	Peacock / Moyse	Roberts / Niblett	Kearney / Barney	Chilcott / Fisher	Thomas / Edelston M	Clark / Henley	Williams C / Blackman	Hargreaves / Deverall	W	3-0	5-2	10,140 (£570.4.9)	8	39
31	22/3	A	WALSALL	Lewis / Mathley	Guy / Skidmore	Fox / Robinson	Peacock / Skidmore	Roberts / Foulkes	Kearney / Newman	Chilcott / Maund	Thomas / Walsh	Clark / Darby	Williams C / Lishman	Hargreaves / Wishaw	L	0-1	0-3	11,952	11	39

Scorers, Times, and Referees

22 — BRIGHTON (A): Thomas 36 / *James 48.*
In a fast-moving game at the Goldstone ground, City cause the Brighton defence many headaches. Clark is denied by the bar before City take the lead when Thomas fires the loose ball into an empty net. A poor punch out by Eddolls sets up David James to shoot in Brighton's leveller.

23 — IPSWICH (H): Thomas 31 / *Little 20, Day 29.* Ref: P Baker.
City prove unable to adapt to the muddy conditions at the Gate, where John Little proves too hot to handle. The winger fires past Eddolls to open the scoring, then lays on Albert Day's headed goal with one of his centres. Thomas dives full-length to head in City's spectacular reply.

24 — EXETER (H): Williams 1, Clark 56 / *Regan 30, Ebdon 84.* Ref: J Wiltshire.
Exeter set up the first attack, but City soon make headway when Williams fires in the early opener. Regan levelled with a well-placed shot, but after the break, Clark's drive into the corner of the net puts City back in front. Richard Ebdon's fierce first-timer brings Exeter their point saver.

25 — BRISTOL ROV (H): Thomas 1, 29, Clark 52, 65. Ref: G Clark.
After a three-inch blanket of snow had been cleared from the pitch the referee, Commander George Clark, declares it fit for play. A view certainly endorsed by Bill Thomas who, after just 30 seconds, fires in the close-range opener in what proves to be an easy City success.

26 — SWINDON (H): Williams C 52, 60, Thomas 70 / *Owen 88.* Ref: F Milner.
This ballet in the blinding snow at Ashton Gate is won by City, very much against the run of play. With Bill Thomas taking over in goal for the injured Cousins for a 15-minute spell City do well to go in on level terms at the break. Williams shoots in the opener, then tucks away a header.

27 — BOURNEMOUTH (A): Ref: C Wakley.
On a frozen pitch that causes a certain amount of trouble, City play in white shirts. They start well and Clark sends in a terrific shot, which Ken Bird does well to turn away, but as Bournemouth come into the game Peacock saves City by hooking John Currie's job off of the goal-line.

28 — PORT VALE (A): Clark 60 / *Pointon 2, Triner 30.* Ref: F Milner.
City are certainly out of luck at Hanley where, as well as Ferguson's hesitation gifting Vale both of their goals, they strike the woodwork no less than four occasions. Following Bill Pointon's headed opener and Don Triner's acute-angled drive, Clark's header is City's sole consolation.

29 — TORQUAY (H): Shaw 20 (og), Clark 34, 75, 85p, 87. Ref: J Wiltshire.
After Ron Shaw, whilst attempting to clear Peacock's free-kick, pushes the ball into his own goal, it is easy for City. Ferguson hardly has a shot worthy of the name to save throughout. Clark's goals are all with his feet, except his second, which he heads in from Chilcott's centre.

30 — READING (H): Thomas 4, 40, Chilcott 27, Clark 52, 65 / *Ed'stn 57, Henley 85.*
The hardy City fans who turned out in a snowstorm are rewarded by one of the finest shots of the season as Chilcott, closing in from the wing, finds the back of the net with terrific force. Clark's second, fired in wide of Cyril O'Sullivan, takes his League campaign tally so far to 32.

31 — WALSALL (A): *Newman 42, Maund 88, [Wilshaw 90].* Ref: R Greenwood.
Gilbert Alsop, hero of Walsall's famous FA Cup win versus Arsenal 14 years ago, is present at Fellows Park. Despite dominating the play, City are thwarted by the outstanding display of ex-pilot Reg Foulkes. Albert Newman shoots through a crowd of players to open the scoring.

Matches 32–42

No	Date	Venue	Opponent	Div	Res	Score	Pos	Pts	Attendance	Receipts	City Scorers / Opponent Scorers	Referee
32	29/3	H	WATFORD	3	L	1:2	16	39	13,851	(£788.15.0)	Clark 87 / Dunderdale 17, 50	Ref: J Tregallis
33	4/4	H	CARDIFF	3	W	2:1	1	41	32,535	(£2,209)	Clark 35, Collins 54 / Rees 73	Ref: C Wakley
34	5/4	A	IPSWICH	3	L	2:3	6	41	16,006		Thomas 37, Collins 44 / Pole 13, Parker S 38, Lang 76	Ref: P Baker
35	7/4	A	CARDIFF	3	D	1:1	1	42	49,310		Williams S 23 / Richards 80	Ref: C Wakley
36	12/4	H	LEYTON ORIENT	3	W	3:0	20	44	16,751	(£981.19.3)	Clark 14, 57, Williams S 85 /	Ref: W Plyer
37	19/4	A	QP RANGERS	3	L	0:1	2	44	19,665		/ McEwan 21	Ref: W Plyer
38	26/4	H	SOUTHEND	3	W	2:0	5	46	12,816	(£516.7.9)	Dymond 73, Williams S 88 /	Ref: A Devine
39	3/5	H	NOTTS CO	3	D	1:1	18	47	12,210	(£675.17.0)	Kearney 12 / Houghton 87	Ref: F Green
40	10/5	H	QP RANGERS	3	D	1:1	2	48	20,861	(£1,205.12.9)	Kearney 70p / Durrant 49	Ref: W Plyer
41	17/5	A	MANSFIELD	3	W	3:1	21	50	7,012		Williams C 27, 31, 33, Bryant 3 /	Ref: G Appleyard
42	24/5	A	CRYSTAL PALACE	3	D	0:0	18	51	11,634		/	

Home Average 18,847 Away 14,618

Line-ups (City above / Opponent below in italics)

No	1	2	3	4	5	6	7	8	9	10	11
32	Ferguson	Guy	Bailey	Morgan	Roberts	Kearney	Chilcott	Thomas	Clark	Williams C	Hargreaves
	Rigg	*Morgan*	*Malpass*	*Ross*	*Farnen*	*Harper*	*Davis*	*Chase*	*Dunderdale*	*Evans*	*Harris*
33	Ferguson	Guy	Bailey	Morgan	Roberts	Peacock	Collins	Thomas	Clark	Williams C	Williams S
	Canning	*Lever*	*Sherwood*	*Williams*	*Stansfield*	*Baker*	*Gibson*	*Hollyman*	*Rees*	*Allen*	*Clarke*
34	Ferguson	Guy	Bailey	Morgan	Roberts	Peacock	Collins	Thomas	Clark	Williams C	Williams S
	Burns	*Bell*	*Rumbold*	*Perrett*	*O'Mahony*	*Baird*	*Little*	*Pole*	*Parker S*	*Parker T*	*Lang*
35	Ferguson	Guy	Bailey	Morgan	Roberts	Kearney	Collins	White	Clark	Williams C	Williams S
	Canning	*Lever*	*Sherwood*	*Hollyman*	*Stansfield*	*Baker*	*Gibson*	*Allen*	*Richards*	*Hill*	*Clark*
36	Ferguson	Guy	Bailey	Morgan	Roberts	Kearney	Collins	White	Clark	Williams C	Williams S
	Tolliday	*Fullbrook*	*Ritson*	*Bacon*	*Bartlett*	*Davidson*	*Roberts*	*Hunt*	*Morran*	*Pullen*	*Baynham*
37	Ferguson	Guy	Bailey	Morgan	Roberts	Kearney	Collins	White	Dymond	Williams C	Williams S
	Allen	*Dudley*	*Jefferson*	*Smith*	*Powell*	*Chapman*	*McEwan*	*Parkinson*	*Durrant*	*Hatton*	*Pattison*
38	Ferguson	Guy	Bailey	Morgan	Roberts	Kearney	Collins	White	Dymond	Williams C	Williams S
	Hankey	*Jackson*	*Walton*	*Harris*	*Montgomery*	*Linton*	*Pritchard*	*Smirk*	*Dudley*	*Thompson*	*Lane*
39	Ferguson	Guy	Bailey	Morgan	Roberts	Kearney	Collins	White	Dymond	Williams C	Williams S
	Whittaker	*Southwell*	*Corkhill*	*Gannon*	*Baxter*	*Dickson*	*Lunn*	*Parkes*	*Jayes*	*Sewell*	*Houghton*
40	Ferguson	Guy	Bailey	Morgan	Roberts	Kearney	Dymond	White	Collins	Williams C	Williams S
	Allen	*Dudley*	*Jefferson*	*Smith*	*Powell*	*Heath*	*McEwan*	*Hatton*	*Durrant*	*Mills*	*Pattison*
41	Ferguson	Guy	Bailey	Morgan	Roberts	Kearney	Dymond	White	Collins	Williams C	Chilcott
	Wright	*Fox*	*Chessell*	*Smith*	*Dallman*	*Hogg*	*Harper*	*Chadbourne*	*Bryant*	*Oscroft*	*Betts*
42	Clack	Bailey	Morgan	Roberts	Kearney	Collins	Clark	White	Kurz	Williams C	Chilcott
	Graham	*Fox*	*Dawes*	*Lewis J*	*Millbank*	*Reece*	*Mycock*	*Kurz*	*Robson*	*Lewis G*	*Howell*

Match reports

32. City's hopes went with the loss of Chilcott with a first-half ankle injury, but by then they were already trailing to burly Bill Dunderdale's shot past Ferguson. Clark coolly fired in for City near the finish, after Dunderdale's first-timer had put the visitors firmly on top earlier in the half.

33. City emulated the Rovers by beating the Welsh side in this thriller. Clark heads in the opener, then Collins steers in a brilliant goal before Bill Rees nets for Cardiff from a well-placed right-wing corner. In the closing stages both Thomas and Collins are thwarted by the woodwork.

34. City are out of luck early on when the referee, after first awarding a goal when Collins nets from close range, changes his decision to a free-kick. The towering Harry Pole heads Ipswich in front against the run of play, but Thomas nods the ball past Michael Burns for City's equaliser.

35. The gates are closed 15 minutes before the start at Ninian Park, where a record Third Division (South) crowd see City, despite having Peacock hobbling on the right wing from as early as the fifth minute, earn a well-deserved point. Indeed it takes a late goal to deprive them of victory.

36. City strolled to victory over a side that strangely offered very little in their re-election fight. Clark, who hooked in City's opener from a Cyril Williams centre, scored a brilliant second goal. He took a high lob and fired the ball into the back of the net before Stan Tolliday could move.

37. A great contest at Loftus Road, but there is no doubt that the more skilful side wins. Shortly after Dymond had cracked a terrific shot against the bar, Fred Durrant set up the only goal of the game. Seizing on a poor back-pass, he whips the ball across for Bill McEwan to fire home.

38. Southend have their keeper to thank for keeping the score down. Indeed it looked for most of the game that Albert Hankey's brilliance would earn his side a point. It takes Dymond's fine shot to beat him, then Cyril Williams lays the ball on for his namesake Sid to drive in the second.

39. Centre-forward Fred Whittaker demonstrates his versatility by playing between the sticks, due to County's regular custodian missing the train. City give their worst display so far and Eric Houghton's drive in the dying minutes that saves the visitors a point is the very least they deserve.

40. Reg Allen is the star of this game which, despite being played on a Saturday, kicked-off in the evening. He pulls off many fine saves for the Londoners, but even he can nothing about Kearney's coolly taken penalty. Fred Durrant gave Rangers the lead with a great shot from 25 yards.

41. With the tonic of Eric Bryant's close-range shot, the Stags gave the City defence a stern test until Kearney set up Cyril Williams to shoot City level. Williams then fires in a 12-yarder before finishing off Guy's 35-yard free-kick for a six-minute hat-trick and City have it easy thereafter.

42. With Clack, the new signing from Brentford making his debut, City are much the better-balanced side in defence than the homesters. The Robins half-back line is in no end-of-season mood, but, whilst Collins plays brilliantly in attack, Clark is thwarted by Dick Graham in goal.

CUP-TIES

Manager: Bob Hewison

SEASON 1946-47

FA Cup

					F-A	H-T	1	2	3	4	5	6	7	8	9	10	11	Scorers, Times, and Referees
1	H	HAYES	30/11	3 W	9-3	4-2	Ferguson	Allen	Bailey	Morgan	Roberts	Jones	Chilcott	Thomas	Clark	Williams C	Hargreaves	Clark 7,12,47,72, Thomas 8, Ch't 28, Do'55
		21,610 *AL*	(£1,480)				*Simmonds*	*Wilson*	*Codd*	*Hill*	*Atkins*	*Gallacher*	*Dowse*	*Sheen*	*Prout*	*Nolan*	*Patterson*	*No'15, Pr'30* (Wil'44, Har51,90)
																		Ref: C Harbridge

Despite the scoreline Hayes, playing in unnumbered red and white quartered jerseys, put up a good fight. Nolan cracked in a fine effort to open the amateurs' account. After Clark's terrific right-footed effort at the Open end, which started the scoring spree, Thomas headed in a good goal.

					F-A	H-T	1	2	3	4	5	6	7	8	9	10	11	Scorers, Times, and Referees
2	H	GILLINGHAM	14/12	3 L	1-2	0-0	Eddolls	Guy	Bailey	Morgan	Roberts	Jones	Chilcott	Thomas	Clark	Williams C	Hargreaves	Clark 52
		21,623 *SL:1*	(£1,542)				*Collins*	*Marks*	*Poole*	*Boswell*	*Kingsnorth*	*Piper*	*Akers*	*Wilson*	*Russell*	*Briggs*	*Warsap*	*Wilson 55, Russell 70*

After Chilcott is fouled in the box, Clark's low-driven spot-kick is stopped by Collins, but being unable to hold it, City's centre-forward flings himself at the ball to force it in off of a post. Wilson's header and a terrific shot from Russell bring the non-Leaguers a deserved success.

Gloucestershire Cup

					F-A	H-T	1	2	3	4	5	6	7	8	9	10	11	Scorers, Times, and Referees
F	A	BRISTOL ROV	26/5	3 D	2-2	1-1	Ferguson	Bailey	Fox	Morgan	Roberts	Kearney	Chilcott	White	Clark	Williams C	Collins	Clark 32, Collins 80
		17,151 *14*	(£1,253.12.9)				*Weare*	*Bamford*	*Watkins*	*Pitt*	*Warren*	*McArthur*	*Baldie*	*Hodges*	*Leamon*	*Morgan*	*Carr*	*Leamon 17, Hodges 84*
																		Ref: J Tregallis

With time running out, the quick-witted Len Hodges back-heels in the Rovers late equaliser to take this game to a replay. After Fred Leamon steers in Carr's centre, Clark is alert enough, when Kearney's 30-yard free-kick rebounds off the bar, to head City's leveller into an open net.

					F-A	H-T	1	2	3	4	5	6	7	8	9	10	11	Scorers, Times, and Referees
R	H	BRISTOL ROV	7/6	3 W	2-0	0-0	Cousins	Guy	Bailey	Morgan	Roberts	Kearney	Chilcott	Thomas	Clark	Williams C	Carr	Williams S 47, Thomas 50
		11,434 *14*	(£767.19.9)				*Weare*	*Bamford*	*Watkins*	*Pitt*	*Warren*	*McArthur*	*Wookey*	*Hodges*	*Leamon*	*Morgan*	*Carr*	Ref: J Tregallis

A poor first half, but by the finish City run out easy winners. Shortly after the break a long pass drops to the feet of Sid Williams, who coolly places the ball into the top corner of the net. Rovers endeavoured to respond before Thomas strode through to finish them off with a cross-shot.

	P	W	D	L	F	A	W	D	L	F	A	Pts
			Home						**Away**			
1 Cardiff	42	18	3	0	60	11	12	3	6	33	19	66
2 QP Rangers	42	15	2	4	42	15	8	9	4	32	25	57
3 BRISTOL C	42	13	4	4	56	20	7	7	7	38	36	51
4 Swindon	42	15	4	2	56	25	4	7	10	28	48	49
5 Walsall	42	11	6	4	42	25	6	6	9	32	34	46
6 Ipswich	42	11	5	5	33	21	5	9	7	28	32	46
7 Bournemouth	42	12	4	5	43	20	6	4	11	29	34	44
8 Southend	42	9	7	5	38	22	8	3	10	33	38	44
9 Reading	42	11	6	4	53	30	5	5	11	30	44	43
10 Port Vale	42	14	4	3	51	28	3	5	13	17	35	43
11 Torquay	42	11	5	5	33	23	4	7	10	19	38	42
12 Notts Co	42	11	4	6	35	19	6	6	11	28	44	40
13 Northampton	42	11	5	5	46	33	4	5	12	26	42	40
14 Bristol Rov	42	9	6	6	34	26	7	2	12	25	43	40
15 Exeter	42	11	6	4	37	27	4	3	14	23	42	39
16 Watford	42	11	4	6	39	27	6	1	14	22	49	39
17 Brighton	42	8	7	6	31	35	5	5	11	23	37	38
18 Crys Palace	42	9	7	5	29	19	4	4	13	20	43	37
19 Leyton Orient	42	10	5	6	40	28	2	3	16	14	47	32
20 Aldershot	42	6	7	8	25	26	4	5	12	23	52	32
21 Norwich	42	6	3	12	38	48	5	5	12	26	52	28
22 Mansfield	42	8	5	8	31	38	1	5	15	17	58	28
	924	240	109	113	892	566	113	109	240	566	892	924

Odds & ends

Double wins: (4) Bristol Rovers, Mansfield Town, Torquay, Reading.
Double losses: (2) Walsall, Ipswich.

Won from behind: (4) Norwich (h), Exeter (a), Watford (a), Mansfield (a).
Lost from in front: (2) Walsall (h), Northampton (h).

High spots: City's record League win – 9-0 versus Aldershot.
Completing the double over Bristol Rovers.
Winning 3-0 at Meadow Lane on 11 September.
Beating Hayes 9-3 at Ashton Gate in the FA Cup on 30 November.

Low spots: Losing 1-4 at Southend and Orient in successive games.
Failing victim to the giant-killing of non-League Gillingham in FA Cup.

AGM (Ashton Gate, 10 February 1948):
Profit £5,450.2s.5d. Season Ticket Sales £383.3s.6d.

Player of the year: Don Clark.
Ever-presents: (1) Dennis Roberts.
Hat-tricks: (6) Don Clark (4), Jack Hargreaves (1), Cyril Williams (1).
Leading scorer: Overall: Don Clark (42). League: Don Clark (36).

	Appearances Lge	Cup	Goals Lge	Cup	Tot
Allen, Robert	1	1			
Bailey, Jack	34	4			
Chilcott, Ken	31	4	4	1	5
Clack, Frank	1				
Clark, Don	37	4	36	6	42
Collins, Sammy	10	1	2	1	3
Cousins, Ken	3				
Cunningham, Edwin	1				
Dymond, William	8		1		1
Eddolls, John	6	1			
Fox, Ray	12	1			
Ferguson, Alex	32	2			
Guy, Ivor	32	2			
Hargreaves, Jack	26	2	9	2	11
Jones, Ernie	22	2	1		1
Kearney, Sid	16	2	2		2
Morgan, Cliff	32	4	2		2
Oram, Dennis	3				
Peacock, Ernie	16		1		1
Roberts, Dennis	42	4			
Thomas, Bill	35	3	14	2	16
White, Arnie	8	1			
Williams, Cyril	41	4	17	1	18
Williams, Sid	13	1	3	1	4
(own-goals)			2		2
24 players used	**462**	**44**	**94**	**14**	**108**

LEAGUE DIVISION 3 (SOUTH)

Manager: Bob Hewison

SEASON 1947-48

Match details

No		Opponent	Date	Res	F-A	H-T	Att (Receipts)	Pos	Pt	Scorers, Times, and Referees
1	H	SOUTHEND	23/8	W	6-0	3-0	23,874 (£1,473.9.9)		2	Townsend 15, 44, 55, Clark 30, 46, [Williams C 62] Ref: H Williams
2	A	NEWPORT	28/8	L	0-1	0-1	16,565		2	Batty 3
3	A	NOTTS CO	30/8	L	1-3	0-1	18,980	13 (15)	2	Townsend 51; Sewell 44, Houghton 50, Evans 56 Ref: W Wood
4	H	NEWPORT	3/9	W	1-0	1-0	25,706 (£1,601.13.2)	8 (6)	4	Townsend 36
5	H	SWANSEA	6/9	W	3-2	1-2	28,068 (£1,743.1.9)	6 (17)	6	Clark 15, Williams C 55, Thomas 75; James 22, 25 Ref: B Griffiths
6	A	LEYTON ORIENT	11/9	W	2-0	1-0	10,883	4 (18)	8	Williams S 11, Clark 67
7	A	BOURNEMOUTH	13/9	L	0-2	0-0	19,059	7 (2)	8	Milligan 63, Guy 73 Ref: R Burgess
8	H	LEYTON ORIENT	17/9	W	6-0	5-0	16,788 (£1,051.3.6)	5 (22)	10	Townsend 1, 21, Clark 15, 90, [Williams C 23, 36]
9	H	IPSWICH	20/9	W	4-0	1-0	23,483 (£1,462.11.7)	4 (9)	12	Townsend 6, 75, Williams C 65, [Clark 70] Ref: V Rae
10	A	BRISTOL ROV	27/9	W	2-0	0-0	34,165 (£2,557.3.3)	3 (8)	14	Chilcott 65, Clark 89 Ref: N Taylor

Line-ups (City player / *opponent*)

No	1	2	3	4	5	6	7	8	9	10	11
1	Clark / *Hankey*	Guy / *Beach*	Bailey / *Walton*	Morgan / *Goodyear*	Roberts / *Sheard*	Kearney / *Montgomery*	Hopkins / *Pritchard*	Townsend / *Smirke*	Clark / *Dudley*	Williams C / *Thompson*	Williams S / *Whitchurch*
2	Clark / *Smith A*	Guy / *Wilcox*	Bailey / *Oldham*	Morgan / *Hammill*	Roberts / *Pincott*	Kearney / *McBlain*	Hopkins / *Williams H*	Townsend / *Newall*	Clark / *Roffi*	Williams C / *Batty*	Williams S / *Lewis I*
3	Clark / *Brown*	Guy / *Southwell*	Bailey / *Howe*	Morgan / *Gannon*	Roberts / *Baxter*	Kearney / *Corkhill*	Hopkins / *Houghton*	Townsend / *Parkes*	Clark / *Evans*	Williams C / *Sewell*	Williams S / *Cumner*
4	Clark / *Turner*	Guy / *Wilcox*	Bailey / *Oldham*	Morgan / *Hammill*	Roberts / *Pincott*	Kearney / *McBlain*	Hopkins / *Williams H*	Townsend / *Carr*	Clark / *Roffi*	Williams C / *Batty*	Williams S / *Lewis I*
5	Clark / *Parry*	Guy / *Feeney*	Bailey / *Fisher*	Morgan / *Paul*	Roberts / *Weston*	Jones / *Burns*	Hopkins / *O'Driscall*	Thomas / *McCrory*	Clark / *James*	Williams C / *Eastham*	Williams S / *Lockhart*
6	Clark / *Tolliday*	Guy / *Brown*	Bailey / *Ritson*	Morgan / *Waller*	Roberts / *Sales*	Thomas / *Stroud*	Hopkins / *Gray*	White / *Hunt*	Clark / *Chapman*	Williams C / *Naylor*	Williams S / *Baynham*
7	Clark / *Bird*	Guy / *Marsden*	Bailey / *Sanaghan*	Morgan / *Togg*	Roberts / *Wilson*	Thomas / *Woodward*	Hopkins / *Mackenzie*	Townsend / *Gray*	Clark / *Milligan*	Williams C / *Paton*	Williams S / *McDonald*
8	Clark / *Tolliday*	Guy / *Ritson*	Bailey / *Farley*	Peacock / *Bacon*	Roberts / *Brown*	Thomas / *Stroud*	Hopkins / *Gray*	Townsend / *Skelton*	Clark / *Hunt*	Williams C / *Pullen*	Williams S / *Baynham*
9	Clark / *Burns*	Guy / *Bell*	Bailey / *Rumbold*	Peacock / *Perrett*	Roberts / *Green*	Thomas / *Baird*	Hopkins / *Day*	Townsend / *Parker S*	Clark / *Jennings*	Williams C / *Parker T*	Williams S / *Pole*
10	Clark / *Weare*	Guy / *Bamford*	Bailey / *McArthur*	Kearney / *Pitt*	Roberts / *Warren*	Thomas / *Fox*	Hopkins / *Wookey*	Townsend / *Hodges*	Clark / *Leaman*	Williams C / *Chadwick*	Chilcott / *Cranfield*

Match reports

1. After new-boy Townsend put City in front with a diving header, Clark doubled the advantage with a magnificent goal. Receiving a high ball in midfield, Clark headed it forward and ran past two defenders before driving a fierce shot into the left-hand corner of Albert Hankey's net.

2. Against relegated Newport, the City are shocked right at the start when Stan Batty registers with a 25-yard free-kick. Thereafter City showed themselves to be the better footballing side and had only themselves to blame for their defeat. Morgan hits a post with a great 30-yard drive.

3. A thrilling game which saw, especially in the first half, some of the finest soccer at Meadow Lane since the war. City are made to pay for squandering their chances when Jackie Sewell heads in an easy goal to put the Magpies in front. Townsend's fine cross-shot registers for City.

4. Despite Kearney's half-hour absence, after breaking his jaw in the second minute, and the loss of Townsend with concussion, sustained when heading in Clark's overhead kick, City bring off a plucky win over the previously unbeaten visitors. Sid Williams hits the bar in the first half.

5. Swansea have been earning the plaudits with their skilful brand of soccer, but are not having the best of luck on the field of play. Despite outclassing City, the tide of play changes with the award of a goal when Jack Parry looked to have saved a Cyril Williams header on the line.

6. Despite Sid Williams netting the opener after all of his four fellow forwards had made attempts, City, for all their better soccer skills, had to weather much Orient pressure. Fortunately, Clark hit home a fine centre from Hopkins to make sure of City's first away win of the season.

7. Despite being reduced to ten men from the 25th minute, when Joe Sanaghan is carried off following a kick in the face, the Cherries are much too skilful for City. Clark's poor clearance sees Duddley Milligan's 35-yarder cannon off the crossbar and rebound off the keeper into the net.

8. Watched by former boss Alex Raisbeck (1922-28), City find Orient easy victims. At the interval it looked like a double-figure score was in prospect, but then the visitors improved and denied City until the last minute, when Clark ran through to fire in the best goal of the game.

9. City could afford Clark's spot-kick failure near the finish, but prior to Cyril Williams firing in a 25-yard cracker it was looking like being a hard game to win. Thereafter it was easy as Clark ran through unchallenged to crash in number three before Townsend headed in the fourth.

10. One of the dourest local derbies ever staged, with little, except the goals, to choose between the teams. Both centre-halves are veritable towers of strength. Prior to Clark's neat finish making things safe for City, Hopkins raced away to make the opening for Chilcott to fire in the opener.

Match-by-match record (matches 11–21)

No	Venue	Opponent	Date	Attendance	Receipts	Pos	Pos	—	Res	F–A	H–T
11	A	READING	4/10	17,529		15	16	2	W	7-2	3-2
12	H	NORWICH	11/10	27,896	(£1,748.16.3)	22	18	2	W	6-0	2-0
13	A	BRIGHTON	18/10	11,820		20	20	2	W	2-0	1-0
14	H	WATFORD	25/10	31,624	(£1,984.3.0)	16	20	2	L	1-2	1-0
15	A	QP RANGERS	1/11	28,358	(£1,757.6.4)	1	20	3	L	0-2	0-1
16	H	PORT VALE	8/11	27,740		11	22	3	W	2-1	1-0
17	A	SWINDON	15/11	26,401	(£1,919)	18	23	3	D	2-2	1-1
18	H	TORQUAY	22/11	18,368	(£1,138.1.6)	9	23	4	L	1-2	0-1
19	A	SOUTHEND	20/12	7,717	(£1,059.6.6)	9	23	5	L	0-4	0-1
20	A	EXETER	26/12	13,380		6	23	7	L	1-3	0-2
21	H	EXETER	27/12	11,620	(£722.0.3)	5	24	6	D	1-1	1-0

11 — A READING (4/10) W 7-2
City: Clark, Guy, Bailey, Thomas, Roberts, Kearney, Hopkins, Townsend, Clark, Williams C, Osman
Reading: Rickett, Goldberg, Gulliver, Moyse, Young, Henley, Fisher, Edelston, McPhee, Smith, Hargreaves
Scorers: Townsend 25, Clark 31, 32, 50, 70, [Kearney 77, 89]; *McPhee 27, Edelston 29*
Ref: A Haines

Clark's close-range drive gives City a narrow advantage at the end of a first half of the most exciting football of the season. Reading are shattered by Kearney and Clark. From a Hopkins cross, Clark notches up his hat-trick with a first-time shot, before heading in his fourth.

12 — H NORWICH (11/10) W 6-0
City: Clark, Guy, Bailey, Thomas, Roberts, Kearney, Hopkins, Townsend, Clark, Williams C, Osman
Norwich: Nethercott, Tobin, Morgan, Robinson, Low, Williams, Ryder, Hold, Ashman, Eyre, Church
Scorers: Williams C 28, Osman 55, [Townsend 40, 47, 60, 65]
Ref: A Devine

Townsend, ably supported by the diminutive Hopkins performing a 'Stanley Matthews act' on the wing, routs the Canaries. Ex-City Colt Ken Nethercott, between the Norwich sticks, has a torrid time after being unable to hold a fierce shot from Williams which put the Robins in front.

13 — A BRIGHTON (18/10) W 2-0
City: Clark, Guy, Bailey, Thomas, Roberts, Kearney, Hopkins, Townsend, Clark, Williams C, Osman
Brighton: Ball, Marriott, Willemse, Darling, Booth, Dugnolle, Thomas, James, Trainor, Chapman, Whent
Scorers: Townsend 18, Clark 80
Ref: H Williams

Quite a good game to watch as City, with Williams their shining star, provide most of the clever football. Kearney starts the move which puts City in front as, with Brighton appealing vainly for offside, he passes to Osman who in turn sets up Townsend to fire the ball past John Ball.

14 — H WATFORD (25/10) L 1-2
City: Clark, Guy, Bailey, Thomas, Roberts, Kearney, Hopkins, Townsend, Clark, Williams C, Osman
Watford: Rigg, Harris, Jones, Hicklin, Hunt, Usher, Davies, Young, Dunderdale, Nolan, Surtees
Scorers: Guy 23; *Davies 58, Young 70*
Ref: F Milner

Watford's fast and clever play in this game has the fans rating them even higher than championship-chasers Swansea. Despite falling behind to Guy's 45-yard free-kick, headed goals from Bill Davies and George Young sees the Hornets deprive City of their unblemished home record.

15 — A QP RANGERS (1/11) L 0-2
City: Clark, Guy, Bailey, Thomas, Roberts, Kearney, Hopkins, Townsend, Clark, Williams C, Osman
QP Rangers: Allen, Dudley, Jefferson, Powell, Smith, Chapman, Boxshall, McEwan, Durrant, Ramscar, Pattison
Scorers: *Pattison 20p, Boxshall 48*
Ref: L Gibbs

Despite the loss of their skipper as early as the fifth minute following a collision with the burly Fred Durrant, City put up a good fight at Loftus Road. Fred Ramscar is brought down when clean through for the successful spot-kick. Danny Boxshall fires goal number two into an open net.

16 — H PORT VALE (8/11) W 2-1
City: Clark, Guy, Bailey, Thomas, Norris, Kearney, Hopkins, Townsend, Clark, Williams C, Osman
Port Vale: Heppell, Butler, Hubbick, Todd, Eastwood, Hallam, Allen, Smith, Martin, Pointon, Shore
Scorers: Williams C 20, Townsend 47; *Allen 70*
Ref: H Key

It appears that City have found a star in local-lad Ray Norris who more than capably fills the boots of last week's injury victim Dennis Roberts. The Valiants offer very little until after Ronnie Allen had fired in their response to a Williams cross-drive and Townsend's close-range shot.

17 — A SWINDON (15/11) D 2-2
City: Clark, Guy, Bailey, Thomas, Norris, Kearney, Hopkins, Townsend, Clark, Williams C, Osman
Swindon: Ferguson, Preece, Emery, Kaye, Norris, Painter, Dryden, Lucas, Owen, Paterson, Bain
Scorers: Townsend 22, Clark 55; *Dryden 38, Owen 51*
Ref: C Wakley

The best game seen so far on the County ground this season is the verdict. Townsend shoots in a close-range opener, but Jackie Dryden's half-volley levels matters before the break. Clark's breasted in effort saves City a point after Maurice Owen had hooked the Railwaymen in front.

18 — H TORQUAY (22/11) L 1-2
City: Clark, Guy, Bailey, Thomas, Norris, Kearney, Hopkins, Townsend, Clark, Williams C, Osman
Torquay: Joslin, Head, Calland, Towers, Evans, Stuttart, Lewis, Shaw, Conley, Hill, Mercer
Scorers: Townsend 50p; *Lewis 35, Conley 57*
Ref: J Wiltshire

With last season's Cup final referee taking charge of this game, the visitors revel in the wet conditions. After Dennis Lewis had driven in the opener, Torquay secured a deserved victory when the ball ends up in the net following Joe Conley's challenge on Clack for a high centre.

19 — A SOUTHEND (20/12) L 0-4
City: Clark, Guy, Bailey, Thomas, Roberts, Kearney, Chilcott, Townsend, Clark, Williams C, Osman
Southend: Nash, Beach, Linton, Goodyear, Sheard, Montgomery, Pritchard, Dudley, Thompson, Bennett, Lane
Scorers: *Thompson 25, Bennett 75, 88, [Pritchard 83]*
Ref: H Williams

City do well to find themselves only trailing to Cyril Thompson's drive at the break, as they had suffered a difficult and uncomfortable first 45 minutes. Matters improved for a while thereafter, but Ken Bennett's run from halfway to slip the ball past Clack sets up Southend's late blitz.

20 — A EXETER (26/12) L 1-3
City: Clark, Guy, Bailey, Thomas, Roberts, Kearney, Hopkins, Townsend, Clark, Williams C, Williams S
Exeter: Singleton, Thompson, Johnstone, Gibson, Davey, Walker, Dymond, Mackay, Sutherland, Evans, Regan
Scorers: Townsend 88; *Sutherland 12, Mackay 43, [Thompson 70p]*
Ref: C Wakley

City produce some delightful soccer, but unfortunately they lack the end product until right at the finish, when Townsend meets a Thomas free-kick with his head to put the ball past Bernard Singleton from close range. City give away the penalty by bringing down Angus Mackay.

21 — H EXETER (27/12) D 1-1
City: Clark, Guy, Bailey, Peacock, Roberts, Kearney, Hopkins, Townsend, Clark, White, Williams S
Exeter: Singleton, Rowe, Johnstone, Evans, Gibson, Walker, Dymond, Mackay, Sutherland, Wright, Regan
Scorers: Thomas 25; *Dymond 85*
Ref: C Wakley

In the first half Peacock netted, but instead of a goal City were awarded a penalty, which Clark hit straight at Bernard Singleton. Exeter, with Horace Wright taking over from their injured keeper, who went on the wing, earn a point thanks to Bill Dymond's great twelve-yard drive.

LEAGUE DIVISION 3 (SOUTH)

Manager: Bob Hewison

SEASON 1947-48

Match details and statistics (City result first; opponents' figures in *italic*)

No	Date	Venue	Opponents	Att	Receipts	Pos	Opp Pos	Pt	F-A	H-T	Result	Scorers, Times, and Referees
22	3/1	H	NOTTS CO	35,287	(£2,227.16.9)	6	18	26	1-0	1-0	W	Townsend 15. Ref: W Wood
23	17/1	A	SWANSEA	15,866		9	3	26	1-6	1-4	L	White 13 [Scrine 15, McC'y 42, 65] *Rawcliffe 3, 49, Comley 6,* Ref: B Griffiths
24	24/1	A	NORTHAMPTON	7,522	(£651)	7	18	28	4-0	3-0	W	Townsend 5, Clark 15, Kearney 17, [*Williams C 60*] Ref: A Devine
25	31/1	H	BOURNEMOUTH	23,287	(£1,452.14.9)	7	2	28	0-4	0-3	L	*McKenzie 15, Milligan 35, 44, 70* Ref: R Burgess
26	7/2	A	IPSWICH	10,862		9	6	28	0-1	0-0	L	*Parker 82* Ref: V Rae
27	14/2	H	BRISTOL ROV	26,386	(£1,691.11.9)	8	18	30	5-2	3-1	W	Clark 10, 65, 80, Townsend 29, *McArt' 40, Morgan 75* [*Williams C 43*] Ref: N Taylor
28	21/2	H	READING	12,542	(£769.0.9)	8	13	30	0-2	0-0	L	*McPhee 50, Fisher 55* Ref: A Haines
29	28/2	A	NORWICH	22,275		8	22	32	3-2	0-1	W	Clark 57, Townsend 80, Tobin 87 (og) *Hold 20, Morgan 69* Ref: A Devine
30	6/3	H	BRIGHTON	13,383	(£829.0.3)	8	21	32	1-2	0-1	L	Clark 51 *James 16p, 70p* Ref: H Williams
31	13/3	A	WATFORD	13,262		9	20	33	1-1	1-0	D	Townsend 43p *Cheney 72* Ref: F Milner

Line-ups (City row / opponents' row in *italic*)

Match	Team	1	2	3	4	5	6	7	8	9	10	11
22	City	Clack	Guy	Bailey	Morgan	Roberts	Thomas	Collins	Townsend	Clark	White	Williams S
22	Notts Co	*Brown*	*Southwell*	*Howe*	*Gannon*	*Corkhill*	*Baxter*	*Evans*	*Sewell*	*Lawton*	*Marsh*	*Cunner*
23	City	Clack	Guy	Bailey	Morgan	Roberts	Thomas	Collins	Townsend	Clark	White	Williams S
23	Swansea	*Roberts*	*Fisher*	*Keene*	*Paul*	*Weston*	*Burns*	*O'Sullivan*	*McCrory*	*Rawcliffe*	*Comley*	*Scrine*
24	City	Clack	Guy	Bailey	Thomas	Roberts	Kearney	Hopkins	Townsend	Clark	Williams C	Osman
24	Northampton	*Jones*	*Smalley*	*Barron*	*Lowery*	*Dennison*	*Caley*	*English*	*King*	*Morrell*	*Jenkins*	*Roberts*
25	City	Clack	Guy	Bailey	Thomas	Roberts	Kearney	Hopkins	Townsend	Clark	Williams C	Osman
25	Bournemouth	*Bird*	*Marsden*	*Sanaghan*	*Tagg*	*Wilson*	*Percival*	*McKenzie*	*Blair*	*Milligan*	*Rowell*	*McDonald*
26	City	Clack	Guy	Bailey	Thomas	Roberts	Kearney	Collins	Townsend	Clark	Williams C	Osman
26	Ipswich	*Brown*	*Bell*	*Rumbold*	*Perratt*	*O'Mahoney*	*Baird*	*Day*	*Jennings*	*Clarke*	*Parker T*	*Little*
27	City	Clack	Guy	Bailey	Thomas	Roberts	Kearney	Hopkins	Townsend	Clark	Williams C	Osman
27	Bristol Rov	*Weare*	*Bamford*	*Watkins*	*Pitt*	*Warren*	*McArthur*	*Pethebridge*	*Wookey*	*Lambden*	*Morgan*	*Watling*
28	City	Clack	Guy	Bailey	Thomas	Roberts	Kearney	Hopkins	Townsend	Clark	Williams C	Osman
28	Reading	*O'Sullivan*	*Goldberg*	*Gulliver*	*Hanley*	*Ratcliffe*	*Deverall*	*Bertschin*	*Barney*	*McPhee*	*Dix*	*Fisher*
29	City	Clack	Guy	Bailey	Morgan	Roberts	Kearney	Chicott	Townsend	Clark	Williams C	Williams S
29	Norwich	*Davis*	*Robinson*	*Tobin*	*Kinsey*	*Low*	*Dutton*	*Church*	*Driver*	*Hold*	*Eyre*	*Morgan*
30	City	Clack	Guy	Bailey	Morgan	Roberts	Thomas	Chicott	Townsend	Clark	Williams C	Williams S
30	Brighton	*Baldwin*	*Morrad*	*Willemse*	*James*	*Young*	*Darling*	*Willard*	*Lancellotte*	*Hipkin*	*Willis*	*Hanlon*
31	City	Clack	Guy	Bailey	Thomas	Roberts	Jones	Williams S	Townsend	Clark	Williams C	Osman
31	Watford	*Rigg*	*Harris*	*Jones*	*Eggleston*	*Farnon*	*Osbourne*	*Davies*	*Paton*	*Thomas*	*Nolan*	*Cheney*

Match reports

22 — v Notts Co: A massive crowd at the Gate to see England international Tommy Lawton, who has recently joined County from Chelsea for a record £20,000 transfer fee. Fortunately, the great man is relatively subdued and City take the points thanks to Townsend diving full-length to head the ball in.

23 — v Swansea: The Swans supporters are singing in the rain after their side maintains their unbeaten home record with this demolition job. City are completely outclassed after Frank Rawcliffe shot through the early opener from barely six yards. White slides in to push home City's solitary response.

24 — v Northampton: Billy Wedlock accompanied the City team for this match at the County ground, where they played in white. Townsend got the action under way by heading in the opener, then Clark registered with a fierce drive before Kearney's half-volley brought City a commanding advantage.

25 — v Bournemouth: The twinkling toes of the fair-haired John McKenzie and the finishing power of Dudley Milligan prove much too much for a poor City side. McKenzie fired in the opener, before Milligan got in on the act with a close-range effort. A header followed before a shot brought the hat-trick.

26 — v Ipswich: City created many chances with their attractive soccer at Portman Road, but had no one to supply the finishing touch. Ultimately they paid the price when Bailey's hurried clearance went straight to Tom Parker, whose well-placed shot into the corner of the net gave Clack no chance.

27 — v Bristol Rov: An unjust scoreline as Rovers, for whom Ray Warren ensured there was no way back by slicing his 60th-minute spot-kick wide, fully played their part in this entertaining game. An alert Clark fired in to open the scoring for City when Townsend's shot bounced down off of the bar.

28 — v Reading: On the frozen Ashton Gate turf it was Reading's veteran centre-forward Magnus McPhee who gave the crowd its biggest thrill. Following an even first half, McPhee broke the deadlock when, after taking a pass from the right, he races into the area and registers with a cannonball shot.

29 — v Norwich: Bottom of the table Norwich put up a terrific fight before succumbing to a late goal, when Maurice Tobin put into his own net. Oscar Hold's fine drive put the Canaries into the lead, but City levelled when Clark dribbled round Derek Davis before depositing the ball into an empty net.

30 — v Brighton: Many of City's moves are spoilt by faulty passing and poor finishing. It is left to Clark to add a little sparkle by shooting an equaliser through the legs of centre-half Len Young. Roberts concedes both of the penalties that allow Tony James to bring Brighton a slightly fortunate victory.

31 — v Watford: Watford, under new boss Bristolian Eddie Hapgood (ex Arsenal and England), are making great strides in their effort to avoid applying for re-election. Following a 2-1 success at Ipswich last week, Dennis Cheney's great run and fine finish salvages an equaliser in this low-key affair.

No	V	Date	Opponent	Res	FT	HT	City Pos	Opp Pos	Pts	Att	Receipts
32	H	20/3	QP RANGERS	W	2:1	2:1	8	1	35	21,184	(£1,379.6.9)
33	H	26/3	WALSALL	D	0:0	0:0	8	3	36	24,998	(£1,563.7.9)
34	A	27/3	PORT VALE	L	0:1	0:1	8	5	36	12,541	
35	A	29/3	WALSALL	L	0:2	0:2	9	3	36	12,743	
36	H	3/4	SWINDON	D	2:2	1:1	9	15	37	16,859	(£1,059.9.9)
37	A	5/4	CRYSTAL PALACE	L	0:4	0:3	9	16	37	13,405	
38	A	10/4	TORQUAY	W	3:2	0:1	9	16	39	6,697	
39	H	17/4	CRYSTAL PALACE	W	2:0	2:0	6	14	41	12,560	(£774.10.9)
40	A	24/4	ALDERSHOT	D	1:1	1:0	7	21	42	4,892	
41	H	26/4	ALDERSHOT	L	2:4	1:2	7	18	42	9,936	(£594.14.9)
42	H	1/5	NORTHAMPTON	D	1:1	0:0	7	14	43	8,392	(£513.9.6)

Home Average 20,951 — Away 15,472

---

32. QP RANGERS
Scorers: Townsend 14, 34 — Hatton 10
Ref: A Haines
City: Clark, Guy, Bailey, Thomas, Roberts, Jones, Williams S, Townsend, Clark, Williams C, Osman
QPR: Saphin, Powell G, Jefferson, Powell T, Smith G, Smith A, Stewart, Ramscar, Durant, Hatton, Harburn

A hard shot into the roof of the net from just five yards. City hit their best form for months despite falling behind when Clack's poor punch-out set up Cyril Hatton to find the net from just five yards. (Townsend's 25th goal of the season) consigns Rangers to their first League defeat since early November.

33. WALSALL
Ref: H Williams
City: Clark, Guy, Bailey, Jones, Roberts, Thomas, Williams S, White, Clark, Williams C, Osman
Walsall: Lewis, Kelly, Walters, Devlin, Foulkes, Newman, Condie, Walsh, Critchley, Lishman, Davies

The words 'goalless draw' usually tell their own dismal story, and such was the case in this game in which Walsall looked the much better side. Many views are often expressed on Townsend's value to the City team, but there was no doubt that he was much missed in this contest.

34. PORT VALE
Scorers: Pointon 28
Ref: H Key
City: Clark, Guy, Bailey, Morgan, Roberts, Thomas, Williams S, Townsend, Clark, Williams C, Osman
Port Vale: Hoppell, Pursell, Hubbick, McGarry, Hayward, Todd, Allen, Martin, Pointon, Smith, Keeley

Roberts has to be at his best to restrict Vale to just one goal – a Bill Pointon header that brings the win that their play deserved. Just before half-time, Clack makes a great save from the clean-through John Smith, then after the break Guy goes off twice having his studs attended to.

35. WALSALL
Scorers: Devlin 59p, Kelly 78
Ref: H Williams
City: Clark, Guy, Bailey, Morgan, Roberts, Jones, Williams S, Townsend, Clark, Williams C, Osman
Walsall: Lewis, Humphries, Skidmore, Walters, Foulkes, Newman, Condie, Devlin, Kelly, Lishman, Guest

A Walsall side, with no fewer than six changes to the side that drew at the Gate on Good Friday, prove much too good for City. John Devlin's penalty, after Jim Condie is brought down, and Fred Kelly's lob are scant reward for the Saddlers who are let down by some poor finishing.

36. SWINDON
Scorers: White 40, Townsend 60p — Owen 5, 78
Ref: C Wakley
City: Clark, Stone, Bailey, Morgan, Roberts, Jones, Williams S, White, Townsend, Williams C, Fox
Swindon: Boulton, Young, Emery, Lloyd, Ithell, Painter, McGuire, Paterson, Owen, Jones, Bain

George Camsell was present to check the form of Swindon's Maurice Owen, who opens the scoring by heading in Jimmy Bain's cross. White equalises with a half-volley before a handball brings Townsend his spot-kick. Owen has the last say by lashing in Swindon's point-saver.

37. CRYSTAL PALACE
Scorers: Clough 3, Kurz 10, 40, Lewis 67
Ref: F Green
City: Clark, Stone, Bailey, Morgan, Roberts, Kearney, Williams S, **Dimmer**, Townsend, Williams C, Osman
Crystal Palace: Graham, Harding, Dawes, Lewis, Bassett, Buckley, Mycock, Russell, Kurz, Burrell, Clough

City are let down by their faulty offside-trap. Fred Kurz beats their tactics time after time and what is more rounds off his work with successful shots. James Clough beats Stone by sheer pace before firing in the opener, then Kurz gets in on the act prior to Glyn Lewis shooting the fourth.

38. TORQUAY
Scorers: Wil'ms S 75, Towns'd 83, Stone 88 — Whitfield 22p, Griffiths 58
Ref: J Wiltshire
City: Clark, Joslin, Bailey, Peacock, Roberts, Kearney, Williams S, Townsend, Clark, Williams C, Fox
Torquay: Joslin, Keeton, Stuttard, Towers, Whitfield, Pryde, Lewis, Griffiths, Kernick, Hill, Thomas

Not dismayed by having what looked like a perfectly valid Townsend goal disallowed a minute after he had fired in a leveller, the City still manage to complete a tremendous fight-back when Stone shoots in a three-yard winner. The smallest man on the field heads in City's opener.

39. CRYSTAL PALACE
Scorers: Townsend 28, Williams C 37
Ref: F Green
City: Clark, Guy, Bailey, Peacock, Roberts, Kearney, Williams S, Townsend, Clark, Williams C, Fox
Crystal Palace: Graham, Harding, Dawes, Lewis, Bassett, Buckley, Mycock, Kurz, Russell, Reece, Clough

Captain F Green, the referee of this game, which City dominated, was the official in charge of the recent Army Cup match when two players were killed by lightning. Townsend lobs in the opener, then Cyril Williams finds the net with a fierce half-volley to double City's advantage.

40. ALDERSHOT
Scorers: Clark 25 — Sherwood 86
Ref: E Crook
City: Clark, Guy, Bailey, Peacock, Roberts, Kearney, Williams S, Townsend, Clark, Williams C, Fox
Aldershot: Reynolds, Rogers, Sheppard, Sherwood, Rowland, Jales, Hobbs, Hood, Reece, McNichol, Hassell

Clark drives in the opener, but Kearney's miskick allows Henry Sherwood to rush in Aldershot's late equaliser. A somewhat fortunate point for the Shots, despite having most of the play against a City side lacking Peacock for the last 20 minutes owing to his first-half shoulder injury.

41. ALDERSHOT
Scorers: Townsend 23, Clark 88 — White 41, 78, Hood 45, 80
Ref: E Crook
City: Clark, Guy, Bailey, Morgan, Roberts, Kearney, Williams S, Townsend, Clark, Williams C, Fox
Aldershot: Reynolds, Rogers, Sheppard, Sherwood, Rowland, Jales, Hobbs, White, Hood, McNichol, Hassell

A surprise, but deserved, Shots win deposits local rivals Bristol Rovers bottom of the table. Townsend, who missed most the second half due to being injured in a collision with Ron Reynolds, fired in the early opener, but from Clack's fisted clearance Jackie White volleyed a leveller.

42. NORTHAMPTON
Scorers: Townsend 62 — King 50
Ref: L Brown
City: Clark, Stone, Bailey, Thomas, Morgan, Kearney, Williams S, Townsend, Clark, Williams C, Williams S
Northampton: Ansell, Smalley, Fisher, Bowen, Lowery, Blunt, English, King, Hughes, Haselgrave, Fowler

Injured against Aldershot in midweek, Townsend made a successful plea to play in this game in his bid to top the English scoring charts. He shoots in his 34th goal of the season to achieve his aim and earn City a point after Fred King had fired hard and low into the corner of the net.

CUP-TIES

Manager: Bob Hewison

SEASON 1947-48

FA Cup

		F-A	H-T	Scorers, Times, and Referees	1	2	3	4	5	6	7	8	9	10	11
1 A DARTFORD	4 D	0-0	0-0		Clack	Guy	Bailey	Morgan	Roberts	Thomas	Hopkins	Townsend	Clark	Williams C	Osman
7,540 SL:15	aet			Ref: A Ford	*Coombes*	*Stratton*	*Wager*	*Cracker*	*Turner*	*Gee*	*Viles*	*Russell*	*Gibbons*	*Parker*	*Etherton*

Due to a colour clash City play in white on the Watling Street ground where, especially in the first half, their defence is given a hard test by the Southern Leaguers. When Dartford got the ball in the net in the 118th minute, City are saved by the award of a free-kick for a foul on Morgan.

		F-A	H-T	Scorers, Times, and Referees	1	2	3	4	5	6	7	8	9	10	11
R H DARTFORD	5 W	9-2	5-1	Towns'd 14, 44, 75, Wil' 19, 35, 56	Clack	Guy	Bailey	Morgan	Roberts	Thomas	Hopkins	Townsend	Clark	Williams C	Osman
19,785 SL:15 (£1,533)				*Gibbons 40, 80* [Clark 42, 70, 87] Ref: A Ford	*Coombes*	*Stratton*	*Wager*	*Cracker*	*Turner*	*Gee*	*Viles*	*Russell*	*Gibbons*	*Parker*	*Shuter*

The Darts show plenty of spirit and Gibbons follows his headed consolation with a first-class shot past Clack to add some respectability to the score. In contrast to last week's encounter, this time the minnows are completely outclassed after Townsend had headed City into an early lead.

		F-A	H-T	Scorers, Times, and Referees	1	2	3	4	5	6	7	8	9	10	11
2 H CRYSTALPALACE	5 L	0-1	0-0		Clack	Guy	Bailey	Morgan	Roberts	Thomas	Hopkins	Townsend	Clark	Williams C	Osman
22,327 16 (£1,569)	aet			*Robson 115* Ref: P Annette	*Graham*	*Harding*	*Dawes*	*Buckley*	*Millbank*	*Reece*	*Mycock*	*Lewis G*	*Robson*	*Kurz*	*Clough*

City are made to pay for many missed first-half chances when, in extra-time, Albert Robson wins the game for Palace. He brings a high centre quickly under control before shooting past the advancing Clack. Both Clack for City and Robson for Palace have goals disallowed for offside.

Gloucestershire Cup

		F-A	H-T	Scorers, Times, and Referees	1	2	3	4	5	6	7	8	9	10	11
F H BRISTOL ROV	7 L	1-2	0-2	Clark 65	Clack	Guy	Bailey	Morgan	Roberts	Thomas	Williams S	White	Clark	Williams C	Jarvis
15,727 20 (£1,027)				*Morgan 9, Watkins 18* Ref: C Barrick	*Liley*	*Bamford*	*Fox*	*Pitt*	*Warren*	*McArthur*	*Hodges*	*Watkins*	*Lambden*	*Morgan*	*Petherbridge*

The Rovers defence is rock-like, withstanding much pressure after Clark's grounder brings City into the game. Jimmy Morgan's fast, rising effort and an easy finish by Barry Watkins, when George Petherbridge's shot hits the bar, brings Rovers their first County Cup since 1936-37.

Bath Coronation Cup

		F-A	H-T	Scorers, Times, and Referees	1	2	3	4	5	6	7	8	9	10	11
F A BATH CITY	7 W	3-2	1-2	Moon 5, 80, White 85	Morgan S	Walker	Bailey	Morgan C	Roberts	Kearney	Collins	Moon	Clark	White	Jarvis
3,000 SL:11 (at Twerton Park)				*Browne 20, McCulloch 30* Ref: C Wakley	*Woodley*	*Owens*	*Stevens*	*Marshall*	*Smith E*	*Onslow*	*Edwards*	*Browne*	*McCulloch*	*Woodman*	*Ball*

Whilst City were the better side with their neat play and accurate passing, it wasn't until near the finish that they obtained two quick goals to snatch the cup from Bath's grasp. McCulloch had put Bath in front after Browne fired in their leveller following on from Moon's City opener.

Berkeley Hospital Cup

		F-A	H-T	Scorers, Times, and Referees	1	2	3	4	5	6	7	8	9	10	11
F A DURSLEY DIST XI	7 W	5-1	2-0	Coles (3), Clark, Thomas	Morgan S	Guy	Bailey	Kearney	Roberts	Thomas	Williams S	Coles	Clark	Williams C	Collins
(Recreation Field, Dursley)				*Carter* Ref: W Oakley	*Stump*	*Neale*	*Priday*	*Workman*	*Evans*	*Read*	*Phillips*	*Carter*	*Clarke*	*Nash*	*Denning*

City are rarely troubled on the Recreation Field, Dursley, in winning the 12th Berkeley Hospital Cup final. Coles (Horfield Old Boys) had an excellent debut, netting three times for a City side, who played attractive football throughout the whole 90 minutes of this Charity encounter.

League Table

#	Team	P	Home					Away					Pts
			W	D	L	F	A	W	D	L	F	A	
1	QP Rangers	42	16	3	2	44	17	10	6	5	30	20	61
2	Bournemouth	42	13	5	3	42	13	11	4	6	34	22	57
3	Walsall	42	13	5	3	37	12	8	2	12	33	28	51
4	Ipswich	42	16	1	4	42	18	2	6	11	22	43	49
5	Swansea	42	14	6	1	48	14	4	6	11	24	38	48
6	Notts Co	42	12	4	5	44	27	7	4	10	30	32	46
7	BRISTOL C	42	11	4	6	47	26	2	7	11	15	39	43
8	Port Vale	42	14	4	3	48	18	2	7	12	15	36	43
9	Southend	42	11	8	2	32	16	4	5	12	19	42	43
10	Reading	42	10	5	6	37	28	6	6	10	21	30	41
11	Exeter	42	11	6	4	34	22	5	5	12	23	41	41
12	Newport Co	42	9	8	4	38	28	5	5	11	17	45	39
13	Crys Palace	42	12	5	4	32	14	4	8	11	23	35	39
14	Northampton	42	10	5	6	35	28	4	8	11	26	44	38
15	Watford	42	6	6	9	31	37	8	4	9	20	42	38
16	Swindon	42	6	10	5	21	20	6	6	11	20	26	36
17	Leyton Orient	42	6	5	8	31	32	5	5	11	23	41	36
18	Torquay	42	8	5	8	31	29	4	7	10	23	33	35
19	Aldershot	42	7	6	8	40	29	5	5	11	32	41	35
20	Bristol Rov	42	5	10	6	22	26	5	5	10	28	41	34
21	Norwich	42	7	3	11	39	34	6	3	11	17	42	34
22	Brighton	42	8	4	9	26	31	3	8	10	29	42	34
		924	227	116	119	803	524	119	116	227	524	803	924

Appearances and Goals

Player	Appearances		Goals		
	Lge	Cup	Lge	Cup	Tot
Bailey, Jack	42	6		1	1
Chilcott, Ken	4				
Clack, Frank	42	4			
Clark, Don	40	6	22	5	27
Coles, Arthur	6	1	3		3
Collins, Sammy		2			
Dimmer, Hyam	5				
Fox, Ray	4				
Guy, Ivor	38	5		1	1
Hopkins, Idris	24	3			
Jarvis, Mervyn		2			
Jones, Ernie		2			
Kearney, Sid	26		3		3
Moon, Edward		1		2	2
Morgan, Cliff	19	5			
Morgan, Syd		2			
Norris, Ray	3				
Osman, Harry	18	3		1	1
Peacock, Ernie	6				
Roberts, Dennis	38	6			
Russell, Alec	2				
Stone, Fred	4				
Thomas, Bill	30	5	2	1	3
Townsend, Len	39	3	31	3	34
Walker,	1	1	1		1
White, Arnie	6	2	2	1	3
Williams, Cyril	37	5	10	3	13
Williams, Sid	28	2	2		2
(own-goals)			1		1
28 players used	462	66	77	18	95

Odds & ends

Double wins: (3) Leyton Orient, Bristol Rov, Norwich.
Double losses: (1) Bournemouth.

Won from behind: (3) Norwich (a), QPR (h), Torquay (a).
Lost from in front: (2) Watford (h), Aldershot (h).

High spots: Crashing in six goals or more on four occasions.
Beating Bristol Rovers 5-2 on 14 February.
Producing the top scorer in the Third Division (S) for two years running.

Low spots: Losing 0-2 at home to Reading on 21 February.
Succumbing 1-6 at the Vetch on 17 January.

AGM (Grand Hotel, Broad Street, Bristol, 15 March 1949):
Loss £2,222.11s.4d. Season Ticket Sales £2,493.15s.0d.

Player of the year: Len Townsend.
Ever-presents: Jack Bailey and Frank Clack.
Hat-tricks: (8) Len Townsend (3), Don Clark (3), Cyril Williams (1), Arthur Coles (1).
Leading scorer: Overall: Len Townsend (34). League: Townsend (31).

LEAGUE DIVISION 3 (SOUTH) Manager: Bob Hewison SEASON 1948-49

Results summary

No	Date	V	Opponent	Att	Receipts	Pos	Opp Pos	Pt	Res	F-A	H-T
1	21/8	A	SOUTHEND	13,722				0	L	0-1	0-1
2	25/8	H	BRIGHTON	24,432	(£1,549.9.8)			1	D	1-1	0-0
3	28/8	H	NORTHAMPTON	22,663	(£1,455.15.6)	9	21	3	W	3-0	0-0
4	1/9	A	BRIGHTON	17,483		9	6	4	D	0-0	0-0
5	4/9	A	NORWICH	22,667		16	12	4	L	0-4	0-2
6	8/9	H	MILLWALL	16,126	(£1,014.19.9)	14	16	5	D	0-0	0-0
7	11/9	H	EXETER	17,055	(£1,096.0.7)	11	8	7	W	1-0	1-0
8	13/9	A	MILLWALL	19,093		12	5	7	L	1-4	1-3
9	18/9	A	BRISTOL ROV	30,003		19	9	7	L	1-3	0-2
10	25/9	A	SWINDON	22,932		20	4	7	L	1-2	1-2

Scorers, Times, and Referees

1. Grant 21 — Ref: R Carter
2. Clark 61; *Davies 51* — Ref: V Rae
3. Townsend 65, 67, 88 — Ref: A Tolley
4. — Ref: V Rae
5. *Hollis 10, 65, Robinson 14p, [Driver 61]*
6. —
7. Boxshall 42 — Ref: H Hauxwell
8. Boxshall 38; *Hurrell 7, Constantine 37, 40, 77* — Ref: R Burgess
9. Clark 80; *Lambden 28, Watling 31, [Petherbridge 52]* — Ref: R Burgess
10. Clark 30; *Jones 37, 44* — Ref: B Griffiths

Line-ups (positions 1–11; City listed first, opponents in italic)

Match	Side	1	2	3	4	5	6	7	8	9	10	11
1	City	Marks	Guy	Bailey	Edwards	Roberts	Davies	Boxshall	Townsend	Clark	Lewis	Williams S
1	*Southend*	*Nash*	*Beech*	*Walton*	*French*	*Sheard*	*Montgomery*	*Tippett*	*Gray*	*Grant*	*Dudley*	*Edwards*
2	City	Marks	Guy	Bailey	Edwards	Roberts	Davies	Boxshall	Townsend	Clark	Lewis	Williams S
2	*Brighton*	*Baldwin*	*Gutteridge*	*Willense*	*Tennant*	*Booth*	*Whent*	*Willard*	*Lancelotte*	*Lewis*	*McNicholls*	*Davies*
3	City	Marks	Guy	Bailey	Edwards	Roberts	Kearney	Boxshall	Townsend	Clark	Thomas	Williams S
3	*Northampton*	*Williams*	*Smalley*	*Barron*	*Coley*	*Lowery*	*Bowen*	*King*	*Smith*	*Frieman*	*Hughes*	*Fowler*
4	City	Marks	Guy	Bailey	Edwards	Roberts	Kearney	Boxshall	Townsend	Clark	Thomas	Lewis
4	*Brighton*	*Baldwin*	*Gutteridge*	*Willense*	*Tennant*	*Young*	*Whent*	*Willard*	*McNichol*	*Lewis*	*Willis*	*Davies*
5	City	Marks	Guy	Bailey	Edwards	Roberts	Davies	Boxshall	White	Clark	Chilcott	Lewis
5	*Norwich*	*Nethercott*	*Robinson*	*Kilbin*	*Pickwick*	*Low*	*Armes*	*Ryder*	*Driver*	*Hollis*	*Hold*	*Church*
6	City	Marks	Guy	Bailey	Edwards	Roberts	Davies	White	Townsend	Clark	Lewis	Jarvis
6	*Millwall*	*Finlayson*	*Evans*	*Tyler*	*Reeves*	*McMillen*	*Brolly*	*Johnson*	*Hurrell*	*Constantine*	*Brown*	*Fisher*
7	City	Marks	Guy	Bailey	Edwards	Roberts	Davies	Boxshall	Townsend	Clark	White	Jarvis
7	*Exeter*	*Hoyle*	*Johnstone*	*Rowe*	*Bartholomew*	*Walker*	*Evans*	*Dymond*	*Smart*	*Smith*	*Mackay*	*Regan*
8	City	Marks	Guy	Bailey	Edwards	Roberts	Davies	Russell	White	Townsend	Boxshall	Jarvis
8	*Millwall*	*Finlayson*	*Evans*	*Tyler*	*Reeves*	*McMillen*	*Brolly*	*Johnson*	*Hurrell*	*Constantine*	*Brown*	*Fisher*
9	City	Marks	Guy	Bailey	Edwards	Roberts	Davies	Russell	Chilcott	Clark	Thomas	Boxshall
9	*Bristol Rov*	*Weare*	*Bamford*	*Fox*	*Pitt*	*Warren*	*McArthur*	*Petherbridge*	*Hodges*	*Lambden*	*Morgan*	*Watling*
10	City	Clark	Guy	Corbett	Edwards	Roberts	Davies	Lewis	Thomas	Clark	Boxshall	Williams
10	*Swindon*	*Bouton*	*Hunt*	*Young*	*Cowie*	*Ithell*	*Kaye*	*Lunn*	*Baynham*	*Owen*	*Jones*	*Bain*

Match reports

1. SOUTHEND — With five new players in their side, City are slow to settle in the first half. New-boy Davies (Plymouth) errs shortly before 3 o'clock when, in endeavouring to pass back to his keeper, he places the ball too near Cyril Grant, who races through to fire past Marks for the game's only goal.

2. BRIGHTON — City fail to take a leaf out of Brighton's book as, despite a tricky cross-wind, they fail to keep the ball on the ground. Brighton play all the football, but their goal is a lucky break. Marks misjudges a high centre and the ball falls for Ken Davies to shoot in, but Clark heads City level.

3. NORTHAMPTON — In the brilliant first-half sunshine, both Townsend and Fred King have shots disallowed. After the interval, Boxshall also has an effort struck-off before Townsend drives in a left-footed effort that counts. Another fierce drive soon follows before he wraps up a hat-trick near the finish.

4. BRIGHTON — Shortly after the break, Ken Davies almost breaks the deadlock for Brighton with a header that hits the crossbar. A 55th-minute injury to Len Young, which sees him move to inside-right, disrupts the Seasiders and allows City to gain the initiative without ever looking likely to score.

5. NORWICH — The Canaries, in their new silk shirts, put on a dashing display against the City, who are weakened by the absence of Lowrie due to his wife's illness. Roberts handles the ball to give away the penalty, then after the break Allenby Driver volleys in a great goal to leave City no way back.

6. MILLWALL — Little fault can be found with City's defence in this contest where not much in the way of scientific football is on display. In contrast, City's attack, missing Boxshall, offers little. Despite controlling most of the play, they only manage six shots for Malcolm Finlayson to deal with.

7. EXETER — Boxshall's brilliant header, which wins the game for City is in marked contrast to their disappointing display. Despite being handicapped by an injury to Richard Smart, Exeter look much the better side and City have cause to be thankful that at least Marks and Guy are on form for them.

8. MILLWALL — The margin of defeat would have been much greater against the rampant Lions if it hadn't been for a great display by Marks between the sticks and the form of centre-half Roberts. Bill Hurrell headed Millwall's opener, whilst, from Russell's pass, Boxshall obtained City's solitary reply.

9. BRISTOL ROV — The Rovers, who had most of the play, fully deserve their success. Vic Lambden's daisy-cutter opens the scoring, then Josser Watling's shot high into the net doubles the advantage. Following the break, George Petherbridge registers with a cross-shot before Clark heads in for City.

10. SWINDON — Despite Clark heading them in front, City find themselves trailing at the interval. Bill Jones bundles Clark over the line for a hotly disputed equaliser before heading Swindon in front. In the second-half sunshine, City are subjected to a gruelling time by their opponents' fast attack.

No	Date	V	Opponent	Positions	Att	Receipts	Res	FT	HT	Scorers	Ref
11	2/10	H	LEYTON ORIENT	19 / 20 / 9	13,414	(£861.9.6)	W	3:0	2:0	Morgan 20, Deverall 41 (og), Boxshall 70	F Green
12	9/10	H	TORQUAY	20 / 11 / 9	15,134	(£973.3.6)	L	0:2	0:1	Lewis 13, Collins 50	W Edwards
13	16/10	A	WALSALL	20 / 17 / 11	13,979		W	1:0	0:0	Clark 50	N Taylor
14	23/10	H	CRYSTAL PALACE	17 / 22 / 13	14,913	(£954.2.3)	W	2:0	1:0	Morgan 44, Davies 51	H Key
15	30/10	A	READING	18 / 9 / 13	18,069		L	1:2	1:1	Clark 14, Edelston 40, 68	C Wakley
16	6/11	H	BOURNEMOUTH	16 / 2 / 15	21,414	(£1,385.11.0)	W	2:1	2:0	Boxshall 22, Townsend 25, McGibbon 50	J Wiltshire
17	13/11	A	WATFORD	16 / 18 / 16	12,360		D	1:1	0:1	Barney 83, Cumner 31	A Smith
18	20/11	H	NOTTS CO	12 / 9 / 18	29,663	(£1,932.16.6)	W	3:1	2:0	Barney 1, Clark 30, Williams S 57, Johnston 60	V Rae
19	18/12	H	SOUTHEND	11 / 19 / 20	13,900	(£878.14.6)	W	2:1	1:1	Townsend 30, Boxshall 75, Tippett 25	R Carter
20	25/12	A	ALDERSHOT	11 / 18 / 21	5,117		D	0:0	0:0		N Taylor
21	27/12	H	ALDERSHOT	10 / 18 / 22	19,541	(£1,244.6.9)	D	1:1	0:0	Townsend 53, Rawcliffe 70	N Taylor

Line-ups (City player / opponent)

No	1	2	3	4	5	6	7	8	9	10	11
11	Clark / *Newton*	Guy / *Banner*	Bailey / *Davidson*	Morgan / *Bacon*	Roberts / *Hales*	Fox / *Deverall*	Boxshall / *Dryden*	Thomas / *Connelly*	Clark / *Neary*	Davies / *Taylor*	Lewis / *McBeachy*
12	Clark / *McFeat*	Guy / *Stuttard*	Bailey / *Calland*	Morgan / *Towers*	Roberts / *Head*	Fox / *Hill*	Boxshall / *Lewis*	Thomas / *Collins*	Clark / *Conley*	Davies / *Griffiths*	Lewis / *Cameron*
13	Clark / *Lewis*	Guy / *Lethey*	Bailey / *Male*	Morgan / *Walters*	Roberts / *Foulkes*	Davies / *Newman*	Williams / *Condie*	Townsend / *Devlin*	Clark / *Milligan*	Barney / *Morgan*	Lewis / *Ross*
14	Clark / *Graham*	Guy / *Harding*	Bailey / *Dawes*	Morgan / *Lewis*	Roberts / *Bassett*	Davies / *Buckley*	Williams / *Clough*	Townsend / *Beresford*	Clark / *Kurz*	Barney / *Davidson*	Lewis / *Sille*
15	Clark / *Marks*	Guy / *Gaunt*	Bailey / *Gulliver*	Morgan / *Henley*	Roberts / *Brice*	Davies / *Reeve*	Williams / *Jordan*	Townsend / *Edelston*	Clark / *MacPhee*	Barney / *Dix*	Lewis / *Amor*
16	Clark / *Bird*	Guy / *Cunningham*	Bailey / *Sanaghan*	Morgan / *Woodward*	Roberts / *Stirling*	Davies / *Percival*	Boxshall / *Rampling*	Townsend / *Blair*	Clark / *McGibbon*	Barney / *Bennett*	Williams / *Cheney*
17	Clark / *Rigg*	Guy / *Harris*	Bailey / *Oliver*	Morgan / *Egleston*	Roberts / *Ratcliffe*	Davies / *Paton*	Boxshall / *Davies*	Townsend / *Drury*	Clark / *Thomas*	Barney / *Osborne*	Williams / *Cumner*
18	Clark / *Mowl*	Guy / *Southwell*	Bailey / *MacDonald*	Morgan / *Gannon*	Roberts / *Brown A*	Davies / *Baxter*	Boxshall / *Freeman*	Townsend / *Sewell*	Clark / *Lawton*	Barney / *Hold*	Williams / *Johnston*
19	Clark / *Nash*	Guy / *Lindsay*	Bailey / *Pritchard*	Morgan / *Goodyear*	Roberts / *Sheard*	Kearney / *Pryde*	Boxshall / *Butler*	Townsend / *McAlinden*	Clark / *Dudley*	Barney / *French*	Tippett / *Tippett*
20	Clark / *Reynolds*	Guy / *Rogers*	Bailey / *Sheppard*	Morgan / *Sherwood*	Roberts / *Rowland*	Kearney / *Cropley*	Boxshall / *Hobbs*	Townsend / *White*	Clark / *Rawcliffe*	Barney / *McNichal*	Lewis / *Sinclair*
21	Clark / *Reynolds*	Guy / *Rogers*	Bailey / *Sheppard*	Morgan / *Sherwood*	Roberts / *Rowland*	Kearney / *Cropley*	Boxshall / *Hobbs*	Townsend / *White*	Clark / *Rawcliffe*	Barney / *McNichal*	Lewis / *Sinclair*

Match reports

11 — Boxshall's fierce shot, which crashes into the net to tie up City's success, is the one bright spot of this poor affair. Morgan opens the scoring with a low-driven deflected free-kick then, shortly before half-time, Harry Deverall hits a back-pass wide of his keeper to put City two up.

12 — Though scheduled to play at the Gate, Townsend turns out for the reserves at Charlton because he missed his train connection. City could have done with him in this poor game, which saw many fans leave well before the end. Ex-City player Sammy Collins fired in Torquay's second.

13 — At Fellows Park, spirited dashes by new man Vic Barney, and Clark's low-driven goal prove a real tonic for City fans, including Frank Peters their old pre-war winger. A deserved first away win of the season for City, as well as their first victory over the Saddler's since the war.

14 — City's half-back line has the time to supplement their attack in this game and come up trumps with both goals. Morgan shot in the opener through a crowd of players, then Davies sends in a 20-yard sizzler that sails in just under the bar. Fred Kurz has a goal disallowed for offside.

15 — City played quite well in the first half at Elm Park, where they find themselves facing George Marks, their recently transferred goalkeeper. Townsend shoots the opener into the roof of the net, but Maurice Edelston hits Reading's leveller, before striding through to fire in the winner.

16 — Doug McGibbon (ex-Fulham and Soton) brings groans from the City fans when he scores with a weak four-yard shot just after the interval. From then on, City have a hard task to retain the advantage given them by Boxshall's fierce opener and Townsend's shot into an empty net.

17 — A poor City show at Vicarage Road, where Barney's shot into an empty net after Clark headed the ball over Tommy Rigg, produces a rather lucky point. Ex-Arsenal men, George Drury and Horace Cumner, combine for Watford's goal, which sees the unmarked winger fire past Clack.

18 — Such was the allure of the illustrious visitors that even the Lord Mayor (Alderman Chas. R Gill) was among the large crowd who witnessed a sensational start. Barney flung himself at the ball and headed it just inside the post to give City an early lead. Clark volleyed in number two.

19 — City make hard work of this win over a poor Southend side who go in front thanks to Tommy Tippett's close-range shot. Sid Williams, who leaves the field with a knee injury shortly before half-time, returns after the interval and provides the pass for Boxshall to hit the winner.

20 — The City do well to share the spoils on the Recreation Ground against a slick Aldershot side. However, they are most fortunate in the closing minutes when Jackie White, the home inside-right, strikes an upright. A hard struggle, during which City produce some spells of good play.

21 — City hold the territorial advantage, but are often all at sea in dealing with a heavy ball on a slippery pitch, which cuts up badly. The advantage of Townsend's unstoppable left-footed drive, crashing in just under the bar, is cancelled out by Frank Rawcliffe shooting in the Shots leveller.

LEAGUE DIVISION 3 (SOUTH)   Manager: Bob Hewison   SEASON 1948-49

Match results

No	Date	Att	•	Pos	Pt	Res	F-A	H-T	Scorers, Times, and Referees
22	A NORTHAMPTON 1/1	6,901 (£580)	16	12	22	L	1-3	0-0	Townsend 88 / *Garrett 51, Fowler 84, King 87.* Ref: A Tolley
23	H NORWICH 15/1	10,989 (£677.4.9)	8	13	22	L	1-6	0-1	Barney 83 / *[Ashman 57, Eyre 73] Kinsey 30, 48, 86, Morgan 50,*
24	A EXETER 22/1	10,066	16	13	23	D	1-1	0-1	Clark 47 / *Regan 18.* Ref: H Hauxwell
25	A IPSWICH 29/1	11,189	10	14	23	L	0-2	0-0	*Parker S 77, Jennings 86.* Ref: A Bond
26	H BRISTOL ROV 5/2	27,543 (£1,813.17.0)	3	13	24	D	1-1	0-0	Clark 78 / *Hodges 55.* Ref: R Burgess
27	H SWINDON 19/2	15,728 (£1,035.5.3)	5	15	24	L	1-3	0-0	Townsend 50p / *Owen 52, 80, Bain 54.* Ref: B Griffiths
28	A LEYTON ORIENT 26/2	8,989	16	17	24	L	1-3	0-2	Barney 53 / *Connelly 12, Neary 25, Naylor 85.* Ref: F Green
29	A TORQUAY 5/3	5,230	11	13	26	W	2-0	1-0	Townsend 14, 82. Ref: W Edwards
30	H WALSALL 12/3	12,263 (£769.7.9)	11	15	27	D	2-2	1-2	Townsend 30, 51 / *Clark 27, Chapman 40.* Ref: N Taylor
31	A CRYSTAL PALACE 19/3	11,840	22	17	27	L	0-4	0-1	*[Chivers 64, Roberts 82 (og)] Lewis 35, McCormick 63,* Ref: H Key

Line-ups (Bristol City player / *opponent*)

No	1	2	3	4	5	6	7	8	9	10	11
22	Clack / *Ansell*	Guy / *Smalley*	Bailey / *Barron*	Edwards / *Smith D*	Peacock / *McCoy*	Davies / *Blunt*	Boxshall / *English*	Townsend / *King*	Clark / *Garrett*	Barney / *Hughes*	Williams / *Fowler*
23	Clack / *Nethercott*	Bailey / *Robinson*	Bailey / *Morgan B*	Morgan / *Pickwick*	Roberts / *Low*	Davies / *Dutton*	Williams / *Morgan G*	Townsend / *Kinsey*	Clark / *Ashman*	Barney / *Eyre*	Jarvis / *Church*
24	Clack / *Hoyle*	Guy / *Johnstone*	Bailey / *Clark*	Peacock / *Bartholomew*	Roberts / *Davey*	Davies / *Gibson*	Lewis / *Dymond*	Townsend / *Smart*	Clark / *Smith*	Barney / *Harrower*	Eveleigh / *Regan*
25	Brown T / *Rumbold*	Guy / *Parry*	Bailey /	Peacock / *Perrett*	Roberts / *Ball*	Morgan / *Baird*	Lewis / *Brown J*	Townsend / *Parker S*	Clark / *Jennings*	Barney / *Parker T*	Eveleigh / *Little*
26	Clack / *Weare*	Guy / *Bamford*	Bailey / *Fox*	Peacock / *Pitt*	Roberts / *Warren*	Peacock / *McArthur*	Townsend / *Petherbridge*	Mullen / *Hodges*	Clark / *Lambden*	Barney / *Morgan*	Lewis / *Watling*
27	Clack / *Burton*	Bailey / *White*	Bailey / *Young*	Morgan / *Kaye*	Roberts / *Hudson*	Davies / *Foxton*	Peacock / *Lum*	Townsend / *Dawson*	Clark / *Owen*	Barney / *Jones*	Mullen / *Bain*
28	Clack / *Gerula*	Bailey / *Banner*	Bailey / *Davidson*	Mullen / *Bacon*	Roberts / *Sales*	Davies / *Deverall*	White / *Gray*	Townsend / *Connelly*	Clark / *Neary*	Barney / *Naylor*	Tovey / *Brinton*
29	Morgan / *Davis*	Stone / *Topping*	Bailey / *Calland*	Mullen / *Towers*	Roberts / *Head*	Davies / *Lester*	White / *Rae*	Townsend / *Lewis*	Peacock / *Conley*	Barney / *Collins*	Tovey / *Shaw*
30	Morgan / *Lewis*	Stone / *Jones*	Bailey / *Methley*	Mullen / *Walters*	Roberts / *Faulkes*	Davies / *Newman*	White / *Condie*	Townsend / *Mullard*	Peacock / *Chapman*	Barney / *Devlin*	Tovey / *Clark*
31	Bumstead / *George*	Stone /	Bailey / *Wyatt*	Mullen / *Lewis*	Roberts / *Chase*	Davies / *Chivers*	Lewis / *Clough*	White / *McCormick*	Townsend / *Kurz*	Barney / *Thomas*	Tovey / *Gaillard*

Match reports

22 — Not a good start to the New Year for the City, as they succumb to their first defeat since the end of October. Archie Garrett (ex-Birmingham), who guested for the Robins during the war, has the entire City defence appealing for offside as he races through to fire in the opening goal.

23 — The skill and speed of the visitors make City look decidedly third-rate in this game. Trailing to Noel Kinsey's fired in opener, City are exposed by the Canaries off the ball running after the break. Kinsey notches his hat-trick when he runs through to shoot past Clack just before the end.

24 — Making his debut as a winger, Gordon Eveleigh switches to the half-back line when Davies injuries his elbow in making a 13th-minute tackle. It takes a fierce drive by Clark, reported as his best goal of the season, as well as Clack saving of a late penalty, to earn City their point.

25 — Twenty minutes from the finish, Clack saves George Rumbold's penalty low to his right, but Ipswich soon make amends when Stan Parker heads in from John Brown's cross. A great shot by Bill Jennings completes the scoring, before Clark fires his spot-kick straight at Tom Brown.

26 — Jackie Pitt's long pass splits the City defence and produces a bout of inter-passing between Vic Lambden and Len Hodges, who takes the ball on the volley to fire in the opener. Clark's angled-shot, fumbled into the net by Jack Weare, brings City an extremely fortunate point indeed.

27 — Despite scoring first when Townsend - after picking himself up - nets from the spot, City find the Railwaymen too hot to handle. Maurice Owen equalises with a shot into the far corner, then Jimmy Bain's high centre creeps in before Owen again finds the target with a fine shot.

28 — City put up a good fight at Brisbane Road, despite losing the services of Clark with a strained ligament barely a minute after Ted Connelly had headed Orient in front. Barney dribbles 20 yards before beating Stan Gerula with a fine shot, but Bill Naylor heads in to end City's fight-back.

29 — The new boys star in City's first victory in eleven games. Local lad Syd Morgan pulls off a number of good saves on his debut, whilst 17-year-old Bill Tovey, in only his second game, engineers the first goal with a pass to Peacock, who squares the ball for Townsend to prod home.

30 — A fortunate point for City, as the Sadlers attack gives them a hectic afternoon. Twice Walsall take the lead, firstly when Tom Clark fires in a terrific shot from eight-yards range, and then Phil Chapman puts away an easy chance when John Devlin's long-range shot cannons off the bar.

31 — City have problems before the game with Peacock having to withdraw after suffering a bilious attack. Captained by ex-Palace player Glyn Lewis, matters didn't improve on the field of play. In the opening ten minutes City concede as many free-kicks and it is downhill all the way.

Football season match-log (Bristol City), matches 32–42.

32. H READING — 26/3
Att 11,622 (£747.15.3) | Pos 18 | L 0-2 (HT 0-1) | 4 | Pts 27
Scorers: *Blackman 18, Gliddon 50* | Ref: C Wakley
City: Clack, Guy, Stone, Peacock, Roberts, Kearney, Mullen, White, Townsend, Barney, Bailey
Reading: Marks, Clover, Gulliver, Henley, Brice, Green, Fisher, Edelston, Blackman, Glidden, Allison

Despite having most of the opening play, City fall away after Ron Blackman fires in the Biscuitmen opener. They are unlucky just before the break, though, when Marks puts a point-blank drive around a post (the best save seen so far this season at Ashton Gate) to keep them out.

33. A BOURNEMOUTH — 2/4
Att 14,004 | Pos 17 | D 0-0 (HT 0-0) | 3 | Pts 28
Ref: J Wiltshire
City: Clack, Guy, Stone, Kearney, Roberts, Davies, Mullen, Townsend, Boxshall, Barney, Bailey
Bournemouth: Bird, Cunningham, Sanaghan, Young, Wilson, Woodward, Stephens, Blakeman, McGibbon, Lunn, Hanlon

Whilst Boxshall had a goal disallowed for offside before the break, long-playing City do well to hold the skilful close-passing Cherries side to a draw. Roberts has a stirring game at the heart of the defence, but the City forwards spurn three quite easy chances early in the second half.

34. A NEWPORT — 7/4
Att 10,278 | Pos 16 | W 2-0 (HT 0-0) | 15 | Pts 30
Scorers: **Mullen 50, 75** | Ref: R Aldridge
City: Clack, Guy, Stone, Kearney, Roberts, Davies, Mullen, Townsend, Boxshall, Barney, Bailey
Newport: Matthews, Bradford, Hayward, Roffi, Wilcox, Morrall, Williams H, Lewis W, Parker, Carr, Shergold

Despite fielding ten of the side that created such a stir in this season's FA Cup, County are no match for City, who switched their wingers for the second half. After scoring direct from his flag-kick, Mullen makes sure of victory with a fierce left-footed shot into the corner of the net.

35. H WATFORD — 9/4
Att 12,459 (£788.16.11) | Pos 16 | D 1-1 (HT 1-1) | 21 | Pts 31
Scorers: **Boxshall 5**, *Davies 44* | Ref: A Smith
City: Clack, Guy, Stone, Peacock, Roberts, Davies, Bailey, Townsend, Boxshall, Barney, Mullen
Watford: Morton, Hooper, Oliver, Paton, Hunt, Fisher, Drury, Woodruff, Thomas, Davies, Cumner

Boxshall's early shot into the corner of the net fails to inspire City. For Watford, Graham Davies nets from close range to conclude the scoring just before the interval. Even though Mullen is denied by the bar after the break, Watford are the more dangerous side and deserve their point.

36. A PORT VALE — 15/4
Att 13,571 | Pos 16 | L 2-4 (HT 0-2) | 12 | Pts 31
Scorers: **Townsend 60p, Guy 75**, *Allen 15, 25, Martin 47, Hulligan 89*
City: Morgan, Stone, Bailey, Edwards, Roberts, Davies, Boxshall, Townsend, Guy, Barney, Mullen
Port Vale: Heppell, Cheadle, Potts, McGarry, Hayward, Todd, Allen, Martin, Polk, Aveyard, Hulligan

Guy shows plenty of aptitude and ability in his unfamiliar centre-forward role and thoroughly deserved his well-taken goal. The skilful and quick-tackling Valiants extinguish City's fight-back when Mick Hulligan fires in his make-sure goal just 30 seconds before the finish.

37. A NOTTS CO — 16/4
Att 27,149 | Pos 16 | L 1-2 (HT 0-0) | 9 | Pts 31
Scorers: **Townsend 57**, *Sewell 58, 81* | Ref: V Rae
City: Morgan, Stone, Bailey, Kearney, Roberts, Davies, Boxshall, Townsend, White, Barney, Mullen
Notts Co: Smith, Southwell, Purvis, Chapman, Brown A, Pimbley, Houghton, Sewell, Hold, Jackson, Johnston

Townsend fires City (in their new shirts) ahead on a hot afternoon at Meadow Lane, but Jackie Sewell decides the game in County's favour with a daisy-cutter after earlier lobbing in a leveller. Without the injured James Jackson for the second half, Notts do well to claim both points.

38. H PORT VALE — 18/4
Att 11,094 (£707.7.9) | Pos 16 | D 1-1 (HT 1-1) | 12 | Pts 32
Scorers: **Stone 14**, *Polk 8*
City: Morgan, Stone, Bailey, Kearney, Roberts, Davies, Boxshall, Townsend, Guy, Barney, Fox
Port Vale: Prince, Butler, Potts, McGarry, Hayward, Todd, Allen, Martin, Polk, Aveyard, Hulligan

With City handicapped with injuries to Davies and Townsend, this game degenerates after the interval. Reserve keeper Harry Prince allows City to level Stan Polk's cross-driven opener. Put off by Guy's challenge, he can only help Stone's free-kick from halfway into his own net.

39. H IPSWICH — 23/4
Att 10,229 (£623.16.0) | Pos 16 | W 2-0 (HT 1-0) | 8 | Pts 34
Scorers: **Boxshall 44, 89** | Ref: A Bond
City: Morgan, Stone, Bailey, Kearney, Roberts, Fox, Boxshall, White, Guy, Barney, Mullen
Ipswich: Brown T, Bell, Mitchell, Perrett, Baird, Neilson, Little, Dempsey, Parker S, Parker T, Brown J

A much-improved display brings its due reward and Boxshall twice heads in for City to notch up their first home win since mid-December. In consequence of the Easter Monday fire, stand patrons are requested to make sure all matches and cigarettes ends are put out before leaving.

40. H SWANSEA — 27/4
Att 14,054 (£891.14.6) | Pos 15 | D 0-0 (HT 0-0) | 1 | Pts 35
City: Morgan, Guy, Bailey, Kearney, Roberts, Fox, Boxshall, White, Edwards, Barney, Mullen
Swansea: Canning, Ewell, Keane, Paul, Weston, Burns, O'Driscoll, McCrory, Scrine, Lucas, Payne

City have the territorial advantage, but despite their enthusiasm there is no doubting the superior craft and ability of the Swansea side. Frank Scrine, in place of the injured Stan Richards, makes the miss of the game with a soft shot following on from Sam McCrory's 30-yard run.

41. A SWANSEA — 30/4
Att 18,958 | Pos 15 | L 0-2 (HT 0-1) | 1 | Pts 35
Scorers: *Scrine 35, O'Driscoll 80*
City: Morgan, Guy, Bailey, Kearney, Roberts, Edwards, Boxshall, White, Townsend, Barney, Mullen
Swansea: Canning, Ewell, Keane, Paul, Weston, Burns, O'Driscoll, McCrory, Scrine, Lucas, Payne

The City have some amazing escapes on a sunny day at the Vetch. Both sides play some fine soccer and Edwards fires City's best chance over the bar before Frank Scrine heads the opener. Roberts is outstanding, but is unable to prevent John O'Driscoll doubling Swansea's advantage.

42. H NEWPORT — 7/5
Att 12,757 (£813.11.6) | Pos 16 | D 1-1 (HT 1-0) | 15 | Pts 36
Scorers: **Townsend 5**, *Roffi 75* | Ref: R Aldridge
City: Morgan, Stone, Bailey, Kearney, Roberts, Edwards, Boxshall, White, Townsend, Barney, Mullen
Newport: Matthews, Bradford, Hayward, Murall, Wilcox, Newell, Williams, Comley, Roffi, Lewis, Shergold

City go all out in their efforts to complete a double over the Ironsides, but, despite much pressure and firing in shot after shot, they are unable to add to Townsend's early drive. With the barrage continuing after the break, Guido Roffi's header brings Newport reward for their resilience.

Home Average 16,573 — Away 14,933

CUP-TIES

Manager: Bob Hewison

SEASON 1948-49

FA Cup

				F-A	H-T	Scorers, Times, and Referees
1	A	CRYSTAL PALACE 12	W	1-0	0-0	Townsend 106
		16,700 22				Ref: R Aldridge
		(£1,450)				

1	2	3	4	5	6	7	8	9	10	11
Clack	Guy	Bailey	Morgan	Roberts	Davies	Boxshall	Townsend	Clark	Barney	Williams
Graham	*Harding*	*Dawes*	*Lewis*	*Chase*	*Buckley*	*Broughton*	*Mullen*	*Howells*	*Mulheron*	*Clough*

A thrilling cup-tie at Selhurst where the action is filmed by the Palace chairman Percy Harper. Townsend's header in extra-time gives City passage to the next round. Justice for City who are robbed of a first-half goal when Dick Graham carried Morgan's shot over his line.

				F-A	H-T	Scorers, Times, and Referees
2	H	SWANSEA 13	W	3-1	2-1	Boxshall 17, Townsend 33,
		11/12				O'Driscoll 15 [Barney 55]
		22,136 1				Ref: G Reader
		(£1,610)				

1	2	3	4	5	6	7	8	9	10	11
Clack	Guy	Bailey	Morgan	Roberts	Davies	Boxshall	Townsend	Clark	Barney	Williams
Parry	*Feeney*	*Keane*	*Paul*	*Weston*	*Burns*	*Wookey*	*Lucas*	*Powell*	*Scrine*	*O'Driscoll*

An almost cast-iron defence and an ability to play the right type of football under bad conditions are the key features of City's victory over star-studded Swansea. John O'Driscoll fired the visitors in front, but City quickly equalised when Boxshall sent his grounder past Jack Parry.

				F-A	H-T	Scorers, Times, and Referees
3	H	CHELSEA 12	L	1-2	1-0	Clark 20
		8/1				Bentley 80, 86, Jones 81
		36,454 1:16				Ref: R Burgess
		(£4,252.1.9)				

1	2	3	4	5	6	7	8	9	10	11
Clack	Guy	Bailey	Morgan	Roberts	Davies	Boxshall	Townsend	Clark	Barney	Williams
Pickering	*Winters*	*Lewis*	*Armstrong*	*Harris*	*McCauley*	*Campbell*	*Bowie*	*Bentley*	*Williams*	*Jones*

Roy Bentley achieved his ambition by scoring against his old club. Clark fired City in front, but they had a number of escapes before Bentley headed in to inspire Chelsea's late revival. Benny Jones shoots into an empty net, then Bentley's magnificent header ties up his side's success.

Gloucestershire Cup

				F-A	H-T	Scorers, Times, and Referees
F	A	BRISTOL ROV 16	L	0-2	0-2	Lambden 5, Morgan 12
		14/5				Ref: R Mortimer
		15,111 5				

1	2	3	4	5	6	7	8	9	10	11
Morgan	Stone	Bailey	Tovey	Roberts	Edwards	Boxshall	White	Townsend	Kearney	Mullen
Liley	*Bamford*	*Fox*	*Pitt*	*Warren*	*McArthur*	*Petherbridge*	*Hodges*	*Lambden*	*Morgan*	*Watling*

Despite a stomach upset bringing about goalkeeper Jack Weare's late withdrawal, the Rovers retain the County Trophy with this easy success. Vic Lambden dribbled around the City keeper before tapping in the opener prior to Jimmy Morgan's 30-yarder doubling Rover's advantage.

James Howell Cup

				F-A	H-T	Scorers, Times, and Referees
F	A	CARDIFF 15	L	0-1	0-0	Baker 60
		2/5				
		8,000 2:4				
		(£500)				

1	2	3	4	5	6	7	8	9	10	11
Morgan	Guy	Stone	Kearney	Roberts	Edwards	Boxshall	White	Bailey	Barney	Mullen
Morris	*Stittall R*	*Sherwood*	*Williams G*	*Montgomery*	*Blair*	*Baker*	*Rees*	*Best*	*Stevenson*	*Edwards G*

A good turn-out at Ninian Park for this game in aid of the National Institute For The Blind. The play didn't reach a particularly high standard and Bill Baker's shot from a pass by Ernie Stevenson proves enough to ensure that Cardiff become the first holders of the handsome silver cup.

	P	W	D	L	F	A	W	D	L	F	A	Pts
			Home					**Away**				
1 Swansea	42	20	1	0	60	11	7	7	7	27	23	62
2 Reading	42	17	3	1	48	18	8	4	9	29	32	55
3 Bournemouth	42	15	2	4	42	17	7	6	8	27	31	52
4 Swindon	42	11	9	1	38	20	7	6	8	26	36	51
5 Bristol Rov	42	13	5	3	42	23	6	5	10	19	28	48
6 Brighton	42	11	5	5	32	26	6	4	13	23	29	48
7 Ipswich	42	14	3	4	53	30	4	6	11	25	47	45
8 Millwall	42	12	7	2	42	23	5	4	12	21	41	45
9 Torquay	42	12	5	4	45	26	5	6	10	20	44	45
10 Norwich	42	11	6	4	32	10	5	6	10	35	39	44
11 Notts Co	42	15	3	3	68	19	4	2	15	34	49	43
12 Exeter	42	12	5	4	45	26	3	5	13	18	50	40
13 Port Vale	42	11	3	7	32	21	3	8	10	19	33	39
14 Walsall	42	9	5	7	34	28	6	3	12	22	36	38
15 Newport Co	42	8	8	7	41	35	6	3	12	27	57	37
16 BRISTOL C	42	8	6	7	28	24	3	5	13	16	38	36
17 Watford	42	8	9	4	24	21	4	6	11	17	33	36
18 Southend	42	5	10	6	18	18	4	6	11	23	28	35
19 Leyton Orient	42	9	6	6	36	29	2	6	13	22	51	34
20 Northampton	42	9	6	6	33	20	3	3	15	18	42	33
21 Aldershot	42	6	5	10	26	29	5	6	10	22	30	33
22 Crys Palace	42	7	8	6	27	27	1	3	17	11	49	27
	924	241	119	102	846	501	102	119	241	501	846	924

Odds & ends

Double wins: (0).

Double losses: (3) Norwich, Swindon, Reading.

Won from behind: (2) Southend (h), Swansea (FAC) (h).

Lost from in front: (4) Swindon (a), Reading (a), Swindon (h), Notts Co (a).

High spots: England star Tommy Lawton visiting with Notts Co.

Beating Swansea Town in the FA Cup.

Thrilling 5-5 draw in a friendly at Merthyr on 12 February.

Low spots: The sad saga which saw the departure of chairman George Jenkins and manager Bob Hewison.

Losing 1-6 at home to Norwich on 15 January.

Chelsea's late revival, which knocked City out of the FA Cup.

Succumbing to Bristol Rovers in the final of the Gloucestershire Cup.

AGM (Grand Hotel, Broad Street, Bristol, 4 April 1950): Loss £12,055.4s.1d. Season Ticket Sales £2,402.5s.2d.

Player of the year: Dennis Roberts.

Ever-presents: (0).

Hat-tricks: (1) Len Townsend (1).

Leading scorer: Overall: Len Townsend (17). League: Townsend (15).

	Appearances		Goals		
	Lge	Cup	Lge	Cup	Tot
Bailey, Jack	41	5			
Barney, Vic	28	4	4	1	5
Boxshall, Danny	28	5	8	1	9
Chilcott, Ken	2				
Clack, Frank	24	3			
Clark, Don	27	3	8	1	9
Corbett, William	1				
Davies, John	30	3	1		1
Edwards, Cliff	14	2			
Eveleigh, Gordon	2				
Fox, Ray	5				
Guy, Ivor	36	4	1		1
Jarvis, Mervyn	4				
Kearney, Sid	15	2			
Lewis, Glyn	18				
Marks, George	9				
Morgan, Cliff	15	3	2		2
Morgan, Syd	9	2			
Mullen, James	16	2	2		2
Peacock, Ernie	8				
Roberts, Dennis	41	5			
Russell, Alec	1				
Stone, Fred	15	2	1		1
Thomas, Bill	6				
Tovey, Bill	4	1			
Townsend, Len	35	4	15	2	17
White, Arnie	15	2	1		1
Williams, Sid	13	3	1		1
(own-goals)					
28 players used	462	55	44	5	49

LEAGUE DIVISION 3 (SOUTH)   Manager: Bob Wright   SEASON 1949-50

Table columns (per match): No | Date | Att | Pos | Pt | F-A | H-T | Scorers, Times, and Referees | 1 | 2 | 3 | 4 | 5 | 6 | 7 | 8 | 9 | 10 | 11

---

1 — H NORTHAMPTON — 20/8
Att 27,463 (£1,633.8.9) · W · F-A 3-1 · H-T 2-0 · Pt 2
Scorers: White 20, Edwards 30, Williams 80 / King 88 · Ref: F Overton

1	2	3	4	5	6	7	8	9	10	11
Coombs	Stone	Bailey	Freeman	Roberts	Edwards	Williams	White	Clark	Eisentrager	Rudkin
Ansell	*Wooley*	*Southam*	*Candlin*	*McCoy*	*Coley*	*King*	*Smith D*	*Garrett*	*Murphy*	*Mitchell*

Despite losing Clark with a knee injury midway through the first half, City win without too much trouble. White volleys in the opener, then a 20-yard Edwards free-kick doubles City's advantage before Williams back-heads a third prior to Fred King firing the ball in from close range.

---

2 — A NOTT'M FOR — 24/8
Att 27,043 (£2,247) · L · F-A 0-3 · H-T 0-1 · Pt 2
Scorers: Kaile 25, 87, Ardron 65p · Ref: G Clark

1	2	3	4	5	6	7	8	9	10	11
Coombs	Stone	Bailey	Freeman	Roberts	Edwards	Williams	White	McCarthy	Eisentrager	Rudkin
Walker	*Thomas*	*McCall*	*Burkitt*	*Gager*	*Morley*	*Scott*	*Love*	*Ardron*	*Kaile*	*Laverton*

The City are comprehensively outplayed in every phase of this game. Gordon Kaile, a late inclusion for Forest, opens the scoring after Wally Ardron hits the crossbar. Bailey's handball allows Ardron to register from the spot before Kaile wraps things up with a shot from close range.

---

3 — A NORWICH — 27/8
Att 25,870 · L · F-A 0-3 · H-T 0-2 · Pos 18 · Pt 2
Scorers: Eyre 25, 35, Kinsey 80 · Ref: H Williams

1	2	3	4	5	6	7	8	9	10	11
Coombs	Stone	Bailey	Freeman	Roberts	Edwards	Williams	White	McCarthy	Eisentrager	Rudkin
Nethercott	*Morgan D*	*Tobin*	*Pickwick*	*Low*	*Dutton*	*Gavin*	*Kinsey*	*Driver*	*Jones*	*Eyre*

City play some good football at Carrow Road, but lack zip in front of goal. Norwich take the lead in a breakaway, which sees Les Eyre driving the ball out of the reach of Coombs. Noel Kinsey wraps up the Canaries' success near the close when he easily finds the net from close range.

---

4 — H NOTT'M FOR — 30/8
Att 25,924 (£1,550.5.9) · L · F-A 0-2 · H-T 0-0 · Pos 19 · Pt 2
Scorers: Ardron 49, 68 · Ref: G Clark

1	2	3	4	5	6	7	8	9	10	11
Coombs	Stone	Bailey	Freeman	Roberts	Edwards	Mullen	White	McCarthy	Eisentrager	Rudkin
Walker	*Thomas*	*McCall*	*Burkitt*	*Gager*	*Knight*	*Scott*	*Love*	*Ardron*	*Ashman*	*Kaile*

Wally Ardron makes amends for having placed a weak 38th-minute spot-kick wide. Hooking in the opener from a right-wing cross that three City players fail to deal with, he then takes advantage of hesitancy between Coombs and Roberts to dash between them and head in the second.

---

5 — H NEWPORT — 3/9
Att 20,007 (£1,166.6.0) · W · F-A 6-0 · H-T 3-0 · Pos 14 · Pt 4
Scorers: Eisentrager 12, 29, 35, 73, White 55, Hawkins 85 · Ref: A Tolley

1	2	3	4	5	6	7	8	9	10	11
Coombs	Stone	Bailey	Freeman	Roberts	Kearney	Boxshall	White	Hawkins	Eisentrager	Rudkin
Hodge	*Wilcox*	*Hayward*	*Staples*	*Depear*	*Williams G*	*Bowen*	*Roffi*	*Parker*	*Newall*	*Harper*

An easy win for City is rounded off when Hawkins shoots in past Guido Roffi, who had taken over between the sticks for the last 15 minutes, when Eric Hodge was injured. Eisentrager, who made a prodigious leap to head in White's cross for his second goal, has a game to remember.

---

6 — A BRISTOL ROV — 10/9
Att 34,463 (£2,387.4.6) · W · F-A 3-2 · H-T 1-0 · Pos 13 · Pt 6
Scorers: Hawkins 11, Rudkin 47, Lowrie 84, Roost 54, Hodges 62 · Ref: A Tarratt

1	2	3	4	5	6	7	8	9	10	11
Weare	Bamford	Fox	Freeman	Roberts	Kearney	White	Eisentrager	Hawkins	Lowrie	Rudkin
			Pitt	*Warren*	*McCourt*	*Bush*	*Hodges*	*Roost*	*James*	*Watling*

Lowrie (£18,000 ex-Newcastle), who turned out once for City during the war, fires in a brilliant late winner. The Rovers great fight-back deserved better, especially as Len Hodges had what looked like a perfectly valid goal disallowed not long after having fired in an equaliser.

---

7 — H SWINDON — 13/9
Att 27,255 (£1,663.1.3) · W · F-A 1-0 · H-T 1-0 · Pos 10 · Pt 8
Scorers: Eisentrager 42 · Ref: B Griffiths

1	2	3	4	5	6	7	8	9	10	11
Coombs	Stone	Bailey	Freeman	Roberts	Kearney	Boxshall	Eisentrager	Hawkins	Lowrie	Rudkin
Boulton	*Cowie*	*Young*	*Kaye*	*Hudson*	*Foxton*	*Lumn*	*Dawson*	*Owen*	*Jones*	*Bain*

Andrew Cowie's ill-judged back-pass to keeper Frank Boulton settles this game. Hawkins, Rudkin and Eisentrager challenged for the ball, which the latter placed into an open net. Both sides contrived to play attractive soccer, but by the finish the pace had dropped considerably.

---

8 — A BRIGHTON — 17/9
Att 16,687 · L · F-A 1-2 · H-T 1-1 · Pos 11 · Pt 8
Scorers: Lowrie 44p / Tennant 35p, Lancelott 75 · Ref: R Burgess

1	2	3	4	5	6	7	8	9	10	11
Ball	Stone	Mitchelson	Freeman	Roberts	Kearney	Boxshall	White	Hawkins	Lowrie	Rudkin
Morrad	*Mansell*	*Willard*	*Whent*		*Tennant*	*Reed*	*McNichol*	*Pinchbeck*	*Lancelotte*	*Morris*

City had enough chances to have won at the Goldstone, where Freeman's half-hearted tackle, that allows Eric Lancelotte to shoot in from close range, consigns them to defeat. Whilst City's approach work is attractive, they tended to dwell on the ball when chances presented themselves.

---

9 — A BOURNEMOUTH — 21/9
Att 8,899 · L · F-A 1-3 · H-T 0-0 · Pos 11 · Pt 8
Scorers: Stone 50 / Cheney 55, Lunn 82, McGibbon 89 · Ref: W Edwards

1	2	3	4	5	6	7	8	9	10	11
Duke	Stone	Mitchelson	Thomas	Roberts	Kearney	Boxshall	Eisentrager	Hawkins	Lowrie	Rudkin
	Cunningham	*Drummond*	*Woodward*	*Stirling*	*Martin*	*Stephens*	*Blair*	*McGibbon*	*Lunn*	*Cheney*

Despite the torrential rain, some surprisingly good football is witnessed. Stone's goal is the highlight, finding the net with his free-kick from just inside the opposition half. Dennis Cheney headed in a leveller, but it is Doug McGibbon's unstoppable shot that is the Cherries best effort.

---

10 — H WALSALL — 24/9
Att 21,691 (£1,284.19.3) · W · F-A 2-1 · H-T 1-0 · Pos 10 · Pt 10
Scorers: Rudkin 41, Hawkins 70 / Morris 52 · Ref: W Muller

1	2	3	4	5	6	7	8	9	10	11
Coombs	Stone	Mitchelson	Thomas	Roberts	Kearney	Boxshall	Eisentrager	Hawkins	Lowrie	Rudkin
Lewis	*Jones*	*Mathley*	*Walters*	*Foulkes*	*Russan*	*Medds*	*Morris*	*Chapman*	*Devlin*	*Betts*

After Gordon Morris had fired in Walsall's great leveller, Eisentrager engineered the move that lead to Hawkins firing in the close-range winner. A deserved City success, but they are fortunate shortly before the close. The ball rolls across the goal with Coombs out of position.

11 A MILLWALL 1/10 L 1:3 11 / 14 / 10 23,894
Hawkins 20 / [Constantine 62]
Hodgetts 5, Simmonds 35,
Ref: E Crook

Coombs	Stone	Bailey	Kearney	Bicknell	Thomas	Boxshall	Eisentrager	Hawkins	Lowrie	Rudkin
Finlayson	*Fisher*	*Tyler*	*Reeves*	*McMillen*	*Forrest*	*Johnson*	*Simmonds*	*Constantine*	*Hurrell*	*Hodgetts*

City missed Dennis Roberts in this hard struggle at the Den; his deputy Roy Bicknell does not have the answer to the wandering tactics of Jim Constantine. Bert Hawkins is indebted to the linesman for signalling his fired in equaliser after Frank Hodgetts had shot through the opener.

---

12 H SOUTHEND 8/10 D 1:1 12 / 9 / 11 20,221 (£1,195.14.9)
Eisentrager 57
Wakefield 77
Ref: H Williams

Coombs	Guy	Mitchelson	Kearney	Roberts	Edwards	Boxshall	Eisentrager	Hawkins	White	Rudkin
Hankey	*Loughran*	*Walton*	*Wallbanks*	*Sheard*	*French*	*Jones L*	*McAlinden*	*Wakefield*	*Morris*	*Tippett*

Albert Wakefield's leveller (Southend's first away goal of the season), fired through from close range, proves enough to earn them a point at Ashton Gate. Eisentrager had earlier scored for City when, after beating two defenders for possession, he registered with a great left-foot shot.

---

13 A NOTTS CO 15/10 L 1:4 12 / 1 / 11 38,055
Rodgers 61 / [Lawton 54]
Sewell 3, 35, Southwell 44,
Ref: G Pankhurst

Coombs	Guy	Mitchelson	Bicknell	Roberts	Edwards	Boxshall	Eisentrager	Rodgers	White	Rudkin
Smith R	*Deans*	*Rigby*	*Chapman*	*Baxter*	*Adamson*	*Sewell*	*Lawton*	*Evans*	*Johnson*	*Southwell*

County's £60,000 forward line proves too much for City for whom Rodgers makes a scoring debut with a cross-shot on the turn after the break. Tommy Lawton, after appearing to handle the ball when beating Roberts, ties up County's comprehensive success with a left-footed effort.

---

14 H PORT VALE 22/10 W 2:0 11 / 8 / 13 19,855 (£1,147.19.0)
Rodgers 3, Rudkin 31
Ref: A Bond

Coombs	Guy	Mitchelson	Kearney	Roberts	Edwards	Boxshall	Eisentrager	Rodgers	White	Rudkin
King R	*Hamlett*	*Butler*	*McGarry*	*Cheadle*	*Todd*	*Barber*	*Aveyard*	*King G*	*Polk*	*Hulligan*

Rodgers celebrates his Ashton Gate debut with a fine header to put City into the lead. Rudkin then increases the Robins advantage with a low shot before half-time, but after the break the goals do not come, despite City putting together one of their best performances so far this season.

---

15 A IPSWICH 29/10 D 0:0 12 / 16 / 14 12,717 (£1,273.7.0)
Ref: V Rae

Coombs	Guy	Mitchelson	Kearney	Roberts	Edwards	Boxshall	White	Rodgers	Eisentrager	Rudkin
Brown T	*Bell*	*Mitchell*	*Baird*	*Smith*	*Parker T*	*Brown J*	*Little*	*Parker S*	*Dobson*	*O'Brien*

Two strong defences dominated this game at Portman Road, where City manage to keep a clean sheet on their travels for the first time this season. Boxshall dribbled some 50 yards early in the second half, but he fires across the face of goal instead of finding the unmarked Rudkin.

---

16 H EXETER 5/11 W 1:0 11 / 20 / 16 21,568 (£1,...)
Rodgers 22
Ref: R Carter

Coombs	Guy	Mitchelson	Kearney	Roberts	Edwards	Boxshall	Lowrie	Rodgers	White	Rudkin
Hoyle	*Johnstone*	*Rowe*	*Doyle*	*Davey*	*Greenwood*	*Hutchings*	*Smart*	*Smith*	*McClelland*	*Murphy*

Inspired by the return of George Lowrie, City play some brilliant football, but, despite much pressing, their only reward is a goal from Arnold Rodgers after a mistake by the Exeter keeper Bert Hoyle. Rodgers, though, has the ball in the net twice more, but offside rules out both efforts.

---

17 A LEYTON ORIENT 12/11 L 0:1 11 / 16 / 16 9,269
Wood 13
Ref: P Annette

Coombs	Guy	Mitchelson	Kearney	Roberts	Edwards	Boxshall	Lowrie	Rodgers	White	Rudkin
Gerula S	*Walton*	*Banner*	*Taylor*	*Rooney*	*Trailor*	*Dryden*	*Bacon*	*Sherratt*	*Wood*	*McGeachy*

City waste their chances on a glue-pot pitch at Brisbane Road, where their keeper's poor punch-out gifts Ted Wood an easy goal. Despite the advantage of a strong wind after the break, City's failure to shoot on sight has the home side frequently looking the more dangerous outfit.

---

18 H READING 19/11 D 2:2 12 / 5 / 17 19,507 (£1,173.10.9)
Brewster 50, Rodgers 70
Brice 55, Edelston 62
Ref: Rev S Davis

Coombs	Guy	Mitchelson	Kearney	Roberts	Edwards	White	Lowrie	Rodgers	**Brewster**	Rudkin
Marks	*Moyse*	*Wicks*	*Henley*	*Brice*	*Reeve*	*Fisher*	*Edelston*	*Blackman*	*Allen*	*Ellison*

Fortunately, the thick fog lifted sufficiently to allow this game to start on time. Brewster's fierce shot livened things up after the interval with City thankful for a Rodgers slammed in effort after Reading had gone in front with Gordon Brice's header and Maurice Edelston's placed shot.

---

19 H CRYSTAL PALACE 3/12 W 2:0 12 / 17 / 19 15,304 (£830.19.9)
Lowrie 65, Rodgers 75
Ref: G Pankhurst

Coombs	Guy	Mitchelson	Kearney	Roberts	Edwards	White	Lowrie	Rodgers	Brewster	Williams
Graham	*Delaney*	*Edwards*	*Chase*	*Watson*	*Ross*	*Blackshaw*	*Mulhurn*	*Rooks*	*Thomas*	*Howells*

After an unmarked Bill Blackshaw had managed to lift the ball over a vacant net not long after the break, Lowrie puts the City in front with a great drive, then later supplies the cross for Rodgers to head neatly home. Unlucky Palace, who had been much the better side in the first half.

---

20 A NORTHAMPTON 17/12 L 2:4 12 / 2 / 19 11,141 (£...)
Edwards 25, Eisentrager 30
Murphy 7, McCul'A 41, 80, Smith 67
Ref: F Overton

Coombs	Guy	Mitchelson	Bicknell	Roberts	Edwards	Boxshall	Eisentrager	Rodgers	Lowrie	Brewster
Ansell	*Smalley*	*Southam*	*Candlin*	*McCoy*	*Coley*	*McCulloch T*	*Smith D*	*McCulloch A*	*Murphy*	*Mitchell*

City pay the cost of their defensive errors at the County ground, where their play is often superior to that of the home side. Ted Murphy lobbed in the opener, but City fought back and, after Edwards had netted with a fine drive, took the lead when Eisentrager fired in from close range.

---

21 H NORWICH 24/12 L 1:2 12 / 3 / 19 23,728 (£1,441.13.0)
Rodgers 67
Eyre 32, Kinsey 70
Ref: H Williams

Coombs	Guy	Mitchelson	Bicknell	Roberts	Edwards	Boxshall	Eisentrager	Rodgers	Lowrie	Brewster
Nethercott	*Morgan*	*Lewis*	*Pickwick*	*Low*	*Dutton*	*Ryder*	*Kinsey*	*Hollis*	*Jones*	*Eyre*

The Canaries, who owed much to their defence, took the lead when Les Eyre ran through from the halfway line before lobbing the ball over Coombs. Rodgers headed the City level, but Noel Kinsey knocked in Norwich's winner when Terry Ryder's effort cannoned off the crossbar.

LEAGUE DIVISION 3 (SOUTH) Manager: Bob Wright SEASON 1949-50

No	Date			Att	Pos	Pt	F-A	H-T	1	2	3	4	5	6	7	8	9	10	11	Scorers, Times, and Referees
22	H	TORQUAY	26/12	24,162 (£1,443.19.9)	11 / 4	D / 20	0-0	0-0	Coombs / *Davis*	Guy / *Topping*	Mitchelson / *Stuttard*	Bicknell / *Towers*	Roberts / *Head*	Edwards / *Whitfield*	Boxshall / *Shaw*	Eisentrager / *Lewis*	Rodgers / *Conley*	Lowrie / *Collins*	Williams / *Cameron*	Ref: W Edwards
23	A	TORQUAY	27/12	12,258	11 / 4	D / 21	3-3	1-2	Coombs / *Davis*	Guy / *Topping*	Mitchelson / *Stuttard*	Bicknell / *Towers*	Roberts / *Head*	Edwards / *Whitfield*	Boxshall / *Shaw*	Eisentrager / *Lewis*	Rodgers / *Conley*	Lowrie / *Mills*	Thomas / *Cameron*	Boxshall 14, Rodgers 60, Eisentr' 83; *Shaw, Conley, Lewis 46* Ref: W Edwards
24	A	NEWPORT	31/12	13,208	11 / 16	L / 21	4-6	1-2	Coombs / *Fearnley*	Guy / *Williams M*	Mitchelson / *Hayward*	Bicknell / *Roffi*	Roberts / *Stansfield*	Edwards / *Newall*	Boxshall / *Bowen*	Eisentrager / *Comley*	Rodgers / *Parker*	Lowrie / *Griffiths*	Thomas / *Harper*	Thomas 23, Rod' 62, 81, Edwards 64; *Bow' 27, 29, 47, Park' 49,60, Com' 79* Ref: A Tolley
25	H	BRISTOL ROV	14/1	36,550 (£2,270.13.9)	14 / 15	L / 21	1-2	1-2	Morgan / *Weare*	Guy / *Bamford*	Bailey / *Fox*	Bicknell / *Pitt*	Roberts / *Warren*	Edwards / *McCourt*	Boxshall / *Petherbridge*	Eisentrager / *James*	Rodgers / *Roost*	Lowrie / *Morgan*	Rudkin / *Watling*	Lowrie 30; *James 8, Roost 16* Ref: R Tarratt
26	H	BRIGHTON	21/1	14,811 (£819.0.9)	17 / 11	L / 21	1-2	1-0	Morgan / *Baldwin*	Guy / *Tennant*	Bailey / *Vitty*	Bicknell / *Whent*	Roberts / *Wilkins*	Edwards / *Brennan*	Boxshall / *Reed*	Eisentrager / *McNichol*	Rodgers / *Leamon*	White / *Kavanagh*	Williams / *Davies*	Rodgers 44; *Leamon 46, Kavanagh 86* Ref: R Burgess
27	A	WALSALL	4/2	9,060	16 / 14	D / 22	1-1	0-0	Morgan / *Lewis*	Guy / *Jones*	Stone / *Walters*	Peacock / *Crutchley*	Roberts / *Russon*	White / *Devlin*	Boxshall / *McLaughlin*	Eisentrager / *Corbett*	Rodgers / *Chapman*	Lowrie / *Green*	Rudkin / *Betts*	White 71; *Devlin 73*
28	H	MILLWALL	18/2	19,021 (£1,108.2.0)	16 / 20	W / 24	2-1	1-1	Morgan / *Hinton*	Guy / *Evans*	Stone / *Fisher*	Peacock / *Hencher*	Roberts / *Reeves*	White / *Forrest*	Spalding / *Hodgetts*	Eisentrager / *Simmonds*	Rodgers / *Constantine*	Lowrie / *Short A*	Rudkin / *Monkhouse*	Rodgers 16, Lowrie 46; *Simmonds 14* Ref: E Crook
29	A	SOUTHEND	25/2	9,397	16 / 7	L / 24	0-2	0-2	Morgan / *Hankey*	Guy / *Loughran*	Stone / *Walton*	Peacock / *Wallbanks*	Roberts / *Sheard*	White / *French*	Spalding / *Jones*	Eisentrager / *McAlinden*	Rodgers / *Wakefield*	Lowrie / *Lawler*	Rudkin / *Clough*	*Wallbanks 20, 27* Ref: H Williams
30	H	NOTTS CO	4/3	32,491 (£2,049.19.0)	16 / 1	W / 26	4-0	1-0	Smith / *Deans*	Guy / *Rigby*	Stone / *Chapman*	Peacock / *Simpson*	Roberts / *Adamson*	White / *Sewell*	Brewster / *Broome*	Eisentrager / *Lawton*	Rodgers / *Evans W*	Lowrie / *Johnston*	Williams	Rodgers 37, Eisentrager 68, 80, [Lowrie 78] Ref: G Pankhurst
31	A	PORT VALE	11/3	11,444	16 / 8	W / 28	2-0	0-0	Morgan / *Heppell*	Guy / *Hamlett*	Stone / *Potts*	Peacock / *McGarry*	Roberts / *Cheadle*	White / *Todd*	Spalding / *Martin*	Eisentrager / *Aveyard*	Rodgers / *Pinchbeck*	Lowrie / *Polk*	Williams / *Hulligan*	White 50, Rodgers 54 Ref: A Bond

Match reports:

22 — Poor Boxing Day fare at Ashton Gate where City and Torquay contrived to put on one of the poorest games seen at the ground so far this season. Injuries, though, do not help with Sid Williams, playing in place of Saturday's injury victim George Brewster, also being hurt.

23 — City, the last team to beat Torquay on their own patch, come within an ace of repeating the feat. Following their recovery from a 1-3 deficit, Lowrie forced Derek Davis to save at the foot of a post, after earlier having outpaced the home defence to put Eisentrager in for the leveller.

24 — Against the club with the worst defensive record in the whole of the Football League, City have no trouble in finding the back of the net. Unfortunately, though, four goals are not enough on the slippery Somerton Park pitch as City's rearguard has an off day and lets in six.

25 — Tony James, a late replacement for the injured Vic Lambden, is the Rovers hero of their deserved victory. He slams in the opener, then his header against the crossbar sets up Bill Roost to breast the winner over the goal-line. Lowrie registers for City with a powerful free-kick.

26 — A defensive misunderstanding costs City a share of the points when Roberts puts the ball over his advancing goalkeeper and Mike Kavanagh runs in to head Brighton's late winner into an open net. Rodgers fired City in front, but ex-Rover Fred Leamon headed Brighton's equaliser.

27 — Despite Arnie White putting City in front with a right-footed shot late on, the Robins (playing in white shirts) still await their first travelling success since September. Arthur Corbett's back-heel sets up John Devlin to fire in the Saddler's equaliser from the edge of the penalty area.

28 — Despite falling behind to a controlled lob from Chris Simmonds, much improved form brings City their first League victory in almost two months. Rodgers hammers in a rip-snorting shot to quickly bring City level, then Lowrie races through to slip in the winner just after the break.

29 — City are left bewildered at the seaside by Southend's swift moving attack and a strong wind. Losing the toss and kicking off against the wind, City are soon up against it with Harold Wallbanks registering with a grand shot, and seven minutes later crashing in a great first-time drive.

30 — City pull off the surprise of the day with this comprehensive victory, which produces the heaviest reverse of the season for the leaders. Notts though are handicapped in being reduced to ten men following Jackie Sewell's 25th-minute thigh injury. Rodgers toe-poked in City's opener.

31 — City's first away victory over Vale since the 1938-39 season sees them become the first side to win at Hanley this season. After White wins a race for possession to slam in the opener shortly after half-time, the pre-war Wolves keeper George Heppell is beaten by a Rodgers low drive.

#	Match	Date	Att	Pos	P	Pts	Result	HT	Scorers / Notes
32	H IPSWICH	18/3	15,963 (£897.7.0)	14	19	30	W 4-2	2-0	Eisentr' 27, Williams 34, Lowrie 60, O'Brien 75, 83 [Rodgers 82] — Ref: V Rae
33	A EXETER	25/3	10,878	15	17	31	D 0-0	0-0	Ref: R Carter
34	H LEYTON ORIENT	1/4	18,908 (£967.19.9)	14	20	32	D 0-0	0-0	Ref: P Annette
35	H ALDERSHOT	7/4	21,592 (£1,267.12.3)	14	21	34	W 2-0	1-0	Williams 37, Rodgers 85 — Ref: E Greig
36	A READING	8/4	14,675	14	6	34	L 0-1	0-0	Glidden 47 — Ref: Rev S Davis
37	A ALDERSHOT	10/4	6,352	14	21	36	W 1-0	0-0	Rodgers 68 — Ref: E Greig
38	H WATFORD	15/4	15,066 (£836.3.0)	14	8	36	L 0-1	0-1	Davies 33 — Ref: A Smith
39	A WATFORD	20/4	8,977 (£603)	14	6	36	L 0-2	0-2	Eggleston 28, Hartburn 31 — Ref: A Smith
40	A CRYSTAL PALACE	22/4	11,263	14	7	37	D 1-1	1-0	Boxshall 13, Kurz 89 — Ref: G Pankhurst
41	H BOURNEMOUTH	29/4	11,350 (£590.1.9)	15	12	39	W 3-2	1-0	Rodgers 25, 67, Peacock 59, Cross 46, Woodward 88 — Ref: W Edwards
42	A SWINDON	6/5	10,401 (£590.1.9)	15	14	40	D 1-1	0-1	Lowrie 49p, Sinner 17 — Ref: B Griffiths

Lineups (City / Opponents):

32 — IPSWICH: Morgan, Guy, Stone, Peacock, Roberts, White, Spalding, Eisentrager, Rodgers, Lowrie, Williams / *Brown, Feeney, Mitchell, Baird, Bell, Fletcher, Brown J, McCrory, Parker, Driver, O'Brien*

City take the lead when Eisentrager's speculative cross, held up in the strong wind, curls back into the net. Little Sid Williams puts City firmly in control by racing in to crack home a second. Despite Joe O'Brien shooting in a double for Town following the break, City are not troubled.

33 — EXETER: Morgan, Guy, Stone, Peacock, Roberts, White, Spalding, Eisentrager, Rodgers, Lowrie, Williams / *Singleton, Johnstone, Clark, Fallon, Goddard, Davey, Mackay, Smart, Smith, McClelland, Regan*

City's defence, particularly the brilliance of keeper Morgan, earns them a point. Shortly before the interval, City are fortunate when the cross-bar twice comes to their rescue. Disappointment for the travelling fans just after the change of ends when Lowrie nets, only to be ruled offside.

34 — LEYTON ORIENT: Morgan, Guy, Stone, Peacock, Roberts, White, Spalding, Eisentrager, Rodgers, Lowrie, Williams / *Welton, Walton, Banner, Adams, Rooney, Deverall, McEwan, Campbell, Sutherland, Blair, Pattison*

Far from convincing playing against a fierce wind in the first half, City find the Orient defence unyielding after the break. On a day when the light blues win the boat race, the most interesting thing at Ashton Gate is the wind loosening a Covered End loudspeaker from its moorings.

35 — ALDERSHOT: Morgan, Guy, Stone, Peacock, Roberts, White, Spalding, Eisentrager, Rodgers, Lowrie, Williams / *Searle, Rogers, Jefferson, White, Billington, Woodward, Sinclair, McNichol, Vickers, Cropley, Durkin*

City owe much to George Lowrie, despite an injury that leaves him hobbling on the wing at the whistle, for making it six games without defeat. Williams beats three men before unleashing a fast-rising opener, then, just before the finish, Rodgers fires off an unstoppable drive.

36 — READING: Morgan, Guy, Stone, Peacock, Roberts, White, Boxshall, Eisentrager, Rodgers, Thomas, Rudkin / *McBride, Moyse, Gulliver, Hanley, Brice, Bewley, Fisher, Brooks, Blackman, Glidden, Allison*

On level terms at the interval, City were hoping to reap the advantage of a high wind in the second half. Reading, however, had other ideas and Gilbert Glidden jumped high to breast the ball in within two minutes of the restart. Despite much pressing, City fail to get what they deserved.

37 — ALDERSHOT: Morgan, Guy, Stone, Peacock, Roberts, White, Williams, Eisentrager, Rodgers, Steeds, Rudkin / *Reynolds, Rogers, Jefferson, White, Billington, Woodward, Sinclair, McNichol, Mortimore, Cropley, Durkin*

A Rodgers header brings City a holiday double over Aldershot, who share with Fulham the unenviable distinction of losing all three of their Easter games. City fully deserved their success as they were the more workmanlike side throughout and rarely looked like forfeiting their lead.

38 — WATFORD: Morgan, Guy, Stone, Peacock, Roberts, White, Williams, Eisentrager, Rodgers, Steeds, Rudkin / *Morton, Eggleston, Harper, Paton, Oliver, Fisher, Davies, Brown, Thomas, Cumner, Hartburn*

Watford just about deserved to win a game that was without any particular distinction. A strong hard-tackling defence gives the Hornets complete control over the City forwards. Eleven minutes after missing an open net, Bill Davies makes amends by registering with a rising shot.

39 — WATFORD: Morgan, Guy, Stone, Peacock, Roberts, White, Spalding, Eisentrager, Rodgers, Steeds, Rudkin / *Morton, Eggleston, Harper, Paton, Oliver, Fisher, Pilkington, Brown, Thomas, Cumner, Hartburn*

In a game lacking in both excitement and quality, City lose out to two first-half goals. Morgan, who is left completely bewildered by Tom Eggleston's vicious shot that opens the scoring, is further undone when a David Thomas header between the backs put John Hartburn away.

40 — CRYSTAL PALACE: Morgan, Guy, Stone, Peacock, Bicknell, White, Spalding, Eisentrager, Boxshall, Brewster, Rudkin / *Graham, Harding, George, Chase, Watson, Buckley, Blackshaw, Kelly, Kurz, Rooke, Hanlon*

Boxshall headed City into an early lead and it looked likely to be enough to grab both points until Fred Kurz hooked in a late equaliser when nine Palace men went into the box for a corner. A draw is a fair result as the City are indebted to goalkeeper Morgan for keeping Palace at bay.

41 — BOURNEMOUTH: Morgan, Mitchelson, Bailey, Peacock, Roberts, White, Boxshall, Eisentrager, Rodgers, Lowrie, Williams / *Bird, Cunningham, Fisher, Woodward, Stirling, Lewis, Stephens, McGibbon, Cross, Haigh, Cheney*

In a contest marked more by determination than finesse, the fans are treated to a feast of goals. Rodgers hooked in City's opener, but Jack Cross shot in the Cherries equaliser. Peacock headed the City back in front before Laurie Woodward's long-range effort concluded the scoring.

42 — SWINDON: Morgan, Mitchelson, Bailey, Peacock, Roberts, White, Spalding, Eisentrager, Boxshall, Lowrie, Williams / *Burton, Foxton, Lloyd, Cowie, Hudson, Kaye, Wheeler, Simner, Onslow, Jones, Bain*

It looked bleak for City at the break as, following Joe Simner's cross-shot which gave Swindon the lead, they were under much pressure. The spot-kick, awarded for George Hudson's foul on Boxshall, changed that and thereafter it is the home side who find themselves under the cosh.

Home Average 21,449
Away 15,808

CUP-TIES

Manager: Bob Wright

SEASON 1949-50

FA Cup

				F-A	H-T	Scorers, Times, and Referees	1	2	3	4	5	6	7	8	9	10	11
1	A	NOTT'M FOR	13	0-1	0-0		Coombs	Guy	Mitchelson	Bicknell	Roberts	Edwards	White	Lowrie	Rodgers	Brewster	Rudkin
26/11			L 2			*Kaile 48*	*Walker*	*Thomas*	*Hutchinson*	*Anderson*	*Gager*	*Burkitt*	*Scott*	*Love*	*Ardron*	*Capel*	*Kaile*
		15,567				(£1,685.16.2)											

A brilliant 50-yard run by ex-bomber pilot John Love DFC enables Forest to score the vital goal. The tall inside-forward beats almost all of City's defenders before passing for Gordon Kaile to fire in from close range. Forest's second-half control brings them a well-deserved success.

Gloucestershire Cup

				F-A	H-T	Scorers, Times, and Referees	1	2	3	4	5	6	7	8	9	10	11
F	H	BRISTOL ROV	15	2-0	2-0	Williams 13, 38	Morgan	Guy	Bailey	Peacock	Roberts	White	Spalding	Eisentrager	Boxshall	Lowrie	Williams
13/5			W 9				*Liley*	*Bamford*	*Fox*	*Pitt*	*Warren*	*McCourt*	*Tippett*	*Bradford*	*Lambden*	*Watkins*	*Watling*
		16,560				Ref: H Pearce											
		(£1,150)															

Williams, who opens the scoring with a shot from ten yards, doubles City's advantage with a header. The Rovers, despite Josser Watling's injury, set up a series of attacks following the interval, but are unable to find the net - Harry Bamford even managing to put a spot-kick wide.

James Howell Cup

				F-A	H-T	Scorers, Times, and Referees	1	2	3	4	5	6	7	8	9	10	11
F	H	CARDIFF	15	2-0	0-0	Lowrie 82p, 84	Morgan	Mitchelson	Bailey	Peacock	Roberts	Steeds	Spalding	Eisentrager	Boxshall	Lowrie	Williams
10/5			W 2:10				*Joslin*	*Rutter*	*Stirfall A*	*Baker*	*Williams G*	*Hollyman*	*Grant*	*Williams R*	*Lever*	*Blair*	*Lamie*
		8,250															
		(£692.6.6)															

Doug Blair could have sewn up this exhilarating contest for Cardiff ten minutes from time but, with only Morgan to beat, his ten-yard shot barely has the strength to reach the keeper. They paid dearly by conceding a penalty in the scramble following Eisentrager's shot hitting a post.

			P		Home						Away				Pts
			P	W	D	L	F	A	W	D	L	F	A		Pts
1	Notts Co		42	17	3	1	60	12	8	5	8	35	38		58
2	Northampton		42	12	6	3	43	21	8	5	8	29	29		51
3	Southend		42	15	4	2	43	15	4	9	8	23	33		51
4	Nott'm For		42	13	0	8	37	15	7	9	5	30	24		49
5	Torquay		42	13	6	2	40	23	6	4	11	26	40		48
6	Watford		42	10	6	5	26	13	6	7	8	19	22		45
7	Crys Palace		42	12	5	4	35	21	3	9	9	20	33		44
8	Brighton		42	9	8	4	32	24	3	4	10	25	45		44
9	Bristol Rov		42	12	5	4	34	18	7	0	14	17	33		43
10	Reading		42	15	2	4	48	21	2	6	13	22	43		42
11	Norwich		42	11	5	5	44	21	5	1	11	21	42		42
12	Bournemouth		42	11	6	4	38	19	5	4	12	19	37		42
13	Port Vale		42	12	6	3	33	13	3	5	13	14	29		41
14	Swindon		42	9	7	5	41	30	6	4	11	18	32		41
15	BRISTOL C		42	12	4	5	38	19	3	6	12	22	42		40
16	Exeter		42	9	8	4	37	27	5	3	13	26	48		39
17	Ipswich		42	9	6	6	36	36	5	5	13	21	50		35
18	Leyton Orient		42	9	6	6	33	30	2	5	14	20	55		35
19	Walsall		42	8	8	5	37	25	1	8	12	24	37		34
20	Aldershot		42	10	5	6	30	16	3	3	15	18	44		34
21	Newport		42	11	5	5	50	34	2	3	16	17	64		34
22	Millwall		42	11	1	9	39	29	3	3	15	16	34		32
			924	251	112	99	854	482	99	112	251	482	854		924

Odds & ends

Double wins: (2) Port Vale, Aldershot.

Double losses: (4) Nott'm Forest, Norwich, Brighton, Watford.

Won from behind: (1) Millwall (h).

Lost from in front: (2) Newport (a), Brighton (h).

High spots: Beating Newport 6-0 at Ashton Gate.

George Lowrie's brilliant late winner at Eastville on 10 September.

Defeating leaders Notts Co 4-0 in front of 32,491 Ashton Gate crowd.

Low spots: Failing to complete the double over Bristol Rovers.

Losing 4-6 at Newport on New Year's Eve.

Don Clark's failed comeback from serious injury.

AGM (Grand Hotel, Broad Street, Bristol, 10 August 1951):

Loss £24,328.13s.7d. Season Ticket Sales £4,289.7s.0d.

Player of the year: Alec Eisentrager.

Ever-presents: (0).

Hat-tricks: (2) George Lowrie (1), Alec Eisentrager (1).

Leading scorer: Overall: Arnold Rodgers (18). League: Rodgers (18).

Appearances and Goals

Player	Appearances		Goals		
	Lge	Cup	Lge	Cup	Tot
Bailey, Jack	14	2			
Bicknell, Roy	17	1			
Boxshall, Danny	24	2	2		2
Brewster, George	6	1	1		1
Clark, Don	1				
Coombs, Frank	24				
Edwards, Cliff	19	1	3		3
Eisentrager, Alec	37	2	11		11
Freeman, Don	8				
Guy, Ivor	28	2			
Hawkins, Bertram	8		4		4
Kearney, Sid	8				
Lowrie, George	26	3	8	2	10
McCarthy, John	3				
Mitchelson, Ken	19	2			
Morgan, Syd	18	2			
Mullen, James	1				
Peacock, Ernie	16	2	1		1
Roberts, Dennis	39	3			
Rodgers, Arnold	28	1	18		18
Rudkin, Tom	27	1	3		1
Spalding, Billy	9	2			
Steeds, Cecil	4	1			
Stone, Fred	23				
Thomas, Bill	6		1		1
White, Arnie	32	2	4		1
Williams, Sid	17	2	3	2	5
27 players used	462	33	60	4	64

LEAGUE DIVISION 3 (SOUTH)

Manager: Pat Beasley

SEASON 1950-51

Match summary

No	H/A	Opponent	Date	Att	Pos		Res	F-A	H-T	Pt	Scorers, Times, and Referees
1	A	BOURNEMOUTH	19/8	21,398 (£1,500)			L	0-1	0-0	0	Evans 49 — Ref: A Smith
2	H	EXETER	23/8	23,598 (£1,786.18.9)			W	3-1	0-0	2	Johnstone 67 (og), Lowrie 76, 87 / Smith 52
3	H	GILLINGHAM	26/8	21,531 (£1,622.4.9)	6	23	W	2-0	2-0	4	Rodgers 20, Beasley 25 — Ref: R Burgess
4	A	EXETER	30/8	9,571 (£671)	7	9	L	0-1	0-1	4	Smith 20
5	H	BRISTOL ROV	2/9	29,916 (£2,355.10.10)	6	5	W	1-0	0-0	6	Lowrie 57 — Ref: C Curtis/B Griffiths
6	H	CRYSTAL PALACE	6/9	13,422 (£1,013.0.9)	3	24	W	2-0	0-0	8	Williams 49, Rodgers 52 — Ref: R Carter
7	A	MILLWALL	9/9	22,761	8	3	L	3-5	1-2	8	Beasley 30, Lowrie 55, Thomas 65 / Const' 25, 27, 53, Neary 58, Short 72p — Ref: W Rogers
8	A	CRYSTAL PALACE	13/9	12,937	10	23	L	0-1	0-0	8	Stevens 90 — Ref: R Carter
9	H	WATFORD	16/9	19,383 (£1,457.10.10)	9	20	W	3-0	2-0	10	Brewster 31, Lowrie 44p, 75 — Ref: A Tolley
10	A	WALSALL	23/9	8,593	11	24	L	1-3	1-0	10	Brewster 12 / Dearson 54, 56, Morris 63 — Ref: H Pearce
11	H	LEYTON ORIENT	30/9	16,286 (£1,224.17.9)	7	11	W	4-1	2-0	12	Eisent'er 23, Lowrie 27, 62, White 74 / Blair 60 — Ref: S Law

Line-ups (City = top line; opponents in italics)

No	Team	1	2	3	4	5	6	7	8	9	10	11
1	City	Morgan	Guy	Bailey	Peacock	Roberts	Beasley	Thomas	Eisentrager	Rodgers	Lowrie	Rudkin
1	*Bournemouth*	*Bird*	*Cunningham*	*Fisher*	*Woodward*	*Gripton*	*Casey*	*Boxshall*	*Haigh*	*McGibbon*	*Evans*	*Cheney*
2	City	Morgan	Singleton	Johnstone	Peacock	Roberts	Beasley	Thomas	Eisentrager	Rodgers	Lowrie	Williams S
2	*Exeter*	*Singleton*	*Johnstone*	*Rowe*	*Fallon*	*Doyle*	*Davey*	*Mackay*	*Dunlop*	*Smith*	*Lynn*	*McClelland*
3	City	Morgan	Guy	Bailey	Peacock	Roberts	Beasley	Thomas	Eisentrager	Rodgers	Lowrie	Williams S
3	*Gillingham*	*Gage*	*Marks*	*Lewin*	*Boswell*	*Skivington*	*Collins*	*Burtenshaw C*	*Burtenshaw W*	*Russell*	*Briggs*	*Veck*
4	City	Morgan	Guy	Bailey	Peacock	Roberts	Beasley	Thomas	Eisentrager	Rodgers	Lowrie	Williams S
4	*Exeter*	*Singleton*	*Johnstone*	*Rowe*	*Fallon*	*Goddard*	*Davey*	*Harrower*	*Dunlop*	*Smith*	*Lynn*	*McClelland*
5	City	Morgan	Guy	Bailey	Peacock	Bicknell	Beasley	Thomas	Eisentrager	Rodgers	Lowrie	Williams S
5	*Bristol Rov*	*Hoyle*	*Bamford*	*Fox*	*Pitt*	*Warren*	*Sampson*	*Petherbridge*	*Bradford*	*Lambden*	*Roast*	*Bush*
6	City	Morgan	Guy	Bailey	Peacock	Bicknell	Beasley	Thomas	Eisentrager	Rodgers	Lowrie	Williams S
6	*Crystal Palace*	*Bumstead*	*Harding*	*George*	*Smith*	*Watson*	*Whittaker*	*Blackshaw*	*Jones*	*Thomas*	*Kelly*	*Hanlon*
7	City	Morgan	Guy	Bailey	Peacock	Bicknell	Beasley	Thomas	Eisentrager	Rodgers	Lowrie	Williams S
7	*Millwall*	*Jardine*	*Fisher*	*Fisher*	*Short*	*Bowler*	*Reeves*	*Johnston*	*Neary*	*Constantine*	*Morgan*	*Jones J*
8	City	Morgan	Guy	Bailey	Peacock	Roberts	Beasley	Thomas	Eisentrager	Rodgers	White	Rudkin
8	*Crystal Palace*	*Bumstead*	*Harding*	*George*	*Ross*	*Briggs*	*Whittaker*	*Stevens*	*Jones*	*Morgan*	*Kelly*	*Hanlon*
9	City	Morgan	Guy	Bailey	Peacock	Roberts	White	Thomas	Eisentrager	Lowrie	Brewster	Beasley
9	*Watford*	*Morton*	*Eggleston*	*Harper*	*Paton*	*Oliver*	*Fisher*	*Laing*	*Nolan*	*Thomas*	*Varty*	*Hartburn*
10	City	Morgan	Guy	Bailey	Peacock	Roberts	Beasley	Thomas	Eisentrager	Rodgers	Brewster	Williams S
10	*Walsall*	*Lewis*	*Jones*	*Methley*	*Walters*	*Russon*	*Green*	*Morris*	*Bowen*	*Dearson*	*Devlin*	*Knowles*
11	City	Morgan	Guy	Bailey	Peacock	Roberts	Beasley	Thomas	Eisentrager	Lowrie	White	Williams S
11	*Leyton Orient*	*Welton*	*Evans*	*Banner*	*Robb*	*Blizzard*	*Brown*	*Davies*	*Rees*	*Sutherland*	*Blair*	*Pattison*

Match reports

1. Despite a 6.15pm kick-off for this game, because of the local cricket festival, City put up a good performance at Dean Court. Player-manager Pat Beasley makes an impressive debut, but is unable to counter a Hugh Evans low cross-shot, which brings the Cherries a fortunate victory.

2. An Exeter side, with three reserves, gave City the shock of their lives in the second half. After Archie Smith easily beats Morgan from six-yards to put the visitors in front, City are very much up against until Cyril Johnstone, challenged by Williams, puts the ball into his own net.

3. A great Rodgers header and a powerful 25-yard shot from player-manager Beasley inspires City's much-improved display. Both sides miss from the spot, Lowrie hitting the upright for City midway through the second half, and Hugh Russell firing high three minutes from time.

4. Considering the heavy and slippery conditions at St James Park, both City and Exeter put on a commendable display. The Grecians, though, deserve their success courtesy of a left-footed 20-yard strike by Archie Smith. City stage a fine second-half rally but are unable to find the net.

5. A delayed kick-off as the referee and linesman (G Hancock) are held up in the Severn Tunnel. For the first-half the other linesman (C Curtis) takes over in the middle with Messrs Strange & Dunning running the line. Lowrie's belter consigns Rovers to their first defeat of the season.

6. A much deserved success for City, despite the heavy rain and a blustery wind. Denied a first-half penalty when the referee changed his mind and gave a free kick instead, City took command just after the break. Williams volleyed in the first, then Rodgers headed home the second.

7. After Jimmy Constantine heads in the opener it becomes a goalrush at the Den. Within a couple of minutes Constantine shoots past Morgan to double his account, then, after Beasley's 20-yarder for City, the hat-trick is completed by a full-length launch to head in Frank Neary's centre.

8. City are undone in the final 15 seconds, when keeper Morgan makes his only error in an otherwise flawless exhibition. He fails to hold a Les Stevens corner-kick and the ball ends up in the net for the only goal of the game. Twice in the first-half, Palace defenders clear off of the line.

9. Sid Thomas is the star as he had the Watford defence under his spell throughout. Lowrie was unlucky to have what looked a perfectly good goal disallowed on the half-hour mark, but within a minute Brewster fired in off an upright. Lowrie blasted in a loose ball for City's third.

10. Ever the fall guys, City present Walsall with their first win of the season. It seemed all so easy following Brewster's headed opener, but in a two-minute spell after the break a remarkable change came over the game. Don Dearson walked in a leveller, then netted from close-range.

11. City maintain their perfect home record this season with an easy victory, but they have cause to thank Guy for heading a fifth minute Bill Rees effort off of the line. Eisentrager opens the scoring with a first-time grounder, then Lowrie doubles City's advantage with a typical power shot.

12 — A BRIGHTON, 7/10 — Att 11,557 — D 1-1 (HT 0-1) — Pos 20 — Pts 13

Bristol City: Morgan, Guy, Bailey, Peacock, Roberts, Beasley, Thomas, Eisentrager, Lowrie, White, Williams S
Brighton: Baldwin, Tennant, Mansell, Willard, South, Wilson, McCurley, McNichol, Thompson, Morrad, Keene

Scorers: Peacock 60 / Thompson 15. Ref: A Bond

After falling behind to a crazy goal, when Cyril Thompson returns a poor Morgan goal-kick straight into the net, City recover to deservedly draw level, thanks to an alert linesman. He spots that Peacock's retaken free-kick had bounced down over the line after hitting the crossbar.

13 — H NEWPORT, 14/10 — Att 22,930 — W 2-1 (HT 2-1) — Pos 12 — Pts 15 — (£1,796.5.3)

Bristol City: Morgan, Guy, Bailey, Peacock, Roberts, Beasley, Thomas, Eisentrager, Lowrie, White, Boxley
Newport: Fearnley, Staples, Hayward, Stroud, Wilcox, Lester, Birch, Beattie, Parker, Moore, Aston

Scorers: White 15, Lowrie 45p / Parker 34. Ref: G Clark

City hold onto their perfect home record thanks to Lowrie's spot-kick after debut boy Boxley had been pushed off the ball. They faded badly after the break and are fortunate near the end when Reg Parker, who had hooked in County's leveller, hit an easy chance straight at Morgan.

14 — A NORWICH, 21/10 — Att 27,130 — D 0-0 (HT 0-0) — Pos 3 — Pts 16

Bristol City: Morgan, Guy, Bailey, Peacock, Roberts, Beasley, Williams S, Eisentrager, Lowrie, Rodgers, Boxley
Norwich: Nethercott, Duffy, Lewis, Pickwick, Foulkes, Ashman, Gavin, Kinsey, Hollis, Eyre, Doherty

Ref: E Baker

The City defence has a busy time, but, apart from a lucky escape early on when Les Eyre hits the crossbar, they hold out splendidly. A hard-earned point for City, for whom Bailey does well in the last minute to block John Gavin's shot. Beasley, Roberts and Peacock are outstanding.

15 — H NORTHAMPTON, 28/10 — Att 20,798 — W 1-0 (HT 0-0) — Pos 11 — Pts 18 — (£1,584.3.6)

Bristol City: Morgan, Guy, Bailey, Peacock, Roberts, Beasley, Williams S, Eisentrager, Lowrie, Rodgers, Boxley
Northampton: Feehan, Smalley, Barron, Candlin, Collins, Davis, English, Dixon, McCulloch, Murphy, Mitchell

Scorer: Lowrie 66p. Ref: F Fiander

Amazing scenes at Ashton Gate after Rodgers takes the ball right through a wall of Northampton defenders to walk the ball into the net. The referee awards a goal, but after protests by the visiting players he changes his decision to a penalty, which Lowrie dispatches with aplomb.

16 — A PORT VALE, 4/11 — Att 11,603 — W 3-1 (HT 2-0) — Pos 15 — Pts 20

Bristol City: Morgan, Guy, Bailey, Peacock, Roberts, Beasley, Williams S, Eisentrager, Lowrie, Rodgers, Boxley
Port Vale: Heppell, Hamlett, Butler, Polk, Cheadle, McGarry, Hulligan, Poppitt, Pinchbeck, Martin, Bennett

Scorers: Boxley 32, Lowrie 44, Rodgers 62 / Hulligan 78. Ref: A Tolley

Under the cosh early on, City take control following Boxley's notching of his first goal for the club with a right-footed shot just inside the post. Lowrie's cunningly curled lob doubles the advantage, then, after the interval, a Rodgers drive brings City their first away win of the season.

17 — H NOTT'M FOR, 11/11 — Att 32,878 — L 0-3 (HT 0-0) — Pos 1 — Pts 20 — (£2,684.12.0)

Bristol City: Morgan, Guy, Bailey, Peacock, Roberts, Beasley, Thomas, Eisentrager, Lowrie, White, Boxley
Nott'm Forest: Walker, Whare, Thomas, Morley, Gager, Burkett, Scott, Johnson, Ardron, Capel, Collindridge

Scorers: Collindridge 70, 84p, Scott 80. Ref: R Reden

The loss of Lowrie, after hurting his leg in a collision with George Walker just before the interval, brings defeat after the Robins had done all the first-half attacking. Colin Collindridge slams in a grand shot to put Forest on the path to depriving City of their untarnished home record.

18 — A TORQUAY, 18/11 — Att 7,323 — L 1-4 (HT 0-2) — Pos 16 — Pts 20

Bristol City: Morgan, Guy, Bailey, Peacock, Roberts, Beasley, Williams S, Eisentrager, Lowrie, Rodgers, Boxley
Torquay: Davis, Topping, Dowan, Brown, McGuiness, Whitfield, Thomas, Shaw, Conley, Collins, Cameron

Scorers: Rodgers 49 / Collins 10, 24, Shaw 58, Conley 80. Ref: W Edwards

Torquay completed the signing of Hugh Brown, Partick Thistle's Scottish international wing-half in time to play in this game at Plainmoor, where City's defence is too easily penetrated. Sammy Collins has his old club on the ropes by twice firing in during the opening 24 minutes.

19 — A SWINDON, 2/12 — Att 13,079 — L 0-1 (HT 0-1) — Pos 14 — Pts 20 — (£1,050.19.3)

Bristol City: Morgan, Guy, Bailey, Peacock, Roberts, Beasley, Spalding, Eisentrager, Lowrie, Rodgers, Williams S
Swindon: Burton, Hunt, May, Kaye, Hudson, Batchelor, Lunn, Wheeler, Onslow, Simner, Bain

Scorer: Simner 23. Ref: A Bond

Swindon are indebted to Sam Burton for his great display between the sticks and a rather fortunate goal for their success. It is mainly all City, but an inspired keeper stands between them and at least a point after Joe Simner takes advantage when Beasley's back-pass sticks in the mud.

20 — H BOURNEMOUTH, 16/12 — Att 15,438 — W 2-0 (HT 0-0) — Pos 12 — Pts 22 — (£1,119.18.0)

Bristol City: Sullivan, Guy, Bailey, Peacock, Roberts, Beasley, Boyd, Eisentrager, Clark, Rodgers, Williams S
Bournemouth: Bird, Cunningham, Drummond, Woodward, Lewis, Casey, Stroud, McGibbon, Cross, Buchanan, Boxshall

Scorers: Rodgers 57, Clark 80. Ref: A Smith

Clark fires against an upright early on, whilst Boxley has his 72nd-minute penalty saved. On the snow covered pitch, a low shot by Rodgers and a Clark effort that takes a fortunate bounce bring City a well-deserved success over opponents who had endured a fraught railway journey.

21 — A GILLINGHAM, 23/12 — Att 8,579 — W 2-1 (HT 1-1) — Pos 22 — Pts 24

Bristol City: Sullivan, Guy, Bailey, Peacock, Roberts, Beasley, Boyd, Eisentrager, Clark, Rodgers, Williams S
Gillingham: Gage, Marks, Lewin, Boswell, Skivington, Ayres, Burtenshaw C, Burtenshaw W, Thomas, Lewis, Carr

Scorers: Boyd 1, Rodgers 65 / Burtenshaw W 4. Ref: R Burgess

Despite Boyd's fine-angled shot putting City in front early on, the Gills are the better side before the break. William Burtenshaw combines well with David Thomas before firing in their leveller, but after the interval City take control and Rodgers hooks in from Clark's headed pass.

22 — H PLYMOUTH, 25/12 — Att 21,158 — W 1-0 (HT 0-0) — Pos 5 — Pts 26 — (£1,695.10.9)

Bristol City: Sullivan, Guy, Bailey, Peacock, Roberts, Beasley, Boyd, Eisentrager, Clark, Rodgers, Williams S
Plymouth: Shortt, Ratcliffe, Jones, Rundle, Chisholm, Porteous, Strauss, Dougal, Tadman, Dews, Govan

Scorer: Boyd 50. Ref: R Rundle

Argyle are much the better footballing side, but their forwards have an off-day at the Gate, whilst City have an intelligent, though somewhat slow-moving, leader in Clark. A perfectly timed run by Boyd allows him to head in a Williams cross for a spectacular winner at the far post.

23 — A PLYMOUTH, 26/12 — Att 26,230 — L 0-2 (HT 0-1) — Pos 8 — Pts 26

Bristol City: Sullivan, Guy, Bailey, Peacock, Roberts, Beasley, Boyd, Eisentrager, Clark, Rodgers, Williams S
Plymouth: Shortt, Silk, Jones, Rundle, Chisholm, Porteous, Astall, Dougal, Tadman, Dews, Govan

Scorers: Astall 8, Dews 82.

A thrill-packed, cut and thrust affair. Whilst Eisentrager has a shot kicked off the line, it is Argyle who score the goals. Delightful play between Alex Govan and Neil Dougal sets up Gordon Astall to shoot in the opener, then after the break George Dews finds the net with a 19-yard drive.

LEAGUE DIVISION 3 (SOUTH)

SEASON 1950-51 — Manager: Pat Beasley

No	V	Opponents	Date	Att (Receipts)	Pos	Pt	Res	F-A	H-T	Scorers, Times, and Referees
24	A	Bristol Rov (3)	30/12	31,680	9	26	L	1-2	0-1	Rodgers 63 / Lambden 22, 80 — Ref: B Griffiths
25	H	Millwall (5)	13/1	21,723 (£1,701.11.9)	9	28	W	2-1	1-1	Rudkin 9, Rodgers 63 / Roberts 25 (og) — Ref: W Rogers
26	H	Southend (6)	17/1	7,745 (£569.12.3)	10	28	L	0-3	0-2	Stubbs 7, 40, Tippett 90 — Ref: A Smith
27	A	Watford (21)	20/1	9,032	7	30	W	2-1	0-1	White 47, Boyd 88 / Brown 34 — Ref: A Tolley
28	A	Southend (9)	31/1	4,216	7	31	D	1-1	1-1	Rodgers 17 / Sibley 39 — Ref: A Smith
29	H	Walsall (20)	3/2	15,508 (£1,264.8.6)	6	32	D	3-3	2-2	Boyd 14, 22, Williams 75 / Dearson 4, 6, Skidmore 76p — Ref: H Pearce
30	H	Brighton (19)	24/2	12,748 (£1,050.19.9)	8	34	W	2-0	1-0	Rodgers 38, 67 — Ref: A Bond
31	A	Newport (13)	3/3	11,494	8	36	W	1-0	1-0	Rogers 21 — Ref: G Clark
32	H	Norwich (3)	10/3	22,079 (£1,761.17.0)	9	37	D	2-2	1-2	Rodgers 19, 83 / Gavin 11, Kinsey 24 — Ref: W Baker
33	A	Northampton (14)	17/3	8,042	8	38	D	2-2	1-0	Eisentrager 38, White 80 / English 54, 68 — Ref: F Fiander
34	A	Reading (9)	23/3	20,065 (£1,741)	9	38	L	2-4	1-0	Eisentrager 35, Rodgers 54 / Blackman 60, 72, 88, Simpson 80p — Ref: A Williams

Line-ups (City player / *opponent* by position)

No	1	2	3	4	5	6	7	8	9	10	11
24	Sullivan / *Hoyle*	Guy / *Bamford*	Peacock / *Pitt*	Bailey / *Fox*	Roberts / *Warren*	Beasley / *Sampson*	Boyd / *Pethebridge*	Eisentrager / *Bradford*	Rodgers / *Lambden*	Brewster / *Roost*	Williams S / *Watling*
25	Sullivan / *Finlayson*	Guy / *Jardine*	Peacock / *Lyons*	Bailey / *Hencher*	Roberts / *Bowler*	Beasley / *Reeves*	Boyd / *Johnson*	Eisentrager / *Constantine*	Clark / *Neary*	Rodgers / *Morgan*	Rudkin / *Jones*
26	Sullivan / *Scannell*	Guy / *Loughan*	Peacock / *Anderson*	Bailey / *French*	Roberts / *Stirling*	White / *Lawler*	Williams S / *Sibley*	Eisentrager / *McAlinden*	Boyd / *Grant*	Rodgers / *Stubbs*	Rudkin / *Tibbett*
27	Sullivan / *Morton*	Guy / *Eggleston*	Peacock / *Jones*	Bailey / *Paton*	Roberts / *Oliver*	Beasley / *Fisher*	Boyd / *Laing*	White / *Brown*	Eisentrager / *Case*	Rodgers / *Varty*	Rudkin / *Hartburn*
28	Sullivan / *Scannell*	Guy / *Loughan*	Peacock / *Anderson*	Bailey / *French*	Roberts / *Stirling*	Beasley / *Lawler*	Boyd / *Sibley*	Eisentrager / *McAlinden*	Bicknell / *Grant*	Rodgers / *Stubbs*	Rudkin / *Davies*
29	Sullivan / *Lewis*	Guy / *Jones*	Peacock / *Skidmore*	Bailey / *Walters*	Roberts / *Russon*	Beasley / *Devlin*	Williams S / *Bowen*	Eisentrager / *Dearson*	Boyd / *Winter*	Rodgers / *O'Neill*	Rudkin / *Allison*
30	Sullivan / *Baldwin*	Guy / *Tennant*	Peacock / *Mansell*	Bailey / *Brennan*	Roberts / *McCoy*	Beasley / *Thompson*	Boyd / *Reed*	White / *McNichol*	Rodgers / *Bennett*	Eisentrager / *Willard*	Boxley / *Morris*
31	Sullivan / *Pope*	Guy / *Staples*	Peacock / *Stroud*	Bailey / *Hayward*	Roberts / *Wilson*	Beasley / *Newall*	Boyd / *Birch*	White / *Beattie*	Rogers / *Parker*	Rodgers / *Shregold*	Boxley / *Moore*
32	Sullivan / *Nethercott*	Guy / *Duffy*	Peacock / *Pickwick*	Bailey / *Arnold*	Roberts / *Foulkes*	Beasley / *Ashman*	Boyd / *Gavin*	White / *Kinsey*	Rodgers / *Hollis*	Eisentrager / *Bradley*	Boxley / *Docherty*
33	Morgan / *Feehan*	Guy / *Southam*	Peacock / *Davis*	Bailey / *Woollard*	Roberts / *Duckhouse*	Beasley / *Hughes*	Boyd / *English*	White / *Dixon*	Rodgers / *McCulloch*	Eisentrager / *Garrett*	Boxley / *Mitchell*
34	Morgan / *McBride*	Guy / *Moyse*	Peacock / *Wicks*	Bailey / *McLean*	Roberts / *Brice*	Beasley / *Johnston*	Boyd / *Simpson*	White / *Edelston*	Rodgers / *Blackman*	Eisentrager / *Henley*	Boxley / *Bainbridge*

Match reports

24. The Rovers deservedly win this thrilling derby as City do not have anyone to match the speed and guile of Vic Lambden. He opens the scoring with a low cross-shot, then, after Rodgers had hooked in to bring City level, wins the game with a drive that takes a bounce before going in.

25. Rudkin puts City into an early lead when slamming the ball in from two yards, but Roberts deflects a John Johnson shot into his own net for the Lions' equaliser. Fortunately, Rodgers races through after the break to ram a splendid winner past Malcolm Finalyson from a narrow angle.

26. On a slippery pitch Southend are quicker to the ball. Danger-man Les Stubbs seizes on Peacock's poor back-pass to fire in the opener, then shortly before half-time produces a prodigious leap to head in the second. Tommy Tippett drives in the third after Guy had cleared off the line.

27. After Tom Brown heads the home side in front, White's tap-in and Boyd's slammed-in effort seal the victory that City's splendid second-half recovery fully deserves. However, City's experiment of playing Eisentrager at centre-forward is not a success in what was a poor game overall.

28. City have much the better of the early play and open the scoring with a clever Rodgers header. Thereafter, though, they fall away and it is no surprise when Albert Sibley notched Southend's equaliser. Following the interval, City are fortunate that United have two goals disallowed.

29. Boyd gives City two early goals in the No 9 shirt and inspires City after Don Dearson had twice struck with powerful cross-shots. Two headed goals take City into the break on level terms, but, after Williams forces the ball in to put them in front, a Roberts foul brings Walsall their spot-kick.

30. City's experimental forward line demonstrate much early slickness and it is no surprise when Boxley gets away to put over a perfect centre which Rodgers, running in at full tilt, heads past keeper Harry Baldwin. Following the break, the duo repeat the trick with the self-same result.

31. Jimmy Rogers scores his first League goal for City when, with the side of his boot, he stabs in Boyd's cross high over keeper Terry Pope. This goal proves enough to consign Newport to their first League defeat in over two months, but it is never easy as City are often on the defensive.

32. A worthy point for City against high-riding Norwich. Failing behind when John Gavin gives Sullivan no possible chance from a few yards out, City equalise with a Rodgers header before Noel Kinsey nods the Canaries back in front. Rodgers fires in from close range to save the day.

33. Despite Eisentrager celebrating his last game as a single man by hitting a storming 18-yarder to put City in front, it took White's scrambled-in effort shortly before the finish to salvage a point. Jack English, with a close-range shot followed by a header, twice registers for Northampton.

34. City dominated matters in the first half, but are unfortunate when Eisentrager, who had steered in the opener from a free-kick, hit the crossbar with a spot-kick shortly before the break. Unfortunately, they faded after Rodgers shot in to double their advantage shortly after the interval.

No	Venue	Opponent	Date	Att	Pos	Opp Pos	Pts	Res	Score	HT	Gate
35	H	PORT VALE	24/3	17,301	9	14	40	W	3-1	2-0	(£1,312.10.6)
36	H	READING	26/3	23,778	9	3	41	D	3-3	1-2	(£1,915.14.0)
37	A	NOTT'M FOR	31/3	16,811	8	1	42	D	0-0	0-0	
38	H	ALDERSHOT	4/4	11,369	8	17	43	D	1-1	0-0	(£747.16.4)
39	H	TORQUAY	7/4	13,975	9	16	43	L	0-2	0-1	(£1,037.10.0)
40	A	ALDERSHOT	14/4	6,231	9	16	44	D	0-0	0-0	(£796.6.9)
41	H	IPSWICH	18/4	12,026	8	9	46	W	2-1	2-1	(£796.6.9)
42	H	SWINDON	21/4	16,129	8	15	48	W	2-0	2-0	(£1,167.1.9)
43	A	COLCHESTER	25/4	12,802	8	16	48	L	0-2	0-0	(£849.9.6)
44	A	COLCHESTER	28/4	7,202	10	16	49	D	1-1	1-1	
45	A	LEYTON ORIENT	3/5	6,479	7	18	51	W	2-0	0-0	
46	A	IPSWICH	5/5	10,728	10	8		L	0-2	0-1	

Home Average 18,457 — Away 13,597

---

35. PORT VALE (H) — Rodgers 29, 87, White 31 / Hulligan 58 — Ref: A Tolley

Teams (City / Vale): Morgan/King, Guy/Hamlett, Bailey/Hayward, Peacock/Leake, Roberts/Cheadle, Beasley/Polk, Boyd/Hulligan, White/Aveyard, Rodgers/Pinchback, Eisentrager/Martin, Boxley/Bennett

An easy victory for City over a lifeless and ragged Vale side. Rodgers headed through from a Beasley free-kick to put City in the lead and White smashed in a second shortly after. Mick Hulligan's fierce drive reduced the arrears, but Rodgers shot in another before the final whistle.

36. READING (H) — Rodgers 38, Boyd 65, White 78 / Edelston 7, 25, Simpson 60p — Ref: A Williams/C Gregory

Teams (City / Reading): Morgan/McBride, Guy/Moyse, Bailey/Wicks!, Peacock/McLean, Roberts/Brice, Beasley/Johnston, Boyd/Simpson, White/Edelston, Rodgers/Blackman, Brewster/Henley, Boxley/Farquhar

A torrid time for the senior linesman who took over at half-time when the referee pulled a calf muscle. The game became a rough-house which eventually saw the 87th-minute dismissal of Stan Wicks. A thrice-taken penalty for Reading, but shots from Rodgers and White save a point.

37. NOTT'M FOREST (A) — Ref: R Reden

Teams (City / Forest): Morgan/Walker, Guy/Whare, Bailey/Thoman, Peacock/Burkitt, Roberts/Gager, Beasley/Morley, Boyd/Scott, White/Laverton, Rodgers/Ardron, Brewster/Capel, Boxley/Collingbridge

With Morgan, Guy, Bailey and Roberts in grand form, City thoroughly deserved this sharing of the spoils with the League leaders. Despite having to withstand much pressure, City's reorganised attack, with Rogers at centre-forward, give the home defence some anxious moments.

38. ALDERSHOT (H) — Rogers 48 / Menzies 56 — Ref: N Taylor

Teams (City / Aldershot): Morgan/Purdie, Guy/Rogers, Bailey/Wilson, Peacock/White, Roberts/Billington, Beasley/Woodward, Boyd/Hobbs, Eisentrager/Menzies, Rogers/Raine, Brewster/Durkin, Boxley/Greenwood

Not a particularly good game, but City should have won with something to spare. Beasley has a left-footed drive disallowed early on and it is not until just after the break that City go in front. A through ball sets up Rogers to shoot home, but Norman Menzies levels with a 25-yarder.

39. TORQUAY (H) — Pembery 10, 80 — Ref: W Edwards

Teams (City / Torquay): Morgan/Webber, Guy/Topping, Bailey/Calland, Peacock/Brown, Roberts/McGuiness, Beasley/Towers, Boyd/Cameron, Eisentrager/Shaw, Lyons/Reid, Rodgers/Evans, Boxley/Pembery

On a pitch covered with pools of water following the morning's storms, City never really recover from Morgan's failure to punch-out a high dropping ball. Gordon Pembery charged him and the ball over the line and later, looking offside, he raced clear to fire the leather into the net.

40. ALDERSHOT (A) — Ref: N Taylor

Teams (City / Aldershot): Sullivan/Purdie, Guy/Rogers, Bailey/Jefferson, Presley/Woodward, Roberts/White, Beasley/Cropley, Boyd/Bonnar, White/Menzies, Rodgers/Raine, Eisentrager/Greenwood, Boxley/Flint

City do well to hold the Shots to a draw as they were without Roberts after he was carried off with a leg injury three minutes prior to the interval. The nearest City come to scoring is near the finish when Arthur Jefferson's back-pass eludes James Purdie and strikes an upright.

41. IPSWICH (H) — Beasley 37, Rodgers 42 / Brown 35 — Ref: E Grieg

Teams (City / Ipswich): Sullivan/Burns, Guy/Harrison, Stone/Deacon, Presley/Baird, Peacock/Rees, Beasley/Parker T, Boyd/Brown, Eisentrager/McCrory, Rodgers/Warne, Brewster/Driver, Boxley/Roberts

John Brown's shot takes a deflection off of Presley's chest and the ball ends up in the back of the net to give Ipswich the lead. Beasley soon fired a 25-yarder leveller that hit the underside of the bar before bouncing down over the line. Rodgers shot in the winner just before the break.

42. SWINDON (H) — Rodgers 1, 40 — Ref: A Bond

Teams (City / Swindon): Sullivan/Burton, Guy/Lloyd, Stone/May, Presley/Kaye, Peacock/Hudson, Beasley/Hill, Boyd/Lunn, White/Onslow, Rodgers/Owen, Eisentrager/Millar, Boxley/Bain

Peacock's mastery of Maurice Owen helps City to a deserved success. Rodgers drives in the opener, then doubles City's advantage with a shot which nearly hits out the roof of the net. Unfortunately, after the break City are unable to repeat the form that had so baffled Swindon earlier.

43. COLCHESTER (A) — Rowlands 67, Keeble 87

Teams (City / Colchester): Sullivan/Wright, Guy/Harrison, Stone/Rowlands, Presley/Bearryman, Roberts/Stewart, Beasley/Layton, Boyd/Jones, Eisentrager/McKim, Rogers/Keeble, Brewster/Elder, Boxley/Church

Colchester, who fail to get in a shot during the opening hour, make City pay for squandering many chances. After surviving a real pounding, the U's grab the points. Trevor Rowlands fires in a second-half opener and Vic Keeble runs through to shoot past Sullivan to tie up the points.

44. COLCHESTER (A) — Eisentrager 24 / Church 44

Teams (City / Colchester): Sullivan/Wright, Guy/Harrison, Stone/Rowlands, Presley/Bearryman, Roberts/Stewart, Beasley/Layton, Williams S/Jones, Eisentrager/McKim, Rogers/Keeble, Brewster/Elder, Boxley/Church

A somewhat dull game, but none the less a deserved point for City, courtesy of Eisentrager's drive that opened the scoring. John Church fired in a splendid equaliser, but despite the U's wind advantage after the break, Sullivan only has to be alert to pull off a save at Jim Elder's feet.

45. LEYTON ORIENT (A) — Eisentrager 81, Boxley 88 — Ref: S Law

Teams (City / Orient): Sullivan/Welton, Guy/Evans, Stone/Banner, Peacock/Blizzard, Roberts/Aldous, White/Brown, Williams S/Jackson, Beasley/Rees, Rogers/Walton, Eisentrager/Blair, Boxley/McBeachy

This typical end of season affair, with little in the way of good play, is settled by City's late strikes. Eisentrager fires the first into the roof of the net when Pat Welton can only parry the ball, then a mix up between John Evans and his goalkeeper allows Boxley to net with an 18-yarder.

46. IPSWICH (A) — Driver 29, Brown 88 — Ref: E Grieg

Teams (City / Ipswich): Sullivan/Burns, Guy/Feeney, Stone/Tyler, Peacock/Baird, White/Rees, Roberts/Parker T, Boyd/Brown, Williams S/McCrory, Rogers/Dobson, Eisentrager/Driver, Boxley/Roberts

At Portman Road, the smart play of the Ipswich attack makes it no surprise when Allenby Driver heads the ball into the roof of the net to put them in front. Following the break, City show to better advantage, but Sullivan spills Tom Parker's free-kick to make a home victory certain.

CUP-TIES

Manager: Pat Beasley

SEASON 1950-51

FA Cup

			F-A	H-T	1	2	3	4	5	6	7	8	9	10	11	Scorers, Times, and Referees
1 H GLOUCESTER 25/11	9 W		4-0	2-0	Morgan	Guy	Bailey	Peacock	Roberts	Beasley	Spalding	Eisentrager	Rogers	Rodgers	Williams S	Rodgers 38, Guy 42, Rodgers 50, [Peacock 65]
17,058 SL:4 (£1,580.11.9)					*King*	*Lawson*	*Peacock*	*Myers*	*Trengett*	*Canavan*	*Boyd*	*Haydon*	*Jenkins*	*Bury*	*Buist*	Ref: J Marsh

Despite being well below their best against the Southern League Championship-chasers, City gain an easy passage into the next round. After a rather fortunate deflection allows Arnold Rodgers to head in the opener, Ivor Guy finds the net with a freak 50-yard lob just prior to the break.

			F-A	H-T	1	2	3	4	5	6	7	8	9	10	11	Scorers, Times, and Referees
2 H WREXHAM 9/12	10 W		2-1	0-1	Morgan	Guy	Bailey	Peacock	Roberts	Beasley	Spalding	Eisentrager	Rogers	Rodgers	Williams S	Williams 72, Rodgers 86
18,514.3N:16 (£1,670.3.3)					*Ferguson*	*Tunney*	*Kelsall*	*Spruce*	*Wilson*	*McCallum*	*Grainger*	*Beynon*	*Lawrence*	*Graham*	*Tunnicliffe*	Lawrence 43, Ref: A Tolley

It looked like City's atrocious finishing would cost them a place in the next round. After Cyril Lawrence's 15-yarder put Wrexham in front, it takes Archie Ferguson's poor punch out to enable Williams to drive in an equaliser. A Rodgers pull-back sets up Rogers to bang in the winner.

			F-A	H-T	1	2	3	4	5	6	7	8	9	10	11	Scorers, Times, and Referees
3 H BLACKBURN 6/1	10 W		2-1	2-1	Sullivan	Guy	Bailey	Peacock	Roberts	Beasley	Williams S	Eisentrager	Clark	Rodgers	Rudkin	Rodgers 37, 44
23,245 2:7 (£2,149.3.0)					*Patterson*	*Stuart*	*Higgins*	*Horton*	*Holliday*	*Ball*	*Wharton*	*Campbell*	*Graham*	*Todd*	*Fenton*	Wharton 16, Ref: F Chadwick

Against the run of play John Wharton puts the visitors in front with a dropping shot, but Rodgers registers with two headers to put City firmly in control. John Patterson, who was the busiest man on the field, does well to keep out one of Guy's long-distance specials just after the break.

			F-A	H-T	1	2	3	4	5	6	7	8	9	10	11	Scorers, Times, and Referees
4 H BRIGHTON 27/1	7 W		1-0	0-0	Sullivan	Guy	Bailey	Peacock	Roberts	Beasley	Williams S	Eisentrager	Clark	Rodgers	Rudkin	Clark 86p
28,763 17 (£2,593.1.8)					*Baldwin*	*Wilkins*	*Mansell*	*Tennant*	*McCoy*	*Wilson*	*Williard*	*McNichol*	*Thompson*	*Bennett*	*Keene*	Ref: H Pearce

A historic day for Bristol soccer as, with Rovers winning at Luton, for the first time both clubs are through to the last sixteen. It was a close-run thing at Ashton Gate though, where it takes Clark's late penalty against a goalkeeper renowned for his spot-kick saves to bring victory.

			F-A	H-T	1	2	3	4	5	6	7	8	9	10	11	Scorers, Times, and Referees
5 A BIRMINGHAM 10/2	8 L		0-2	0-1	Sullivan	Guy	Bailey	Peacock	Roberts	Beasley	Williams S	Eisentrager	Clark	Rodgers	Rudkin	
47,831 2:9 (£4,241.19.3)					*Merrick*	*Badham*	*Martin*	*Boyd*	*Atkins*	*Ferris*	*Stewart*	*Higgins*	*Trigg*	*Smith*	*Berry*	Stewart 28, Trigg 82, Ref: P Power

The gates are shut 45 minutes before kick-off at St Andrew's where City pay the price for wasting their chances. They are the more assertive side, but John Stewart's fierce drive puts the Blues in front in their first attack, then shortly before time, Cyril Trigg nets with a low-drive.

Gloucestershire Cup

			F-A	H-T	1	2	3	4	5	6	7	8	9	10	11	Scorers, Times, and Referees
F A BRISTOL ROV 12/5	10 D		1-1	1-0	Sullivan	Guy	Stone	Peacock	Roberts	Beasley	Eisentrager	Rogers	Rodgers	White	Boxley	Boxley 12
16,673 6					*Hoyle*	*Watkins*	*Fox*	*Pitt*	*Warren*	*Sampson*	*Petherbridge*	*Bradford*	*Lambden*	*Roost*	*Watling*	Lambden 82, Ref: N Taylor

After a perfectly placed drive puts City in front, the crowd stand silent during the interval when the Fishponds British Legion Band plays the march past of the Gloucestershire Regiment in honour of their gallant stand in Korea. Vic Lambden's first-time drive brings the Rovers level.

			Home					Away				
	P	W	D	L	F	A	W	D	L	F	A	Pts
1 Nott'm For	46	16	6	1	57	17	14	4	5	53	23	70
2 Norwich	46	16	6	1	42	14	6	8	9	40	31	64
3 Reading	46	15	6	2	57	17	6	9	8	31	36	57
4 Plymouth	46	16	5	2	54	19	8	4	11	31	36	57
5 Millwall	46	15	6	2	52	23	8	4	11	28	34	56
6 Bristol Rov	46	15	7	1	46	18	5	8	10	18	24	55
7 Southend	46	15	4	4	64	27	6	6	11	28	42	52
8 Ipswich	46	15	4	4	48	24	6	2	13	21	34	52
9 Bournemouth	46	17	5	1	49	16	5	2	16	16	41	51
10 BRISTOL C	46	15	4	4	41	25	5	7	11	23	34	51
11 Newport	46	13	4	6	48	25	6	5	12	29	45	47
12 Port Vale	46	13	6	4	35	24	5	7	13	25	41	45
13 Brighton	46	13	8	4	51	31	1	2	9	20	48	43
14 Exeter	46	11	4	8	33	30	7	2	14	29	55	42
15 Walsall	46	12	4	7	32	20	3	6	14	20	42	40
16 Colchester	46	12	5	6	43	25	2	7	14	20	51	40
17 Swindon	46	15	4	4	38	17	1	3	20	17	50	40
18 Aldershot	46	11	8	4	37	20	4	2	17	19	68	40
19 Leyton Orient	46	13	2	8	36	28	2	6	15	17	47	38
20 Torquay	46	13	2	8	47	39	1	7	15	17	42	37
21 Northampton	46	8	9	6	39	30	3	2	18	16	37	36
22 Gillingham	46	10	7	6	41	30	3	2	18	28	71	35
23 Watford	46	8	5	10	29	28	1	6	16	25	60	29
24 Crys Palace	46	6	5	12	18	39	2	6	15	15	45	27
	1104	311	126	115	1037	586	115	126	311	586	1037	1104

Odds & ends

Double wins: (5) Gillingham, Watford, Leyton Orient, Newport, Port Vale.

Double losses: (1) Torquay.

Won from behind: (5) Exeter (h), Watford (a) Ipswich (h), Wrexham (h) (FAC), Blackburn (h) (FAC).

Lost from in front: (2) Walsall (a), Reading (a).

High spots: Beating Leyton Orient on 30 September.
Reaching the 5th Round of the FA Cup.

Low spots: The injury that saw City lose the services of George Lowrie just before half-time against Nottingham Forest on 11 November.
The squandered chances at St Andrew's in the FA Cup.

AGM (Grand Hotel, Broad Street, Bristol, 13 May 1951):
Loss £483.13s.4d. Season Ticket Sales £4,484.10s.10d.

Player of the year: Ivor Guy and Ernie 'Ginger' Peacock.

Ever-presents: (1) Ivor Guy.

Hat-tricks: (0).

Leading scorer: Overall: Arnold Rodgers (23). League: Rodgers (20).

	Appearances		Goals		
	Lge	Cup	Lge	Cup	Tot
Bailey, Jack	39	5	3		3
Beasley, Pat	43	6	3		3
Bicknell, Roy	4				
Boxley, Jack	23	1	2	1	3
Boyd, John	24		6		6
Brewster, George	7		2		2
Clark, Don	5	3	1	1	2
Eisentrager, Alec	42	6	5		5
Guy, Ivor	46	6		1	1
Lowrie, George	16		11		11
Lyons, Mike	1				
Morgan, Syd	26	2			
Peacock, Ernie	44	6	1	1	2
Presley, Derek	4				
Roberts, Dennis	41	6			
Rodgers, Arnold	39	6	20	3	23
Rogers, Jimmy	8	3	2	2	4
Rudkin, Tom	7	3	1		1
Spalding, Billy	1	2			
Stone, Fred	7	1			
Sullivan, Cornelius	20	4			
Thomas, Sid	13				
White, Arnie	21	1	1		1
Williams, Sid	25	5	6		6
(own-goals)					
24 players used	506	66	64	10	74

LEAGUE DIVISION 3 (SOUTH)

Manager: Pat Beasley   **SEASON 1951-52**

No	Date	Venue / Opponent	Att	Pos	Pt	F-A	H-T	Scorers, Times, and Referees
1	18/8	H NEWPORT	30,048 (£2,652.8.4)	—	W, 2	3-1	3-1	Rodgers 1, Atyeo 11, Williams 24 / Parker 26 — Ref: H Ball
2	22/8	A BOURNEMOUTH	16,659	—	D, 3	0-0	0-0	
3	25/8	A READING	21,856 (£2,111)	14 / 1	L, 3	0-3	0-1	Edelston 28, 86, Blackman 85 — Ref: G Roden
4	28/8	H BOURNEMOUTH	19,750 (£1,737.2.3)	3 / 14	W, 5	1-0	1-0	Boxley 33
5	1/9	A NORTHAMPTON	14,152 (£1,173)	3 / 23	W, 7	2-1	2-0	Williams 35, Beasley 41p / Ramscar 78p — Ref: A Mann
6	8/9	A PORT VALE	14,472	11 / 12	L, 7	0-1	0-1	Martin 14 — Ref: G Pankhurst
7	11/9	H MILLWALL	20,602 (£1,794.13.0)	5 / 11	W, 9	2-1	1-0	Atyeo 27, Eisentrager 47 / Neary 67 — Ref: S Law
8	15/9	H BRISTOL ROV	31,497 (£2,969.17.9)	9 / 2	D, 10	1-1	0-0	Atyeo 89 / Lambden 77 — Ref: N Taylor
9	19/9	A MILLWALL	14,620 (£1,269.6.6)	10 / 6	L, 10	2-3	1-1	Eisentrager 21, Atyeo 84 / Neary 30, 62, 80 — Ref: S Law
10	22/9	H IPSWICH	20,664 (£1,838.7.0)	12 / 8	L, 10	0-2	0-0	Garneys 54, 59 — Ref: W Thompson
11	29/9	A TORQUAY	8,359 (£689)	13 / 22	W, 12	2-1	1-1	Eisentrager 29, Atyeo 67 / Shaw 5 — Ref: W Edwards

Line-ups (1–11) — Bristol City above, opponents in italic

1 H NEWPORT

1	2	3	4	5	6	7	8	9	10	11
Sullivan	Guy	Stone	Peacock	Roberts	Beasley	Eisentrager	Williams C	Atyeo	Rodgers	Boxley
Pope	*Staples*	*Hayward*	*Stroud*	*Wilcox*	*Newall*	*Birch*	*Beattie*	*Parker*	*Shergold*	*Moore*

Using his head to good effect, Atyeo has a great start to his City career. He nods the ball down for Rodgers to slam it first time into the net after just 45 seconds, then dispatches a cross to get off the mark himself. Williams fires in the third before County's Reg Parker shoots in low.

2 A BOURNEMOUTH

1	2	3	4	5	6	7	8	9	10	11
Sullivan	Guy	Stone	Presley	Roberts	Beasley	Eisentrager	Williams C	Atyeo	Rodgers	Boxley
Bird	*Cunningham*	*Drummond*	*Woodward*	*Gripton*	*Casey*	*Stroud*	*Marsh*	*Cheney*	*Gaynor*	*Boxshall*

A match of attractive soccer, but neither forward line could make much impression on two quick-tackling defences. The Cherries, who have not been beaten at home in almost a year, start the better, but City take control following a spell that sees them force four quick corners.

3 A READING

1	2	3	4	5	6	7	8	9	10	11
Sullivan	Guy	Stone	Presley	Roberts	Beasley	Eisentrager	Williams C	Atyeo	Rodgers	Boxley
Marks	*Moyse*	*Wicks*	*Lewis*	*Brice*	*Johnston*	*Simpson*	*Edelston*	*Blackman*	*Hanley*	*Bainbridge*

City, forcing the game in their endeavours to respond to Maurice Edelston's first-half shot into an open goal, are hit by Reading's late blitz. After a 40-yard ball sets up Ron Blackman to head in, the centre-forward lays on an easy chance for Edelston to tap the ball into City's net.

4 H BOURNEMOUTH

1	2	3	4	5	6	7	8	9	10	11
Sullivan	Guy	Bailey	Presley	Roberts	Beasley	Eisentrager	Williams C	Atyeo	Rodgers	Boxley
Bird	*Cunningham*	*Drummond*	*Woodward*	*Gripton*	*Neave*	*Stroud*	*Marsh*	*Cheney*	*Casey*	*Boxshall*

After Boxley runs through to fire the ball home with terrific force from just inside the penalty area, Bournemouth fight back well and City are somewhat lucky to survive. Fortunately, Sullivan is in fine form as, aided by a strong wind after the break, the visitors take up the offensive.

5 A NORTHAMPTON

1	2	3	4	5	6	7	8	9	10	11
Sullivan	Guy	Bailey	Presley	Roberts	Beasley	Eisentrager	Williams C	Atyeo	Rodgers	Boxley
Ansell	*Connell*	*Wilson*	*Canlin*	*Duckhouse*	*Davis*	*English*	*Payne*	*O'Donnell*	*Ramscar*	*Staroscik*

This was not the most polished game of football, but City deserve great credit as Guy was a virtual passenger with a knee injury for most of the second half. A fast-rising shot finds the top corner of the Cobblers net for the City opener, then Peter Connell handles to concede the penalty.

6 A PORT VALE

1	2	3	4	5	6	7	8	9	10	11
Sullivan	Stone	Bailey	Presley	Roberts	Beasley	Eisentrager	Williams C	Atyeo	Rodgers	Boxley
Heppell	*Hamlett*	*Hayward*	*Turner*	*Cheadle*	*Sproson*	*Hulligan*	*Martin*	*Pinchbeck*	*Aveyard*	*Bennett*

Not even the masterly guidance of player-boss Pat Beasley at his best can spur City to a share of the points in this game that is chosen by BBC for their second secret broadcast. Despite dominating and creating plenty of chances, City prove unable to reply to Alan Martin's high-drive.

7 H MILLWALL

1	2	3	4	5	6	7	8	9	10	11
Sullivan	Stone	Bailey	Peacock	Roberts	Beasley	Eisentrager	Williams C	Atyeo	Rodgers	Boxley
Hinton	*Quinn*	*Fisher*	*Reeves*	*Bowler*	*White*	*Johnson*	*Constantine*	*Neary*	*Morgan*	*Hartburn*

City come out triumphant at the end of one of the best games of football seen at the Gate for many a day. Atyeo weaves his way through in fine style before pushing the opener past Ted Hinton, then, following the break, Eisentrager finds the net with one of his pile-drivers from 16 yards.

8 H BRISTOL ROV

1	2	3	4	5	6	7	8	9	10	11
Sullivan	Stone	Bailey	Peacock	Roberts	Beasley	Eisentrager	Williams C	Atyeo	Rodgers	Boxley
Hoyle	*Bamford*	*Fox*	*Pitt*	*Warren*	*Sampson*	*Petherbridge*	*Bradford*	*Lambden*	*Roost*	*Watling*

The early stages of the Bristol derby consist of fast, exciting soccer, but the goals do not come until near the end. The honours are deservedly shared at half time, but, following, the break Vic Lambden heads Rovers into a deserved lead. Atyeo equalises at the death with a fine shot.

9 A MILLWALL

1	2	3	4	5	6	7	8	9	10	11
Sullivan	Hinton	Bailey	Peacock	Roberts	Beasley	Eisentrager	Williams C	Atyeo	Rodgers	Boxley
Hinton	*Jardine*	*Fisher*	*Short*	*Bowler*	*White*	*Johnson*	*Constantine*	*Neary*	*Morgan*	*Hartburn*

Boxley becomes the third City player to be laid up this season. Leading thanks to Eisentrager's snap-shot, City's winger is later left hobbling for the remainder of the half before going off. Following Stone's eighth-minute handling offence, Frank Neary puts the resultant penalty wide.

10 H IPSWICH

1	2	3	4	5	6	7	8	9	10	11
Sullivan	Stone	Bailey	Peacock	Roberts	Beasley	Eisentrager	Williams C	Atyeo	Rodgers	Boxley
Burns	*Green*	*Tyler*	*Baird*	*Rees*	*Parker*	*Myles*	*McCrory*	*Garneys*	*Drivers*	*Roberts*

City's defence pay the price for their casual attitude when Tom Garneys, Ipswich's new signing from Brentford, notches a quick double. He scores with a brilliant 25-yarder, before finding the net again shortly after by driving in Tom Parker's cross following a muddled clearance.

11 A TORQUAY

1	2	3	4	5	6	7	8	9	10	11
Sullivan	Webber G	Bailey	Tovey	Roberts	Beasley	Eisentrager	Williams C	Atyeo	Rodgers	Boxley
Topping	*Calland*	*Brown*	*Warren*	*Towers*	*Lewis*	*Shaw*	*Edds*	*Collins*	*Thomas*	*Boyd*

Atyeo's rocket-like shot brings City the points in a hard, fast game at Plainmoor, where Tovey takes the eye with his dynamic display. Both sides miss many chances following Ron Shaw's cannonball opener. After his first shot hits an upright, Eisentrager fires in City's equaliser.

12 A NORWICH 6/10 — 15 L 0-1 0-1

Hollis 25
Ref: R Hall
28,302 1 12

Sullivan	Stone	Bailey	Peacock	Roberts	Beasley	Eisentrager	Williams C	Atyeo	Rodgers	Boyd
Nethercott	*Duffy*	*Lewis*	*Pickwick*	*Foulkes*	*Dutton*	*Gavin*	*Kinsey*	*Hollis*	*Ashman*	*Docherty*

At one stage towards the finish, City have ten men in the opposition box, but are unable get the ball past Ken Nethercott. After Noel Kinsey sent Roy Hollis away to fire Norwich in front, City almost totally dominate the proceedings only to be let down by some abject finishing.

---

13 H EXETER 13/10 — 15 D 1-1 1-1

Rodgers 3
Mackay 37
Ref: H Wright
19,053 23 13
(£1,674.1.0)

Sullivan	Stone	Bailey	Peacock	Roberts	Beasley	Boyd	Williams C	Atyeo	Rodgers	Boxley
Leary G	*Warren*	*Clark*	*Fallon*	*Goddard*	*Davey*	*Regan*	*Smart*	*Smith*	*Mackay*	*McClelland*

Despite the encouragement of an early-headed strike from Rodgers, City disappoint. Yet again they squander many openings and allow themselves to be upset by the visitors more forceful style. Angus Mackay bundles Sullivan and the ball over the line for the equaliser.

---

14 A COLCHESTER 20/10 — 15 L 0-2 1-4

Williams 80
Cutting 4, Keeble 21, 75, 87
Ref: R Burgess
9,552 19 13

Sullivan	Stone	Bailey	Tovey	Roberts	Steeds	Eisentrager	Williams C	Rodgers	Beasley	Boxley
Wright	*Harrison*	*Rowlands*	*Bearryman*	*Stewart*	*Elder*	*Jones*	*Scott*	*Keeble*	*Cutting*	*Church*

The U's fast-moving forwards hold sway at Layer Road. A Len Jones centre sets up Fred Cutting to fire in a three-yard opener, then Vic Keeble runs onto flick in the first of his hat-trick. George Wright's spilling of Beasley's shot sees Williams obtain City's consolation.

---

15 H CRYSTAL PALACE 27/10 — 14 W 2-0 2-0

Atyeo 65, Lowrie 82
Ref: Rev S Davis
18,887 20 15
(£1,633.0.6)

Sullivan	Guy	Bailey	Peacock	Roberts	Beasley	Rogers	Williams C	Atyeo	Lowrie	Eisentrager
Anderson	*Scott*	*Macdonald*	*McGeachie*	*Briggs*	*Price*	*Broughton*	*Rainford*	*Evans*	*Burgess*	*Devonshire*

Despite being handicapped by Peacock's injury, City take a deserved lead when Atyeo seizes onto Beasley's deflected drive to thump the ball high into the roof of the Palace net. Lowrie marks his comeback by controlling an awkward ball and beating Bob Anderson with a fierce effort.

---

16 A SWINDON 3/11 — 13 D 0-0 0-0

Ref: N Taylor
16,296 9 16

Sullivan	Uprichard	Bailey	Williams C	Roberts	Beasley	Rogers	Eisentrager	Atyeo	Lowrie	Williams S
Hunt	*Gulliver*	*Kaye*	*Hudson*	*Batchelor*	*Lunn*	*Onslow*	*Owen*	*Betteridge*	*Bain*	

City certainly earn their point in this hard and fast encounter, which attracts the largest crowd of the season to the County ground. Whilst Maurice Owen and Atyeo are the outstanding forwards, City have cause to be thankful for Sullivan's brilliant display between the sticks.

---

17 H LEYTON ORIENT 10/11 — 13 D 1-1 1-1

Atyeo 9
Rees 21
Ref: R Carter
19,607 9 17
(£1,719.8.9)

Sullivan	Welton	Bailey	Peacock	Roberts	Beasley	Eisentrager	Williams C	Atyeo	Lowrie	Boyd
Evans	*Banner*	*Blizzard*	*Aldous*	*Deverall*	*Woan*	*Cater*	*Rees*	*Blair*	*Blatchford*	

City fail to maintain the promising start given them by Atyeo's brilliant shot. Loose marking allows Welsh international William Rees to run through and equalise with a rising shot. The visitors are much the better side after the break and City have a hard battle to hang on to a point.

---

18 A WALSALL 17/11 — 14 L 0-2 0-1

Giles 14, Bridgett 88
Ref: J Jackson
6,549 9 17

Sullivan	Lewis	Bailey	Williams C	Roberts	Beasley	Eisentrager	Rodgers	Lowrie	Jones
Holding	*Green*	*Dean*	*Russon*	*Walker*	*Bowen*	*O'Neill*	*Bridgett*	*Evans*	*Giles P*

Walsall's dash proves too much for City at Fellows Park, where new £5,000 winger Ernie Jones switches flanks to try and ginger up their lack lustre attack. After Philip Giles opens the scoring with a cross-drive, the City never look remotely capable of pulling the game out of the fire.

---

19 A ALDERSHOT 1/12 — 15 L 0-1 0-0

White 71
Ref: N Taylor
6,781 21 17

Sullivan	Nichol	Bailey	Tovey	Roberts	Beasley	Jones	Eisentrager	Atyeo	Williams C	Boyd
Laird	*Jefferson*	*Gormley*	*Billington*	*White*	*Durkin*	*Taggart*	*Raine*	*Menzies*	*Flint*	

City spurn their chances in a poor game and are made to pay the price when Jack White finds the back of the net with a shot from just inside the area. For Aldershot, who claim their first home win over City in four years, George Nichol pulls off a great save from Atyeo on half-time.

---

20 H WATFORD 8/12 — 17 L 1-3 0-1

Jones 70
Haigh 17, Thompson 46, 87
Ref: W Elliott
10,228 13 17
(£890.2.6)

Sullivan	Saphin	Bailey	Tovey	Roberts	Beasley	Eisentrager	Williams C	Atyeo	Lowrie	Masters
Eastway	*Jones B*	*Eggleston*	*Patan*	*Meadows*	*Cook*	*Haigh*	*Thompson*	*Jones M*	*Collins*	

Mistakes in defence against a lively attack cost City this game. Gordon Haigh is allowed to run through unchallenged to shoot in the opener, then, after the interval, Sullivan fails to come out for a corner and Cyril Thompson heads in Watford's second. Jones smashes in for the City.

---

21 H READING 22/12 — 21 L 1-3 0-0

[Blackmore 88]
Eisentrager 89
Bainbridge 57, Simpson 87,
Ref: G Roden
14,680 6 17
(£1,248.15.9)

Sullivan	Marks	Bailey	Tovey	Roberts	Beasley	Jones	Eisentrager	Atyeo	Rodgers	Masters
Moyes	*Wicks*	*Lewis*	*Brice*	*Johnston*	*Simpson*	*Edelston*	*Blackman*	*Henley*	*Bainbridge*	

Ken Bainbridge notches the opener with a fierce close-range shot in this fast and interesting game at the Gate, where Reading take the biscuit with a well-deserved victory. A thrilling finale with three goals in the dying minutes, including Eisentrager hooking in from Peacock's centre.

---

22 A PLYMOUTH 25/12 — 19 D 2-2 2-2

Atyeo 12, Rogers 17
Rattray 2, 40
Ref: G Sawyer
16,911 2 18

Sullivan	Shortt	Bailey	Peacock	Roberts	Tovey	Jones	Eisentrager	Atyeo	Williams C	Rodgers
Ratcliffe	*Jones*	*Dougall*	*Chisholm*	*Perteous*	*Astall*	*Dews*	*Tadman*	*Rattray*	*Govan*	

A clever goal by Atyeo counters Peter Rattray's early opener, then Rogers puts City ahead before Rattray heads in Argyle's leveller. A muddy pitch makes things difficult after the break, but Rogers misses, what would have been a deserved City winner, by heading over a vacant net.

---

23 H PLYMOUTH 26/12 — 17 D 1-1 0-0

Roberts 90
Tadman 83
Ref: G Sawyer
27,092 2 19
(£2,643.19.5)

Sullivan	Shortt	Bailey	Peacock	Roberts	Tovey	Jones	Eisentrager	Atyeo	Williams C	Rogers
Ratcliffe	*Jones*	*Dougall*	*Chisholm*	*Porteous*	*Astall*	*Dews*	*Tadman*	*Rattray*	*Govan*	

Maurice Tadman fires Argyle ahead from a free-kick, but Roberts, on moving upfield to supplement the attack, saves City right at the finish. Jones gets away on the right and centres to Rogers who heads onto Roberts to fire the ball, through a mass of defenders, past William Shortt.

No	Date	Opponent	1	2	3	4	5	6	7	8	9	10	11	Scorers, Times, and Referees	Att	Pos	Pt	F-A	H-T
24	29/12	H NORTHAMPTON	Sullivan / Wood	Guy / Collins	Bailey / Connell	Peacock / Candlin	Roberts / Duckhouse	Tovey / Dodgin	Masters / English	Eisentrager / Payne	Atyeo / McCulloch	Williams C / Ramscar	Rogers / Fowler	Eisentrager 36p, Rogers 77 — Ref: H Mann	18,733 (£1,658.14.9)	16 / 6	21	W 2-0	1-0
25	5/1	H PORT VALE	Sullivan / Heppell	Guy / Turner	Bailey / Hayward	Peacock / Todd	Roberts / Cheadle	Tovey / Polk	Masters / Barber	Eisentrager / Hallam	Atyeo / Aveyard	Williams C / Mullard	Rogers / Hulligan	Rogers 39 — Ref: G Pankhurst	17,598 (£1,533.0.9)	15 / 24	23	W 1-0	1-0
26	12/1	H GILLINGHAM	Sullivan / Rigg	Guy / Marks	Bailey / Lewin	Peacock / Boswell	Roberts / Niblett	Tovey / Ayres	Jones / Russell	Eisentrager / Burtenshaw	Atyeo / Thomas	Williams C / Lewis	Rogers / Briggs	Williams C 20, Eisenstr' 39p, Tovey 77 / Thomas 15, Russell 46 — Ref: C Bucknall	13,567 (£1,113.12.3)	14 / 17	25	W 3-2	2-1
27	19/1	A BRISTOL ROV	Sullivan / Hoyle	Guy / Bamford	Bailey / Fox	Peacock / Pitt	Roberts / Warren	Tovey / Sampson	Jones / Petherbridge	Eisentrager / Roost	Atyeo / Lambden	Williams C / Bradford	Rogers / Bush	Bradford 7, Petherbridge 86 — Ref: N Taylor	34,612 (£2,722)	15 / 6	25	L 0-2	0-1
28	26/1	A IPSWICH	Sullivan / Parry	Guy / Feeney	Bailey / Deacon	Peacock / Murchison	Roberts / Rees	Beasley / Parker	Jones / Warne	Williams C / McCrory	Atyeo / Garneys	Rodgers / Dobson	Rogers / Roberts	Atyeo 22 / Garneys 47 — Ref: W Clapton	9,146	15 / 20	26	D 1-1	1-0
29	6/2	H SOUTHEND	Sullivan / Scannell	Guy / Pritchard	Bailey / Anderson	Peacock / French	Roberts / Sheard	Tovey / Lawler	Jones / Sibley	Rodgers / Thompson	Atyeo / Wakefield	Lowrie / Grant	Rogers / Stubbs	Rodgers 25, 75, Rogers 60, Lowrie 64, [Atyeo 77, Jones 80] — Ref: F Williams	8,638 (£709.9.0)	13 / 14	28	W 6-0	1-0
30	9/2	A TORQUAY	Sullivan / Webber G	Guy / Topping	Bailey / Calland	Peacock / Brown	Roberts / Webber E	Tovey / Towers	Jones / Shaw	Rodgers / Lewis	Atyeo / Northcott	Lowrie / Collins	Rogers / Edds	Rodgers 37, 38 / Edds 28, 67 — Ref: W Edwards	19,787 (£1,831.18.0)	14 / 19	29	D 2-2	2-1
31	16/2	H NORWICH	Sullivan / Nethercott	Stone / Morgan	Bailey / Lewis	Peacock / Pickwick	Roberts / Holmes	Tovey / Ashman	Masters / Gavin	Williams C / McCrohan	Atyeo / Hollis	Beasley / Kinsey	Rogers / Summers	Beasley 13, Rodg' 36 [Roberts 80 (og)] / Gavin 21, 30, 60, McCrohan 74 — Ref: R Hall	19,825 (£1,849.3.0)	14 / 4	29	L 2-5	2-2
32	27/2	A SOUTHEND	Sullivan / Morton	Guy / Loughran	Bailey / Anderson	Peacock / French	Roberts / Sheard	Steeds / Lawler	Masters / Sibley	Eisentrager / McAlinden	Atyeo / Grant	Rodgers / Thompson	Rogers / Stubbs	Rodgers 75 [Grant 65, Thompson 88] / Sibley 3, French 55, Stubbs 56 — Ref: F Williams	3,806	14 / 9	29	L 1-5	0-1
33	1/3	A EXETER	Sullivan / Singleton	Guy / Warren	Bailey / Rowe	Peacock / Davey	Roberts / Doyle	Beasley / Harrower	Eisentrager / Hutchins	Steeds / Smart	Atyeo / McClelland	Rodgers / MacKay	Boyd / Regan	— Ref: H Wright	8,284	14 / 21	30	D 0-0	0-0
34	8/3	H COLCHESTER	Sullivan / Coombes	Guy / Harrison	Bailey / Rookes	Peacock / Bearryman	Roberts / Stewart	Steeds / Elder	Rogers / Aitchison	Rogers / Scott	Atyeo / Rowlands	Rodgers / McKim	Williams S / Church	Rogers 39, Williams C 45 — Ref: R Burgess	14,373 (£1,227.14.6)	14 / 12	32	W 2-0	2-0

Match reports

24 — Northampton: City's improved display brings them a double and their first League win in over three months. Rogers (later to run in City's second) misses an open goal by heading against the crossbar in the very first minute, but a foul on City's left-winger brings the spot-kick that puts them in front.

25 — Port Vale: Opportunist Rogers is City's match-winner. Master's dropped a centre into the goalmouth that looked like the keeper's all the way, but Rogers had other ideas. He challenged George Heppell for the high ball and, when the custodian dropped it, he was able to stab it into the open net.

26 — Gillingham: Falling behind early on when Hugh Russell beats Sullivan from close range following a corner, City recover to level with a Williams header and then take the lead with a spot-kick following a foul on Atyeo. Russell heads the visitors back on terms, but Tovey fires in City's winner.

27 — Bristol Rov: Following Geoff Bradford's left-footed drive that opens the scoring, it is goodbye City, who are caught out in their attempts to force a leveller. The Rovers punt the ball upfield and George Petherbridge races through to fire in a masterly effort that makes sure of the Pirates' success.

28 — Ipswich: Atyeo culminates a run down the right from halfway with a neat flick over the advancing goalkeeper to put City in front with a brilliant goal. Unfortunately, Tom Garneys heads in an equaliser to deprive City of a deserved success. Ipswich owe much to Jack Parry's display in goal.

29 — Southend: At a minute's silence in memory of the late King George VI, the City forwards set about Southend in determined fashion. However, at the interval all they have to show for their dominance is a close-in shot from Rodgers at the Covered End that gave Tommy Scannell no chance.

30 — Torquay: City only have themselves to blame for failing to end the Torquay post-war Ashton bogey. Despite Rodgers levelling the cross-driven opener with a header, and then almost immediately netting with real rasper, a grand header by Ernie Edds makes City pay for missing their chances.

31 — Norwich: Thanks to Rodgers firing past Ken Nethercott, City go in level at the half-time interval, but thereafter they are outpaced by superior opponents. Beasley puts City in front with a low-drive before John Gavin wins in his hat-trick. Roy McCrohan runs through to fire in a brilliant goal.

32 — Southend: Just prior to Southend's fourth goal, City are reduced to ten men for the rest of the match when winger Rogers is injured. It did not make any difference to the result as City are outplayed throughout, though Rodgers does manage to capitalise on a defensive error to pull one goal back.

33 — Exeter: City play well in the early stages, but their attack, especially Atyeo, spurn many chances. By the finish they are indebted to their defence, particularly Sullivan, Guy, Peacock and Roberts, for securing a point. Bailey finds Dennis Hutchins to be a handful in this scrappy game.

34 — Colchester: The City are not impressive, but they are good enough to claim their first ever success over the Layer Road club. Taking the lead with a fine cross-shot that the referee awards even though John Harrison hooks the ball out, victory is made almost certain right on the stroke of half-time.

Bristol City Match Records 35–46

35 — A, 15/3 — CRYSTAL PALACE
Position 14 · Att. 13,906 (15) · **L 1:2** · Pts 32

Scorers: Rogers 31, Bennett 60, Thomas 72
Ref: Rev S Davis

City: Sullivan, Guy, Bailey, Peacock, Roberts, Williams C, Jones, Rogers, Atyeo, Rodgers, Williams S
Opp: *Hughes, Edwards, McDonald, McGeachie, Briggs, Chivers, Evans, Rainford, Thomas, Rundle, Bennett*

A Rogers shot on the run brings City a deserved first-half advantage at Selhurst Park, but, shortly after the interval Ron Bennett flings himself full-length to head an equaliser. Thereafter, City offer little and Palace's winner, courtesy of a 20-yard drive by John Thomas, is no surprise.

36 — H, 22/3 — SWINDON
Position 11 · Att. 14,823 (12) · **W 2:1** · Pts 34 · (£1,294.5.6)

Scorers: Atyeo 57, Rodgers 81p, Onslow 7
Ref: N Taylor

City: Sullivan, Roberts, Bailey, Peacock, Compton, Williams C, Jones, Rogers, Atyeo, Rodgers, Williams S
Opp: *Upichard, Hunt, May, Kaye, Hudson, Gray, Lunn, Onslow, Owen, Betteridge, Boyd*

City's lucky day as the winning penalty, scored by Rodgers, who had earlier been taken off unconscious, is awarded for George Hudson's supposed push on Atyeo as they challenged for a ball. Roy Onslow's lobbed centre-cum-shot, is equalised by Atyeo's high-dropping effort.

37 — H, 5/4 — WALSALL
Position 13 · Att. 8,558 (24) · **W 2:0** · Pts 36 · (£677.10.6)

Scorers: Rogers 12, Rodgers 83
Ref: J Jackson

City: Sullivan, Guy, Bailey, Peacock, Roberts, Williams C, Jones, Rogers, Atyeo, Rodgers, Masters
Opp: *Lewis, Jones, Montgomery, Walters, Green, Millington, Bowen, Dean, Winter, Devlin, Barber*

City attacked throughout, but after an early opener when Rogers picked his spot to hit a powerful right-footed shot into the far corner of the net, no further goals come until near the end. Rodgers makes victory certain when, from Atyeo's centre, he is able to walk the ball into the net.

38 — H, 11/4 — BRIGHTON
Position 11 · Att. 18,915 (3) · **W 4:1** · Pts 38 · (£1,730.19.6)

Scorers: Williams 13, Masters 17, Rodgers 71, Garbutt 81, [Rogers 77]
Ref: R Carter

City: Sullivan, Guy, Bailey, Peacock, Roberts, Williams C, Jones, Rogers, Atyeo, Rodgers, Masters
Opp: *Ball, Tennant, Mansell, Willard, McCoy, Wilson, Reed, McNichol, Garbutt, Bennett, Howard*

City's forwards show they mean business with Atyeo netting after barely 20 seconds. Unfortunately, this effort is disallowed as is another of his after the interval. Following an eight-yard Williams opener and Masters registering direct from a corner, Brighton are totally outplayed.

39 — A, 12/4 — SHREWSBURY
Position 11 · Att. 11,119 (21) · **L 0:2** · Pts 38

Scorers: McCulloch 2, 70
Ref: A Smith

City: Sullivan, Guy, Bailey, Peacock, Roberts, Tovey, Jones, Williams C, Atyeo, Rodgers, Masters
Opp: *Eggleston, Halpin, Potter, Bullions, Ashworth, Butler, Reagan, Jackson, McCulloch, Beynon, Roberts*

City are unlucky with shots that hit the bar, but they are undone by Adam McCulloch. The centre-forward registers the opener with a fierce drive, then, after the interval, makes sure of the points by throwing himself full-length to head in a grand goal from Arnold Jackson's cross.

40 — A, 14/4 — BRIGHTON
Position 12 · Att. 17,519 (4) · **D 1:1** · Pts 39

Scorers: Eisentrager 33, Sirrel 36
Ref: R Carter

City: Sullivan, Ball, Bailey, Peacock, Roberts, Williams C, Jones, Eisentrager, Atyeo, Rodgers, Williams S
Opp: *Tennant, Mansell, Willard, South, Wilson, Reed, McNichol, Higgins, Sirrel, Howard*

Whilst City open the scoring against the run of play when Eisentrager drives in a great first-time shot from 20 yards, Albion quickly respond when Jimmy Sirrel runs onto a Ron Higgins flick to fire past Sullivan. A draw is a fair result of a match that only came to life in fits and starts.

41 — H, 19/4 — ALDERSHOT
Position 13 · Att. 12,540 (19) · **D 1:1** · Pts 40 · (£1,030.3.6)

Scorers: Rodgers 50, Stewart 54
Ref: N Taylor

City: Sullivan, Guy, Bailey, Peacock, Roberts, Williams C, Jones, Eisentrager, Atyeo, Rodgers, Williams S
Opp: *Houston, Rogers, Jefferson, Laird, White, Cropley, Durkin, Menzies, Gormley, Stewart, Flint*

It is of no credit this draw against the Shots, as playing against a poor side City play like a poor side themselves. A dreary game, without polish and without a worthwhile ball-player on view, is only redeemed by the goals. A cool side-foot effort is countered by William Stewart's header.

42 — H, 22/4 — SHREWSBURY
Position 11 · Att. 9,502 (23) · **W 3:0** · Pts 42 · (£724.10.3)

Scorers: Jones 29, Rogers 42, Atyeo 53
Ref: A Smith

City: Sullivan, Eggleston, Bailey, Peacock, Roberts, Williams C, Jones, Atyeo, Jackson, Rodgers, Boxley
Opp: *Halpin, Potter, Bullions, Ashworth, Butler, Dodd, McCulloch, Beynon, Roberts*

The visitors find themselves completely outclassed, but nothing goes right for Rodgers. Denied a goal in the tenth minute when John Halpin handles on the line, Rodgers fires the resultant penalty straight at the keeper, a feat he repeats with another spot-kick not long before the end.

43 — A, 26/4 — WATFORD
Position 12 · Att. 6,078 (20) · **L 1:3** · Pts 42

Scorers: Rogers 49, Thompson 74, Brown 82, Tovey 88(og)
Ref: W Elliott

City: Sullivan, Guy, Bailey, Peacock, Roberts, Williams C, Jones, Tovey, Atyeo, Rogers, Boxley
Opp: *Saphin, Eastway, Jones, Eggleston, Nolan, Kelly, Cook, Haigh, Thompson, Brown, Collins*

Against enthusiastic opponents fighting the threat of re-election, City's defence suddenly looked weary in the latter stages and succumbed to Tom Brown's shot and Tovey's own goal. After Rogers had headed City into the lead, Cyril Thompson shot through a fine Watford equaliser.

44 — A, 28/4 — NEWPORT
Position 12 · Att. 7,714 (6) · **L 0:1** · Pts 42

Scorers: Nelson 2
Ref: H Ball

City: Sullivan, Guy, Bailey, Peacock, Roberts, Williams C, Jones, Steeds, Atyeo, Rogers, Eisentrager
Opp: *Fernley, Staples, Hayward, Evans, Wilcox, Newall, Birch, Beattie, Nelson, Shergold, Moore*

With City still contriving to spurn easy chances this game is over almost before it begins. Danny Newall's neat through ball gives Anthony Nelson, the young Welsh amateur international who proves to be a real handful for Roberts, the opening to fire the only goal past Sullivan.

45 — A, 1/5 — LEYTON ORIENT
Position 14 · Att. 5,239 (18) · **L 0:2** · Pts 42

Scorers: Pacey 44, 67
Ref: R Carter

City: Sullivan, Guy, Bailey, Peacock, Roberts, Williams C, Jones, Eisentrager, Atyeo, Rogers, Boxley
Opp: *Welton, Evans, Banner, Blizard, Aldous, Deverall, Woan, Pacey, Bryant, Rees, Blatchford*

Orient owe their win to the opportunism of Dennis Pacey, who only joined them this season. He opens the scoring shortly before the interval when he heads in from Don Woan's corner, then sends Arthur Banner's free-kick into the net to make the game safe midway through the second half.

46 — A, 3/5 — GILLINGHAM
Position 15 · Att. 12,017 (22) · **L 0:5** · Pts 42

Scorers: Burtenshaw 13, 80, Forrester 25, [Thomas 48, 73]
Ref: C Bucknall

City: Sullivan, Guy, Bailey, Peacock, Roberts, Williams C, Lyons, Rogers, Atyeo, Rodgers, Tovey
Opp: *Rigg, Marks, Lewin, Boswell, Niblett, Scarth, Ayres, Burtenshaw, Thomas, Forrester, Briggs*

With this demolition, Gillingham escape having to apply for re-election on goal-average at the expense of Exeter. After Bill Burtenshaw side-foots in the opener, City are comprehensively beaten on all points. A glorious 20-yard drive by David Thomas, is the best score of the game.

Home Average 17,780
Away 13,215

FA Cup

			F-A	H-T	Scorers, Times, and Referees
1 A BRIGHTON	14	W	2-1	2-1	Atyeo 5, 12
	17,740	4			Bennett 44
	(£1,910.7.9)				Ref: G Baker

1	2	3	4	5	6	7	8	9	10	11
Sullivan	Guy	Bailey	Tovey	Roberts	Beasley	Eisentrager	Williams C	Atyeo	Lowrie	Boyd
Baldwin	*Tennant*	*Mansell*	*Willard*	*McCoy*	*Wilson*	*Reed*	*McNichol*	*Bennett*	*Sirrel*	*Keene*

An FA Cup surprise at the Goldstone ground, where the best player on the field netted twice to bring City passage through to the next round. Shortly after he had put City in front with a low-drive, Atyeo's prodigious leap allows him to head a long free-kick into the Seagulls' nest.

			F-A	H-T	Scorers, Times, and Referees
2 A COLCHESTER	16	L	1-2	0-2	Rodgers 64
	9,988	18			Scott 7, Davidson 29
	(£913.10.6)				Ref: H Wright

1	2	3	4	5	6	7	8	9	10	11
Sullivan	Guy	Bailey	Tovey	Roberts	Beasley	Jones	Eisentrager	Atyeo	Rodgers	Masters
Wright	*Harrison*	*Rookes*	*Bearryman*	*Stuart*	*Elder*	*Davidson*	*Scott*	*Keeble*	*Cutting*	*Church*

Trailing to August Scott's simple shot and Adam Davidson's curling corner that Sullivan can only help into the net, City's rally comes too late against a superior opponents. Rodgers races in to hammer home a great shot, but time proves City's enemy as they suddenly turn on the style.

Gloucestershire Cup

			F-A	H-T	Scorers, Times, and Referees
F A BRISTOL ROV	15	W	2-1	2-1	Williams 38, Rodgers 43
	16,214	7			Petherbridge 20
	(£1,672)				Ref: B Griffiths

1	2	3	4	5	6	7	8	9	10	11
Sullivan	Guy	Bailey	Peacock	Roberts	Williams C	Jones	Rogers	Atyeo	Rodgers	Boxley
Radford	*Watkins*	*Fox*	*Pitt*	*Warren*	*Sampson*	*Petherbridge*	*Micklewright*	*Lambden*	*Bradford*	*Watling*

In contrast to last season's dire contest this game is marked by football of the highest standard. City rally well after falling behind when George Petherbridge side-foots in the opener. Williams beats Howard Radford all ends up with a first-time grounder, before Rogers lobs in the winner.

St Dunstan's Charity Cup

			F-A	H-T	Scorers, Times, and Referees
F A CHIPPENHAM TOWN	15	W	9-1	4-0	Norman 7,50,55, Evans 35, Jones 44,
	2,531	WL:1			Davies 87 [Atyeo 40, 70, Beasley 75, 80]
	(£148)				

1	2	3	4	5	6	7	8	9	10	11
Morgan	Tovey	Wilcox	Goulding	Peacock	Beasley	Jones	Norman	Atyeo	Eisentrager	Evans

City annihilate the newly crowned Western League Champions in this contest for the St Dunstan's Charity Cup. Against a rampant City outfit, the only respite for gallant Chippenham comes almost on time when left-winger Davies fires in the only shot good enough to beat Morgan.

		Home					Away					
	P	W	D	L	F	A	W	D	L	F	A	Pts
1 Plymouth	46	19	3	1	70	19	10	5	8	37	34	66
2 Reading	46	19	2	2	73	23	10	1	12	39	37	61
3 Norwich	46	18	1	4	55	15	8	8	7	34	35	61
4 Millwall	46	16	5	2	46	21	7	7	9	28	32	58
5 Brighton	46	15	4	4	57	24	9	6	8	30	39	58
6 Newport	46	13	7	3	45	26	8	5	10	32	50	54
7 Bristol Rov	46	14	5	4	60	20	6	7	10	29	33	52
8 Northampton	46	17	1	5	65	31	5	4	14	28	43	49
9 Southend	46	16	6	1	56	17	3	4	16	19	49	48
10 Colchester	46	12	7	4	32	22	5	5	13	24	55	46
11 Torquay	46	10	3	10	53	42	7	7	9	33	56	44
12 Aldershot	46	11	7	5	40	27	4	7	12	38	62	44
13 Port Vale	46	11	5	7	33	16	3	4	16	17	50	43
14 Bournemouth	46	11	4	8	42	30	5	6	12	27	45	42
15 BRISTOL C	46	13	6	4	44	26	2	6	15	14	43	42
16 Swindon	46	9	9	5	29	22	5	5	13	22	46	42
17 Ipswich	46	12	4	7	45	31	5	5	14	18	43	41
18 Leyton Orient	46	12	5	6	39	26	4	4	15	16	42	41
19 Crys Palace	46	9	7	7	32	28	6	2	15	29	52	39
20 Shrewsbury	46	11	3	9	35	29	2	7	14	27	57	36
21 Watford	46	7	7	9	34	37	6	3	14	23	44	36
22 Gillingham	46	10	7	6	47	31	6	1	16	24	50	35
23 Exeter	46	10	4	9	40	36	3	5	15	25	50	35
24 Walsall	46	11	1	3	38	31	2	2	19	17	63	31
	1104	306	118	128	1110	630	128	118	306	630	1110	1104

	Appearances		Goals		
	Lge	Cup	Lge	Cup	Tot
Atyeo, John	44	4	12	4	16
Bailey, Jack	43	3			
Beasley, Pat	23	3	2	2	4
Boxley, Jack	16	1	1		1
Boyd, Jack	7	1			
Compton, Terry	1				
Eisentrager, Alec	32	3	7		7
Evans, Leslie*		1		1	1
Goulding, Brian		1			
Guy, Ivor	36	3			
Jones, Ernie	22	3	3	1	4
Lowrie, George	6	1	2		2
Lyons, Michael	1				
Masters, Graham	9	1	1		1
Morgan, Syd		1			
Norman, Griffith*		1		3	3
Peacock, Ernie	34	2			
Presley, Derek	5				
Roberts, Dennis	46	3	1		1
Rodgers, Arnold	36	2	12	1	13
Rogers, Jimmy	22	1	10	1	11
Steeds, Cecil	5				
Stone, Fred	12				
Sullivan, Cornelius	46	3			
Tovey, Bill	17	3	1		1
Wilcox, Caradoc*		1			
Williams, Cyril	39	2	6	1	7
Williams, Sid	4				
28 players used	506	44	58	14	72

Odds & ends

Double wins: (1) Northampton.

Double losses: (3) Reading, Norwich, Watford.

Won from behind: (2) Torquay (a), Gillingham (h).

Lost from in front: Millwall (a), Norwich (h), C Palace (a), Watford (a).

High spots: Putting six goals into the Southend net on 6 February.

Winning at Brighton in the FA Cup.

Beating Bristol Rovers in the Gloucestershire Cup final.

Low spots: The losing trips to Essex, going down 1-4 at Colchester and 1-5 at Southend.

Conceding three second-half goals at home to Norwich.

AGM (Grand Hotel, Broad Street, Bristol, 20 April 1953): Profit £2,228.3s.6d. Season Ticket Sales £5,265.19s.0d.

* Cardiff players.

Player of the year: Cyril Williams.

Ever-presents: (2) Dennis Roberts, Cornelius Sullivan.

Hat-tricks: (1) Griffith Norman (1).

Leading scorer: Overall J Atyeo (16). League J Atyeo and A Rodgers (12).

LEAGUE DIVISION 3 (SOUTH) — Manager: Pat Beasley — SEASON 1952-53

No	Date	Att (receipts)	Pos	Pt	Res	F-A	H-T	Scorers, Times, and Referees	1	2	3	4	5	6	7	8	9	10	11
1	A WATFORD 23/8	22,409 (£2,255.16.6)		0	L	1-4	1-2	Williams 8 / Paton 11, Bowie 35, Thompson 69, 76 Saphin / Ref: F Overton	Sullivan	Mitchelson	Bailey	Peacock	Roberts	Williams	Jones	Rogers	Atyeo	Rogers	Boxley
										Gallogly	Croker	Eddlestone	Phipps	Mitchell	Paton	Bowie	Thompson	Paterson	Collins
2	H MILLWALL 26/8	20,975		1	D	0-0	0-0	Ref: C Bucknall	Morgan	Mitchelson	Bailey	Peacock	Roberts	Williams	Jones	Rogers	Atyeo	Rogers	Boxley
									Finlayson	Jardine	Fisher	Reeves	Bowler	Short	Johnson	Stabbart	Neary	Morgan	Hartburn
3	H BRIGHTON 30/8	17,352 (£1,809.12.6)	19	2	D	2-2	0-1	Rodgers 66, Boxley 74 / Keene 44, Sirrel 80 / Ref: F Williams	Morgan	Mitchelson	Bailey	Peacock	Roberts	Williams	Jones	Rogers	Atyeo	Rogers	Boxley
									Ball	Tennant	Mansell	McIlvenny	McCoy	South	Reed	Sirrel	Owens	Leadbeater	Keene
4	A MILLWALL 3/9	18,453	16	3	D	1-1	0-0	Atyeo 88 / Neary 62 / Ref: C Bucknall	Morgan	Mitchelson	Bailey	Peacock	Roberts	Williams	Jones	Rogers	Atyeo	Rogers	Tovey
									Finlayson	Jardine	Fisher	Reeves	Bowler	Short	Johnson	Stabbart	Neary	Morgan	Mansfield
5	A NEWPORT 6/9	9,573	18	3	L	3-4	1-3	Roberts 32p, Rodg's 52, 59 [Moore 85] / Sherg'd 17, Roberts 18 (og), Nelson 29, Pope / Ref: H Ball	Morgan	Mitchelson	Bailey	Peacock	Roberts	Williams	Rogers	Atyeo	Rogers	Eisentrager	Boxley
									Pope	Staple	Newall	Haines	Wilcox	Stroud	Birch	Beattie	Nelson	Shergold	Moore
6	H IPSWICH 9/9	7,622 (£783.13.9)	15	5	W	4-2	2-1	Williams 22, 88, Rodgers 30, Eisen'r 88 / Mitchelson 40 (og), Garneys 69	Sullivan	Newman	Bailey	Peacock	Roberts	Tovey W	Eisentrager	Atyeo	Rogers	Williams	Boxley
									Feeney	Snell	Rees	Myles	Rees	Parker	Gaynor	Dobson	Garneys	Callaghan	Ball
7	H CRYSTAL PALACE 13/9	17,163 (£1,807.4.3)	12	7	W	5-0	3-0	Williams 9, 15, 50, Rodgers 40 [Atyeo 77] / Ref: G Thorpe	Sullivan	Guy	Bailey	Peacock	Roberts	Tovey W	Eisentrager	Atyeo	Rogers	Williams	Boxley
									Anderson	Scott	Macdonald	Nelson	Briggs	Andrews	Devonshire	Thomas	Broughton	Burgess	Hanlon
8	A IPSWICH 17/9	7,153	13	7	L	0-1	0-1	Elsworthy 23	Sullivan	Newman	Bailey	Peacock	Compton	Tovey W	Eisentrager	Atyeo	Rogers	Williams	Boxley
									Feeney	Deacon	Myles	Rees		Parker	Jones	Callaghan	Garneys	Elsworthy	Gaynor
9	A BRISTOL ROV 20/9	29,910	14	8	D	0-0	0-0	Ref: H Ball	Sullivan	Guy	Bailey	Tovey W	Compton	Williams	Eisentrager	Atyeo	Rogers	Rogers	Boxley
									Hoyle	Bamford	Fox	Pitt	Warren	Sampson	McIlveney	Bush	Lambden	Bradford	Petherbridge
10	H COLCHESTER 23/9	13,600 (£1,380.5.6)	11	10	W	3-2	3-2	Rogers 3, Rodgers 13, 29 / Barlow 12, McCurley 30 / Ref: R Hall	Morgan	Guy	Bailey	Peacock	Roberts	Tovey W	Eisentrager	Atyeo	Rogers	Williams	Rogers
									Coombs	Harrison	Rookes	Bearryman	Stewart	Elder	Church	Scott	McCurley	Barlow	Wright
11	A TORQUAY 27/9	7,059	11	12	W	2-1	2-0	Rodgers 24, 28 / Shaw 88 / Ref: W Dellow	Morgan	Guy	Bailey	Peacock	Roberts	Tovey W	Eisentrager	Atyeo	Rogers	Williams	Rogers
									Webber G	Drinkwater	Lewis K	Lewis D	Webber E	Towers	Shaw	Collins	Northcott	Edds	Topping

Match reports

1. Watford's close-season £20,000 spending spree entices the largest post-war crowd to Vicarage Road. Williams lobs City in front, but, despite dominating thereafter, it is the Brewers who find the net. John Paton looked offside when rushing in to put away Cyril Thompson's cross.

2. This hard and robust game, full of incident despite the lack of goals, is well controlled by the referee. City have to battle hard for their point, though they are helped by some inexcusable lapses in front of goal by the impressive visitors who otherwise scarcely exhibited any weak links.

3. Despite Jones being a hobbling passenger for much of the time, City hit back to take the lead. Unfortunately, the euphoria of a Rodgers header and John Ball's fumble that sees Boxley placing the ball into an empty net, is dissipated by Jimmy Sirrel running through Brighton's leveller.

4. City astound the prophets with an accomplished display at the Den, despite Frank Neary flicking the ball in to put Millwall in front following Stan Morgan's quickly taken free-kick. Following a corner, six shots are charged down before Atyeo crashes in City's well-deserved equaliser.

5. William Shergold hammers County in front, then Roberts deflects in John Moore's shot. After Tony Nelson shoots in Newport's third, a push on Roberts allows the City skipper to pull one back from the spot. Rodgers twice shoots in for parity, but Moore drives in County's winner.

6. City are full value for this victory, but Tom Garneys stars for the visitors and his goal, a full-blooded drive on the turn from 20 yards, will be long remembered. Williams heads in City's opener and also notches the last goal of the game when turning in a long ball from Eisentrager.

7. A poor Palace side, seeking their first post-war goal at Ashton Gate, prove no match for brilliant City. Williams' shot, which was beating Bob Anderson all the way, takes a late deflection to put City ahead. Atyeo's cracking right-footed drive sets the seal on a comprehensive City win.

8. A hard-fought and evenly contested game in the cold and wet at Portman Road, where Compton proves an able deputy for the injured Roberts. The frame is frequently struck, but the only goal is obtained by the outstanding John Elsworthy. A great shot that hits the underside of the bar.

9. With the gates shut 25 minutes before kick-off, the crowd hear an appeal from the Lord Mayor (Alderman HV Ross) for funds for the newly formed Hospital Broadcasts. City's hard-pressed defence takes the honours in a contest in which the soccer was enthusiastic more than subtle.

10. City take the spoils in this entertaining game, thanks to Jim Elder hitting the post with his 81st-minute spot-kick, courtesy of Tovey's handball on the line. Herbert Barlow heads in the U's reply to Rogers fired in opener, but Rodgers soon restores City's advantage by hooking the ball in.

11. Despite the 28th minute loss of Rogers – taken unconscious to hospital – and an injury to Bailey that leaves him hobbling out on the wing for three-quarters of this game, City pull off their first away win since success at Plainmoor almost a year ago. Rodgers slams in both City's goals.

12. A LEYTON ORIENT — 2/10 — 7,562 — (£2,390.10.9 n/a)

Pos 8 — W 3-1 — 19 — 14

Boxley 6, Rodgers 7, 69 — 2-1 — *Blizzard 21*
Ref: R Burgess

Morgan	Guy	Stone	Peacock	Roberts	Tovey W	Eisentrager	Atyeo	Rodgers	Williams	Boxley
Groombridge	*Charlton*	*Evans*	*Blizzard*	*Aldous*	*Mansley*	*Woan*	*Blair*	*Pacey*	*Brown*	*Poulton*

City have to fight hard for this win, though it would have been an injustice had they not captured both points. Boxley's wonder shot from a narrow angle gives City the lead, then Rodgers is able to run the ball in before Les Blizzard's high 25-yarder slips through Morgan's fingers.

13. H NORTHAMPTON — 4/10 — 21,785 — (£2,390.10.9)

Pos 10 — L 2-3 — 2 — 14

Atyeo 34, Eisentrager 88 — 1-1 — *Stone 14 (og), O'Donnell 52, English 65* Wood
Ref: A Smith

Morgan	Guy	Stone	Peacock	Roberts	Tovey W	Eisentrager	Atyeo	Rodgers	Williams	Boxley
Southam	*Patterson*	*Hughes*	*Collins*	*McLain*	*English*	*O'Donnell*	*Edelston*	*Ramscar*	*Fowler*	

Sluggish City's misery is summed up when Alf Wood saves Tovey's penalty-kick a minute before Eisentrager's double kick produces their late goal. Stone is unfortunate in diverting Fred Ramscar's cross-shot into his own net, but Atyeo's pile-driver levels matters prior to the interval.

14. H GILLINGHAM — 11/10 — 19,755 — (£2,137.5.6)

Pos 6 — W 4-0 — 18 — 16

Eisentrag' 6, 50, Rodgers 39, Jones 80 — 2-0
Ref: W Elliott

Morgan	Guy	Stone	Peacock	White	Tovey W	Jones	Eisentrager	Rodgers	Williams	Boxley
Rigg	*Blake*	*Lewin*	*Boswell*	*Niblett*	*McKee*	*Scarth*	*Sowden*	*Thomas*	*Lambert*	*Long*

Jackie White is in brilliant form as he captains his new side to a convincing success. Shortly after being denied by the crossbar, Eisentrager puts City in front with a shot high into the top of the net. Later he lobs in another after Rodgers had notched up City's second with a low drive.

15. A WALSALL — 18/10 — 7,229 —

Pos 6 — D 3-3 — 24 — 17

Eisentrager 17, Boxley 70, Jones 75 — 1-2 — *Giles 26, Bridgett 37, Morris 65*
Ref: W Clapton

Morgan	Guy	Stone	Peacock	White	Tovey W	Jones	Eisentrager	Rodgers	Williams	Boxley
Lewis	*Freeman*	*Walters*	*Dean*	*Green*	*Howell*	*Morris*	*Bowen*	*Bridgett*	*Duggins*	*Giles P*

A scrappy game at Fellows Park where, after Eisentrager's left-footed drive puts City in front, it takes Boxley's 25-yarder and a Jones header to salvage a point. The keeper, at fault with all three Saddlers' goals, starts the rot with a poor throw for Philip Giles to shoot Walsall's opener.

16. H SHREWSBURY — 25/10 — 19,950 — (£2,161.17.3)

Pos 5 — W 3-2 — 24 — 19

Rodgers 9, Eisentrager 17, Boxley 60 — 2-1 — *Jackson 25, McCulloch 80*
Ref: B Griffiths

Sullivan	Guy	Bailey	Peacock	White	Tovey W	Rogers	Eisentrager	Rodgers	Williams	Boxley
Eggleston	*Halpin*	*Quinton*	*Beynon*	*Ashworth*	*Butler*	*Fisher*	*Keery*	*McCulloch*	*Jackson*	*Reagan*

Rodgers, with a left-footed drive, gives City an early advantage, which Eisentrager doubles with a great 25-yarder from an almost impossible angle. Goalkeeper Sullivan errs in failing to gather Arnold Jackson's soft lob, but he has no chance with Adam McCulloch's left-footed drive.

17. A QP RANGERS — 1/11 — 14,718 —

Pos 6 — L 1-2 — 15 — 19

Eisentrager 43 — 1-2 — *Mountford 8, Addinall 12*
Ref: G Pankhurst

Sullivan	Guy	Bailey	Peacock	White	Tovey W	Rogers	Eisentrager	Rodgers	Williams	Boxley
Brown	*Poppitt*	*Ingham*	*Nicholas*	*Spence*	*Gilberg*	*Mountford*	*Smith*	*Addinall*	*Quinn*	*Shepherd*

After Boxley has his third-minute shot disallowed for offside, veteran George Mountford fires in from a couple of yards to put Rangers in front. Albert Addinall fires in to double the advantage before Eisentrager registers with a low drive. Hard luck for City who deserved better.

18. H SWINDON — 8/11 — 21,266 — (£2,327.6.3)

Pos 4 — W 4-2 — 21 — 21

Rodgers 4, Rogers 8, Williams 40, Owen 28, 71 — 3-1 — *[Eisentrager 83]*
Ref: W Edwards

Cook	Watkin	Bailey	Peacock	White	Tovey W	Jones	Eisentrager	Rogers	Williams	Boxley
Burton	*Hunt*	*Elwell*	*Betteridge*	*Hudson*	*Prouton*	*Lumn*	*Millar*	*Owen*	*Ryder*	*Bain*

Cook's brilliant display rescues a defence that needs to guard against slackening when ahead. Rodgers forces a centre into the net for City's opener, then his namesake rams in a loose ball for second. Maurice Owen finds the target from a narrow angle and later heads in another.

19. A ALDERSHOT — 15/11 — 5,857 —

Pos 4 — W 2-1 — 19 — 23

Rodgers 53, 66 — 0-1 — *Alison 14*
Ref: L Burfield

Cook	Watkin	Bailey	Peacock	White	Tovey W	Jones	Eisentrager	Rodgers	Williams	Boxley
Huston	*Rogers*	*Jefferson A*	*Reddie*	*Billington*	*Cropley*	*Alison*	*Menzies*	*Bonnar*	*Stewart*	*Flint*

The fog lifts by kick-off, but the light remains as poor as City's first-half display, which leaves them trailing to Jimmy Alison's header. Much improved play after the break sees Rodgers drive in an equaliser before ramming in the winner when Eisentrager's shot is stopped on the line.

20. A NORWICH — 29/11 — 20,020 —

Pos 5 — D 0-0 — 2 — 24

0-0
Ref: R Tarratt

Cook	Guy	Bailey	Peacock	White	Tovey W	Jones	Eisentrager	Rodgers	Williams	Boxley
Nethercott	*Morgan*	*Lewis*	*Dutton*	*Faulkes*	*Ashman*	*Gavin*	*Kinsey*	*Johnston*	*Rattray*	*Summers*

City put on one of their best performances so far this season to secure a point in this fast, exciting game at Carrow Road, which belies the goal-less scoreline. Against a team with the division's best defensive record, City make many threatening raids, but are let down by poor finishing.

21. H EXETER — 6/12 — 18,594 — (£1,998.1.9)

Pos 4 — W 4-1 — 9 — 26

Eisentrager 16p, Rodgers 41, 72, Mackay 10 — 2-1 — *[Walton 79 (og)]* Kelly !
Ref: L Mackay

Cook	Guy	Bailey	Peacock	White	Tovey W	Jones	Eisentrager	Rodgers	Williams	Boxley
Walton	*Rowe*	*Davey*	*Goddard*	*Booth*	*Mitchell*	*Knight*	*Dailey*	*Mackay*	*Regan*	

The Exeter keeper protests too much following City's spot-kick award when Tovey is brought down at the end of a dribble from halfway, and when the kick is ordered to be retaken following his save. Stand-in keeper Jim Dailey is given no chance with Eisentrager's second attempt.

22. A EXETER — 13/12 — 10,597 —

Pos 4 — D 1-1 — 8 — 27

Rodgers 46 — 0-1 — *Mackay 18*
Ref: A Blyth

Cook	Guy	Bailey	Peacock	White	Tovey W	Jones	Eisentrager	Rodgers	Williams	Boxley
Kelly	*Walton*	*Rowe*	*Booth*	*Goddard*	*Davey*	*Mitchell*	*Knight*	*Murphy*	*Mackay*	*Regan*

Cook is City's hero with several saves of international class at St James Park. Angus Mackay puts Exeter in front from a 25-yard free-kick - conjuring up a high lob over the top of the City players lined up in front of goal. Rodgers equalises with a low drive into the corner of the net.

23. H WATFORD — 20/12 — 12,744 — (£1,470.14.0)

Pos 4 — W 5-1 — 13 — 29

Williams 20, Rodgers 24, 57, 71, Meadows 88 — 2-0 — *[Eisentrager 68]* Underwood Croker
Ref: F Overton

Cook	Bailey	Peacock	White	Tovey W	Jones	Eisentrager	Rodgers	Williams	**Regan**
Underwood	*Croker*	*Jones*	*Phipps*	*Mitchell*	*Meadows*	*Nolan*	*Reid*	*Thompson*	*Collins*

Having not beaten Watford at the Gate since the war, City lay their bogey in grand style, despite Eisentrager's 86th-minute spot-kick being saved. Williams heads in from a Jones flag-kick to put City in front, then Rodgers slams in the second when the keeper can only parry a shot.

LEAGUE DIVISION 3 (SOUTH)

Manager: Pat Beasley

SEASON 1952-53

No	Date	V	Opponent	Att (receipts)	Opp Pos	Pos	Pt	F-A	H-T	Scorers, Times, and Referees
24	26/12	H	SOUTHEND	30,332 (£3,428.10.0)	14	4	W 31	5-0	2-0	Rodgers 1, Williams 41, Regan 65, [Tovey 71, Peacock 84] — Ref: W Dellow
25	3/1	A	BRIGHTON	15,905	7	3	W 33	1-0	1-0	Williams 20 — Ref: F Williams
26	10/1	H	READING	22,676 (£2,541.3.9)	12	3	D 34	1-1	0-1	Atyeo 89 [Blackman 26] — Ref: J Edwards
27	17/1	H	NEWPORT	20,756 (£2,306.17.9)	16	4	W 36	2-0	1-0	Williams 19, Rodgers 46 — Ref: H Ball
28	24/1	A	CRYSTAL PALACE	12,296	22	2	W 38	3-1	0-1	Rodgers 47, Williams 60, 81 [George 43p] — Ref: G Thorpe
29	31/1	A	READING	11,178	14	4	L 38	0-4	0-2	[Brooks 6, Blackman 38, Parker 61, Reeves 84p] — Ref: F Read
30	7/2	H	BRISTOL ROV	35,606 (£4,089.1.9)	1	4	D 39	0-0	0-0	— Ref: H Ball
31	14/2	A	TORQUAY	15,138 (£1,641.3.0)	19	4	D 40	4-4	1-0	Wil'ms 21, Atyeo 57, Eis' 60, Regan 88 [March't 50, Collins 55, 69, Thomas 87] — Ref: W Dellow
32	21/2	A	NORTHAMPTON	15,291 (£1,626)	3	2	W 42	2-0	1-0	Regan 22, 53p — Ref: A Smith
33	28/2	A	GILLINGHAM	12,571	11	2	W 44	1-0	0-0	Atyeo 71 — Ref: E Elliott
34	7/3	H	WALSALL	16,864 (£1,802.15.9)	24	2	W 46	6-1	4-0	Rodgers 7, Atyeo 22, 31, Regan 32, 73p, Williams 60 [Green 89] — Ref: W Clapton

Line-ups (City player / *opponent*)

No	1	2	3	4	5	6	7	8	9	10	11
24	Cook / *Scannell*	Guy / *Loughran*	Bailey / *Duggins*	Peacock / *O'Neil*	White / *Sheard*	Tovey W / *Lawler*	Jones / *Sibley*	Eisentrager / *McAllinden*	Rodgers / *Marsden*	Williams C / *Grant*	Regan / *Thompson*
25	Cook / *Ball*	Guy / *Tennant*	Bailey / *McLafferty*	Peacock / *McIlvenny*	White / *McCoy*	Tovey W / *Wilson*	Jones / *Reed*	Atyeo / *Leadbeater*	Rodgers / *Owens*	Williams / *Bennett*	Regan / *Howard*
26	Cook / *Kirkwood*	Guy / *Smith*	Bailey / *Reeves*	Peacock / *McLean*	White / *Wicks*	Tovey W / *Johnston*	Davis / *Simpson*	Atyeo / *Anderton*	Eisentrager / *Blackman*	Williams / *Brookes*	Regan / *Hinshelwood*
27	Cook / *Pope*	Guy / *Waite*	Bailey / *Hayward*	Peacock / *Newall*	White / *Wilcox*	Tovey W! / *Donaldson*	Jones / *Birch*	Atyeo / *Beattie!*	Rodgers / *Shergold*	Williams / *Morrey*	Regan /
28	Cook / *Macdonald*	Guy / *George*	Bailey / *McDonald*	Peacock / *Grimshaw*	White / *Briggs*	Tovey W / *Chilvers*	Regan / *Fell*	Atyeo / *Hancox*	Rodgers / *Evans*	Williams / *Devonshire*	Boxley / *Bennett*
29	Cook / *Kirkwood*	Guy / *Smith*	Bailey / *Reeves*	Peacock / *McLean*	White / *Wicks*	Tovey W / *Johnston*	Rodgers / *Simpson*	Eisentrager / *Brooks*	Watkin / *Blackman*	Williams / *Parker*	Regan / *Bainbridge*
30	Cook / *Hoyle*	Guy / *Bamford*	Bailey / *Fox*	Peacock / *Pitt*	White / *Warren*	Tovey W / *Sampson*	Boxley / *McIlvenny*	Atyeo / *Bush*	Rodgers / *Lambden*	Williams / *Bradford*	Regan / *Petherbridge*
31	Cook / *Webber G*	Guy / *Stilfall*	Bailey / *Drinkwater*	Peacock / *Lewis*	White / *Webber E*	Tovey W / *Norman*	Eisentrager / *Shaw*	Atyeo / *Collins*	Rodgers / *Marchant*	Williams / *Mills*	Regan / *Thomas*
32	Cook / *Wood*	Guy / *Southam*	Bailey / *Patterson*	Peacock / *Hughes*	White / *Candlin*	Tovey W / *Dodgin*	Eisentrager / *English*	Atyeo / *Baxter*	Rodgers / *O'Donnell*	Williams / *Ramscar*	Regan / *Fowler*
33	Cook / *Rigg*	Guy / *Marks*	Bailey / *Lewin*	Peacock / *Boswell*	White / *Niblett*	Tovey W / *Forester*	Eisentrager / *Lewis*	Rogers / *Scarth*	Atyeo / *King*	Williams / *Lambert*	Regan / *Long*
34	Cook / *Lewis*	Guy / *Rowe*	Bailey / *Walters*	Peacock / *Millington*	White / *Horne*	Tovey W / *Green*	Eisentrager / *Bowen*	Atyeo / *Knight*	Rodgers / *McIntosh*	Williams / *Wright*	Regan / *Giles P*

24 SOUTHEND — With Rodgers netting after just six seconds and a Williams chip over Tommy Scannell shortly before the half-time break, this turns into a City romp. Regan's dropping shot, followed by Tovey's scorching volley and Peacock's cleverly placed 30-yard free-kick bring up the nap hand.

25 BRIGHTON — Cook's last-minute saving of Des Tennant's spot-kick, following Guy's misplaced tackle on Ken Bennett, ensures that the first-half shot that Williams put past John Ball brings City a deserved success. A fast and exciting game with near misses and goal-line clearances at both ends.

26 READING — Prior to kick-off Billy Pocock presented Harry Dolman with a £600 contribution for building the last section of the grandstand. Atyeo salvages a point by coolly side-footing a last-minute goal after Ron Blackman had seized on White's poor clearance to fire in the first with a low shot.

27 NEWPORT — Despite occasions of unnecessarily robust play, it still comes as a surprise when the referee, whilst awarding City a free-kick, orders Tovey and George Beattie off the field of play midway through the second-half. City go in front when keeper Terry Pope lets slip a Williams ground shot.

28 CRYSTAL PALACE — Tovey brings down Ron Bennett, which allows Bristolian Ron George to fire George ahead from the spot against the run of play. Rodgers levels with a screw-shot directly after the interval and then Williams cracks in two goals - the first completing a brilliant move - to secure the points.

29 READING — With Atyeo missing with influenza, City create a surprise by playing full-back Cyril Watkin in his place. On winning the toss City take advantage of the boisterous wind, but despite being camped almost inclusively in Reading's half, find themselves two down at the break.

30 BRISTOL ROV — This great Bristol derby at Ashton Gate has everything except goals. A good result for City, who have their skipper Jackie White handicapped with a leg injury from the 20th minute. Prior to the kick-off the vast crowd sing *Abide With Me* in memory of the East Coast flood victims.

31 TORQUAY — For the first time Cook turns out in a blue jersey rather than his lucky, but faded, green one. On a muddy pitch, Williams puts City in front with a delightful header, but after the break Marwood Marchant is on hand to crack in an equaliser when Ron Shaw's shot rebounds off the post.

32 NORTHAMPTON — City are able to take advantage of schemer Maurice Edleston's absence from this game to deprive the Cobblers of their unbeaten home record. Atyeo's strong run sets up Regan to fire City in front, then after the interval a foul on Rodgers sees the winger make no mistake from the spot.

33 GILLINGHAM — In front of the President of the Football League, Arthur Drewry, making his first visit to the Priestfield Stadium, the City are full value for their victory. Atyeo has the simplest of tasks in tapping the ball into the net when Regan's low first-time shot rebounds off the foot of the post.

34 WALSALL — Walsall are completely outplayed by a City side wearing black armbands in memory of director Percy Bennett. Released by the Bristol University rag students just before kick-off, Rodgers (in goal for ten minutes in the second half) responds by driving in City's early opener.

Bristol City — season match record (games 35–46)

No.		Opponent	Date		Res	Score	HT	Pos	Pts	Att	Receipts	Ref
35	A	SHREWSBURY	14/3	2	W	1-0	0-0	18	48	11,093		B Griffiths
36	H	QP RANGERS	21/3	2	D	4-4	1-3	15	49	20,052	£2,215.9.3.	G Pankhurst
37	A	SWINDON	28/3	2	D	0-0	0-0	22	50	10,026	£1,104	W Edwards
38	H	BOURNEMOUTH	3/4	2	D	1-1	1-0	12	51	25,403	£2,887.15.9	F Fiander
39	H	ALDERSHOT	4/4	2	D	0-0	0-0	19	52	16,177	£1,841.0.0	L Burfield
40	A	BOURNEMOUTH	6/4	4	L	1-4	1-2	10	52	13,892	£1,932.19.6	F Fiander
41	A	COLCHESTER	11/4	5	L	1-3	0-0	13	52	7,519	£925.15.3	R Hall
42	H	NORWICH	18/4	5	L	0-1	0-0	4	52	17,650		R Tarratt
43	H	LEYTON ORIENT	21/4	5	W	2-1	0-1	13	54	9,527		R Burgess
44	A	COVENTRY	25/4	5	D	2-2	1-0	6	55	11,009		Rev S Davis
45	H	COVENTRY	28/4	5	W	1-0	1-0	6	57	10,562	£1,061.10.0	Rev S Davis
46	A	SOUTHEND	29/4	4	W	4-0	2-0	8	59	6,555		W Dellow

Home Average 18,763 — Away 12,516

---

35. A SHREWSBURY — Rogers 53

City: Cook, Guy, Bailey, Peacock, White, Tovey W, Eisentrager, Rogers, Atyeo, Williams, Regan
Opp: Birkett, Bannister, Lewis, Beynon, Bullons, Crutchley, Fisher, Jackson, Marsden, Brown, Roberts

On a hard pitch at Gay Meadow, City deserve their win, which comes courtesy of Rogers, who calmly side-foots in the only goal of the game. There should have been more goals, however, as City created many chances and Atyeo hit the post with a brilliant header in the 17th minute.

36. H QP RANGERS — Rogers 32, White 71, Aty' 72, Wil'ms 82 / Smith 14, 38, Cameron 22, Mount'd 90

City: Cook, Guy, Bailey, Peacock, White, Tovey W, Eisentrager, Rogers, Atyeo, Williams, Regan
Opp: Brown, Poppitt, Ingham, Nicholas, Chapman, Clayton, Mountford, Smith, Tomkys, Cameron, Shepherd

A thriller at Ashton, right from when William Smith hooked in the opener until George Mountford's low-shot equaliser right on time. White inspired City's fight-back when coming forward to drive the ball in. Atyeo's great cross-shot brings City level and Williams fires them in front.

37. A SWINDON — 0-0

City: Cook, Guy, Bailey, Peacock, White, Tovey W, Eisentrager, Rogers, Atyeo, Williams, Regan
Opp: Burton, Hunt, Elwell, Betteridge, Batchelor, Bines, Ryder, Lumn, Owen, Parker, Bain

At the County Ground, sparkling City do everything but score. Only the brilliance of the Swindon goalkeeper Sam Burton stands between them and victory in a fast and exciting game, that saw, prior to the kick-off, a minute's silence being observed in memory of the late Queen Mary.

38. H BOURNEMOUTH — Atyeo 44 / Cross 55

City: Cook, Guy, Bailey, Peacock, White, Tovey W, Eisentrager, Rogers, Atyeo, Williams, Regan
Opp: Godwin, Drummond, Thompson, Woodward, Hardy, Neave, Buchanan, Cross, Cheney, Harrison

Disappointment at the Gate where City drop yet another point to find themselves trailing eight points behind Rovers. Atyeo's left-footed drive puts City in front, but the Cherries level when Jack Cross outpaces White to fizz in a shot which Cook gets a hand to but is unable to stop.

39. H ALDERSHOT — 0-0

City: Cook, Mitchelson, Bailey, Peacock, White, Tovey W, Eisentrager, Rogers, Atyeo, Williams, Regan
Opp: Houston, Rogers, Jefferson, Reddie, Laird, Cropley, Hobbs, McCulloch, Raine, Durkin, Flint

Both teams appear tired in this poor game littered with mistakes and the squandering of easy chances. City even fail with a 73rd-minute spot-kick after Reagan's shot is handled. The City winger takes the kick himself, but Joe Houston anticipates the direction and saves at full stretch.

40. A BOURNEMOUTH — Tovey R 55 / Buchanan 22, Cross 38, Cheney 83, Godwin 84

City: Cook, Guy, Bailey, Peacock, White, Tovey W, Eisentrager, Tovey R, Atyeo, Williams, Regan
Opp: Godwin, Drummond, Thompson, Woodward, Hardy, Neave, Gaynor, Buchanan, Cross, Cheney, Harrison

After a headed goal from Cameron Buchanan and a shot from Jack Cross, new-boy Ron Tovey inspires City after the interval by scoring with a great left-footed shot. Unfortunately, Buchanan's shrewd pass that puts Dennis Cheney through for the first of his two goals quells City's fire.

41. A COLCHESTER — Tovey R 53 / Edwards 9, 57, Barlow 70

City: Cook, Wright G, Bailey, Peacock, White, Tovey W, Regan, Tovey R, Atyeo, Williams, Boxley
Opp: Wright G, Harrison, Rookes, Hill, Stewart, Elder, McCurley, Scott, Edwards, Barlow, Wright P

City, with Bill Tovey off with a knee injury from the tenth minute, put on a brave display. Ron Tovey drives in a fierce equaliser to the melee opener by Stan Edwards. Unfortunately, a fine Edwards header and Herbert Barlow's effort, when White loses control, brings the U's victory.

42. H NORWICH — Gavin 50

City: Cook, Guy, Mitchelson, Peacock, White, Tovey W, Eisentrager, Tovey R, Atyeo, Williams, Regan
Opp: Nethercott, Proctor, Lewis, Faulkes, Holmes, Ashman, Gavin, Kinsey, Ackerman, McCrohan, Docherty

It is real end-of-season stuff at Ashton Gate, where John Gavin's goal early in the second half settles a scrappy game in which City squander their chances. Alf Ackerman runs down the left flank and, after Cook partially parries his shot, Gavin runs in to hook the loose ball into the net.

43. H LEYTON ORIENT — White 53, Boxley 56 / Rees 33

City: Cook, Guy, Mitchelson, Peacock, White, Tovey W, Regan, Tovey R, Atyeo, Eisentrager, Boxley
Opp: Welton, Banner, Charlton, Blizzard, Aldous, Deverall, Facey, Listed, Pacey, Rees, Whiteley

City obtain their first win in over a month, but their performance leaves much to be desired. William Rees calmly picks his spot from 18 yards to fire in the game's opener, but City improve somewhat after the interval and firstly White then Boxley shoot in to secure a long-awaited win.

44. A COVENTRY — White 44, Tovey 65 / Hill P 48, Thomas 73

City: Cook, Guy, Bailey, Peacock, White, Tovey W, Regan, Tovey R, Atyeo, Williams, Boxley
Opp: Matthews, Timmins, Mason, Harvey, McDonnell, Simpson, Nutt, Lowrie, Thomas, Hill P, Hill J

Despite being carried off with an early leg injury, White returns to hobble on the left wing and head City in front. Tovey's acute-angled drive restores City's lead after Peter Hill had hooked Coventry level. Bryn Thomas, with an innocuous header, deprives the City of their win bonus.

45. H COVENTRY — White 13

City: Cook, Guy, Bailey, Peacock, White, Tovey W, Jones, Tovey R, Atyeo, Eisentrager, Boxley
Opp: Matthews, Quinney, Mason, Harvey, McDonnell, Austin, Nutt, Dorman, Thomas, Hill P, Hill J

Whilst City are unfortunate when Peacock's 19-yard free-kick that finds the net is ordered to be retaken, White quickly heads them in front. City, despite making all the early running, are soon made to fight all the way by a Coventry side with eight players under 22 years of age.

46. A SOUTHEND — Regan 18, Atyeo 22, Boxley 54, [Williams 59]

City: Cook, Guy, Bailey, Peacock, White, Jones, Jones, Eisentrager, Atyeo, Williams, Regan
Opp: Scannell, Lawler, Duggins, Burns, Sterling, Bridge, Sibley, Grant, McAlinden, Thompson, Bainbridge

United make all of the early running before City wake up with goals from Regan and Atyeo. After the break the referee gets stick for not using a white ball in the gathering gloom, but further strikes from Eisentrager (a grand drive) and Williams bring the City a well-deserved success.

CUP-TIES

Manager: Pat Beasley

SEASON 1952-53

FA Cup

				F-A	H-T	Scorers, Times, and Referees	1	2	3	4	5	6	7	8	9	10	11
1	A	COVENTRY	4	L 0-2	0-1	Brown 1, Hill 81	Cook	Guy	Bailey	Peacock	White	Tovey W	Jones	Eisentrager	Rodgers	Williams	Boxley
		22/11	5			Ref: S Rogers	Spencer	McDonnell	Mason	Cook	Kirk	Simpson	Warner	Dorman	Brown	Hill P	Johnson
		17,062															
		(£2,195.14.3)															

In front of 1,000 travelling fans, City hit back strongly following Coventry's early opener when Ted Brown pounces on Richard Mason's cross to net from close in. Unfortunately, in being unable to get the ball past Derek Spencer they are further undone by Peter Hill's close-range shot.

Gloucestershire Cup

				F-A	H-T	Scorers, Times, and Referees	1	2	3	4	5	6	7	8	9	10	11
F	A	BRISTOL ROV	5	W 2-0	2-0	Atyeo 17, Eisentrager 20	Cook	Guy	Bailey	Peacock	Roberts	White	Eisentrager	Atyeo	Tovey R	Williams	Boxley
		8/5	1			Ref: B Griffiths	Radford	Allcock	Fox	Pitt	Warren	Sampson	Petherbridge	Bush	Lambden	Bradford	Watling
		19,214															
		(£2,000+)															

Although City have Ron Tovey as a virtual passenger for more than half the game, they are much the better side. A low cross-shot by Atyeo puts City in front, then Eisentrager fires in from 18 yards to double the advantage. Rovers improve after the break, but still fail to impress.

	P	W	D	L	F	A	W	D	L	F	A	Pts
			Home						Away			
1 Bristol Rov	46	17	4	2	55	19	9	8	6	37	27	64
2 Millwall	46	14	7	2	46	16	10	7	6	36	28	62
3 Northampton	46	18	4	1	75	30	8	6	9	34	40	62
4 Norwich	46	16	6	1	56	17	9	4	10	43	38	60
5 BRISTOL C	46	13	8	2	62	28	9	7	7	33	33	59
6 Coventry	46	15	5	3	52	22	4	7	12	25	40	50
7 Brighton	46	12	6	5	48	30	7	6	10	33	45	50
8 Southend	46	15	5	3	41	21	3	8	12	28	53	49
9 Bournemouth	46	15	3	5	49	23	4	6	13	25	46	47
10 Watford	46	12	8	3	39	21	3	9	11	23	42	47
11 Reading	46	17	3	3	53	18	2	5	16	16	46	46
12 Torquay	46	15	4	4	61	28	3	5	15	26	60	45
13 Crys Palace	46	12	7	4	40	26	3	6	14	26	56	43
14 Leyton Orient	46	12	7	4	52	28	4	3	16	16	45	42
15 Newport	46	12	4	7	43	34	4	6	13	27	48	42
16 Ipswich	46	10	7	6	34	28	3	8	12	26	41	41
17 Exeter	46	11	8	4	40	24	2	6	15	21	47	40
18 Swindon	46	9	5	9	38	33	5	7	11	26	46	40
19 Aldershot	46	8	8	7	36	29	4	7	12	25	48	39
20 QP Rangers	46	9	9	5	37	34	3	6	14	24	48	39
21 Gillingham	46	10	7	6	30	26	3	6	13	25	48	39
22 Colchester	46	9	9	5	40	29	3	5	15	19	47	38
23 Shrewsbury	46	11	5	7	38	35	1	7	15	30	56	36
24 Walsall	46	5	9	9	35	46	2	1	20	21	72	24
	1104	297	148	107	1100	645	107	148	297	645	1100	1104

Odds & ends

Double wins: (5) Crystal Palace, Leyton Orient, Gillingham, Shrewsbury, Southend.

Double losses: (0).

Won from behind: (4) Aldershot (a), Exeter (h), Crystal Palace (a), Leyton Orient (h).

Lost from in front: (1) Watford (a).

High spots: Beating Bristol Rovers 2-0 in the Gloucestershire Cup.
The visit of First Division Wolves to inaugurate City's first floodlights.

Low spots: The dropping of ten points in a winless seven game run, straddling the Easter period, that blew away City's promotion quest.

AGM (Grand Hotel, Broad Street, Bristol, 15 March 1954):
Loss £2,346.7s.9d. Season Ticket Sales £5,159.15s.0d.

Player of the year: Cyril Williams and Arnold Rodgers.

Ever-presents: Ernie 'Ginger' Peacock.

Hat-tricks: (2) Arnold Rodgers (1), Cyril Williams (1).

Leading scorer: Overall: Arnold Rodgers (26). League: Rodgers (26).

	Appearances		Goals		
	Lge	Cup	Lge	Cup	Tot
Atyeo, John	33	1	11	1	12
Bailey, Jack	41	2			
Boxley, Jack	25	2	4		4
Compton, Terry	1				
Cook, Tony	29	2			
Davis, Ken	1				
Eisentrager, Alec	38	2	12	1	13
Guy, Ivor	37	2			
Jones, Ernie	17	1	3		3
Mitchelson, Ken	9				
Morgan, Syd	10				
Peacock, Ernie	46	2	1		1
Regan, Doug	21		7		7
Roberts, Dennis	17	1	1		1
Rodgers, Arnold	33	1	26		26
Rogers, Jimmy	18		4		4
Stone, Fred	3				
Sullivan, Cornelius	7				
Tovey, Bill	36	1	1		1
Tovey, Ron	6	1	3		3
Watkin, Cyril	3				
White, Jack	33	2	4		4
Williams, Cyril	42	2	17		17
(own-goals)			1		1
23 players used	506	22	95	2	97

LEAGUE DIVISION 3 (SOUTH)　　Manager: Pat Beasley　　SEASON 1953-54

No	Date	Att Pos	Pt	F-A	H-T	Scorers, Times, and Referees	1	2	3	4	5	6	7	8	9	10	11
1	H GILLINGHAM 19/8	19,506	D	1-1	0-1	Atyeo 90 / Millar 31 / Ref: A Smith	Cook *Rigg*	Guy *Marks*	Bailey *Lewin*	**Regan J** *Boswell*	Peacock *Niblett*	White *Forrester*	Eisentrager *Scarth*	Atyeo *Evans*	Rodgers *Morgan*	Williams *Millar*	Regan D *Long*
		(£2,118.10.6)				After frittering away their chances in this evening affair, it takes Atyeo's well-placed corner in the dying seconds to salvage a point for City. A poor contest in which a corner also brings the visitors their goal - Jimmy Scarth crossing for Bill Millar to head in.											
2	H QP RANGERS 22/8	20,819	L	1-2	0-1	Rodgers 62 / Petchey 9, Cameron 67 / Ref: H Ball	Cook *Brown*	Guy *Poppitt*	Bailey *Ingram*	Peacock *Spence*	Roberts *Taylor*	White *Clayton*	Eisentrager *Mountford*	Atyeo *Cameron*	Rodgers *Hawkins*	Tovey R *Petchey*	Regan D *Shepherd*
		(£2,167.15.0)				City improve on their previous display, but again spurn their chances after falling behind to George Petchey's cleverly hooked shot on the turn. Robert Cameron's 35-yarder brings the visitors the points after Rodgers, with a neat over-the-head following a corner, had levelled for City.											
3	A WALSALL 27/8	15 / 15,158	20	0-0	0-0	Ref: R Hall	Cook *Flack*	Guy *Holding*	Bailey *Green*	Peacock *Dean*	White *Bridgett*	Williams *Woodward*	Eisentrager *Grubb*	Atyeo *Bromley T*	Rodgers *Finlay*	Tovey R *Scarlett*	Boxley *Morris*
						All City's good work in this game, which they dominated, is wasted by a lack of fire-power. Doug Flack in the Saddlers goal has five times as much work to do than Cook and deserves the reception he received at the finish, even though there was no excuse for some of City's misses.											
4	A SOUTHAMPTON 29/8	20 / 17,832	L 2 / 5	2-4	2-2	Micklewright 21, 32 / Hoskins 11, 43, Walker 64, Day 86 / Ref: H Husband	Cook *Christie*	Guy *Ellerington*	Bailey *Gregory*	Peacock *Elliott*	White *Clements*	Williams *Simpson*	Jones *Flood*	Atyeo *Williams*	Rodgers *Day*	**Micklewright** *Walker*	Boxley *Hoskins*
						Indecision between Cook and Guy allows John Hoskins to nip in and shoot home. Micklewright, who notches the equaliser with a fast-rising effort, which John Christie is unable to hold, puts City ahead with a hard drive. Hoskins ends a great 40-yard run by shooting the Saints level.											
5	H WALSALL 1/9	11 / 14,708	W 4 / 24	4-1	1-1	Boxley 41p, 82, Rodgers 55, 73 / Morris 43 / Ref: R Hall	Cook *Flack*	Guy *Horne*	Bailey *Perry*	Peacock *Dean*	White *Bridgett*	Williams *Green*	Jones *Grubb*	Atyeo *Bromley T*	Rodgers *Finlay*	Micklewright *Scarlett*	Boxley *Morris*
		(£1,427.13.3)				City are twice denied by the bar early on in this thrilling game, which sees both Jones and White off injured for spells. A tale of two penalties for Boxley as, despite the keeper getting a hand to the ball, he puts City in front with his first, but in the 80th minute fires his second well wide.											
6	H COLCHESTER 5/9	11 / 17,424	W 6 / 13	3-0	1-0	Rodgers 28, 70, Boxley 67 / Ref: J Jackson	Cook *Wright*	Guy *Harrison*	Bailey *Lewis*	Peacock *Bearryman*	Roberts *Stewart*	Williams *Elder*	Regan D *Grice*	Atyeo *Scott*	Rodgers *McCurley*	Micklewright *Barlow*	Boxley *Keene*
		(£1,757.2.6)				All the goals come at the end of good combination play, as City win almost as they please. Rodgers takes advantage of a rebound to roll in the first, then a great four-man move enables Boxley to put away the second, before he lays on an easy chance for Rodgers to knock in the third.											
7	A EXETER 9/9	8 / 9,870	W 8 / 17	1-0	1-0	Boxley 30 / Ref: L Burfield	Cook *Kelly*	Guy *Walton*	Bailey *Doyle*	White *Booth*	Roberts *Goddard*	Williams *Dodgin*	Regan D *McClelland*	Atyeo *Samuels*	Rodgers *Mitchell*	Micklewright *Murphy*	Boxley *Parker*
		(£920)				Thanks to Boxley's first-half header, City win this defence-dominated struggle. A deserved success in a game fought with the keeness typical of clashes between the clubs. Roberts is magnificent for City, but skipper for the day Duggie Regan has a quiet game against his old club.											
8	A CRYSTAL PALACE 12/9	6 / 18,723	W 10 / 9	2-1	0-1	Rodgers 52, Atyeo 63 / Randall 18 / Ref: C Bucknall	Cook *Bailey*	Guy *George*	White *McDonald*	Peacock *Williams*	Roberts *Briggs*	Williams *Andrews*	Regan D *Fell*	Atyeo *Thomas*	Rodgers *Randall*	Micklewright *Foulds*	Boxley *Devonshire*
						City take Palace's unbeaten home record, despite trailing to Ernie Randall's cool lob and Micklewright putting a 32nd-minute spot-kick over the crossbar. Rodgers hooks in a leveller and Atyeo registers with a low-shot before Cook pushes Ron George's late penalty round the post.											
9	H EXETER 15/9	5 / 15,529	W 12 / 13	5-1	0-0	Regan 50, 88, Rodgers 60, 80, Goddard 85, [Atyeo 70] / Ref: L Burfield	Cook *Kelly*	Guy *Walton*	White *Doyle*	Peacock *Booth*	Roberts *Goddard*	Williams *Dodgin*	Regan D *Mitchell*	Atyeo *MacKay*	Rodgers *Donaldson*	Micklewright *Murphy*	Boxley *McClelland*
		(£1,612.17.9)				City gain an overdue reward for their efforts in this fine game when Hugh Kelly's failure to gather White's free-kick leads to Regan firing in from six yards. Rodgers races past Norman Dodgin to shoot in the second and Atyeo outjumps everyone to head in the best goal of the match.											
10	A LEYTON ORIENT 19/9	7 / 13,225	L 12 / 12	1-4	0-3	Rodgers 81 / Poulton 16, Rees 25, 39, Facey 67 / Ref: H Broadhurst	Cook *Walton*	White *Evans*	White *Charlton*	Peacock *McMahon*	Roberts *Aldous*	Williams *Blizzard*	Rogers *Facey*	Atyeo *Rees*	Rodgers *Pacey*	Micklewright *Morgan*	Regan D *Poulton*
						Despite being soundly beaten, City still had the chances to have saved this game. With the wind at their backs after the break, City are twice denied by the woodwork, and Atyeo misses an open goal before Rodgers nets from close range. Ken Facey's volley is the game's best goal.											
11	A NORWICH 23/9	7 / 20,776	D 13 / 1	1-1	1-0	Rodgers 4 / Brennan 85 / Ref: A Bond	Cook *Nethercott*	Guy *Morgan*	White *Lewis W*	Peacock *Pickwick*	Roberts *Holmes*	Williams *Ashman*	Rogers *Adams*	Atyeo *Brennan*	Rodgers *Ackerman*	Tovey R *Summers*	Boxley *Collins*
						City dominate the play after taking an early lead with a spectacular header. Unfortunately, the latter stages, which sees Robert Brennan head in a leveller, take place in gathering gloom due to the time spent on repairing City's goal when the metal support collapsed just before half-time.											

Match 12 — H ALDERSHOT, 26/9

19,949 (£2,088.5.0)	6	W	4-0	9 / 15

Rodgers 29, Peacock 47, Atyeo 54, 69

Cook	Guy	Bailey	Peacock	White	Williams	Rogers	Atyeo	Rodgers	Tovey R	Boxley
Brown	Rogers	Jefferson	Laird	Billington	Cropley	Gayner	McCulloch	Lacey	Alison	Flint

A high centre from Arnold Rodgers brings the opener, the ball ending up in the net as Fred Brown is put under pressure by Jimmy Rogers. The goalkeeper is again at fault when Peacock's free-kick doubles the advantage, before Atyeo's header and a later shot ties up a flattering victory.

Ref: W Clements

Match 13 — H NORWICH, 30/9

18,706 (£2,106.2.6)	5	W	3-1	3 / 17

Micklewright 2, 77, Atyeo 62 / Ackerman 34

Cook	Guy	White	Peacock	Roberts	Williams	Rogers	Micklewright	Atyeo	Boxley	Watkins
Nethercott	Morgan	Lewis	Pickwick	Holmes	Ashman	Gavin	Brennan	Ackerman	Summers	Collins

After putting a rebound wide on seven minutes, following Cook's save from Robert Brennan's spot-kick, Alf Ackerman makes amends by firing in the leveller to City's headed opener. Atyeo's shot after the break and another Micklewright header ends Norwich's unbeaten record.

Ref: A Bond

Match 14 — A SWINDON, 3/10

15,610	5	L	0-5	8 / 17

Owen 26, Bull 38, Cross 54, Lambert 73 [Lunn 89]

Cook	Guy	Bailey	Peacock	Roberts	Williams	Rogers	Eisentrager	Micklewright	Boxley	Watkins
Burton	Hunt	Hilton	Cross	Hudson	Johnston	Lunn	Betteridge	Owen	Lambert	Bull

City, without the injured Atyeo and Tovey (unable make the ground in time from his army camp), offer little after Maurice Owen heads in the opener. Despite Ken Lambert's 30-yard dribble prior to driving in Town's fourth, the afternoon's best strike is Jim Cross's terrific 20-yarder.

Ref: Rev S Davis

Match 15 — H IPSWICH, 10/10

22,711 (£2,483.6.6)	8	L	2-3	1 / 17

Boxley 34p, 78 / Elsworthy 20, McLuckie 65, 80

Cook	Guy	White	Peacock	Roberts	Williams	Rogers	Micklewright	Atyeo	Tovey R	Boxley
Parry	Acres	Feeney	Myles	Rees	Parker	Reed	Crowe	Garneys	Elsworthy	McLuckie

After John Elsworthy fires the visitors in front, Tom Parker's handball, shortly after City had abandoned their close-passing methods, allows Boxley to level from the spot. City continued to disappoint, however, and flaws in both defence and attack bring about an unsurprising defeat.

Ref: R Hall

Match 16 — A BOURNEMOUTH, 17/10

10,066	9	L	2-5	21 / 17

Atyeo 42, 44 / Guy 27(og), Fidler 28, Cross 58, 82 [Williams 63 (og)]

Cook	Guy	Bailey	Peacock	Roberts	White	Rogers	Atyeo	Rodgers	Williams	Boxley
Godwin	Keetley	Drummond	Macdonald	Hardy	Rushworth	Stephens	Fidler	Cross	Cheney	Harrison

Injuries to Steel, White and Cook hinder City's cause at Dean Court, where they do not deserve to lose by such a heavy margin. Atyeo heads in two fine goals just before half-time to level Frank Fidler's terrific strike and a Peter Harrison effort that is deflected in off of Guy's shoulder.

Ref: G Sawyer

Match 17 — H COVENTRY, 24/10

16,395 (£1,791.5.9)	6	W	1-0	14 / 19

Micklewright 43

Cook	Guy	Bailey	Peacock	Roberts	Williams	Eisentrager	Micklewright	Atyeo	Rodgers	Boxley
Taylor	Jones	Kirk	Jamieson	McDonnell	Austin	Nutt	Dorman	Brown	Hill P	Johnston

A smart move by Williams and Boxley, well finished off by Micklewright who drives a powerful shot past Peter Taylor, brings City the full quota of points. Not a great game on a greasy Ashton Gate surface, but, despite Coventry's dangerous breakaways, City deserve their success.

Ref: R Tarratt

Match 18 — A GILLINGHAM, 31/10

10,968	7	D	2-2	18 / 20

Atyeo 26, 74 / Evans 13, Morgan 71

Cook	Guy	Bailey	Peacock	Roberts	Williams	Eisentrager	Atyeo	Rodgers	Micklewright	Boxley
Rigg	Marks	Lewin	Boswell	Ayres	Forrester	Gurkin	Evans	Scarth	Morgan	Millar

A freak goal puts the City behind - a lofted shot by Bill Evans appeared to going well over the bar before dipping into the top of the net. Atyeo slams City level before the break, and then does the same with a fine shot in the second half after Ernie Morgan tapped the Gills back in front.

Ref: A Smith

Match 19 — H NORTHAMPTON, 7/11

17,380 (£1,851.19.3)	6	W	2-1	10 / 22

Atyeo 67, Rodgers 84 / Smith 50

Cook	Guy	Bailey	Peacock	Roberts	Williams	Eisentrager	Atyeo	Rodgers	Micklewright	Boxley
Wood	Marston	Patterson	Smith	Collins	Hughes	English	Anderson	Cross	Ramscar	Fowler

City made hard work of this victory over the Cobblers, courtesy of a fine Rodgers header near the end. Good approach-work by Williams, Boxley and Atyeo sets up many chances, which are missed, and Smith cracks in a snap goal just after half-time to put the visitors in front.

Ref: W Dellow

Match 20 — A TORQUAY, 14/11

7,480 (£690)	7	L	0-4	16 / 22

Collins 12, 27, Bond 49, 83

Cook	Guy	Bailey	Peacock	Roberts	Williams	Eisentrager	Atyeo	Rodgers	Tovey R	Micklewright
Hayes	Parphitt	Drinkwater	Lewis	Webber	Norman	Shaw	Collins	Dobbie	Mills	Bond

Sammy Collins jumps up high to flick in the opener, though after the break Cook gets some measure of revenge by saving the inside-right's penalty-kick after Williams had fisted away a certain goal. Unfortunately, the ball runs to Graham Bond who notches his first League goal.

Ref: W Clapton

Match 21 — A BRIGHTON, 28/11

19,214	12	L	1-2	4 / 22

Williams 38 / Mundy 52, Gordon 87

Cook	Guy	Bailey	Peacock	Compton	White	Rogers	Atyeo	Micklewright	Williams	Regan D
Gill	Tennant	Langley	McIlvenny	South	Wilson	Gordon	Mundy	Adinall	Leadbeater	Howard

After Williams had opened the scoring with a close-in shot not long before the interval, City take a second-half pounding. Albert Mundy equalises with a three-yard drive, then shortly before time Dennis Gordon blasts a square ball from Jim Leadbeater into an open goal.

Ref: W Elliott

Match 22 — H SOUTHEND, 5/12

14,543	9	W	4-1	20 / 24

Rogers 8, Boxley 44p, 88, Williams 58 / Dicker 3

Cook	Guy	Bailey	Peacock	Compton	White	Rogers	Atyeo	Micklewright	Williams	Boxley
Threadgold	Young	Anderson	Pavitt	Stirling	Lawler	Lockhart	McAlinden	Grant	Dicker	Lowder

Despite taking an early lead when Leslie Dicker's rising shot beats Cook, Southend are well beaten. Rogers finds the top corner of the net with a right-footed effort to level matters, and then Doug Young's handball brings Boxley his penalty before two headers complete City's success.

Ref: H Husband

Match 23 — A QP RANGERS, 19/12

8,126	7	W	1-0	19 / 26

Boxley 37

Cook	Guy	Bailey	Peacock	Compton	Regan J	Rogers	Atyeo	Micklewright	Williams	Boxley
Brown	Woods	Ingham	White	Taylor	Angell	Tomkys	Cameron	Petchey	Hurrell	Shepherd

Atyeo, who had a great effort disallowed for offside after the break, laid on the ball for Boxley to side-foot in the only goal of the game. A deserved victory as City were much the better side, despite Cook being called upon to make a couple of classy saves to keep Rangers out.

Ref: H Ball

LEAGUE DIVISION 3 (SOUTH)

Manager: Pat Beasley — SEASON 1953-54

Match details

No	Date	H/A	Opponent	Att	Receipts	Opp Pos	Result	F-A	H-T	Pos	Pt	Scorers, Times, and Referees
24	25/12	A	NEWPORT	14,836		19	L	2-3	1-1	10	26	Rogers 16, Micklewright 78 / Graham 35, Birch 67, Wharton 86 — Ref: A Smith
25	26/12	H	NEWPORT	24,607	(£2,884.5.6)	22	W	3-0	2-0	8	28	Atyeo 25, 88, Williams 36 — Ref: A Smith
26	2/1	H	SOUTHAMPTON	21,693	(£2,391.11.0)	2	W	1-0	1-0	7	30	Atyeo 7 — Ref: H Husband
27	16/1	A	COLCHESTER	7,931		22	W	2-0	1-0	5	32	Boxley 16, Micklewright 88 — Ref: J Jackson
28	23/1	H	CRYSTAL PALACE	17,552	(£1,828.13.6)	15	W	4-0	1-0	4	34	Regan J 16, White 50, Jones 71, [Micklewright 84] — Ref: C Bucknall
29	30/1	A	SHREWSBURY	6,816		17	L	3-4	1-4	4	34	Micklewright 15, 78, Atyeo 89 / Hud 11, 44, Comp 27 (og), Brennan 43 — Ref: H Ball
30	6/2	H	LEYTON ORIENT	15,846	(£1,629.16.0)	11	W	1-0	0-0	4	36	Micklewright 61 — Ref: H Broadhurst
31	13/2	A	ALDERSHOT	6,044		21	W	5-2	1-0	4	38	White 29, Atyeo 58, 85, Mickle' 87, 89 / Flint 53, McCulloch 63 — Ref: W Clements
32	20/2	H	SWINDON	23,749	(£2,616.10.6)	17	W	5-1	3-1	4	40	Atyeo 3, 32, 52, Micklewright 13, 81 / Onslow 7 — Ref: Rev S Davis
33	27/2	A	IPSWICH	14,182		2	L	1-2	0-1	4	40	Williams 69 / Garneys 28, 71 — Ref: R Hall
34	6/3	H	BOURNEMOUTH	16,821	(£1,853.18.6)	18	D	1-1	0-0	4	41	White 79 / Gayner 68 — Ref: G Sawyer

Line-ups (City player / opponent)

No	1	2	3	4	5	6	7	8	9	10	11
24	Cook / Hughes	Guy / Staples	Bailey / Hayward	Regan J / Thomas	Compton / Wilcox	White / Witcomb	Rogers / Birch	Atyeo / Lucas	Micklewright / Graham	Williams / Newell	Boxley / Wharton
25	Cook / Hughes	Guy / Haines	Bailey / Hayward	Regan J / Thomas	Compton / Wilcox	White / Witcomb	Rogers / Birch	Atyeo / Lucas	Micklewright / Graham	Williams / Newell	Boxley / Wharton
26	Cook / Christie	Guy / Gregory	Bailey / Traynor	Regan J / Elliott	Compton / Clements	White / Wilkins	Rogers / Flood	Atyeo / Williams	Micklewright / Day	Williams / Walker	Boxley / McLaughlin
27	Cook / Wright G	Guy / Harrison	Bailey / Lewis	Regan J / Bearryman	Compton / Bicknell	White / Elder	Jones / Scott	Atyeo / Barlow	Micklewright / Church	Williams / Dale	Boxley / Wright P
28	Cook / Bailey	Guy / Edwards	Bailey / McDonald	Regan J / Moss	Compton / Briggs	White / Simpson	Jones / Berry	Atyeo / Willard	Micklewright / Andrews	Williams / Devonshire	Boxley / Hanlon
29	Cook / McBride	Guy / Bannister	Bailey / Parr	Regan J / Beynon	Compton / Dickinson	White / Crutchley	Jones / Price	Atyeo / Stamps	Micklewright / Hudson	Williams / Brennan	Boxley / McCue
30	Cook / Groombridge	Guy / Evans	Bailey / Charlton	Regan J / Blizzard	Compton / Aldous	White / Mallett	Jones / Facey	Atyeo / Pacey	Micklewright / Davies	Williams / Morgan	Boxley / Poulton
31	Cook / Brown	Guy / Jefferson	Bailey / Banks	Regan J / Alison	Compton / Billington	White / Wood	Jones / Gaynor	Atyeo / Lacey	Micklewright / McCulloch	Williams / Durkin	Boxley / Flint
32	Cook / Burton	Guy / Hunt	Bailey / Elwell	Regan J / Cross	Compton / Hudson	White / Johnston	Jones / Nunn	Atyeo / Onslow	Micklewright / Owen	Williams / Lambert	Boxley / Bull
33	Cook / Parry	Guy / Acres	Bailey / Feeney	Regan J / Myles	Compton / Parker	White / Fletcher	Jones / Reed	Atyeo / Crowe	Micklewright / Garneys	Williams / Brown	Boxley / McLuckie
34	Cook / Godwin	Guy / Cunningham	Bailey / Keetley	Regan J / Rushworth	Compton / Hardy	White / Thompson	Hughes W / Gayner	Atyeo / Hunt	Micklewright / Hunt	Williams / Buchanan	Boxley / Harrison

Match reports

24 — With both sides contriving to play a high-brand of soccer, Rogers opens the scoring. Les Graham brings County level and Cliff Birch puts them in front. City thought Micklewright had saved a point, but Newport's player-manager Billy Lucas lays on the pass for John Wharton's winner.

25 — Atyeo puts the home fans in a good mood as he fires in the opener from a pull-back. Williams then nods in the second, before Atyeo gets in on the scoresheet again. He heads the ball down and turns quickly before shooting into the net as Newport suffer their first reverse in six games.

26 — A slight mist hovering over the ground at the start fails to disguise City's first-half dominance. Atyeo slams in an early shot that beats John Christie, but after the break the Saints improve and it requires Bailey's remarkable goal-line clearance to prevent them from levelling matters.

27 — A hard-fought game in which Boxley's left foot puts City on the way to their first ever win at Layer Road. With City under much pressure in the closing stages, Micklewright makes victory certain by chasing Atyeo's long high pass and lobbing the ball in over keeper George Wright.

28 — Inspired by Boxley playing at the top of his form, City's attack proves much too hot for Palace to handle. After Regan drove in the opener from 16 yards, White's great strike from the edge of the penalty area puts City firmly in control. Jones's bicycle kick produces the goal of the game.

29 — A header levelled matters after John Hudson cracked in the opener. Compton's own-goal, Harry Brennan's shot and Hudson's header leaves City facing a mammoth task at the break. Fortunately, Micklewright's tap-in and Atyeo's header brings some respectability to the scoreline.

30 — As last week, the City are much the better side on a frozen pitch, but this time it is not defensive failings but the failure to convert many excellent chances. Fortunately, Micklewright heads in from a Williams centre to secure all of the points.

31 — Leading thanks to White's volley, City are shocked by Ken Flint's cross-shot that brings the Shots level. Charlie Billington's poor back-pass allows Atyeo to put City back in front, before Adam McCulloch is gifted an easy chance. Atyeo's drive sparks City's late three-goal burst.

32 — Roy Onslow fires in Swindon's reply to Atyeo's headed opener, but thereafter there is only side in it as City have the promotion look about them. Atyeo mesmerises City's emerald green rivals to claim his first ever hat-trick with a hooked in effort, following on from his earlier drive.

33 — Despite an Atyeo header being kept out by a post and Boxley having an effort kicked off the line, City are not at their best at Portman Road. Tom Garneys heads the home side in front, but Williams does likewise to equalise matters, prior to the Ipswich No 9 hooking in the winner.

34 — City, who squander many chances, including Boxley's 75th-minute penalty, which the keeper keeps out with his leg, have to thank an alert linesman for their point. White's 25-yarder, that hit the underside of the bar and rebounded into play, equalises Len Gayner's close-range shot.

35 — 13/3 — A **WATFORD** — 13,048 — 6 3 — **L 0-2** — 41
Brown 51, Bowie 72
Ref: W Clements

City	Cook	Guy	Bailey	Regan J	Compton	White	Jones	Atyeo	Micklewright	Williams	Regan D
Watford	*Bennett*	*Bewley*	*Jones*	*Kelly*	*Nolan*	*Mitchell*	*Cook*	*Bowie*	*Brown*	*Smith*	*Paton*

With Compton a passenger at centre-forward following his early knee injury, City put up a plucky display before succumbing to Roy Brown's header and Jim Bowie's shot. Watford are unlucky when Cook heads against the crossbar, whilst City's appeals for a late spot-kick are denied.

---

36 — 20/3 — H **BRIGHTON** — 22,138 (£2,517.11.9) — 6 1 — **D 1-1** — 42
Regan D 56 / Gordon 44
Ref: W Elliott

City	Cook	Guy	Bailey	Regan J	Peacock	White	Eisentrager	Atyeo	Micklewright	Williams	Regan D
Brighton	*Gill*	*Tennant*	*Langley*	*Burtenshaw*	*South*	*Wilson*	*Mundy*	*Bowie*	*Addinall*	*Leadbeater*	*Howard*

Regan drives in a terrific shot to level Dennis Gordon's swerving centre that had deceived the City keeper. This game is too robust for Cook, who is knocked out and carried off midway through the second half, before coming back to play at centre-forward with Guy between the sticks.

---

37 — 27/3 — A **NORTHAMPTON** — 8,283 — 8 5 — **L 0-3** — 42
O'Donnell 41, English 60, McLain 76
Ref: F Fiander

City	Cook	Guy	Bailey	Regan J	Peacock	White	Boxley	Atyeo	Micklewright	Williams	Regan D
Northampton	*Wood*	*Marston*	*Southam*	*Hughes*	*Collins*	*Upton*	*English*	*O'Donnell*	*McLain*	*Ramscar*	*Fowler*

City are easily beaten, but are unlucky when the referee changes his mind after awarding a 36th-minute penalty. William O'Donnell nets an easy opener and White's poor back-pass allows Jack English to fire in another before Tom McLain's rasper sets the seal on Town's victory.

---

38 — 3/4 — H **TORQUAY** — 14,246 (£1,481.10.6) — 5 10 — **W 3-0** — 44
Boxley 1, Atyeo 12, Eisentrager 64
Ref: W Clapton

City	Cook	Guy	Bailey	Regan J	Peacock	White	Micklewright	Atyeo	Rodgers	Eisentrager	Boxley
Torquay	*Webber G*	*Drinkwater*	*Smith*	*Lewis*	*Webber E*	*Norman*	*Dougan*	*Collins*	*Debbie*	*Mills*	*Thomas*

City cruise to an easy win after Boxley's rising left-footed shot, which the goalkeeper should have saved, gives them a first-minute lead. Atyeo doubles City's advantage with a terrific shot prior to Eisentrager's fine ground level drive that brings up the treble during the second half.

---

39 — 7/4 — A **READING** — 6,829 — 5 8 — **W 2-0** — 46
Eisentrager 35, Micklewright 82
Ref: S Rogers

City	Morgan	Guy	Bailey	Regan J	Peacock	White	Micklewright	Atyeo	Rodgers	Eisentrager	Boxley
Reading	*Jones*	*Mansell*	*Reeves*	*Leach*	*Livingstone*	*Docherty*	*Grieve*	*Hinshelwood*	*Blackman*	*Anderton*	*Quinlan*

Syd Morgan, in goal for City for the first time since 1952, has little to do but takes the eye with his prodigious kicking. Rodgers hooks in the opener from Micklewright's centre, before the right-winger gets in on the act by breaking through Reading's defence to slot in the second.

---

40 — 10/4 — A **SOUTHEND** — 7,729 — 3 14 — **W 1-0** — 48
Burns 20 (og)
Ref: H Husband

City	Morgan	Guy	Bailey	Regan J	Peacock	White	Micklewright	Atyeo	Rodgers	Eisentrager	Boxley
Southend	*Threadgold*	*Pavitt*	*Anderson*	*Duthie*	*Stirling*	*Burns*	*Sibley*	*Thompson*	*Hollis*	*Bainbridge*	*McDonald*

Boxley's low driven curling centre is deflected into his own-goal by Frank Burns to bring City victory. A deserved success as City, despite spurning many chances, play much the better soccer. Regan does well in the first half to head Joe Sibley's terrific drive off the goal-line.

---

41 — 16/4 — A **MILLWALL** — 17,410 — 3 9 — **L 0-1** — 48
White 38 (og)
Ref: R Burgess

City	Morgan	Guy	Bailey	Regan J	Peacock	White	Micklewright	Atyeo	Rodgers	Eisentrager	Boxley
Millwall	*Brewer*	*Jardine*	*Fisher*	*Heydon*	*Hurley*	*Saward*	*Hazlett*	*Smith*	*Shepherd*	*Stobbart*	*Hartburn*

A poor display at the Den, where City skipper White has the misfortune to nod the ball into his own net whilst attempting to clear. The thrills are few in this scrappy affair, made difficult by a fierce wind. In the late stages only the bar prevents John Hartburn from adding to the score.

---

42 — 17/4 — H **READING** — 16,701 (£1,760.16.6) — 3 10 — **W 3-1** — 50
Eisentrager 1, Rodgers 71, 79 / Docherty 29
Ref: S Rogers

City	Morgan	Guy	Bailey	Regan J	Peacock	White	Eisentrager	Atyeo	Rodgers	Williams	Boxley
Reading	*Jones*	*Penford*	*Mansell*	*Davis*	*Reeves*	*Leach*	*Simpson*	*Chung*	*Blackman*	*Docherty*	*Hinshelwood*

Another first-minute goal at Ashton Gate, though this time it is a header, registered by Eisentrager, that puts City in front. Tom Docherty fires in from 15 yards to bring Reading level, but after the break Rodgers twice wellies the ball in for a deserved home success on the hard surface.

---

43 — 19/4 — H **MILLWALL** — 14,618 (£1,522.2.0) — 3 13 — **W 2-1** — 52
Hurley 4 (og), Atyeo 9 / Shepherd 15
Ref: R Burgess

City	Morgan	Guy	Bailey	Regan J	Peacock	White	Eisentrager	Atyeo	Rodgers	Williams	Boxley
Millwall	*Brewer*	*Jardine*	*Fisher*	*Heydon*	*Hurley*	*Thippleton*	*Johnson*	*Smith*	*Shepherd*	*Sawara*	*Hazlett*

John Shepherd's spectacular header ends the scoring with only 15 minutes played, but the thrills continue until the game develops into a scrappy affair after the break. Boxley's shot (cannoning off Charlie Hurley's legs) and Atyeo's hooked effort make sure of the points.

---

44 — 24/4 — A **COVENTRY** — 7,454 — 3 15 — **L 0-3** — 52
Dorman 62, Brown 65, 81
Ref: R Tarratt

City	Morgan	Guy	Bailey	Regan J	Peacock	White	Eisentrager	Atyeo	Micklewright	Williams	Regan D
Coventry	*Taylor*	*Jones*	*Kirk*	*Jamieson*	*McDonnell*	*Austin*	*Nutt*	*Dorman*	*Brown*	*Hill P*	*Hill J*

Atyeo's half-hearted tackle lets Dan Dorman through to crack a grand shot past Morgan, then the City keeper is at fault for the second as he allows the ball to bounce out of his hands for Edward Brown to walk it into the net. City's downfall is completed by Brown's volley.

---

45 — 27/4 — H **WATFORD** — 10,941 (£1,016.14.6) — 3 5 — **W 2-0** — 54
Rodgers 14, Boxley 54, Smith 64
Ref: W Clements

City	Morgan	Guy	Bailey	Regan J	Peacock	White	Eisentrager	Atyeo	Rodgers	Williams	Boxley
Watford	*Bennett*	*Bewley*	*Galogly*	*Kelly*	*Nolan*	*Shipwright*	*Cook*	*Smith*	*Wilson*	*Paterson*	*Adams*

City produce a disappointing display, but they make better use of their scoring opportunities than their opponents. Rodgers fires in the opener when Edward Bennett is only able to parry Eisentrager's shot, then Boxley blasts in from a goalmouth scramble to double City's advantage.

---

46 — 29/4 — H **SHREWSBURY** — 8,129 — 3 21 — **W 3-1** — 56
Boxley 13b, 44, Regan D 76 / Jackson 48
Ref: H Ball (£685.1.6)

City	Morgan	Guy	Bailey	Regan J	Peacock	White	Regan D	Atyeo	Rodgers	Eisentrager	Boxley
Shrewsbury	*McBride*	*Bannister*	*Parr*	*Beynon*	*Candlin*	*Crutchley*	*Price*	*Stamps*	*Hudson*	*Jackson*	*McCue*

Duggie Regan makes up for his namesake's blunder in allowing Arnold Jackson to get Shrewsbury back into the game, with a hard angled shot to wrap up the scoring. A mixed evening for Boxley who, after Maurice Candlin's handball on the line, has his 42nd-minute spot-kick saved.

Home Average 17,596 Away 12,070

CUP-TIES

Manager: Pat Beasley

SEASON 1953-54

FA Cup

1 A TORQUAY 21/11 7 W 3-1 2-1
Attendance 10,042 (16) (£1,130.0.9)
Scorers, Times, and Referees: Atyeo 30, Micklewright 43, 48 / Collins 19p / Ref: W Elliott

	1	2	3	4	5	6	7	8	9	10	11
City	Cook	Guy	Bailey	Peacock	Compton	White	Rogers	Atyeo	Micklewright	Williams	Boxley
Torquay	*Hayes*	*Parphitt*	*Towers*	*Lewis*	*Webber*	*Norman*	*Shaw*	*Collins*	*Dobbie*	*Mills*	*Bond*

City get quick revenge for last week's League defeat as in this game they are much the better side, despite Torquay taking the lead from the spot after White handled a bouncing ball. Atyeo coolly lobbed in a leveller prior to Micklewright's cross-shot on the run putting City in front.

2 A RHYL 12/12 9 W 3-0 2-0
Attendance 9,000 (£1,504.17.6)
Scorers, Times, and Referees: Micklewright 24, Atyeo 37, Williams 72 / Ref: H Ball

	1	2	3	4	5	6	7	8	9	10	11
City	Cook	Guy	Bailey	Regan J	Compton	White	Rogers	Atyeo	Micklewright	Williams	Boxley
Rhyl	*Humphreys*	*Fazackerley*	*Munro*	*McLean*	*Donaldson*	*Rogers*	*Devine*	*Hanlon*	*Spendlove*	*Valentine*	*Stafford*

Set to play down the slope and watched by ex-Rovers boss Capt A Prince-Cox, who is a Rhyl director, City have too much class for their non-League opponents. It might have been more difficult if Munro had not failed from the spot 14 minutes before Williams headed in City's third.

3 H ROTHERHAM 9/1 7 L 1-3 0-0
Attendance 29,216 (2.8) (£3,856.8.3)
Scorers, Times, and Referees: Atyeo 85 / Grainger 58, 80, 89 / Ref: A Smith

	1	2	3	4	5	6	7	8	9	10	11
City	Cook	Guy	Bailey	Regan J	Compton	White	Rogers	Atyeo	Micklewright	Williams	Boxley
Rotherham	*Quainey*	*Selkirk*	*Warner*	*Marshall*	*Noble*	*Williams D*	*Grainger*	*Henderson*	*Burke*	*Guest*	*Wilson*

The Millers do all the early attacking, but it is Boxley who first finds the net with a disallowed 37th-minute effort. Jack Grainger breaks the deadlock by heading the visitors in front and then fires in two more to notch up his hat-trick. Atyeo drives a great goal into the net for City.

Gloucestershire Cup

F H BRISTOL ROV 3/5 3 D 2-2 1-1
Attendance 13,668 (£1,816)
Scorers, Times, and Referees: Williams 12, Eisentrager 54 / Warren 41, Meyer 77 / Ref: A Bond

	1	2	3	4	5	6	7	8	9	10	11
City	Morgan	Guy	Bailey	Regan J	Peacock	White	Eisentrager	Atyeo	Rodgers	Williams	Regan D
Rovers	*Anderson*	*Allcock*	*Fox*	*Cairney*	*Warren*	*Sampson*	*McIlvenny*	*Meyer*	*Hale*	*Roost*	*Petherbridge*

Barrie Meyer beats Morgan all ends up with a great shot on the turn to save the Rovers in one of the best county cup games of recent years. Williams shoots a 15-yard opener, but Ray Warren levels with a 35-yard free-kick, before an Eisentrager header puts City in front once more.

Chippenham Sportsman & Traders Trophy

F N SWINDON 27/4 3 W 2-0 0-0
(19)
Scorers, Times, and Referees: Smith 68, Rogers 80p / (at Chippenham United FC)

	1	2	3	4	5	6	7	8	9	10	11
City	King	Mitchelson	Steel	Tovey W	Hague	McLean	Rogers	Smith	Thresher	Gilbert	Watkins
Swindon	*Reading*	*Tilley R*	*Goddard*	*Jackson*	*Bines*	*Nelson*	*Bain*	*Dean*	*Tilley D*	*Archer*	*Williamson*

At the Firs, both sides in this inaugural Sportsmen & Traders Trophy final are composed of mainly young players. A poor first half, but City, who give a trial to King (RAOC), dominate after the interval. Smith heads them in front and his later felling brings an inevitable penalty.

			Home					Away					
		P	W	D	L	F	A	W	D	L	F	A	Pts
1	Ipswich	46	15	5	3	47	19	12	5	6	35	32	64
2	Brighton	46	17	3	3	57	31	9	6	8	29	30	61
3	BRISTOL C	46	18	3	2	59	18	7	3	13	29	48	56
4	Watford	46	16	3	4	52	23	5	7	11	33	46	52
5	Northampton	46	18	4	1	63	18	2	7	14	19	37	51
6	Southampton	46	17	5	1	51	22	2	8	13	25	41	51
7	Norwich	46	13	5	5	43	28	8	4	11	30	38	51
8	Reading	46	14	3	6	57	33	6	6	11	29	40	49
9	Exeter	46	12	2	9	39	22	8	6	9	29	36	48
10	Gillingham	46	14	3	6	37	22	7	3	13	24	44	48
11	Leyton Orient	46	14	5	4	48	26	2	10	11	31	47	47
12	Millwall	46	15	3	5	44	24	4	6	13	30	53	47
13	Torquay	46	10	10	3	48	33	4	8	11	33	56	46
14	Coventry	46	14	5	4	36	15	4	4	15	25	41	45
15	Newport	46	14	4	5	42	28	5	2	16	19	53	44
16	Southend	46	15	2	6	47	22	3	5	15	23	49	43
17	Aldershot	46	11	5	7	45	31	6	4	13	28	55	43
18	QP Rangers	46	10	5	8	32	25	6	5	12	20	43	42
19	Bournemouth	46	12	5	6	47	27	4	3	16	19	43	40
20	Swindon	46	13	5	5	48	21	2	5	16	17	49	40
21	Shrewsbury	46	12	8	3	48	34	2	4	17	17	42	40
22	Crys Palace	46	11	7	5	41	30	3	5	15	19	56	40
23	Colchester	46	7	7	9	35	29	3	3	17	15	49	30
24	Walsall	46	8	5	10	22	27	1	3	19	18	60	26
		1104	320	112	120	1088	608	120	112	320	608	1088	1104

Odds & ends

Double wins: (6) Colchester, Exeter, Crystal Palace, Aldershot, Southend, Reading.

Double losses: (1) Ipswich.

Won from behind: (4) Crystal Palace (a), Northampton T (h), Southend (h), Torquay (a) (FAC).

Lost from in front: (2) Brighton (a), Newport (a).

High spots: The five successive wins in September that pushed City into the promotion race.

Winning seven of the last nine games.

City's record floodlight friendly attendance of 28,991 on 30 March.

Low spots: The campaign's poor start, only two points from 4 games.

Losing 0-5 at Swindon Town on 3 October.

AGM (Grand Hotel, Broad Street, Bristol, 20 December 1954):
Profit £8,041.12s.5d. Season Ticket Sales £8,419.18s.0d.

Player of the year: John Atyeo.
Ever-presents: (1) Ivor Guy.
Hat-tricks: (1) John Atyeo.
Leading scorer: Overall: John Atyeo (25). League: John Atyeo (22).

	Appearances		Goals		
	Lge	Cup	Lge	Cup	Tot
Atyeo, John	45	4	22	3	25
Bailey, Jack	39	4			
Boxley, Jack	41	3			
Compton, Terry	15	3			
Cook, Tony	38	3	14		14
Eisentrager, Alec	19	1	3	1	4
Gilbert,		1			
Guy, Ivor	46	4			
Hague, Len		1			
Jones, Ernie	11		1		1
King, Roy		1			
McLean, Alec		1			
Micklewright, Andy	36	3	16	3	19
Mitchelson, Ken	8	1			
Morgan, Syd	8				
Peacock, Ernie	32	2	1		1
Regan, Doug	12	1	4		4
Regan, Jimmy	25	3	1		1
Roberts, Dennis	15				
Rodgers, Arnold	23	1	14		14
Rogers, Jimmy	13	4	3	1	4
Smith, David		1		1	1
Steel, Richard	1	1			
Thresher, Mike		1			
Tovey, Bill	6				
Tovey, Ron	2	1			
Watkins, Johnny					
White, Jack	40	4	3		3
Williams, Cyril	39	4	4	2	6
(own-goals)			2		2
29 players used	506	55	88	11	99

LEAGUE DIVISION 3 (SOUTH)

Manager: Pat Beasley

SEASON 1954-55

No	Date	Att	Pos	Pt	F-A	H-T	Scorers, Times, and Referees	1	2	3	4	5	6	7	8	9	10	11
1	A GILLINGHAM 21/8	14,404		D 1	1-1	0-1	Atyeo 55 / Morgan 6 / Ref: A Smith	Cook	Jackson	Bailey	Regan J	Peacock	White	Eisentrager	Atyeo	Rodgers	Williams	Boxley
								Rigg	Marks	Lewin	Boswell	Ayres	McKell	Scarth	Evans W	Adley	Morgan	Millar
2	A TORQUAY 25/8	10,432		D 2	2-2	0-1	White 82, Webber 88 (og) / Shaw 38, Mills 75 / Ref: C Porter	Cook	Guy	Bailey	Regan J	Peacock	White	Eisentrager	Atyeo	Rodgers	Williams	Boxley
								Jefferies	Towers	Smith H	Lewis	Webber	Norman	Shaw	Collins	Dobbie	Mills	Smith J
3	H LEYTON ORIENT 28/8	19,715 (£2,120.10.0)	4 8	W 4	5-0	2-0	Boxley 3p, Rodgers 28, 89, [Blizzard 72 (og), Williams 78] / Ref: E Jennings	Cook	Guy	Bailey	Regan J	Peacock	White	Eisentrager	Atyeo	Rodgers	Williams	Boxley
								Walton	Lee	Charlton	Blizzard	Aldous	McKnight	Facey	Rees	Pacey	Burgess	Hartburn
4	H TORQUAY 31/8	18,773 (£1,972.8.6)	4 9	D 5	1-1	0-1	Rogers 63 / Shaw 33 / Ref: C Porter	Cook	Guy	Bailey	Regan J	Peacock	White	Rogers	Atyeo	Rodgers	Williams	Boxley
								Jefferies	Towers	Smith H	Lewis	Webber	Norman	Shaw	Collins	Smith J	Dougan	Thomas
5	A MILLWALL 4/9	15,603	2 19	W 7	3-1	2-1	Boxley 31, Rogers 38, Williams 69 / Johnson 2 / Ref: G Pankhurst	Cook	Guy	Bailey	Regan J	Peacock	White	Rogers	Atyeo	Rodgers	Williams	Boxley
								Finlayson	Jardine	Fisher	Heydon	Hurley	Saward	Johnson	Smith	Shepherd	Ramscar	Summers
6	A COLCHESTER 9/9	8,522	2 16	W 9	2-0	1-0	Rodgers 43, 68 / Ref: F Gardner	Cook	Guy	Bailey	Regan J	Peacock	White	Rogers	Atyeo	Rodgers	Williams	Boxley
								Kirk	Harrison	Lewis	McCourt	Stewart	Hunt	Birch	Dale	Plant	McKim	Grice
7	H SOUTHAMPTON 11/9	24,809 (£2,884.1.0)	2 11	W 11	2-0	1-0	Atyeo 10, Williams 79 / Ref: R Tarratt	Cook	Guy	Bailey	Regan J	Peacock	White	Rogers	Atyeo	Rodgers	Williams	Boxley
								Kiernan	Wilkins	Traynor	Elliott	Parker	Simpson	Foulkes	Mulgrew	Day	Walker	Hoskins
8	H COLCHESTER 14/9	18,710 (£2,012.18.6)	1 20	W 13	4-0	3-0	Rodgers 11, 34, 68, Atyeo 21 / Ref: F Gardner	Cook	Guy	Bailey	Regan J	Peacock	White	Rogers	Atyeo	Rodgers	Williams	Boxley
								Kirk	Harrison	Lewis	Elder	Stewart	Hunt	McGurley	Dale	Plant	McKim	Leonard
9	A COVENTRY 18/9	29,879	1 3	W 15	3-1	3-1	Atyeo 6, 19, Rogers 13 / Capel 34 / Ref: C Holland	Cook	Guy	Bailey	Regan J	Peacock	White	Rogers	Atyeo	Rodgers	Williams	Boxley
								Taylor	Jones	Kirk	Jameison	McDonnell	Austin	Nutt	Hill	Brown	Capel	Collindridge
10	H WALSALL 21/9	20,394 (£2,204.5.0)	1 24	W 17	5-3	2-0	Box' 33, 37, Fort 76 (og), Rog' 77, Atv' 80 / Goffin 60, Davis 62, Tarrant 71p / Ref: W Dellow	Cook	Guy	Bailey	Regan J	Allen	White	Rogers	Atyeo	Rodgers	Williams	Boxley
								McBride	Fort	Vinnall	Ferriday	Bridgett	Russon	Myerscough	Davies	Morris	Tarrant	Goffin
11	H BRENTFORD 25/9	28,980 (£3,344.19.3)	1 12	W 19	2-1	2-0	Rodgers 26, 28 / Dudley 85 / Ref: T Wood	Cook	Guy	Bailey	Regan J	Peacock	White	Rogers	Atyeo	Rodgers	Williams	Boxley
								Feehan	Coote	Latimer	Harper	Dargie	Rainford	Heath	Stobbart	Dudley	Towers	Robertson

Match 1 — Despite a lush green surface instead of the normal dust bowl conditions at the Priestfield Stadium there is no sign of the much-heralded English soccer revival in this game. Atyeo's header from an impossible position brings City a point in this typical Third Division kick and rush contest.

Match 2 — Atyeo's header, in off the head of Torquay boss Eric Webber, earns City a point in this keenly fought affair. Despite monopolising the first half, City fall behind when Ron Shaw shoots in the opener. Don Mills doubles Torquay's advantage, before White fires in to give City hope.

Match 3 — From the moment Boxley puts his spot-kick into the Covered End net, after Stan Aldous brings down Rodgers, the result of this game is never in doubt. After his first shot is blocked, Rodgers doubles the advantage by seizing on the loose ball and ramming it high into the roof of the net.

Match 4 — City spurn their chances in this hard struggle but are unlucky that the final whistle rules out an Arnold Rodgers scrambled in effort, as well as a push on the keeper depriving Jimmy Rogers in the 78th minute. Rogers cuts in and fires the ball home to level Ron Shaw's left-footed opener.

Match 5 — There is not a weak link in City's impressive win against fashion-conscious Millwall in their blue silk shirts and abbreviated shorts. Malcolm Finlayson in the Lions goal has a hectic time, and he has to thank his crossbar and upright that he didn't have three more goals put past him.

Match 6 — City hand out a soccer lesson to the U's, as their sparkling play produces the victory it deserved. City go in front when Cook's throw-out leads to five passes before reaching Rogers, who fires in from five yards. Rodgers then makes success certain by putting away a centre from Boxley.

Match 7 — The Saints, with lightweight boots and limbering up sessions before games, are another side to have gone Continental this season. They are, however, outplayed by City who give them a real pounding. Goals from the feet of Atyeo and Williams, but there should have been more.

Match 8 — The City are never extended by the often outclassed visitors. Atyeo's goal is a gem, giving the fans a truly memorable moment as he jumps up high in true Tommy Lawton style to head the ball in from Boxley's cross. Rodgers demonstrates all of his old dash as he notches up a hat-trick.

Match 9 — In front of the biggest Highfield Road crowd in more than five years, City soon take control. Following on from his earlier shot and a Rogers header, Atyeo hurls himself at White's cross to head in the opener. Coventry's brief fight-back is rewarded by Tom Capel heading past Cook.

Match 10 — Having performed a near miracle in restricting City to a couple of lashed in Boxley efforts, Walsall suddenly race into a 3-2 lead. Fortunately, City are revived by Sam Fort, who, in his attempt to clear, drills the ball past his own keeper. A debut to remember for 19-year-old Peter Allen.

Match 11 — Rarely has a centre-forward given a defence such a pounding as Rodgers inflicted on a Brentford side previously unbeaten in seven games. He slams in both his goals at the Covered End, where Frank Dudley's high lob over the stranded Cook brings the Bees their late consolation.

#	V	Opponent	Date	Att.				Result	HT
12	A	WALSALL	30/9	8,911	24	21	1 W	3-1	3-0

Atyeo 32, 38, Rodgers 43 / Davis 89 — Ref: W Dellow

City: Cook, Guy, Bailey, Regan J, Peacock, White, Rogers, Atyeo, Rodgers, Williams, Boxley
Walsall: *McBride, Fort, Vinall, Morris, McPherson, Ferriday, Myerscough, Davis, Richards, Tarrant, Meek*

City are never in any danger after Atyeo heads in Boxley's centre to open the scoring. Len Davis also used his head to obtain Walsall's late consolation, but by then Atyeo had run through to glide the ball past Vince McBride and Rodgers had found the net with a crisp drive.

#	V	Opponent	Date	Att.				Result	HT
13	A	BRIGHTON	2/10	21,034	15	23	1 W	1-0	1-0

Rodgers 22 — Ref: F Fiander

City: Cook, Guy, Bailey, Regan J, Peacock, White, Rogers, Atyeo, Rodgers, Williams, Boxley
Brighton: *Gill, Tennant, Langley, Gilberg, McNeil, Wilson, Gordon, Mundy, Moore, Leadbeater, Foreman*

City are fortunate to maintain their unbeaten record let alone win thanks to a goal that Arnold Rodgers, who had earlier been denied by the bar, tries to claim he had headed out of the keeper's hands. To the reporters, however, it was clear that Eric Gill had misjudged Jimmy Rogers' lob.

#	V	Opponent	Date	Att.				Result	HT
14	A	SOUTHEND	9/10	12,930	8	23	1 L	2-3	1-1

Atyeo 43, Boxley 80 / Burns 35, Bambridge 49, Sibley 62 — Ref: H Husband

City: Cook, Guy, Bailey, Regan J, Peacock, White, Rogers, Atyeo, Rodgers, Williams, Boxley
Southend: *Threadgold, Pavitt, Anderson S, Burns, Howe, Lawler, Sibley, Bridge, Hollis, Baron, Bainbridge*

At Southend Stadium, the Shrimpers end the season's last unbeaten record. City make far too many defensive mistakes and are out Coppinged by their trainer's old side. Their only consolation is the fact that Atyeo's goal, which the nets with a waist-high volley, is the best of the game.

#	V	Opponent	Date	Att.				Result	HT
15	H	ALDERSHOT	16/10	21,875	14	25	1 W	6-1	2-0

(£2,521.7.3)

Jefferson S 14 (og), Atyeo 32, 85, McCulloch 87 [Wilms 51, Rogers 64, 68], Brown — Ref: W Clements

City: Cook, Guy, Bailey, Regan J, Peacock, White, Rogers, Atyeo, Rodgers, Williams, Boxley
Aldershot: *Brown, Jefferson S, Jefferson A, Alison, Billington, Sirrell, Ball, Barley, McCulloch, Menzies, Flint*

Rogers is outstanding in City's hammering of Aldershot, which makes them the highest scorers in the League. The Shots, without an away point this season, are never in the hunt as Rogers, with two powerful shots, notches the best goals of the match, as well as laying on two more.

#	V	Opponent	Date	Att.				Result	HT
16	A	SWINDON	23/10	19,880	12	26	1 D	2-2	0-2

Rogers 52, Boxley 68p / Owen 10, Hunter 37 — Ref: G Pankhurst

City: Cook, Guy, Bailey, Regan J, Peacock, White, Rogers, Atyeo, Rodgers, Williams, Boxley
Swindon: *Burton, Hunt, Hilton, Johnston, Hudson, Williams, Hunter, Onslow, Owen, Gemmell, Bull*

Despite Arnold Rodgers going off with a head injury, following a collision with Sam Burton two minutes prior to half-time, he comes back early after the break to inspire City to a share of the spoils. His header rebounds off of the bar to allow Jimmy Rogers to hook in City's opener.

#	V	Opponent	Date	Att.				Result	HT
17	H	EXETER	30/10	26,449	18	28	1 W	2-0	0-0

(£3,003.10.9)

Atyeo 60, Micklewright 80 — Ref: A Howlett

City: Cook, Guy, Bailey, Regan J, Peacock, White, Rogers, Atyeo, Rodgers, Micklewright, Boxley
Exeter: *Kelly, Doyle, Douglas, Mitchell, Davey, Dodgin, Callan, John, Donaldson, Anderson, Kalle*

A scrappy contest which City should have won with ease. New signing Tommy Burden watches from the Stand as City spurn many chances before Atyeo volleys in the opener. The visitors (only four goals in nine away games) offer little and Micklewright makes sure of the points.

#	V	Opponent	Date	Att.				Result	HT
18	A	NORTHAMPTON	6/11	11,608	9	28	1 L	0-2	0-1

(£1,243)

Starocsik 29, 65p — Ref: G Gibson

City: Cook, Guy, Bailey, Regan J, Peacock, White, Rogers, Atyeo, Rodgers, Burden, Boxley
Northampton: *Wood, Southam, Patterson, Smith, Croy, Hughes, Starocsik, Hazledine, McLain, Jones, Fowler*

With White limping with an ankle injury from the early stages City are up against it, but worse is to follow as Bailey breaks his left arm in the last minute. City are well beaten by the Cobblers at the County Ground, for whom ex-Third Lanark players Felix Starocsik and John Croy star.

#	V	Opponent	Date	Att.				Result	HT
19	H	WATFORD	13/11	21,910	14	30	1 W	1-0	0-0

(£2,473.18.6)

Boxley 88 — Ref: E Jennings

City: Cook, Guy, Bailey, Regan J, Peacock, White, Rogers, Atyeo, Rodgers, Williams, **Burden**
Watford: *Bennett, Bateman, Bewley, Meadows, Shipwright, Mitchell, Paton, Bowie, Cook, Smith, Adams*

Ivor is a wonderful guy as he takes over in goal from the injured Cook for all but the opening four minutes of this game. Despite suffering a kick in the face, Guy survives a terrific bombardment to keep Watford at bay and leave the way open for Boxley to fire in City's late decider.

#	V	Opponent	Date	Att.				Result	HT
20	H	QP RANGERS	27/11	17,657	7	31	1 D	1-1	0-1

(£2,035.10.9)

Rogers 85 / Tomkys 39 — Ref: E Hill

City: Cook, Guy, Bailey, Regan J, Peacock, White, Rogers, Atyeo, Rodgers, Williams, Boxley
QPR: *Brown, Wood, Ingham, Nicholas, Powell, Angell, Tomkys, Cameron, Fidler, Smith, Kerrins*

City just manage to salvage a point against a Rangers side, without their keeper for 13 minutes of the first half, thanks to Rodgers, who drives the ball in from ten yards. A fitting reward for almost constant attacking after going behind when Mike Tomkys fired in from close range.

#	V	Opponent	Date	Att.				Result	HT
21	A	NEWPORT	4/12	10,886	20	32	1 D	2-2	0-2

Burden 62, Atyeo 87 / Johnston 40, 44 — Ref: S Perry

City: Cook, Guy, Bailey, Regan J, Peacock, White, Rogers, Atyeo, Burden, Williams, Boxley
Newport: *Pope, Staples, Lewis, Hollyman, Wilcox, Thomas, Hudson, Shergold, Johnston, Harris, Wharton*

City are still struggling to rediscover their form and it is not until they fall behind to Tom Johnston's walk-in goal and his later scrambled in effort that they wake up. Burden turns the ball over the line to set City back into the contest and sets the scene for Atyeo's point-saving header.

#	V	Opponent	Date	Att.				Result	HT
22	A	SHREWSBURY	11/12	8,208	19	34	1 W	2-0	1-0

Rodgers 41, 57 — Ref: L Callaghan

City: Cook, Guy, Bailey, Regan J, Peacock, White, Rogers, Atyeo, Rodgers, Williams, Boxley
Shrewsbury: *Crossley, Bannister, Parr, Candlin, Atkins, Maloney, Price, O'Donnell, Hudson, Brennan, Weigh*

On a heavy pitch, both sides give a good display, but the City forwards have the luck that deserted Shrewsbury. Rodgers, who taps in the opener when goalkeeper Russell Crossley can only push out Boxley's shot, makes the points safe by heading in Atyeo's perfect centre.

#	V	Opponent	Date	Att.				Result	HT
23	H	GILLINGHAM	18/12	17,880	11	34	2 L	1-4	1-1

(£1,935.1.3)

Atyeo 4 / Morgan 12, 57, 69, Sowden 79 — Ref: A Smith

City: Cook, Guy, Bailey, Regan J, Peacock, White, Rogers, Atyeo, Rodgers, Williams, Boxley
Gillingham: *Rigg, Marks, West, Boswell, Nibbett, Riggs, Sowden, Evans, Scarth, Morgan, Miller*

City's 14-month unbeaten home record is wrecked, but the crowd get the plaudits from visiting boss Archie Clarke for their sportsmanlike behaviour in defeat. Atyeo slams in the opening goal at the Covered End, but City are undone by Morgan's treble (shot, tap-in and header).

LEAGUE DIVISION 3 (SOUTH)

Manager: Pat Beasley

SEASON 1954-55

No	Date	Scorers, Times, and Referees	Att	Pos	Pt	F-A	H-T	1	2	3	4	5	6	7	8	9	10	11
24	H READING 25/12	Rodgers 3, Eisentrager 21, Wheeler 64, Ref: F Read	16,800 (£1,931.16.6)	1	W 36	2-1	2-0	Anderson / *Meeson*	Guy / *Penford*	Jackson / *Mansell*	Burden / *Davis J*	Peacock / *Davies W*	White / *Leach*	Rodgers / *Simpson*	Atyeo / *Hinshelwood*	Rodgers / *Campbell*	Eisentrager / *Uphill*	Regan D / *Wheeler*
25	A READING 27/12	Rodgers 25, Atyeo 78, Ref: F Read	18,929	1	W 38	2-0	1-0	Anderson / *Meeson*	Guy / *Penford*	Thresher / *Mansell*	Regan J / *Davis J*	Peacock / *Davies W*	White / *Leach*	Rodgers / *Simpson*	Atyeo / *Chung*	Rodgers / *Livingstone*	Eisentrager / *Uphill*	Regan D / *Wheeler*
26	A LEYTON ORIENT 1/1	Boxley 29 *(Blizzard 63)*, Groves 32, Hartburn 38, 51, Ref: E Jennings	20,327	1 (2)	L 38	1-4	1-2	Anderson / *Welton*	Guy / *Lee*	Thresher / *Charlton*	Burden / *Blizzard*	Peacock / *Aldous*	White / *McKnight*	Rodgers / *Groves*	Atyeo / *Facey*	Rodgers / *Rees*	Eisentrager / *Morgan*	Boxley / *Hartburn*
27	H NORWICH 8/1	Chung 48, Ref: W Dellow	16,332 (£1,736.16.6)	2	L 38	0-1	0-0	Anderson / *Nethercott*	Guy / *Holmes*	Thresher / *Lewis*	Peacock / *McCrohan*	White / *Foulkes*	Burden / *Ashman*	Rodgers / *Gordon*	Atyeo / *Brennan*	Rodgers / *Kearns*	Williams / *Chung*	Boxley / *Reagan*
28	A SOUTHAMPTON 22/1	Atyeo 88, Flood 26, Day 48p, Ref: R Tarratt	18,334	2 (3)	L 38	1-2	0-1	Anderson / *Kiernan*	Guy / *Turner*	Thresher / *Traynor*	Regan J / *McLaughlin*	White / *Wilkins*	Burden / *Simpson*	Rodgers / *Flood*	Micklewright / *Williams R*	Atyeo / *Day*	Williams / *Walker*	Boxley / *Hoskins*
29	A NORWICH 29/1	Burden 12, Ref: W Dellow	24,189	2 (6)	W 40	1-0	1-0	Anderson / *Nethercott*	Guy / *Holmes*	Thresher / *Lewis*	White / *McCrohan*	Peacock / *Foulkes*	Williams / *Ashman*	Eisentrager / *Gordon*	Atyeo / *Brennan*	Rogers / *Kearns*	Burden / *Chung*	Boxley / *Reagan*
30	H COVENTRY 5/2	White 13, Rogers 83, Ref: C Holland	21,758 (£2,444.13.0)	2 (9)	W 42	2-0	1-0	Anderson / *Matthews*	Guy / *Jones*	Thresher / *Kirk*	White / *Jamieson*	Peacock / *McDonnell*	Williams / *Simpson*	Eisentrager / *Johnson*	Atyeo / *Lee*	Rogers / *Moore*	Burden / *Capel*	Boxley / *Collimbridge*
31	A BRENTFORD 12/2	Atyeo 34, Eisentrager 60, Rainford 8, Robertson 42, Ref: T Wood	11,563	2 (19)	D 43	2-2	1-2	Anderson / *Feehan*	Guy / *Horne*	Thresher / *Coote*	White / *Harper*	Peacock / *Latimer*	Williams / *Bristow*	Eisentrager / *Robertson*	Atyeo / *Rainford*	Rogers / *Stoddart*	Burden / *Perrin*	Boxley / *Dudley*
32	H BRIGHTON 19/2	Rogers 4, 70, Atyeo 43p, Gordon 34, 83, Ref: F Fiander	24,649 (£2,800.16.0)	2 (13)	W 45	3-2	2-1	Anderson / *Gill*	Guy / *Tennant*	Thresher / *Langley*	White / *Gilberg*	Peacock / *McNeill*	Williams / *Wilson*	Milton / *Gordon*	Atyeo / *Mundy*	Rogers / *Moore*	Burden / *Foreman*	Boxley / *Howard*
33	H SOUTHEND 26/2	Rogers 29, 62, Atyeo 67, Bridge 12, Hollis 42, Ref: R Mann	20,837 (£2,313.19.3)	1 (12)	W 47	3-2	1-2	Anderson / *Scannell*	Guy / *Pavitt*	Thresher / *Anderson*	White / *Burns*	Peacock / *Howe*	Williams / *Lawler*	Milton / *Sibley*	Atyeo / *Duthie*	Rogers / *Hollis*	Burden / *Baron*	Boxley / *Bridge*
34	A ALDERSHOT 5/3	Burden 2, Rogers 73, Ref: W Clements	6,832	1 (16)	W 49	2-0	1-0	Anderson / *Brown*	Guy / *Monk*	Thresher / *Banks*	White / *Alison*	Peacock / *Billington*	Williams / *Sirrell*	Milton / *Gaynor J*	Atyeo / *Gaynor L*	Rogers / *Lacey*	Burden / *Menzies*	Boxley / *Flint*

24 — *City made really hard work of winning this game, the highlight of which is a spectacular goal. From a corner, which White heads on into the goalmouth, Eisentrager jumps high into the air and with a deft overhead kick sends the ball speeding into the top corner of the Open End net.*

25 — *In a game more noteworthy for its vigour than its skill, City fully merit their win at Elm Park despite a lucky opener when David Meeson lets a simple Rodgers header trickle through his legs. Atyeo is the best man on the field and a defensive mix up lets him register with an easy goal.*

26 — *Despite taking the lead when Boxley's shot deflects in off of Stan Aldous, sluggish City are routed by Orient's pace and skill. Vic Groves nips past Thresher to flick in a 35-yard cross for the equaliser, then John Hartburn's half-volley and his later toe-ender put Orient firmly in control.*

27 — *Rodgers, who is injured for most of this game, manages to get the ball in the net but is given offside. City had the chances to have won, but Norwich ride their luck to secure their first away win in seven games, thanks to a lob from new boy Sammy Chung - £5,000 from Reading.*

28 — *Anderson's acrobatics keep the score down as City's worrying decline shows no sign of ending. The Saints are in charge throughout and deserve the win, courtesy of John Flood's lob and Eric Day's spot-kick after John Hoskins is brought down in the penalty area by Thresher.*

29 — *At last, City rediscover promotion form with a top-quality soccer display at Carrow Road, where Burden's half-volley, after Eisentrager had beaten two men to create the chance, proves enough to defeat a Norwich side that had gained seven points from their previous four games.*

30 — *Despite a quagmire pitch, City conjure up another top display as Coventry's Young England keeper Reg Matthews is beaten by White's header and a Rogers tap-in. Matthews is busy indeed, pulling off thirteen saves and dealing with eleven back-passes from his overworked defenders.*

31 — *With any luck City would have won this game, but they have to be satisfied with sharing the spoils. Rogers is unfortunate to have what would have been the winning goal disallowed, but no doubt about City's opener. Wilf Copping says he had never seen better than Atyeo's grand shot.*

32 — *Despite Rogers firing in from close range to put City into an early lead, Dennis Gordon fires in a Brighton leveller from barely a yard out. Atyeo puts City back in front, netting from the spot after being brought down by Wilson, but it takes another Rogers effort to calm the nerves.*

33 — *The roar almost raises the roof after this game, when the fans are informed of promotion rivals Leyton Orient losing at home to Watford. An important City win over their bogey side. A delighted Atyeo, who had a first-half shot disallowed, performs a somersault following his decider.*

34 — *Milton impresses with his long passing ability, but it is the courage and determination of Rogers, dwarfed by Charlie Billington, that takes the eye. Despite his lack of polish he proves ideal for the centre-forward role, slotting in Boxley's low ball after Burden headed City into the lead.*

Bristol City season match record — matches 35–46

Match 35 — MILLWALL (H) 9/3 · Result: W 5-1 · Pos 4 · Pts 51 · Att 13,264 · (£1,445.13.3.)
Scorers: Atyeo 13, 69p, Boxley 37, Summers 58 [Rogers 84, 88] · Ref: G Pankhurst

City	Anderson	Guy	Thresher	White	Peacock	Williams	Milton	Atyeo	Rogers	Burden	Boxley
Millwall	*Findlayson*	*Jardine*	*Anslow*	*Short*	*Hurley*	*Saward*	*Johnson*	*Smith*	*Pacey*	*Ramscar*	*Summers*

A brilliant display by City as they annihilate the Lions, who prior to this game had the Division's best defence. Atyeo leaves three opponents sprawling before cracking in the 20-yard opener. Toothache sufferer Rogers completes the scoring with a stinging right-footed drive.

Match 36 — SWINDON (H) 12/3 · Result: W 3-0 · Pos 20 · Pts 53 · Att 24,380 · (£2,789.18.3)
Scorers: Burden 11, 53, Boxley 50 · Ref: G Pankhurst

City	Anderson	Guy	Thresher	White	Peacock	Williams	Milton	Atyeo	Rogers	Burden	Boxley
Swindon	*Burton*	*Hunt*	*Hilton*	*Cross*	*Hudson*	*Williams G*	*Gibson*	*Sampson*	*Owen*	*Williams H*	*Beards*

Despite the bitter north-east wind, a good crowd sees City continue their promotion surge. Burden's great 20-yard rising shot ties up a convincing success, even though in the second half Atyeo has his penalty kept out by a post, whilst offside rules out a great Rogers goal.

Match 37 — EXETER (A) 19/3 · Result: W 1-0 · Pos 19 · Pts 55 · Att 12,112 · (£1,150)
Scorers: Rogers 67 · Ref: A Howlett

City	Anderson	Guy	Thresher	White	Peacock	Williams	Milton	Atyeo	Rogers	Burden	Boxley
Exeter	*Kelly*	*Doyle*	*Dunne*	*Harvey*	*Collins*	*Davey*	*Thomas*	*Houghton*	*Mitchell*	*Murphy*	*John*

City fail to find their best form on a bumpy pitch, but they are still good enough to take the points. A goal from out of the blue does the trick, a powerful right-footed 18-yard drive into the top corner that many felt Exeter's Irish International keeper Hugh Kelly could have saved.

Match 38 — NORTHAMPTON (H) 26/3 · Result: W 5-1 · Pos 13 · Pts 57 · Att 20,955 · (£2,468.3.0)
Scorers: Atyeo 42, Milton 44, Rogers 67, 84, Patterson 10 [Boxley 88] · Ref: C Gibson

City	Anderson	Guy	Thresher	White	Peacock	Williams	Milton	Atyeo	Rogers	Burden	Boxley
Northampton	*Wood*	*Marston*	*Patterson*	*Hughes*	*Collins*	*McLain*	*Mills*	*Smith EW*	*Adams*	*Jones*	*Fowler*

After Ron Patterson runs through to shoot the Cobblers in front, desperate defending keeps City out until just before the half-time interval. Alf Wood's poor punch-out allows Atyeo to fire in, then Milton promptly pings another into the Covered End net to put the City firmly in control.

Match 39 — WATFORD (A) 2/4 · Result: W 2-0 · Pos 6 · Pts 59 · Att 15,850
Scorers: Milton 42, Atyeo 62 · Ref: E Jennings

City	Anderson	Guy	Thresher	White	Peacock	Williams	Milton	Atyeo	Rogers	Burden	Boxley
Watford	*Bennett*	*Bateman*	*Bewley*	*Meadows*	*Shipwright*	*Mitchell*	*Brown*	*Catleugh*	*Cook*	*Bowie*	*Adams*

With Guy a limping passenger of the right wing in the second half, City pull off a great win at Vicarage Road to put themselves five points clear of Orient, who have two games in hand. Milton heads City in front just before the break, then Atyeo's lob makes sure of the points.

Match 40 — BOURNEMOUTH (H) 9/4 · Result: D 2-2 · Pos 10 · Pts 60 · Att 33,302 · (£3,801.1.9)
Scorers: Atyeo 19p, 44, Siddall 8, Hobbs 40 · Ref: A Howlett

City	Anderson	Guy	Thresher	White	Peacock	Williams	Milton	Atyeo	Rogers	Burden	Boxley
Bournemouth	*Godwin*	*Cunningham*	*Drummond*	*Rushworth*	*Crossland*	*Brown*	*Murray*	*Siddall*	*Hobbs*	*Newsham*	*Harrison*

Denied an early penalty when Rogers is brought down, City fall behind when Barry Siddall shoots in soon after. Atyeo is fouled to bring his spot-kick leveller, but John Hobbs stabs the Cherries back in front. Atyeo's hard drive secures the draw that puts City six points clear of Orient.

Match 41 — SHREWSBURY (H) 11/4 · Result: W 4-1 · Pos 18 · Pts 62 · Att 26,208 · (£3,013.0.0)
Scorers: Rogers 7, Burden 14, 80, Atyeo 88p, Russell 76 · Ref: L Callaghan

City	Anderson	Guy	Thresher	White	Peacock	Williams	Milton	Atyeo	Rogers	Burden	Boxley
Shrewsbury	*McBride*	*Bannister*	*Parr*	*Wallace*	*Maloney*	*Candlin*	*Price*	*O'Donnell*	*Weigh*	*Russell*	*McCue*

After their flying start, when both Rogers and Burden fire into the Covered End net, City do little of note until being shocked by Ray Russell's goal for the visitors. City's Easter's haul of three points from their two games is made even better by Leyton Orient losing all three of theirs.

Match 42 — QP RANGERS (A) 16/4 · Result: D 1-1 · Pos 9 · Pts 63 · Att 12,498
Scorers: Rogers 58, Shepherd 89p · Ref: W Gaiger

City	Anderson	Guy	Thresher	White	Peacock	Williams	Milton	Atyeo	Rogers	Burden	Boxley
QP Rangers	*Brown*	*Wood*	*Ingham*	*Nicholas*	*Rutter*	*Angell*	*Pounder*	*Longbottom*	*Clark*	*Cameron*	*Shepherd*

City's magnificent defence is breached right at the finish to leave them five points clear of Orient, and needing just four points from four games to clinch promotion. Williams trips Albert Pounder to give Ernie Shepherd the last-gasp spot-kick that equalises a Rogers stabbed in effort.

Match 43 — CRYSTAL PALACE (H) 19/4 · Result: W 3-0 · Pos 20 · Pts 65 · Att 27,657 · (£3,136.12.3)
Scorers: Rogers 10, Atyeo 22, 50 · Ref: F Stringer

City	Anderson	Guy	Thresher	White	Peacock	Williams	Milton	Atyeo	Rogers	Burden	Boxley
Crystal Palace	*Macdonald*	*Edwards*	*Greenwood*	*Belcher*	*Saunders*	*Andrews*	*Grieve*	*Berry*	*Hyatt*	*Tilston*	*Gunning*

Rogers is in the right place to shoot in the opener when the keeper can only push out a fierce drive. Atyeo then gets in on the act with a neat header and an easy tap in to leave City needing just two points to be sure of the promotion prize, which will be theirs if Orient lose tomorrow.

Match 44 — NEWPORT (H) 23/4 · Result: D 0-0 · Pos 18 · Pts 66 · Att 27,726 · (£3,203.10.0)
Ref: H Vickers

City	Anderson	Guy	Thresher	White	Peacock	Williams	Milton	Atyeo	Rogers	Burden	Boxley
Newport	*Hughes*	*Lever*	*Lewis*	*Lucas*	*Wilcox*	*Thomas*	*Hudson*	*Graham*	*Johnston*	*Harris*	*Shergold*

No goals but the large crowd at Ashton Gate are happy as they see their heroes presented with the Championship Shield by Arthur Oakley, a senior vice-president of the League. City controlled most of the game, but their forwards failed to click with their customary fluency.

Match 45 — BOURNEMOUTH (A) 27/4 · Result: W 1-0 · Pos 16 · Pts 68 · Att 9,679
Scorers: Milton 33 · Ref: A Howlett

City	Anderson	Guy	Thresher	White	Peacock	Williams	Milton	Atyeo	Rogers	Burden	Boxley
Bournemouth	*Godwin*	*Cunningham*	*Drummond*	*McDonald*	*Crosland*	*Brown*	*Siddall*	*Newsham*	*Hobbs*	*Hunt*	*Allen*

Milton races past Ian Drummond and fires in a grand low cross-shot to secure City's first win at Dean Court since Oct 1924. Despite Atyeo being unlucky with a shot that hits the bar, the Robins are fortunate to survive a rousing second half. A new record points total for the club.

Match 46 — CRYSTAL PALACE (A) 30/4 · Result: W 2-1 · Pos 20 · Pts 70 · Att 14,425
Scorers: Burden 21, Rogers 87, Tilston 44 · Ref: F Stringer

City	Anderson	Guy	Thresher	White	Peacock	Williams	Eisentrager	Atyeo	Rogers	Burden	Boxley
Crystal Palace	*Macdonald*	*Edwards*	*Greenwood*	*Choules*	*Saunders*	*Andrews*	*Barry*	*Belcher*	*Deakin*	*Tilston*	*Gunning*

A seven-yard header secures the win that enables City to equal Nottingham Forest's points record for the Division that was set up four years ago. Burden rolled in City's opener, but Tom Tilston fired a leveller past Anderson (captain against his old club) from a couple of yards out.

Home Average 22,219 · Away 14,654

CUP-TIES

Manager: Pat Beasley

SEASON 1954-55

FA Cup

			F-A	H-T	Scorers, Times, and Referees	1	2	3	4	5	6	7	8	9	10	11
1	H	SOUTHEND	1 L 1:2	1-0	Rodgers 20	Cook	Guy	Jackson	Regan J	Peacock	White	Rogers	Atyeo	Rodgers	Williams	Boxley
	20/11	20,594 8			Hollis 57, 73	Threadgold	Pavitt	Anderson	Burns	Howe	Lawler	Sibley	Bridge	Hollis	Baron	Bainbridge
		(£2,774.1.3)			Ref: W Clements											

City have the day's best Cup crowd, but their fans are unable to inspire them as they give their worst display of the season. The better side early on, Rodgers shooting City in front, the Robins fall away after the break and Roy Hollis fires a double to bring the visitors a deserved win.

Gloucestershire Cup

			F-A	H-T	Scorers, Times, and Referees	1	2	3	4	5	6	7	8	9	10	11
F	A	BRISTOL ROV	1 L 1:2	0-1	Atyeo 89	Anderson	Guy	Thresher	White	Peacock	Williams	Eisentrager	Atyeo	Rogers	Burden	Boxley
	2/5	20,097 2:9			Warren 43, Peacock 58 (og)	Radford	Bamford	Allcock	Pitt	Warren	Sampson	Petherbridge	Biggs	Bradford	Roost	Watling
					Ref: Rev S Davis											

City are out of luck, with Atyeo having his 24th-minute shot struck off as Rogers is offside, then eight minutes from time Harry Bamford hooks out a ball that the visitors claim was over the line. Atyeo heads in brilliantly from White's free-kick, but by then it is very much too late.

	P	W	D	L	F	A	W	D	L	F	A	Pts
			Home					Away				
1 BRISTOL C	46	17	4	2	62	22	13	6	4	39	25	70
2 Leyton Orient	46	16	2	5	48	20	10	7	6	41	27	61
3 Southampton	46	16	6	1	49	19	8	5	10	26	32	59
4 Gillingham	46	12	8	3	41	28	8	7	8	36	38	55
5 Millwall	46	14	6	3	44	25	6	5	12	28	43	51
6 Brighton	46	14	4	5	47	27	6	6	11	29	36	50
7 Watford	46	11	9	3	45	26	5	5	11	26	36	50
8 Torquay	46	12	6	5	51	39	6	6	11	31	43	48
9 Coventry	46	15	5	3	50	26	5	3	13	17	33	47
10 Southend	46	13	5	5	48	28	4	7	12	35	52	46
11 Brentford	46	11	6	6	44	36	5	8	10	38	46	46
12 Norwich	46	13	5	5	40	23	5	13	5	20	37	46
13 Northampton	46	13	5	5	47	27	6	3	14	26	54	46
14 Aldershot	46	12	6	5	44	23	4	7	12	31	48	45
15 QP Rangers	46	13	7	3	46	25	2	7	14	23	50	44
16 Shrewsbury	46	14	5	4	49	24	5	4	16	21	54	42
17 Bournemouth	46	7	8	8	32	29	5	10	8	25	36	42
18 Reading	46	7	10	6	32	26	6	6	12	33	47	41
19 Newport	46	8	8	7	32	29	3	8	12	28	44	38
20 Crys Palace	46	9	11	3	32	24	2	5	16	20	56	38
21 Swindon	46	10	8	5	30	19	1	7	15	16	45	37
22 Exeter	46	9	7	7	30	31	2	8	13	17	42	37
23 Walsall	46	9	6	8	49	36	1	8	14	26	50	34
24 Colchester	46	7	6	10	33	40	2	7	14	20	51	31
	1104	282	153	117	1025	652	117	153	282	652	1025	1104

Odds & ends

Double wins: (11) Millwall, Colchester, Coventry, Walsall, Brighton, Aldershot, Exeter, Watford, Shrewsbury, Reading, Crystal Palace.
Double losses: (0).

Won from behind: (3) Millwall (a), Southend (h), Northampton (h).
Lost from in front: (2) Gillingham (h), Leyton Orient (a).

High spots: Achieving the promotion prize and equalling the record of 70 points set by Nottingham Forest four years ago. The 18-match unbeaten run that concluded the season.

Low spots: Losing at home to Gillingham on 18 December. Being outplayed at Brisbane Road on New Year's Day. The poor spell in January which knocked City off the top of the table. Losing at home to Southend United in the FA Cup.

AGM (Royal Hotel, College Green, Bristol, 30 December 1955): Profit £4,289.8s.0d. Season Ticket Sales £9,095.0s.0d.

Player of the year: John Atyeo and Tommy Burden.
Ever-presents: (1) John Atyeo.
Hat-tricks: (1) Arnold Rodgers.
Leading scorer: Overall John Atyeo (29). League Atyeo (28).

	Appearances		Goals		
	Lge	Cup	Lge	Cup	Tot
Allen, Peter	1				
Anderson, Bob	23	1			
Atyeo, John	46	2	28	1	29
Bailey, Jack	18				
Boxley, Jack	43	2	11		11
Burden, Tommy	27	1	8		8
Cook, Tony	23	1			
Guy, Ivor	45	2			
Eisentrager, Alec	10	1	2		2
Jackson, Norman	7	1			
Micklewright, Andy	3		1		1
Milton, Arthur	14		3		3
Peacock, Ernie	44	2			
Regan, Doug	3				
Regan, Jimmy	22	1			
Rodgers, Arnold	26	1	13	1	14
Rogers, Jimmy	44	2	25		25
Thresher, Mike	22	1			
White, Jack	46	2	2		2
Williams, Cyril	39	2	4		4
(own-goals)			4		4
20 players used	506	22	101	2	103

LEAGUE DIVISION 2

Manager: Pat Beasley

SEASON 1955-56

No	Date	V	Opponent	Res	F-A	H-T	Att (Gate)	Pos	Pt	1	2	3	4	5	6	7	8	9	10	11	Scorers, Times, and Referees
1	20/8	H	SWANSEA	W	2:1	1:0	31,618 (£3,475.18.0)	2	2	Anderson	Guy	Thrasher	White	Peacock	Williams	Regan D	Atyeo	Rogers	Burden	Boxley	Rogers 13, Williams 53 — Ref: R Mann
										King	*Willis*	*Thomas*	*Charles*	*Kiley*	*Burgess*	*Allchurch L*	*Griffiths*	*Medwin*	*Allchurch I*	*Jones C*	*Jones 82*
2	22/8	A	ROTHERHAM	W	3:1	1:0	15,409 (£1,735.18.0)	4	4	Anderson	Guy	Thrasher	White	Peacock	Williams	Eisentrager	Atyeo	Rogers	Burden	Boxley	Eisentrager 35, Rogers 64, Atyeo 65 — Ref: E Hill
										Quairney	*Selkirk*	*Warner*	*Marshall*	*Noble*	*Morgan*	*Grainger*	*Moore*	*Farmer*	*Guest*	*Wilson*	*Farmer 74*
3	27/8	A	NOTTS CO	L	2:3	1:2	14,596	6	4	Anderson	Guy	Thrasher	White	Peacock	Williams	Regan D	Atyeo	Rogers	Burden	Boxley	Williams 11, Atyeo 88p — Ref: J Mitchell
										Bradley	*Southwell*	*Cruikshank*	*Adamson*	*Chatham*	*McGrath*	*Wills*	*Roby*	*Jackson*	*Wylie*	*Crookes*	*Roby 5, Wills 24, Cruikshank 52p*
4	30/8	H	ROTHERHAM	W	5:2	5:1	27,142 (£2,945.0.10)	4	6	Anderson	Guy	Thrasher	White	Peacock	Williams	Eisentrager	Atyeo	Rogers	Burden	Boxley	E'trager 4, Rogers 9, 27, Atyeo 23, [White 39] — Ref: E Hill
										Quairney	*Selkirk*	*Johnston*	*Marshall*	*Noble*	*Keyworth*	*Grainger*	*Moore*	*Farmer*	*Guest*	*Wilson*	*Farmer 21, Grainger 63*
5	3/9	H	LEEDS	L	0:1	0:0	31,060 (£3,445.17.6)	7	6	Anderson	Guy	Thrasher	White	Peacock	Williams	Smith	Eisentrager	Rogers	Burden	Boxley	— Ref: A Smith
										Wood	*Dunn*	*Hair*	*Gibson*	*Charles*	*Kerfoot*	*Williams*	*Ripley*	*Brook*	*Forrest*	*Meek*	*Forrest 81*
6	6/9	H	WEST HAM	W	3:1	2:0	25,993 (£2,827.10.6)	3	8	Cook	Guy	Thrasher	White	Peacock	Williams	Eisentrager	Atyeo	Rodgers	Burden	Boxley	Atyeo 19, Rodgers 25, [Cantwell 68(og)] — Ref: H Haworth
										Taylor	*Wright*	*Cantwell*	*Malcolm*	*Allison*	*O'Farrell*	*Hooper*	*Andrews*	*Dare*	*Dick*	*Tucker*	*Tucker 62*
7	10/9	A	FULHAM	L	0:3	0:1	25,876	8	8	Cook	Guy	Thrasher	White	Peacock	Williams	Eisentrager	Atyeo	Rodgers	Burden	Boxley	— Ref: R Hartley
										Black	*Chenhall*	*Lawler*	*Stapleton*	*Greenwood*	*Lowe E*	*Stevens*	*Robson*	*Jezzard*	*Haynes*	*Milton*	*Haynes 14, Jezzard 80, 85*
8	17/9	H	BURY	W	3:1	2:0	22,949 (£2,493.10.6)	8	10	Cook	Guy	Thrasher	White	Peacock	Williams	Eisentrager	Atyeo	Rodgers	Burden	Boxley	Atyeo 30p, 35, 78 — Ref: A Burnham
										Conway	*Fairclough*	*Massey*	*May*	*Neilson*	*Cockburn*	*Robinson*	*Daniel*	*Kelly*	*Pearson*	*Law*	*Pearson 53*
9	24/9	A	BARNSLEY	D	0:0	0:0	19,545	9	11	Cook	Guy	Thrasher	White	Peacock	Williams	Eisentrager	Atyeo	Rodgers	Burden	Boxley	— Ref: A Bond
										Hough	*Swift*	*Betts*	*Jackson*	*Spruce*	*Jarman*	*Kaye*	*Lumley*	*Brown R*	*Wood*	*Bartlett*	
10	1/10	H	MIDDLESBROUGH	W	2:0	1:0	28,788 (£3,214.2.6)	7	13	Cook	Guy	Thrasher	White	Peacock	Williams	Eisentrager	Atyeo	Rodgers	Burden	Boxley	Atyeo 1, Rodgers 69 — Ref: K Collinge
										Ugolini	*Barnard*	*Stonehouse*	*Harris*	*Robinson*	*Dicks*	*Delapenha*	*Scott*	*Clough*	*Fitzsimmons*	*Mitchell*	

Match reports

1. City are well on top in this game, though Swansea are weakened by the 32nd-minute departure of their player-manager Ronnie Burgess with a leg injury. Burden's perfect pass gives Rogers all the time in the world to fire in the opener. Cliff Jones cleverly back-heels in for the Swans.

2. City have too much pace for the Millers, who are let down by wayward finishing. A lightning 25-yard drive puts City in front. Then after the break Rogers heads in from Regan's free-kick.

3. Atyeo's spot-kick, after John McGrath handles to keep out a shot, comes too late to save City from their first defeat since January. Levelling when a Williams shot deflects into the net off Frank Cruikshank, City should have done better, but are undone by County's disputed penalty.

4. Despite being reduced to nine men late on in the first half (Atyeo 36 & Rogers 43), City romp to a scintillating success. Keeper John Quairney mishandles a lob for Eisentrager to shoot in the first goal at the Open End, then finds himself yorked by White's half-volley for City's fifth.

5. After a silence in memory of former City Chairman George Jenkins, who died this morning, Smith's terrific left-footed 15th-minute drive has Royden Wood needing to produce a great leap to push the ball out for a corner. Robert Forrest runs through to flick in the contest's only goal.

6. The Hammers create plenty of chances and should have salvaged a point. Fortunately, City prove the better finishers - Atyeo's 16-yarder into the Open End net, Rodgers firing home off Noel Cantwell into his own net.

7. In this robust affair City are poor near goal, though Rodgers is unfortunate to head onto the bar before Johnny Haynes nets for the home side with a low left-footed drive. Bedford Jezzard's double (a great cross-shot and a 15-yard cracker) bring Fulham a somewhat flattering scoreline.

8. Atyeo punishes Henry Cockburn for pushing him off of the ball by dispatching the resultant spot-kick to Chris Conway's right, then darts through to crash a great effort into the Bury net. Stan Pearson drives in a response, but Atyeo claims his hat-trick with a close-range shot.

9. City's forwards disappoint in this meeting of last season's Champions of the Northern and Southern Sections of the Third Division. Barnsley play some polished football, but their bustling forwards find themselves constantly thwarted by Cook's brilliance between the sticks for City.

10. With tickets on sale for the local derby, there are still 5,000 fans clamouring to get in at kick-off. Despite both managers requesting a delayed start the referee refuses and Atyeo cracks in a right-footed opener. A lucky goal for Rodgers - the ball just bouncing off of him into the net.

11 H LIVERPOOL 8/10 — 4 W 2:1 — 13 15 — 25,496 (£2,823.14.3)
Atyeo 63, 84 / Rowley 38 / Ref: H Broadhurst — 0-1

Cook	Guy	Thresher	White	Peacock	Williams	Eisentrager	Atyeo	Rogers	Burden	Boxley
Rudham	Molyneux	Moran	Saunders	Hughes	Twentyman	Payne	Rowley	Bimpson	Evans	A'Court

Tony Rowley's pushed in opener from Louis Bimpson's centre is matched by Atyeo's in-off-the-crossbar-shot that brings protests that the ball had not crossed the line. Against a good Liverpool side, there's no doubt about the winner as Atyeo dribbles through to fire past Doug Rudham.

12 A LEICESTER 15/10 — 4 D 2:2 — 12 16 — 28,254
Atyeo 31, Rogers 50 / Rowley 15p, 24 / Ref: W Clements — 1-2

Cook	Guy	Thresher	White	Peacock	Williams	Eisentrager	Atyeo	Rogers	Burden	Boxley
Anderson	Cunningham	Webb	Froggatt	Fincham	Russell	Griffiths	Morris	Hines	Rowley	Hogg

England boss Walter Winterbottom sees Atyeo in great form as City make a fine recovery. Arthur Rowley puts Leicester into the lead with a disputed spot-kick, then heads in to double the advantage. Atyeo nets from a narrow angle, before Rogers hooks the ball in from a few yards.

13 H BRISTOL ROV 22/10 — 5 D 1:1 — 7 17 — 39,583 (£4,503.9.0)
Rogers 78 / Meyer 62 / Ref: R Mann — 0-0

Cook	Guy	Thresher	White	Peacock	Williams	Eisentrager	Atyeo	Rogers	Burden	Boxley
Radford	Bamford	Allcock	Pitt	Warren	Sampson	Petherbridge	Ward	Meyer	Bradford	Hooper

The Rovers have the slight edge in this local derby played before an Ashton Gate record League crowd, but City are handicapped, with the injured White playing up front in the second half. Rogers slams the ball in for City after Barrie Meyer's cross-shot had opened the scoring.

14 A BLACKBURN 29/10 — 2 W 6:4 — 12 19 — 24,695
At'14,81, Eis'18, Box'28, Rog'43, Bur'78 / Briggs 1, 35, Langton 55, Crossan 70 Elv / Ref: H Husband — 4-2

Cook	Guy	Thresher	White	Peacock	Williams	Eisentrager	Atyeo	Rogers	Burden	Boxley
Smith	Eckersley	Clayton R	Binns	Clayton K	Douglas	Crossan	Briggs	Quigley	Langton	

City play great attacking football in this game, which is a thriller right from the outset when Tom Briggs fires in from six yards after just 30 seconds. Atyeo drives in a powerful equaliser before Eisentrager's cracking shot puts City in front. Atyeo's header rounds off a fine display.

15 H HULL 5/11 — 2 W 5:2 — 22 21 — 22,776 (£2,515.0.0)
Pea'26, Aty'42, Rog'51, 80, Eis'64 / Jensen 35p, Cripsey 62 / Ref: L Hamer — 2-1

Cook	Guy	Thresher	White	Peacock	Williams	Eisentrager	Atyeo	Rogers	Burden	Boxley
Fisher	Dennison	Jensen	Martin	Franklyn	Davidson	Smith	Bradbury	Duncan	Patterson	Cripsey

Despite the score and the fact that Atyeo (2) and Eisentrager have goals disallowed, City make hard work of this success. Peacock's free-kick is missed by everyone as it sails high into the net, whilst Guy's handling of Bill Bradbury's header bring the Tigers their equalising penalty.

16 A NOTT'M FOR 12/11 — 2 W 2:0 — 19 23 — 14,295
Atyeo 15, McKinlay 52 (og) / Ref: F Cowan — 1-0

Cook	Guy	Thresher	White	Peacock	Williams	Eisentrager	Atyeo	Rogers	Burden	Boxley
Nicholson	Whare	Thomas	Morley	McKinlay	Regan J / Burkitt	Imlach	Barrett	Higham	Alexander	Jones

City do not have to be at their best to win this contest, the highlight of which is Atyeo's side-footed opener, following a brilliant bout of combination play. A somewhat fortunate second as Harry Nicholson is wrong footed when a Rogers 15-yarder is deflected by Bob McKinlay.

17 H SHEFFIELD WED 19/11 — 1 W 3:2 — 3 25 — 32,731 (£3,675.10.6)
Atyeo 19, Rogers 35, 51 / Broadbent 5, Shiner 47p / Ref: H Vickers — 2-1

Cook	Guy	Thresher	White	Peacock	Williams	Eisentrager	Atyeo	Rogers	Burden	Boxley
Williams !	McEvoy	Bingley	Gibson	Swan	Kay	Wilkinson	Quixall	Shiner	Froggatt	Broadbent

A classic first half, but this game gets over-keen after the break. Albert Broadbent fires Wednesday into an early lead, but Atyeo soon drives in a six-yarder prior to City's contentious winner. Keeper Leslie Williams, in catching Atyeo's header, is bundled over the goal-line by Rogers.

18 A DONCASTER 26/11 — 1 L 2:3 — 16 25 — 11,144
Burden 16, Rogers 22 / McMorran 46, 82, Mooney 48 / Ref: J Jenkins — 2-0

Cook	Guy	Thresher	White	Peacock	Williams	Eisentrager	Atyeo	Rogers	Burden	Boxley
Hardwick	Makepeace	Gavin	Kilkenny	Williams	Teesdale	Mooney	Jeffrey	McMorran	Tindill	Walker

Burden's long shot and a six-yard drive by Rogers in finishing off his great dribble should have had this game won for City, but by the finish they are well-beaten. Ted McMorran's fast low-drive gets Rovers back into the match, and another of his low efforts brings deserved success.

19 H LINCOLN 3/12 — 1 W 5:1 — 11 27 — 26,329 (£2,896.16.0)
Rog'7, Wil'ms 12, Atyeo 25, 59, 62 / Compton 54 (og) / Ref: F Stringer — 3-0

Cook	Guy	Thresher	White	Peacock	Williams	Eisentrager	Atyeo	Rogers	Burden	Boxley
Downie	Graham	Troops	Middleton	Emery	Neal	Munro	Garvie	Northcott	Bannan	Finch

Compton, on his return in place of the injured Peacock, has the misfortune to head the ball into his own net whilst attempting to clear a centre. This, the only headed goal of the game, brings Lincoln, trailing to efforts past Mitchell Downie by Rogers and Williams, back into the contest.

20 A STOKE 10/12 — 1 L 2:4 — 8 27 — 17,042
Rogers 36, Atyeo 69p (Oscroft 60) / Bowyer 15, Graver 23, King 30, / Ref: R Tarratt — 1-3

Cook	Guy	Thresher	White	Peacock	Williams	Eisentrager	Atyeo	Rogers	Burden	Boxley
Robertson	Short	McCue	Mountford	Thomson	Sellars	Coleman	Bowyer	Graver	King	Oscroft

Frank Bowyer is allowed to run through unchallenged to put on the opener with a swerver, then both Andy Graver and John King register with fierce shots before Rogers responds for City with a diving header from Boxley's cross. John McCue's foul on Eisentrager brings the penalty.

21 A SWANSEA 17/12 — 1 L 1:2 — 2 27 — 22,067
Eisentrager 30 / Griffiths 2, Hennings 29 / Ref: R Mann — 1-2

Cook	Guy	Thresher	White	Peacock	Williams	Eisentrager	Atyeo	Rogers	Burden	Boxley
King	Willis	Thomas	Hennings	Charles	Jones B	Allchurch L	Griffiths	Medwin	Allchurch I	Jones C

Over 1,000 City fans see the Swans kick off with a white ball which Harry Griffiths soon heads into the net. Robert Hennings then fires in from 25 yards before Eisentrager registers for City with a clever double-kick. City are unlucky to lose this game of much skill and excitement.

LEAGUE DIVISION 2   Manager: Pat Beasley   SEASON 1955-56

No	Date		Att Pos Pt	F-A	H-T	Scorers, Times, and Referees	1	2	3	4	5	6	7	8	9	10	11
22	24/12	H NOTTS CO	3 L / 24,075 14 27 (£2,659.5.0)	1-3	1-0	Rogers 43 / Taylor 47, 55, Roby 81 / Ref: J Mitchell	Cook	Guy	Thresher	White	Peacock	Williams	Eisentrager	Atyeo	Rogers	Burden	Boxley
							Smith	*Cruikshank*	*Groome*	*Loxley*	*Chatham*	*Johnston*	*Roby*	*Wyllie*	*Jackson*	*Taylor*	*Crookes*
23	26/12	A PLYMOUTH	4 L / 22,983 21 27	0-5	0-2	[Williams 78] / Davis 8, Crawford 38, 71, Davies 56 / Ref: C Porter	Cook	Guy	Thresher	White	Peacock	Regan J	Eisentrager	Atyeo	Rogers	Burden	Boxley
							Shortt	*Robertson*	*Jones*	*Dougall*	*Langman P*	*Wetton*	*Davies*	*Williams*	*Davis*	*Crawford*	*Twissell*
24	27/12	H PLYMOUTH	2 W / 27,716 21 29 (£3,113.16.9)	6-0	3-0	Atyeo 2, 18, Rogers 42, 55, 77, [Burden 72] / Ref: C Porter	Anderson	Guy	Thresher	White	Peacock	Regan J	Virgin	Atyeo	Rogers	Burden	Boxley
							Shortt	*Robertson*	*Jones*	*Dougall*	*Langman P*	*Wetton*	*Davies*	*Williams*	*Davis*	*Crawford*	*Twissell*
25	31/12	A LEEDS	5 L / 31,751 3 29	1-2	0-2	Rogers 46 / Hutchinson 26, Brook 31 / Ref: A Smith	Anderson	Guy	Thresher	White	Peacock	Regan J	Virgin	Eisentrager	Rogers	Burden	Boxley
							Wood	*Dunn*	*Hair*	*Gibson*	*Charlton*	*Kerfoot*	*Hutchinson*	*Brook*	*Charles*	*Vickers*	*Overfield*
26	14/1	H FULHAM	3 W / 27,798 10 31 (£3,105.4.3)	2-1	0-0	Eisentrager 53, Atyeo 64 / Haynes 88 / Ref: F Stringer	Anderson	Guy	Thresher	White	Compton	Williams	Eisentrager	Atyeo	Rogers	Burden	Boxley
							Black	*Wilson*	*Lawler*	*Smith*	*Brice*	*Lowe*	*Hill*	*Robson*	*Jezzard*	*Haynes*	*Mitten*
27	21/1	A BURY	2 D / 13,820 16 32	1-1	0-0	Rogers 47 / Fairclough 82 / Ref: A Burnham	Anderson	Guy	Thresher	White	Peacock	Williams	Eisentrager	Atyeo	Rogers	Burden	Boxley
							McLaren	*Fairclough*	*Massey*	*Daniel*	*Melson*	*Tilley*	*Robinson*	*May*	*Kelly*	*Pearson*	*Lawson*
28	4/2	H BARNSLEY	3 W / 19,581 18 34 (£2,063.17.0)	2-0	1-0	Boxley 17, Atyeo 70 / Ref: A Bond	Anderson	Guy	Thresher	White	Peacock	Williams	Eisentrager	Atyeo	Rogers	Burden	Boxley
							Hough	*Swift*	*Betts*	*Archer*	*Sharp*	*Walters*	*Kaye*	*Brawn R*	*Duggins*	*Graham*	*Bartlett*
29	11/2	A MIDDLESBROUGH	3 L / 15,412 14 34	1-2	1-1	Atyeo 21 / Delapenha 2, Clough 70 / Ref: K Collinge	Anderson	Guy	Thresher	White	Peacock	Williams	Eisentrager	Atyeo	Rogers	Burden	Boxley
							Ugolini	*Barnard*	*Corbett*	*Harris*	*Robinson*	*Dicks*	*Day*	*Scott*	*Clough*	*Fitzsimmons*	*Delapenha*
30	18/2	A SHEFFIELD WED	5 L / 21,925 1 34	1-2	1-1	Burden 4 / Quixall 14, 52 / Ref: H Vickers	Anderson	Jackson	Thresher	White	Peacock	Williams	Hinshelwood	Atyeo	Rogers	Burden	Boxley
							McIntosh	*Staniforth*	*Curtis*	*McAnearney*	*McEvoy*	*O'Donnell*	*Finney*	*Quixall*	*Shiner*	*Froggatt*	*Broadbent*
31	25/2	H LEICESTER	4 D / 27,654 2 35 (£3,069.1.0)	1-1	1-1	Burden 34 / Riley 17 / Ref: W Clements	Anderson	Guy	Thresher	White	Peacock	Williams	Hinshelwood	Atyeo	Rogers	Burden	Boxley
							Anderson	*Cunningham*	*Ogilvie*	*Froggatt*	*Fincham*	*Ward*	*Riley*	*Morris*	*Gardiner*	*Rowley*	*Hogg*

22 — A minute's silence at the start in memory of County star Leon Leuty who died during the week. Rogers crashes in a terrific effort to give City the lead but then County take control with their clever and direct play. John Taylor shoots County level, then puts them ahead with a fine drive.

23 — In the muddy conditions, City's persistence with a close-passing game destroys any chance of a first-ever success at Home Park. Against opponents who fling the ball about and make good use of the wings, City find that Regan's 75th-minute move to centre-forward has no effect.

24 — Argyle contribute much to this fast, accurate game. Atyeo, although not fully recovered from a badly bruised big toe, side-foots in the opener past William Shortt and adds another with a fierce drive. Prior to Rogers crashing in City's third, Eric Davis nets, only to be ruled offside.

25 — City deserved at least a point from this hard-fought match in which they played the more polished football. Rogers heads in from a corner just after the break to celebrate his 25th birthday, but by then both George Hutchinson and Harold Brook had tapped in easy chances for Leeds.

26 — Eisentrager dummies Robin Lawler and runs on to beat Ian Black with a tremendous grounder into the far corner of the net to put City on the way to a deserved victory. Johnny Haynes screws in a late goal for Fulham, but by then Atyeo had headed in from a Rogers centre for City.

27 — As a snowstorm sweeps Gigg Lane, Cyril Fairclough, looking well offside, runs forward to drive the ball past Anderson and rob City of the win that their play deserved. Rogers had given City the lead - hammering in a rebound when Roy McLaren parried his first shot against a post.

28 — Boxley's shot that puts City ahead after Atyeo's header cannons off a defender, brings an acrobatic roll of celebration from skipper White. On a treacherous, ice-bound surface that produces many mistakes, Atyeo's low cross-drive makes sure of the City's well-deserved success.

29 — In his home town, Anderson gives a magnificent display, but cannot save City from defeat. Atyeo's hammer drive, before having a 55th-minute strike disallowed, levels Lloyd Delapenha fired in opener. Brian Clough races on to head in Middlesbrough's deserved winner.

30 — Burden's low first-time shot from Atyeo's knock-down gives City a great start, but they are worn down in the second half. Albert Quixall races through to fire Wednesday level with a perfect ground-shot, then after the half-time break he has all the time in the world to slot in the winner.

31 — Whilst a draw is a fair result of this hard game on a frozen pitch, Hinshelwood, the liveliest of the home forwards, is unfortunate in having his 31st-minute shot struck off for offside. Howard Riley's first-time shot puts the visitors in front, but Burden coolly lobs in City's equaliser.

Bristol City — Match Record (matches 32–42)

No	Date	Venue	Opponent	Pos	Res	FT	HT	Attendance	LgPos	Pts	Receipts	Scorers (City / *opponent*)	Referee
32	3/3	A	BRISTOL ROV	3	W	3:0	1:0	35,198	4	37		Atyeo 41, 73, Rogers 64	Ref: N Taylor
33	10/3	H	STOKE	4	L	0:1	0:1	28,275	12	37	(£3,126.3.0)	*Oscroft 17*	Ref: R Tarratt
34	17/3	A	HULL	4	W	3:1	1:0	11,174	22	39	(£1,019)	Rodgers 29, Atyeo 55, Hinshelw'd 89 / *Jensen 88p*	Ref: L Hamer
35	24/3	H	NOTT'M FOR	4	D	0:0	0:0	22,824	10	40	(£2,468.10.6)		Ref: F Cowan
36	30/3	A	PORT VALE	6	L	0:2	0:1	24,900	3	40		*Smith 43, 78*	Ref: R Tarratt
37	31/3	A	LIVERPOOL	7	L	1:2	1:0	46,713	2	40		Atyeo 18 / *Arnell 74, Evans 88p*	Ref: H Broadhurst
38	2/4	H	PORT VALE	8	D	0:0	0:0	24,348	4	41	(£2,643.1.0)		Ref: R Tarratt
39	7/4	H	DONCASTER	5	W	4:1	0:1	20,777	17	43	(£2,192.5.6)	Rogers 53, 64, 87, Atyeo 76 / *Tindill 17*	Ref: E Jennings
40	14/4	A	LINCOLN	8	L	0:2	0:1	10,313	12	43		*Withers 19, Gibson 79*	Ref: F Stringer
41	21/4	H	BLACKBURN	7	W	2:0	2:0	20,554	8	45	(£2,184.12.0)	Rogers 3, Burden 35	Ref: H Husband
42	28/4	A	WEST HAM	8	L	0:3	0:1	13,534	15			*Blackburn 41, Sexton 65, 68*	Ref: H Haworth

Home Average 26,575   Away 20,983

Line-ups (City players, *opponents in italic*)

No	1	2	3	4	5	6	7	8	9	10	11
32	Anderson	Guy	Thresher	White	Peacock	Williams	Hinshelwood	Atyeo	Rogers	Burden	Boxley
32	*Nicholls*	*Bamford*	*Allcock*	*Pitt*	*Hale*	*Sampson*	*Petherbridge*	*Biggs*	*Meyer*	*Ward*	*Watling*
33	Anderson	Guy	Thresher	White	Peacock	Williams	Hinshelwood	Atyeo	Rogers	Burden	Boxley
33	*Robertson*	*Whiston*	*McCue*	*Cairns*	*Thomson*	*Sellars*	*Coleman*	*Bowyer*	*Graver*	*Kelly*	*Oscroft*
34	Anderson	Guy	Thresher	White	Peacock	Williams	Hinshelwood	Atyeo	Rodgers	Burden	Smith
34	*Bly*	*Neal*	*Jensen*	*Davidson*	*Feasey*	*Bulless*	*Smith*	*Bradbury*	*Mortensen*	*Clarke*	*Cripsey*
35	Anderson	Guy	Thresher	White	Peacock	Williams	Hinshelwood	Atyeo	Rodgers	Burden	Boxley
35	*Nicholson*	*Whare*	*Thomas*	*Morley*	*McKinlay*	*Burkitt*	*Small*	*Scott*	*Higham*	*Lishman*	*Imlach*
36	Anderson	Guy	Thresher	White	Peacock	Williams	Hinshelwood	Atyeo	Rogers	Burden	Boxley
36	*King*	*Turner*	*Potts*	*Leake*	*Hayward*	*Sproson*	*Cunliffe*	*Stephenson*	*Smith*	*Baily*	*Bennett*
37	Anderson	Guy	White	White	Peacock	Williams	Hinshelwood	Atyeo	Rogers	Burden	Boxley
37	*Underwood*	*Molyneux*	*Moran*	*Twentyman*	*Hughes*	*Simpson*	*Anderson*	*Arnell*	*Evans*		*A'Court*
38	Anderson	Guy	Thresher	White	Peacock	Williams	Hinshelwood	Atyeo	Rogers	Burden	Boxley
38	*King*	*Turner*	*Potts*	*Leake*	*Hayward*	*Sproson*	*Cunliffe*	*Baily*	*Stephenson*	*Griffiths*	*Bennett*
39	Anderson	Guy	Bailey	White	Peacock	Burden	Hinshelwood	Atyeo	Rogers	Eisentrager	Boxley
39	*Gregg*	*Makepeace*	*Graham*	*Hunt*	*Williams*	*Teasdale*	*Mooney*	*Jeffrey*	*McMorran*	*Tindill*	*Walker G*
40	Anderson	Guy	Bailey	White	Peacock	Burden	Hinshelwood	Atyeo	Rogers	Eisentrager	Boxley
40	*Downie*	*Graham*	*Troops*	*Middleton*	*Emery*	*Brown*	*Munro*	*Gibson*	*Northcott*	*Bannan*	*Withers*
41	Cook	Steel	Bailey	White	Peacock	Compton	Hinshelwood	Eisentrager	Rogers	Burden	Boxley
41	*Elvy*	*Taylor*	*Eckersley*	*Clayton R*	*Bell*	*Kelly*	*Douglas*	*Smith*	*Briggs*	*Quigley*	*Langton*
42	Cook	Steel	Bailey	White	Peacock	Compton	Hinshelwood	Eisentrager	Rogers	Burden	Boxley
42	*Gregory*	*Bond*	*Cantwell*	*Parker*	*Brown*	*Lansdowne*	*Dare*	*Sexton*	*Blackburn*	*Smith*	*Tucker*

Match reports

32. No complaints from the Rovers when Atyeo bundled Ron Nicholls and the ball over the line to put City in front. Atyeo's great 15-yard right-foot effort ties up a decisive victory, after having earlier seen his shot bounce off of the bar for Rogers to rush in and head the ball into the net.

33. After the Lord Mayor's show again as City never recovered from a slow start. Harry Oscroft shoots the Potters into an early lead and thereafter City are never good enough to beat the visiting defence. The City up the tempo after the interval, but Stoke hold out by pulling everyone back.

34. City's hard-pressed defence is much indebted to Anderson in this poor game. Rodgers calmly shoots the opener into the corner of the net, then Atyeo's blasts in from 12 yards, before a supposed foul by Peacock brings Hull their spot-kick. Hinshelwood ends the scoring from 12 yards.

35. City's attack is badly off form in this game, which is well below the standard that is required of two teams in the promotion hunt. Jack Burkitt has his name taken for his first-half tackle on Boxley. Disappointment two minutes from time when offside rules out Atyeo's great header.

36. Skilful City have the edge, but Vale go ahead with their only first-half effort of note. Anderson drops Roy Sproson's shot to give Stan Smith his easy tap in. Denied by the woodwork and defenders on the line, City are further undone - Anderson caught out by Smith's half-hit effort.

37. Despite being down to ten men throughout the whole of the second half (Eric Anderson missing, following his injury), Liverpool secure the points. Alan Arnell hooks home to level Atyeo's rolled-in opener, then Peacock punches the ball out give John Evans his spot-kick winner.

38. With only one goal to show for some fine football over the three Easter games, City have practically dropped out of the promotion race. They make and waste many chances in this game, even Atyeo firing wide from the spot in the 38th minute after being brought down by Reg Potts.

39. Trailing to Bert Tindill's rolled-in effort, City are fortunate that Alick Jeffrey shoots straight at Anderson when clean through just before half-time. Rogers has plenty of time to hit the leveller when a Rodgers header comes back off of a post. Two more shots bring Rogers his hat-trick.

40. Below-form City are hard pressed at Sincil Bank, where Lincoln run out easy winners. Burden has to clear off the line early on before Alan Withers nets with a grand shot from ten yards. City look well beaten before the finish and it is no surprise when Colin Gibson heads in.

41. City's bright first-half display brings victory over a Blackburn side whose promotion hopes disappear with this defeat. Rogers put City in front when he darts past William Kelly and hooks the ball round Reg Elvy into an open net. Burden turns in City's second from a Rogers pass.

42. City are well beaten at dusty Upton Park, where hardly a blade of grass is in evidence. Cook makes a number of great saves before Alan Blackburn heads in the opener just before the interval. Two unstoppable shots from Dave Sexton wrap up West Ham's end of season stroll.

CUP-TIES

Manager: Pat Beasley

SEASON 1955-56

FA Cup

			F-A	H-T	Scorers, Times, and Referees	1	2	3	4	5	6	7	8	9	10	11
3	A EVERTON	5 L	1:3	0-1	Atyeo 88 [Harris J 80]	Anderson	Guy	Thresher	White	Peacock	Williams	Virgin	Atyeo	Rogers	Burden	Boxley
	7/1				Eglington 12, Wainwright 75,	O'Neill	Moore	Tansley	Farrell	Jones	Leila	Harris B	Wainwright	Harris J	Fielding	Eglington
	46,493 1:7				Ref: J Williams											
	(£6,488.17.6)															

Superior skill brings Everton a rather flattering victory against a City side who spurn many chances. Star man Tom Eglington thumps the Toffees into an early lead. Ted Wainwright heads in a second and Jimmy Harris fires in another, before Atyeo powers in City's late reply.

Gloucestershire Cup

			F-A	H-T	Scorers, Times, and Referees	1	2	3	4	5	6	7	8	9	10	11
F	H BRISTOL ROV	11 L	0-1	0-1	Meyer 10	Cook	Guy	Bailey	White	Peacock	Williams	Hinshelwood	Atyeo	Rogers	Eisentrager	Boxley
	30/4	11,952 6			Ref: R Mann	Radford	Bamford	Edwards	Sykes	Hale	Sampson	Petherbridge	Biggs	Roost	Meyer	Hooper
	(£1,711)															

Rovers have the edge in this keen tussle. They twice come close to scoring before Barrie Meyer registers with a right-footed shot at the Open End from George Petherbridge's corner. Prior to the break, Bill Roost fires against a post and Howard Radford does well to save from Atyeo.

	P	W	D	L	F	A	W	D	L	F	A	Pts
			Home						Away			
1 Sheffield Wed	42	13	5	3	60	28	6	3	12	41	34	55
2 Leeds	42	17	3	1	51	18	6	3	12	29	42	52
3 Liverpool	42	14	4	3	52	25	7	3	11	33	38	48
4 Blackburn	42	13	4	4	55	29	8	2	11	29	36	48
5 Leicester	42	15	3	3	63	23	6	3	12	31	55	48
6 Bristol Rov	42	13	3	5	53	33	8	3	10	31	37	47
7 Nottm Forest	42	9	5	7	30	26	10	4	7	38	37	46
8 Lincoln	42	14	5	2	49	17	4	5	12	30	48	46
9 Fulham	42	15	2	4	59	27	5	4	12	30	52	46
10 Swansea	42	14	4	3	49	23	6	2	13	34	58	45
11 BRISTOL C	42	14	4	3	49	20	5	3	13	31	44	45
12 Port Vale	42	12	4	5	38	21	4	9	8	22	37	45
13 Stoke	42	13	2	6	47	27	7	2	12	24	35	44
14 Middlesboro	42	11	4	6	46	31	5	4	12	30	47	40
15 Bury	42	9	5	7	44	39	7	3	11	42	51	40
16 West Ham	42	12	4	5	52	27	7	2	12	22	42	39
17 Doncaster	42	11	5	5	45	30	1	6	14	24	66	35
18 Barnsley	42	10	5	6	33	35	1	7	13	14	49	34
19 Rotherham	42	7	5	9	29	34	5	4	12	27	41	33
20 Notts Co	42	8	5	8	39	37	3	4	14	16	45	31
21 Plymouth	42	7	6	8	33	25	4	2	16	21	62	28
22 Hull	42	6	4	11	32	45	4	2	15	21	52	26
	924	257	90	115	1008	620	115	90	257	620	1008	924

Odds & ends

Double wins: (3) Rotherham, Blackburn, Hull.
Double losses: (2) Notts Co, Leeds, Stoke.

Won from behind: (4) Liverpool (h), Blackburn (a), Sheffield Wed (h), Doncaster (h).
Lost from in front: (3) Doncaster (a), Sheffield Wed (a), Liverpool (a).

High spots: City's play up until the turn of the year, when they looked a good bet for further promotion.
The thrilling 6-4 success at Ewood Park on 29 October.
Beating Sheffield Wednesday on 19 November to go top of the table.

Low spots: Dropping out of the promotion race in the spring.
The poor performance at Upton Park that concluded the season.

AGM (Royal Hotel, College Green, Bristol, 2 April 1957):
Profit £7,699.10s.5d. Season Ticket Sales £16,869.0s.0d.

Player of the year: John Atyeo and Jimmy Rogers.
Ever-presents: (0).
Hat-tricks: (4) John Atyeo (2), Jimmy Rogers (2).
Leading scorer: Overall: John Atyeo (31). League: John Atyeo (30).

	Appearances		Goals		
	Lge	Cup	Lge	Cup	Tot
Anderson, Bob	22				
Atyeo, John	39	2	30	1	31
Bailey, Jack	6	1			
Boxley, Jack	40	2	2		2
Burden, Tommy	41	1	6		6
Compton, Terry	4				
Cook, Tony	20	1			
Guy, Ivor	39	2			
Eisentrager, Alec	32	1	6		6
Hinshelwood, Wally	10	1	1		1
Jackson, Norman	1				
Peacock, Ernie	40	2	1		1
Regan, Doug	3				
Regan, Jimmy	4				
Rodgers, Arnold	10		3		3
Rogers, Jimmy	34	2	25		25
Smith, David	3				
Steel, Richard	2				
Thresher, Mike	35	1			
Virgin, Derek	2	1			
White, Jack	41	2	1		1
Williams, Cyril	34	2	3		3
(own-goals)			2		2
22 players used	462	22	80	1	81

LEAGUE DIVISION 2

Manager: Pat Beasley

SEASON 1956-57

Match results

No	Date	Pos	Res	F-A	H-T	Att	Receipts	Pt	Scorers, Times, and Referees
1	A LINCOLN 18/8		D	1-1	0-0	12,727		1	Atyeo 55 / *Bannan 52*, Ref: W Hickson
2	H NOTT'M FOR 21/8		L	1-5	0-2	27,898	(£3,020.10.4)	1	Atyeo 84 / *Morley 11, Lishman 19, 82, [Barrett 59, 73]* Ref: J Hunt
3	H ROTHERHAM 25/8	12 / 20	W	2-1	2-0	21,241	(£2,260.5.6)	3	Atyeo 8, 29 / *Hunter 72*, Ref: A Bond
4	A NOTT'M FOR 30/8	14 / 2	D	2-2	1-1	23,172		4	Smith 25, Atyeo 88 / *Wilson 17, McKinlay 80*, Ref: J Hunt
5	A PORT VALE 1/9	17 / 16	L	1-3	0-2	17,645		4	Rogers 61 / *Done 9, Smith 42, 46*, Ref: R Mann
6	H FULHAM 4/9	18 / 16	L	0-3	0-3	22,675	(£2,482.4.6)	4	/ *Chamb'in 6, Stevens 28, Dwight 36*, Ref: K Collinge
7	H BARNSLEY 8/9	20 / 13	L	1-2	1-1	19,863	(£2,095.17.6)	4	Atyeo 1 / *Brown 15, McCann 57*, Ref: J Mitchell
8	A FULHAM 12/9	20 / 10	L	1-2	1-1	15,110		4	Hinshelwood 32 / *Chamberlain 40, Hill 66*, Ref: K Collinge
9	A SHEFFIELD UTD 15/9	20 / 2	D	1-1	0-0	22,490		5	Atyeo 83 / *Wilkinson 85*, Ref: L Clarke
10	H BRISTOL ROV 22/9	18 / 7	W	5-3	1-1	37,207	(£4,117.18.0)	7	Atyeo 22, 68, Williams 46, 48, *Ward 3, 74, Biggs 60* [Hinsh'wood 77], Ref: N Taylor

Line-ups (City player / *opponent*)

No	1	2	3	4	5	6	7	8	9	10	11
1	Cook A / *Downie*	Baillie / *Graham*	Thresher / *Troops*	White / *Middleton*	Peacock / *Emery*	Williams C / *Neal*	Hinshelwood / *Munro*	Eisentrager / *Gibson*	Atyeo / *Northcott*	Burden / *Bannan*	Boxley / *Finch*
2	Cook A / *Farmer*	Baillie / *Whare*	Thresher / *Thomas*	White / *Morley*	Peacock / *McKinlay*	Williams C / *Burkitt*	Hinshelwood / *Small*	Eisentrager / *Barrett*	Atyeo / *Wilson*	Burden / *Lishman*	Boxley / *Imlach*
3	Cook A / *Scrivens*	Baillie / *Selkirk*	Thresher / *Morgan*	White / *Neilson*	Peacock / *Noble*	Williams C / *Williams*	Eisentrager / *Grainger*	Atyeo / *Moore*	Rogers / *Farmer*	Burden / *Slater*	Smith / *Hunter*
4	Cook A / *Farmer*	Baillie / *Whare*	Thresher / *Thomas*	White / *Morley*	Compton / *McKinlay*	Williams C / *Burkitt*	Hinshelwood / *Small*	Atyeo / *Barrett*	Rogers / *Wilson*	Eisentrager / *Lishman*	Smith / *Imlach*
5	Cook A / *King*	Baillie / *Turner*	Thresher / *Potts*	White / *Poole*	Compton / *Hayward*	Williams C / *Sproson*	Eisentrager / *Askey*	Atyeo / *Smith*	Rogers / *Bally*	Burden / *Done*	Smith / *Stephenson*
6	Anderson / *Black*	Guy / *Collins*	Thresher / *Lawler*	White / *Stapleton*	Compton / *Lampe*	Baillie / *Lowe*	Eisentrager / *Stevens*	Atyeo / *Hill*	Rogers / *Dwight*	Burden / *Haynes*	Smith / *Chamberlain*
7	Anderson / *Hough*	Guy / *Thomas*	Thresher / *Swift*	White / *Smith*	Peacock / *Spruce*	Burden / *Walters*	Hinshelwood / *Kaye*	Atyeo / *Storey*	Rogers / *Brown*	Eisentrager / *Graham*	Boxley / *McCann*
8	Cook A / *Black*	Guy / *Collins*	Thresher / *Lawler*	White / *Stapleton*	Compton / *Lampe*	Burden / *Lowe*	Hinshelwood / *Stevens*	Atyeo / *Hill*	Rogers / *Dwight*	Williams C / *Haynes*	Smith / *Chamberlain*
9	Cook A / *Burgin*	Guy / *Shaw G*	Thresher / *Mason*	White / *Hoyland*	Compton / *J Shaw*	Burden / *Iley*	Hinshelwood / *Hawksworth*	Atyeo / *Spencer*	Rogers / *Wilkinson*	Williams C / *Howitt*	Smith / *Grainger*
10	Cook A / *Radford*	Guy / *Bamford*	Thresher / *Lawrence*	White / *Pitt*	Compton / *Hale*	Burden / *Sampson*	Hinshelwood / *Petherbridge*	Atyeo / *Biggs*	Rogers / *Meyer*	Williams C / *Ward*	Smith / *Hooper*

Match reports

1. A fine goal by Atyeo, coolly beating the keeper after racing clear on Hinshelwood's pass, brings City a deserved point at Sincil Bank. City create the better chances, but it is the Imps who go in front when Tommy Bannan's header finds the net despite Baille's great effort to clear.

2. City are unable to match the speed and skill of the visitors, who have lost just once away since December. Cook is surprised by Bill Morley's shot and then Doug Lishman fires through before Atyeo has his 25th-minute spot-kick saved. The best of the game is City's 18-yard cracker.

3. Handicapped by Peacock's first-half injury, which leaves him a limping passenger, City hold on grimly to win this hard-fought game. Atyeo's pair (a side-footed effort followed by a thunderbolt) secures the points, despite John Hunter's clever angled drive into the far corner of the net.

4. After Bill McKinlay's half-volley appeared to have won the game for Forest, Atyeo earns City a well-deserved point. Seizing on Eisentrager's pass down the middle he races past two defenders before slipping the ball past William Farmer to deprive the home side of their 100% record.

5. Against winless Vale, City are up against it when Cook makes no attempt to save Cyril Done's 16-yard angled drive. Rogers hooks in when the ball cannons off the crossbar, but it is City's only response to Stan Smith's low shot just before the break, and his acute-angled lob soon after.

6. With the floodlights coming on City's play improves in this their first ever League game to be completed under artificial lighting. City not only hold rampant Fulham to their half-time advantage, but should have got among the goals. Eisentrager fires a 79th-minute spot-kick over the bar.

7. Despite the encouragement of Atyeo beating Harry Hough with a perfectly judged shot after just 30 seconds, City are no match for Barnsley. Anderson makes a mess of trying to punch-out Bob Brown's 20-yarder and ragged City get the jeers when John McCann runs clear on goal.

8. Attack-minded City are twice thwarted by the crossbar as well as having shots kicked off the line. Hinshelwood shoots City in front with a low right-footed effort, but Jimmy Hill gets through to secure the points for Fulham after Tosh Chamberlain levelled with a narrow-angled swerver.

9. City's fine display is rewarded by a share of the spoils thanks to Cook saving Colin Grainger's 75th-minute spot-kick, when John Wilkinson is tripped by White. After Atyeo had rolled the ball past Ted Burgin, Wilkinson's slammed in effort prevents City from taking all the points.

10. A record eight-goal haul for the Bristol derby finds City triumphant at the finish, despite the shock of going behind to Dai Ward's right-footed cross-drive. After Atyeo heads City level, they take the lead when Smith's header, which is going wide, is diverted into the net off of Williams.

City Match Record (Matches 11–21)

11 — H BLACKBURN, 29/9 — Pos 15 — W 3-0 — 19/9 — Att 23,323 (£2,514.0.6)
Scorers: Rogers 20, 88, Atyeo 52
Ref: S Barker

City	Cook A	Guy	Thresher	White	Compton	Burden	Hinshelwood	Rogers	Atyeo	Boxley	Smith
Blackburn	*Leyland*	*Taylor*	*Bell*	*Clayton R*	*Binns*	*Clayton K*	*Douglas*	*Briggs*	*Dobing*	*Crossan*	*McLead*

Atyeo burst through the middle before setting Rogers up to crash in the opener, then Rogers returns the compliment by heading back for the City's No 8 to slam in another. Atyeo's firmly placed shot just before the finish ties up a success in which Hinshelwood is City's mainstay.

12 — A NOTTS CO, 6/10 — Pos 13 — D 1-1 — 22/10 — Att 12,005
Scorers: Williams 9; Lane 43
Ref: W Clements

City	Cook A	Guy	Thresher	Peacock	Compton	Burden	Hinshelwood	Rogers	Atyeo	Williams C	Smith
Notts Co	*Smith*	*Southwell*	*Maddison*	*Loxley*	*Chatham*	*Jackson*	*Lane*	*Roby*	*Russell*	*Carver*	*Wills*

Both teams wear black armbands and observe a minute's silence in memory of City reserve Colin Read, who was shot and killed in an ambush in Cyprus last week. In a poor game, a first-time drive gives City the advantage, but John Lane rams in an equaliser for a raged County side.

13 — H LIVERPOOL, 13/10 — Pos 12 — W 2-1 — 14/12 — Att 26,263 (£2,867.9.0)
Scorers: Williams 15, Rogers 89; Wheeler 8
Ref: A Bond

City	Cook A	Guy	Thresher	White	Compton	Burden	Hinshelwood	Rogers	Atyeo	Williams C	Smith
Liverpool	*Younger*	*Molyneux*	*Moran*	*Wilkinson*	*Hughes*	*Saunders*	*Simpson*	*Wheeler*	*Liddell*	*Anderson*	*A'Court*

Liverpool forfeit their unbeaten away record in the dying seconds, when Tom Younger gets his hands to, but fails to hold Rogers' full-powered drive. A deserved City success as Williams had a goal disallowed barely two minutes earlier. Both first-half goals in this thriller are headed in.

14 — A MIDDLESBROUGH, 20/10 — Pos 14 — L 1-4 — 7/12 — Att 23,824
Scorers: Rogers 68; Clough 37, 55, Delapenha 69
Ref: F Collinge

City	Cook A	Baillie	Thresher	White	Compton	Burden	Hinshelwood	Rogers	Atyeo	Williams	Smith
Middlesbrough	*Million*	*Bernard*	*Stonehouse*	*Harris*	*Robinson*	*Dicks*	*Delapenha*	*McLean*	*Clough*	*Fitzsimmons*	*Burbeck*

Brian Clough gives City due warning with several terrific shots before firing in a twelve-yard opener. Rogers slams in for City after a well-judged ground shot had doubled Middlesbrough's advantage, but almost immediately Lloyd Delaphena crashes in an unstoppable six-yarder.

15 — H HUDDERSFIELD, 27/10 — Pos 12 — W 2-1 — 9/14 — Att 25,111 (£2,730.16.0)
Scorers: Atyeo 61, Burden 69; Hickson 89 [Harris 85]
Ref: A Westwood

City	Cook A	Guy	Thresher	White	Compton	Burden	Hinshelwood	Rogers	Atyeo	Williams C	Smith
Huddersfield	*Kennon*	*Conwell*	*Wilson*	*McGarry*	*Taylor*	*Quested*	*Marriott*	*Watson*	*Hickson*	*Simpson*	*Metcalfe*

Huddersfield are slightly the more impressive side before the break, but Atyeo's powerful header and a magnificent shot by Burden puts City in control. Dave Hickson heads in Town's close-range reply, but it comes much too late to deny City a deserved win over the skilful visitors.

16 — A BURY, 3/11 — Pos 11 — W 3-2 — 22/16 — Att 9,641
Scorers: Hinshelwood 5, 75, Williams 84; Cleadell 23, Pearson 40
Ref: E Jennings

City	Cook A	McLaren	Thresher	White	Compton	Burden	Hinshelwood	Rogers	Atyeo	Williams C	Smith
Bury	*McLaren*	*Tilley*	*Massey*	*Daniel*	*Nielson*	*Quigley*	*Robinson*	*Gleadell*	*May*	*Pearson*	*Robertson*

The Shakers, without a home win since August, provide City with their first away win. Hinshelwood crashes in the early opener, then – after Eddie Gleadall's 25 yarder and Stan Pearson's header – puts City back on par with a rare header. An innocent looking shot wins the game.

17 — H GRIMSBY, 10/11 — Pos 15 — L 0-2 — 16/16 — Att 19,202 (£2,029.0.0)
Scorers: Scott 42, Maddison 68
Ref: J Kelly

City	Cook A	Guy	Thresher	White	Compton	Burden	Hinshelwood	Rogers	Atyeo	Williams C	Boxley
Grimsby	*Williams*	*Brown*	*De Gruchy*	*Conner*	*Johnston*	*Richardson*	*Scott*	*Evans*	*Hodgson*	*Priestley*	*Maddison*

City are well beaten by much quicker opponents, who move the ball accurately. At a time when the game badly needed a goal, John Scott hammered in from nine yards to put the Mariners in front, then James Maddison has all the time he needed to shot past Cook from close in.

18 — A DONCASTER, 17/11 — Pos 15 — L 1-4 — 7/16 — Att 12,472 (£1,863.5.6)
Scorers: White 2p; Walker R 20, Walker G 58, 71, [McMorran 80]
Ref: H Haworth

City	Cook A	Guy	Bailey	White	Compton	Burden	Hinshelwood	Walker	Rogers	Burden	Boxley
Doncaster	*Gregg*	*Makepeace*	*Graham*	*Gavin*	*Williams*	*Ewing*	*Mooney*	*Walker R*	*McMorran*	*Cavanagh*	*Walker G*

Despite taking an early lead, courtesy of Charlie Williams felling Walker, City are unable to match their determined opponents. Geoff Walker knows little when he deflects Tommy Ewing's cross into the net to put his side ahead at the break when Harry Gregg is off receiving treatment.

19 — H STOKE, 24/11 — Pos 16 — L 1-2 — 7/16 — Att 18,022
Scorers: Watkins 80; Kelly 10, Coleman 40
Ref: K Aston

City	Cook A	Guy	Thresher	White	Compton	Burden	Hinshelwood	Eisentrager	Rogers	Williams C	Watkins
Stoke	*Robertson*	*Mountford*	*McCue*	*Sellars*	*Thomson*	*Cairns*	*Coleman*	*Bowyer*	*King*	*Kelly*	*Oscroft*

City's slide continues, but they show plenty of fight in the second half when Watkins finds the net with a powerful first-timer. George Kelly side-foots the visitors in front from John King's centre, then Thresher deflects the ball to Neville Coleman, who fires in the Potters second.

20 — A LEYTON ORIENT, 1/12 — Pos 16 — D 2-2 — 8/17 — Att 17,752
Scorers: Walker 8, Hinshelwood 10; White 11, Johnson 89
Ref: N Hough

City	Cook A	Guy	Thresher	White	Compton	Burden	Hinshelwood	Walker	Atyeo	Baillie	Watkins
Leyton Orient	*Groombridge*	*Gregory*	*Willemse*	*Facey*	*Aldous*	*McKnight*	*White*	*Sexton*	*Johnston*	*Heckman*	*Smith*

With Ron Heckman hobbling after the break, Tom Johnston's saves the home side with a late goal, which is allowed to stand despite protests for pushing. Walker bundles in the opener and Hinshelwood's first-timer doubles City's advantage, before Phil White fires in for Orient.

21 — H LEICESTER, 8/12 — Pos 16 — L 0-1 — 1/17 — Att 24,757 (£2,702.19.0)
Scorers: McNeill 17, 75
Ref: E Jennings

City	Cook A	Guy	Thresher	White	Compton	Burden	Hinshelwood	Rogers	Curtis	Baillie	Watkins
Leicester	*Anderson*	*Milburn*	*Ogilvie*	*Morris*	*Froggatt*	*Ward*	*McDonald*	*McNeill*	*Hines*	*Rowley*	*Hogg*

The Filberts go top of the table after this convincing success at Ashton Gate, where Eire international Dermot Curtis makes his City debut. Ian McNeill heads the ball down into the corner of the net for Leicester's opener, then, after the break, stabs the ball in to make sure of the points.

LEAGUE DIVISION 2   Manager: Pat Beasley   SEASON 1956-57

Match details

No	Date	V	Opponents	Result	F–A	H–T	Att	Opp Pos	Pt	Pos	City scorers	Opp scorers	Referee
22	15/12	H	LINCOLN	W	**5-1**	1-1	**12,772** (£1,286.18.6)	14	19	15	Watkins 35, Hinshelwood 62, 68, Atyeo 71, Curtis 75	Northcott 29	W Hickson
23	22/12	A	ROTHERHAM	L	**1-6**	1-2	**4,669** (£459)	18	19	19	Peacock 12	Johnson 53, 70, Slater 22, 81, Grainger 27, 56	A Bond
24	26/12	A	SWANSEA	L	0-5	0-1	**17,954**	14	19	19	—	Charles 35, 48, Allchurch I 50, Palmer 72, Allchurch L 74	B Griffiths
25	29/12	H	PORT VALE	D	3-3	3-2	**18,561** (£1,913.11.6)	20	20	19	Etheridge 3, Curtis 16, Burden 42	Hayward 43p, Poole 44, 66	R Mann
26	12/1	A	BARNSLEY	L	0-3	0-1	**13,517**	15	20	19	—	Edgar 32, Bartlett 67, Kaye 84	J Mitchell
27	19/1	H	SHEFFIELD UTD	W	**5-1**	3-1	**19,968** (£2,087.5.0)	7	22	19	Etheridge 24, Williams 32, Atyeo 33, 80, 85	Hawksworth 35	J Baxter
28	2/2	A	BRISTOL ROV	D	0-0	0-0	**32,055**	9	23	19	—	—	N Taylor
29	9/2	A	BLACKBURN	L	1-3	1-1	**25,986**	4	23	19	Williams C 25	McLeod 27, Douglas 71, Dobing 73	S Barker
30	20/2	H	NOTTS CO	W	3-0	3-0	**19,288** (£1,969.1.6)	22	25	18	Atyeo 16, Williams C 18, Watkins 25p	—	W Clements
31	2/3	H	MIDDLESBROUGH	W	2-1	2-1	**22,402** (£2,353.6.6)	10	27	18	Etheridge 10, Watkins 43p	McLean 21	F Collinge

Line-ups (Bristol City)

No	1	2	3	4	5	6	7	8	9	10	11
22	Cook A	Guy	Thresher	Peacock	Compton	Burden	Hinshelwood	Atyeo	Curtis	**Etheridge**	Watkins
23	Cook A	Guy	Thresher	Peacock	Compton	Burden	Hinshelwood	Atyeo	Curtis	Etheridge	Watkins
24	Anderson	Guy	Bailey	Peacock	Compton	Burden	Hinshelwood	Eisentrager	Curtis	Etheridge	Watkins
25	Anderson	Guy	Bailey	White	Peacock	Burden	Hinshelwood	Eisentrager	Curtis	Etheridge	Watkins
26	Anderson	Guy	Bailey	White	Peacock	Burden	Hinshelwood	Atyeo	Curtis	Etheridge	Watkins
27	Anderson	Guy	Bailey	White	Peacock	Burden	Hinshelwood	Williams C	Atyeo	Etheridge	Watkins
28	Anderson	Bailey	Thresher	White	Peacock !	Burden	Hinshelwood	Williams C	Atyeo	Etheridge	Watkins
29	Anderson	Guy	Bailey	Burden	White	Williams C	Hinshelwood	Williams C	Atyeo	Etheridge	Watkins
30	Anderson	Guy	Bailey	Burden	White	Williams A	Hinshelwood	Williams C	Atyeo	Etheridge	Watkins
31	Anderson	Bailey	Thresher	Burden	White	Williams A	Hinshelwood	Williams C	Atyeo	Etheridge	Watkins

Line-ups (Opponents, italic in original)

No	1	2	3	4	5	6	7	8	9	10	11
22	*Downie*	*Graham*	*Troops*	*Middleton*	*Emery*	*Neal*	*Munro*	*Bannan*	*Northcott*	*Watson*	*Finch*
23	*Quairney*	*Selkirk*	*Morgan*	*Keyworth*	*Noble*	*Williams*	*Grainger*	*Stephenson*	*Johnson*	*Slater*	*Bambridge*
24	*Evans*	*Thomas*	*Jones B*	*Charles*	*Peake*	*Brown*	*Allchurch L*	*Griffiths*	*Palmer*	*Allchurch I*	*Jones C*
25	*King*	*Turner*	*Potts*	*Mountford*	*Hayward*	*Sproson*	*Askey*	*Spurdle*	*Stephenson*	*Poole*	*Cunliffe*
26	*Hough*	*Short*	*Swift*	*Bartlett*	*Sharp*	*Walters*	*Kaye*	*Holmes*	*Chappell*	*Edgar*	*McCann*
27	*Hodgkinson*	*Coldwell*	*Shaw G*	*Hoyland*	*Barrass*	*Iley*	*Waldock*	*Laverty*	*Hawksworth*	*Spencer*	*Grainger*
28	*Nicholls*	*Bamford*	*Edwards*	*Pitt !*	*Hale*	*Sampson*	*Petherbridge*	*Sykes*	*Biggs*	*Ward*	*Hooper*
29	*Leyland*	*Taylor*	*Eckersley*	*Clayton R*	*Woods*	*Clayton K*	*Douglas*	*Dobin*	*Briggs*	*Vernon*	*McLeod*
30	*Linton*	*Southwell*	*Cruikshank*	*Bulch*	*Russell*	*Carver*	*Roby*	*Taylor*	*Jackson*	*Wylie*	*Wills*
31	*Taylor*	*Bilcliff*	*Brown*	*Harris*	*Phillips*	*Dicks*	*Day*	*McLean*	*Clough*	*Fitzsimons*	*Burbeck*

Match reports

22 — Lincoln (H): A low crowd in the heavy rain at the Gate see City recover well after going behind to Tommy Northcott's 15-yard pile-driver, then Hinshelwood puts City ahead with a shot that barely trickles in. Watkins levels with a left-footed blaster, which finishes off his run through the middle.

23 — Rotherham (A): Unfortunately for City, despite a quagmire pitch and low-lying fog, the referee rules this game to go ahead. After eluding both Atyeo and John Quairney, Peacock's lobbed 40-yard free-kick bobs in to give City the lead, but following John Slater's headed leveller they are outclassed.

24 — Swansea (A): City are well-beaten side at the Vetch, where Swansea notch up their best win of the season. Anderson pulls off some miraculous saves to prevent an even heavier defeat, though his failure to hold a hard drive by Mel Charles just after the break puts the Swans into a 2-0 lead.

25 — Port Vale (H): Shots from Etheridge, Curtis and Burden have City cruising, but the award of a penalty, when Peacock is surprisingly ruled to have fouled, changes everything. Harry Poole, who lobbed in Vale's second, taps in Port Vale's point-saver when Anderson fails to hold his initial shot.

26 — Barnsley (A): Arthur Kaye and John McCann are outstanding in Barnsley's young attack. They carve City apart, following Atyeo's disallowed 17th-minute offside goal. John Edgar, after completely missing the ball, recovers to conjure up Barnsley opener with a low-angled drive into the net.

27 — Sheffield Utd (H): After notching his first two goals with his feet, Atyeo celebrates with a somersault the great header that brings up his hat-trick. Etheridge heads in the opener and Williams doubles City's advantage with a shot into the corner of the net, before Derek Hawksworth heads in for the Blades.

28 — Bristol Rov (A): Plenty of mud, but no goals at Eastville. A hard, but not over-robust game, it was a pity that Peacock and Jackie Pitt were both ordered off after coming to blows five minutes from the end. An unfortunate game for Peacock who injured his thigh early on and was left a limping passenger.

29 — Blackburn (A): City's low-shot opener comes completely against the run of play. Ally McLeod drives in Blackburn's immediate leveller, but City survive much pressure before Brian Douglas fires Rovers in front. Peter Dobing deflects in Ronnie Clayton's pass to wrap up Blackburn's success.

30 — Notts Co (H): In City's first full League game under lights, only Jimmy Linton stands between them and a hatful of goals. Atyeo skilfully diverts in with his foot a Watkins shot and Cyril Williams stretches out a leg to put away the second. Peter Russell handles a high lob to gift City the spot-kick.

31 — Middlesbrough (H): Etheridge's expert lob and Watkins sending the keeper the wrong way with his a fiercely struck spot-kick following Tom Brown's tackle on Hinshelwood, brings City a hard fought win. Anderson is at fault with the equaliser, spooning Ron Burbeck's shot into Derek McLean's path.

No	V	Date	Opponent	Pos	Res	Score	Att	Pts	Gate Receipts
32	A	9/3	HUDDERSFIELD	18	L	1:2	14,218	27 / 11	
33	H	16/3	BURY	18	W	2:0	15,167	29 / 20	(£1,540.15.6)
34	A	23/3	GRIMSBY	16	W	3:0	12,692	31 / 15	
35	H	30/3	DONCASTER	16	W	4:0	18,848	33 / 12	(£1,949.10.6)
36	A	6/4	STOKE	15	W	2:0	13,399	35 / 6	
37	H	13/4	LEYTON ORIENT	14	W	4:2	19,350	37 / 15	(£2,001.18.0)
38	H	19/4	WEST HAM	14	D	1:1	24,731	38 / 7	(£2,635.18.0)
39	A	20/4	LEICESTER	14	D	1:1	32,653	39 / 1	
40	A	22/4	WEST HAM	16	L	1:3	9,343	39 / 8	
41	H	27/4	SWANSEA	13	W	3:1	19,344	41 / 10	(£1,977.19.0)
42	A	1/5	LIVERPOOL	13	L	1:2	15,108	41 / 3	

Home Average 21,714   Away 17,068

Scorers and Referees

- 32: Atyeo 50 / Taylor 52, Metcalfe 65p. Ref: E Hill
- 33: Atyeo 1, 76. Ref: E Jennings
- 34: Curtis 6, 74, De Gruchy 50 (og). Ref: J Kelly
- 35: Etheridge 8, 9, Curtis 15, Atyeo 34. Ref: H Haworth
- 36: Watkins 85, Atyeo 89. Ref: K Aston
- 37: Curtis 38, 53, Etheridge 58, Atyeo 86 / Andrews 39, Woosnam 54. Ref: N Hough
- 38: Curtis 55 / Allison 35. Ref: W Hickson
- 39: Curtis 4 / Hines 4. Ref: E Jennings
- 40: Atyeo 32 / Dick 24, Lewis 75, Dare 80. Ref: W Hickson
- 41: Curtis 23, 64, 84 / Peake 82. Ref: B Griffiths
- 42: Curtis 70 / Rowley 33, Liddell 54. Ref: A Bond

Line-ups (City players in bold, opponents in italics)

No	1	2	3	4	5	6	7	8	9	10	11
32	**Anderson** *Kennon*	**Bailey** *Conwell*	**Thresher** *Gibson*	**Peacock** *McGarry*	**White** *Cockerill*	**Burden** *Quested*	**Hinshelwood** *McHale*	**Williams C** *Massie*	**Atyeo** *Taylor*	**Etheridge** *Simpson*	**Watkins** *Metcalfe*
33	**Anderson** *Garam*	**Bailey** *Robertson*	**Thresher** *Conroy*	**Peacock** *May*	**White** *McGrath*	**Burden** *Neill*	**Hinshelwood** *Robinson*	**Williams C** *Tilley*	**Atyeo** *Kelly*	**Etheridge** *Reid*	**Watkins** *Lockhart*
34	**Anderson** *Williams*	**Bailey** *Brown*	**Thresher** *De Gruchy*	**Peacock** *Conner*	**White** *Tucker*	**Burden** *Jobling*	**Hinshelwood** *Scott*	**Williams A** *Priestley*	**Curtis** *Crosbie*	**Etheridge** *Rafferty*	**Watkins** *Maddison*
35	**Anderson** *Gregg*	**Bailey** *Makepeace*	**Thresher** *Graham*	**Peacock** *Hunt*	**White** *Williams*	**Burden** *Gavin*	**Hinshelwood** *Mooney*	**Williams A** *Tindill*	**Curtis** *Brown*	**Etheridge** *Cavanagh*	**Watkins** *Walker*
36	**Anderson** *Robertson*	**Bailey** *Mountford*	**Thresher** *McCue*	**Peacock** *Asprey*	**White** *Thomson*	**Burden** *Sellars*	**Hinshelwood** *Coleman*	**Williams A** *Ward*	**Curtis** *Hutton*	**Etheridge** *Kelly*	**Watkins** *Oscroft*
37	**Anderson** *Groombridge*	**Bailey** *Gregory*	**Thresher** *Willense*	**Peacock** *Facey*	**White** *Aldous*	**Cook C** *Cook*	**Hinshelwood** *White*	**Williams A** *Woosnam*	**Curtis** *Johnston*	**Etheridge** *Sexton*	**Watkins** *Andrews*
38	**Anderson** *Gregory*	**Bailey** *Bond*	**Thresher** *Cantwell*	**Peacock** *Malcolm*	**White** *Allison*	**Burden** *Lansdowne*	**Hinshelwood** *Musgrove*	**Williams A** *Smith J*	**Curtis** *Dare*	**Etheridge** *Lewis*	**Watkins** *Dick*
39	**Anderson** *MacLaren*	**Bailey** *Milburn*	**Thresher** *Webb*	**Peacock** *Morris*	**White** *Froggatt*	**Burden** *Ward*	**Hinshelwood** *Wright*	**Williams A** *Moran*	**Curtis** *Hines*	**Etheridge** *Rowley*	**Watkins** *Hogg*
40	**Anderson** *Gregory*	**Bailey** *Bond*	**Thresher** *Cantwell*	**Peacock** *Pyke*	**White** *Brown*	**Burden** *Allison*	**Hinshelwood** *Dare*	**Williams A** *Smith*	**Atyeo** *Lewis*	**Etheridge** *Dick*	**Watkins** *Musgrove*
41	**Anderson** *King*	**Bailey** *Thomas*	**Terris** *Jones B*	**Peacock** *Charles*	**White** *Peake*	**Burden** *Pearson*	**Hinshelwood** *Allchurch L*	**Williams A** *Griffiths*	**Curtis** *Palmer*	**Etheridge** *Allchurch I*	**Watkins** *Jones C*
42	**Anderson** *Younger*	**Bailey** *Molyneux*	**Thresher** *Moran*	**Peacock** *Campell D*	**White** *Hughes*	**Emery** *Twentyman*	**Hinshelwood** *Jackson*	**Williams A** *Rowley*	**Curtis** *Liddell*	**Etheridge** *Melia*	**Watkins** *A'Court*

Match reports

32 — In a game of much good football and some incredible misses by both sides, City are beaten when Vic Metcalfe registers from the spot after Peacock is penalised for pushing. Atyeo heads City into the lead, but within minutes Ken Taylor crashes in a terrific shot to level matters up.

33 — The reporters clock Atyeo's opening goal (a low shot into the corner of the net) at a new League record time of six seconds, but the referee says nine, just two more than the record. Atyeo's terrific drive into the roof of the net in the second half make sure of two precious points.

34 — City's neat, attacking football is soon rewarded. Curtis kneels down to head the ball into an empty net when the Grimsby keeper misjudges a long centre, but 27 minutes later he isn't so lucky as his shot is disallowed. Ray De Gruchy hooks into his own net to double City's lead.

35 — Spring is in the air as City make merry against Doncaster. Etheridge picks his spot when heading the opener into the far corner of the net from Hinshelwood's centre, then he screws in another when a shot is stopped almost on the line. A Curtis shot and an Atyeo header end the scoring.

36 — It looked as though City would have to pay for spurning many chances at the Victoria ground, but two late strikes secure the points. Watkins hammers in the first and another of his pile-drivers cannons off of Bill Robertson's chest for Atyeo to ram the second into the back of the net.

37 — After an unstoppable four-yard drive from Curtis enlivens this game, Jimmy Andrews levels with an angled shot from six yards as the City defenders just stand and watch. Curtis cracks City back in front but Phil Woosnam heads Orient level before Atyeo's header secures the points.

38 — In the Easter sunshine at Ashton Gate, Curtis volleys in a great leveller under the watchful eye of the Eire selectors. The Hammers' strolling tempo put City right out of their stride early on and it is no surprise when Malcolm Allison runs in to head a corner into the roof of the net.

39 — Things looked ominous for City when Derek Hines races on to Arthur Rowley's through pass to fire in an 18-yard cross-shot, but Curtis outstrips Jack Froggatt to level with a toe-poke past Dave MacLaren. On top in the first half, City have to weather much second-half pressure.

40 — Failure to clear sees both John Dick and Bill Dare firing in for the Hammers, whilst Ted Lewis slips past White to slam his goal in off of the crossbar. Watched by England boss Walter Winterbottom, Atyeo traps the ball and turns before firing in a shot that gives the keeper no chance.

41 — It's a great day for the Irish at Ashton Gate, where Curtis secures his first City hat-trick. Starting off with a first-time drive into the roof of the net, he follows with an acute-angled volley and a right-footed effort that finds the net. The Swans only reply is Dudley Peake's pivot shot.

42 — Anderson keeps City in the game before the interval, but he can do nothing about the Pools' freak opener. White's clearance hits Tony Rowley and rebounds into the net. Curtis brings City some reward for their rousing second-half display by putting both ball and goalkeeper into the net.

FA Cup

		F-A	H-T	Scorers, Times, and Referees	1	2	3	4	5	6	7	8	9	10	11
3 H ROTHERHAM 5/1	19 W	4-1	2-1	Curtis 14, Atyeo 17, 60, Stephenson 19 [Hinshelwood 48] 25,048 18 (£3,586.0.0) Ref: R Warnke	Anderson *Quairney*	Guy *Selkirk*	Bailey *Morgan*	White *Keyworth*	Peacock *Noble*	Burden *Williams D*	Hinshelwood *Grainger*	Atyeo *Stephenson*	Curtis *Dixon*	Etheridge *Slater*	Wakins *Bambridge*
4 H RHYL 26/1	19 W	3-0	2-0	Etheridge 3, Atyeo 6, 52 29,438 CL (£4,112.7.6) Ref: N Hough	Anderson *Hanson*	Bailey *Spruce*	Thresher *Reynolds*	White *Roberts*	Peacock *Rogers*	Burden *Donaldson*	Hinshelwood *Hughes*	Williams C *Russell*	Atyeo *Williams J*	Etheridge *Williams H*	Watkins *Meakin*
5 A ASTON VILLA 16/2	19 L	1-2	0-1	Atyeo 50 Pace 36, Sewell 72 63,099 1:13 Ref: J Williams	Anderson *Sims*	Bailey *Lynn*	Thresher *Aldis*	White *Crowther*	Peacock *Dugdale*	Burden *Saward*	Hinshelwood *Smith*	Williams C *Sewell*	Atyeo *Pace*	Etheridge *Dixon*	Watkins *McParland*

With Atyeo back after injury, City come back to form against skilful opponents to make progress in the Cup for the first time in three years. Curtis drives in City's opener, then Atyeo registers with a rising- shot before Roy Stephenson's 25-yard free-kick gets through for the Millers.

After clearing away the leeks which littered the pitch, City start this game against the giant-killers, who had beaten Notts County 3-1 away, with a bang. A magnificent Etheridge header and a shot by Atyeo has City firmly in control. Rhyl fight hard but are let down by their finishing.

City get back on terms when Peacock's long pass through the middle finds Atyeo who, after sending Jim Dugdale the wrong way with a body swerve, crashes in a wonder goal. Unfortunately, Jackie Sewell's diving header finishes off a City side who have Peacock limping at the finish.

Gloucestershire Cup

		F-A	H-T	Scorers, Times, and Referees	1	2	3	4	5	6	7	8	9	10	11
F A BRISTOL ROV 29/4	13 W	2-1	1-1	Atyeo 19, Curtis 84 Bradford 33 14,648 9 Ref: B Griffiths	Anderson *Radford*	Bailey *Bamford*	Thresher *Edwards*	Burden *Pitt*	White *Hale*	Williams A *Sykes*	Hinshelwood *McIlvenny*	Atyeo *Biggs*	Curtis *Bradford*	Etheridge *Meyer*	Watkins *Hooper*

The international selection of Atyeo and Curtis has the crowd hopeful of seeing some class soccer. Unfortunately, apart from Atyeo's 25-yard opener, there is little to enthuse over other than the sportsmanship on display. Rovers leveller is mis-hit, but Curtis slams in a 15-yard winner.

Abandoned League Fixture

		F-A	H-T	Scorers, Times, and Referees	1	2	3	4	5	6	7	8	9	10	11
31 A LIVERPOOL 23/2	18 A	A	1-0	Etheridge 42 17,492 8 Ref: A Bond Abandoned at half-time	Anderson *Younger*	Bailey *McNulty*	Thresher *Moran*	White *White*	Compton *Hughes*	Williams A *Twentyman*	Hinshelwood *Jackson*	Eisentrager *Wheeler*	Curtis *Liddell*	Etheridge *Evans*	Watkins *A'Court*

Heavy rain following on from a three-hour snowstorm makes the conditions difficult, but it is still a surprise when the referee abandons the game at half-time. Liverpool look the stronger side, but Etheridge puts City in front when forcing the ball over the goal line in a scramble.

	P	W	D	L	F	A	W	D	L	F	A	Pts
			Home						Away			
1 Leicester	42	14	5	2	68	36	11	6	4	41	31	61
2 Nott'm For	42	13	4	4	50	29	9	6	6	44	26	54
3 Liverpool	42	16	1	4	53	26	5	10	6	29	28	53
4 Blackburn	42	12	6	3	49	32	9	4	8	34	43	52
5 Stoke	42	16	2	3	64	18	4	6	11	19	40	48
6 Middlesboro	42	12	5	4	51	29	7	5	9	33	31	48
7 Sheffield Wed	42	11	6	4	45	28	7	4	10	42	48	46
8 West Ham	42	12	4	5	31	24	7	4	10	28	39	46
9 Bristol Rov	42	12	5	4	47	24	6	4	11	34	48	45
10 Swansea	42	12	3	6	53	34	7	4	10	37	56	45
11 Fulham	42	13	1	7	53	32	6	3	12	31	44	42
12 Huddersfield	42	10	3	8	33	27	8	3	10	35	47	42
13 BRISTOL C	42	13	2	6	49	21	3	7	11	25	47	41
14 Doncaster	42	12	5	4	51	21	3	5	13	26	56	40
15 Leyton Orient	42	7	8	6	34	38	8	2	11	32	46	40
16 Grimsby	42	12	4	5	41	26	5	1	15	20	36	39
17 Rotherham	42	9	7	5	37	28	4	4	13	37	49	37
18 Lincoln	42	9	4	8	34	27	5	2	14	20	53	34
19 Barnsley	42	8	7	6	39	35	4	3	14	20	54	34
20 Notts Co	42	7	6	8	34	32	2	6	13	24	54	30
21 Bury	42	5	3	13	37	47	4	4	13	23	49	25
22 Port Vale	42	7	4	10	31	42	1	2	18	26	59	22
	924	242	95	125	984	660	125	95	242	660	984	924

Appearances / Goals

	Appearances		Goals		
	Lge	Cup	Lge	Cup	Tot
Anderson, Bob	22	5			
Atyeo, John	37	4	23	6	29
Bailey, Jack	19	5			
Baillie, Joe	10				
Boxley, Jack	5				
Burden, Tommy	40	4			
Compton, Terry	21	1	2		2
Cook, Charles	1				
Cook, Tony	21				
Curtis, Dermot	16	3	13	2	15
Eisentrager, Alec	11	1			
Emery, Terry	1				
Etheridge, Bobby	22	5	6	2	8
Guy, Ivor	21	1			
Hinshelwood, Wally	41	5	7	1	8
Peacock, Ernie	19	3	1		1
Rogers, Jimmy	16		5		5
Smith, David	15		1		1
Terris, James	1				
Thresher, Mike	37	4			
Walker, George	2				
Watkins, Johnny	24	5	1		1
White, Jack	37	5	5		5
Williams, Alan	12	2			
Williams, Cyril	22	2	8		8
(own-goals)			1		1
25 players used	**473**	**55**	**74**	**11**	**85**

Odds & ends

Double wins: (1) Bury.
Double losses: (2) Fulham, Barnsley.

Won from behind: (3) Bristol Rovers (h), Liverpool (h), Lincoln (h).
Lost from in front: (6) Barnsley (h), Fulham (a), Doncaster (a), Rotherham (a), Blackburn (a), Huddersfield (a).

High spots: Beating Bristol Rovers 5-3 at the Gate on 22 September.
Banging in five goals at the Gate against both Lincoln and Sheffield Utd.
Knocking giant-killers Rhyl out of the FA Cup.
John Atyeo's FA Cup goal at Villa Park on 16 February.
John Atyeo and Dermot Curtis being opposing centre-forwards in the
England v Eire World Cup games.

Low spots: The poor start to the season, only one win in nine games.
Losing 1-6 at Millmoor against Rotherham United on 22 December.
The Boxing Day debacle at Swansea.

AGM (Brecknell, Dolman & Rogers, Pennywell Road, 15 April 1958):
Profit £1,233.0s.0d. Season Ticket Sales £17,031.0s.0d.

Note: The League details (right) include the abandoned game at Anfield.

Player of the year: John Atyeo.
Ever-presents: (0).
Hat-tricks: (2) John Atyeo (1), Dermot Curtis (1).
Leading scorer: Overall: John Atyeo (29). League: John Atyeo (23).

LEAGUE DIVISION 2

Manager: Beasley ⇨ Peter Doherty   SEASON 1957-58

No	Date	Venue / Opponent	Att	Pos	Res	Pt	F-A	H-T	Scorers, Times, and Referees	1	2	3	4	5	6	7	8	9	10	11
1	24/8	H LIVERPOOL	28,431 (£3,082.3.0)		L	0	1:2	1-0	Watkins 43 / *Rowley 57, 85* / Ref: H Husband	Anderson	Bailey	Thresher	Burden	White	Williams A	Hinshelwood	Atyeo	Curtis	Etheridge	Watkins
										Younger	*Molyneux*	*Moran*	*Wheeler*	*White*	*Campbell*	*Jackson*	*Rowley*	*Liddell*	*Melia*	*A'Court*
2	26/8	A STOKE	23,001		L	0	0:3	0-2	*Bowyer 17, Kelly 39, King 73*	Anderson	Bailey	Thresher	Peacock	White	Williams A	Hinshelwood	Atyeo	Curtis	Etheridge	Watkins
										Robertson	*Mountford*	*McCue*	*Asprey*	*Thomson*	*Sellars*	*Coleman*	*Bowyer*	*King*	*Kelly*	*Oscroft*
3	31/8	A MIDDLESBROUGH	21,834	19 *16*	D	1	0:0	0-0	Ref: E Crawford	Anderson	Bailey	Thresher	Peacock	White	Williams A	Hinshelwood	Burden	Atyeo	Etheridge	Watkins
										Taylor	*Bilcliff*	*Robinson*	*Harris*	*Phillips*	*Dicks*	*Day*	*McLean*	*Clough*	*Peacock*	*Burbeck*
4	3/9	H STOKE	25,817 (£2,782.14.6)	14 *3*	W	3	2:1	2:1	Burden 1, Atyeo 21 / *Kelly 9* / Ref: R Smith	Anderson	Bailey	Thresher	Peacock	White	Williams A	Hinshelwood	Burden	Atyeo	Etheridge	Watkins
										Robertson	*Mountford*	*McCue*	*Asprey*	*Thomson*	*Sellars*	*Coleman*	*Bowyer*	*King*	*Kelly*	*Oscroft*
5	7/9	H LEYTON ORIENT	23,283 (£2,457.0.0)	16 *18*	D	4	2:2	0-2	Hinshelwood 58, Etheridge 65 / *Heckman 32, Johnston 40* / Ref: J Pickles	Anderson	Bailey	Thresher	Peacock	Compton	Williams A	Hinshelwood	Burden	Atyeo	Etheridge	Watkins
										Welton	*Gregory*	*Willemse*	*Facey*	*Bishop*	*McKnight*	*Nicholson*	*Woosam*	*Julians*	*Johnston*	*Heckman*
6	10/9	H GRIMSBY	20,127 (£2,187.15.0)	13 *4*	W	6	3:2	2:1	Atyeo 6, 84, Watkins 42p / *Rafferty 19, Stockin 88* / Ref: R Mann	Anderson	Bailey	Thresher	Peacock	White	Williams A	Hinshelwood	Burden	Atyeo	Etheridge	Watkins
										Tinsley	*Fleming*	*Richardson*	*Conner*	*Tucker*	*Walker*	*Priestley*	*Evans*	*Rafferty*	*Stockin*	*Fell*
7	14/9	A CHARLTON	22,354	17 *1*	L	6	0:1	0-1	*Summers 30* / Ref: J Barradell	Anderson	Bailey	Thresher	Peacock	White	Williams A	Hinshelwood	Burden	Atyeo	Etheridge	Watkins
										Duff	*Edwards*	*Hewie*	*Hammond*	*Jago*	*Ufton*	*Lawrie*	*Ayre*	*Leary*	*Summers*	*Kiernan*
8	17/9	A GRIMSBY	12,004	15 *8*	D	7	1:1	0-0	Atyeo 81 / *Priestley 50* / Ref: K Tuck	Anderson	Bailey	Thresher	Peacock	White	Williams C	Hinshelwood	Atyeo	Curtis	Etheridge	Watkins
										Tinsley	*Brown*	*Richardson*	*Conner*	*Tucker*	*Walker*	*Priestley*	*Evans*	*Rafferty*	*Stockin*	*Fell*
9	21/9	H DONCASTER	21,476 (£2,292.7.6)	17 *21*	D	8	2:2	1:2	Atyeo 35, 89 / *Walker 30, Kelly 31* / Ref: M Horner	Anderson	Bailey	Thresher	Peacock	White	Williams A	Hinshelwood	Burden	Atyeo	Williams C	Watkins
										Gregg	*Gavin*	*Graham*	*Kilkenny*	*Williams*	*Ewing*	*Mooney*	*Tindill*	*Kelly*	*Cavanagh*	*Walker*
10	28/9	A ROTHERHAM	8,850	18 *10*	L	8	1:4	0-1	Etheridge 75 *(Farmer 57, 86)* / *Webster 42, Stephenson 48* / Ref: K Dagnall	Anderson	Bailey	Thresher	Peacock	White	Williams A	Eisentrager	Burden	Atyeo	Etheridge	Watkins
										Quairney	*Johnson*	*Silman*	*Lambert*	*Noble*	*Keyworth*	*Webster*	*Kettleborough*	*Farmer*	*Stephens*	*Stephenson*

Match reports

1. From a high Watkins free-kick, Atyeo harasses the Liverpool keeper, who can only help the leather into the Open End net, to put City into the lead against the run of play. The head of striker Tony Rowley brings Liverpool the success that their superior play throughout fully deserved.

2. Whilst Curtis is denied by the bar before Frank Bowyer blasts in Stoke's opener, City are a side lacking in punch, confidence or poise against a veteran Stoke outfit possessing a virile attack. City though have their moments, especially early on, but are let down by their poor finishing.

3. A deceptive scoreline as both sides have their chances at Ayresome Park, where Atyeo's cultured play sets up many opportunities for his colleagues to spurn. Resolute defending keeps the potent home attack at bay and, fortunately for City, Brian Clough adopts a deep-lying role.

4. At last City find their form and knock Stoke off the top of the table with sweeping forward movements. Atyeo beats three defenders before firing in a sizzling shot past William Robertson. If they played like this every game, few could rival them for footballing ability and elegance.

5. After Burden has a header disallowed for offside early on, City find themselves in deep trouble at half-time. Poor defending probably has both satisfied with a point at the end after a fine move, involving Thresher, Watkins and Burden, sends in the unmarked Etheridge to level matters.

6. Even though Atyeo shot them ahead early on, City fail, in the incessant rain, to equal last week's heights. Fortunate to be awarded a spot-kick when Malcom Tucker collides with Atyeo, City struggle to hold onto the points during the final minutes after Ron Stockin bundles the ball in.

7. City are robbed when the officials failed to spot that White's 20th minute 20-yarder bounces down a good foot over the line after hitting the bar. Johnny Summers fires Charlton ahead from Bob Ayre's pass, then after the break offside deprives both Bill Kiernan and Ayre of goals.

8. In the 13th minute Ron Rafferty sends both the ball and Anderson into the net, but fortunately for City the goal is disallowed. Gerald Priestley's narrow-angled shot puts Grimsby deservedly ahead, but from a Williams pass Atyeo steers the ball beneath Colin Tinsley.

9. Atyeo's goals – a shot straight and true from outside the penalty area and an 18-yard injury-time drive – brings City a share of the points in a game they should have won. Unfortunately, defensive frailties present Ron Walker with a simple tap-in and allows Walter Kelly a free header.

10. City's superior football in the opening half-hour has Rotherham reeling under grey skies at Millmoor. Atyeo is denied by the bar before Barry Webster shoots the Millers ahead, then City's centre-forward is again thwarted when his 44th-minute shot on the turn is disallowed for offside.

11 H HUDDERSFIELD 5/10 — Pos 19 — L 1-3 — 10 / 8 — Att 21,636 (£2,301.1.0)
Watkins 40p
Massie 44, Wilson 83, Bain 88
Ref: E Jennings

	1	2	3	4	5	6	7	8	9	10	11
City	Anderson	Cook C	Thresher	Burden	Peacock	Williams A	Hinshelwood	Atyeo	Curtis	Etheridge	Watkins
Huddersfield	Kennon	Conwell	Wilson	Cockerill	Taylor	McGarry	McHale	Massie	Bain	Simpson	Metcalfe

City look set for a deserved point until England international Vic Metcalfe turns on the style in the closing stages. He sets up Ray Wilson to shoot past Cook, then Alex Bain scrambles his cross over the line. Ken Taylor's foolish hand-ball sees Watkins put City ahead from the spot.

---

12 H BRISTOL ROV 12/10 — Pos 18 — W 3-2 — 9 / 10 — Att 33,746 (£3,696.12.6)
Atyeo 23, 53, Walker 59
Ward 54, Hooper 70
Ref: W Clements

	1	2	3	4	5	6	7	8	9	10	11
City	Anderson	White	Thresher	Burden	Peacock	Williams A	Hinshelwood	Walker	Atyeo	Eisentrager	Watkins
Rovers	Nicholls	Bamford	Watling	Ricketts	Biggs	Sampson	Mabbutt	Meyer	Bradford	Ward	Hooper

Despite Peter Hooper's volley into the net via the bar, Walker's header proves decisive for City in this hard-fought derby against injury-hit Rovers, playing Alfie Biggs at centre-half. In front of the cameras filming for the BBC Sportsview programme, Atyeo fired City into the lead.

---

13 H NOTTS CO 26/10 — Pos 15 — W 3-1 — 21 / 12 — Att 18,394 (£1,973.5.0)
Watkins 13p, Atyeo 21, 67
Carver 44
Ref: D Blues

	1	2	3	4	5	6	7	8	9	10	11
City	Anderson	Rae	Thresher	Burden	Peacock	Williams A	Hinshelwood	Walker	Atyeo	Eisentrager	Watkins
Notts Co	Linton	Cruickshank	Maddison	Sheridan	Loxley	Carver	Gissing	Lane	Russell	Newsham	Wills

Apart from Gerry Carver's surprise shot that finds the net off an upright, City are rarely troubled by a County side including debutant John Gissing. Walker gets brought down for the penalty and Atyeo fires in a rebound before his second-half header clinches an impressive win.

---

14 A IPSWICH 2/11 — Pos 17 — L 2-4 — 13 / 12 — Att 17,681
Atyeo 35, Eisentrager 57
Phillips 4, 25p, 80, Garneys 37
Ref: J Williams

	1	2	3	4	5	6	7	8	9	10	11
City	Anderson	White	Thresher	Burden	Peacock	Williams A	Hinshelwood	Walker	Atyeo	Eisentrager	Watkins
Ipswich	Bailey	Acres	Malcolm	Pickett	Rees	Johnstone	Reed	Millward	Garneys	Phillips	Leadbeater

Williams has a nightmare game for City. At fault when Tom Garneys sent Ted Phillips through for the opener, he then handles to concede the spot-kick. Atyeo's strike is certainly the best goal of the game, crashing the ball home from Hinshelwood's pull-back from the by-line.

---

15 H BLACKBURN 9/11 — Pos 18 — D 0-0 — 2 / 13 — Att 23,276 (£2,492.3.0)
Ref: K Aston

	1	2	3	4	5	6	7	8	9	10	11
City	Anderson	White	Thresher	Burden	Peacock	White	Hinshelwood	Walker	Atyeo	Eisentrager	Watkins
Blackburn	Leyland	Taylor	Eckersley	Clayton	Woods	McGrath	Douglas	Vernon	Dobing	Stephenson	MacLeod

A deserved point against the leaders. City are frustrated when Hinshelwood's goal direct from a corner is disallowed because of the obstruction of keeper Harry Leyland. White and Walker have shots cleared off the goal-line, whilst after the break a Watkins shot is touched onto a post.

---

16 A SHEFFIELD UTD 16/11 — Pos 15 — W 3-0 — 10 / 15 — Att 15,222
Atyeo 24, 49, 82
Ref: F Collinge

	1	2	3	4	5	6	7	8	9	10	11
City	Anderson	Hodgkinson	Thresher	Burden	Peacock	White	Hinshelwood	Walker	Atyeo	Eisentrager	Watkins
Sheffield Utd	Hodgkinson	Coldwell	Shaw G	Richardson	Shaw J	Summers	Ringstead	Hamilton	Howitt	Russell	Hawksworth

Discarded by England in midweek, Atyeo shows the selectors what they are missing. After Atyeo's headed opener, Joe Shaw's faulty back-pass allows him to notch his second before a low shot across Alan Hodginson brings up his hat-trick as City pull off the shock of the day.

---

17 H WEST HAM 23/11 — Pos 15 — D 1-1 — 5 / 16 — Att 22,305 (£2,388.5.0)
Walker 25
Dick 86
Ref: A Westwood

	1	2	3	4	5	6	7	8	9	10	11
City	Anderson	Gregory	Thresher	Burden	Peacock	Williams A	Hinshelwood	Walker	Atyeo	Eisentrager	Watkins
West Ham	Gregory	Bond	Cantwell	Malcolm	Brown	Lansdowne	Dare	Smith	Keeble	Dick	Musgrove

The Hammers live up to their ball-playing reputation, but over-do it to such an extent that it almost cost them the game. Falling behind when John Dick chips them level from Bill Dare's cross. Ernie Gregory could only parry Atyeo's shot for Walker to shoot in, it is near the end when...

---

18 A BARNSLEY 30/11 — Pos 17 — L 1-4 — 6 / 16 — Att 13,508 (£1,795.17.6)
Atyeo 38
Graham 20, 87, McCann 57, [Kaye 75p]
Ref: H Haworth

	1	2	3	4	5	6	7	8	9	10	11
City	Anderson	Hough	Thresher	Burden	Peacock	Williams A	Hinshelwood	Walker	Atyeo	Curtis	Watkins
Barnsley	Hough	Short	Gillott	Wood	Sharp	Bartlett	Kaye	Smith	Chappell	Graham	McCann

Despite having slightly the better of the early play, City fall behind to a fine volley. Atyeo levels from close in, but John McCann has time to place his shot past Anderson. Peacock concedes the spot-kick converted by Arthur Kaye, and Malcolm Graham places in Barnsley's fourth.

---

19 H FULHAM 7/12 — Pos 18 — L 0-5 — 6 / 16 — Att 16,983
Haynes 12, Dwight 15, 61, Hill 23, [Chamberlain 34]
Ref: W Hickson

	1	2	3	4	5	6	7	8	9	10	11
City	Anderson	Macedo	Thresher	Burden	Peacock	Williams A	Hinshelwood	Atyeo	Curtis	Etheridge	Watkins
Fulham	Macedo	Cohen	Langley	Bentley	Lampe	Lowe	Barton	Hill	Dwight	Haynes	Chamberlain

A nonchalant daisy cutter from Johnny Haynes puts Fulham in rampant mood. Roy Dwight slots in the visitors' second, then his perfect pass sets Jimmy Hill to net with a cross-shot. Tosh Chamberlain's header ends the early blitz and Dwight's second-half tap-in completes the rout.

---

20 A SWANSEA 14/12 — Pos 20 — L 1-5 — 22 / 16 — Att 10,147
Curtis 69
Jones C 2, 12p, Price 40, White 55 (og), [Allchurch L 64]
Ref: E Hill

	1	2	3	4	5	6	7	8	9	10	11
City	Anderson	King	Thresher	Burden	Peacock	Williams A	Hinshelwood	Atyeo	Curtis	Etheridge	Watkins
Swansea	King	Griffiths	Jones B	Charles	Peake	Nurse	Allchurch L	Lewis	Price	Allchurch I	Jones C

Despite having lost their six previous home games, the Swans prove far too good for out of touch City. Cliff Jones shoots in the opener when his first effort rebounds off Rae. The right-back brings down Ivor Allchurch to gift Jones his penalty. Curtis nets for City with a great drive.

---

21 A LIVERPOOL 21/12 — Pos 21 — L 3-4 — 1 / 16 — Att 38,051
Burden 50, Watkins 71, Curtis 75
Rowley 1, 55, McNam'a 9, A'Court 86
Ref: G Black

	1	2	3	4	5	6	7	8	9	10	11
City	Anderson	Younger	Thresher	Burden	Peacock	Williams A	Hinshelwood	Atyeo	Curtis	Etheridge	Watkins
Liverpool	Younger	Molyneux	Moran	Wheeler	White	Campbell	McNamara	Rowley	Liddell	Melia	A'Court

City's stirring rally just fails as Alan A'Court shoots home a late winner at the second attempt after Anderson's fine save. Burden's first-time 20-yard drive brings City into the game after Tony Rowley had flicked the Pool ahead after just 45 seconds. Watkins scores with a rare header.

LEAGUE DIVISION 2 — Manager: Beasley ⇨ Peter Doherty — SEASON 1957-58

No	Date	Att	Gate	Pos	Res	Pt	F-A	H-T
22	H DERBY 25/12	17,090	(£1,742.5.0)	18	W	16 / 18	2-1	1-1
23	A DERBY 26/12	25,630		19	L	16 / 18	2-5	1-2
24	H MIDDLESBROUGH 28/12	23,124	(£2,489.17.0)	18	D	14 / 19	0-0	0-0
25	A LEYTON ORIENT 11/1	15,662	(£2,125.15.6)	20	L	11 / 19	0-4	0-1
26	H CHARLTON 18/1	19,526		20	L	2 / 19	1-2	1-0
27	A DONCASTER 1/2	9,752	(£2,810.3.6)	21	L	17 / 19	1-2	1-1
28	H ROTHERHAM 8/2	25,639		21	L	18 / 19	0-1	0-0
29	A HUDDERSFIELD 19/2	5,971		21	D	7 / 20	0-0	0-0
30	A WEST HAM 22/2	22,795		21	L	1 / 20	2-3	1-2
31	H LINCOLN 1/3	20,041	(£2,087.4.0)	20	W	22 / 22	4-0	3-0

22 — H DERBY 25/12

Line-up (1–11): Anderson, Rae, Thresher, Burden, Peacock, Williams A, Hinshelwood, Atyeo, Curtis, Etheridge, Watkins
Opponents: Orford, Barrowcliffe, Davies, Clark, McDonnell, Upton, Powell, Parry, Darwin, Ryan, Woodhead

Scorers, Times, and Referees: Atyeo 24, 65; Ryan 36; Ref: B Griffiths

After spurning three good chances in the opening 20 minutes, City are fortunate with Atyeo's opener as the referee ignores his linesman's raised offside flag. Fortunately, his second is more satisfying as he fires in a pull-back from Curtis to clinch a deserved Christmas Day success.

23 — A DERBY 26/12

Line-up (1–11): Anderson, Rae, Thresher, Burden, White, Williams A, Hinshelwood, Atyeo, Curtis, Etheridge, Watkins
Opponents: Orford, Barrowcliffe, Davies, Clark, McDonnell, Upton, Powell, Parry, Darwin, Ryan, Woodhead

Scorers, Times, and Referees: Curtis 23, Atyeo 77 (Darwin 85); Ryan 14, Whead 25, Parry 65, 68

Anderson is well and truly beaten by Reg Ryan's shot, but somewhat against the run of play Curtis equalises for City after beating Martin McDonnell in the air. George Darwin runs nearly three-quarters of the field to tie up Derby's well-deserved revenge for yesterday's defeat.

24 — H MIDDLESBROUGH 28/12

Line-up (1–11): Cook A, Thresher, Burden, —, White, Parr, Hinshelwood, Atyeo, Curtis, Munroe, Watkins
Opponents: Taylor, Blcliff, Brown, Harris, Phillips, Birbeck, Day, McLean, Clough, Peacock, Holliday

Scorers, Times, and Referees: Ref: A Bond

Both sets of forwards rarely looked like scoring in this poor game. Middlesbrough, though, had cause to feel aggrieved with Brian Clough having his goal struck off on 34 minutes for supposedly fouling Thresher, not long after Eddie Holliday's drive had been kept out by a post.

25 — A LEYTON ORIENT 11/1

Line-up (1–11): Cook A, Bailey, Rae, Burden, Compton, White, Hinshelwood, Atyeo, Curtis, Eisentrager, Smith D
Opponents: George, Eagles, Gregory, McKnight, Bishop, Carey, White, Woosam, Johnston, Andrews, Hartburn

Scorers, Times, and Referees: Johnston 28, 76, 82, Woosam 63; Ref: B Buckle

Controversy at Brisbane Road as City claim that not only did Tom Johnston, the League top scorer, put the opener in with his hand, but the ball was cleared off the line. A push on Compton saw Johnston tuck away another, but no dispute over his third as he soared high to nod in a cross.

26 — H CHARLTON 18/1

Line-up (1–11): Anderson, Burden, Thresher, Emery, Compton, White, Hinshelwood, Walker, Atyeo, Etheridge, Summers
Opponents: Duff, Firmani, Townsend, Hewie, Jago, Kiernan, White, Lucas, Ryan, Leary, Summers

Scorers, Times, and Referees: Atyeo 34; Summers 46, White 74 (og); Ref: R Chandler

City deservedly lead at half-time, thanks to Atyeo slamming the ball home. Unfortunately, Johnny Summers scrambled in an equaliser straight after the break, then White headed a cross into his own net. Shortly after Walker was denied by a post, then Atyeo had a header disallowed.

27 — A DONCASTER 1/2

Line-up (1–11): Anderson, Terris, Thresher, Emery, Williams A, White, Hinshelwood, Walker, Atyeo, Etheridge, Watkins
Opponents: McIntosh, Makepeace, Graham, Cavanagh, Williams, Jago, Tindill, Callan, Kelly, Nicholson, Walker

Scorers, Times, and Referees: Walker 5; Tindill 8, Callan 53; Ref: K Collinge

A quick return to Bellevue for new City boss Peter Doherty, where neither City, who wore their new high-necked white shirts, or Doncaster performed like relegation candidates. Walker's first-time shot is helped into the net by Atyeo, but Bert Tindill soon levels with a header.

28 — H ROTHERHAM 8/2

Line-up (1–11): Anderson, Terris, Thresher, Emery, Williams A, Burden, Hinshelwood, Walker, Atyeo, Etheridge, Tindill
Opponents: Quairney, Silman, Morgan, Williams, Madden, Keyworth, Webster, Kettleborough, Noble, Jones, Broadbent

Scorers, Times, and Referees: Broadbent 88; Ref: D Howell

After a two-minute silence for the victims of the Manchester United Air Disaster, atrocious finishing costs City this game. Albert Broadbent takes full advantage of a poor defensive wall to fire in a free-kick from just outside the area after Williams had fouled Keith Kettleborough.

29 — A HUDDERSFIELD 19/2

Line-up (1–11): Anderson, Peacock, Thresher, Emery, Williams A, Burden, Hinshelwood, Tindill, Atyeo, Etheridge, Watkins
Opponents: Kennon, Gibson, Wilson, McGarry, Taylor, Connor, McHale, France, Massie, Simpson, Metcalfe

Scorers, Times, and Referees: Ref: K Howley

With a little more luck, City would have been celebrating their first League win since Christmas. In the gusty wind their determination and hard tackling surprised the smallest Leeds Road crowd of the season. City's football after the interval matched that of Town prior to the break.

30 — A WEST HAM 22/2

Line-up (1–11): Anderson, Peacock, Thresher, Emery, Williams A, Burden, Hinshelwood, Tindill, Atyeo, Etheridge, Watkins
Opponents: Gregory, Bond, Cantwell, Malcolm, Brown, Pyke, Dare, Smith, Keeble, Dick, Grice

Scorers, Times, and Referees: Tindill 24, Hinshelwood 81; Dare 17, Keeble 30, Williams 55 (og); Ref: F Cohen

Wearing black armbands in memory of director John Saywell, who died during the week, City fall behind when Bill Dare prods the ball home. Tindill's equaliser was the goal of the game – a glorious 20-yard drive in-off the post. No dishonour in this defeat as City fought all the way.

31 — H LINCOLN 1/3

Line-up (1–11): Cook A, Terris, Thresher, Emery, Williams A, Burden, Hinshelwood, Tindill, Atyeo, Etheridge, Watkins
Opponents: Thompson, Jackson, Smith, Middleton, Emery, Linnecor, Smillie, Hannah, Neale, Chapman, Withers

Scorers, Times, and Referees: Etheridge 14, 19, Watkins 44, 75p; Ref: P Smyth

An easy success for City over the bottom of the table visitors, for whom Jeff Smith (ex-Sheffield Utd) is making his debut. Two headed goals from Etheridge, before a Watkins scorcher flashes into the net off of Robert Jackson. Smith's handball sets up Watkins with his spot-kick.

Bristol City — Season results (matches 32–42)

No	V	Opponent	Date	Pos	Res	FT	HT	Scorers	Opposition scorers	Att		Referee
32	A	NOTTS CO	8/3	19	W	1-0	1-0	Tindill 8		10,042	20 24	Ref: A Bond
33	H	IPSWICH	15/3	18	W	1-0	0-0	Tindill 78		20,101	9 26	Ref: J Mitchell (£2,113.17.6)
34	A	BLACKBURN	24/3	18	L	0-5	0-0		Douglas 48, Dobing 51, 54, 80, 82p	8,825	4 26	Ref: A Westwood
35	H	SHEFFIELD UTD	29/3	18	L	1-4	0-2	Atyeo 46	Russell 4, 20, 89, Hawksworth 59	20,215	6 26	Ref: R Mann (£2,115.16.0)
36	A	CARDIFF	4/4	18	W	3-2	2-2	Etheridge 22, Atyeo 36, Tindill 89	Hewitt 4, 5	15,567	15 28	Ref: D Blues
37	A	BRISTOL ROV	5/4	18	D	3-3	3-3	Etheridge 5, Pyle 41 (og), H'wood 28	Bradford 23, 38, Hooper 28	28,005	8 29	Ref: R Smith
38	H	CARDIFF	7/4	17	W	2-0	0-0	Etheridge 59, Atyeo 61		25,723	15 31	Ref: W Hickson (£2,753.9.6)
39	H	BARNSLEY	12/4	17	W	5-0	3-0	Tindill 1, 3, 50, Watkins 22, 55p		18,249	13 34	Ref: F Gerrard (£1,843.10.6)
40	A	FULHAM	19/4	17	W	4-3	4-0	Tindill 1, 34, 44, Atyeo 5	Chamberlain 73, Barton 87, 89	27,042	5 36	Ref: K Stokes
41	A	LINCOLN	23/4	17	L	0-4	0-3		[Harbertson 32, 61] Chapman 8, Smillie 13,	10,011	21 36	Ref: K Collinge
42	H	SWANSEA	26/4	17	L	1-2	1-1	Walker 2	Allchurch L 25, Terry 53	18,029	19 36	Ref: K Aston (£1,872.12.6)

Home Average 22,058
Away 17,236

Line-ups (City / opposition in italics) and match reports

32 — Notts Co: Cook A (*Linton*), Peacock (*Chatham*), Thresher (*Pritchard*), Emery (*Loxley*), Williams A (*Rawson*), Burden (*Carver*), Hinshelwood (*Roby*), Tindill (*Jackson*), Atyeo (*Lane*), Etheridge (*Newsham*), Watkins (*Wills*).
After Tindill races onto Etheridge's pass to fire City into an early lead, it is all hands to the pumps as they have to resist County's all-out attempts to score. A freak snow-storm after 20 minutes adds to their problems, but as suddenly as it started it had abated before half-time.

33 — Ipswich: Cook A (*Bailey*), Peacock (*Carberry*), Thresher (*Deacon*), Emery (*Pickett*), Williams A (*Rees D*), Burden (*Elsworthy*), Hinshelwood (*Lundstrom*), Tindill (*Millward*), Atyeo (*Garneys*), Etheridge (*Rees W*), Watkins (*Leadbeater*).
Alan Williams dashed from his wedding reception to turn out in this game, in which City exerted almost constant pressure. Tindill clinches two more much-needed points by forcing the ball in when Etheridge's header to Hinshelwood's precision centre rebounds off of the crossbar.

34 — Blackburn: Cook A (*Leyland*), Peacock (*Taylor*), Thresher (*Eckersley*), Emery (*Clayton*), Williams A (*Woods*), Burden (*McGrath*), Hinshelwood (*Douglas*), Tindill (*Dobing*), Atyeo (*Johnston*), Etheridge (*Vernon*), Watkins (*MacLeod*).
Electing to play into the stiff wind, Blackburn made City suffer for not making good use of the elements before the break. No sign of Rovers suffering a FA Cup hangover following Saturday's semi-final defeat against Bolton, a Brian Douglas headed opener has them on the rampage.

35 — Sheffield Utd: Cook A (*Hodgkinson*), Peacock (*Coldwell*), Thresher (*Mason*), Emery (*Richardson*), Williams A (*Shaw J*), Burden (*Summers*), Hinshelwood (*Ringstead*), Tindill (*Russell*), Atyeo (*Pace*), Etheridge (*Hodgson*), Watkins (*Hawksworth*).
At the finish some 200 fans invade the pitch to vent their anger at referee Mann for disallowing four City strikes (Watkins 8 minutes, Etheridge 43, 75 & Tindill 74) for offside. However, only the third decision is questionable as City succumb to a side who take their chances well.

36 — Cardiff: Anderson (*Jones*), Briggs (*Stitfall*), Thresher (*Sullivan*), McCall (*Harrington*), Williams A (*Malloy*), Burden (*Baker*), Hinshelwood (*Walsh*), Tindill (*Hewitt*), Atyeo (*Bonson*), Etheridge (*Nugent*), Watkins (*Hudson*).
After conceding relatively simple early goals to Welsh international Ron Hewitt, City fight back to level before the half-time interval. Tindill tees up Etheridge to nod in and then Atyeo heads home from a Watkins chip. Tempers fray after the break, but Tindill heads in City's winner.

37 — Bristol Rov: Anderson (*Bamford*), Nicholls (*Doyle*), Thresher (*Sykes*), McCall (*Pyle*), Williams A (*Sampson*), Burden (*McIlvenny*), Hinshelwood (*Meyer*), Tindill (*Bradford*), Atyeo (*Ward*), Etheridge (*Hooper*), Watkins.
An exciting first half at Eastville where City score their goals at the Tote End. Wally Hinshelwood's left-footed drive from the centre-forward position secured a valuable point for City to aid their relegation fight, but the Rovers are entitled to feel aggrieved in not winning this contest.

38 — Cardiff: Briggs (*Jones*), Thresher (*Stitfall*), McCall (*Sullivan*), Williams A (*McGuckin*), Burden (*Malloy*), Tindill (*Harrington*), Walker (*Hudson*), Atyeo (*Hewitt*), Etheridge (*Bonson*), Watkins (*Jenkins*), (*Nugent*).
Goals at the Open End bring City a vital victory to make them safe from the threat of relegation. Etheridge speeds in to make sure Walker's header crossed the line, then Atyeo, who gives a vintage display, doubles City's advantage by flicking the ball into the corner of Cardiff's net.

39 — Barnsley: Anderson (*Hough*), Briggs (*Short*), Thresher (*Swift*), McCall (*Bartlett*), Williams A (*Sharp*), Burden (*Wood*), Virgin (*Kaye*), Tindill (*Smith*), Atyeo (*Chappell*), Etheridge (*Graham*), Watkins (*McCann*).
With the relegation pressure off, City make a great start with Tindill's shot hitting Colin Swift and cannoning past Harry Hough after barely 15 seconds. With 22-year-old amateur Derek Virgin in their ranks in place of the unfit Hinshelwood, City achieve their best win of the season.

40 — Fulham: Anderson (*Macedo*), Briggs (*Cohen*), Thresher (*Chenhall*), McCall (*Forbes*), Williams A (*Stapleton*), Burden (*Lowe*), Hinshelwood (*Stevens*), Tindill (*Barton*), Atyeo (*Cook*), Etheridge (*Hill*), Watkins (*Chamberlain*).
Another early goal for City as Tindill nets after just 30 seconds at Craven Cottage. With Johnny Haynes away for England on international duty it all seems so easy for City who are coasting on their 4-0 interval lead, has them hanging on at the finish.

41 — Lincoln: Anderson (*Downie*), Peacock (*Jackson*), Thresher (*Dykes*), McCall (*Green*), Williams A (*Emery*), Burden (*Linnecor*), Virgin (*Smillie*), Tindill (*Hannah*), Atyeo (*Harbertson*), Etheridge (*Chapman*), Watkins (*Withers*).
Peacock and Thresher find Lincoln's wingers too hot to handle. The Imps dominate from the start, and go ahead when Roy Chapman stabs the ball in. Tindill and Atyeo then both have goals disallowed for offside, before Ron Harbertson's low-diving header trebles Lincoln's advantage.

42 — Swansea: Anderson (*King*), Briggs (*Thomas*), Thresher (*Griffiths*), McCall (*Woods*), Williams A (*Daniel*), Burden (*Brown*), **Bevan** (*Smillie*), Walker (*Charles*), Atyeo (*Terry*), Etheridge (*Allchurch I*), Watkins (*Beech*).
Despite Walker's early goal, striking the ball in from eight yards, many City fans are of the opinion that the game is fixed to allow Swansea the victory they required to escape relegation. Len Allchurch appears to control the ball with his hand before shooting in an easy equaliser.

CUP-TIES

Manager: Beasley ⇨ Peter Doherty SEASON 1957-58

FA Cup

No				F-A	H-T	1	2	3	4	5	6	7	8	9	10	11	Scorers, Times, and Referees
3	A ACCRINGTON	18	D	2:2	1:1	Cook A	Bailey	Rae	Burden	Peacock	White	Hinshelwood	Atyeo	Curtis	Eisentrager	Smith D	Hinshelwood 27, Curtis 80
4/1	12,276 3N:8					*McInnes*	*McNichal*	*Harrower*	*Sowden*	*Stones*	*Tighe*	*Anders*	*Mulkerrin*	*Stewart*	*Storey*	*Byrom*	*Stewart 15, Byrom 82*
	(£4,340.10.0)																Ref: W Clements

At a frozen Peel Park, City are fortunate to survive. After George Stewart coolly heads Accrington in front, Hinshelwood, from Atyeo's great pass, fires in a leveller. Ray Byrom's great strike brings the homesters their deserved equaliser not long after Curtis had shot City in front.

No				F-A	H-T	1	2	3	4	5	6	7	8	9	10	11	Scorers, Times, and Referees
3R	H ACCRINGTON	18	W	3:1	1:1	Cook A	Bailey	Rae	Burden	Peacock	White	Hinshelwood	Atyeo	Curtis	Eisentrager	Smith D	Atyeo 40, 86, Curtis 87
7/1	32,196 3N:8					*McInnes*	*McNichal*	*Harrower*	*Hunter*	*Stones*	*Tighe*	*Anders*	*Sowden*	*Stewart*	*Storey*	*Byrom*	*Sowden 15*
	(£4,340.10.0)																Ref: W Clements

Playing in Bristol Rovers kit as they did in the first meeting, City make hard work of this victory in front of a new record Ashton Gate floodlit crowd. Shots from Atyeo and an acute angled effort from Curtis take City through after Peter Sowden headed the visitors into an early lead.

No				F-A	H-T	1	2	3	4	5	6	7	8	9	10	11	Scorers, Times, and Referees
4	A NOTTS CO	20	W	2:1	0:0	Anderson	Bailey	Thresher	Emery	Williams A	Burden	Hinshelwood	Walker	Atyeo	Etheridge	Watkins	Etheridge 77, Hinshelwood 88
25/1	18,395 18					*Bradley*	*Chatham*	*Pritchard*	*Loxley*	*Russell*	*Carver*	*Wills*	*Newsham*	*Jackson*	*Roby*	*Tucker*	*Pritchard 55*
	(£2,545.13.0)																Ref: K Aston

Unlucky when his shot is kicked off the line on 25 minutes, Etheridge makes his mark with his headed leveller after the break. Roy Pritchard's deflected free-kick opens the scoring, but his back-pass brings City's late winner. The ball holds up in the mud for Hinshelwood to tuck away.

No				F-A	H-T	1	2	3	4	5	6	7	8	9	10	11	Scorers, Times, and Referees
5	H BRISTOL ROV	21	L	3:4	1:3	Anderson	Terris	Thresher	Emery	Williams A	Burden	Hinshelwood	Walker	Atyeo	Etheridge	Watkins	Watkins 4, Etheridge 57, Burden 65
15/2	39,160 15					*Nicholls*	*Bamford*	*Watling*	*Sykes*	*Pyle*	*Sampson*	*Petherbridge*	*Meyer*	*Bradford*	*Ward*	*Hooper*	*Syk" 28, Ward 31, Meyer 42, Bradf" 83*
	(£5,439.1.0)																Ref: R Leafe

A classic from the moment Watkins headed City into an early lead. Unfortunately, it is a mixed afternoon for City's left-winger, who has his spot-kick saved by Ron Nicholls just before half-time. Controversy over Geoff Bradford's match-winning shot as many-thought him offside.

Gloucestershire Cup

No				F-A	H-T	1	2	3	4	5	6	7	8	9	10	11	Scorers, Times, and Referees
F	H BRISTOL ROV	17	W	4:1	2:1	Anderson	Peacock	Thresher	McCall	Williams A	Burden	Hinshelwood	Atyeo	Curtis	Etheridge	Watkins	Etheridge 13, 79, Atyeo 36,
29/4	10,590 10					*Radford*	*Bamford*	*Watling*	*Sykes*	*Hale*	*Sampson*	*Mabbutt*	*Biggs*	*Bradford*	*Ward*	*Hooper*	[Curtis 74] *Bradford 6*
																	Ref: R Leafe

Sheer perfection sums up City's display after Geoff Bradford steers the ball in for Rovers' early lead. Etheridge's header soon levels matters, prior to Atyeo hammering City in front. Following the break, Curtis shoots home from six yards, and Etheridge nets with a tremendous drive.

	P	Home W	D	L	F	A	Away W	D	L	F	A	Pts
1 West Ham	42	12	8	1	56	25	11	3	7	45	29	57
2 Blackburn	42	13	7	1	50	18	9	5	7	43	39	56
3 Charlton	42	15	3	3	65	33	9	4	8	42	36	55
4 Liverpool	42	17	3	1	50	13	5	7	9	29	41	54
5 Fulham	42	13	5	3	53	24	7	7	7	44	35	52
6 Sheffield Utd	42	12	5	4	38	22	9	5	7	37	28	52
7 Middlesboro	42	13	3	5	52	29	6	4	11	31	45	45
8 Ipswich	42	13	4	4	45	29	6	2	13	23	40	44
9 Huddersfield	42	9	8	4	28	24	5	8	8	35	42	44
10 Bristol Rov	42	12	5	4	52	31	5	3	13	33	49	42
11 Stoke	42	9	4	8	49	36	9	2	10	26	37	42
12 Leyton Orient	42	14	2	5	53	27	3	5	13	24	52	41
13 Grimsby	42	13	4	4	54	30	4	2	15	32	53	40
14 Barnsley	42	10	6	5	40	25	4	6	11	30	49	40
15 Cardiff	42	10	5	6	44	31	4	4	13	19	46	37
16 Derby	42	11	3	7	37	36	4	3	14	23	45	36
17 BRISTOL C	42	9	5	7	35	31	4	4	13	28	57	35
18 Rotherham	42	8	3	10	38	44	6	2	13	27	57	33
19 Swansea	42	8	3	10	48	45	3	6	12	24	54	31
20 Lincoln	42	6	6	9	33	35	2	9	10	22	47	31
21 Notts Co	42	9	3	9	24	31	3	3	15	20	49	30
22 Doncaster	42	7	5	9	34	40	1	6	14	22	48	27
	924	243	100	119	978	659	119	100	243	659	978	924

Appearances / Goals

	Appearances Lge	Cup	Goals Lge	Cup	Tot
Anderson, Bob	35	3			
Atyeo, John	42	5	23	3	26
Bailey, Jack	12	3			
Briggs, Alec	4				
Burden, Tommy	38	5	2	1	3
Bevan, Brian	1				
Compton, Terry	3				
Cook, Charles	1				
Cook, Tony	7	2			
Curtis, Dermot	11	3	3	3	6
Eisentrager, Alec	8	2	1		1
Emery, Terry	10	2			
Etheridge, Bobby	31	3	7	4	11
Hinshelwood, Wally	38	5	3	2	5
McCall, Peter	7	1			
Munroe, William	1				
Parr, Gordon	2				
Peacock, Ernie	30	3			
Rae, Ian	12	1			
Smith, David	1	2			
Terris, James	3	1			
Thresher, Mike	41	4			
Tindill, Herbert	14		10		10
Virgin, Derek	1				
Walker, George	12	2	4		4
Watkins, Johnny	40	3	9	1	10
White, Jack	20	2			
Williams, Alan	34	3			
Williams, Cyril	3				
(own-goals)			1		1
29 players used	462	55	63	14	77

Odds & ends

Double wins: (2) Notts Co, Cardiff.

Double losses: (4) Liverpool, Charlton, Rotherham, Swansea.

Won from behind: (3) Cardiff (a), Accrington (h) (FAC), Notts Co (a) (FAC).

Lost from in front: (6) Liverpool (h), Huddersfield (h), Charlton (h), Doncaster (a), Swansea (h), Bristol Rov (h) (FAC).

High spots: City's escape from relegation thanks to the appointment of the great Peter Doherty as manager.

The performances of Bert Tindill, signed from Doncaster Rovers.

The 3-3 draw at Eastville on 5 April.

City's first-half play at Craven Cottage on 19 April.

Low spots: Losing 0-5 at home to Fulham on 7 December.

Shipping five goals at Swansea, Derby and Blackburn.

Losing at home to Bristol Rovers in the FA Cup.

AGM (Brecknell, Dolman & Rogers, Pennywell Road, 20 April 1959): Profit £4,839.4s.10d. Season Ticket Sales £17,180.0s.0d.

Player of the year: Bert Tindill.

Ever-presents: (1) John Atyeo.

Hat-tricks: (4) Bert Tindill (3), John Atyeo (1).

Leading scorer: Overall: John Atyeo (26). League: John Atyeo (23).

LEAGUE DIVISION 2

Manager: Peter Doherty

SEASON 1958-59

No	Date		Att	Pos	Pt	F-A	H-T	Scorers, Times, and Referees
1	H ROTHERHAM	23/8	25,253 (£2,651.0.0)		W 2	6-1	1-1	Atyeo 27, Hinshelwood 65, 73, Jones 28 [Tindill 76, 78, Eth'dge 82] Ref: J Hunt
2	A BARNSLEY	27/8	14,283		W 4	7-4	2:1	Eth' 20, Watk' 35, Atyo 53, 80, 87, Chappell 6, 51, 54, 81 [Tindill 67, 82] Ref: J Mitchell
3	A SHEFFIELD UTD	30/8	23,133	5	L 4	0-4	0-2	Hamilton 15, Hodgson 44, Pace 65, [Ringstead 69] Ref: F Stringer
4	H BARNSLEY	2/9	28,530 (£3,024.5.0)	2	W 6	3-1	1-1	Atyeo 24, Tindill 75, Watkins 78, Holmes 8, Ref: A Bond
5	H BRIGHTON	6/9	23,661 (£2,468.2.6)	2	W 8	3-0	2-0	Etheridge 16, McCall 21, Atyeo 76, Ref: K Collinge
6	A HUDDERSFIELD	9/9	13,884	2	W 10	1-0	1-0	Atyeo 42, Ref: K Dagnall
7	A GRIMSBY	13/9	15,606	3	L 10	0-2	0-2	Cockerill 13, Fell 25, Ref: J Barradell
8	H HUDDERSFIELD	16/9	29,428 (£3,171.6.0)	2	W 12	2-1	2-0	Watkins 1, Tindill 5, Massie 75, Ref: E Jennings
9	H LIVERPOOL	20/9	27,162 (£2,900.10.6)	3	L 12	1-3	1-1	Moran 21 (og), Liddell 1, 55, Melia 51, Ref: W Clements
10	A MIDDLESBROUGH	27/9	29,498	3	D 13	0-0	0-0	Ref: R Ryalls

Line-ups (City in roman, opponents in italic)

No	1	2	3	4	5	6	7	8	9	10	11
1	Anderson	Peacock	Thresher	McCall	Williams A	Burden	Hinshelwood	Tindill	Atyeo	Etheridge	Watkins
	Ironside	*Silman*	*Morgan*	*Lambert*	*Madden*	*Williams*	*Webster*	*Layne*	*Waterhouse*	*Jones*	*Broadbent*
2	Anderson	Peacock	Thresher	McCall	Williams A	Burden	Hinshelwood	Tindill	Atyeo	Etheridge	Watkins
	Hough	*Short*	*Swift*	*Bartlett*	*Sharp*	*Barber*	*Kaye*	*Smith*	*Chappell*	*Graham*	*McCann*
3	Anderson	Peacock	Thresher	McCall	Williams A	Burden	Hinshelwood	Tindill	Atyeo	Etheridge	Watkins
	Hodgkinson	*Coldwell*	*Shaw G*	*Richardson*	*Shaw J*	*Summers*	*Ringstead*	*Hamilton*	*Pace*	*Simpson*	*Hodgson*
4	Anderson	Peacock	Thresher	McCall	Williams A	Burden	Hinshelwood	Tindill	Atyeo	Etheridge	Watkins
	Hough	*Short*	*Swift*	*Bartlett*	*Sharp*	*Houghton*	*Whyke*	*Holmes*	*Chappell*	*Graham*	*McCann*
5	Anderson	Peacock	Thresher	McCall	Williams A	Burden	Hinshelwood	Tindill	Atyeo	Etheridge	Watkins
	Gill	*Bisset*	*Jennings*	*Burtenshaw*	*Whitfield*	*Wilson*	*Gordon*	*Bertolini*	*Shepherd*	*Sexton*	*Howard*
6	Cook	Peacock	Thresher	McCall	Williams A	Burden	Hinshelwood	Tindill	Atyeo	Etheridge	Watkins
	Kennon	*Conwell*	*Wilson*	*McGarry*	*Connor*	*Low*	*Howard*	*Law*	*Hawksworth*	*Massie*	*Ledger*
7	Cook	Peacock	Thresher	McCall	Williams A	Burden	Hinshelwood	Tindill	Atyeo	Etheridge	Watkins
	Ball	*Donovan*	*Richardson*	*Connor*	*Jobling*	*Cockerill*	*Scott*	*Briggs*	*Rafferty*	*Cullen*	*Fell*
8	Cook	Peacock	Thresher	McCall	Williams A	Burden	Hinshelwood	Tindill	Atyeo	Etheridge	Watkins
	Kennon	*Gibson*	*Wilson*	*McGarry*	*Coddington*	*Low*	*McHale*	*Law*	*Massie*	*Hawksworth*	*Ledger*
9	Cook	Hopkinson	Thresher	McCall	Williams A	Burden	Hinshelwood	Tindill	Atyeo	Etheridge	Watkins
	Younger	*Byrne*	*Moran*	*Wheeler*	*White*	*Campbell*	*Morris*	*Melia*	*Liddell*	*Harrower*	*A'Court*
10	Cook	Hopkinson	Thresher	McCall	Williams A	Burden	Hinshelwood	Tindill	Atyeo	Etheridge	Watkins
	Taylor	*Bilcliff*	*Stonehouse*	*Harris*	*Philip*	*Dicks*	*McLean*	*Scott*	*Clough*	*Fitzsimmons*	*Burbeck*

Match reports

1. A minute's silence is observed in memory of City vice-chairman Charles Crawford, who died during the week. Watkins is thwarted when Roy Ironside saves his 12th-minute penalty, but Atyeo's brilliant header and a superb Glyn Jones drive gets the scoring underway. What a start!

2. This game ranks as one of City's finest post-war performances. A marvellous contest, which ebbs and flows, but it is not until near the end that City have the comfort of a two-goal advantage. Surely goal of the season - the Watkins shot that hits the net with the speed of a guided missile.

3. City are without Anderson's services for the last 15 minutes of the first half. Fortunately, Etheridge proves to be an able deputy, except for an error of judgement for Billy Hodgson's goal. Anderson, on his return, can do nothing to prevent the Blade's gaining a well-deserved success.

4. City turn on the style in the first half, but are foiled by Barnsley's uncompromising defence. Tom Holmes gives the visitors an early lead, seizing on Cook's clearance to leave the keeper stranded from 30 yards. A typical left-footed Watkins pile-driver secures the points for City.

5. Tom Bisset handles on the line to keep out Atyeo's header, but Watkins has the resultant 55th-minute penalty saved. Pleased when Etheridge nods in the opener, even City supporters are dismayed when Stan Howard's goal for outplayed Brighton is disallowed for offside near the end.

6. City's defence takes the honours at Leeds Road, where they have to battle hard to hold onto the lead given them by Atyeo's chip that just clears keeper Sandy Kennon. When Hinshelwood is booked late on, the crowd voice their disapproval of City's tactics with a barrage of booing.

7. Despite an improved second-half display, City's inability to find the net means they are unable to get anything from this game. Ron Cockerill registers from 25 yards to put Grimsby in front. Jimmy Fell leaves City a mountain to climb, when firing the ball in after slipping past Peacock.

8. In front of the largest crowd for a floodlight League game at the Gate, City put on sparkling display for the opening 40 minutes. Deservedly in front thanks to headers from Watkins on 30 seconds and Tindill shortly after, City lose their way when Peacock pulls his right-thigh muscle.

9. Billy Liddell gets Liverpool off to a great start, registering with his drive after just 15 seconds, but it is goalkeeper Tommy Younger who is their star. After Hinshelwood's shot is deflected in by the helpless Ronnie Moran, it is Younger who has to perform heroics to keep City out.

10. The City defence takes the honours as Boro's four forward changes fail to improve their scoring rate. Centre-half Williams has a fine game against England prospect Brian Clough at Ayresome Park, where City's forwards are unable to put the finishing touch to some crisp moves.

11 — H CHARLTON · 4/10 · Att 23,831 (£2,514.16.0) · Pos 5 · L 2-4 · 6/13
Tindill 23, Etheridge 60 / Ryan 27, Summers 47, 50, 62 · Ref: D Cooper

Cook	Hopkinson	Thresher	McCall	Williams A	Burden	Hinshelwood	Tindill	Atyeo	Etheridge	Watkins
Duff	*Edwards*	*Townsend*	*Hewie*	*Jago*	*Kiernan*	*Lawrie*	*Lucas*	*Leary*	*Ryan*	*Summers*

Charlton boss Jimmy Trotter's half-time talk is responsible for City's defeat. He deploys John Ryan, Stuart Leary and Fred Lucas to draw City's defenders out of position. John Summers quickly takes advantage, back-heading his first and driving in a 10-yarder for his second.

---

12 — H SWANSEA · 11/10 · Att 24,309 (£2,581.17.0) · Pos 5 · W 4-0 · 11/15
Atyeo 40, 69, 87, Watkins 55 · Ref: F Collinge

Cook	Hopkinson	Thresher	McCall	Williams A	Burden	Hinshelwood	Tindill	Atyeo	Etheridge	Watkins
King	*Thomas*	*Lawson*	*Charles*	*Daniel*	*Brown*	*Allchurch*	*Davies Reg*	*Palmer*	*Webster*	*Griffiths*

Hinshelwood turns on the style as his younger son Paul watches his father in action for the first time. A convincing victory for the City in a game in which Watkins, out on the left, meets Hinshelwood's cross from the right to score with a great pile-driver into the Covered End net.

---

13 — A STOKE · 18/10 · Att 22,658 · Pos 5 · L 1-2 · 3/15
Etheridge 70 / King 46p, Thomson 85 · Ref: A Jobling

Cook	Hopkinson	Thresher	McCall	Williams A	Burden	Hinshelwood	Tindill	Atyeo	Etheridge	Watkins
Robertson	*McCue*	*Allen*	*Asprey*	*Thomson*	*Ratcliffe*	*Howitt*	*Bowyer*	*King*	*Wilshaw*	*Oscroft*

This game is enlivened by a debatable penalty when Hopkinson falls on the ball in a tussle with Harry Oscroft. Following Etheridge's leveller, skilful City have Stoke on the rack, but the lack of a sharpshooter is costly. Ken Thomson's headed winner is a cruel and unexpected blow.

---

14 — H SUNDERLAND · 25/10 · Att 25,510 (£2,704.7.6) · Pos 4 · W 4-1 · 22/17
Virgin 5, 28, Atyeo 33, Tindill 80, Grainger 13 · Ref: W Hickson

Cook	Hopkinson	Thresher	McCall	Williams A	Burden	Virgin	Tindill	Atyeo	Etheridge	Watkins
Bollands	*Nelson*	*Ashurst*	*McNab*	*Hurley*	*Pearce*	*Bircham*	*Anderson*	*Kichenbrand*	*O'Neill*	*Grainger*

For this demolition of relegated Sunderland, singer Frankie Vaughan is at Ashton Gate appealing for support for the National Federation of Boys Clubs. Derek Virgin has a scintillating game for City, his second goal - a brilliant shot into the Open End net - caps a great 40-yard run.

---

15 — A BRISTOL ROV · 1/11 · Att 32,129 · Pos 4 · W 2-1 · 6/19
Tindill 68, Atyeo 77 / Sykes 80 · Ref: B Griffiths

Cook	Hopkinson	Thresher	McCall	Williams A	Burden	Virgin	Tindill	Atyeo	Etheridge	Watkins
Radford	*Doyle*	*Watling*	*Sykes*	*Pyle*	*Sampson*	*McIlveny*	*Biggs*	*Bradford*	*Ward*	*Hooper*

A respectful silence in memory of Rovers star Harry Bamford, who died in a scooter accident during the week, is the prelude to a far from clean derby. Mervyn Griffiths has to be at his best to maintain control as City take their chances to win despite Rovers territorial advantage.

---

16 — H FULHAM · 8/11 · Att 32,378 (£3,522.8.6) · Pos 3 · D 1-1 · 2/20
Etheridge 4p / Haynes 8 · Ref: D Howell

Cook	Hopkinson	Thresher	McCall	Williams A	Burden	Hinshelwood	Tindill	Atyeo	Etheridge	Watkins
Macedo	*Cohen*	*Langley*	*Lowe*	*Bentley*	*Lawler*	*Key*	*Hill*	*Cook*	*Haynes*	*Leggat*

McCall has a fine game in curtailing the great genius of Johnny Haynes. Both sides have their chances, but a draw is a fair result. Ex-City man Roy Bentley's trip on Watkins brings Etheridge his spot-kick, but Haynes heads in a leveller to preserve the Cottagers' unbeaten away record.

---

17 — A SHEFFIELD WED · 15/11 · Att 28,652 · Pos 3 · W 3-2 · 2/22
Tindill 27, Williams 89, Atyeo 90 / Finney 11, 17 · Ref: H Haworth

Cook	Hopkinson	Thresher	McCall	Williams A	Burden	Hinshelwood	Tindill	Atyeo	Etheridge	Watkins
Springett	*Martin*	*Curtis*	*McAnearney*	*T Swan*	*Gibson*	*Wilkinson*	*Fraggatt*	*Shiner*	*Fantham*	*Finney*

City's never say die spirit ends Wednesday's run of eight successive league wins at Hillsborough. Williams rams in City's late equaliser, but they are not satisfied and keeping on the offensive, Atyeo crashes home Hinshelwood's ground-level centre to secure a memorable victory.

---

18 — H SCUNTHORPE · 22/11 · Att 20,306 (£2,069.13.0) · Pos 3 · L 0-1 · 18/22
/ Marriott 59 · Ref: R Mann

Cook	Hopkinson	Thresher	McCall	Williams A	Burden	Hinshelwood	Tindill	Atyeo	Etheridge	Watkins
Hardwick	*Hubbard*	*Brownsword*	*Marshall*	*Horstead*	*Sharpe*	*Marriott*	*Haigh*	*Waldock*	*Neale*	*Jones*

If Atyeo had not missed three fine chances in the opening half-hour it is likely that City would have cantered to victory. Thereafter Ronnie Waldock and Jack Marriott, whose slammed in winner brought forth an amazing burst of clapping from the fans, gave City the runaround.

---

19 — A LEYTON ORIENT · 29/11 · Att 9,591 · Pos 4 · L 2-4 · 13/22
Etheridge 55, Atyeo 60 / Elwood 30, 54, 65, 68 · Ref: A Holland

Cook	Hopkinson	Thresher	McCall	Williams A	Burden	Hinshelwood	Tindill	Atyeo	Etheridge	Watkins
George	*Wright*	*Gregory*	*Facey*	*Bishop*	*Lucas*	*White*	*Lazarus*	*Julians*	*Lewis*	*Elwood*

Hopkinson's poor clearances set up Orient for their opening two goals, whilst Etheridge fluffs two easy chances for City prior to the interval. The Orient wingers give Hopkinson and Thresher a torrid afternoon, but City should have done better after Atyeo had jabbed in an equaliser.

---

20 — H DERBY · 6/12 · Att 20,312 (£2,066.10.0) · Pos 7 · L 1-3 · 12/22
Etheridge 47 / Parry 15, Hunt 52, Darwin 56 · Ref: J Mitchell

Cook	Hopkinson	Thresher	McCall	Williams A	Burden	Hinshelwood	Tindill	Atyeo	Rogers	Watkins
Oxford	*Barrowcliffe*	*Martin*	*Upton*	*Young*	*Davies*	*Hannigan*	*Parry*	*Hunt*	*Darwin*	*Cargill*

A not particularly auspicious Ashton Gate return for Jimmy Rogers after three years at Coventry as City are denied by Ken Oxford's star performance in the Derby goal. He pulls off five amazing saves in the first half and one after the break. Etheridge's 16-yarder levels for City.

---

21 — A LINCOLN · 13/12 · Att 7,041 · Pos 5 · W 2-0 · 21/24
Hopkinson 3, Tindill 4 · Ref: A Ellis

Cook	Hopkinson	Thresher	McCall	Williams A	Burden	Hinshelwood	Tindill	Atyeo	Etheridge	Watkins
Heath	*Green*	*Smith*	*Middleton*	*Emery*	*Linnecor*	*McClelland*	*Harbertson*	*Graver*	*Chapman*	*Finch*

Hopkinson, who almost signed for Lincoln in the summer on being released by Doncaster, is the star man in this Sincil Bank clash. Finding himself further upfield than usual after a surging run out of defence, he heeds Etheridge's shout to fire in from 25 yards for his first ever goal.

Match details

No	Date	H/A	Opponents	Att	Pos	Pt	F-A	H-T	Scorers, Times, and Referees
22	20/12	A	ROTHERHAM	6,653	5	26	W 2:1	1:0	Hinshelwood 7, Atyeo 72; *Twidle 67*; Ref: C Sant
23	26/12	H	CARDIFF	27,570 (£2,945.5.0)	6	26	L 2:3	1:1	Etheridge 28, Atyeo 49; *Walsh 32, Bonson 67, 71*; Ref: E Jennings
24	27/12	A	CARDIFF	27,146	6	26	L 0:1	0:1	*Burden 4 (og)*; Ref: R Chandler
25	3/1	H	SHEFFIELD UTD	20,834 (£2,159.11.0)	6	28	W 3:1	2:0	Tindill 22, 51, Atyeo 27; *Pace 63*; Ref: H Husband
26	17/1	A	BRIGHTON	18,246	6	29	D 2:2	1:0	Tindill 19, 65; *Sexton 50, 86*; Ref: J Taylor
27	7/2	A	LIVERPOOL	34,091	9	29	L 2:3	1:2	Tindill 19, Atyeo 76; *Arnell 2, 70, Melia 29*; Ref: P Rhodes
28	14/2	H	MIDDLESBROUGH	18,336 (£1,851.6.0)	8	30	D 2:2	1:0	Atyeo 36, Etheridge 80; *Harris 49p, Clough 73*; Ref: E Hill
29	21/2	A	CHARLTON	11,146	10	30	L 1:4	0:1	Tindill 52; *Leary 28, 89, Ryan 62, Hewie 85*; Ref: J Hunt
30	24/2	H	GRIMSBY	15,440 (£1,485.1.6)	8	32	W 1:0	1:0	Atyeo 23; Ref: F Cowan
31	28/2	A	FULHAM	26,891	9	32	L 0:1	0:1	*Leggat 26*; Ref: R Wood

(opponents' positions shown in original: 22, 9, 8, 5, 14, 2, 16, 9, 19, 2)

Line-ups (City, with opponents in italic)

No	1	2	3	4	5	6	7	8	9	10	11
22	Cook	Hopkinson	Thresher	McCall	Williams A	Burden	Hinshelwood	Atyeo	Tindill	Etheridge	Watkins
	Quairney	*Perry*	*Morgan*	*Lambert*	*Madden*	*Williams*	*Sawyer*	*Webster*	*Twidle*	*Kettleborough*	*Broadbent*
23	Cook	Nicholls	Thresher	McCall	Williams A	Burden	Hinshelwood	Tindill	Atyeo	Etheridge	Watkins
		Milne	*Stitfall*	*Sullivan*	*Malloy*	*Baker*	*Walsh*	*Tapscott*	*Bonson*	*Hewitt*	*Reynolds*
24	Cook	Nicholls	Thresher	McCall	Williams A	Burden	Hinshelwood	Walker	Tindill	Etheridge	Watkins
		Milne	*Stitfall*	*Sullivan*	*Malloy*	*Baker*	*Walsh*	*Tapscott*	*Bonson*	*Hewitt*	*Jenkins*
25	Cook	Hopkinson	Thresher	McCall	Williams A	Burden	Hinshelwood	Tindill	Atyeo	Etheridge	Smith D
		Coldwell	*Shaw G*	*Hoyland*	*Shaw J*	*Summers*	*Lewis*	*Hamilton*	*Pace*	*Russell*	*Simpson*
26	Cook	Hollins	Thresher	McCall	Williams A	Burden	Hinshelwood	Tindill	Atyeo	Etheridge	Smith D
		Bisset	*Little*	*Bertolini*	*Jennings*	*Wilson*	*Tiddy*	*Shepherd*	*Sexton*	*Dixon*	*Jones*
27	Cook	Hopkinson	Thresher	McCall	Williams A	Burden	Hinshelwood	Etheridge	Atyeo	Tindill	Rogers
	Younger	*Molyneux*	*Moran*	*Wheeler*	*White*	*Twentyman*	*Morris*	*Melia*	*Arnell*	*Harrower*	*A'Court*
28	Cook	Taylor	Thresher	McCall	Williams A	Burden	Hinshelwood	Tindill	Atyeo	Etheridge	Rogers
		Barnard	*Stonehouse*	*Yeoman*	*Phillips*	*Harris*	*Fitzsimmons*	*Fernie*	*Clough*	*Peacock*	*Holliday*
29	Cook	Duff	Thresher	McCall	Williams A	Burden	Hinshelwood	Tindill	Atyeo	Etheridge	Rogers
		Sewell	*Townsend*	*Lucas*	*Jago*	*Kiernan*	*White*	*Hewie*	*Leary*	*Ryan*	*Lawrie*
30	Cook	Barnett	Thresher	McCall	Williams A	Burden	Hinshelwood	Tindill	Atyeo	Etheridge	Rogers
		Donovan	*Fleming*	*Welbourne*	*Jobling*	*Cockerill*	*Williams D*	*Scott*	*Barratt*	*Cullen*	*Fell*
31	Cook	Hawkins	Thresher	McCall	Williams A	Burden	Hinshelwood	Tindill	Atyeo	Etheridge	Rogers
		Cohen	*Langley*	*Mullery*	*Bentley*	*Lawler*	*Cook*	*Barton*	*Doherty*	*Haynes*	*Leggat*

Match reports

22 — Rotherham (A): Atyeo thought his strained knee could do with another week's rest, but following a late fitness test he declares himself happy to play. In the ankle-deep mud he proves to be the best forward on the pitch. 'One of my best goals this season,' is his verdict on his match-winning strike.

23 — Cardiff (H): Despite Cardiff's composed football, City are unlucky not to have drawn this fine contest. Cardiff's winner is controversial as Joe Bonson unfairly bundles Cook over the line. Etheridge steered in the opener from Tindill's cross, but Atyeo's 20-yard strike is the goal of the game.

24 — Cardiff (A): City are again unlucky against Cardiff, beaten by Alex Milne's early free-kick which goes in off of Burden's shin. Unfortunately, City are made to pay for failing to take their chances in a game in which they make and fluff twice as many opportunities as their Welsh rivals.

25 — Sheffield Utd (H): On a quagmire of a pitch, City's wing play proves a winning formula against the Blades. Tindill shoots in at the Park End to open the scoring, but both sides fail with spot-kicks. Etheridge hits a post on 44 minutes, whilst Graham Shaw's effort is saved by Cook 14 minutes from the end.

26 — Brighton (A): The much-maligned Hopkinson is the rock in City's rearguard action on the South Coast. City are fortunate, just a few minutes after Dave Sexton had half-volleyed in Brighton's deserved late equaliser, that alert referee Jack Taylor spots Fred Jones fisting the ball into the net.

27 — Liverpool (A): Alan Arnell, with a neat 12-yard left-footer, gets his side off to a good start, but Tindill hooks City level from 15 yards. Jimmy Melia races through to pick his spot, but City again level when Atyeo fires in. Cook gives away a last-minute penalty, but saves Ronnie Moran's kick.

28 — Middlesbrough (H): Whilst the visitors are thrice denied by the woodwork prior to Atyeo putting City ahead, they are gifted their goals. Williams concedes the spot-kick by punching the ball away when Cook fumbles a weak shot, then failure in dealing with a cross makes it easy for Brian Clough.

29 — Charlton (A): John Hewie's offside-looking header and Stuart Leary's grand shot in the final five minutes give an untrue reflection of the play. Tindill, denied early on when the officials fail to spot that his drive, which hits the underside of the bar, drops down over the line, fires in for City.

30 — Grimsby (H): This was Alan Barnett's match as the Grimsby custodian, whom City tried to sign from Pompey until being put off by the £4,000 asking price, often thwarted the home forwards. Atyeo drives in the winner when the goalkeeper is slow to recover after brilliantly saving from Etheridge.

31 — Fulham (A): In ideal spring conditions, Graham Leggat's well-taken goal settles a poor game shortly before Hopkinson is left a hobbling passenger on the wing. Johnny Haynes is unlucky to have his 12-yard drive disallowed midway through the second half and his side given a free-kick instead.

Match 32 — H STOKE — 7/3
Attendance: 15,945 (£1,567.15.0) · League pos 8 · W 2:1 (HT 1-0) · (4, 34)
Scorers: Burden 14, Tindill 46 / *Howitt 75*
Ref: K Aston

Pos	Bristol City	Stoke
1	Cook	*Robertson*
2	Hopkinson	*McCue*
3	Thresher	*Allen*
4	McCall	*Asprey*
5	Williams A	*Thomson*
6	Burden	*Cairns*
7	Hinshelwood	*Bentley*
8	Tindill	*Howitt*
9	Atyeo	*King*
10	Etheridge	*Ratcliffe*
11	Virgin	*Oscroft*

Burden hammers in a fine goal in this narrow victory over a Stoke side who, as well as failing from the spot, have a first-half effort disallowed for offside. Cook dives full length to save Robert Cairns's 73rd-minute spot-kick, but is unable to do anything about Ron Howitt's 18-yarder.

Match 33 — A SUNDERLAND — 14/3
Attendance: 24,049 · League pos 9 · L 1:3 (HT 1-0) · (11, 34)
Scorers: Atyeo 28 / *Taylor 53, 76, Goodchild 87*
Ref: R Ryalls

Pos	Bristol City	Sunderland
1	Cook	*Wakeham*
2	Hopkinson	*Nelson*
3	Thresher	*Ashurst*
4	McCall	*Anderson*
5	Williams A	*Hurley*
6	Burden	*Pearce*
7	Hinshelwood	*Fraser*
8	Tindill	*Goodchild*
9	Atyeo	*Kitchenbrand*
10	Etheridge	*Taylor*
11	Virgin	*Godbold*

City match Charlie Hurley in the air when Atyeo takes over the centre-forward role from Tindill some 20 minutes after the start. Despite Sunderland's domination, it seems for a while that City might hang on, but Ernie Taylor's pair of close-range efforts change all such hopes.

Match 34 — H BRISTOL ROV — 21/3
Attendance: 27,140 (£2,859.3.6) · League pos 10 · D 1:1 (HT 0-1) · (7, 35)
Scorers: Atyeo 60 / *Ward 44*
Ref: R Smith

Pos	Bristol City	Bristol Rovers
1	Cook	*Norman*
2	Hopkinson	*Doyle*
3	Burden	*Watling*
4	McCall	*Sykes*
5	Williams A	*Pyle*
6	**Casey**	*Mabbutt*
7	Hinshelwood	*Smith G*
8	Tindill	*Ward*
9	Atyeo	*Bradford*
10	Etheridge	*Biggs*
11	Watkins	*Hooper*

Controversy over City's Open End equaliser which, despite it appearing that Watkins had scored direct from his corner, was officially awarded to Atyeo. However, a deserved point for City as they fight-back well after Dai Ward had headed Rovers in front shortly before the interval.

Match 35 — H IPSWICH — 27/3
Attendance: 20,117 (£2,030.1.6) · League pos 8 · W 3:0 (HT 1-0) · (16, 37)
Scorers: Etheridge 38, 57p, Watkins 73
Ref: C Sant

Pos	Bristol City	Ipswich
1	Cook	*Bailey*
2	Hopkinson	*Carberry*
3	Thresher	*Malcolm*
4	McCall	*Pickett*
5	Williams A	*Snell*
6	Casey	*Johnstone*
7	Hinshelwood	*Siddall*
8	Tindill	*Rees*
9	Atyeo	*Crawford*
10	Etheridge	*Phillips*
11	Watkins	*Leadbeater*

Etheridge stars, but it is only the fact of Bobby Williams being unfit that enables him to play. Watkins breaks the Covered End net with a great pile-driver to set the seal on City's win, but denies the shot is as powerful as at Barnsley. Cook saves Ray Crawford's 88th-minute spot-kick.

Match 36 — A SWANSEA — 28/3
Attendance: 13,336 · League pos 8 · L 0:1 (HT 0-0) · (11, 37)
Scorers: / *Davies 74*
Ref: F Gerrard

Pos	Bristol City	Swansea
1	Cook	*King*
2	Hopkinson	*Hughes*
3	Thresher	*Griffiths*
4	McCall	*Woods*
5	Williams A	*Nurse*
6	Burden	*Saunders*
7	Hinshelwood	*Allchurch*
8	Tindill	*Davies Reg*
9	Atyeo	*Webster*
10	Etheridge	*Williams H*
11	Watkins	*Williams G*

City's forwards seldom look liked troubling the Swansea custodian in this dull affair, whilst only the crossbar prevents Burden heading in a 20th-minute own-goal. Cook is caught off his line as Reg Davies lobs the ball over his head from 20 yards to clinch the points for the Swans.

Match 37 — A IPSWICH — 30/3
Attendance: 13,549 · League pos 8 · D 1:1 (HT 1-0) · (16, 38)
Scorers: Tindill 13 / *Phillips 64*
Ref: J Williams

Pos	Bristol City	Ipswich
1	Cook	*Bailey*
2	Hopkinson	*Carberry*
3	Thresher	*Malcolm*
4	McCall	*Pickett*
5	Williams A	*Snell*
6	Burden	*Johnstone*
7	Hinshelwood	*Berry*
8	Tindill	*Rees*
9	Atyeo	*Curtis*
10	Etheridge	*Phillips*
11	Watkins	*Leadbeater*

Tindill slams Hinshelwood's centre into the net for City's early lead, but they have to face a savage onslaught especially after the break. Ted Phillips fires in a leveller from the edge of the area. Derek Rees has his 80th-minute effort struck off when the referee consults his linesman.

Match 38 — H SHEFFIELD WED — 4/4
Attendance: 21,495 (£2,213.3.0) · League pos 9 · L 1:2 (HT 1-2) · (2, 38)
Scorers: / *Fantham 12, Kay 20*
Ref: J Hunt

Pos	Bristol City	Sheffield Wed
1	Cook	*MacLaren*
2	Hopkinson	*Staniforth*
3	Thresher	*Curtis*
4	McCall	*McAnearney/T Swan*
5	Williams A	*Kay*
6	Burden	*Wilkinson*
7	Hinshelwood	*Froggatt*
8	Tindill	*Shiner*
9	Atyeo	*Fantham*
10	Etheridge	*Finney*
11	Watkins	

Both sides wear black armbands in memory of Birmingham's Jeff Hall, who died this morning. A fortunate success for First Division bound Wednesday thanks to their early goals. Twice City are frustrated when handling offences by Peter Swan in the penalty area go unpunished.

Match 39 — A SCUNTHORPE — 11/4
Attendance: 11,101 · League pos 8 · D 3:3 (HT 2-1) · (17, 39)
Scorers: Etheridge 10p, Atyeo 39, 59, McCall 13 (og) / *Donnelly 52p, 56p*
Ref: L Tirebuck

Pos	Bristol City	Scunthorpe
1	Cook	*Hardwick*
2	Hopkinson	*Hubbard*
3	Thresher	*Brownsword*
4	McCall	*Haigh*
5	Williams A	*Howard*
6	Casey	*Neale*
7	Hinshelwood	*Marriott*
8	Tindill	*Waldock*
9	Atyeo	*Harburn*
10	Etheridge	*Donnelly*
11	Watkins	*Jones*

If City's spot-kick was dubious, the Iron's first is equally doubtful. Cook pulls off great saves to keep out Jack Brownsword's two efforts, but each time the linesman is not satisfied. Peter Donnelly takes over and registers with a rising shot, before scoring another penalty shortly after.

Match 40 — H LEYTON ORIENT — 18/4
Attendance: 14,708 (£1,391.2.6) · League pos 12 · L 0:1 (HT 0-0) · (18, 39)
Scorers: / *Johnson 76*
Ref: W Clements

Pos	Bristol City	Leyton Orient
1	Cook	*George*
2	Hopkinson	*Wright*
3	Thresher	*Charlton*
4	McCall	*Facey*
5	Williams A	*Bishop*
6	Casey	*Lea*
7	Hinshelwood	*White*
8	Tindill	*Brown*
9	Atyeo	*Johnston*
10	**Williams R**	*Baily*
11		*Elwood*

In front of the lowest home crowd so far this season, Burden wins the toss and City defend the Covered End. Those that stayed away must have had a premonition about this drab and aimless affair. Edward Brown's pull-back for Tom Johnston to net from close in decides the matter.

Match 41 — H LINCOLN — 21/4
Attendance: 10,369 (£843.13.0) · League pos 8 · W 1:0 (HT 1-0) · (19, 41)
Scorers: Atyeo 42
Ref: F Stringer

Pos	Bristol City	Lincoln
1	Cook	*Downie*
2	Hopkinson	*Green*
3	Thresher	*Smith*
4	McCall	*Middleton*
5	Williams A	*McEvoy*
6	Casey	*Linnecor*
7	Hinshelwood	*Fitzsimmons*
8	Tindill	*McClelland*
9	Atyeo	*Graver*
10	Etheridge	*Chapman*
11	Rogers	*Wright*

Switching places with Hinshelwood on the half-hour mark, Rogers at last has the chance to play in his favoured position. He is instrumental in the only goal, his lobbed corner being well headed home by Atyeo. A dour struggle, which the relegation threatened Imps are unlucky to lose.

Match 42 — A DERBY — 25/4
Attendance: 12,034 · League pos 10 · L 1:4 (HT 0-2) · (6, 41)
Scorers: Williams R 49 / *Swallow 22, 39, Powell 54, [Hannigan 80]*
Ref: M Dixon

Pos	Bristol City	Derby
1	Cook	*Mitchell*
2	Hopkinson	*Barrowcliffe*
3	Thresher	*Martin*
4	McCall	*Upton*
5	Williams A	*Moore*
6	Etheridge	*Davies*
7	Hinshelwood	*Powell*
8	Tindill	*Swallow*
9	Atyeo	*Hannigan*
10	Etheridge	*Brown*
11	Rogers	*Scarborough*

A disappointing end to a season that promised so much prior to Christmas, as City's casual defensive display brings a heavy defeat at the Baseball Ground. City youngster Bobby Williams darts onto Atyeo's nod-down to prod the ball into the net for his first ever League goal.

Home Average 22,506
Away Average 18,796

CUP-TIES

Manager: Peter Doherty

SEASON 1958-59

FA Cup

				F-A	H-T	Scorers, Times, and Referees	1	2	3	4	5	6	7	8	9	10	11
3	A	DONCASTER	6 W	2-0	1-0	Watkins 19, Tindill 59	Cook	Hopkinson	Thresher	McCall	Williams A	Burden	Hinshelwood	Etheridge	Atyeo	Tindill	Watkins
		19/1				8,432 3:24	*Nimmo*	*White*	*Gavin*	*Kilkenny*	*Makepeace*	*Cavanagh*	*Mooney*	*Callan*	*Minton*	*Walker*	*Sharp*
						(£1,142)											
						Ref: F Cowan											
4	H	BLACKPOOL	6 D	1-1	1-0	Tindill 17	Cook	Hopkinson	Thresher	McCall	Williams A	Burden	Hinshelwood	Tindill	Atyeo	Etheridge	Watkins
		24/1				Charnley 54	*Farm*	*Armfield*	*Wright*	*Hauser*	*Gratrix*	*Kelly*	*Matthews*	*Mudie*	*Charnley*	*Durie*	*Perry*
						42,594 1:8											
						(£5,569.15.6)											
						Ref: K Aston											
4R	A	BLACKPOOL	6 L	0-1	0-0	Durie 59	Cook	Hopkinson	Thresher	McCall	Williams A	Burden	Hinshelwood	Etheridge	Atyeo	Tindill	Watkins
		28/1				25,933 1:8	*Farm*	*Armfield*	*Garrett*	*Hauser*	*Gratrix*	*Kelly*	*Matthews*	*Mudie*	*Charnley*	*Durie*	*Perry*
						Ref: K Aston											

Despite losing the services of Brian Makepeace with a groin strain following his tenth-minute tackle on Tindill, Doncaster almost make City pay for easing up near the end. A typical power shot by Watkins puts City in front and Tindill is his usual alert self when firing in the second.

City, in the unfamiliar blue of Cardiff, give Blackpool a torrid afternoon. Hinshelwood outshines the great Stanley Matthews - kept quiet by Thresher - and it is his short corner that leads to Tindill shooting City ahead. The Pool hang on for a draw after Ray Charnley forces the ball in.

City put up a stirring defensive display in the fog as well as making Blackpool rock. In the final ten minutes there is enough excitement around the homesters' goal to keep City's 1,000 fans hopeful of an equaliser, but unfortunately David Durie's 12-yard curler is destined to be decisive.

Gloucestershire Cup

				F-A	H-T	Scorers, Times, and Referees	1	2	3	4	5	6	7	8	9	10	11
F	A	BRISTOL ROV	10 D	1-1	0-1	Tindill 76	Cook	Hopkinson	Thresher	Burden	Williams A	Casey	Coggins	Tindill	Atyeo	Etheridge	Hinshelwood
		4/5				Ward 1	*Norman*	*Hillard*	*Watling*	*Sykes*	*Pyle*	*Mabbutt*	*Smith*	*Ward*	*Bradford*	*Biggs*	*Hooper*
						11,022 6											
						Ref: L Callaghan											

After the excitement of Dai Ward's seven second opener - latching onto Ray Mabbutt's through ball to fire past Cook - this contest becomes a very drab affair until Tindill heads in City's equaliser. Thereafter a stirring struggle ensues, but no further goals to separate the two sides.

	P	Home					Away					Pts
		W	D	L	F	A	W	D	L	F	A	
1 Sheffield Wed	42	18	2	1	68	13	10	4	7	38	35	62
2 Fulham	42	18	1	2	65	26	9	5	7	31	35	60
3 Sheffield Utd	42	16	2	3	54	15	7	5	9	28	33	53
4 Liverpool	42	15	3	3	57	25	9	2	10	30	37	53
5 Stoke	42	16	2	3	48	19	5	5	11	24	39	49
6 Bristol Rov	42	13	5	3	46	23	5	7	9	34	41	48
7 Derby	42	15	1	5	46	29	5	7	9	28	42	48
8 Charlton	42	13	3	5	53	33	5	4	12	39	57	43
9 Cardiff	42	12	2	7	37	26	6	5	10	28	39	43
10 BRISTOL C	42	11	3	7	43	27	6	4	11	31	43	41
11 Swansea	42	12	5	4	52	30	5	2	14	27	51	41
12 Brighton	42	10	9	2	46	29	3	6	12	28	61	41
13 Middlesboro	42	9	7	5	51	26	6	3	12	36	45	40
14 Huddersfield	42	12	3	6	39	20	4	5	12	23	35	40
15 Sunderland	42	13	4	4	42	23	3	4	14	22	52	40
16 Ipswich	42	12	4	5	37	27	4	4	14	25	50	40
17 Leyton Orient	42	9	4	8	43	30	5	4	12	28	48	36
18 Scunthorpe	42	7	6	8	32	37	5	3	13	23	47	33
19 Lincoln	42	10	5	6	45	37	2	2	18	18	56	29
20 Rotherham	42	9	5	7	32	28	1	4	16	10	54	29
21 Grimsby	42	7	7	7	41	36	2	3	16	21	54	28
22 Barnsley	42	8	4	9	34	34	3	3	16	21	57	27
	924	265	87	110	1011	593	110	87	265	593	1011	924

Odds & ends

Double wins: (4) Barnsley, Huddersfield, Rotherham, Lincoln.
Double losses: (5) Cardiff, Liverpool, Charlton, Leyton Orient, Derby.

Won from behind: (3) Barnsley (a), Barnsley (h), Sheffield Wed (a).
Lost from in front: (3) Charlton (h), Cardiff (h), Sunderland (a).

High spots: The 13 goal salvo in the opening two games.
Wally Hinshelwood's display in beating Swansea 4-0 on 11 October.
Derek Virgin's fine form as City beat Sunderland 4-1 on 25 October.
Beating Bristol Rovers 2-1 at Eastville on 1 November.
The exciting top of the table draw with Fulham on 8 November.
Depriving Sheffield Wed of their unbeaten home record on 15 November
The brilliant cup-tie against Blackpool at Ashton Gate on 24 January.

Low spots: Losing at home to struggling Scunthorpe.

AGM (Brecknell, Dolman & Rogers, Pennywell Road, 26 January 1960):
Loss £13,050.0s.0d. Season Ticket Sales £17,500.0s.0d.

Player of the year: Tony Cook & Wally Hinshelwood.

Ever-presents: (1) Bert Tindill.
Hat-tricks: (2) John Atyeo (2).
Leading-scorer: Overall: John Atyeo (25). League: John Atyeo (25).

	Appearances		Goals		
	Lge	Cup	Lge	Cup	Tot
Anderson, Bob	5				
Atyeo, John	40	4	25		25
Burden, Tommy	41	4	1		1
Casey, Tommy	8	1			
Coggins, Phil		1			
Cook, Tony	37	4			
Etheridge, Bobby	41	4			
Hinshelwood, Wally	40	4	13		13
Hopkinson, Gordon	34	4	3		3
McCall, Peter	38	3	1		1
Peacock, Ernie	8		1		1
Rogers, Jimmy	9				
Smith, David	2				
Thresher, Mike	41	4			
Tindill, Bert	42	4	20	3	23
Virgin, Derek	4		2		2
Walker, George	1				
Watkins, Johnny	30	3	5	1	6
Williams, Alan	39	4	1		1
Williams, Bobby	2		1		1
(own-goals)			1		1
20 players used	462	44	74	4	78

LEAGUE DIVISION 2 — SEASON 1959-60

Manager: Doherty ⇨ Les Bardsley

Match results

No		Opponent	Date	Att	Pos	Res	Pt	F-A	H-T	Scorers, Times, and Referees
1	A	SCUNTHORPE	22/8	10,863		D	1	1:1	0:1	Rogers 63 / Brownsword 43p / Ref: N Hough
2	A	LIVERPOOL	26/8	33,071		L	1	2:4	1:2	Atyeo 35, Rogers 47 / Liddell 4, 30, Melia 52p, A'Court 65 / Ref: E Crawford
3	H	ROTHERHAM	29/8	20,407 (£2,132.12.6)	18	L	1	2:3	0:1	Cavanagh 56p, Hinshelwood 65 / Kirkman 18, 47, Robinson 61 / Ref: I Rosekilly
4	H	LIVERPOOL	1/9	22,776 (£2,515.14.6)	14	W	3	1:0	1:0	Rogers 13 / Ref: E Jennings
5	A	CARDIFF	5/9	22,545	18	L	3	2:4	1:4	Atyeo 38, Hinshelwood 67 / Hudson 4, 19, Watkins 20, Baker 24 / Ref: J Taylor
6	A	CHARLTON	9/9	13,461	20	L	3	2:4	0:2	Williams R 74, Taylor 89 [Lawrie 88] / Summers 9, 82, Leary 40 / Ref: L Hamer
7	H	HULL	12/9	16,427 (£1,648.5.0)	22	L	3	0:1	0:0	Coates 61 / Ref: P Brandwood
8	H	CHARLTON	15/9	19,717 (£2,113.19.6)	22	L	3	1:2	1:0	Etheridge 6 / Casey 68 (og), Leary 77 / Ref: R Mann
9	A	SHEFFIELD UTD	19/9	17,777	22	L	3	2:5	1:2	Rogers 15, Virgin 55 [Russell 81] / Shiels 10, 34, Hamilton 70, Pace 73 / Ref: K Howley
10	H	MIDDLESBROUGH	26/9	21,640 (£2,360.6.0)	18	W	5	2:0	1:0	Rogers 5, Williams A 54 / Ref: J Pickles

---

Line-ups (City / opponent)

1 — A Scunthorpe

	1	2	3	4	5	6	7	8	9	10	11
City	Cook	Collinson	Thresher	Burden	Williams A	Casey	Hinshelwood	Cavanagh	Atyeo	Rogers	McCann
Scunthorpe	Hardwick	John	Brownsword	Sharp	Horstead	Neale	Marriott	Waldock	Harburn	Haigh	Donnelly

A humid day for the shirt-sleeved crowd who see City youngster Roger Collinson give a cultured display on his League debut in place of the injured Hopkinson. City's improved second-half performance earns a share of the points, thanks to Rogers side-footing in McCann's centre.

2 — A Liverpool

	1	2	3	4	5	6	7	8	9	10	11
City	Cook	Hopkinson	Thresher	McCall	Williams A	Casey	Hinshelwood	Cavanagh	Atyeo	Rogers	McCann
Liverpool	Slater	Molyneux	Moran	Wilkinson	White	Twentyman	Morris	Melia	Liddell	Harrower	A'Court

City are fortunate not to concede more in this thrilling clash. Despite being outplayed, City fight-back to draw level when Rogers soars high to expertly head in Hinshelwood's cross. Unfortunately, Thresher's hand-ball allows Jimmy Melia to put Liverpool back in front from the spot.

3 — H Rotherham

	1	2	3	4	5	6	7	8	9	10	11
City	Cook	Hopkinson	Thresher	Burden	Etheridge	Casey	Hinshelwood	Cavanagh	Atyeo	Rogers	McCann
Rotherham	Ironside	Silman	Morgan	Lambert	Madden	Waterhouse	Webster	Kirkman	Myerscough	Robinson	Bambridge

Rotherham, after winning the toss and electing to defend the Covered End, give City a soccer lesson on the new £12,000 pitch. City, who abandon their system of using Atyeo and Rogers as a twin spearhead, are completely out of sorts, and both their goals are fortuitous affairs.

4 — H Liverpool

	1	2	3	4	5	6	7	8	9	10	11
City	Cook	Hopkinson	Thresher	Burden	Williams A	Casey	Hinshelwood	Rogers	Atyeo	Etheridge	McCann
Liverpool	Rudham	Molyneux	Moran	Wilkinson	White	Twentyman	Morrissey	Melia	Liddell	Harrower	A'Court

What a difference a few days make as City turn in a stirring performance against the impressive visitors. Rogers is on hand to slam the ball into the net when Doug Rudham touches Hinshelwood's effort onto a post, but City have to weather much Liverpool pressure to take the points.

5 — A Cardiff

	1	2	3	4	5	6	7	8	9	10	11
City	Cook	Hopkinson	Thresher	Burden	Williams A	Casey	Hinshelwood	Rogers	Atyeo	Etheridge	McCann
Cardiff	Vearncombe	Harrington	Milne	Gammon	Malloy	Baker	Hudson	Stitfall	Moore	Bonson	Watkins

Johnny Watkins stars in captaining Cardiff for the day against his old club. City are a shambles at the back early on and all but the opening Cardiff strike should have been prevented. A freakish goal for Hinshelwood - volleying McCann's cross into the ground and high into the net.

6 — A Charlton

	1	2	3	4	5	6	7	8	9	10	11
City	Cook	Hopkinson	Briggs	Burden	Williams A	Casey	Hinshelwood	Taylor	Atyeo	Williams R	McCann
Charlton	Duff	Sewell	Townsend	Hinton	Ufton	Kiernan	Lawrie	Lucas	Summers	Leary	Werge

Whilst Doherty's decision to throw in City's talented youngsters fails to produce any points, both Bobby Williams and Archie Taylor get on the scoresheet. Williams registers with a soaring header, whilst Taylor finishes off his run from the halfway line with a great left-foot shot.

7 — H Hull

	1	2	3	4	5	6	7	8	9	10	11
City	Cook	Hopkinson	Briggs	Burden	Williams A	Casey	Hinshelwood	Taylor	Atyeo	Williams R	McCann
Hull	Fisher	Harrison	Bulless	Davidson	Feasey	Garvey	Bowering	Collinson	Coates	Bradbury	Crickmore

City are well on top before a breakaway by the Tigers leaves the unmarked David Coates with the fairly simple task of shooting past Cook. The 75th-minute departure of the injured Les Collinson gives City hope, but the visitors, somewhat fortuitously, withstand much late pressure.

8 — H Charlton

	1	2	3	4	5	6	7	8	9	10	11
City	Cook	Hopkinson	Thresher	Williams A	Williams A	Casey	Rogers !	Atyeo	Virgin	Etheridge	McCann
Charlton	Duff	Sewell	Townsend !	Hewie	Ufton	Kiernan	Lawrie	Lucas	Summers	Leary	White

City are in commanding form early on during which time Etheridge headed them in front and they are extremely unlucky to be denied a penalty. Unfortunately, the sending off of Rogers and Don Townsend for a skirmish just before half-time, changes the complexion of the game.

9 — A Sheffield Utd

	1	2	3	4	5	6	7	8	9	10	11
City	Cook	Hopkinson	Thresher	Williams A	McCall	Casey	Rogers	Atyeo	Virgin	Etheridge	McCann
Sheffield Utd	Hodgkinson	Coldwell	Shaw G	Hoyland	Shaw J	Summers	Shiels	Hamilton	Pace	Russell	Simpson

A 58th-minute clash of heads with Derek Pace, has McCall (turning out in place of fibrosis victim Burden) off the field for 16 minutes, before coming back to play on the right wing. Williams handles to concede a 68th-minute penalty, but Graham Shaw slams the spot-kick over the bar.

10 — H Middlesbrough

	1	2	3	4	5	6	7	8	9	10	11
City	Cook	Hopkinson	Thresher	Burden	McCall	Casey	Rogers	Atyeo	Williams A	Etheridge	McCann
Middlesbrough	Taylor	Barnard	McNeil	Harris	Phillips	Yeoman	Day	Fernie	Clough	Peacock	Holliday

A welcome return over opponents handicapped by losing Ray Barnard with a broken leg after just six minutes. Alan Williams does well in the unfamiliar centre-forward role – running onto Burden's through ball to shoot past Peter Taylor after having an earlier effort disallowed.

Match 11

A DERBY — 3/10 | Pos 20 | L | 18 | 5 | Att 16,270 | 0-3 | HT 0-2
Scorers: Upton 6, Thompson 36, Hannigan 72 *Oxford*
Ref: T Cooper

Cook | Hopkinson | Thresher | Burden | McCall | Casey | Rogers | Atyeo | Williams A | Etheridge | McCann
(Barrowcliffe | Martin | Upton | Moore | Davies | Swallow | Hall | Thompson | Darwin | Hannigan)

In contrast to the last match, Alan Williams looks sadly out of place at centre-forward. Rogers is denied by an upright just prior to the interval, and Casey's header is disallowed in the 65th minute, but City can have no complaints as Derby fully deserve their first home win of the season.

Match 12

H BRISTOL ROV — 10/10 | Pos 19 | W | 10 | 7 | Att 26,253 (£2,997.17.6) | 2-1 | HT 0-0
Scorers: Atyeo 59, 83; Biggs 53
Ref: H Horner

Cook | Hopkinson | Thresher | Burden | McCall | Casey | Hinshelwood | Cavanagh | Atyeo | Etheridge | McCann
(Norman | Hillard | Watling | Sykes | Pyle | Mabbutt | Smith | Biggs | Bradford | Jones | Hooper)

City show that they have the spirit for survival in what is surely one of the best local derbies. There is little to choose between the sides, but an Atyeo double (a great 15-yard shot, that equalises Alfie Biggs' brilliant headed opener, and a diving header) secure the precious points for City.

Match 13

H BRIGHTON — 24/10 | Pos 20 | L | 10 | 7 | Att 18,093 (£1,916.7.6) | 0-1 | HT 0-0
Scorers: Thorne 81
Ref: C Sant

Cook | Hopkinson | Thresher | Burden | McCall | Casey | Hinshelwood | Cavanagh | Atyeo | Etheridge | McCann
(Hollins | McNicol | Little | Bertolini | Jennings | Wilson | Tiddy | McNeil | Curry | Thorne | Gordon)

Brighton, with Glen Wilson a passenger for all but the first minute and off the field completely after the break, snatch victory after City waste numerous opportunities. Burden loses possession and City's defence is caught cold as Bill Curry lays on the pass for Adrian Thorne's winner.

Match 14

A STOKE — 31/10 | Pos 20 | W | 10 | 9 | Att 14,441 | 3-1 | HT 1-1
Scorers: Graham 22, 81, Atyeo 60; Newlands 16
Ref: A Jobling

Cook | Collinson | Thresher | Cavanagh | Williams A | **Jacobs** | **Coggins** | Etheridge | Atyeo | **Graham** | McCann
(Robertson | McCue | Allen | Asprey | Andrew | Ratcliffe | Newlands | Bowyer | King | Wilshaw | Cunliffe)

City will be hoping that Malcolm Graham's injury problems are behind him as he marks his long-awaited debut with two fine goals and has a hand in the other. Stoke have to endure the boos of their fans at the close, but good debuts for City youngsters Frank Jacobs and Phil Coggins.

Match 15

H PORTSMOUTH — 7/11 | Pos 18 | W | 22 | 11 | Att 21,298 (£2,295.16.6) | 2-0 | HT 1-0
Scorers: Atyeo 25, Graham 74
Ref: D Howell

Cook | Collinson | Thresher | Cavanagh | Williams A | Jacobs | Coggins | Etheridge | Atyeo | Graham | McCann
(Beattie | Gunter | Dickinson | Howells | Hayward | Carter | Campbell | Newman | Saunders | Harris | Cutler)

City's revival continues against fellow strugglers Pompey. Cook is City's hero with one of his best ever saves in keeping out a Derek Harris header, as well as stopping Jimmy Dickinson's 30-yarder. Graham registers with a neat header, whilst his earlier nod-down had set up Atyeo.

Match 16

A SUNDERLAND — 14/11 | Pos 20 | L | 7 | 11 | Att 21,025 | 2-3 | HT 1-1
Scorers: McNab 34 (og), Graham 71; Grainger 41, Fogarty 55, 62
Ref: R Windle

Cook | Collinson | Thresher | Cavanagh | Williams A | Jacobs | Coggins | Etheridge | Atyeo | Graham | McCann
(Wakeham | Nelson | Ashurst | Anderson | Hurley | McNab | Fraser | Fogarty | Lawther | Taylor | Grainger)

Graham continues his rich vein of form against a Sunderland side unbeaten at home since last December. Deprived of a goal when Jim McNab helps his shot into the net, Graham makes no mistake from McCann's pull-back. Williams and Etheridge are both booked in this rugged clash.

Match 17

H ASTON VILLA — 21/11 | Pos 21 | L | 1 | 11 | Att 29,985 (£3,465.12.0) | 0-5 | HT 0-2
Scorers: [McParland 87] Hitchens 40, 42, 86, Wylie 56
Ref: F Gerrard

Cook | Collinson | Thresher | Cavanagh | Williams A | Jacobs | Coggins | Atyeo | Hill | Graham | McCann
(Sims | Lynn | Neal | Crowe | Dugdale | Saward | MacEwan | Thomson | Hitchens | Wylie | McParland)

City do quite well for 40 minutes until Villa find the form that netted them eleven goals against Charlton last week. Villa's short-corner routine at the East End is City's undoing. Peter McParland's great strike is consolation for him having earlier been booked for a foul on Cavanagh.

Match 18

A LINCOLN — 28/11 | Pos 22 | L | 15 | 11 | Att 10,667 | 1-3 | HT 0-0
Scorers: Cavanagh 71; Linnecor 63, McClelland 75, 86
Ref: F Collinge

Cook | Collinson | Thresher | Cavanagh | Williams A | Casey | Hinshelwood | Atyeo | Rogers | Etheridge | **Derrick**
(Thompson | Allen | Smith | Middleton | Grattan | Jackson | McClelland | Harbertson | Graver | Linnecor | Smillie)

With McCann being on the injury list, Jantzen Derrick becomes Bristol City's youngest debutant at sixteen years 324 days. City, playing in white, are caught out by John McClelland's narrow angled drive following Cook's failure in dealing with Jeff Smith's swerving free-kick.

Match 19

H LEYTON ORIENT — 5/12 | Pos 21 | D | 5 | 12 | Att 14,126 (£1,386.7.0) | 1-1 | HT 1-1
Scorers: Etheridge 31; Johnston 2
Ref: W Clements

Cook | Collinson | Thresher | Cavanagh | Williams A | Casey | Hinshelwood | Atyeo | Rogers | Etheridge | McCann
(Groombridge | Wright | Charlton | Facey | Bishop | Sorrell | White | Brown | Johnston | Foster | McDonald)

Despite mounting a second-half onslaught in one of the most exciting matches of the season, City can do no more that notch up their first draw in 18 games. Spurred on by the shock of Tom Johnston's headed opener, Etheridge thumps in a 12-yarder to have City all-square at the break.

Match 20

A HUDDERSFIELD — 12/12 | Pos 22 | L | 5 | 12 | Att 10,705 | 1-6 | HT 0-5
Scorers: Rogers 87 [Taylor 44, Cod'gton 47p] Dinsdale 5, Law 23, Massie 31, 41, [Wood]
Ref: K Seddon

Cook | Collinson | Thresher | Cavanagh | Williams A | Casey | Hinshelwood | Atyeo | Rogers | Etheridge | McCann
(Wood | Gibson | Wilson | Taylor | Coddington | McGarry | McHale | Law | Dinsdale | Massie | Hawksworth)

But for Cook it would have been even worse for City as Huddersfield deserved even more in their well-merited win. The Town have two penalties, but Cook moves smartly to his left to save John Coddington's 66th-minute effort after Williams had brought down Peter Dinsdale.

Match 21

H SCUNTHORPE — 19/12 | Pos 22 | L | 12 | 12 | Att 9,099 (£819.14.6) | 0-1 | HT 0-1
Scorers: Marriott 19, Middleton 67
Ref: J Finney

Cook | Collinson | Thresher | Burden | Williams A | Casey | Rogers | Atyeo | Etheridge | Rogers | McCann
(Jones | John | Brownsword | Haigh | Heward | Sharp | Marriott | Thomas | Middleton | Donnelly | Baker)

It is little wonder, given their insistence in ploughing through the mud in the centre of the pitch, that City lost. Scunthorpe used the wings and go in front when John Marriott nips in when Cook fails to hold Len Sharp's free-kick. Rogers has his jack-knife header turned against a post.

No	Date	Att	Pos (City/Opp)	Pt	Res	F-A	H-T	1	2	3	4	5	6	7	8	9	10	11
22	A PLYMOUTH 26/12	18,377	21 / 19	14	W	4-1	2-1	Cook	Collinson	Thresher	McCall	Williams A	Burden	Rogers	Cavanagh	Atyeo	Williams R	McCann
								Barnsley	Robertson	Bellett	Williams J S	Wyatt	Casey	Penk	Carter	Waldock	Jenkins	Wright

22. Williams R 6, Atyeo 44, 65, [Rogers 67]; Waldock 16. Ref: A Thorpe

Christmas is a time of snow, singing and presents, and at Home Park, City have all three. Their happy fans burst forth into song, whilst a freak storm supplies the snow. The present of a much-needed win is reward for a fine display, despite McCann's broken leg just after the interval.

No	Date	Att	Pos (City/Opp)	Pt	Res	F-A	H-T	1	2	3	4	5	6	7	8	9	10	11
23	H PLYMOUTH 28/12	22,644 (£2,549.17.6)	21 / 20	16	W	2-1	2-0	Cook	Collinson	Thresher	McCall	Williams A	Burden	Rogers	Cavanagh	Atyeo	Williams R	Derrick
								Barnsley	Stacey	Fulton	Williams J S	Fincham	Casey	Penk	Carter	Waldock	Dann	Wright

23. Atyeo 12, Rogers 21; Waldock 51. Ref: J Taylor

When Derrick's shot spins off of Terry Stacey's boot, Atyeo heads in his 200th League and Cup goal. It all seems so easy when Rogers steers in City's second, but Ron Waldock's shot on the turn produces a torrid time before they are able to claim a double against the spirited Pilgrims.

No	Date	Att	Pos (City/Opp)	Pt	Res	F-A	H-T	1	2	3	4	5	6	7	8	9	10	11
24	A ROTHERHAM 2/1	13,719	21 / 3	16	L	1-3	1-2	Cook	Collinson	Thresher	McCall	Williams A	Burden	Rogers	Cavanagh	Atyeo	Williams R	Bevan
								Ironside	Perry	Morgan	Lambert	Madden	Williams	Webster	Kettleborough	Sawyer	Myerscough	Kirkman

24. Cavanagh 21 [Collinson 80 (og)]; Webster 12, Williams A 39 (og). Ref: R Reddaway

Despite the limping Rogers, City give the Millers a hard game. Cavanagh lashes in a fine individual effort to level Barry Webster's brilliant shot, but poor finishing and a couple of own goals (Williams deflecting in a cross and Collinson's back-pass eluding Cook) bring defeat.

No	Date	Att	Pos (City/Opp)	Pt	Res	F-A	H-T	1	2	3	4	5	6	7	8	9	10	11
25	H CARDIFF 16/1	18,184 (£1,953.19.6)	21 / 2	16	L	0-3	0-1	Cook	Collinson	Thresher	McCall	Williams A	Burden	Hinshelwood	Cavanagh	Atyeo	Etheridge	Derrick
								Vearncombe	Milne	Stitfall	Sullivan	Malloy	Baker	Walsh	Tapscott	Moore	Bonson	Watkins

25. Bonson 4, McCall 51 (og), Moore 89. Ref: F Cowan

City have the relegation look in this defeat by promotion chasing Cardiff. It is a wonder that the visitors did not score more as they have many chances. Brian Walsh's dazzling right-wing burst sets up Graham Moore to complete Cardiff's win with a diving header at the Open End.

No	Date	Att	Pos (City/Opp)	Pt	Res	F-A	H-T	1	2	3	4	5	6	7	8	9	10	11
26	A HULL 23/1	12,605	21 / 22	17	D	1-1	1-1	Cook	Collinson	Thresher	McCall	Williams A	Burden	Hill	Cavanagh	Atyeo	Casey	Hinshelwood
								Bly	Davidson	Bulless	Bennion	Garvey	Collinson	Clarke	Sewell	Shiner	Gubbins	Bowering

26. Atyeo 36; Clarke 19. Ref: R Leafe

Atyeo levels Doug Clarke's cross-shot opener by flicking Thresher's 40-yard ball into the goalmouth through his legs into the opposite corner of the net. A surprise strike maybe, but inspired by this City's fighting spirit gives hope that this might be the turning point in their fortunes.

No	Date	Att	Pos (City/Opp)	Pt	Res	F-A	H-T	1	2	3	4	5	6	7	8	9	10	11
27	H SHEFFIELD UTD 6/2	16,248 (£1,647.3.0)	21 / 7	18	D	2-2	2-1	Cook	Collinson	Thresher	McCall	Williams A	Burden	Hill	Cavanagh	Atyeo	Graham	Hinshelwood
								Hodgkinson	Coldwell	Shaw G	Richardson	Finnigan	Summers	Lewis	Hamilton	Pace	Hodgson	Simpson

27. Cavanagh 21, Graham 44; Lewis 42, Simpson 57. Ref: P Carr

Cavanagh's shot on the turn and Atyeo's head-down for Graham to easily fire home has City deservedly in front at the break, despite Cook letting in a weak Kevin Lewis shot. Unfortunately, following Ron Simpson's fired in equaliser the Blades took control and should have won.

No	Date	Att	Pos (City/Opp)	Pt	Res	F-A	H-T	1	2	3	4	5	6	7	8	9	10	11
28	A MIDDLESBROUGH 13/2	17,871	21 / 4	18	L	3-6	1-3	Cook	Briggs	Thresher	McCall	Williams A	Burden	Rogers	Cavanagh	Atyeo	Graham	Hinshelwood
								Taylor	Stonehouse		Harris	Thomson	Yeoman	McLean	Fernie	Clough	Waldock	Holliday

28. Rogers 40, Graham 54, Cav'agh 85p; Clough 6, 68, 89, Ha' 27p, McL' 32, 70 Taylor. Ref: L Tirebuck

With Briggs in place of the injured Thresher, and Rogers taking over from Hill, City respond well to a three-goal deficit. A Rogers header and Graham's shot raise hopes of an equaliser, but Brian Clough's volley on the turn and Derek McLean's header restore Boro's advantage.

No	Date	Att	Pos (City/Opp)	Pt	Res	F-A	H-T	1	2	3	4	5	6	7	8	9	10	11
29	H DERBY 20/2	14,055 (£1,482.18.0)	21 / 17	18	L	0-1	0-1	Cook	Collinson	Thresher	McCall	Williams A	Burden	Rogers	Cavanagh	Atyeo	Graham	Hinshelwood
								Orford	Conwell	Martin	Mays	Young	Upton	Swallow	Powell	Hannigan	Darwin	Cargill

29. Swallow 37. Ref: C Rogers

Heavy rain just before the start leaves the pitch resembling a lake. City, with Burden hitting the bar and Cavanagh having what looked like a perfectly valid goal disallowed, are well on top in the early stages. Ray Swallow runs through to chip Cook from 20 yards for Derby's winner.

No	Date	Att	Pos (City/Opp)	Pt	Res	F-A	H-T	1	2	3	4	5	6	7	8	9	10	11
30	A BRISTOL ROV 27/2	27,039	21 / 11	18	L	1-2	1-2	Cook	Collinson	Thresher	McCall	Williams A	Burden	Rogers	Cavanagh	Atyeo	Graham	McCann
								Radford	Hillard	Watling	Sykes	Pyle	Mabbutt	Petherbridge	Biggs	Bradford	Ward	Hooper

30. Graham 43; Hooper 8, Biggs 18. Ref: K Collinge

An entertaining game with City taking control following the break. Unfortunately, poor finishing means they are unable to add to Graham's first-half shot which, after hitting the foot of a post, trickles over the line at the Muller Road End. Cook's fumble gifts Rovers their opener.

No	Date	Att	Pos (City/Opp)	Pt	Res	F-A	H-T	1	2	3	4	5	6	7	8	9	10	11
31	H SWANSEA 5/3	14,368 (£1,411.7.0)	21 / 13	19	D	2-2	1-1	Cook	Collinson	Thresher	McCall	Williams A	Burden	Rogers	Cavanagh	Atyeo	Graham	Hinshelwood
								King	Sanders	Griffiths	Saunders	Nurse	Williams H	Jones B	Davies R	Reynolds	Webster I	Williams G

31. Rogers 27, 69; Williams G 2, Jones 80. Ref: A Rowbottom

City should have won easily against opponents with a limping Alan Sanders following a first-half injury and Colin Webster sent off in the 54th minute for bringing down Graham. Unfortunately, Barrie Jones rolls a through ball between Cook's legs to bring Swansea a share of the spoils.

32 A BRIGHTON 12/3 21 L 1-5 15,976 17 19

Cavanagh 41 [Jennings 70p]
Clayton 4, Curry 38, 53, 89p,
Ref: J Cooke

| Cook | Collinson | McCall | Williams A | Casey | Rogers | Virgin | Atyeo | Cavanagh | Hinshelwood |
| Hollins | Bisset | Bertolini | Jennings | Abbiss | Tiddy | McNeill | Curry | Clayton | Gordon |

City have some brisk early attacks, but after Ron Clayton's three-yard tap-in is allowed, despite offside protests, they find Bill Curry much too hot to handle. Even with Roy Little a limping passenger after the interval, City can make no impression and relegation now appears inevitable.

---

33 H LINCOLN 19/3 21 W 1-0 16,221 14 21 (£1,655.13.0)

Rogers 23
Ref: T Cooper

| Cook | Collinson | Thresher | Etheridge | Williams A | Rogers | Virgin | Atyeo | Burden | Derrick |
| Heath | Allen | Smith | Middleton | Jackson | McClelland | Linnecor | Hawksworth | Chapman | Dunwell |

Following the sacking of manager Peter Doherty, City dominate the play and turn up trumps against the unchanged Imps. There is only one goal though; Rogers latching onto skipper Burden's through pass and sliding the ball through the mud past the advancing William Heath.

---

34 A PORTSMOUTH 26/3 21 L 0-2 15,697 19 21

Harris 9, Chapman 14
Ref: K Stokes

| Cook | Collinson | Thresher | Etheridge | Williams A | Rogers | Virgin | Atyeo | Burden | McCann |
| Beattie | Thomas | Dickinson | Chapman | Carter | Wilson | Saunders | Newman | Harris | Cutler |

In front of a large gathering of City fans, Burden wins the toss and elects to attack the Open End. Against a Pompey side who obtained a shock win at Cardiff last Saturday, Cook is a fault with both the headed opener and Sammy Chapman's half-hit 25-yarder which dips inside the post.

---

35 H SUNDERLAND 2/4 21 W 1-0 13,437 20 23 (£1,320.3.6)

Atyeo 44
Ref: W Clements

| Cook | Collinson | Thresher | Etheridge | Williams A | Rogers | Burden | Atyeo | Graham | McCann |
| Wakeham | Nelson | Jones | Anderson | Hurley | McNab | Davison | Lawther | Taylor | Grainger |

City pepper the Sunderland goal with long-range shots, but it is Atyeo's short-range header past Peter Wakenham that secures the points. On losing the toss, City defend the Open End and Graham is unlucky on seven minutes with a terrific 25-yard drive that thumps against the bar.

---

36 A ASTON VILLA 9/4 21 L 1-2 33,556 1 23

Collinson 14
Lynn 48p, 87p
Ref: H Callaghan

| Cook | Collinson | Thresher | Etheridge | Williams A | Rogers | Burden | Atyeo | Graham | McCann |
| Sims | Lynn | Neal | Crowe | Dugdale | Saward | Adam | Thomson | Wylie | McParland |

On a day that an attempt is made to assassinate South African Premier Hendrik Verwoerd, City are desperately unlucky to lose at Villa Park. Collinson's great shot from near the halfway line hits the underside of the crossbar and bounces down over the line to give City a shock lead.

---

37 A IPSWICH 15/4 21 W 3-1 13,055 8 25

Atyeo 50, 56, Rogers 83
Rees 87
Ref: A Moore

| Cook | Collinson | Thresher | Etheridge | Williams A | Rogers | Burden | Atyeo | Graham | Virgin |
| Bailey | Carberry | Acres | Pickett | Nelson | Owen | Rees | Crawford | Phillips | Leadbeater |

Atyeo, who had the ball in the net on 38 minutes, only for the referee to rule that he had fouled Andy Nelson, makes amends with two scoring shots after the break. Following intense Ipswich pressure, Rogers secured City's third goal by slamming the ball in from Collinson's free-kick.

---

38 H HUDDERSFIELD 16/4 21 L 2-3 17,722 4 25 (£1,819.15.6)

Wilson 2 (og), Atyeo 84 [Massey 89]
Etheridge 16 (og), McHale 86,
Ref: P Brandwood

| Cook | Collinson | Thresher | Etheridge | Williams A | Rogers | Burden | Atyeo | Graham | Virgin |
| Wood | Gibson | Wilson | Taylor | Coddington | McGarry | McHale | Sinclair | Connor | Massie | Ledger |

Ray Wilson celebrates his first call-up for England by misjudging Graham's low centre and side-footing the ball into his own net past a surprised custodian. Graham is unlucky to have his shot, which would have put City 3-1 ahead, disallowed for pushing as he burst through.

---

39 H IPSWICH 18/4 21 W 5-1 11,140 9 27 (£987.13.0)

Atyeo 3, 87, Williams R 18,
Curtis 7 [Rogers 53, 711]
Ref: R Mann

| Cook | Collinson | Thresher | Etheridge | Williams A | Rogers | Burden | Atyeo | Williams R | Virgin |
| Bailey | Carberry | Acres | Pickett | Nelson | Owen | Rees | Curtis | Phillips | Leadbeater |

City's biggest win of the season comes courtesy of jittery Ipswich keeper Roy Bailey, who is to blame for four of the goals. Given the fact that Rogers looked offside when scoring his first and that Ipswich have two rejected penalty appeals, it seems that City have some luck at long last.

---

40 A LEYTON ORIENT 23/4 22 L 1-3 9,153 11 27

Williams R 30
Brown 5, 15, McDonald 63
Ref: R Jordan

| Cook | Collinson | Thresher | Etheridge | Williams A | Rogers | Burden | Atyeo | Williams R | Derrick |
| Nicholson | Eagles | Lewis | Carey | Bishop | Sorrell | White | Waites | Johnston | Brown | McDonald |

This defeat makes relegation inevitable as City again have cause to rue their lack of luck this season. 'We shall be back – and quickly,' says Chairman Dolman. The over-theatrical referee disallows a perfectly good Williams goal and ignores his linesman flagging for a City penalty.

---

41 A SWANSEA 26/4 22 L 1-6 7,920 13 27

Graham 42 [Dodson 83, Williams 84]
Jones 19, 85, Wil's A 33 (og), All' 44,
Ref: J Taylor

| Cook | Collinson | Thresher | Etheridge | Williams A | Rogers | Williams R | Atyeo | Graham | Derrick |
| King | Hughes | Purcell | Johnson | Nurse | Allchurch | Reynolds | Dodson | Williams H | Jones |

Swansea's youngest ever side put City to the sword in this thrilling match, which as well as producing seven goals, sees three shots hitting the woodwork and the keepers making great saves. Despite losing heavily, City fully play their part with some sparkling and delightful football.

---

42 H STOKE 30/4 22 L 0-2 9,013 18 27

Rogers 49
King 33, Williams A 35 (og)
Ref: K Aston (£720.10.0)

| Cook | Briggs | Thresher | Etheridge | Williams A | Rogers | Burden | Atyeo | Williams R | Derrick |
| Younger | Allen | Wilson | Howitt | Andrews | Cairns | Anderson | Bentley | King | Cunliffe |

Against a poor Stoke side – reduced to ten men with the loss of the injured Dennis Wilson after just eight minutes – City are even worse. Denied a penalty when Robert Cairns appears to handle, City get some scant consolation from this abysmal game when Rogers fires in.

Home 17,755
Away 16,943
Average

CUP-TIES

Manager: Doherty ⇨ Les Bardsley

SEASON 1959-60

FA Cup

				F-A	H-T	Scorers, Times, and Referees	1	2	3	4	5	6	7	8	9	10	11
3	H	CHARLTON	21 L	2:3	2:0	Atyeo 40, Cavanagh 42	Cook	Collinson	Thresher	McCall	Williams A	Burden	Rogers	Cavanagh	Atyeo	Etheridge	Derrick
9/1		18,400 11				Lawrie 54, 59p, 84	*Duff*	*Edwards*	*Townsend*	*Hewie*	*Jago*	*Lucas*	*Lawrie*	*White*	*Leary*	*Kiernan*	*Summers*
		(£2,972.17.3)				Ref: R Warnke											

On a bitterly cold afternoon a shot from Atyeo and a Cavanagh header seemed to have this cup-tie won for City, but Sam Lawrie had other ideas. Scrambling the ball in soon after the break, he added a penalty when Burden fouled John Summers, before firing in an 18-yard winner.

Gloucestershire Cup

				F-A	H-T		1	2	3	4	5	6	7	8	9	10	11
F	A	BRISTOL ROV	22 W	3:2	0:1	Atyeo 49, 64, Rogers 53	Cook	Collinson	Thresher	Etheridge	Williams A	Casey	Rogers	Burden	Atyeo	Williams R	Virgin
2/5		7,195 9				Biggs 34, 78	*Radford*	*Hillard*	*Watling*	*Sykes*	*Frowen*	*Mabbutt*	*Petherbridge*	*Biggs*	*Bradford*	*Ward*	*Hooper*
						Ref: G Pullin											

After falling behind to Alfie Biggs' right-footed opener, City find the form that has eluded them for much of the season. A narrow-angled Rogers effort is sandwiched between a couple of Atyeo headers as City turn on the style, before a Biggs screamer sets up a hectic finale.

		Home					Away					
	P	W	D	L	F	A	W	D	L	F	A	Pts
1 Aston Villa	42	17	3	1	62	19	8	6	7	27	24	59
2 Cardiff	42	15	2	4	55	36	8	10	3	35	26	58
3 Liverpool	42	15	3	3	59	28	5	7	9	31	38	50
4 Sheffield Utd	42	12	5	4	43	22	7	7	7	25	29	50
5 Middlesboro	42	14	4	2	56	21	5	5	11	34	43	48
6 Huddersfield	42	13	3	5	44	20	6	6	9	29	32	47
7 Charlton	42	12	7	2	55	28	5	6	10	35	59	47
8 Rotherham	42	9	9	3	31	23	8	4	9	30	37	47
9 Bristol Rov	42	12	6	3	42	28	6	5	10	30	50	47
10 Leyton Orient	42	12	4	5	47	25	3	10	8	29	36	44
11 Ipswich	42	12	5	4	48	24	7	1	13	30	44	44
12 Swansea	42	12	6	3	54	32	3	4	14	28	52	40
13 Lincoln	42	11	3	7	41	25	5	4	12	34	53	39
14 Brighton	42	7	8	6	35	32	6	4	11	32	44	38
15 Scunthorpe	42	9	7	5	38	26	4	3	14	19	45	36
16 Sunderland	42	8	6	7	35	29	6	1	11	17	36	36
17 Stoke	42	8	8	5	40	38	6	4	11	26	45	35
18 Derby	42	9	4	8	31	28	5	3	13	30	49	35
19 Plymouth	42	10	6	5	42	36	3	3	15	19	53	35
20 Portsmouth	42	6	6	9	36	36	4	6	11	23	41	32
21 Hull	42	7	6	8	27	30	3	4	14	21	46	30
22 BRISTOL C	42	8	3	10	27	31	3	2	16	33	66	27
	924	238	110	114	948	617	114	110	238	617	948	924

Odds & ends

Double wins: (2) Plymouth, Ipswich.

Double losses: (7) Rotherham, Cardiff, Charlton, Derby, Brighton, Aston Villa, Huddersfield.

Won from behind: (3) Bristol Rov (h), Stoke (a), Bristol R (a) (GC).

Lost from in front: (5) Charlton (h), Sunderland (a), Aston Villa (a), Huddersfield (h), Charlton (h) (FAC).

High spots: The home win over Liverpool on 1 September.

Defeating Middlesbrough 2-0 Ashton Gate on 26 September.

Beating Bristol Rovers at Ashton Gate on 10 October.

The 3-1 success at the Victoria Ground on 31 October.

Low spots: Conceding six at Huddersfield, Middlesbrough and Swansea.

The dire performance against Stoke in the last game of the season.

The FA Cup defeat by Charlton.

The injury problems that kept Malcolm Graham out of the side.

The acrimony that divided the club and resulted in relegation.

AGM (Brecknell, Dolman & Rogers, Pennywell Road, 7 March 1961):

Profit £43,009.0s.0d. Season Ticket Sales £17,350.0.0.

Player of the year: Roger Collinson.

Ever-presents: (2) John Atyeo and Tony Cook.

Hat-tricks: (0).

Leading scorer: Overall: John Atyeo (19). League: Atyeo and Rogers (16).

	Appearances			Goals			
	Lge	FAC	GC	Lge	FAC	GC	Tot
Atyeo, John	42	1		16	1	2	19
Bevan, Brian	1						
Briggs, Alec	4						
Burden, Tommy	30	1	1				
Casey, Tommy	25		1				
Cavanagh, Tommy	24	1		6	1		7
Coggins, Phil	4						
Collinson, Roger	29	1	1	1			1
Cook, Tony	42	1	1				
Derrick, Jantzen	6						
Etheridge, Bobby	27	1	1	2			2
Graham, Malcolm	14			8			8
Hill, Ally	3						
Hinshelwood, Wally	20			2			2
Hopkinson, Gordon	12						
Jacobs, Frank	4						
McCall, Peter	20	1					
McCann, John	26						
Rogers, Jimmy	31	1	1	16			17
Taylor, Archie	2					1	1
Thresher, Mike	40	1	1	1			1
Virgin, Derek	8		1	1			1
Williams, Alan	39	1	1	4			4
Williams, Bobby	9			2			2
(own-goals)							2
24 players used	462	11	11	60	2	3	65

LEAGUE DIVISION 3   Manager: Fred Ford   SEASON 1960-61

No	Date		Att	Pos	Pt	F-A	H-T	Scorers, Times, and Referees	1	2	3	4	5	6	7	8	9	10	11
1	20/8	A BRADFORD C	11,034		L	0-2	0-0	Jackson D 68, Reid 72 / Ref: K Seddon	Cook	Collinson	Thresher	Burden	Williams A	Casey	Taylor	Atyeo	Virgin	Ryan	Derrick
									Downie	Flockett	Currie	Jackson P	Lawlor	Mollett	Webb	Jackson D	Devanney	Reid	Howard
2	23/8	H BOURNEMOUTH	14,455 (£1,945.16.0)		W	1-0	0-0	Derrick 87 / Ref: A Rowbottom	Cook	Collinson	Thresher	Burden	Williams A	Casey	Taylor	Williams R	Virgin	Ryan	Derrick
					2				Lynne	Standley	Woollard	Arnott	Burgess	King	Lovie	Gibbs	Jones	Dowsett	Smith
3	27/8	H BARNSLEY	8,495 (£1,072.6.0)	5	W	4-0	1-0	Taylor 35, Rogers 47, Casey 53, [Williams 73] / Ref: D Howell	Cook	Collinson	Thresher	Burden	Etheridge	Casey	Taylor	Rogers	Tait	Williams R	Derrick
				8	4				Leeson	Swift	Bennett	Barber	Sharp	Wood	Smillie	Tindill	Hopkins	Beaumont	Lunn
4	31/8	A BOURNEMOUTH	9,642	8	D	2-2	1-1	Burden 35, Rogers 64, Dowsett 9, Evans 14 / Ref: A Sturgeon	Cook	Collinson	Thresher	Burden	Etheridge	Casey	Taylor	Rogers	Tait	Williams R	Derrick
				17	5				Lynne	Standley	Woollard	Arnott	Burgess	King	Bumstead	Dowsett	Evans	Bolton	Smith
5	3/9	A NEWPORT	8,538	15	L	1-4	0-2	Williams R 48, McPherson 5, 51, 64, Fry 18 / Ref: E Jennings	Cook	Collinson	Thresher	Burden	Etheridge	Casey	Taylor	Rogers	Tait	Williams R	Derrick
				10	5				Weare	Bird	Sherwood	Riggs	Peake	Rowland	Fry	McSeveney	McPherson	Singer	Smith
6	6/9	H SWINDON	16,550 (£2,360.7.6)	12	D	1-1	0-1	Rogers 89, Hunt 2 / Ref: P Carr	Cook	Collinson	Thresher	Burden	Etheridge	Casey	Taylor	Rogers	Tait	Williams R	Derrick
				4	6				Burton	Wollen	Trollope	Morgan	Owen	Woodruff	Summerbee	Hunt	Layne	Jackson	D'Arcy
7	10/9	H COLCHESTER	11,842 (£1,420.17.0)	6	W	5-0	3-0	Etheridge 27, Rogers 30, Tait 40, [Casey 71, Derrick 84] / Ref: H New	Cook	Collinson	Thresher	Burden	Etheridge	Casey	Taylor	Rogers	Tait	Williams R	Derrick
				12	8				Ames	Rumney	Fowler	Parker	Milligan	Hammond	Williams	Hill	Langman	King	Howe
8	17/9	A GRIMSBY	11,956	13	L	2-5	1-4	Tait 6, 73 [Williams 29, Fell 43] / Scott 15, Rafferty 20, 58 / Ref: A Luty	Cook	Collinson	Thresher	Burden	Etheridge	Casey	Taylor	Rogers	Tait	Williams R	Derrick
				1	8				White	Donovan	Keeble	Pearce	Jobling	Welbourne	Scott	Rafferty	Cullen	Williams	Fell
9	20/9	H NOTTS CO	14,839 (£1,904.6.6)	9	W	2-1	2-1	Atyeo 25, 35, Roby 24 / Ref: A Mason	Cook	Collinson	Thresher	Burden	Williams A	Casey	Rogers	Atyeo	Tait	Williams R	Derrick
				7	10				Smith	Butler	Noon	Sheridan	Loxley	Gibson	Roby	Joyce	Hateley	Forrest	Withers
10	24/9	H HULL	14,889 (£1,880.4.0)	13	L	1-2	1-2	Atyeo 6 / Price 13, Gubbins 40p / Ref: K Dagnall	Cook	Collinson	Thresher	Burden	Williams A	Casey	Rogers	Atyeo	Tait	Williams R	Derrick
				10	10				Fisher	Davidson	Garvey	Collinson	Milner	Bulless	Clarke	Price	Chilton	McMillan	Gubbins
11	29/9	A NOTTS CO	14,230	15	L	0-3	0-1	Forrest 7, Roby 80, Hateley 82 / Ref: J Carr	Cook	Hopkinson	Thresher	McCall	Quinlan	Casey	Rogers	Etheridge	Williams A	McCann	Boxley
				6	10				Smith	Noon	Sheridan	Loxley	Carver		Roby	Joyce	Hateley	Forrest	Withers

Match reports:

1. City start well and Casey shakes a post with his drive. Unfortunately, Atyeo sustains a bad ankle sprain on 19 minutes, which, not only disrupts City's rhythm, but also reduces them to ten men some three minutes prior to the half-time break. David Jackson's 18-yarder opens the scoring.

2. Fred Ford's decision to move winger Derrick inside with just ten minutes of the game remaining transforms City. What had been a fumbling and stumbling outfit is suddenly one of movement and invention. An eight-yard lob settles matters as the Cherries are almost overwhelmed.

3. The hardy spectators who had to brave the monsoon rain as well as thunder and lightning to see this match are rewarded by a thrilling contest. After withstanding early Barnsley pressure, Tait's 29th-minute tap-in is ruled offside, but, not long after, Taylor registers with a 20-yard rocket.

4. After Gilbert Dowsett heads the Cherries in front, attack-minded City are stunned when Ray Evans forces in number two. Refusing to panic, they keep on the offensive and Burden nets with a brilliant 35-yarder. The equaliser though is not so memorable – just a scramble over the line.

5. City play the better football, but their defence is torn apart by Newport's long-ball style. For the opener, Ken McPherson just manages to poke the ball in as Cook attempts to grasp it. City's sole response sees Williams put away the rebound when a Rogers header cannons off of the bar.

6. Swindon are robbed at Ashton Gate as a neat Rogers header from Taylor's cross deprives them of the win that their play deserved. Off to a great start with Ernie Hunt crashing the ball home from ten yards, it is a surprise that the visitors' stylish play fails to produce further goals.

7. Colchester, barren of skill, speed, urgency, and even it seems, interest, prove unworthy opponents. Unfortunately, City can only take about one-fifth of their opportunities, but the fans are happy enough with a five-goal haul, despite Etheridge having his 57th-minute penalty saved.

8. A glorious Collinson/Taylor/Rogers/Tait move, which brings City the opener, has the Grimsby fans murmuring in tones of trepidation, but four goals in 28 minutes by the home side change all that. City play well in this entertaining contest, but, by the finish, are beaten by the better side.

9. All the goals come in an exciting first half when Atyeo, on his return from injury, scores twice to inspire City's recovery after conceding Don Roby's powerful cross-shot. Atyeo follows his first, a powerful 15-yard header, with a run into the box and a toe-poke past George Smith.

10. Alan Williams, who has his worst game in a long while, upends Chris Chilton to concede the spot-kick from which the Tigers obtain their winning goal. A deserved Hull success as they are the better side, coming back well after Atyeo had turned in Tait's pass to put City ahead.

11. Casey is in brilliant form, but he concedes a free-kick on the edge of the penalty area from which Chris Joyce chips up for an offside looking Robert Forrest to put the ball into the net. City, with 19 year-old Quinlan making a good debut, play well but are let down by poor finishing.

City Match Record (Games 12–23)

Game 12 — A READING — 1-1 (HT 0-0)
Position 16, D · 19 11 · Att: 7,360 (£1,801.19.0)
Scorers: Williams R 89 / Wheeler 53
Ref: J Finney

City	Reading
Cook	*Meeson*
Hopkinson	*Goodall*
Briggs	*Vallard*
McCall	*Spiers*
Quinlan	*Davies*
Casey	*Evans*
Rogers	*McIlvenny*
Etheridge	*Whitehouse*
Ryan	*Wheeler*
Williams R	*Webb*
McCann	*Buck*

Bobby Williams thumps the ball into the net for City to salvage a last-minute point. In truth, this late effort should not have been necessary, as in the first half City waste their chances. Following the break, though, it is Reading who are ascendant and James Wheeler heads them in front.

Game 13 — H COVENTRY — 2-0 (HT 1-0)
Position 13, W · 17 13 · Att: 14,108 (£1,801.19.0)
Scorers: Etheridge 9, Casey 72
Ref: G Thorpe

City	Coventry
Cook	*Lightening*
Hopkinson	*Kletzenbauer*
Thresher	*Bennett*
McCall	*Kearns*
Connor	*Curtis*
Casey	*Jones*
Taylor	*Stiffle*
Atyeo	*Ryan*
Tait	*Satchell*
Etheridge	*Farmer*
Boxley	*Hill*

Etheridge's accurate header to Tait's cross gets City on the goal trail, but seeking to add further he then has the misfortune to have two more headers cleared off the line. City make sure of victory when Taylor's centre is met by Casey's left foot, to send a 20-yard screamer into the net.

Game 14 — H PORT VALE — 3-4 (HT 2-0)
Position 16, L · 12 13 · Att: 8,803 (£1,073.18.0)
Scorers: Atyeo 6, 66, Tait 25 [Whalley 80] / Jackson 57p, Portwood 72, 77
Ref: L Callaghan

City	Port Vale
Cook	*Hancock*
Hopkinson	*Raine*
Thresher	*Sproston*
McCall	*Poole*
Connor	*Ford*
Casey	*Miles*
Taylor	*Jackson*
Atyeo	*Portwood*
Tait	*Whalley*
Etheridge	*Steele*
Boxley	*Fidler*

On a day that sees the wind blow off part of the main stand roof, City are also blown away by the visitors' comeback. It was all so easy until a disputed spot-kick, but even so Atyeo nodded in to restore City's advantage. Selwyn Whalley beats the offside trap to walk in Vale's winner.

Game 15 — A SOUTHEND — 0-1 (HT 0-0)
Position 16, L · 17 13 · Att: 8,805 (£871.16.6)
Scorers: — / Laverty 59
Ref: A Sturgeon

City	Southend
Cook	*Threadgold*
Collinson	*Anderson*
Thresher	*Holton*
McCall	*Costello*
Connor	*Dicks*
Casey	*Whale*
Rogers	*Stenhouse*
Atyeo	*Corthine*
Tait	*Houghton*
Burden	*Laverty*
Boxley	*Nutt*

City find Alan Dicks in fine form at Roots Hall, where they fail to take their chances. Burden hits a post just before half-time, but the City defence is all at sea when Pat Laverty, on receiving Brian Houghton's knock-down, is completely unmarked in beating Cook from ten yards.

Game 16 — A SWINDON — 1-3 (HT 0-1)
Position 16, L · 10 13 · Att: 16,618
Scorers: Atyeo 64 / Layne 22, 86, 89
Ref: F Reid

City	Swindon
Cook	*Burton*
Collinson	*Wollen*
Thresher	*Trollope*
McCall	*Morgan*
Connor	*Owen*
Casey	*Woodruff*
Rogers	*Summerbee*
Atyeo	*Hunt*
Tait	*Layne*
Burden	*Jackson*
Boxley	*Darcy*

The Swindon starlets appeared to be fading after Atyeo fired in City's equaliser, but they discover fresh reserves of strength to snatch two late goals. A thrilling end to a game played in a cup-tie like atmosphere in front of the largest County ground attendance so far this season.

Game 17 — H CHESTERFIELD — 3-0 (HT 2-0)
Position 16, W · 23 15 · Att: 7,796 (£880.10.0)
Scorers: Tait 30, Derrick 44, Rogers 80
Ref: J Taylor

City	Chesterfield
Cook	*Powell*
Collinson	*Clarke*
Thresher	*Sears*
Connor	*Smallwood*
Williams A	*Blakey*
Etheridge	*Frear*
Rogers	*Bowering*
Atyeo	*Havenhand*
Williams Ad	*Foley*
Derrick	*Rackstraw*
Maddison	*Maddison*

Chesterfield are undone as early as the sixth minute when keeper Ron Powell suffers a head injury. After going off for treatment, he comes back just before Tait notches a two-yard opener. Playing on the wing until half-time, he resumes in goal from Terry Foley after the interval.

Game 18 — A BURY — 0-1 (HT 0-1)
Position 16, L · 1 15 · Att: 10,856
Scorers: — / Jackson 11
Ref: J Bellwood

City	Bury
Cook	*Adams*
Collinson	*Robertson*
Thresher	*Conroy*
Connor	*Turner*
Williams A	*McGrath*
Etheridge	*Atherton*
Tait	*Calder*
Atyeo	*Holden*
Williams R	*Watson*
Derrick	*Jackson*
Boxley	*Hubbard*

Cook, whose fine display between the sticks prevents a heavy City defeat, receives a fine ovation from the Gigg Lane crowd. Bury, despite the handicap of Donald Watson's early injury, are firmly in control throughout. Alan Jackson's header sees Bury deservedly take the points.

Game 19 — A SHREWSBURY — 2-4 (HT 1-4)
Position 17, L · 18 15 · Att: 7,998
Scorers: Williams R 44, Tait 68 [Hobson 35] / Rowley 18p, Starkey 33, 34
Ref: J Powell

City	Shrewsbury
Cook	*Gibson*
Collinson	*Walter*
Thresher	*Skeech*
Connor	*Wallace*
Williams A	*Pountney*
Etheridge	*Harley*
Tait	*Hobson*
Atyeo	*Starkey*
Williams Ad	*Baker*
Williams R	*Rowley*
Boxley	*McLaughlin*

Collinson's bringing down James McLaughlin, which leads to player-manager Arthur Rowley putting his side ahead from the spot, heralds a three goals in a three minute spell that has City reeling. Fighting back it is a pity that offside rules out a 75th-minute Bobby Williams effort.

Game 20 — H HALIFAX — 3-2 (HT 0-0)
Position 15, W · 5 17 · Att: 10,910 (£1,303.11.0)
Scorers: Williams R 47, Atyeo 83, Casey 86 / Large 53, Blackburn 78
Ref: P Brandwood

City	Halifax
Nicholson	*Knowles*
Collinson	*Stanley*
Thresher	*Hudson*
Connor	*Tilley*
Williams A	*South*
Etheridge	*Fagan*
Casey	*Priestley*
Atyeo	*Sinclair*
Tait	*Whitelaw*
Williams R	*Large*
Derrick	*Blackburn*

City do not wake up until Alan Blackburn's scrambled in effort puts the visitors into a 2-1 lead. There is little of distinction, but Casey's ferocious left-foot effort into the Halifax net, following hot on the heels of Atyeo's opportunist one, is a shot worthy of winning any game.

Game 21 — A BRENTFORD — 0-2 (HT 0-0)
Position 17, L · 16 17 · Att: 5,205
Scorers: — / Towers 55, Francis 86
Ref: J Carr

City	Brentford
Cook	*Cakebread*
Collinson	*Wilson*
Thresher	*Coote*
Connor	*Goundry*
Etheridge	*Dargie*
Derrick	*Higginson*
Atyeo	*Docherty*
Rogers	*Rainford*
Connor	*Francis*
Williams R	*Towers*
Virgin	*Hales*

Connor looks like he might solve City's centre-half problem, as he is brilliant in this game. He keeps City in with the chance of a point until Cook's lapse just before the end. The keeper misjudges a long-kick to leave George Francis with the simple task of lobbing the ball in the net.

Game 22 — H BRADFORD C — 1-2 (HT 0-1)
Position 18, L · 21 17 · Att: 7,833 (£871.16.6)
Scorers: Connor 48 / Reid 36, 90p
Ref: R Mann

City	Bradford C
Cook	*Downie*
Collinson	*Flackett*
Thresher	*Storton*
Connor	*Jackson P*
Williams A	*Currie*
Etheridge	*Webb*
Rogers	*Roberts*
Atyeo	*Duncan*
Connor	*Reid*
Burden	*Smith*
Boxley	

With Connor at centre-forward, City have the best of a poor game, but Williams brings down James Duncan for Bradford's penalty winner just 20 seconds from time. Connor has the satisfaction of getting City's goal, however inelegantly he manages to turn McCall's centre over the line.

Game 23 — H QP RANGERS — 1-1 (HT 1-0)
Position 18, D · 3 18 · Att: 10,794 (£1,384.16.6)
Scorers: Tait 1 / Bedford 49
Ref: G Thorpe

City	QP Rangers
Cook	*Drinkwater*
Hopkinson	*Woods*
Thresher	*Ingham*
McCall	*Keen*
Connor	*Rutter*
Casey	*Angell*
Rogers	*Lazarus*
Atyeo	*Bedford*
Tait	*Evans*
Williams R	*Andrews*
Derrick	*Longbottom*

Despite the benefit of Tait's lucky opener – his tentative cross glancing off of Keith Rutter's boot to curl away into the net — City are unable to capitalise in this boring draw. Ranger's equaliser comes from a goalmouth melee, which has City vainly protesting that Cook had been fouled.

LEAGUE DIVISION 3

Manager: Fred Ford — SEASON 1960-61

No 24 — A QP RANGERS — 27/12
Att 15,391 · Pos 18 (*3*) · Pt D 19 · F-A 1-1 · H-T 0-1
Scorers: Tait 63, Woods 35p · Ref: R Windle

	1	2	3	4	5	6	7	8	9	10	11
City	Cook	Hopkinson	Thresher	Etheridge	Connor	Casey	Rogers	Atyeo	Tait	Williams R	Boxley
QPR	Drinkwater	Woods	Ingham	Keen	Rutter	Angall	Lazarus	Bedford	Evans	Andrews	Clark

A hostile atmosphere develops at Loftus Road due to City's tackling on Mark Lazarus and Clive Clark. At one stage some spectators get onto the pitch to remonstrate with the referee over his lenient approach. It is Thresher's tackle on Lazarus that brings Pat Woods his spot-kick.

No 25 — A BARNSLEY — 31/12
Att 8,043 · Pos 19 (*11*) · Pt L 19 · F-A 0-2 · H-T 0-1
Scorers: Houghton 8, Oliver 85 · Ref: J Bullough

	1	2	3	4	5	6	7	8	9	10	11
City	Cook	Hopkinson	Thresher	Etheridge	Connor	Casey	Rogers	Atyeo	Tait	Williams R	Boxley
Barnsley	Leeson	Swift	Brookes E	Barber	Sharp	Houghton	Smillie	Bartlett	Tindill	Oliver	Brookes C

City play entertaining football in a fine game at Oakwell, but are let down by their poor finishing. There are no slackers or non-triers in City's side and Cook has no chance with either of the snappy shots that bring Barnsley their goals. William Houghton's 25-yard drive is unstoppable.

No 26 — H NEWPORT — 14/1
Att 12,172 (£1,468.3.0) · Pos 19 (*10*) · Pt W 21 · F-A 3-0 · H-T 2-0
Scorers: Casey 2, Tait 6, 76 · Ref: F Reid

	1	2	3	4	5	6	7	8	9	10	11
City	Cook	Hopkinson	Thresher	Etheridge	Connor	Casey	Rogers	Atyeo	Tait	Williams R	Derrick
Newport	Weare	Sherwood	Rowland	Burton	Peake	Riggs	Fry	McPherson	Ford	Meyer	McSeveney

Two early goals put City in charge, but County have their chances. Casey's 25-yarder, that bounds down over the line after hitting both the bar and the inside of a post, opens the scoring, then Tait taps in a rebound, before notching a second-half header to see off County's challenge.

No 27 — A COLCHESTER — 21/1
Att 5,099 · Pos 18 (*23*) · Pt W 23 · F-A 1-0 · H-T 1-0
Scorers: Atyeo 10 · Ref: H New

	1	2	3	4	5	6	7	8	9	10	11
City	Cook	Hopkinson	Thresher	Etheridge	Connor	Casey	Rogers	Atyeo	Tait	Williams R	Wright
Colchester	Ames	Eagles	Fowler	Harris	Milligan	Hunt R N	Williams	McLeod	Langman	Hunt R R	

On a glue-pot pitch, City's first away League win of the season is chiefly due to a resolute defence, ably marshalled by the outstanding Connor. It is Atyeo, though, who settles the contest on receiving a Rogers pass, side-footing a 15-yarder just inside the far-post past Percy Ames.

No 28 — H GRIMSBY — 4/2
Att 11,141 (£1,304.19.6) · Pos 18 (*5*) · Pt W 25 · F-A 2-1 · H-T 2-1
Scorers: Atyeo 20p, 25, Cullen 40 · Ref: K Seddon

	1	2	3	4	5	6	7	8	9	10	11
City	Cook	Hopkinson	Thresher	Etheridge	Connor	Casey	Virgin	Atyeo	Tait	Williams R	Derrick
Grimsby	White	Donovan	Keeble	Welbourne	Cockerill	Pearce	Scott	Rafferty	Cullen	Williams	Fell

Promotion-chasing Grimsby slump to their third consecutive defeat. Donal Donovan's check on Tait brings City their Open End spot-kick and Brian Keeble's poor control allows Virgin to set up Atyeo to fire in. A measured shot from the edge of the area is the Mariners' sole response.

No 29 — A HULL — 13/2
Att 7,077 · Pos 16 (*13*) · Pt D 26 · F-A 3-3 · H-T 2-2
Scorers: Derrick 34, 35, Atyeo 88, Chilton 10, Clarke 44, Gubbins 82 · Ref: K Stokes

	1	2	3	4	5	6	7	8	9	10	11
City	Cook	Hopkinson	Thresher	Etheridge	Connor	Casey	Rogers	Atyeo	Tait	Williams R	Derrick
Hull	Fisher	Davidson	Garvey	Collinson	Feasey	Bulless	Clarke	Price	Chilton	Gubbins	Crickmore

A thriller at Boothferry Park, where Cook concedes a 40th-minute spot-kick for manhandling Chris Chilton. Fortunately, Ralph Gubbins blasts over the bar. Atyeo earns City a deserved point, cutting in onto a Williams pass and placing a narrow angled shot into the far corner of the net.

No 30 — H READING — 18/2
Att 11,606 (£1,397.1.6) · Pos 14 (*20*) · Pt W 28 · F-A 2-0 · H-T 1-0
Scorers: Rogers 42, Tait 83 · Ref: W Clements

	1	2	3	4	5	6	7	8	9	10	11
City	Cook	Briggs	Thresher	Etheridge	Connor	Casey	Rogers	Atyeo	Tait	Williams R	Derrick
Reading	Meeson	Neate	Reeves	Spiers	Davies	Evans	Head	Whitehouse	Lacey	Buck	Travers

Atyeo's 18-yarder at the Covered End, which David Meeson turns aside in fine style after 29 minutes, is the only full-blooded shot of note. Fortunately, with Gordon Neate's clearance allowing Rogers a tap-in and Tait nipping onto Casey's centre to fire through, the points are City's.

No 31 — H WALSALL — 21/2
Att 12,029 (£1,480.5.0) · Pos 13 (*5*) · Pt W 30 · F-A 2-0 · H-T 2-0
Scorers: Atyeo 28, 35 · Ref: J Finney

	1	2	3	4	5	6	7	8	9	10	11
City	Cook	Hopkinson	Thresher	Etheridge	Connor	Casey	Rogers	Atyeo	Tait	Williams R	Derrick
Walsall	Christie	Palin	Sharples	Hill	McPherson	Dudley	Askey	Hopkinson	Wilson	Richards	Taylor

City are doubly fortunate, as not only did the referee fail to spot Thresher's hand keeping out Colin Askey's shot, but straight away they race upfield where Atyeo meets Tait's centre 15 yards out to fire in a left-footed opener. An Atyeo header soon increases City's advantage.

No 32 — A WATFORD — 25/2
Att 7,630 · Pos 13 (*12*) · Pt W 32 · F-A 1-0 · H-T 0-0
Scorers: Porter 86 (og) · Ref: N Hough

	1	2	3	4	5	6	7	8	9	10	11
City	Cook	Hopkinson	Thresher	Etheridge	Connor	Casey	Rogers	Atyeo	Tait	Williams R	Derrick
Watford	Underwood	Bell	Nicholas	Holton	McNeice	Porter	Gregory	Harmer	Fairbrother	Smith	Bunce

Watford's costly side never look better than mediocre in this contest. The points should have been safely in City's pockets before half-time, but it takes an own-goal from left-half Andy Porter (deflecting Atyeo's effort over the line) near the call of time to secure a deserved away success.

No 33 — A TRANMERE — 27/2
Att 11,477 · Pos 13 (*22*) · Pt L 32 · F-A 2-3 · H-T 1-0
Scorers: Rogers 33, Williams 65, Arnell 73, 78, Williams 86 · Ref: H Hackney

	1	2	3	4	5	6	7	8	9	10	11
City	Cook	Hopkinson	Thresher	Etheridge	Connor	Casey	Rogers	Atyeo	Tait	Williams R	Derrick
Tranmere	Payne	Frith	Brown	Neill	McGugan	King	Finney	Williams	Rowley	Arnell	Eglington

A thriller at Prenton Park, where Tranmere's hotly disputed equaliser helps end City's proud unbeaten League run this year. Cook appeared to pull off a spectacular save from Alan Arnell's header, but, much to City's amazement, the linesman flags that the ball had crossed the line.

No 34 — H SOUTHEND — 4/3
Att 11,379 (£1,341.3.6) · Pos 11 (*17*) · Pt W 34 · F-A 2-0 · H-T 1-0
Scorers: Williams R 34, Tait 54 · Ref: H New

	1	2	3	4	5	6	7	8	9	10	11
City	Cook	Hopkinson	Thresher	Etheridge	Connor	Casey	Rogers	Atyeo	Tait	Williams R	Derrick
Southend	Gay	Williamson	Anderson	Kellard	Watson	Dicks	Corthine	Laverty	Fryatt	McKinven	Duncan

Played at a funeral pace, City easily win this drab affair. Bobby Williams is the star performer and is involved in both goals. His fierce ground shot into the corner of the net opens the scoring and, after the break, his mazy defence-splitting dribble sets up Tait for what is an easy tap-in.

League Results (matches 35–46)

No	Date	V	Opponent	Pos	Res	Score		Pts	Att	Receipts	Scorers	Referee
35	11/3	A	CHESTERFIELD	14	L	0-3	24	34	4,451		Havenhand 68, 86, Mays 90	F Cowan
36	14/3	H	WATFORD	10	W	4-1	12	36	12,141	(£1,442.17.6)	Rogers 22, Tait 53, Etheridge 54, [Atyeo 76], Walker 90	L Hamer
37	18/3	H	BURY	11	L	1-2	1	36	12,764	(£1,562.4.0)	Adams 12 (og), Holden 24, 31	P Brandwood
38	25/3	A	WALSALL	14	L	**0-4**	3	36	10,115		Richards 11, 75, Thresher 53 (og), [Faulkner 59]	A Luty
39	31/3	H	TORQUAY	13	D	2-2	7	37	13,713	(£1,695.16.6)	Bush 1, 11, Northcott T 44, Hancock 68	J Finney
40	1/4	H	SHREWSBURY	14	D	0-0	15	38	8,805	(£1,001.3.6)		E Jennings
41	3/4	A	TORQUAY	13	D	0-0	5	39	6,863			C Rogers
42	8/4	A	HALIFAX	15	L	1-2	11	39	4,883		Virgin 75, Holmes 40, 54	F Cowan
43	15/4	H	TRANMERE	14	W	2-0	21	41	8,504	(£920.1.0)	Atyeo 68, Tait 75	F Clarke
44	22/4	A	PORT VALE	13	D	1-1	6	42	4,068		Tait 3, Llewellyn 34	N Hough
45	24/4	A	COVENTRY	15	L	1-2	13	42	8,340		Atyeo 50, Allen 24, Hill 63	M Fussey
46	29/4	H	BRENTFORD	14	W	3-0	17	44	8,656	(£936.11.6)	Atyeo 27p, 37, 79	J Kelly

Home Average 11,488 Away 8,943

Team line-ups (City player / opponent)

No	Cook	Hopkinson	Thresher	Etheridge	Connor	Jacobs	Rogers	Atyeo	Tait	Williams R	Derrick
35	Cook / Powell	Hopkinson / Clarke	Thresher / Sears	Etheridge / Mays	Connor / Blakey	Jacobs / Frear	Rogers / Bowering	Atyeo / Havenhand	Tait / Frost	Williams R / Rackstraw	Derrick / Maddison
36	Cook / Underwood	Hopkinson / Bell	Thresher / Nicholas	Etheridge / Catleugh	**Low** / McNeice	Casey / Chung	Rogers / Benning	Atyeo / Harmer	Tait / Holton	Williams R / Walker	Derrick / Bunce
37	Cook / Adams	Hopkinson / Robertson	Thresher / Conroy	Etheridge / Turner	Low / Stokoe	Casey / Atherton	Rogers / Calder	Atyeo / Holden	Tait / Watson	Williams R / Jackson	Derrick / Hubbard
38	Cook / Christie	Hopkinson / Palin	Thresher / Sharples	Etheridge / Hill	Connor / Eden	Casey / Dudley	Rogers / Davies	Atyeo / Faulkner	Tait / Wilson	Williams R / Richards	Derrick / Taylor
39	Cook / Gill	Collinson / Bettany	Briggs / Smith	Etheridge / Hancock	Williams A / Northcott G	Casey / Rawson	Rogers / Lewis	Atyeo / Cox	**Bush** / Northcott T	Williams Ad / Mills	Boxley / Pym
40	Cook / Gibson	Collinson / Waiters	Briggs / Skeech	McCall / Wallace	Etheridge / Pountney	Casey / Harley	Virgin / Cornfield	Atyeo / Dolby	**Bush** / Baker	Derrick / Starkey	Derrick / McLaughlin
41	Cook / Gill	Collinson / Bettany	Briggs / James	McCall / Hancock	Etheridge / Northcott G	Casey / Rawson	Derrick / Lewis	Atyeo / Cox	Bush / Northcott T	Williams R / Mills	Boxley / Pym
42	Cook / Knowles	Collinson / Stanley	Briggs / Hudson	Etheridge / Harrison	Low / South	Casey / Tilley	Derrick / Sinclair	Atyeo / Smith	Rogers / Allan	Williams A / Holmes	Virgin / Ringer
43	Cook / Leyland	Briggs / Frith	Thresher / Brown	Etheridge / Neill	Connor / McGugan	Casey / King	Low / Murray	Atyeo / Arnell	Tait / Amell	Williams K / Gubbins	Virgin / Eglington
44	Cook / Hancock	Briggs / Raine	Thresher / Sproson	Etheridge / Poole	Connor / Ford	Casey / Miles	Derrick / Hall	Atyeo / Calland	Tait / Llewellyn	Williams R / Fidler	Rogers / Oscroft
45	Cook / Wesson	Hopkinson / Kletzenbauer	Thresher / Austin	Etheridge / Kearns	Connor / Curtis	Casey / Farmer	Rogers / Imlach	Atyeo / Hewitt	Tait / Holder	Williams R / Hill	Derrick / Allen
46	Cook / Cakebread	Briggs / Wilson	Thresher / Coote	Burden / Bristow	Connor / Dargie	Low / Higgenson	**Peters** / Hales	**Clark** / Rainford	Atyeo / Summers	Williams R / Towers	Derrick / McLeod

Match reports

35 – Chesterfield (a): Connor is little more than a passenger after a fifth-minute knee injury and he finally leaves the field four minutes from time. Keith Havenhand takes advantage of City's poor defending to stab his side in front before heading in a second. Albert May's 20-yarder gives Cook little chance.

36 – Watford (h): There is no holding City as they sweep confidently, and often brilliantly, to a double over Watford. Rogers finishes off a seven-man move with a header to open the scoring. Tait doubles City's advantage by dribbling through the visitors defence and slotting the ball into an open net.

37 – Bury (h): The BBC Saturday night highlights programme does little to clear up the many controversial decisions of this game. City are lucky with their goal as it seemed that the ball had not crossed the line, but near the end the citing of Tait for dangerous play to rule out Atyeo's goal is absurd.

38 – Walsall (a): Hopkinson's 25th minute knee injury, which has him off the field for a while, and hobbling on the wing thereafter, doesn't help matters as shoddy City suffer their worst defeat of the season. Tony Richards becomes Walsall's record goalscorer - his second raising his total to 166.

39 – Torquay (h): Bush marks his League debut with a lobbed shot from the edge of the area after just 65 seconds, then adds another with a fierce eight-yard drive. Tommy Northcott's 30-yard lob gets Torquay back into the game and they are worthy of the point earned by David Hancock's shot.

40 – Shrewsbury (h): Nine out of ten goalless draws are colourless, lifeless affairs. Regretfully, this match was not the exception. Colourless and lifeless are two of the more polite adjectives that can be applied to this shocking exhibition. For City only Cook, Briggs and Etheridge distinguished themselves.

41 – Torquay (a): Derrick dazzles, but City waste many chances against a Torquay side - down to nine men for the last seven minutes. David Lewis makes a good save during his spell between the sticks, exited three minutes earlier - with Mervyn Gill following the concussed Colin Rawson, who had

42 – Halifax (a): Alan Williams is given a surprise outing at inside-left and plays well enough to justify another opportunity against Tranmere on Saturday. A full-strength City would probably have won this game. Tom Holmes shoots in both Halifax goals, whilst for City, Virgin nets from 20 yards.

43 – Tranmere (h): The Butlins Beauties entertain before the start of this game, in which Bobby Williams takes the place of his namesake Alan. Harry Leyland, the ex-Blackburn Rovers goalkeeper who played in last year's FA Cup final, prevents a rout. Atyeo's shoots in on the turn to put City in front.

44 – Port Vale (a): Considering the heavy downpour and the lack of atmosphere from Vale's lowest crowd of the season, this was not a bad match by any means. Tait applies the finishing touch to a Rogers shot, but thereafter City are often caught offside before Bert Llewellyn heads the homesters level.

45 – Coventry (a): City are robbed by the referee who gives offside against Tait 20 minutes from time, when Frank Kletzenbauer puts a Williams cross into his own net. A determined display, deserving at least a draw, City are unfortunate to be beaten by Peter Hill's shot, which trickles over the line.

46 – Brentford (h): A decorous end to the League season, listening to the band play musical honours for Tommy Burden on the occasion of his last game. With next week's FA Cup final referee in charge of this leisurely affair, the fans are treated to a classic Atyeo goal that gives City a two-nil lead.

CUP-TIES

Manager: Fred Ford   SEASON 1960-61

League Cup

			F-A	H-T	Scorers, Times, and Referees	1	2	3	4	5	6	7	8	9	10	11
2 A ALDERSHOT 10/10	16	D	1-1	1-0	Boxley 38, Hasty 62 — Ref: K Aston — 5,700 4:5	Cook *Brodie*	Hopkinson *Bannister*	Thresher *Jackson*	McCall *Mundy*	Williams A *Shipwright*	Jacobs *Tyrer*	Rogers *Taylor*	Atyeo *Hasty*	Tait *Kirkup*	Etheridge *Lawlor*	Boxley *Parnell*

Down to ten men following Hopkinson's 18th-minute departure on a stretcher with torn ligaments, City put on a magnificent display to earn a replay. From just inside the penalty area Boxley puts City in front - his shot going in off an upright - but Paddy Hasty fires in a great leveller.

			F-A	H-T	Scorers, Times, and Referees	1	2	3	4	5	6	7	8	9	10	11
2R H ALDERSHOT 25/10 (£1,349.12.0)	16	W	3-0	2-0	Atyeo 28, 39, Williams Ad 87 — Ref: J Finney — 9,229 4:5	Cook *Brodie*	Collinson *Bannister*	Thresher *Jackson*	Connor *Lennan*	Williams A *Shipwright*	Etheridge *Tyrer*	Tait *Taylor*	Williams A *Hasty*	Tait *Kirkup*	Williams Ad *Humphries*	Derrick *Lawlor*

Despite Etheridge shooting wide from a first-half spot-kick after Tait is brought down, this game is easy for City. Atyeo's first-half goals - a shot followed by a header - put City in charge. Adrian Williams crowns his fine display by nodding in from Collinson's 35-yard free-kick.

			F-A	H-T	Scorers, Times, and Referees	1	2	3	4	5	6	7	8	9	10	11
3 A NOTT'M FOR 15/11	17	L	1-2	0-1	Atyeo 83, Quigley 40, Williams A 84 (og) — Ref: K Collinge — 3,690 1:22	Cook *Grummitt*	Collinson *Patrick*	Thresher *McDonald*	Connor *Palmer*	Williams A *McKinlay*	Etheridge *Iley*	Tait *Gray*	Atyeo *Booth*	Williams R *Vowden*	Williams Ad *Quigley*	Derrick *Le Flem*

A low crowd as this game is played on a midweek afternoon, owing to Forest not having floodlights. Tragedy for Alan Williams who, pressed by John Quigley, puts the ball into his own net almost immediately after being involved in the move that saw Atyeo firing in City's leveller.

FA Cup

			F-A	H-T	Scorers, Times, and Referees	1	2	3	4	5	6	7	8	9	10	11
1 H CHICHESTER CITY 5/11 (£2,074.10.0)	16	W	11-0	8-0	Wil's Ad 5, 42, 50, Tait 10, Bailey 21(og), [Atyeo 25, 30, 37, 54, 74, Wil's R 44] — Ref: R Reddaway — 12,588 SCL	Cook *Thomas*	Collinson *Cunningham*	Thresher *Knotts*	Connor *Rumsey*	Williams A *Bailey*	Etheridge *Aburrow*	Tait *Green*	Williams R *Hillier*	Atyeo *Gilfillan*	Williams Ad *Blythman*	Derrick *Harris*

A stroll against the Sussex amateurs, who had forfeited home advantage. Complacency creeps in after the interval, City spurning many chances in their desire to set up Derrick (the only forward who fails to score). Atyeo's lob into the net for his second goal is the best of the afternoon.

			F-A	H-T	Scorers, Times, and Referees	1	2	3	4	5	6	7	8	9	10	11
2 A KINGS LYNN 26/11 (£.)	15	D	2-2	2-0	Atyeo 9, Rogers 11, Sewell 84, Dunn 90 — Ref: N Hough — 6,762 SP-20	Cook *Manning*	Collinson *Mackay*	Thresher *Wilson*	Etheridge *Dunn*	Connor *Cleary*	Casey *Johnson*	Rogers *Baxter*	Atyeo *Chilleystone*	Tait *Dixon*	Williams R *Sewell*	Derrick *Sharp*

Despite scoring twice in three minutes - Atyeo flicking in Tait's centre and Rogers spectacularly shooting in off a post - City have a torrid time. Lynn sense their chance after Casey's 60th-minute injury, but it takes until Dunn's shot in the dying seconds to snatch a deserved replay.

			F-A	H-T	Scorers, Times, and Referees	1	2	3	4	5	6	7	8	9	10	11
2R H KINGS LYNN 29/11 (£2,228.14.6)	15	W	3-0	2-0	Atyeo 2, Rogers 22, 65 — Ref: P Carr — 14,471 SP-20	Cook *Manning*	Collinson *Mackay*	Thresher *Wilson*	McCall *Dunn*	Connor *Cleary*	Etheridge *Johnson*	Rogers *Baxter*	Atyeo *Chilleystone*	Bush *Dixon*	Ryan *Sewell*	Derrick *Sharp*

The City manager banks on strength and the long-ball game to make sure that City will not be as troubled as they were on Saturday by their skilful Southern League opponents. Bush's flick-on from Derrick's centre brings Atyeo an early goal, but the visitors do not ever give up.

			F-A	H-T	Scorers, Times, and Referees	1	2	3	4	5	6	7	8	9	10	11
3 A PLYMOUTH 7/1	19	W	1-0	1-0	Williams R 38 — Ref: H New — 13,087 2:9	Cook *MacLaren*	Hopkinson *Robertson*	Thresher *Stacey*	Etheridge *Williams*	Connor *Fincham*	Casey *Newman*	Rogers *Carter*	Atyeo *Brown*	Tait *Kirby*	Williams R *Jackson*	Boxley *Wright*

A thriller in the rain and mud at Home Park, this game ends with the Argyle goalkeeper Dave MacLaren playing on the wing after suffering a fractured cheekbone in the 62nd minute. Williams nets the only goal (a 12-yarder into the rigging) on ploughing forward to hit Boxley's centre.

			F-A	H-T	Scorers, Times, and Referees	1	2	3	4	5	6	7	8	9	10	11
4A A LEICESTER 28/1 (£5,900)	18	A-A	0-0		Abandoned at half-time due to a waterlogged pitch — Ref: G McCabe — 26,109 1:8	Cook *Banks*	Hopkinson *Chalmers*	Thresher *Norman*	Etheridge *McLintock*	Connor *King*	Casey *Appleton*	Rogers *Riley*	Atyeo *Walsh*	Tait *Leek*	Williams R *Keyworth*	Derrick *Wills*

Leicester have more of the play, but the flooded conditions make sure that this 45-minute exercise bears little resemblance to a football match. For City, Atyeo has a header smothered at the foot of a post, whilst Tait might have scored if he had shot rather than passed the ball to Derrick.

			F-A	H-T	Scorers, Times, and Referees	1	2	3	4	5	6	7	8	9	10	11
4 A LEICESTER 31/1 (£5,600)	18	L	1-5	1-5	Norman 23 (og), Wills 25, Leek 32, 33, Walsh 41, 45 — Ref: G McCabe — 27,710 1:8	Cook *Banks*	Hopkinson *Chalmers*	Thresher *Norman*	Etheridge *McLintock*	Connor *King*	Casey *Appleton*	Virgin *Riley*	Atyeo *Walsh*	Tait *Leek*	Williams R *Keyworth*	Derrick *Wills*

Brief highlights of this game are shown on BBC, but there is little to cheer for City fans other than Norman's back-pass own-goal, which gave them the lead. Whilst Leicester's goal rush puts paid to any giant-killing hopes, City, to their credit, give a spirited showing after the interval.

Gloucestershire Cup

			F-A	H-T	Scorers, Times, and Referees	1	2	3	4	5	6	7	8	9	10	11
F A BRISTOL ROV 1/5	14	W	3-1	0-0	Atyeo 61, 63, Derrick 87, Jarman 51 — Ref: S Yates — 12,109 2:17	Cook *Norman*	Briggs *Hilliard*	Thresher *Frowen*	Etheridge *Stone*	Connor *Davis*	Casey *Mabbutt*	Rogers *Jarman*	Atyeo *Jones R*	Tait *Bradford*	Williams R *Hooper*	Derrick *Watkins*

Super-City outplay the Rovers after going behind when Harold Jarman races onto Ray Mabbutt's through-ball to flick the leather wide of Cook's left-hand. Derrick is City's star and he climaxes his great 50-yard dribble with a fierce shot between Malcolm Norman and the far post.

			Home					Away					
		P	W	D	L	F	A	W	D	L	F	A	Pts
1	Bury	46	18	3	2	62	17	12	5	6	46	28	68
2	Walsall	46	19	4	0	62	20	9	4	12	36	40	62
3	QP Rangers	46	18	4	1	58	23	7	6	10	35	37	60
4	Watford	46	12	7	4	52	27	8	5	10	33	45	52
5	Notts Co	46	16	3	4	52	24	5	6	12	30	53	51
6	Grimsby	46	14	4	5	48	32	6	6	11	29	37	50
7	Port Vale	46	15	3	5	63	30	2	12	9	33	49	49
8	Barnsley	46	15	5	3	56	30	6	2	15	27	50	49
9	Halifax	46	14	7	2	42	22	7	2	10	29	56	49
10	Shrewsbury	46	13	7	3	54	26	2	9	12	29	49	46
11	Hull	46	13	6	4	51	28	4	6	13	22	45	46
12	Torquay	46	8	12	3	37	26	6	5	12	38	57	45
13	Newport	46	12	7	4	51	30	5	4	14	30	60	45
14	BRISTOL C	46	15	4	4	50	19	2	6	15	20	49	44
15	Coventry	46	14	6	3	54	25	2	6	15	26	58	44
16	Swindon	46	13	6	4	41	16	3	7	13	21	39	43
17	Brentford	46	10	9	4	41	28	3	8	12	15	42	43
18	Reading	46	13	5	5	48	29	1	7	15	24	54	40
19	Bournemouth	46	8	7	8	34	39	7	3	13	24	37	40
20	Southend	46	10	8	5	38	26	4	3	16	22	50	39
21	Tranmere	46	11	5	7	53	50	4	3	16	26	65	38
22	Bradford C	46	8	8	7	37	36	3	6	14	28	51	36
23	Colchester	46	8	5	10	40	44	3	6	14	28	57	33
24	Chesterfield	46	9	6	8	42	29	1	6	16	25	58	32
		1104	306	141	105	1166	676	105	141	306	676	1166	1104

Odds & ends

Double wins: (2) Colchester, Watford.
Double losses (2): Bradford C, Bury.

Won from behind: (2) Notts Co (h), Bristol Rov (a) (GC).
Lost from in front: (6) Grimsby (a), Hull (h), Port Vale (h), Tranmere (a), Bury (h), Leicester (a) (FAC).

High spots: The first away League win of the season on 21 January.
The victory over Barnsley on 27 August.
Tommy Burden's farewell against Brentford on 29 April.
Beating Chichester City 11-0 in the FA Cup.
Winning at Plymouth in the FA Cup.

Low spots: Port Vale's late goals at Ashton Gate on 8 October.
Only scoring three times in the second-half against Chichester City.
Losing at Leicester in the FA Cup after opening the scoring.

AGM (Brecknell, Dolman & Rogers, Pennywell Road, 5 March 1962):
Loss £10,075.0s.0d. Season Ticket Sales £10,744.0s.0d.

Note: The FAC details include the abandoned match at Leicester.

Player of the year: Alex Tait.
Ever-presents: (0).
Hat-tricks: (3) John Atyeo (2), Adrian Williams (1).
Leading scorer: Overall: John Atyeo (31). League: John Atyeo (19).

	Appearances				Goals				
	Lge	FLC	FAC	GC	Lge	FLC	FAC	GC	Tot
Atyeo, John	37	3	6	1	19	3	7	2	31
Boxley, Jack	12	1	1				1		1
Briggs, Alec	9			1					
Burden, Tommy	14				1				1
Bush, Terry	2		1		2				2
Casey, Tommy	36		4		5				5
Clark, Brian	1								
Collinson, Roger	21	2	3		1				1
Connor, Jack	28	2	6	1					
Cook, Tony	45	3	6	1					
Derrick, Jantzen	32	2	5	1	5			1	6
Etheridge, Bobby	38	3	6	1	3				3
Hopkinson, Gordon	21	1	3						
Jacobs, Frank	1								
Low, Gordon	7								
McCall, Peter	11		1						
McCann, John	4								
Nicholson, Harry	1								
Peters, Rogers	1								
Quinlan, Mike	2								
Rogers, Jimmy	37	1	4	1	8		3		11
Ryan, John	3		1						
Tait, Alex	35	3	5	1	15		1		16
Taylor, Archie	10				1				1
Thresher, Mike	41	3	6	1					
Virgin, Derek	6		1		1				1
Williams, Adrian	4	2	2	1		2	2		4
Williams, Alan	11	3	1						
Williams, Bobby	36	2	5	1	7		2		9
(own-goals)					2		2		4
29 players used	506	33	66	11	70	5	18	3	96

LEAGUE DIVISION 3

Manager: Fred Ford — SEASON 1961-62

No	Date	V	Opponent	Att (receipts)	Pos	Pt	Res	F-A	H-T	Scorers, Times, and Referees	1	2	3	4	5	6	7	8	9	10	11
1	19/8	A	NOTTS CO	10,203		0	L	0-1	0-0	Horobin 90p / Ref: J Pickles	Cook	Briggs	Thresher	Etheridge	Connor	Low	Rogers	Clark	Atyeo	Williams R	Peters
											Smith	*Edwards*	*Noon*	*Sheridan*	*Loxley*	*Carver*	*Joyce*	*Horobin*	*Hateley*	*Forrest*	*Withers*
2	22/8	H	NORTHAMPTON	14,415 (£1,857.17.6)		2	W	1-0	0-0	Atyeo 57 / Ref: H New	Cook	Briggs	Thresher	Etheridge	Connor	Low	Rogers	Clark	Atyeo	Williams R	Derrick
											Coe	*Foley*	*Claypole*	*Leck*	*Branston*	*Everitt*	*Spelman*	*Wright*	*Moran*	*Lines*	
3	26/8	H	SHREWSBURY	12,033 (£1,471.5.0)	18	2	L	0-1	0-0	Rowley 80 / Ref: K Aston	Cook	Briggs	Thresher	Etheridge	Connor	Low	Rogers	Clark	Atyeo	Williams R	Peters
											Gibson	*Walters*	*Skeech*	*Pountney*	*Wallace*	*Harley*	*Kenning*	*Starkey*	*Baker*	*Rowley*	*McLaughlin*
4	29/8	A	NORTHAMPTON	12,832	12	4	W	1-0	0-0	Williams 62 / Ref: E Crawford	Nicholls	Briggs	Thresher	Etheridge	Connor	Low	Rogers	Williams R	Atyeo	Casey	Peters
											Coe	*Foley*	*Claypole*	*Everitt*	*Branston*	*Leck*	*Dixon*	*Clayton*	*Terry*	*Moran*	*Fowler*
5	2/9	A	PETERBOROUGH	14,758	10	6	W	4-3	3-2	Low 2, Etheridge 17, Williams 43, 80 / Hails 25, McNamee 28, Emery 89 / Ref: A Holland	Nicholls	Briggs	Thresher	Etheridge	Connor	Low	Rogers	Williams R	Atyeo	Casey	Peters
											Walls	*Whittaker*	*Walker*	*Rayner*	*Rigby*	*Ripley*	*Hails*	*Emery*	*Bly*	*Smith*	*McNamee*
6	5/9	H	NEWPORT	15,915 (£2,078.15.0)	11	6	L	1-2	0-0	Williams 69 / Smith 65, Bowman 77 / Ref: D Howell	Nicholls	Briggs	Thresher	Etheridge	Connor	Low	Tait	Williams R	Atyeo	Casey	Peters
											Weare	*Bird*	*Herrity*	*Bowman*	*Evans*	*Rowlands*	*Fry*	*Robertson*	*Buchanan*	*Finlay*	*Smith*
7	9/9	H	PORT VALE	10,670 (£1,277.8.0)	18	6	L	0-1	0-0	Poole 53 / Ref: J Finney	Nicholls	Briggs	Thresher	Etheridge	Connor	Low	Derrick	Williams R	Atyeo	Casey	Peters
											Hancock	*Whalley*	*Sproson*	*Ford*	*Nicholson*	*Miles*	*Longbottom*	*Poole*	*Llewellyn*	*Steele*	*Edwards*
8	16/9	A	LINCOLN	4,090	16	7	D	1-1	0-0	Williams 88 / McClelland 62 / Ref: L Tirebuck	Cook	Briggs	Thresher	Etheridge	Connor	Low	Smith	Williams R	Meyer	Casey	Peters
											Greaves	*Jackson*	*Smith*	*Heward*	*Haines*	*Drysdale*	*McClelland*	*Linnecor*	*Harbertson*	*Buick*	*Tracey*
9	18/9	A	SOUTHEND	9,338	18	7	L	0-1	0-1	Kellard 15 / Ref: L Mason	Cook	Briggs	Thresher	Etheridge	Connor	Low	Tait	Clark	Meyer	Williams R	Peters
											Guy	*Sheils*	*Anderson*	*Costello*	*Watson*	*Grieveson*	*Bentley*	*Jones*	*Brand*	*McKinven*	*Kellard*
10	23/9	A	BRADFORD PA	10,432	19	7	L	0-2	0-1	Atkinson 6, Spratt 88 / Ref: A Sparling	Cook	Briggs	Thresher	Etheridge	Connor	Low	Rogers	Williams R	Meyer	Casey	Derrick
											Gebbie	*Walker*	*March*	*Scauler*	*McCalman*	*Dick*	*Atkinson*	*Spratt*	*Hannigan*	*Gibson*	*Bird*
11	26/9	H	SOUTHEND	10,679 (£1,290.4.0)	17	9	W	3-2	2-1	Meyer 24p, Griev'n 34 (og), Williams 52 / Brand 14, Jones 70 / Ref: W Haynes	Cook	Briggs	Thresher	Etheridge	Connor	Casey	Rogers	Atyeo	Meyer	Williams R	Derrick
											Guy	*Sheils*	*Anderson*	*Costello*	*Watson*	*Grieveson*	*Bentley*	*Jones*	*Brand*	*Gibson*	*Kellard*

1. City sparkled with their sprightly, attractive brand of football at Meadow Lane. Unfortunately, one commodity is missing, as their shooting left much to de desired. Connor's tackle on Alan Withers allows Notts to open their centenary season with a win thanks to a last-minute penalty.

2. Atyeo must have been red-faced as he obtained City's winner. Standing a good ten yards offside, he is the recipient of the Cobblers captain Jimmy Moran's attempted 30-yard back-pass. Onto the chance in a flash, Atyeo deposits the ball in the net to bring City an undeserved win.

3. Shrewsbury's 35-year-old player-manager Arthur Rowley conducts as his side call the tune. His splendid headed goal takes his League scoring record to 380 and his total for Shrewsbury to 102 in just a little over three years. Atyeo races clear to shoot in near the end but is given offside.

4. The Cobblers must be glad to see the back of City as once again they lose a game in which they are the better side. Nicholls, who almost joined Northampton from Cardiff in the summer, is City's hero with many fine saves. Williams lobs the ball over Norman Coe to clinch City's win.

5. City make the most of their chances to take Peterborough's unblemished record and inflict on them their first home defeat for a year. From a Rogers flag-kick, Low rams the ball in to get City off to a great start. A well-controlled acute angled shot by Williams secures the points.

6. Andy Bowman, signed from Hearts in the summer and reputed to be the highest paid player in the Third Division, notches Newport's deserved winner with a scorching right-footed volley from 30 yards. The City are run off their feet by County's breathtaking all-action brand of football.

7. City give the points away at Ashton Gate, where the visitors notch up their first win of the season. On the lush playing surface City, despite a fairly lifeless performance, monopolised much of the play. Connor's miskicked clearance allows Harry Poole to slot in Vale's winner.

8. Even with full-back Harry Smith on the wing for the injured Derrick, City fully deserve the point earned by Williams's late angled reply to John McClelland's headed opener. In front of the day's lowest attendance, City are frustrated by the Lincoln woodwork no less than four times.

9. Bobby Kellard's hammered in shot that enters the net off the underside of the bar - Southend's first goal in four games – proves enough to win this game. City's attack must take the blame for this defeat as they had the chances in this match, but again find that the killer touch is lacking.

10. Park Avenue's player-manager Jimmy Scoular provides the only class in this poor advert for Third Division soccer. His immaculate positional play and authoritative use of the ball enables his side to control the majority of the play, even though the City both start and finish the stronger.

11. An amazing miss by Williams, set up just three yards out he fires against a post, has City on the back-foot a minute later when Ken Jones sends a 20-yarder speeding into the net. Thereafter, most of the action takes place in City's half, but they just manage to hold on to their advantage.

Football results table — matches 12 to 23. Each entry shows, left-to-right: match number, venue (H/A), opponent, date; City's league position / opponent's league position / City's points; result and score; City scorers / opponent scorers; referee; attendance (and gate receipts); both teams' line-ups (City player first, opponent second) and a match report.

12. H GRIMSBY — 29/9 — Pos 13 / Opp 5 / Pts 11 — W 3-0 (1-0)
Scorers: Atyeo 13, 54, 60
Ref: K Dagnall — Att: 11,256 (£1,350.17.0)

	City	Grimsby
1	Cook	Barnett
2	Briggs	Donovan
3	Thresher	Keeble
4	Etheridge	Welbourne
5	Connor	Jobling
6	Casey	Cockerill
7	Rogers	Scott
8	Atyeo	Williams
9	Meyer	Rafferty
10	Williams R	Cullen
11	Derrick	Jones

City's experiment with Friday night soccer proves little, as the attendance is little more than that for a normal midweek game. Grimsby's powerful attacking play at the outset is quelled by Atyeo's rather fortunate opener, his mis-hit shot being misjudged by keeper Alan Barnett.

13. H BRENTFORD — 3/10 — Pos 10 / Opp 24 / Pts 13 — W 3-0 (2-0)
Scorers: Williams 32, 78, Etheridge 44
Ref: K Burns — Att: 10,717 (£1,291.6.6)

	City	Brentford
1	Cook	Cakebread
2	Briggs	Wilson
3	Thresher	Gitcham
4	Etheridge	Belcher
5	Connor	Dargie
6	Casey	Coote
7	Rogers	Rainford
8	Atyeo	Brooks
9	Tait	Higginson
10	Williams R	O'Donnell
11	Derrick	McLeod

There is a look of inevitable failure about Brentford, playing like a side marking time until the formalities of relegation are complete. Bobby Williams shows some honest-to-goodness cheek to add to his undoubted skill in waltzing around an opponent before flicking in City's opener.

14. H HULL — 7/10 — Pos 11 / Opp 8 / Pts 14 — D 1-1 (0-1)
Scorers: Atyeo 46 / Connor 20 (og)
Ref: F Cowan — Att: 10,088 (£1,260.13.0)

	City	Hull
1	Cook	Fisher
2	Briggs	Davidson
3	Thresher	Garvey
4	Etheridge	Collinson
5	Connor	Feasey
6	Casey	McMillan
7	Rogers	Clarke
8	Atyeo	Henderson
9	Tait	Chilton
10	Williams R	Bulless
11	Peters	Crickmore

Bernard Fisher's superb goalkeeping keeps City at bay. His great second-half save at full-length from a fierce header by Jimmy Rogers will remain unchallenged as a vivid memory of the season. Connor gifts Hull their goal, the ball spinning off his head into the roof of the net.

15. A BRENTFORD — 10/10 — Pos 7 / Opp 23 / Pts 16 — W 2-0 (2-0)
Scorers: Williams 6, Tait 31
Ref: F Stringer — Att: 8,579

	City	Brentford
1	Cook	Cakebread
2	Briggs	Wilson
3	Thresher	Gitshen
4	Etheridge	Higginson
5	Connor	Dargie
6	Casey	Coote
7	Rogers	Summers
8	Atyeo	Rainford
9	Tait	Francis
10	Williams R	Brooks
11	Peters	McLeod

Brentford's second-half fight-back peters out when Johnny Brooks fails with a 76th-minute spot-kick, awarded following Thresher's handball. He blasts his penalty against the bar and, whilst he put the rebound away, this is correctly disallowed as no other player had touched the ball.

16. A WATFORD — 14/10 — Pos 8 / Opp 11 / Pts 17 — D 1-1 (0-1)
Scorers: Tait 68 / Walker 1
Ref: J Taylor — Att: 11,860

	City	Watford
1	Cook	Underwood
2	Briggs	Bell
3	Thresher	Meldrum
4	Etheridge	Ryden
5	Connor	McNeice
6	Casey	Gregory
7	Rogers	Benning
8	Atyeo	Crisp
9	Tait	Fairbrother
10	Williams R	Walker
11	Peters	Bunce

Trailing to Peter Walker's 30-second shot, City find themselves reduced to ten men throughout the second half with Peters missing due to an ankle injury just before the interval. Tait secures a share of the spoils by running from near halfway and rolling the ball past Dave Underwood.

17. A NEWPORT — 16/10 — Pos 9 / Opp 23 / Pts 17 — L 1-3 (0-1)
Scorers: Atyeo 90 / Harris 5, 58, 63
Ref: J Loynton — Att: 7,006

	City	Newport
1	Cook	Clarke
2	Briggs	Bird
3	Thresher	Herritty
4	Etheridge	Evans
5	Connor	Peake
6	Casey	Rowland
7	Rogers	Robertson
8	Atyeo	Thomas
9	Tait	Harris
10	Williams R	Finlay
11	Peters	Smith

A big let-down as, instead of the expected win to take them into fourth place, City are humiliated. Bottom of the table Newport, apart from an inspired spell after the break, do not play particularly well themselves but are good enough to gain their first win since beating City last month.

18. H SWINDON — 21/10 — Pos 7 / Opp 20 / Pts 19 — W 5-3 (3-2)
Scorers: Williams 13, 40, Atyeo 19, Tait 29 / Hunt E 14p, McPher' 24 [Noake 54]
Ref: A Edge — Att: 13,158

	City	Swindon
1	Cook	Burton
2	Briggs	Jones
3	Thresher	Trollope
4	Etheridge	Morgan
5	Connor	Owen
6	Casey	Woodruff
7	Rogers	Summerbee
8	Atyeo	Hunt E
9	Tait	McPherson
10	Williams R	Hunt R
11	Noake	Darcy

Goals galore as City cash in on Swindon's mistakes, especially when Tait forces Sam Burton to take Casey's free-kick over the line. Etheridge nets with a spectacular header, only to have it disallowed due to an infringement. Ernie Hunt surprises City with his goal from a free-kick.

19. A TORQUAY — 28/10 — Pos 5 / Opp 23 / Pts 21 — W 3-1 (1-0)
Scorers: Casey 44p, Rogers 48, Atyeo 61 / Hancock 63
Ref: A Sturgeon — Att: 5,052

	City	Torquay
1	Cook	Gill
2	Briggs	Bettany
3	Thresher	Eckersall
4	Etheridge	Hancock
5	Connor	Northcott G
6	Casey	Spencer
7	Rogers	Baxter
8	Atyeo	Cox
9	Tait	Northcott T
10	Williams R	Laraman
11	Noake	Pym

Rising to fifth place, the City players get £2 on top of their £4 win bonus. Larry Baxter fires Torquay's early penalty wide, but Casey has no such problem netting his first ever City spot-kick. Rogers cracks in from 20 yards, but City are on the rack when Dave Hancock hammers in.

20. A BARNSLEY — 11/11 — Pos 9 / Opp 15 / Pts 21 — L 3-7 (1-4)
Scorers: Connor 40, Wil's 46, Tait 76 [Smillie 89/Nicholls 89] / Oliv' 5, 42, 48, Swin' 7, 79, Con' 25 (og), Turner
Ref: G Hartley — Att: 5,618

	City	Barnsley
1	Cook	Hopper
2	Briggs	Brookes
3	Thresher	Wood
4	Etheridge	Sharp
5	Connor	Houghton
6	Casey	Smillie
7	Rogers	Tindill
8	Atyeo	Swindells
9	Tait	Oliver
10	Williams R	Jagger
11	Noake	

Even with City 1-4 behind at half-time, few would have felt inclined to predict the result of this exciting game at Oakwell. City are unlucky with Etheridge having a 25-yard shot disallowed because Tait is offside, whilst one of Barnsley's goals should have suffered the same fate.

21. H QP RANGERS — 18/11 — Pos 8 / Opp 6 / Pts 23 — W 2-0 (2-0)
Scorers: Williams 18, 23
Ref: R Mann — Att: 10,892 (£1,322.4.0)

	City	QP Rangers
1	Cook	Drinkwater
2	Briggs	Bentley
3	Thresher	Williams
4	Etheridge	Keen
5	Connor	Rutter
6	Casey	Angell
7	Rogers	McClelland
8	Atyeo	Bedford
9	Tait	Evans
10	Williams R	Collins
11	Noake	Barber

Rangers' manager Alec Stock, in stating that this was his side's worst display of the season, queried whether star man Tait ever stops running. Williams opens the scoring with a great 25-yard drive, but his second is but a simple shot after the ball skids off the head of Mike Keen.

22. H BOURNEMOUTH — 2/12 — Pos 6 / Opp 1 / Pts 25 — W 2-1 (0-1)
Scorers: Atyeo 47, 62 / Bumstead 22
Ref: A Sturgeon — Att: 14,285 (£1,892.14.0)

	City	Bournemouth
1	Cook	Best
2	Briggs	Woollard
3	Thresher	Jones
4	Etheridge	McGarry
5	Connor	Brown
6	Casey	Stanley
7	Rogers	Bumstead
8	Atyeo	Gibbs
9	Tait	Dowsett
10	Williams R	Archer
11	Derrick	Coxon

Losing to Ray Bumstead's fierce 25-yarder, and fortunate that offside rules out a Brian Gibb effort, City storm back after the interval against opponents who have lost but once in the League this season. Atyeo twice jabs in from close range as City's fine form brings the fans to life.

23. A CRYSTAL PALACE — 9/12 — Pos 5 / Opp 7 / Pts 27 — W 3-2 (1-2)
Scorers: Atyeo 37, 70, Derrick 77 / Allen 11, Uphill 35
Ref: K Seddon — Att: 17,365

	City	Crystal Palace
1	Cook	Rouse
2	Briggs	Long
3	Thresher	McNichol
4	Etheridge	Summersby
5	Connor	Evans
6	Casey	Petchey
7	Rogers	Allen
8	Atyeo	Byrne
9	Tait	Uphill
10	Williams R	Smillie
11	Derrick	Heckman

City demonstrate great spirit in overcoming a two-goal deficit. Inspired by Connor in defence and the mercurial skills of Derrick in attack, this is a game to cherish for the small band of City fans. Appropriately it is Derrick, with a neatly placed shot, who secures a well-deserved winner.

LEAGUE DIVISION 3

Manager: Fred Ford

SEASON 1961-62

No	V	Opponent	Date	Att (Receipts)	Pos	Pt	Res	F-A	H-T	Scorers, Times, and Referees
24	H	NOTTS CO	16/12	12,805 (£1,600.12.6)	3	29	W	6-0	3-0	Tait 15, 18, Atyeo 42, 60, 74, 82 — Ref: E Jennings
25	A	SHREWSBURY	23/12	4,408	4	30	D	2-2	1-0	Derrick 14, Tait 86 / Skeech 53, Hines 82 — Ref: G Hartley
26	A	READING	26/12	11,399	4	31	D	2-2	1-1	Atyeo 20, Etheridge 84 / Lacey 41, Whitehouse 59 — Ref: R Mann
27	H	PETERBOROUGH	13/1	17,123 (£2,278.7.0)	7	31	L	1-2	1-1	Atyeo 40 / Bly 15, 75 — Ref: W Clements
28	A	PORT VALE	20/1	7,662	5	33	W	2-0	0-0	Rogers 76, Williams 85 — Ref: A Luty
29	A	HALIFAX	27/1	5,777	3	35	W	4-3	2-3	Etheridge 4, Atyeo 27, Connor 70, [Tait 82] / Redfearn 11, 14, Hopper 32 — Ref: G Hartley
30	H	LINCOLN	3/2	12,190 (£1,600.12.0)	3	37	W	2-0	1-0	Williams 43, Jackson 67 (og) — Ref: J Mitchell
31	H	READING	6/2	18,590 (£2,547.15.0)	3	39	W	5-0	3-0	Derrick 4, Tait 11, Atyeo 44, Casey 79 [Williams 82] — Ref: K Tuck
32	H	BRADFORD PA	10/2	16,217 (£2,137.14.0)	2	41	W	6-1	6-1	Rogers 12, Atyeo 16, Williams 23, 34, [Casey 38p, Tait 40] / Spratt 26p — Ref: P Brandwood
33	A	GRIMSBY	17/2	11,793	3	41	L	0-1	0-1	Rafferty 44 — Ref: V James
34	A	HULL	24/2	3,876	3	41	L	2-3	1-1	Garvey 38 (og), Connor 87 / Henderson 37, Price 65, McSeveney 69 — Ref: K Dagnall

Team line-ups

No	1	2	3	4	5	6	7	8	9	10	11
24 City	Cook	Briggs	Thrasher	Etheridge	Connor	Casey	Rogers	Atyeo	Tait	Williams R	Derrick
24 Notts Co (17)	Smith	Butler	Noon	Sheridan	Loxley	Carver	Moore	Harobin	Hateley	Forrest	Withers
25 City	Cook	Briggs	Thrasher	Etheridge	Connor	Casey	Peters	Atyeo	Tait	Williams R	Derrick
25 Shrewsbury (13)	Gibson	Walters	Skeech	Harley	Wallace	Pountney	Kenning	Hines	Starkey	Rowley	McLaughlin
26 City	Cook	Briggs	Thrasher	Etheridge	Connor	Casey	Peters	Atyeo	Tait	Williams R	Derrick
26 Reading (3)	Meeson	Goodall	High	Walker	Spiers	Evans	Wheeler	Whitehouse	Lacey	Norton	Allen
27 City	Cook	Briggs	Thrasher	Etheridge	Connor	Casey	Rogers	Atyeo	Tait	Williams R	Derrick
27 Peterborough (3)	Walls	Whittaker	Walker	Rayner	Hopkins	Ripley	Hails	Smith	Bly	Hudson	Senior
28 City	Cook	Briggs	Thrasher	Etheridge	Connor	Casey	Rogers	Atyeo	Tait	Williams R	Derrick
28 Port Vale (10)	Hancock	Whalley	Sproson	Poole	Nicholson	Miles	Jackson	Longbottom	Hunt	Steele	Grainger
29 City	Cook	Briggs	Thrasher	Etheridge	Connor	Casey	Rogers	Atyeo	Tait	Williams R	Derrick
29 Halifax (19)	Knowles	Stanley	Roscoe	Harrison	South	Large	Priestley	Barnett	Hopper	Smith	Redfearn
30 City	Cook	Briggs	Thrasher	Etheridge	Connor	Casey	Rogers	Atyeo	Tait	Williams R	Derrick
30 Lincoln (21)	Graves	Green	Smith	Franks	Jackson	Middleton	Bannister	Tracey	Punter	Linnecor	Broadbent
31 City	Cook	Briggs	Thrasher	Etheridge	Connor	Casey	Rogers	Atyeo	Tait	Williams R	Derrick
31 Reading (5)	Wilkie	Goodall	High	Walker	Spiers	Evans	Batt	Whitehouse	Lacey	Webb	Allen
32 City	Cook	Briggs	Thrasher	Etheridge	Connor	Casey	Rogers	Atyeo	Tait	Williams R	Derrick
32 Bradford PA (17)	Alexander	Walker	March	Scoular	McCalman	Dick	Atkinson	Spratt	Buchanan	Gibson	Hannigan
33 City	Cook	Briggs	Thrasher	Etheridge	Connor	Casey	Rogers	Atyeo	Tait	Williams R	Derrick
33 Grimsby (4)	Barnett	Donovan	Keeble	Pearce	Jobling	Knights	Scott	Cullen	Portwood	Rafferty	Jones
34 City	Cook	Briggs	Thrasher	Etheridge	Connor	Casey	Rogers	Atyeo	Tait	Clark	Derrick
34 Hull (15)	Fisher	Garvey	Bulless	Collinson	Feasey	McMillan	Clarke	Price	King	Henderson	McSeveney

Match reports

24 — NOTTS CO: George Smith, the Notts goalkeeper, confesses after this confident City display that he could not recall when he last had such a hectic game. Tait takes his early goals well, particularly the headed opener, whilst Atyeo's last couple are well executed in City's fifth successive victory.

25 — SHREWSBURY: Derrick thumped City into an early lead, but Connor and Cook's fatal hesitation in dealing with Gordon Skeech's lobbed 45-yarder, which rolls behind them into the net, gets the Shrews back into the game. Derek Hines nudges the homesters in front, but Tait fires in City's point-saver.

26 — READING: This pulsating match has everything, but City are convinced that they are robbed of victory. When they were losing 1-2 a shot by Atyeo is only half-stopped by the Reading keeper and the referee fails to notice Maurice Evans hooking the ball out from behind the goal-line with his arm.

27 — PETERBOROUGH: City are made to pay for missing a host of chances (only Atyeo registering with a Covered End header) when Terry Bly shoots in the visitors' winner. Goalkeeper Cook is adamant that Bly's effort, which hits the underside of the crossbar and bounces down, does not cross the goal-line.

28 — PORT VALE: Early on in this keenly contested battle in the mud at Vale Park, offside rules out both a Ralph Hunt header and a shot by Atyeo. After surviving intense Port Vale pressure, a hard drive from Rogers puts City in front before a neat shot by Williams doubles their advantage.

29 — HALIFAX: Keeper David Knowles errs in his side's defeat in this exciting, error-strewn, affair. Glaringly to blame for City's first three goals, he should have made more effort with Tait's narrow-angled winner. The City defence is almost as bad as they are at fault for all three Halifax goals.

30 — LINCOLN: City are not dismayed when Atyeo's tenth-minute effort is disallowed due to the ball accidentally hitting Tait's arm. The Lincoln citadel has many amazing escapes, but Williams fires City in front and Robert Jackson deflects the ball into his own net to make City's win secure.

31 — READING: City for promotion is the unanimous verdict of the managers and scouts present at this demolition of one of their main rivals. Derrick's low shot into the far corner gets City's show on the road. Atyeo's header leaves no way back for Reading after Tait had fired in from a few yards.

32 — BRADFORD PA: Despite the goals, all seven of which come in the first half, City's play does not approach the high standard of last Tuesday night's match with Reading. Atyeo, who looked offside when turning in his goal at the Open End, has a poor game and contributes little to the City success.

33 — GRIMSBY: City's defence has rarely played better than in this defeat at Blundell Park. Cook was deceived when Ron Rafferty completely missed his kick before recovering to fire in the only goal. Connor gets the ball in the net, but is offside, whilst Atyeo puts City's best chance over the crossbar.

34 — HULL: Cook incurs wrath after lashing out on being fouled by Dave King on 75 minutes and John McSeveney shortly after. Uproar ensues and at the end of this slip-shod affair, City have to run a gauntlet of blows from the home fans. Clark is unlucky with a 25-yard drive that hits an upright.

Season match-by-match record (matches 35–46).

No	Date	Venue	Opponents	W/D/L	Result	HT	—	Pts	Attendance	Receipts
35	3/3	H	WATFORD	W	2-1	0-0	7	43	11,883	(£1,510.16.0)
36	6/3	H	PORTSMOUTH	L	0-4	0-3	1	43	22,124	(£3,202.0.0.0)
37	10/3	A	SWINDON	W	4-0	1-0	17	45	12,936	
38	17/3	H	TORQUAY	W	4-1	1-0	21	47	11,946	(£1,456.16.0)
39	24/3	A	PORTSMOUTH	L	0-5	0-2	1	47	20,584	
40	31/3	H	BARNSLEY	D	0-0	0-0	20	48	8,506	(£973.2.6)
41	7/4	A	QP RANGERS	L	1-4	0-2	4	48	11,482	
42	14/4	A	HALIFAX	W	4-3	2-1	18	50	6,807	(£727.13.0)
43	21/4	A	BOURNEMOUTH	L	1-2	0-0	2	50	12,922	
44	23/4	A	COVENTRY	D	1-1	0-1	16	51	5,965	
45	24/4	H	COVENTRY	W	3-2	1-0	16	53	6,674	(£696.18.0)
46	28/4	H	CRYSTAL PALACE	D	2-2	1-1	15	54	7,199	(£768.11.6)

Home Average 12,447 · Away 9,823

Line-ups (position columns 1–11; City first, opponents in italics)

Match	Team	1	2	3	4	5	6	7	8	9	10	11
35	City	Cook	Briggs	Thresher	Etheridge	Connor	Casey	Rogers	Atyeo	Tait	Williams R	Derrick
35	Watford	*Underwood*	*Bell*	*Nicholas*	*Catleugh*	*McNeice*	*Gregory*	*Williams T*	*Crisp*	*Brown*	*Harmer*	*Bunce*
36	City	Cook	Briggs	Thresher	Etheridge	Connor	Casey	Rogers	Atyeo	Tait	Williams R	Derrick
36	Portsmouth	*Beattie*	*Rutter*	*Wilson*	*Brown*	*Snowdon*	*Dickinson*	*Barton*	*Gordon*	*Saunders*	*Blackburn*	*Dodson*
37	City	Cook	Ford	Briggs	Etheridge	Connor	Casey	Rogers	Atyeo	Tait	Williams R	Derrick
37	Swindon	*O'Hara*	*Wollen*	*Trollope*	*Smart*	*Owen*	*Woodruff*	*Summerbee*	*Hunt*	*Smith*	*Atkins*	*Weaver*
38	City	Cook	Ford	Briggs	Etheridge	Connor	Casey	Rogers	Atyeo	Tait	Williams R	Derrick
38	Torquay	*Marsh*	*Bettany*	*Allen*	*Spencer*	*Smith*	*Hancock*	*Astall*	*Jenkins*	*Northcott*	*Mills*	*Pym*
39	City	Cook	Briggs	Thresher	Etheridge	Connor	Casey	Rogers	Atyeo	Tait	Williams R	Derrick
39	Portsmouth	*Beattie*	*Rutter*	*Wilson*	*Brown*	*Snowdon*	*Dickinson*	*Barton*	*Gordon*	*Saunders*	*Blackburn*	*Dodson*
40	City	Williams C	Briggs	**Palmer**	Etheridge	Connor	Casey	Rogers	Atyeo	Tait	Williams R	Noake
40	Barnsley	*Hopper*	*Green*		*Wood*	*Sharp*	*Houghton*	*Smillie*	*Bartlett*	*Tindill*	*Oliver*	*Ring*
41	City	Cook	Briggs	Williams W	Etheridge	Connor	Casey	Rogers	Atyeo	Tait	Williams R	Noake
41	QP Rangers	*Drinkwater*	*Ingham*		*Keen*	*Rutter*	*Angell*	*McClelland*	*Bedford*	*Evans*	*Collins*	*Lazarus*
42	City	Cook	Briggs	Williams W	Etheridge	Connor	Casey	Rogers	Atyeo	Tait	Williams R	Noake
42	Halifax	*Downsborough*	*Stanley*	*Fagan*	*Harrison*	*South*	*Burgess*	*Priestley*	*Barnett*	*Large*	*Smith*	*Redfearn*
43	City	Cook	Ford	Briggs	Etheridge	Connor	Casey	Rogers	Atyeo	Tait	Williams R	Noake
43	Bournemouth	*Best*	*Farmer*	*Jones*	*Arnott*	*Nelson*	*Bolton*	*Spelman*	*Weller*	*Dowsett*	*Archer*	*Coxon*
44	City	Cook	Ford	Briggs	McCall	Connor	Casey	Rogers	Atyeo	Tait	Williams R	Noake
44	Coventry	*Lightening*	*Kletzenbauer*	*Austin*	*Kearns*	*Curtis*	*Bruck*	*Dwight*	*Farmer*	*Satchwell*	*McCann*	*Imlach*
45	City	Cook	Ford	Briggs	McCall	Connor	Casey	Rogers	Clark	Tait	Williams R	Noake
45	Coventry	*Lightening*	*Kletzenbauer*	*Austin*	*Bruck*	*Curtis*	*Allen*	*Imlach*	*Holder*	*Turner*	*Farmer*	*Bassett*
46	City	Nicholls	Ford	Briggs	Etheridge	Connor	Casey	Peters	Clark	Bush	Williams R	Noake
46	Crystal Palace	*Rouse*	*McNichol*	*Little*	*Long*	*Wood*	*Patchey*	*Wedge*	*Summersby*	*Cartwright*	*Smillie*	*Heckman*

Scorers and referees

- **35** — Atyeo 60, Casey 85 / *Gregory 89*. Ref: K Collinge
- **36** — *Blackburn 3, Dodson 36, Saunders 40, [Barton 58]*. Ref: P Bye
- **37** — Atyeo 30, 57, 73, Tait 82. Ref: E Jennings
- **38** — Tait 8, Rogers 53, Williams 61, [Derrick 73] / *Northcott 80*. Ref: N Hough
- **39** — *Barton 32, Blackburn 43, Connor 54 (og), [Dodson 58, 70]*. Ref: P Brandwood
- **40** — Ref: F Stringer
- **41** — Noake 57 / *Evans 4, 58, Bedford 22, 83*. Ref: H New
- **42** — Atyeo 12, Noake 34, Tait 83, Connor 90 / *Smith 19, Large 77, Redfearn 89*. Ref: K Aston
- **43** — Connor 58 / *Weller 49*, Etheridge 88 (og). Ref: C Woan
- **44** — Atyeo 62 / *Farmer 41*. Ref: H Richards
- **45** — Williams 40, Clark 53, 66 / *Holder 48, Farmer 52*. Ref: A Jobling
- **46** — Etheridge 23, Peters 70 / *Smillie 31, 52*. Ref: R Windle

Match reports

35. Despite the hard frost-bound pitch, the early play gives false promise of a good game. Derrick starts with three glorious shoots - one shaving the bar, another saved by the keeper, and a third headed off the goal-line. Atyeo barges Dave Underwood over before tapping in City's opener.

36. The chimes ring out as Pompeys pace, skill and all-action style proves too much for City. Keith Blackburn fires in an angled shot off Cook's legs to put the visitors in front, David Dodson then heads in a rebound before Ron Saunders fires home from close range, all before the break.

37. A three-goal haul, which would have been more if a late effort had not been controversially disallowed for offside, allied to his probing and chasing, clearly marks Atyeo as the star man of a superb City performance. A marvellous 15-yard shot-on-the-turn brings Atyeo his hat-trick.

38. Torquay's defensive mistakes help lethargic City to victory in this typical end of season game. Tait displays his usual tenacity in running through to fire City in front, whilst both Williams and Derrick take their chances well. Rogers, the best player, obtains his 100th City goal.

39. Field Marshall Lord Montgomery makes a rare visit to Fratton Park and, as a fighting man, he must have been shocked by City's spiritless second-half display. With Thresher limping on the wing, City offer little after a Ron Saunders shot is diverted by Connor into his own net.

40. The Grand National and the fine sunny weather kept the attendance down at Ashton Gate. Those who stayed away are fortunate, as this was a frustrating game, with City failing to break down opponents who remain firmly entrenched in their own half of the field throughout the contest.

41. Old-fashioned boot and rush tactics are too much for City at Loftus Road. The driving wind favours Rangers before the break and they take full advantage. A six-man move enables Noake to shoot City back into the game, but Bernard Evans heads in to restore the homesters' advantage.

42. A repeat of three months ago, and again it is the Halifax custodian, albeit a different one in Peter Downsborough, who is at fault with three of City's goals. A thrilling finish with Brian Redfearn's angled drive 30 seconds from the finish being countered by Connor's last-kick winner.

43. Etheridge ends City's promotion hopes. With no home player in sight he has the misfortune to deposit Chris Weller's rolled ball into his own net with a fantastic shot. Earlier, Connor had headed City level after Weller had run onto Brian Farmer's pass to put Bournemouth in front.

44. Rarely can a side defend so desperately as Coventry did in the second half and still emerge with a point. Heroic keeping by 6ft 2in South African Arthur Lightening, who prevents five certain goals. City score when McCall heads the ball back for Atyeo to side-foot the ball in.

45. City's lowest League crowd since the war see their favourites play some scintillating football. The scoreline hardly suggests a handsome win, but it would have been if Cook had not blundered badly for Coventry's two goals. Clark's brilliant right-foot shot brings a deserved success.

46. City, with Briggs limping on the wing after going off for quarter-of-an-hour in the first-half, wilt in the sun against polished Palace. Even without Brian Wood, due to a 37th-minute cartilage injury, Palace look much the better side, and only woeful finishing prevents them winning.

CUP-TIES

Manager: Fred Ford

SEASON 1961-62

League Cup

			F-A	H-T	Scorers, Times, and Referees	1	2	3	4	5	6	7	8	9	10	11
1 A YORK 13/9	17	L	0-3	0-0	Weir 46, Stainsby 62, Wragg 78 Ref: M Parkinson 8,379 4:4	Nicholls	Briggs	Thrasher	Etheridge	Connor	Low	Derrick	Atyeo	Tait	Williams R	Peters
						Forgan	Bingley	Heron	Woods	Jackson	Fountain	Weir	Wragg	Stainsby	Wilkinson	Gould

Early injuries to Atyeo and Nicholls are no excuse as City are deservedly beaten by a quick, slick and thrustful York side. 'The best team we have played so far this season,' say the City players, who are not helped by the woeful finishing that spoils some delightful approach play.

FA Cup

			F-A	H-T	Scorers, Times, and Referees	1	2	3	4	5	6	7	8	9	10	11
1 H HEREFORD 4/11	5	D	1-1	0-1	Tait 53 / Biggs 13 Ref: A Mason 14,518 SP:7 (£2,349.15.6)	Cook	Briggs	Thrasher	Etheridge	Connor	Casey	Rogers	Atyeo	Tait	Williams R	Noake
						Isaac	Layton	Powell	Masters	Daniel	Styles	Hardiman	Morris	Biggs	Smith	Dixon

After this game, City can have no illusions about the difficulties facing them in the replay. There were times when the class came from the visitors, for whom Roy Smith's perfect pass sets up Tony Biggs to thump them into an early lead. Tait's close-in shot saved City's bacon.

			F-A	H-T	Scorers, Times, and Referees	1	2	3	4	5	6	7	8	9	10	11
1R A HEREFORD 8/11	5	W	5-2	2-0	Williams 25, Atyeo 36, 66, Tait 78, Daniel 63p, Smith 72 [Etheridge 88] Ref: A Mason 11,222 SP:7 (£1,362.8.0)	Cook	Briggs	Thrasher	Etheridge	Connor	Casey	Rogers	Atyeo	Tait	Williams R	Noake
						Isaac	Layton	Powell	Masters	Daniel	Styles	Hardiman	Morris	Biggs	Smith	Dixon

On a night that the improved floodlighting at Edgar Street is switched on, the Hereford part-timers are cruelly treated by the final result in this seven-goal thriller. Twice they come back to within a goal of City before finally cracking. Tait's narrow-angled goal is the game's highlight.

			F-A	H-T	Scorers, Times, and Referees	1	2	3	4	5	6	7	8	9	10	11
2 H DARTFORD 25/11	8	W	8-2	4-0	Tait 9, 44, 61, Der'k 21, 26, Con'r 72, Fletcher 75, Pacey 88 [Aty' 80, Rog' 86] Ref: H Horner 13,086 S1:3 (£2,100.3.6)	Cook	Briggs	Thrasher	Etheridge	Connor	Casey	Rogers	Atyeo	Tait	Williams R	Derrick
						Bourne	Redmond	Newstead	White	Mabey	Howells	Pacey	Taylor	Ackerman	Fletcher	Adams

Despite catching City offside 21 times in the opening 65 minutes, it does the Darts little good. Of all the goals, only Derrick's, when shooting in his first, looked offside. The visitors are a shambles, but they get some consolation with first Briggs, then Casey being at fault for their goals.

			F-A	H-T	Scorers, Times, and Referees	1	2	3	4	5	6	7	8	9	10	11
3 H WALSALL 6/1	6	D	0-0	0-0	Ref: J Cattlin 22,535 2:12 (£3,647.11.6)	Cook	Briggs	Thrasher	Etheridge	Connor	Casey	Rogers	Atyeo	Tait	Williams R	Derrick
						Boswell	Sharples	Guttridge	Hill	Eden	Dudley	Meek	Hodgkisson	Wilson	Richards	Taylor

In an exciting cup-tie, the plan to give Tait freedom to roam is not a success, even though he was faced by a stop-gap centre-half. City fail to take their many chances and, as the fog descends after the break, they are thrice denied by Walsall's raw 18-year-old goalkeeper Alan Boswell.

			F-A	H-T	Scorers, Times, and Referees	1	2	3	4	5	6	7	8	9	10	11
3R A WALSALL 9/1	6	L	1-4	0-1	Derrick 84 [Taylor 90] / Richards 6, 81, Hodgkisson 75, Ref: J Cattlin 15,420 2:12 (£2,481.3.6)	Cook	Briggs	Thrasher	Etheridge	Connor	Casey	Rogers	Atyeo	Tait	Williams R	Derrick
						Boswell	Sharples	Guttridge	Hill	McPherson	Dudley	Meek	Hodgkisson	Wilson	Richards	Taylor

Derrick scores with a 25-yard curler at Fellows Park, but by then City had crumbled against the Saddlers second-half onslaught. Surprisingly, it is City who provide most of the finesse, but Walsall have the fire-power to build on the fiercely struck opener from the foot of Tony Richards.

Welsh Cup

			F-A	H-T	Scorers, Times, and Referees	1	2	3	4	5	6	7	8	9	10	11
5 H MERTHYR TYDFIL 23/1	6	W	4-2	4-2	Atyeo 10, Briggs 15, Williams 30, Godsall 42, Ford 44 (og) [Stacey 35] Ref: G Powell 3,134 SP:17	Cook	Ford	Briggs	Etheridge	Connor	Casey	Stacey	Atyeo	Bush	Williams R	Derrick
						Crump	Davies	Steel	Jones	O'Carroll	Bowkett	Godsall	Hancox	O'Halloran	Derrick	Watkins

Stacey marks his debut with ferocious angled cross-shot into the far corner and City, with their early swift, telling, football, are cruising 4-0 up. Complacency then set in and Godsall hit in a scorcher from 12 yards, and Ford sliced in a low centre from the same player into his own net.

			F-A	H-T	Scorers, Times, and Referees	1	2	3	4	5	6	7	8	9	10	11
6 H CARDIFF 20/2	3	L	0-2	0-1	Ward 44, 46 Ref: R Smith 13,579 1:19	Cook	Ford	Thrasher	Etheridge	Connor	Casey	Rogers	Atyeo	Tait	Williams R	Derrick
						John	Stittall	Milne	Hole	Rankmore	Baker	King P	Tapscott	King J	Ward	McIntosh

Ex-Rover Dai Ward could have notched a hat-trick but his second-half shot hits the bar. His first is fortunate, deflecting in John King's shot with his leg, but his second is a fantastic narrow-angled drive. No luck for City, for whom Derrick and Williams are thwarted by the crossbar.

Gloucestershire Cup

			F-A	H-T	Scorers, Times, and Referees	1	2	3	4	5	6	7	8	9	10	11
F H BRISTOL ROV 1/5	6	W	3-1	0-1	Clark 57, 63, 76 / Williams K 40 Ref: G Walker 9,201 2:21	Cook	Ford	Smith	Etheridge	Connor	Casey	Peters	Clark	Tait	Williams R	Derrick
						Hall	Bradford	Hillard	Sykes	Frowen	Bumpstead	Jarman	Hamilton	Williams K	Jones R	Hooper

At the end of an even first half, Keith Williams's low-level centre finds the far corner when Cook fails to make contact with his fly-kick. After Clark's ten-yard leveller, Rovers lack the spirit to counter City's speed and artistry. A header and an 18-yard volley complete Clark's hat-trick.

	P	W	D	L	F (Home)	A (Home)	W	D	L	F (Away)	A (Away)	Pts
1 Portsmouth	46	15	6	2	48	23	12	5	6	39	24	65
2 Grimsby	46	18	3	2	49	18	10	3	10	31	38	62
3 Bournemouth	46	14	8	1	42	18	7	9	7	27	27	59
4 QP Rangers	46	15	3	5	65	31	9	8	6	31	42	59
5 Peterborough	46	16	0	7	60	38	10	6	7	47	44	58
6 BRISTOL C	46	15	3	5	56	27	8	5	10	38	45	54
7 Reading	46	14	5	4	46	24	8	4	11	31	42	53
8 Northampton	46	12	6	5	52	24	8	5	10	33	33	51
9 Swindon	46	11	8	4	48	26	6	7	10	30	45	49
10 Hull	46	15	2	6	43	20	5	6	12	24	34	48
11 Bradford PA	46	13	5	5	47	27	7	2	14	33	51	47
12 Port Vale	46	12	4	7	41	23	5	7	11	24	35	45
13 Notts Co	46	14	5	4	44	23	3	4	16	23	51	43
14 Coventry	46	11	6	6	38	26	5	5	13	26	45	43
15 Crys Palace	46	8	8	7	50	41	6	6	11	33	39	42
16 Southend	46	10	7	6	31	26	3	9	11	26	43	42
17 Watford	46	10	9	4	37	26	4	4	15	26	48	41
18 Halifax	46	9	5	9	34	35	6	5	12	28	49	40
19 Shrewsbury	46	8	7	8	46	37	5	5	13	27	47	38
20 Barnsley	46	9	6	8	45	41	4	6	13	26	54	38
21 Torquay	46	9	4	10	48	44	6	2	15	28	56	36
22 Lincoln	46	4	10	9	31	43	5	7	11	26	44	35
23 Brentford	46	11	3	9	34	29	2	5	16	19	64	34
24 Newport Co	46	6	5	12	29	38	1	3	19	17	64	22
	1104	279	128	145	1064	708	145	128	279	708	1064	1104

Odds & ends

Double wins: (5) Northampton, Brentford, Swindon, Torquay, Halifax.
Double losses: (2) Newport, Portsmouth.

Won from behind: (4) Southend (h), Bournemouth (h), Crystal Palace (a). Bristol Rov (h) (GC).
Lost from in front: (0).

High spots: The thrilling win at Peterborough on 2 September.
The scintillating performance at Selhurst Park on 9 December.
Bagging six goals against Notts Co on 16 December.
Beating Bradford 6-1 on 10 February.
Winning 4-0 at Swindon on 10 March.
The electric FA Cup atmosphere at Hereford on 8 November.
The 8-2 FA Cup success against Dartford on 25 November.

Low spots: The last-minute penalty at Notts Co on 19 August.
Succumbing 3-7 at Barnsley on 11 November.

AGM (Brecknell, Dolman & Rogers, 4 December 1962):
Profit £4,512.0s.0d. Season Ticket Sales £9,067.0s.0d.

Player of the year: Jack Connor/Bobby Williams.
Ever-presents: (3) Alec Briggs, Jack Connor, Bobby Etheridge.
Hat-tricks: (5) John Atyeo (3), Alex Tait (1), Brian Clark (1).
Leading scorer: Overall: John Atyeo (31). League: John Atyeo (27).

Appearances and Goals

	Appearances Lge	Appearances Cup	Goals Lge	Goals Cup	Goals Tot
Atyeo, John	42	8	27	4	31
Briggs, Alec	46	7	1		1
Bush, Terry	1	1			
Casey, Tommy	40	8	4		4
Clark, Brian	8	1	2	3	5
Connor, Jack	46	9	5	1	6
Cook, Tony	40	8			
Derrick, Jantzen	26	7	4	3	7
Etheridge, Bobby	46	9	5	1	6
Ford, Tony	8	3			
Low, Gordon	10	1	1		1
McCall, Peter	2				
Meyer, Barrie	5		1		1
Nicholls, Ron	6	1			
Noake, David	11	2	3		3
Palmer, Geoff	1				
Peters, Roger	13	2	1		1
Rogers, Jimmy	38	6	4	1	5
Smith, Harry	1	1			
Stacey, Steve				1	1
Tait, Alex	34	8	13	5	18
Thresher, Mike	37	7			
Williams, Bobby	45	9	21	2	23
(own-goals)			3		4
23 players used	506	99	94	22	116

LEAGUE DIVISION 3 — SEASON 1962-63

Manager: Fred Ford

---

1. H MILLWALL — 18/8
D 2-2 (H-T 1-2) · Pt 1 · Att 14,049 (£2,078.2.3)
Scorers: Atyeo 11, 64 / *Gilchrist 5, Terry 29* · Ref: K Dagnall

	1	2	3	4	5	6	7	8	9	10	11
City	Cook	Briggs	Thresher	Connor	Pyle	Low	Savino	Atyeo	Tait	Lythgoe	Derrick
Millwall	Davies	Gilchrist	Brady P	Obeney	Brady R	Wilson	Broadfoot	Townsend	Terry	Towers	McQuade

After Cook makes a hash of John Gilchrist's 35-yard drive to gift the visitors their early goal, City could have done with the adventurous attacking style of the missing Casey. The move of the game involves six players and ends with Atyeo firing City level with his usual aplomb.

---

2. A COLCHESTER — 20/8
L 0-1 (H-T 0-1) · Pt 1 · Att 6,824
Scorers: *Hunt RR 44* · Ref: D Howell

	1	2	3	4	5	6	7	8	9	10	11
City	Cook	Briggs	Thresher	Connor	Pyle	Etheridge	Savino	Lythgoe	Tait	Williams	Derrick
Colchester	Ames	Griffiths	Fowler	Harris	Forbes	Hunt RM	Grice	Hill	King	Hunt RR	Wright

With Atyeo absent due to illness, City find newly promoted Colchester in resilient mood. On receiving Mike Grice's pass, Bobby Hunt stabs the ball past Cook to secure all the points for the U's, who do well to withstand almost constant second-half pressure as City turn on the style.

---

3. A SHREWSBURY — 25/8
D 3-3 (H-T 1-1) · Pt 2 · Pos 17/13 · Att 6,097
Scorers: Atyeo 33, 52, Lythgoe 69 / *Rowley 28, 60, Middleton 61* · Ref: J Parkinson

	1	2	3	4	5	6	7	8	9	10	11
City	Cook	Briggs	Thresher	Connor	Pyle	Etheridge	Savino	Clark	Atyeo	Lythgoe	Derrick
Shrewsbury	Gibson	Walters	Skeech	Harley	Morrall	Pountney	Middleton	Nixon	Starkey	Rowley	McLaughlin

A swirling wind and a bobbing ball dominate the first half, the highlight of which is Arthur Rowley's well-placed 22-yarder which opens the scoring. City take control after the break and, but for Gibson brilliantly saving Lythgoe's shot, should have won in the dying seconds.

---

4. H COLCHESTER — 28/8
L 1-2 (H-T 1-1) · Pt 2 · Pos 19/3 · Att 12,508 (£1,876.5.0)
Scorers: Etheridge 18p / *King 16, 86* · Ref: J Taylor

	1	2	3	4	5	6	7	8	9	10	11
City	Cook	Briggs	Thresher	Connor	Pyle	Etheridge	Savino	Atyeo	Tait	Lythgoe	Derrick
Colchester	Ames	Griffiths	Fowler	Harris	Forbes	Hunt RM	Grice	Hunt RR	King	Hill	Wright

City are stumped by Martyn King (ex-Oxford Blue and Pegasus), who adds to his first-half hammer shot by dribbling past Pyle and Connor to slip in the late winner. Etheridge's twice (both successful) taken penalty, following Ron Hunt's handling offence, is City's sole response.

---

5. H PORT VALE — 1/9
W 2-0 (H-T 1-0) · Pt 4 · Pos 13/8 · Att 9,626 (£1,338.11.6)
Scorers: Atyeo 7, Clark 61 · Ref: T Dawes

	1	2	3	4	5	6	7	8	9	10	11
City	Cook	Briggs	Thresher	Parr	Connor	Etheridge	Tait	Clark	Atyeo	Lythgoe	Derrick
Port Vale	Hancock	Lowe	Sproson	Ford	Nicholson	Miles	Rowland	Steele	Llewellyn	Longbottom	Grainger

City are well worth their first win of the season, though Vale (playing in an all yellow strip) are unlucky in being thrice denied by the frame of the goal. On a warm, sunny day, Atyeo fires in City's opener at the Covered End and after the interval Clark registers with a 15-yard drive.

---

6. A BOURNEMOUTH — 5/9
D 1-1 (H-T 1-0) · Pt 5 · Pos 13/14 · Att 11,502
Scorers: Atyeo 23 / *Gibbs 65* · Ref: K Aston

	1	2	3	4	5	6	7	8	9	10	11
City	Cook	Briggs	Thresher	Parr	Connor	Etheridge	Tait	Clark	Atyeo	Lythgoe	Derrick
Bournemouth	Best	Farmer	Jones	McGarry	Nelson	Bolton	Spelman	Bumstead	Thompson	Gibbs	Coxon

Derrick runs rings round the Cherries by giving his best display to date. Etheridge is unlucky with the referee ruling a penalty when the ball hit his elbow, but Cook saves Ron Spelman's 50th-minute spot-kick. Quite how Bournemouth survive City's final ten minutes blitz is a mystery.

---

7. A READING — 8/9
W 3-0 (H-T 0-0) · Pt 7 · Pos 10/19 · Att 6,848
Scorers: Atyeo 50, 53, Clark 82 · Ref: M Fussey

	1	2	3	4	5	6	7	8	9	10	11
City	Nicholls	Briggs	Thresher	Parr	Connor	Etheridge	Tait	Clark	Atyeo	Williams	Derrick
Reading	Dixon	Walker	High	Travers	Spiers	Evans	Palethorpe	Lacey	Martin	Wheeler	Allen

For Reading it is only a mixture of poor finishing, bad luck (twice hitting the woodwork) and City's dogged defence (Thresher clearing off the line) that prevents them from taking the lead. Atyeo's quick goals transform the contest and Clark's delightful header is the icing on the cake.

---

8. H BOURNEMOUTH — 11/9
W 1-0 (H-T 1-0) · Pt 9 · Pos 8/14 · Att 13,283 (£2,015.8.6)
Scorers: Atyeo 17 · Ref: W Clements

	1	2	3	4	5	6	7	8	9	10	11
City	Nicholls	Briggs	Thresher	Parr	Connor	Etheridge	Tait	Clark	Atyeo	Williams	Derrick
Bournemouth	Best	Farmer	Jones	McGarry	Nelson	Standley	Bumstead	Archer	Thompson	Gibbs	Crickmore

The Cherries live up to their reputation of being a hard side to beat, but luck is with City who have to withstand a terrific pounding in the final stages. In this game, which only shines in fits and starts, Atyeo slips past David Best to gently place the only goal into an empty net.

---

9. A BRISTOL ROV — 15/9
W 2-1 (H-T 0-0) · Pt 11 · Pos 3/18 · Att 20,664
Scorers: Etheridge 56p, Clark 74 / *Williams K 78* · Ref: N Hough

	1	2	3	4	5	6	7	8	9	10	11
City	Nicholls	Briggs	Thresher	Parr	Connor	Etheridge	Tait	Clark	Atyeo	Williams	Derrick
Bristol Rov	Million	Bradford	Jones G	Stone	Sykes	Mabbutt	Jarman	Williams K	Oldfield	Hamilton	Jones R

Etheridge's spot-kick, after Williams is upended by the onrushing Esmond Million, sets City on the way to taking the Rovers' unbeaten home record. Clark's header from Tait's high centre secures the points, despite Keith Williams registering with an angled drive not long afterwards.

---

10. A NOTTS CO — 20/9
L 2-3 (H-T 2-2) · Pt 11 · Pos 8/6 · Att 5,993
Scorers: Tait 7, Atyeo 14 / *Jones 8, Fry 40, Loxley 88* · Ref: W Haynes

	1	2	3	4	5	6	7	8	9	10	11
City	Nicholls	Briggs	Thresher	Parr	Connor	Etheridge	Tait	Clark	Atyeo	Williams	Derrick
Notts Co	Smith	Hampton	Bircumshaw	Sheridan	Gibson	Loxley	Fry	Brown	Jones	Astle	Tait

Bert Loxley's brilliant header rewards County's fight-back. Tait, put clear by Atyeo's neat header, gives City an early lead, but Barrie Jones quickly sweeps in a leveller. Atyeo's hooked shot restores City's advantage, but Connor's poor back-pass allows Keith Fry to restore parity.

---

11. H WATFORD — 22/9
D 3-3 (H-T 1-0) · Pt 12 · Pos 7/1 · Att 13,426 (£1,981.18.6)
Scorers: Atyeo 44, Williams 69, McNeice 88 (og) / *Larkin 54, Ward 71, Howfield 74* · Ref: K Burns

	1	2	3	4	5	6	7	8	9	10	11
City	Nicholls	Briggs	Thresher	Parr	Connor	Etheridge	Tait	Clark	Atyeo	Williams	Derrick
Watford	Linton	Bell	Nicholas	Larkin	McNeice	Gregory	Howfield	Fraser	Fairbrother	Ward	Harris

Vince McNeice, who had stood between the super-playing City attack and a bag full of goals, makes his one mistake barely two minutes prior to the final whistle. His mistimed left-footed clearance sees the ball spin high into the air before nestling firmly in the centre of his own net.

Match 12 — A BRADFORD PA, 29/9

12	A BRADFORD PA	4	W	5-2	3-1	8.917	18 14

(£2,000.7.0)

Clark 15, 26, Derrick 29, 74, Tait 63
Buchanan 9, Maxwell 68
Ref: A Sparling

Nicholls	Briggs	Thresher	Parr	Connor	Etheridge	Tait	Clark	Atyeo	Williams	Derrick
Gebbie	Walker	March	Scoular	McCalman	Dick	Hannigan	Buchanan	Green	Maxwell	Bird

Despite being shocked by John Buchanan's 20-yarder that goes in off a post, City recover to take Avenue's unbeaten home record. Cultured play soon has them level when an unmarked Clark hits the ball past Bert Gebbie. A rare Derrick header rounds off a brilliant performance.

Match 13 — H COVENTRY, 2/10

13	H COVENTRY	5	D	1-1	1-0	13.422	11 15

Derrick 11
Whitehouse 57
Ref: R Smith

Nicholls	Briggs	Thresher	Parr	Connor	Etheridge	Tait	Clark	Atyeo	Williams	Derrick
Meeson	Sillett	Kletzenbauer	Hill	Curtis	Bruck	Humphries	Barr	Bly	Whitehouse	Rees

City start at a breathless pace, but after Derrick hammers them into the lead they squander their chances. Hard-battling Coventry obtain their equaliser courtesy of a terrible mix-up in front of goal. Connor and Low fail to clear and Jim Whitehouse takes the chance to fire the ball in.

Match 14 — A CARLISLE, 5/10

14	A CARLISLE	3	W	5-2	3-2	8.229	23 17

Peters 1, Clark 27, Williams 29, 64, Tait 63
Davies 10, Dagger 38 [Derrick 89]
Ref: K Howley

Cook	Briggs	Thresher	Etheridge	Connor	Casey	Peters	Clark	Atyeo	Williams	Derrick
Dean	Neil	McBain	Oliphant	McConnell	Thompson	Dagger	Davies	Stark	Walker	Taylor

City boss Fred Ford's first return to Carlisle (trainer nine years ago) brings a reprimand from the referee for coaching from the line. An odd feature of this game is the fact that corner-kicks lead to four of the first five goals. City's brilliant display has the crowd gasping in admiration.

Match 15 — H SWINDON, 13/10

15	H SWINDON	6	D	2-2	0-2	21,864	5 18

(£3,563.9.0)

Williams 54, Atyeo 87
Jackson 7, Hunt 39p
Ref: J Cattin

Cook	Briggs	Thresher	Etheridge	Connor	Casey	Peters	Clark	Atyeo	Williams	Derrick
Turner	Wollen	Trollope	Morgan	Owen	Woodruff	Summerbee	Hunt	Smith	Jackson	Darcy

City fail to heed Fred Ford's warnings regarding Swindon's long throw-ins and pay the price. Keith Morgan's throw leads to Cliff Jackson scrambling in the six-yard opener, whilst another sees Thresher tripping Ernie Hunt to concede the penalty. Atyeo stabs in City's late leveller.

Match 16 — A PETERBOROUGH, 20/10

16	A PETERBOROUGH	7	L	1-3	1-1	12.760	2 18

Etheridge 17p
Hudson 15, 67, Horobin 48
Ref: R Aldous

Cook	Briggs	Thresher	Etheridge	Connor	Casey	Peters	Clark	Atyeo	Williams	Derrick
Ronson	Singleton	Walker	Jackson	Hopkins	Simpson	Sheavills	Rayner	Hudson	Horobin	McNamee

Following manager Jimmy Hagan's controversial dismissal last week, the Posh, who are helped by City's poor shooting, give their best display of the season. The turning point in this thrilling contest is early in the second half, when the unfortunate Williams twice muffs open goals.

Match 17 — A COVENTRY, 23/10

17	A COVENTRY	8	L	2-4	2-3	11.390	11 18

Atyeo 13, 38
Farmer 1p, Barr 8, Bly 12 [Whitehouse 56]
Ref: S Stokes

Cook	Briggs	Thresher	Etheridge	Connor	Casey	Peters	Clark	Atyeo	Williams	Derrick
Meeson	Sillett	Kletzenbauer	Hill	Curtis	Farmer	Humphries	Barr	Bly	Whitehouse	Dwight

The Sky Blues are off to a flier starting with a 45-second spot-kick when Casey, with his hands at his side, is penalised. Not long after, from the game's first corner Hugh Barr heads in and from yet another Bill Humphries flag-kick, Terry Bly repeats the feat with just 12 minutes gone.

Match 18 — H BARNSLEY, 27/10

18	H BARNSLEY	6	W	5-2	3-2	10.034	19 20

(£1,421.17.6)

Atyeo 3, Clark 6, 87, Etheridge 20p,
Leighton 4, Kerr 41 [Williams 65]
Ref: V Batty

Cook	Briggs	Thresher	Etheridge	Connor	Casey	Peters	Clark	Atyeo	Williams	Derrick
Hill	Hopper	Brookes	Nicol	Winstanley	Wood	Hosie	Kerr	Leighton	Oliver	O'Hara

Clark impresses the watching scouts with his skill and scoring prowess. Notching the first of his two goals with a header at the Covered End, he also makes the opening for another. City control the majority of the play, mainly thanks to the midfied prompting of Casey and Etheridge.

Match 19 — H QP RANGERS, 10/11

19	H QP RANGERS	13	L	2-4	1-1	13.262	5 20

(£1,980.3.6)

Bush 3, Williams 46 [McClelland 89]
Bedford 15, 73, Barber 80,
Ref: J Loynton

Cook	Briggs	Thresher	Etheridge	Connor	Casey	Peters	Clark	Bush	Williams	Derrick
Drinkwater	Bentley	Ingham	Malcolm	Dugdale	Angell	McClelland	Bedford	Large	Collins	Barber

After the match disturbances with the City fans unhappy about losing Cook, his deputy Etheridge performing brilliantly, with a broken arm in the 50th minute, being further incensed by the visitors' highly controversial third goal, as the ball appeared to have gone out for a goal-kick.

Match 20 — A HULL, 17/11

20	A HULL	14	L	0-4	0-2	7.367	15 20

Chilton 22, 86, 88, McSeveney 36
Ref: J Bullough

Nicholls	Davidson	Thresher	Etheridge	Connor	Casey	Peters	Savino	Bush	Williams	Derrick
Williams	Sharpe	Collinson	Garvey	McMillan	Clarke	Henderson	Chilton	Cummins	McSeveney	

John McSeveney fires home a 20-yarder to double the Tigers' advantage after an offside looking Ray Henderson had set up Chris Chilton to run in the opener. Despite City's impressive early second-half display, Chilton's cross-shot squeezes in at the far post to bring up his hat-trick.

Match 21 — A WREXHAM, 1/12

21	A WREXHAM	14	L	1-2	1-2	10.923	10 20

Meyer 23
Whitehouse 35, Phythian 39
Ref: J Carr

Nicholls	Ford	Briggs	Etheridge	Connor	Savino	Low	Clark	Meyer	Williams	Peters
Keelan	Jones P	McGowan	Barnes K	Fox	Jones T	Barnes R	Griffiths	Phythian	Whitehouse	Colbridge

City, with six of their side having played the majority of their football this term for the reserves, are not good enough to hang onto Meyer's neat opener. Low's slip presents Ernie Phythian with the winner after a well-worked goal by Brian Whitehouse had brought Wrexham level.

Match 22 — H HALIFAX, 8/12

22	H HALIFAX	15	D	2-2	1-2	6.244	22 21

(£857.3.0)

Clark 14, Meyer 51
Priestley 29, Tait 35
Ref: H New

Nicholls	Ford	Briggs	Etheridge	Connor	Low	Tait	Clark	Meyer	Williams	Peters
Downsborough	Stanley	Roscoe	Tilley	South	Harrison	Priestley	Tait	Richardson	Carlin	Holden

Defensive errors again prove costly. Gerald Priestley beats the offside trap to level Clark's rolled in effort and Barry Tait fires in from eight yards to put the visitors in front. Meyer's towering header restores parity, but he has an 87th minute effort disallowed for tripping Alex South.

Match 23 — A MILLWALL, 15/12

23	A MILLWALL	15	L	2-4	2-2	8.151	16 21

Meyer 17, 40
Broadfoot 23, Jones 34, 55p, Spears 83
Ref: E Jennings

Nicholls	Briggs	Smith DB	Etheridge	Connor	Low	Clark	Tait	Meyer	Williams	Peters
Davies	John	Cripps	Anderson	Brady	Wilson	Spears	Broadfoot	Terry	Jones	Haverty

The good news is that Atyeo, playing for the reserves on his comeback from injury, has scored twice. Certainly City need him as in the five games he has missed just one point has been secured, but who will be left out on his return? Hopefully not Meyer, who is City's best player.

LEAGUE DIVISION 3

Manager: Fred Ford

SEASON 1962-63

No	Date	Match	Att / Receipts	Pos	Pt	Res	F-A	H-T	1	2	3	4	5	6	7	8	9	10	11
24	22/12	H SHREWSBURY	6,656 (£891.14.0)	14/12	23	W	3-1	0-0	Nicholls	Briggs	Smith DB	Etheridge	Connor	Casey	Peters	Clark	Tait	Meyer	Derrick
									Miller	*Wright*	*Walters*	*Hemsley*	*Dolby*	*Pountney*	*McLauchlin*	*Harley*	*Middleton*	*Rowley*	*French*
25	26/12	H BRIGHTON	9,096 (£1,291.9.6)	14/20	23	L	1-2	0-2	Nicholls	Briggs	Smith DB	Etheridge	Connor	Casey	Tait	Clark	Atyeo	Meyer	Peters
									Baker	*Jest*	*Baxter*	*Bertolini*	*Jennings*	*Cassidy*	*Waites*	*Collins*	*Donelly*	*Goodchild*	*Franks*
26	16/2	H BRADFORD PA	7,805 (£1,007.1.0)	14/19	25	W	4-2	3-0	Nicholls	Briggs	Thresher	Parr	Connor	Etheridge	Tait	Clark	Atyeo	Williams	Derrick
									Dine	*Walker*	*Lawton*	*Flynn*	*McCalman*	*Atkinson*	*Hannigan*	*Hector*	*Williams*	*Williamson*	*Bird*
27	23/2	H CARLISLE	8,413 (£1,124.17.6)	14/24	26	D	2-2	0-0	Nicholls	Briggs	Thresher	Parr	Connor	Etheridge	Tait	Clark	Atyeo	Davies	Peters
									Dean	*Caldwell*	*McBain*	*Oliphant*	*Marsden*	*McConnell*	*Taylor*	*Brayton*	*Livingstone*	*Davies*	*Kirkup*
28	2/3	A SWINDON	16,919	15/2	26	L	2-3	1-0	Nicholls	Briggs	Thresher	Parr	Connor	Etheridge	Tait	Clark	Atyeo	Williams	Derrick
									O'Hara	*Dawson*	*Trollope*	*Morgan*	*McPherson*	*Woodruff*	*Summerbee*	*Hunt*	*Smith*	*Jackson*	*Darcy*
29	9/3	H PETERBOROUGH	7,347 (£1,056.5.0)	14/2	27	D	1-1	1-0	Nicholls	Briggs	Thresher	Parr	Connor	Etheridge	Tait	Clark	Atyeo	Williams	Derrick
									Ranson	*Stafford*	*Jackson*	*Sissons*	*Hopkins*	*Simpson*	*Senior*	*Horobin*	*Hudson*	*Moulden*	*McNamee*
30	16/3	A BARNSLEY	6,131	15/18	28	D	1-1	1-0	Nicholls	Briggs	Thresher	Parr	Connor	Etheridge	Tait	Clark	Atyeo	Williams	Peters
									Ogley	*Hopper*	*Murphy*	*Nicol*	*Winstanley*	*Houghton*	*Hosie*	*Oliver*	*Leighton*	*Kerr*	*O'Hara*
31	19/3	A BRIGHTON	5,418	15/17	28	L	0-1	0-1	Nicholls	McGonigal	Briggs	Thresher	Pyle	Etheridge	Tait	Clark	Atyeo	Williams	Peters
									Saunders	*Burtenshaw*	*Bertolini*	*Jennings*	*Cassidy*	*Waites*	*Collins*	*Donnelly*	*Jackson*	*Cooper*	
32	23/3	H NORTHAMPTON	9,642 (£1,346.12.9)	14/3	30	W	3-1	1-1	Nicholls	Briggs	Thresher	Parr	Pyle	Etheridge	Tait	Clark	Atyeo	Williams	Peters
									Brodie	*Foley*	*Everitt*	*Leck*	*Branston*	*Kurila*	*Hails*	*Smith*	*Large*	*Reid*	*Lines*
33	26/3	A WATFORD	5,972	11/13	32	W	4-1	3-0	Nicholls	Briggs	Thresher	Parr	Pyle	Casey	Tait	Clark	Atyeo	Williams	Peters
									Underwood	*Bell*	*Nicholas*	*Catleugh*	*Larkin*	*Gregory*	*Howfield*	*Chung*	*Ward*	*Harris*	
34	30/3	A QP RANGERS	5,716	13/11	32	L	1-3	1-1	Nicholls	Briggs	Thresher	Etheridge	Low	Casey	Tait	Clark	Atyeo	Williams	Peters
									Smith	*Taylor*	*Ingham*	*Malcolm*	*Williams W*	*Keen*	*Barber*	*Bedford*	*Lazarus*	*Leary*	*Collins*

Scorers, Times, and Referees

24 Clark 73, 89, Walters 82 (og) / McLaughlin 55 — Ref: H Horner
City give a pathetic display in the fog, but somehow still manage to beat more skilful opponents. It takes the booking of Etheridge for his protests over the visitors goal to wake City up. Clark runs almost the full length of the field with the ball, before ramming home the final goal.

25 Clark 60 / Goodchild 24, Donelly 41 — Ref: L Callaghan
On a peat-covered pitch, Clark's spectacular diving header is City's only reward. Brighton's shoot-on-sight policy, as well as producing the stabbed in opener and Peter Donnelly's rammed in effort, sees them hit the crossbar, have a shot cleared off the line, and a goal disallowed.

26 Derrick 13, Williams 32, Tait 40, [Eth'ridge 52] / Hector 76, McCalman 78 — Ref: W Clements
Despite trailing to Derrick's ram shot, a Williams header, Tait's dribble, and Etheridge's 25-yarder, Avenue's late revival has City hanging on. Kevin Hector's zig-zag run finishes with a cross-shot into the corner of the net, before Parr's error allows Don McCalman to run the ball in.

27 Clark 70, Peters 87 / Brayton 54, 77 — Ref: J Cattlin
City are thwarted by Alan McBain's three goal-line clearances and Joe Dean's fine display between the sticks. Shocked by Barry Brayton's slipped in opener, Clark nods City level, before Brayton's well-placed shot puts the visitors back in front. Peters' low ten-yarder saves the day.

28 Williams 35, Clark 46 / Hunt 54p, Summerbee 65, Smith 81 — Ref: J Pickles
Fred Ford is incensed by three of the referee's decisions. The first is the award of Ernie Hunt's well-taken spot-kick following Thresher's tussle with Jack Smith, then City are denied a penalty of their own when Tait is brought down, and finally the free-kick leading to Swindon's winner.

29 Tait 36 / Jackson 90 — Ref: W Handley
Cliff Jackson's crisp 25-yarder injury-time leveller deprives City of the win that they deserve. The referee gives cause for complaint, throughout, with dubious free-kick decisions that flow in City's favour, except when failing to award a penalty on the hour.

30 Clark 1 / O'Hara 65 — Ref: W Crossley
Despite Barnsley's offside tactics and a swirling wind, City collect their first away point for five months. With the encouragement of Clark's ten-yarder after 15 seconds, City should have done better, but missed chances prove costly when Ted O'Hara heads in from Jim Hosie's cross.

31 Donnelly 23 — Ref: A Moore
City only have themselves to blame for this defeat as, despite pegging Brighton back into their own half after the break, they are unable to put away their chances. Nicholls, whose poor place-kicking was of concern throughout, sends a kick to Peter Donnelly who fires in the only goal.

32 Tait 25, Williams 54, Clark 82 / Reid 15 — Ref: N Hough
City's livewire attack is inspired by Clark and Tait, although the winger's goal is fortunate as his centre is misjudged by the Northampton keeper as it curls in at the Covered end. Following John Reid's opener, Nicholls pulls off a couple of super saves to keep the Cobblers at bay.

33 Williams 12, Clark 25, 33, 55 / Howfield 67 — Ref: R Aldous
Clark's opportunism secures the points for super City. After Bunny Larkin brings down Peters on 54 minutes, Etheridge side-foots the ball in at a prodigious pace from the edge of the box.

34 Tait 15 / Collins 20, Leary 48, Barber 88 — Ref: G Roper
The small crowd in the 60,000-capacity White City Stadium watch two lethargic sides serve up a match quite out of keeping with the plush surroundings. Tait notches a cracking opener, but a mix-up between Low and Casey allows John Collins to stroke home an equaliser.

Season fixtures 35–46

No	Date	Venue	Opponent	Pos	Res	(n)	Pts	FT	HT	Attendance	Receipts	Scorers (City / Opponents)	Referee
35	6/4	H	HULL	12	W	10	34	3-1	2-1	8,794	(£1,207.13.0)	Clark 12p, 17, 61p / McSeveney 2	K Seddon
36	8/4	A	NORTHAMPTON	12	L	2	34	1-5	1-2	12,366		Foley 6 (og) / Large 3, 59, Smith 33, 88, Mills 68	K Dagnall
37	13/4	A	CRYSTAL PALACE	13	L	14	34	2-3	1-0	14,645		Savino 1, Tait 54 / Burridge 49, Dowsett 81, Holton 89	A Jobling
38	15/4	A	SOUTHEND	15	D	6	35	2-2	0-1	12,717		Derrick 54, 83 / Wall 3, Bradbury 85	T Dawes
39	16/4	H	SOUTHEND	12	W	6	37	6-3	4-1	9,815	(£1,346.10.6)	Williams 1, 29, 49, Meyer 26, 37, 51 / McNeill 9, Wall 61, Jones 65	J Mitchell
40	23/4	H	BRISTOL ROV	12	W	20	39	4-1	3-0	22,739	(£3,564.8.6)	Williams 2, Derrick 41, Clark 42, Williams K 71 [Waterhouse 58]	J Finney
41	27/4	A	HALIFAX	12	W	24	41	5-2	1-2	2,297		Williams 42, 50, 74, 78, Tait 79 / Tait 4, Holden 38	J Parkinson
42	30/4	H	NOTTS CO	12	D	6	42	1-1	1-0	12,197	(£1,755.16.0)	Derrick 32 / Whitehouse 73 (og)	N Matthews
43	3/5	H	WREXHAM	13	L	11	42	0-2	0-1	9,795	(£1,313.0.0)	— / Metcalf 33, Barnes 88	K Burns
44	7/5	H	CRYSTAL PALACE	12	D	13	43	1-1	1-1	8,732	(£1,185.5.0)	Williams 15 / Burridge 25	P Brandwood
45	11/5	A	PORT VALE	14	L	4	43	1-3	0-2	5,337		Etheridge 59 / Richards 2, 39, Rowland 80	J Bullough
46	18/5	H	READING	14	W	20	45	4-2	1-1	7,043	(£896.3.0)	Atyeo 32, Derrick 53, Tait 68, 71 / Wheeler 21, 51p	A Atherton

Home Average 11,121 Away 9,269

Line-ups (City / Opponents)

No	1	2	3	4	5	6	7	8	9	10	11
35 City	Nicholls	Briggs	Thresher	Etheridge	Low	Casey	Tait	Clark	Atyeo	Williams	Peters
35 Hull	Williams	Davidson	Bulless	Collinson	Garvey	McMillan	Clarke	King	Chilton	Cummins	McSeveney
36 City	Nicholls	Briggs	Thresher	Etheridge	Low	Casey	Tait	Clark	Atyeo	Williams	Peters
36 Northampton	Brodie	Foley	Everitt	Kurila	Branston	Mills	Hails	Smith	Large	Reid	Lines
37 City	Nicholls	Briggs	Thresher	Etheridge	Low	Waterhouse	Savino	Clark	Tait	Williams	Derrick
37 C. Palace	Glazier	Howe	Townsend	Petchey	Wood	Long	Werge	Holton	Dowsett	Burridge	Allen
38 City	Nicholls	Briggs	Thresher	Etheridge	Low	Waterhouse	Savino	Clark	Tait	Williams	Derrick
38 Southend	Goy	Costello	Neal	Bentley	Watson	Bradbury	Wall	Jones	Fryatt	Kellard	McKinven
39 City	Nicholls	Briggs	Thresher	Etheridge	Low	Waterhouse	Meyer	Clark	Tait	Williams	Derrick
39 Southend	Goy	Costello	Neal	Bentley	Watson	Bradbury	Wall	Jones	Fryatt	McNeill	McKinven
40 City	Nicholls	Briggs	Thresher	Etheridge	Low	Savino	Williams K	Clark	Tait	Williams	Derrick
40 Bristol Rov	Million	Hilliard	Jones G	Mabbutt	Davis	Oldfield	Jarman	Biggs		Jones R	Muxworthy
41 City	Nicholls	Briggs	Thresher	Etheridge	Low	Waterhouse	Savino	Clark	Tait	Williams	Derrick
41 Halifax	Downsborough Russell	Tilley	Roscoe	South	Harrison	Strodder	Tait	Holden	Carlin		Fiddler
42 City	Cook	Briggs	Thresher	Etheridge	Low	Waterhouse	Savino	Clark	Tait	Williams	Derrick
42 Notts Co	Smith	Edwards	Bircumshaw	Sheridan	Gibson	Loxley	Moore	Astle	Hateley	Tait	Flower
43 City	Cook	Briggs	Thresher	Etheridge	Low	Savino	Barnes K	Clark	Whitehouse	Williams	Williams
43 Wrexham	Keelan	Jones P	Holland	Barnes K	Fox	Jones T	Barnes R	Griffiths		Metcalf	Colbridge
44 City	Gibson	Briggs	Thresher	Etheridge	Low	Waterhouse	Savino	Clark	Savino	Williams	Derrick
44 C. Palace	Glazier	Howe	Wood	Townsend	Long	Holton	Werge	Lewis	Dowsett	Burridge	Allen
45 City	Gibson	Briggs	Thresher	Etheridge	Low	Savino	Savino	Clark	Savino	Williams	Derrick
45 Port Vale	Hancock K	Whalley	Sproson	Poole	Nicholson	Miles	Rowland	Steele	Richards	Hancock B	Edwards
46 City	Cook	Briggs	Thresher	Etheridge	Low	Waterhouse	Tait	Clark	Atyeo	Williams	Derrick
46 Reading	Wilkie	Walker	Meldrum	Evans	Spiers	Travers	Wheeler	Petts	Allen	Shreeve	Webb

Match reports

35 — Hull: Despite the shock of John McSeveney's jabbed in 90-second opener – a record 27th goal of a season for a Hull winger – City recover. A lucky penalty award, put away by Clark, gets them going, though they are fortunate when Les Collinson's scoring free-kick is ordered to be retaken.

36 — Northampton: Despite going behind to Frank Large's narrow-angled drive, City look the better side in the early stages after Theo Foley turns Clark's sliced shot into his own net. Ray Smith's low header puts the Cobblers in charge and Roly Mills caps his fine game by firing in from 15 yards.

37 — Crystal Palace: A heartening City display at Selhurst where keeper Nicholls is the star. He does the lot in this thriller, even saving Ronnie Allen's penalty, but boobs at the close to let in Cliff Holton's half-hit shot. City dispute Gilbert Dowsett's header, which is ruled over the line before Briggs clears.

38 — Southend: Derrick is one of those rare soccer individuals – a left-winger with a stronger shot in his right boot than his left. In this game it is two right-footed shots that bring City a deserved point. On top after the break, City are denied a win by Terry Bradbury rolling the ball into a vacant net.

39 — Southend: Williams gets City off to a grand start in this entertaining encounter with a perfectly placed shot into the Covered End net. Ian McNeill's 18-yard dropping-shot brings the Shrimpers level, but Meyer blasts in on his way to a hat-trick, which he completes with two great headers.

40 — Bristol Rov: Williams shoots City into an early lead at the Covered End and Derrick hammers in another before Clark rolls in the third. The crossbar denies Alfie Biggs on the interval, but Keith Williams does manage to fire through for the Rovers after Waterhouse's 20-yard registers for City.

41 — Halifax: It has been a season of near misses for Bobby Williams, but not this match in which he registers on four occasions. Two of his goals are great, but the best is his first, which gets City back into the game. Etheridge's header-on is dispatched into the back of the net with a first-time volley.

42 — Notts Co: After going behind, a well-disciplined County defence ensures that City's scoring spree comes to an end in this drab game. Derrick heads in Tait's perfect centre, but Waterhouse boots Bob Tait's low speculative pass into the Covered End net to gift the visitors a share of the spoils.

43 — Wrexham: Wrexham's offside tactics brings them the points but not the plaudits. Their second goal illustrates the irony of the game as Ron Barnes is well offside, but despite being flagged, he is allowed to continue and plant the ball in the City net. Mike Metcalf slams in the opener from ten yards.

44 — Crystal Palace: A poor game in which the visitors negative 3-3-4 formation incurs the wrath of the crowd. A move involving Derrick, Tait and Clark ends with Williams running in City's goal, but Palace's equaliser from Peter Burridge's overhead-kick sets the scene for a really frustrating evening.

45 — Port Vale: A game of mixed fortunes for Gibson, whose failure to hold efforts from first John Rowland and then Stan Edwards allows Tony Richards to fire in his two goals. Etheridge dribbles through for City, before Rowland's snap-shot from the edge of the area makes Vale's victory complete.

46 — Reading: After Atyeo's low six-yard drive levels James Wheeler's fired in opener, Low's pull on Dennis Allen's jersey results in Reading's spot-kick. Derrick's low ten-yard drive at the Open End, and Tait's double (a ten-yard hammer shot, and then a header) brings up City's century of goals.

CUP-TIES

Manager: Fred Ford

SEASON 1962-63

League Cup

					F-A	H-T	Scorers, Times, and Referees	1	2	3	4	5	6	7	8	9	10	11
2	H	ROTHERHAM	7	L	1-2	0-0	Etheridge 88p, Taylor 46, 54, Ref: W Handley	Nicholls	Briggs	Thresher	Parr	Connor	Etheridge	Peters	Clark	Atyeo	Williams	Derrick
25/9		(7,469 2:14) (£1,263.9.0)						Ironside	Cassidy	Morgan	Lambert	Madden	Lancaster	Kirkman	Casper	Bennett	Weston	Taylor

City make a nonsense of their lower status against the Millers, but are let down by poor shooting and errors by goalkeeper Nicholls. Deceived by the 25-yard opener, he later punches a centre-cum-shot into his own net. Bill Cassidy's mild clash with Williams brings about the spot-kick.

FA Cup

					F-A	H-T	Scorers, Times, and Referees	1	2	3	4	5	6	7	8	9	10	11
1 H		WELLINGTON	6	W	4-2	1-1	Atyeo 34, 62, Etheridge 65p, Russell 13, Rodgers 87 [Derrick 73], Ref: K Aston	Cook	Briggs	Thresher	Etheridge	Connor	Casey	Peters	Clark	Atyeo	Williams	Derrick
3/11		(9,379 SP:6) (£1,620.7.6)						Brown	Whitehouse	Rodgers	Timmins	Dunn	Davis	Jones M	Cocker	Deakin	Russell	Laverty

Ex-City skipper Jack White returned to Ashton Gate as boss of Wellington, but is unable to inspire a shock victory, despite his side taking a surprise lead with the goal of the game. Gary Brown's mishandling presents Atyeo with both of his goals, and thereafter it is easy for City.

					F-A	H-T	Scorers, Times, and Referees	1	2	3	4	5	6	7	8	9	10	11
2 H		WIMBLEDON	14	W	2-1	2-0	Clark 7, 32, Peters 60 (og), Ref: J Finney	Nicholls	Briggs	Thresher	Etheridge	Connor	Low	Peters	Clark	Bush	Williams	Derrick
24/11		(13,778 IL:1) (£2,454.6.6)						McAlpine	Rudge	Coote	Hamm	Law	Ardrey	Brown	Martin	Reynolds	Moore	Williams N

Against one of the best amateur sides, City's first-half display is crisp and penetrative. It is different after the break, though, as the Dons make a spirited comeback aided and abetted by an amazing own-goal by Peters – his best ever strike – as he attempts to put the ball out for a corner.

					F-A	H-T	Scorers, Times, and Referees	1	2	3	4	5	6	7	8	9	10	11
3 H		ASTON VILLA	14	D	1-1	1-0	Clark 10, Burrows 62p, Ref: K Aston	Nicholls	Briggs	Thresher	Parr	Connor	Etheridge	Tait	Clark	Atyeo	Williams	Derrick
16/1		(22,176 1:6) (£6,173.13.6)						Sidebottom	Fraser	Aitken	Crowe	Sleeuwenhoeck	Deakin	MacEwan	Thomson	Dougan	Woosam	Burrows

Rubber-booted City are full value for the half-time lead, given them when Clark hammers home a low shot from 20 yards. Villa's extra pace and ability shows after the break when they change their footwear. Thresher scoops out James McEwan's corner to concede the penalty.

					F-A	H-T	Scorers, Times, and Referees	1	2	3	4	5	6	7	8	9	10	11
3R A		ASTON VILLA	15	L	2-3	2-1	Williams 5, Etheridge 25, Burrows 4, Baker 67, Thomson 86, Ref: N Hough	Nicholls	Briggs	Thresher	Parr	Connor	Etheridge	Tait	Clark	Atyeo	Williams	Derrick
7/3		(23,718 1:7) (£4,489.11.0)						Sidebottom	Lee	Aitken	Crowe	Sleeuwenhoeck	Deakin	MacEwan	Baker	Thomson	Woosam	Burrows

Magnificent City should have won this cup-tie after fighting back following a Harry Burrows blaster on the edge of the box. Williams levels with a shot from an almost impossible angle and Etheridge's 15-yarder puts them in front. Bob Thomson's late header is a cruel blow for City.

Gloucestershire Cup

					F-A	H-T	Scorers, Times, and Referees	1	2	3	4	5	6	7	8	9	10	11
F A		BRISTOL ROV	14	L	1-2	0-1	Derrick 89, Hamilton 23, Jones R 54, Ref: D Smith	Cook	Briggs	Thresher	Etheridge	Low	Waterhouse	Savino	Clark	Atyeo	Williams	Derrick
23/5		(8,018 19)						Hall	Hillard	Jones G	Oldfield	Davis	Mabbutt	Jarman	Jones R	Biggs	Hamilton	Bradford

Two brilliant Rovers goals take the steam out of City, whose only reply is Derrick's stabbed in effort when both the scorer and provider Atyeo are offside - just one of many curious refereeing decisions. A deserved success for Rovers, who win the Cup for the first time in seven years.

	P	W	D	L	F	A	W	D	L	F	A	Pts
		Home					Away					
1 Northampton	46	16	6	1	64	19	10	4	9	45	41	62
2 Swindon	46	18	2	3	60	22	7	12	4	27	34	58
3 Port Vale	46	16	4	3	47	25	7	4	12	25	33	54
4 Coventry	46	14	6	3	54	28	4	11	8	29	41	53
5 Bournemouth	46	11	12	0	39	16	7	4	12	24	30	52
6 Peterborough	46	11	5	7	48	33	9	6	8	45	42	51
7 Notts Co	46	15	3	5	46	29	4	10	9	27	45	51
8 Southend	46	11	7	5	38	24	8	5	10	37	53	50
9 Wrexham	46	14	6	3	54	27	6	3	14	30	56	49
10 Hull	46	12	6	5	40	22	7	4	12	34	47	48
11 Crys Palace	46	10	7	6	38	22	6	10	7	27	36	47
12 Colchester	46	11	6	6	41	35	5	5	11	32	58	47
13 QP Rangers	46	9	8	6	44	36	8	5	10	41	40	45
14 BRISTOL C	46	10	9	4	54	38	6	4	13	46	54	45
15 Shrewsbury	46	13	4	6	57	41	3	8	12	26	40	44
16 Millwall	46	11	6	6	50	32	4	7	12	32	55	43
17 Watford	46	12	3	8	55	40	5	5	13	27	45	42
18 Barnsley	46	12	6	5	39	25	3	5	15	24	46	41
19 Bristol Rov	46	11	8	4	45	29	4	3	16	25	59	41
20 Reading	46	13	4	6	51	30	3	4	16	23	48	40
21 Bradford PA	46	10	9	4	43	36	4	3	16	36	61	40
22 Brighton	46	7	6	10	28	38	5	6	12	30	46	36
23 Carlisle	46	12	4	7	41	37	1	5	17	20	52	35
24 Halifax	46	8	3	12	41	51	1	9	13	23	55	30
	1104	287	138	127	1117	735	127	138	287	735	1117	1104

Odds & ends

Double wins: (3) Reading, Bristol Rov, Bradford.

Double losses: (4) Colchester, QPR, Wrexham, Brighton.

Won from behind: (7) Bradford (a), Shrewsbury (h), Northampton (h), Hull (h), Halifax (a), Reading (h), Wellington (h) (FAC).

Lost from in front: (7) Notts Co (a), QPR (h), Wrexham (a), Millwall (a), Swindon (a), QPRs (a), Crystal Palace (a).

High spots: Winning 5-2 at Park Avenue on 29 September.
The 6-3 success over Southend United on 16 April.
Beating Bristol Rovers 4-1 at Ashton Gate on 23 April.
Scoring four goals against Reading in the last game of the season to post up a century of League goals.

Low spots: Losing 1-5 at Northampton on 8 April.
The poor showing against Wrexham on 3 May.

AGM (Brecknell, Dolman & Rogers, 23 December 1963):
Loss £25,000.0s.0d. Season Ticket Sales £7,231.0s.0d.

Player of the year: Brian Clark.
Ever-presents: (1) Alec Briggs.
Hat-tricks: (5) Brian Clark (2), Bobby Williams (2), Barrie Meyer (1).
Leading scorer: Overall: Brian Clark (26). League: Brian Clark (23).

Appearances / Goals

	Appearances				Goals				
	Lge	FLC	FAC	GC	Lge	FLC	FAC	GC	Tot
Atyeo, John	30	1	3	1	16		2		18
Briggs, Alec	46	1	4	1					
Bush, Terry	2				1				1
Casey, Tommy	13		1						
Clark, Brian	42	1	4	1	23	3			26
Connor, Jack	29		4						
Cook, Tony	15		1						
Derrick, Jantzen	35	1	4	1	10		1	1	12
Etheridge, Bobby	45	1	4	1	6	1	2		9
Ford, Tony	2								
Gibson, Mike	2								
Low, Gordon	17		1	1					
Lythgoe, Derek	6				1				1
Meyer, Barrie	6				7				7
Nicholls, Ron	29	1	3						
Parr, Gordon	16	1	2						
Peters, Roger	19	1	2		2				2
Pyle, David	8								
Savino, Ray	15			1	1				1
Smith, David	3								
Tait, Alex	37		2		10				10
Thresher, Mike	41	1	4	1					
Waterhouse, Ken	10				1				1
Williams, Bobby	38	1	4	1	19		1		20
(own-goals)					3				3
24 players used	506	11	44	11	100		9	1	110

LEAGUE DIVISION 3

Manager: Fred Ford

SEASON 1963-64

Match details

No		Date	Att (Receipts)	W/D/L	Pos	Pt	F-A	H-T	Scorers, Times, and Referees
1	H BRISTOL ROV	24/8	20,697 (£3,312.17.0)	W	2	2	3-0	1-0	Derrick 2, Atyeo 52, Hooper 87 — Ref: W Handley
2	A BRENTFORD	27/8	16,843	W	4	4	2-1	0-0	Atyeo 52, Lythgoe 64 / Dick 59 — Ref: K Burns
3	A PORT VALE	31/8	10,363	L	9 (5)	4	1-4	0-1	Clark 73 / Richards 6, 85, 89, Rowland 54 — Ref: J Parkinson
4	H NOTTS CO	7/9	9,440 (£1,346.9.0)	W	6 (24)	6	2-0	1-0	Atyeo 4, 75 — Ref: P Brandwood
5	H BRENTFORD	10/9	12,689 (£1,864.7.0)	D	5 (7)	7	3-3	3-2	Clark 22, Atyeo 27, Hooper 36 / Dick 20, 65, Kurila 24 (og) — Ref: W Clements
6	A CREWE	14/9	5,841	L	9 (13)	7	0-2	0-1	King 27, 82 — Ref: D Brady
7	A SHREWSBURY	18/9	7,152	L	13 (4)	7	0-2	0-0	Rowley 49, Boardman 68
8	H CRYSTAL PALACE	21/9	9,782 (£1,386.18.0)	D	15 (5)	8	1-1	0-0	Williams 57 / Burridge 52 — Ref: H Horner
9	A WALSALL	28/9	6,312	D	15 (20)	9	1-1	0-0	Atyeo 53 / Smith 70 — Ref: S Kayley
10	H SHREWSBURY	1/10	9,247 (£1,280.2.0)	D	14 (6)	10	2-2	0-2	Atyeo 62, Derrick 70 / Clarke 8, 10 — Ref: P Bye
11	H READING	5/10	7,585 (£1,060.16.6)	L	16 (17)	10	0-2	0-1	Wheeler 27, Walker 78 — Ref: D Lyden

Line-ups (Bristol City / opponents in italic)

No	1	2	3	4	5	6	7	8	9	10	11
1	Cook	Briggs	Thresher	Etheridge	Connor	Waterhouse	Derrick	Clark	Atyeo	Williams	**Hooper**
1	*Hall*	*Hillard*	*Jones G*	*Bumpstead*	*Davis*	*Sykes*	*Jarman*	*Biggs*	*Jones R*	*Hamilton*	*Jenkins*
2	Cook	Briggs	Thresher	Etheridge	Connor	Waterhouse	Derrick	Clark	Atyeo	Williams	Lythgoe
2	*Rycraft*	*Coote*	*Jones*	*Higginson*	*Scott*	*Crowe*	*Black*	*Brooks*	*McAdams*	*Dick*	*McLeod*
3	Cook	Briggs	Thresher	Etheridge	Connor	Waterhouse	Derrick	Clark	Atyeo	Williams	Lythgoe
3	*Hancock*	*Whalley*	*Sproson*	*Steele*	*Nicholson*	*Rawlings*	*Bingham*	*Poole*	*Richards*	*Cheesbrough*	*Rowland*
4	Gibson	Briggs	Thresher	Etheridge	Connor	**Kurila**	Tait	Clark	Atyeo	Williams	Hooper
4	*Smith*	*Hampton*	*Bircumshaw*	*Edwards*	*Gibson*	*Carver*	*Povey*	*Astle*	*Bly*	*Tait*	*Jones*
5	Gibson	Briggs	Thresher	Etheridge	Connor	Kurila	Tait	Clark	Atyeo	Lythgoe	Hooper
5	*Rycraft*	*Coote*	*Jones*	*Higginson*	*Scott*	*Crowe*	*Black*	*Fielding*	*McAdams*	*Dick*	*McLeod*
6	Gibson	Briggs	Thresher	Etheridge	Connor	Kurila	Tait	Clark	Atyeo	Lythgoe	Hooper
6	*Hickson*	*Whelan*	*Leigh*	*Keery*	*Barnes*	*Riggs*	*Wheatley*	*Shepherd*	*Lord*	*King*	*Smith*
7	Gibson	Briggs	Thresher	Etheridge	Connor	Waterhouse	Derrick	Clark	Atyeo	Williams	Hooper
7	*Boswell*	*Wright*	*Turner*	*Harley*	*Dolby*	*Pountney*	*Gregson*	*Boardman*	*Middleton*	*Rowley*	*Taylor*
8	Gibson	Briggs	Thresher	Etheridge	Connor	Waterhouse	Derrick	Clark	Atyeo	Williams	Derrick
8	*Glazier*	*Long*	*Townsend*	*Petchey*	*Wood*	*Howe*	*Werge*	*Holton*	*Dowsett*	*Burridge*	*Allen*
9	Gibson	Ford	Briggs	Parr	Connor	Kurila	Tait	Clark	Atyeo	Lythgoe	Derrick
9	*White*	*Raper*	*Gregg*	*Palin*	*Howells*	*Wills*	*Smith*	*Matthews*	*O'Neill*	*Newton*	*Fell*
10	Gibson	Ford	Briggs	Parr	Connor	Kurila	Derrick	Clark	Atyeo	Lythgoe	Hooper
10	*McLaughlin*	*Wright*	*Turner*	*Harley*	*Dolby*	*Pountney*	*Gregson*	*Ross*	*Clarke*	*Brodie*	*Middleton*
11	Gibson	Briggs	Parr		Connor	Kurila	Derrick	Clark	Atyeo	Lythgoe	Hooper
11	*Wilkie*	*Walker*	*Meldrum*	*Evans*	*Spiers*	*Travers*	*Jones*	*Wheeler*	*Martin*	*Norton*	*Allen*

Match reports

1. This lethargic curtain-raiser leaves the crowd unimpressed as they watch the colourless football with condemning silence. Even after Derrick's tapped in opener the goals are greeted with just polite applause. Only Bobby Jones rouses the fans when he fires his 62nd-minute penalty wide.

2. At half-time City should have been beaten out of sight by a dominant Brentford side costing £80,000 to put together, but following the break Atyeo's two-yard header puts them in front. Lythgoe side-foots home City's winner after John Dick strode through to net the Bees' leveller.

3. Already trailing to Tony Richards's 15-yarder and John Rowland's half-hit effort that somehow ends up in the net, Clark volleys in from the edge of the area for the City. Richards then blasts in his 200th League goal and completes his hat-trick in the third minute of injury-time.

4. Marksmanship is the big difference between the sides. Notts, with just one goal in five games and despite Jeff Astle and Terry Bly's presence, are woefully short in this department. As well as his scoring headers, Atyeo is denied by a post, and has a couple of shots cleared off the line.

5. The Bees, left dazed when Atyeo heads City level, is off the field receiving treatment when his deputy George McLeod is beaten by Hooper's fierce drive. John Dick notches Brentford's point-saver after the break when he cuts past Gibson and shoots into an empty net.

6. Except for Lythgoe hitting the base of an upright and a weak Atyeo header cleared off the line, City are outplayed in the first half. With the wind in their favour they make a bright start after the break, but the game turns when offside rules out Lythgoe's fine 63rd-minute header.

7. Gibson makes a hero's return to his former club. It is his acrobatics and supreme courage that saves a poor City side, who create and offer little, from complete and utter annihilation. George Boardman rounds off Shrewsbury's success by stabbing in Harry Middleton's touch-on.

8. In spite of an injured Thresher and Glazier's magnificent save of Clark's 63rd-minute penalty, City salvage a point from this poor affair thanks to Williams's neat-footed effort. Peter Burridge, who slammed Palace in front, has his 35th-minute barge of Gibson over the line disallowed.

9. A less than full-strength City take the lead when an interception by Briggs sets up Atyeo to put a splendid shot past Malcolm White. Indecision between Gibson and Connor allows Roger Smith to scramble in an equaliser, the same player firing wide of an open goal in the dying seconds.

10. A Jekyll and Hyde performance as City's worst first-half display for years leaves them trailing to a couple of headers. After the break, though, their form is sensational and they come close to victory. Derrick blasts home a leveller after Atyeo's header had got City back into the game.

11. Struggling before the interval, City reverse the tables in the second half with Reading under constant siege. Unfortunately, being unable to break down a packed defence, the Biscuitmen take the points thanks to James Wheeler's 25-yard free-kick and John Walker's low drive.

Match-by-match records (matches 12–23)

12 — A COVENTRY — 8/10
Pos 17 · 23,884 · 1 / 10
Score 0-2 (HT 0-2) · L · 1-2
Hooper 82 / *Hale 8, Hudson 34*
Ref: H Hackney
City: Gibson, Ford, Briggs, Parr, Connor, Low, Derrick, Clark, Atyeo, Williams, Hooper
Coventry: Wesson, Sillett, Kearns, Hill, Curtis, Farmer, Humphries, Hale, Hudson, Machin, Rees
Coventry are the better team, but City give the leaders a fright after going behind to Ken Hale's lashed in effort and George Hudson's fierce drive. Unfortunately, it is not until late on, when Hooper takes advantage of Weeson's mishandle, that they are able to get the ball in the net.

13 — H PETERBOROUGH — 11/10
Pos 14 · 10,770 · 7 / 12 · (£1,491.15.0)
Score 3-1 (HT 1-1) · W
Williams 10, 87, Derrick 67 / *Moulden 32*
Ref: H New
City: Gibson, Ford, Briggs, Parr, Connor, Low, Derrick, Clark, Atyeo, Williams, Hooper
Peterborough: Duff, Hopkins, Walker, Wright, Rankmore, Pearce, Moulden, Horobin, Dougan, Smith, McNamee
After Williams slams City in front from 15 yards, it is only poor finishing that keeps Posh in this contest. Tony Moulden runs the ball in for the visitors' leveller, but Willie Duff's error in letting Derrick's shot through his legs restores City's advantage, before Williams drives in another.

14 — H COVENTRY — 15/10
Pos 18 · 13,582 · 1 / 12 · (£2,060.16.0)
Score 0-1 (HT 0-1) · L
Hale 4
Ref: J Finney
City: Gibson, Briggs, Thresher, Parr, Connor, Low, Derrick, Clark, Atyeo, Williams, Hooper
Coventry: Wesson, Sillett, Kearns, Hill, Curtis, Farmer, Humphries, Hale, Hudson, Machin, Rees
Ken Hale's 16-yard shot, which is deflected off Connor's foot and spins over Gibson into the net, allows Coventry to stretch their lead at the top of the table. A lucky goal perhaps, but not their performance as the Sky Blues team possess far too much skill, power and pace for City.

15 — H BOURNEMOUTH — 19/10
Pos 17 · 11,272 · 4 / 14
Score 1-0 (HT 0-0) · W
Atyeo 62
Ref: G Davis
City: Gibson, Briggs, Thresher, Parr, Connor, Low, Derrick, Clark, Atyeo, Williams, Tait
Bournemouth: Best, Farmer, MacDonald, Standley, Gater, Bolton, Bumstead, Woods, Coughlin, Singer, Crickmore
City are worthy winners at Dean Court, where they bring to an end Bournemouth's 33-match, 18-month, unbeaten home run. Atyeo's headed goal is a poor return for City's overall superiority. The Cherries' keeper David Best is man of the match, pulling off a dozen remarkable saves.

16 — A LUTON — 23/10
Pos 15 · 5,107 · 21 / 16
Score 4-1 (HT 1-0) · W
Morton 26 (og), Atyeo 60, Derrick 77, [Clark 83] / *Walden 85*
Ref: D Lyden
City: Gibson, Briggs, Thresher, Parr, Connor, Low, Derrick, Clark, Atyeo, Williams, Tait
Luton: Baynham, Morton, Bramwell, Pacey, Fincham, Lownds, Walden, Smith, McKechnie, Salisbury, Weir
A post keeps out David Pacey's 25-yarder early on, but Luton are unsettled by Robert Morton's own-goal. After having a shot disallowed following the break, Atyeo's low effort puts City firmly on top. Derrick and Clark shoot in, before Harry Walden heads Luton's consolation.

17 — H HULL — 26/10
Pos 11 · 10,568 · 16 / 18 · (£1,551.8.0)
Score 1-0 (HT 0-0) · W
Williams 49
Ref: W Haynes
City: Gibson, Briggs, Thresher, Parr, Connor, Low, Derrick, Clark, Atyeo, Williams, Tait
Hull: Swan, Davidson, Butler, Garvey, Feasey, McMillan, Clarke, Wilkinson, Chilton, Henderson, McSeveney
A poor game not worthy of the occasion of the FA's 100th anniversary. The Tigers, with John McSeveney and Eric McMillan limping at the conclusion, have a good share of the play, but are let down by poor finishing. Williams heads the winner, diverting in Tait's goalbound drive.

18 — H LUTON — 29/10
Pos 9 · 10,269 · 21 / 20 · (£1,428.12.0)
Score 5-1 (HT 3-0) · W
Atyeo 8, Clark 21, Hooper 32, Turner 49, [Williams 78, 80]
Ref: D Howell
City: Gibson, Briggs, Thresher, Parr, Connor, Low, Derrick, Clark, Atyeo, Williams, Hooper
Luton: Baynham, Morton, Bramwell, Pacey, Fincham, McGuffie, Walden, Salisbury, Turner, McKechnie, Weir
An easy success for brilliant City who are denied by the exploits of ex-England keeper Ron Baynham. All the goals come from feet, Clark's power-driven 20-yarder and Gordon Turner's 25-yarder being the highlights. Atyeo's 15-yard shot-on-the-turn gets the action under way.

19 — A BARNSLEY — 2/11
Pos 7 · 6,124 · 20 / 22
Score 4-2 (HT 2-1) · W
Williams 26, Atyeo 32, Clark 86p, 90 / *Briggs 35 (og), Leighton 60*
Ref: W Grundy
City: Gibson, Briggs, Thresher, Parr, Connor, Low, Derrick, Clark, Atyeo, Williams, Hooper
Barnsley: Hopper, Brookes, Wood, Winstanley, Houghton, Sheavills, Clarke, Byrne, Leighton, Kerr, O'Hara
A dramatic finale with Bill Houghton's handball at the end of normal time. Clark's mis-hit penalty finds the net, then in injury-time he strokes the ball in from a Williams pass. In a game spoilt by Barnsley's tactics, the Tykes fight back well after Williams and Atyeo fired in for City.

20 — H MILLWALL — 9/11
Pos 8 · 10,332 · 22 / 23 · (£1,812.9.6)
Score 0-0 (HT 0-0) · D
Ref: J Taylor
City: Gibson, Briggs, Thresher, Parr, Connor, Low, Derrick, Clark, Atyeo, Williams, Hooper
Millwall: Stepney, John, Gilchrist, Harper, Snowden, Obeney, Foster, McLaughlin, Terry, Jones, Haverty
Alex Stepney is applauded off the field at Ashton Gate after he had prevented City extending their winning run to six games. His brilliance, allied to some ineffective finishing, costs City this game, which is late in starting because of emergency repairs being required to a goal net.

21 — H WATFORD — 23/11
Pos 6 · 9,962 · 9 / 25 · (£1,435.13.6)
Score 2-0 (HT 0-0) · W
Atyeo 52, Clark 75p
Ref: D Corbett
City: Gibson, Briggs, Thresher, Parr, Connor, Low, Derrick, Clark, Atyeo, Williams, Hooper
Watford: Jennings, Bell, McCready, Welbourne, Mancini, Catleugh, Spelman, Larkin, Livesey, Oliver, Harris
The performance of Watford goalkeeper Pat Jennings exceeds even that of Stepney in the previous home match, but he is unable to prevent City's success. Atyeo's drive is deflected off a defender to put City in front, whilst Tom McCready brings down Williams for the spot-kick.

22 — A SOUTHEND — 30/11
Pos 6 · 6,801 · 18 / 26
Score 1-1 (HT 0-0) · D
Thresher 53 / *McKinven 89*
Ref: R Tinkler
City: Gibson, Briggs, Thresher, Parr, Connor, Low, Derrick, Clark, Atyeo, Williams, Hooper
Southend: Goy, Costello, Neal, Bentley, Watson, Ashworth, Slater, Gilfillan, Conway, Beesley, McKinven
John McKinven hammers in Malcom Slater's corner in the very last minute to foil City in this poor game. City create the better chances, but Gibson had to be brave to save at the feet of Robert Gilfillan early on. Thresher's left-footed drive from the edge of the area is his first for City.

23 — A BRISTOL ROV — 14/12
Pos 7 · 19,451 · 12 / 26
Score 0-4 (HT 0-3) · L
Gibson 4og, Jarman 9, Biggs 11, [Bradford 85]
Ref: J Finney
City: Gibson, Briggs, Thresher, Parr, Connor, Low, Derrick, Clark, Atyeo, Williams, Hooper
Bristol Rov: Hall, Hillard, Jones G, Oldfield, Davis, Mabbutt, Jarman, Brown, Biggs, Hamilton, Bradford
After Gibson knocks the ball over his own goal-line before Geoff Bradford makes sure, nervous City are carved apart by an incisive Rovers team. Harold Jarman's 20-yard cross-shot is followed by an Alfie Biggs rasper, and City are down and out almost before the game has started.

LEAGUE DIVISION 3

Manager: Fred Ford

SEASON 1963-64

Column positions: 1 Gibson | 2 | 3 Thresher | 4 Parr | 5 Connor | 6 Low | 7 Derrick | 8 Clark | 9 Atyeo | 10 Williams | 11 Hooper

---

No 24 — H PORT VALE — 21/12
Att 6,021 (£763.6.0) — Pos 13 — Pt 27 — F-A 0-0 — H-T 0-0
Scorers, Times and Referees: Ref: B Setchell

1	2	3	4	5	6	7	8	9	10	11
Gibson	Briggs	Thresher	Parr	Connor	Low	Derrick	Clark	Atyeo	Williams	Hooper
Hancock	*Whalley*	*Wilson*	*Rawlings*	*Nicholson*	*Sproson*	*Bingham*	*Steele*	*Richards*	*Mudie*	*Smith*

Defenders rule supreme on an icy pitch at Ashton Gate, where the soccer is played at a pedestrian pace. Briggs is City's star, but Atyeo, wearing canvas boots, adapted to the conditions better than most. The game's final move sees Derrick fail with an easy heading opportunity.

No 25 — A QP RANGERS — 28/12
Att 6,916 — Pos 17 — Pt 29 — F-A 2-0 — H-T 1-0
Scorers, Times and Referees: Low 33, Williams 80 — Ref: R Harper

1	2	3	4	5	6	7	8	9	10	11
Gibson	Briggs	Thresher	Parr	Connor	Low	Derrick	Clark	Atyeo	Williams	Hooper
Springett	*Angell*	*Brady P*	*Malcolm*	*Brady R*	*Keen*	*Lazarus*	*Bedford*	*Gibbs*	*Leary*	*McQuade*

A game of two contrasting halves at Loftus Road, where City's performance prior to the break is a triumph for their skilful football. Low's 30-yarder gives them the lead, but after the interval City are forced back by a furious onslaught before Williams dribbles past Peter Springett.

No 26 — A NOTTS CO — 11/1
Att 5,824 — Pos 23 — Pt 30 — F-A 1-1 — H-T 1-1
Scorers, Times and Referees: Williams 36 / Edwards 19 — Ref: F Cowen

1	2	3	4	5	6	7	8	9	10	11
Gibson	Briggs	Thresher	Parr	Connor	Low	Derrick	Clark	Atyeo	Williams	Hooper
Smith	*Bircumshaw*	*Agnew*	*Edwards*	*Gibson*	*Lowe*	*Fry*	*Astle*	*Bly*	*Carver*	*Barber*

It looked like Clark's 55th-minute drive, which hits both posts, had spun over the goal-line before trickling back into play. Notts, in front with a deflected 25-yarder, are handicapped by Keith Fry's half-time departure following an earlier injury. Williams slips in Atyeo's knock-down.

No 27 — H CREWE — 18/1
Att 8,117 (£1,105.0.0) — Pos 17 — Pt 31 — F-A 1-1 — H-T 0-1
Scorers, Times and Referees: Clark 58 / Gowans 14 — Ref: E Jennings

1	2	3	4	5	6	7	8	9	10	11
Gibson	Etheridge	Thresher	Parr	Connor	Waterhouse	Derrick	Clark	Atyeo	Williams	Tait
Mailey	*Whelan*	*Leigh*	*Bodell*	*Barnes*	*Riggs*	*Gowans*	*Haydock*	*King*	*Keery*	*Kemp*

Injuries prevent City beating their 1955 record, which they equalled last week, of being unchanged for 14 games. After Clark's superb drive equalises a Peter Gowans first-time left-footed strike, the City are thwarted by the many brilliant saves of the lightly built Willie Mailey.

No 28 — A CRYSTAL PALACE — 1/2
Att 16,539 — Pos 2 — Pt 31 — F-A 0-1 — H-T 0-0
Scorers, Times and Referees: Kellard 47 — Ref: P Brandwood

1	2	3	4	5	6	7	8	9	10	11
Gibson	Briggs	Thresher	Parr	Connor	Low	Derrick	Clark	Atyeo	Williams	Hooper
Glazier	*Sewell*	*Townsend*	*Stephenson*	*Wood*	*Howe*	*Imlach*	*Brooks*	*Holton*	*Burridge*	*Kellard*

Low's failure to spot Bobby Kellard steaming in as he decides to let Connor's back-pass trickle through to Gibson, costs City a point in this poor game and surely ends their promotion hopes. The Palace winger was able to get to the ball before Gibson and slip the leather into the net.

No 29 — H WALSALL — 8/2
Att 7,503 (£1,002.16.6) — Pos 16 — Pt 33 — F-A 5-1 — H-T 1-1
Scorers, Times and Referees: Clark 8, Williams 50, Atyeo 57, 62, 80 / Wiggin 13 — Ref: J Cooke

1	2	3	4	5	6	7	8	9	10	11
Gibson	Briggs	Thresher	Parr	Connor	Low	Derrick	Clark	Atyeo	Williams	Hooper
Tennant	*Gregg*	*Sharples*	*Roper*	*McPherson*	*Dudley*	*Meek*	*Matthews*	*Wiggin*	*Mason*	*Foster*

Just a day after Atyeo's 32nd birthday, the Ashton crowd rise to acclaim the maestro when, after Clark's effort had been blocked, he puts City 3-1 ahead with an easy shot, to register his 300th league and cup goal. He inspires City to inflict on Walsall their heaviest defeat of the season.

No 30 — H WREXHAM — 11/2
Att 8,905 (£1,184.12.0) — Pos 24 — Pt 35 — F-A 4-0 — H-T 1-0
Scorers, Times and Referees: Hooper 42, Atyeo 68, Clark 79, 86 — Ref: J Loynton

1	2	3	4	5	6	7	8	9	10	11
Gibson	Briggs	Thresher	Parr	Connor	Low	Derrick	Clark	Atyeo	Williams	Hooper
Jones A	*Robertson*	*McGill*	*Powell*	*Jones P*	*Johnson*	*Mayers*	*Myerscough*	*Phythian*	*McMillan*	*Colbridge*

City dominate this affair and with more steadiness would surely have reached double figures. Hooper's 15-yarder blaster in completing a swift, dazzling passing move is the best goal, but Williams is unlucky at the finish. The whistle sounds just as his shot was on its way into the net.

No 31 — A READING — 15/2
Att 9,873 — Pos 6 — Pt 36 — F-A 1-1 — H-T 0-1
Scorers, Times and Referees: Atyeo 68 / Webb 1 — Ref: G Davis

1	2	3	4	5	6	7	8	9	10	11
Gibson	Briggs	Thresher	Parr	Connor	Low	Derrick	Clark	Atyeo	Williams	Hooper
Wilkie	*Walker*	*Meldrum*	*Evans*	*Spiers*	*Travers*	*Jones*	*Kerr*	*Grant*	*Webb*	*Allen*

Reading deservedly lead at half-time thanks to Doug Webb's 25 second opener, which City hotly disputed for offside. After the break, Derrick, that lean, long-legged enigma, inspires City with a star performance. Leading Reading a merry dance, he sets up Atyeo to volley in the leveller.

No 32 — A PETERBOROUGH — 22/2
Att 7,400 — Pos 13 — Pt 36 — F-A 2-4 — H-T 1-2
Scorers, Times and Referees: Hooper 19, Williams 51 / Turley 3, Smith 30, McNamee 48, 78 — Ref: H Hackney/S Dent

1	2	3	4	5	6	7	8	9	10	11
Gibson	Briggs	Thresher	Parr	Connor	Low	Derrick	Clark	Atyeo	Williams	Hooper
Duff	*Hopkins*	*Sissons*	*Jackson*	*Rankmore*	*Cooper*	*Moulden*	*Horobin*	*Turley*	*Smith*	*McNamee*

The start of the second half is delayed for five minutes when senior linesman S J Dent taking over from H Hackney who pulls his hamstring. Following the resignation of manager Jack Fairbrother, Peterborough notch up their first win of the year and their first goal in six games.

No 33 — A COLCHESTER — 24/2
Att 4,803 — Pos 9 — Pt 37 — F-A 1-1 — H-T 0-0
Scorers, Times and Referees: Atyeo 52 / Docherty 61 — Ref: D Wells

1	2	3	4	5	6	7	8	9	10	11
Gibson	Briggs	Thresher	Parr	Connor	Low	Derrick	Clark	Atyeo	Williams	Hooper
Ames	*Woods*	*Fowler*	*McCrohan*	*Rutter*	*Docherty*	*Hill*	*McColl*	*Hunt*	*Stark*	*Grice*

John Doherty's 20-yarder, which takes a wicked deflection off of Low, enables Colchester to notch up their 14th draw of the season with this hard-fought encounter. Denied a penalty when Keith Rutter handles just inside the area, City take the lead with Atyeo's fine shot on the turn.

No 34 — H OLDHAM — 29/2
Att 9,900 (£1,386.6.0) — Pos 10 — Pt 39 — F-A 3-1 — H-T 2-0
Scorers, Times and Referees: Clark 17, Branagan 38 (og), Williams 64 / Sievewright 83 — Ref: L Callaghan

1	2	3	4	5	6	7	8	9	10	11
Gibson	Briggs	Thresher	Parr	Connor	Low	Derrick	Clark	Atyeo	Williams	Hooper
Halsall	*Branagan*	*Marshall*	*Frizzell*	*Williams*	*Sievewright*	*Ledger*	*Johnstone*	*Colquhoun*	*Bowie*	*Whitaker*

City, who twice in the opening minutes have goals disallowed, demonstrate too much speed and guile for an Oldham side making seven changes. Clark fires in a 12-yard opener, then the ball skids off Ken Branagan's head into his own net before Williams slams in City's third.

Season results log (matches 35–46). City (Bristol City) players listed first in each cell; opponents' players second.

#	V	Opponent	Date	HT	FT	Res	(5)/Pos	Pts	Attendance	Receipts
35	A	HULL	7/3	1:3	4:4	D	5 / 13	40	4,726	—
36	H	QP RANGERS	10/3	1:1	2:1	W	5 / 18	42	8,869	(£1,180.2.6)
37	H	BARNSLEY	14/3	2:1	5:2	W	5 / 19	44	6,950	(£946.7.0)
38	A	OLDHAM	21/3	2:0	2:1	W	5 / 8	46	7,556	—
39	H	MANSFIELD	27/3	0:3	2:3	L	5 / 7	46	13,914	(£2,028.11.0)
40	H	COLCHESTER	28/3	0:0	3:1	W	5 / 13	48	7,779	(£1,040.18.0)
41	A	MANSFIELD	30/3	0:3	0:4	L	5 / 6	48	8,736	—
42	A	WATFORD	4/4	1:1	2:2	D	5 / 3	49	9,907	—
43	H	SOUTHEND	11/4	0:0	2:2	D	5 / 13	50	7,314	(£929.13.6)
44	A	WREXHAM	18/4	0:1	1:1	D	5 / 23	51	2,875	(£929.13.6)
45	A	MILLWALL	20/4	0:0	1:0	W	5 / 19	53	12,264	—
46	H	BOURNEMOUTH	25/4	3:0	3:1	W	5 / 4	55	7,787	(£1,055.9.6)

Home Average 9,912 — Away 9,416

Scorers, referees and line-ups

35 — A HULL, 7/3 (4:4)
Scorers: Hooper 30p, Williams 51, 85, Clark 73 / *Low 3 (og), Garvey 18, Wilk'n 40, Dav 63p Swan*
Ref: J Pickles
City: Gibson, Briggs, Thresher, Parr, Connor, Low, Derrick, Clark, Atyeo, Williams, Hooper
Hull: Swan, Davidson, Butler, Garvey, Milner, Simpkin, Chilton, Wilkinson, Rafferty, Henderson, McSeveney
The first six goals are all the consequence of bad play or infringements. After William Wilkinson shoots Hull 3-1 ahead, Williams heads in for City. Briggs fouls Wilkinson to give the Tigers their penalty, but Clark's screamer sets the scene for Williams to slam in City's point-saver.

36 — H QP RANGERS, 10/3 (2:1)
Scorers: Hooper 45, Parr 65 / *McLeod 44*
Ref: K Burns
City: Nicholls, Briggs, Thresher, Parr, Connor, Low, Derrick, Clark, Atyeo, Williams, Hooper
QPR: Smith, Brady P, Angell, Malcolm, Keen, Gibbs, Sibley, Bedford, Leary, Graham, McLeod
Hooper's prodigious shooting enlivens this poor affair. His 30-yarder right on half-time, levelling George McLeod's shot 45 seconds earlier, is followed by a 23-yard free-kick (kept out by a post), and a 35-yard rocket. Parr's half-volley from the edge of the area is his first ever goal.

37 — H BARNSLEY, 14/3 (5:2)
Scorers: Will's 30, Atyeo 31, 82, Hooper 67p, [Clark 68] / *Leighton 14, Shevills 77*
Ref: D Howell
City: Nicholls, Briggs, Thresher, Parr, Connor, Bush, Derrick, Clark, Atyeo, Williams, Hooper
Barnsley: Hill, Hopper, Brookes, Wood, Winstanley, Houghton, Shevills, Kerr, Leighton, Byrne, O'Hara
Despite injuries to Derrick and Williams, City's strength in the mud is sufficient to overcome the Tykes. Williams stabs in the leveller to Tony Leighton's steered in opener from John Byrne's pass, prior to Atyeo nodding City in front. Bill Houghton brings down Hooper for his penalty.

38 — A OLDHAM, 21/3 (2:1)
Scorers: Williams 17, Low 40 / *Lister 90p*
Ref: R Egan
City: Nicholls, Briggs, Thresher, Parr, Connor, Low, Tait, Clark, Atyeo, Williams, Hooper
Oldham: Bollands, Branagan, Taylor, Williams, Jackson, Sievwright, Ledger, Frizzell, Lister, Craig, Whitaker
A comfortably win over an Oldham side still struggling to find their early season form. It was easy for City, especially in the first half, with Williams netting a 18-yard drive and Low's 25-yard chip in off the far post. Briggs's push on Bob Craig gives away the injury-time penalty.

39 — H MANSFIELD, 27/3 (2:3)
Scorers: Hooper 69, Clark 83 / *Wagstaff 26, 39, Tyrer 41*
Ref: J Mitchell
City: Nicholls, Briggs, Thresher, Parr, Connor, Low, Derrick, Clark, Atyeo, Williams, Hooper
Mansfield: Treharne, Jones, Humble, Chapman S, Gill, Morris, Tyrer, Coates, Wagstaff, Chapman R, Scanlon
In the sunshine, an outstanding Mansfield side run City ragged in the first half. Ken Wagstaff is the star, beating three defenders he strolls through to shoot in the opener. Hooper's blasted in free-kick gives City some hope, but, despite Clark firing in, the deficit proves too great.

40 — H COLCHESTER, 28/3 (3:1)
Scorers: Clark 46, Williams 61, Atyeo 73 / *Stark 87*
Ref: W Gow
City: Gibson, Briggs, Etheridge, Parr, Low, Bush, Savino, Clark, Atyeo, Williams, Hooper
Colchester: Ames, Woods, Fowler, McGraham, Rutter, Trevis, Hill, McCall, King, Stark, Grice
City dominate the first half, but it is not until after the break that the goals come. Clark hammers in from 18 yards to break the deadlock, Williams hooks in the second, then Atyeo heads home from close range, before Billy Stark's rocket from near the corner flag deceives Gibson.

41 — A MANSFIELD, 30/3 (0:4)
Scorers: — / *Coates 3, 17, 27, Chapman S 89*
Ref: K Seddon
City: Gibson, Briggs, Thresher, Parr, Connor, Bush, Savino, Clark, Atyeo, Williams, Hooper
Mansfield: Treharne, Jones, Humble, Chapman S, Gill, Morris, Tyrer, Coates, Wagstaff, Chapman R, Scanlon
City control the second-half play, putting in 15 shots, but are frustrated by great saves, as well as the post. Unfortunately, by then the game is already lost, as, despite Gibson saving Peter Morris's 26th-minute penalty, two shots and a header from David Coates have Mansfield coasting.

42 — A WATFORD, 4/4 (2:2)
Scorers: Williams 25, Hooper 47 / *Harris 15p, Livesey 71*
Ref: A Jobling
City: Gibson, Ford, Thresher, Parr, Connor, Bush, Savino, Clark, Atyeo, Williams, Hooper
Watford: Jennings, Bell, Jones, Crisp, Chung, Catleugh, Spellman, McAnearney, Livesey, Oliver, Harris
Following George Harris's controversial penalty (being 'felled outside the box), Hooper's classic-strike puts City ahead after the break. Ford's back-pass sticks in the mud to allow Charlie Livesey to hook the ball in off the underside of the bar for Watford's rather fortunate point-saver.

43 — H SOUTHEND, 11/4 (2:2)
Scorers: Williams 64, Bush 85 / *Bradbury 72, 86*
Ref: L Faulkner
City: Gibson, Ford, Thresher, Parr, Connor, Bush, Savino, Clark, Atyeo, Williams, Hooper
Southend: Goy, Neal, King, Bentley, Watson, Bradbury, Slater, Smith, Gilfillan, Beesley, McKinven
City are lethargic in the first half, but after the break they take command and during one ten-minute spell of sustained pressure Williams slips the ball in at the Open End. Bush's fierce shot looked to have secured a late win, but Terry Bradbury's cross-shot leaves Gibson baffled.

44 — A WREXHAM, 18/4 (1:1)
Scorers: Clark 67 / *Jones 21p*
Ref: P Hackney
City: Gibson, Ford, Thresher, Parr, Connor, Bush, Savino, Clark, Atyeo, Williams, Hooper
Wrexham: Fleet, Robertson, McGill, Powell, Morrall, Johnson, Mayers, Phythian, Jones, Bent, Colbridge
Atyeo will want to forget this match as he misses four open goals after the interval. Following a few early scares, City over-run the poor Welsh side, but all they have to show is Clark's run-in goal, which equalises Wrexham's spot-kick – given for Thresher's trip on Derek Mayers.

45 — A MILLWALL, 20/4 (1:0)
Scorers: Hooper 65p / —
Ref: —
City: Gibson, Ford, Thresher, Parr, Connor, Bush, Savino, Clark, Atyeo, Williams, Hooper
Millwall: Stepney, Gilchrist, John, Jones, Leedham, Wilson, Senior, Whitehouse, Terry, Townsend, Gray
City come to the aid of their ex-coach Bill Harvey, now boss of relegation-threatened Luton Town. A deserved success, courtesy of Hooper's typically fierce penalty-kick after Savino is tripped. Both sides are denied by the woodwork, which thwarts Hooper as well as Pat Terry.

46 — H BOURNEMOUTH, 25/4 (3:1)
Scorers: Williams 3, Parr 24, Clark 25 / *Coughlin 72*
Ref: G Davis
City: Gibson, Ford, Thresher, Parr, Connor, Bush, Savino, Clark, Atyeo, Williams, Hooper
Bournemouth: Best, Farmer, Keith, Groves, Gater, Bolton, Bumstead, Woods, Coughlin, Archer, Crickmore
No end of season apathy in a game of contrasting halves. City's non-stop attacking display before the break is rewarded by an early three-goal avalanche, but the second half degenerates into an ill-tempered affair. The referee fails to spot a handling offence keeping out a Williams shot.

CUP-TIES

Manager: Fred Ford

SEASON 1963-64

League Cup

					F-A	H-T	Scorers, Times, and Referees
1	A	GILLINGHAM	4/9	9 L	2-4	0-2	Atyeo 48, 62 *(Waldock 58)*
							Stringfellow 2, 66, Gibbs 38,
			5,940 4:5				Ref: D Wells

1	2	3	4	5	6	7	8	9	10	11
Cook	Briggs	Thresher	Etheridge	Connor	Waterhouse	Tait	Clark	Atyeo	Williams	Hooper
Simpson	*Hudson*	*Hunt*	*Arnott*	*Burgess*	*Farrall*	*Ridley*	*Stringfellow*	*Waldock*	*Gibbs*	*Pulley*

Peter Stringfellow's header gives the Gills an early lead, but City have their chances before a Brian Gibbs curler doubled the advantage. Atyeo's header and his rolled-in effort keep City in touch, but Ron Waldock's close-in shot and Stringfellow's blaster prove too much.

FA Cup

					F-A	H-T	Scorers, Times, and Referees
1	A	CORBY	16/11	8 W	3-1	2-1	Low 35, Williams 43, Clark 88
							Crawley 27
			4,904 £1:5				Ref: J Taylor
			(£858.11.0)				

1	2	3	4	5	6	7	8	9	10	11
Gibson	Biggs	Thresher	Parr	Connor	Low	Derrick	Clark	Atyeo	Williams	Hooper
Alexander	*Rodgers*	*Pollard*	*Rennie*	*Parsons*	*Curran*	*Stenhouse*	*Stanley*	*Hukin*	*Crawley*	*Jagger*

Crawley drives the ball in from six yards to celebrate his 28th birthday, but Low's 25-yarder levels for City. In the face of Corby's relentless attacks after the break, it is a struggle for City's hard-pressed defenders, but Clark's rasping left-footed drive from Derrick's cross brings relief.

					F-A	H-T	Scorers, Times, and Referees
2	A	EXETER	7/12	6 W	2-0	1-0	Atyeo 4, 88
			15,077 4:4				Ref: J Finney
			(£2,430.1.0)				

1	2	3	4	5	6	7	8	9	10	11
Gibson	Biggs	Thresher	Parr	Connor	Low	Derrick	Clark	Atyeo	Williams	Hooper
Barnett	*Smyth*	*Macdonald*	*Mitchell*	*Harvey*	*Anderson*	*Rees*	*Northcott*	*Curtis*	*Grace*	*Phoenix*

Gibson demonstrates just why he is the best goalkeeper in the Third Division at present. After City had snatched an early lead he makes at least eight fine saves to keep dominant Exeter at bay. Clark fails with a 44th-minute penalty, but Atyeo takes his goals with characteristic coolness.

					F-A	H-T	Scorers, Times, and Referees
3	A	DONCASTER	4/1	8 D	2-2	1-0	Atyeo 2, Clark 88
							Taylor 64, Ripley 84
			18,050 4:15				Ref: G Grundy
			(£2,722.17.6)				

1	2	3	4	5	6	7	8	9	10	11
Gibson	Biggs	Thresher	Parr	Connor	Low	Derrick	Clark	Atyeo	Williams	Hooper
Potter	*Raine*	*Meadows*	*Windross*	*White*	*Ripley*	*Robinson*	*Booth*	*Hale*	*Jeffrey*	*Taylor*

Clark saves City's bacon by jabbing in an untidy equaliser just two minutes from the end of this thrilling cup-tie. Doncaster's Alick Jeffrey is the star performer on the field, but, just before half time, Clark is unlucky to have a City goal disallowed after having it first awarded.

					F-A	H-T	Scorers, Times, and Referees
3R	H	DONCASTER	7/1	8 W	2-0		Hooper 20p, Atyeo 64
			20,269 4:15				Ref: G Grundy
			(£3,599.5.6)				

1	2	3	4	5	6	7	8	9	10	11
Gibson	Biggs	Thresher	Parr	Connor	Low	Derrick	Clark	Atyeo	Williams	Hooper
Potter	*Raine*	*Meadows*	*Windross*	*Crompton*	*Ripley*	*Robinson*	*Booth*	*Hall*	*Jeffrey*	*Taylor*

It is somewhat ironic that, in his third comeback game, Alick Jeffrey has to return to the ground where in an international nearly eight years earlier a broken leg brought his career to a shattering halt. Thankfully, there are no problems this time, except that his side bows out of the Cup.

					F-A	H-T	Scorers, Times, and Referees
4	A	SUNDERLAND	25/1	10 L	1-6	1-3	Hooper 31 *(Crossan 84, 85)*
							Herd 5, 40, Hurley 35, Sharkey 55,
			46,201 2:2				Ref: W Crossley
			(£9,008.1.0)				

1	2	3	4	5	6	7	8	9	10	11
Gibson	Briggs	Thresher	Parr	Connor	Low	Derrick	Clark	Atyeo	Williams	Hooper
Montgomery	*Irwin*	*Ashurst*	*Harvey*	*Hurley*	*McNab*	*Usher*	*Herd*	*Sharkey*	*Crossan*	*Mulhall*

Despite a Williams shot that raps the post in the seventh minute and Hooper's rocket shot, City are outclassed by a Sunderland side that never stops running for each other. City's 800 travelling fans have to see their side often dazzled and mesmerised by Sunderland's sensational soccer.

Gloucestershire Cup

					F-A	H-T	Scorers, Times, and Referees
F	H	BRISTOL ROV	28/4	5 D	2-2	1-0	Low 13, Williams 79
							Munro 60, Brown 68
			7,693 12				Ref: S Turnnell

1	2	3	4	5	6	7	8	9	10	11
Gibson	Ford	Thresher	Parr	Low	Bush	Savino	Clark	Atyeo	Williams	Hooper
Hall	*Hillard*	*Davis*	*Oldfield*	*Stone*	*Mabbut*	*Jarman*	*Brown*	*Biggs*	*Hamilton*	*Munro*

Williams fires in from close range to save City from a surprise defeat. Following Low's lobbed opener, City enjoy the better of the early play, but the Rovers dominate the middle period. After Alex Munro's controversial equaliser, John Brown darts through to put Rovers in front.

Abandoned League Game

					F-A	H-T	Scorers, Times, and Referees
25	H	QP RANGERS	26/12	8	A A	3-0	Clark 9, Derrick 20, Hooper 23p
							Abandoned at half-time due to fog
			10,681 17				Ref: K Burns
			(£1,570.6.6)				

1	2	3	4	5	6	7	8	9	10	11
Gibson	Briggs	Thresher	Parr	Connor	Low	Derrick	Clark	Atyeo	Williams	Hooper
Springett	*Angell*	*Brady P*	*Malcolm*	*Brady R*	*Keen*	*Lazarus*	*Bedford*	*Gibbs*	*Leary*	*McQuade*

City's brilliant attacking football brings a series of goalmouth thrills and scrambles. Clark's great 18-yard shot into the top corner of the net opens the scoring, then Derrick rounds the keeper to tap in City's second before Hooper dispatches the penalty following the tripping of Atyeo.

League Table

		P	W	D	L	F	A	W	D	L	F	A	Pts
			Home					**Away**					
1	Coventry	46	14	7	2	62	32	8	9	6	36	29	60
2	Crys Palace	46	17	4	2	38	14	6	10	7	35	37	60
3	Watford	46	16	6	1	57	28	7	6	10	22	31	58
4	Bournemouth	46	17	4	2	47	15	7	4	12	32	43	56
5	BRISTOL C	46	13	7	3	52	24	7	8	8	32	40	55
6	Reading	46	15	5	3	49	26	6	5	12	30	36	52
7	Mansfield	46	15	8	0	51	20	5	3	15	25	42	51
8	Hull	46	11	9	3	45	27	8	5	10	28	41	49
9	Oldham	46	13	3	7	44	35	7	5	11	29	35	48
10	Peterborough	46	13	6	4	52	27	5	5	13	23	43	47
11	Shrewsbury	46	13	6	4	43	19	5	5	13	30	61	47
12	Bristol Rov	46	9	6	8	52	34	5	2	11	39	45	46
13	Port Vale	46	13	6	4	35	13	3	8	12	18	36	46
14	Southend	46	9	10	4	42	26	6	5	12	35	52	45
15	QP Rangers	46	13	4	6	47	34	5	5	13	29	44	45
16	Brentford	46	11	4	8	54	36	4	10	9	33	44	44
17	Colchester	46	10	8	5	45	26	2	11	10	25	42	43
18	Luton	46	12	2	9	42	41	4	8	11	22	39	42
19	Walsall	46	7	9	7	34	35	6	5	12	25	41	40
20	Barnsley	46	9	9	5	34	29	3	6	14	34	65	39
21	Millwall	46	9	4	10	33	29	5	6	12	20	38	38
22	Crewe	46	10	5	8	29	26	1	7	15	21	51	34
23	Wrexham	46	9	4	10	50	42	4	2	17	25	65	32
24	Notts Co	46	7	8	8	29	26	2	1	20	16	66	27
		1104	285	144	123	1066	664	123	144	285	664	1066	1104

Odds & ends

Double wins: (5) Bournemouth, Luton, Barnsley, QPR, Oldham.
Double losses: (2) Coventry, Mansfield.

Won from behind: (3) QPR (h), Barnsley (h), Corby (a) (FAC).
Lost from in front: (0).

High spots: The win at Brentford on 27 August.
City's brilliant performance in beating Luton 5-1 on 29 October.
The frantic finale at Barnsley on 2 November.
Beating Walsall at Ashton Gate on 8 February.
Victory at Oldham on 21 March.
Peter Hooper's FA Cup goal at Sunderland, where City are overrun.

Low spots: The lack of atmosphere at Ashton Gate in the first game.
Losing 0-4 at Eastville on 14 December.
The ending of City's promotion hopes at Mansfield on 30 March.

AGM (Brecknell, Dolman & Rogers, Pennywell Rd, 1 December 1964):
Loss £3,860.0s.0d. Season Ticket Sales £8,186.0s.0d.
Note: The details (right) include the abandoned League game v QPR.

Player of the year: John Atyeo and Bobby Williams.
Ever-presents: (2) John Atyeo, Brian Clark.
Hat-tricks: (1) John Atyeo.
Leading scorer: Overall: John Atyeo (27). League: John Atyeo (21).

Appearances and Goals

	Appearances		Goals		
	Lge	Cup	Lge	Cup	Tot
Atyeo, John	47	7	21	6	27
Briggs, Alec	39	6	1		1
Bush, Terry	9	1			
Clark, Brian	47	7	19	2	21
Connor, Jack	40	6			
Cook, Tony	3	1			
Derrick, Jantzen	34	5	5		5
Etheridge, Bobby	10	1			
Ford, Tony	14	1			
Gibson, Mike	40	6			
Hooper, Peter	39	7	13	2	15
Kurila, John	6				
Low, Gordon	33	6	2	2	4
Lythgoe, Derek	7		1		1
Nicholls, Ron	4				
Parr, Gordon	39	6	2		2
Savino, Ray	8	1			
Tait, Alex	11	1			
Thresher, Mike	39	7			
Waterhouse, Ken	6	1			
Williams, Bobby	42	7	20	2	22
(own-goals)			2		2
21 players used	517	77	87	14	101

LEAGUE DIVISION 3 — Manager: Fred Ford — SEASON 1964-65

No	Venue / Opponent	Date	Att	Pos	Pt	F-A	H-T	Scorers, Times, and Referees	1	2	3	4	5	6	7	8	9	10	11
1	A SCUNTHORPE	22/8	5,702		0	L 2-5	1-1	Clark 17, 82 / (Sloan 69, 73) Lawther 31, 70, Kirkman 49. Ref: J Parkinson	Gibson	Ford	Thresher	Parr	Low	Bush	Savino	Clark	Atyeo	Williams	Peters
	Scunthorpe								Reeves	Horstead	Betts	Lindsey	Neale	Bannister	Hutton	Kirkman	Lawther	Sloan	Ratcliffe
2	H BARNSLEY	25/8	10,491 (£1,829.10.0)	2	2	W 5-1	4-0	Clark 4, 14, 32, Hopper 10 (og), 58 (og), Leighton 59. Ref: P Brandwood	Gibson	Ford	Thresher	Parr	Low	Drury	Savino	Clark	Atyeo	Williams	Peters
	Barnsley								Hill	Hopper	Brookes	Swallow	Winstanley	Cunningham	Sheavills	Kerr	Leighton	Byrne	O'Hara
3	H WALSALL	29/8	9,478 (£1,594.11.6)	7	4	W 5-1	2-0	Atyeo 44, 47, 83, Ford 37p, Clark 57 / Matthews 46. Ref: V Batty	Gibson	Ford	Thresher	Parr	Low	Bush	Savino	Clark	Atyeo	Williams	Peters
	Walsall								Carling	Gregg	Kletzenbauer	Roper	Leedham	Hodgkisson	Meek	Matthews	Llewellyn	Clarke	Foster
4	A WATFORD	5/9	9,418	10	5	D 2-2	1-2	Peters 34, Williams 57 / Saunders 15, 20. Ref: W Clements	Gibson	Ford	Thresher	Parr	Low	Bush	Savino	Clark	Atyeo	Williams	Peters
	Watford								George	Nicholas	Jones	Welbourne	Chung	Catleugh	Bond	McAnearney	Saunders	Owen	Harris
5	H SOUTHEND	8/9	11,737 (£2,115.12.6)	3	7	W 4-0	1-0	Williams 44, Atyeo 50, 63, 65. Ref: D Lyden	Gibson	Ford	Thresher	Parr	Low	Bush	Savino	Clark	Atyeo	Williams	Peters
	Southend								McKechnie	Neal	King	Banks	Bradbury	Ashworth	Woodley	Friel	Gilfillan	Beesley	Slater
6	H WORKINGTON	12/9	10,536 (£1,834.6.6)	4	9	W 5-0	1-0	Bush 8, 46, Clark 57, 62, 64. Ref: D Wells	Gibson	Ford	Thresher	Parr	Low	Bush	Savino	Clark	Atyeo	Williams	Peters
	Workington								Owen	Furphy	Lumsden	Hale	Brown	Birkinshaw	Lowes	Carr	Napier	Moran	Martin
7	A SOUTHEND	14/9	8,780	1	11	W 4-0	1-0	Williams 35, Bush 47, Clark 67, 85. Ref: J Osborne	Gibson	Ford	Briggs	Parr	Connor	Low	Savino	Clark	Bush	Williams	Peters
	Southend								McKechnie	Neal	King	Banks	Metcalf	Bradbury	Slater	Smith	Conway	Friel	Woodley
8	A HULL	19/9	7,485	4	11	L 2-3	1-1	Williams 10, Clark 74 / Corner 34, McSeveney 50, 85p. Ref: K Dagnall	Gibson	Ford	Briggs	Parr	Connor	Low	Derrick	Clark	Bush	Williams	Peters
	Hull								Swan	Davidson	Butler	Collinson	Feasey	Summers	Clarke	Wilkinson	Corner	Henderson	McSeveney
9	H GILLINGHAM	26/9	11,556 (£2,084.0.0)	6	11	L 1-2	0-1	Bush 56 / Gibbs 15, Farrall 58. Ref: G Martin	Gibson	Ford	Briggs	Parr	Connor	Low	Peters	Clark	Bush	Williams	Hooper
	Gillingham								Simpson	Arnott	Hudson	Riggs	Burgess	Farrall	Godfrey	Gibbs	Green	White	Meredith
10	H READING	29/9	11,981 (£2,148.10.6)	5	13	W 2-0	0-0	Low 53, Bush 55. Ref: A Weller	Gibson	Ford	Briggs	Parr	Connor	Low	Savino	Clark	Bush	Williams	Peters
	Reading								Wilkie	Walker	Meldrum	Norton	Spiers	Evans	Allen	Thornhill	Terry	Webb	Travers
11	A BRISTOL ROV	3/10	25,370	2	14	D 1-1	1-1	Peters 1 / Biggs 9. Ref: K Burns	Gibson	Ford	Briggs	Parr	Connor	Low	Savino	Clark	Bush	Williams	Peters
	Bristol Rov								Hall	Hillard	Jones G	Oldfield	Davis	Mabbutt	Jarman	Brown	Biggs	Hamilton	Jones R

1 — Scunthorpe: A deceptive looking score as City, apart from being undone by three goals in four second-half minutes, play well. Atyeo has a powerful header cleared off the goal-line, whilst twice the Scunthorpe woodwork is struck, and their keeper Brian Reeves pulls of four quite outstanding saves.

2 — Barnsley: An outstanding first-half display from City, which starts with Clark, in the very first minute, and Atyeo later, being denied by a post. Alan Hopper puts City well in charge when, challenged by Peters, he heads into his own net not long after Clark's fierce drive had put them ahead.

3 — Walsall: Against a weakened Walsall side, following the loss of their captain Frank Kletzenbauer with a broken leg after just 15 minutes, City run riot. However, it is not until a disputed penalty - Low checked by Frank Gregg - that the floodgates are unlocked for yet another five-goal haul.

4 — Watford: With injuries to Hooper and Derrick this season, lightweight wingers Savino and Peters are now playing well enough to deserve their place on merit. They inspire City's recovery after block-busting strikes by Ron Saunders - Watford's £15,000 newcomer - threaten to blow City away.

5 — Southend: Atyeo shows his critics that he is far from finished with a superbly taken hat-trick - all with his feet - that match anything he produced in his pomp. After a Williams bullet-like shot finds the top corner of the net right on half-time, United are completely destroyed by Atyeo's display.

6 — Workington: With Gibson making three quite outstanding saves, as well as the intervention of the bar, to keep the visitors at bay, City are rather fortunate to be in front at the interval. It takes Bush's magnificent second-half header, a replica of his first goal, to quell Workington's tremendous spirit.

7 — Southend: Despite Savino's leg injury which means he is a virtual passenger for all but the opening 15 minutes, City produce one of their best displays since relegation. Clark wraps up this comprehensive victory with a great drive from the edge of the area after running right through the middle.

8 — Hull: Having saved Andy Davidson's weak 20th-minute spot-kick, Gibson is unable to repeat the feat when John McSeveney crashes in Hull's late penalty winner when the referee is conned by Doug Clarke's dramatic fall. Williams squeezes City ahead in what is a rather poor contest.

9 — Gillingham: Against defensively minded Gillingham, City are bereft of ideas. The crowd, incensed by the visitors' blanket-defence, as well as their time-wasting and negative back-passing, frequently give vent to their feelings. Bush's diving header from a Peters cross is City's only bright spot.

10 — Reading: The City wingers have the beating of their markers in this game. Gibson has little to do, except from picking out from the back of the net Pat Terry's first-half offside header. Low's 30-yard right-footed pile-driver breaks the deadlock before Bush's low drive makes the points secure.

11 — Bristol Rov: Bernard Hall's early blunder gifts Peters a rare headed goal, but the Rovers response is not long delayed. The Baron (Alfie Biggs) deposits his header into the back of City's net to set the stage for a rough, tough contest, containing plenty of thrills, if but little in the way of good football.

Match Log (entries 12–23)

---

12 · A · READING — 7/10
Att. 11,856 · (£1,773.15.6) · 6 D 4 15 · FT 1-1 (HT 1-0)
Parr 24 / Travers 60p · Ref: B Setchell

Pos	City	Reading
1	Gibson	Wilkie
2	Ford	Walker
3	Briggs	Meldrum
4	Parr	Norton
5	Connor	Spiers
6	Low	Evans
7	Savino	Allen
8	Clark	Thornhill
9	Bush	Terry
10	Williams	Webb
11	Peters	Travers

For most of this bone-crunching clash, City's goal is under constant pressure, but in their first attack Parr heads in from Savino's corner-kick to put them in front. Mike Travers nets with a disputed penalty, but fails with his second six minutes later when the upright repels his shot.

---

13 · H · COLCHESTER — 10/10
Att. 9,983 · 6 D 24 16 · FT 1-1 (HT 1-1)
Atyeo 10 / Longbottom 3 · Ref: D Corbett

Pos	City	Colchester
1	Gibson	Buck
2	Ford	Rumney
3	Briggs	Fowler
4	Parr	Trevis
5	Connor	Forbes
6	Low	Jones
7	Savino	Grice
8	Clark	Longbottom
9	Bush	Stark
10	Williams	Salsbury
11	Peters	Aitchison

Arthur Longbottom's early drive proves enough for the U's to get away with larceny. All City have to show for their dominance is Atyeo's right-footed ten-yarder. Clark fluffs two open goals, whilst both he and Williams have efforts cleared off the line and Atyeo is denied by a post.

---

14 · H · QP RANGERS — 13/10
Att. 11,133 · (£1,952.15.0) · 3 W 16 18 · FT 2-0 (HT 0-0)
Atyeo 79, 85 · Ref: W Handley

Pos	City	QP Rangers
1	Gibson	Springett
2	Ford	Brady P
3	Briggs	Nash
4	Parr	Hazell
5	Connor	Brady R
6	Low	Keen
7	Savino	Morgan I
8	Clark	Collins
9	Atyeo	McAdams
10	Williams	Bedford
11	Peters	Morgan R

A shoddy display under the refurbished lights before Atyeo enlivens matters. From Low's free-kick the City No 9 looks yards offside as he breasts the ball down before placing it into the net. Six minutes later he makes sure of victory, outjumping Ray Brady to head in a fine goal.

---

15 · A · PORT VALE — 17/10
Att. 5,564 · 4 W 20 20 · FT 2-1 (HT 1-1)
Atyeo 43, Savino 85 / Cheesbrough 8 · Ref: G Hartley

Pos	City	Port Vale
1	Gibson	Hancock
2	Ford	Alcock
3	Briggs	Wilson
4	Parr	Steele
5	Connor	Nicholson
6	Low	Sproson
7	Savino	Trafford
8	Clark	Cheesbrough
9	Atyeo	Poole
10	Bush	Miles
11	Hooper	Rowland

Taking up the offensive at Vale Park, City are shocked by Albert Cheesbrough's early opportunist goal. Stung by this reversal, City dominate, but it is not until near half-time that Atyeo slides in the leveller from Hooper's driven cross. Savino's unstoppable shot secures a deserved win.

---

16 · A · QP RANGERS — 19/10
Att. 5,560 · 4 L 14 20 · FT 0-1 (HT 0-1)
Bedford 22 · Ref: E Wallace

Pos	City	QP Rangers
1	Gibson	Springett
2	Ford	Brady P
3	Briggs	Nash
4	Parr	Hazell
5	Connor	Brady R
6	Low	Keen
7	Savino	Morgan I
8	Clark	Collins
9	Atyeo	Leary
10	Bush	Bedford
11	Hooper	Morgan R

Despite Atyeo's early disallowed effort and Clark being deprived by City's award of a free-kick near the end, youthful Rangers have matters very much their own way. City are caught napping by a quickly taken throw and Brian Bedford's two-yard header extracts full punishment.

---

17 · H · CARLISLE — 23/10
Att. 10,303 · (£1,754.17.6) · 4 L 7 20 · FT 1-2 (HT 0-1)
Atyeo 76 / Evans 24, Kirkup 47 · Ref: R Paine

Pos	City	Carlisle
1	Gibson	Ross
2	Ford	Neil
3	Briggs	Caldwell
4	Parr	McConnell
5	Connor	Passmoor
6	Low	Harland
7	Savino	Brayton
8	Clark	Evans
9	Atyeo	Large
10	Bush	Blain
11	Hooper	Kirkup

The visitors' precise play has City struggling and they fall behind when John Evans jabs the ball in. An offside-looking Frank Kirkup beats Gibson from a narrow angle to double the advantage, but Alan Ross lets an Atyeo header slip through his hands to get City back into the game.

---

18 · A · OLDHAM — 28/10
Att. 8,013 · 11 L 20 20 · FT 3-7 (HT 2-3)
Sh' 23, 33, Clk 83 (Bart' 50, 59, Har' 65) / Colqu'n 7, Frizell 26, 70, Branagan 34, Swan · Ref: J Thacker

Pos	City	Oldham
1	Gibson	—
2	Ford	—
3	Briggs	—
4	Parr	McCall
5	Connor	Williams A
6	Low	Martin
7	Savino	Colquhoun
8	Clark	Frizell
9	Atyeo	Harris
10	Sharpe	Bowie
11	Sharpe	Bartley

Clark's diving header concludes the scoring in this ten-goal thriller at Boundary Park, that saw another five attempts striking the woodwork, as well as many great saves and missed chances. John Colquhoun picks his spot for the opener, whilst City respond with Sharpe's low shot.

---

19 · A · LUTON — 31/10
Att. 5,385 · 8 D 20 21 · FT 0-0 (HT 0-0)
Ref: T Dawes

Pos	City	Luton
1	Gibson	Tinsley
2	Ford	McBain
3	Briggs	Jardine
4	Parr	Pacey
5	Connor	Caleb
6	Low	Bramwell
7	Derrick	Hails
8	Clark	Pleat
9	Atyeo	McKechnie
10	Sharpe	Reid
11	Sharpe	Whittaker

The Hatters keeper is kept busy, pulling off brilliant saves from Atyeo as City pile on the pressure. It is an hour before Luton get a look in, when Gibson keeps out David Pleat's hooked shot. With 13 minutes left Sharpe races clear, but Colin Tinsley saves at point-blank-range.

---

20 · A · BARNSLEY — 3/11
Att. 3,982 · 6 W 21 23 · FT 2-1 (HT 0-1)
Sharpe 48, Clark 84 / Kerr 25 · Ref: J Cattlin

Pos	City	Barnsley
1	Gibson	Wilcox
2	Ford	Hopper
3	Briggs	Murphy
4	Parr	Byrne
5	Connor	Swallow
6	Low	Cunningham
7	Savino	Sheavills
8	Clark	Kerr
9	Derrick	Leighton
10	Sharpe	Graham
11	Sharpe	O'Hara

City are torn apart by Barnsley's rapier-like thrusts. Fortunately, Gibson is at the top of his form, but even he can do nothing about George Kerr's 25-yarder. Sharpe's half-volley brings City level and Clark secures an unlikely victory with a well-timed leap to head in a Peters corner.

---

21 · H · MANSFIELD — 7/11
Att. 9,653 · (£1,663.1.0) · 6 D 5 24 · FT 1-1 (HT 0-0)
Hooper 47 / Scanlon 64 · Ref: P Bye

Pos	City	Mansfield
1	Gibson	Treharne
2	Ford	Jones
3	Briggs	Toon
4	Bush	Hall
5	Connor	Gill
6	Low	Morris
7	Derrick	Anderson
8	Clark	Wagstaff
9	Derrick	Graham
10	Sharpe	Chapman
11	Sharpe	Scanlon

Despite dominating the first half, when Colin Toon's clear hand-ball inside the area is ignored, it is not until after the break that City take the lead - Hooper toeing the ball in before colliding with Colin Treharne. Albert Scanlon's 15-yard right-footer levels this undistinguished match.

---

22 · H · PETERBOROUGH — 21/11
Att. 9,222 · (£1,576.1.0) · 5 W 12 26 · FT 3-1 (HT 1-0)
Atyeo 17, Rankmore 52 (og), Ford 86p / Crawford 71 · Ref: G Davis

Pos	City	Peterborough
1	Gibson	Sims
2	Ford	Cooper
3	Briggs	Birks
4	Bush	Bolton
5	Connor	Rankmore
6	Low	Orr
7	Savino	Crawford
8	Clark	Moulden
9	Atyeo	Dougan
10	Sharpe	Deakin
11	Peters	McNamee

A well-deserved half-time ovation for City, leading thanks to Atyeo stroking the ball home after gliding onto Low's pass. Frank Rankmore's headed own-goal and his trip on the City No 9 for Ford's spot-kick, brings a convincing success, despite Ian Crawford's drive for the Posh.

---

23 · A · BOURNEMOUTH — 28/11
Att. 9,016 · 4 W 11 28 · FT 2-1 (HT 1-0)
Clark 33, Peters 52 / Archer 89 · Ref: J Lowry

Pos	City	Bournemouth
1	Gibson	Best
2	Ford	Farmer
3	Briggs	Compton
4	Bush	Bolton
5	Connor	Gater
6	Low	Naylor
7	Savino	Bumstead
8	Clark	Archer
9	Atyeo	Hodgson
10	Sharpe	O'Neill
11	Peters	Coxon

Set to face the sun, City in white spurn early chances before Clark hammers in from ten yards. Following the interval, Peters stabs the ball home to double City's advantage. Bill Coxon has his effort disallowed for pushing, before John Archer drives in a late Cherries consolation.

LEAGUE DIVISION 3 — Manager: Fred Ford — SEASON 1964-65

Match details

No	Date	Venue	Opponent (pos)	Att	Pos	Pt	Res	F-A	H-T	Referee
24	12/12	H	SCUNTHORPE (16)	**8,387** (£1,445.19.6)	4	29	D	2-2	1-1	B Setchell
25	19/12	A	WALSALL (24)	5,213	3	31	W	4-2	2-1	K Seddon
26	26/12	A	BRENTFORD (2)	16,065	7	31	L	1-2	1-1	G Roper
27	2/1	H	WATFORD (15)	10,758 (£1,876.11.6)	7	32	D	1-1	0-0	W Gow
28	15/1	A	WORKINGTON (15)	3,380	8	32	L	0-1	0-0	K Howley
29	23/1	H	HULL (2)	14,131 (£2,614.13.0)	8	32	L	1-2	0-0	D Wells
30	30/1	H	EXETER (19)	8,450 (£1,435.14.6)	7	33	D	1-1	0-0	K Burns
31	6/2	A	GILLINGHAM (2)	10,867	9	33	L	0-2	0-2	R Spittle
32	13/2	H	BRISTOL ROV (4)	23,053 (£4,497.1.0)	7	35	W	2-1	0-0	D Lyden
33	20/2	A	COLCHESTER (22)	**2,898**	7	37	W	3-2	1-0	R Paine
34	27/2	H	PORT VALE (24)	8,552 (£1,425.8.0)	7	39	W	3-0	1-0	G Roper

Scorers and times

No	City scorers	Opponent scorers
24	Atyeo 9, Bush 50	Thomas 30, 52
25	Bush 41, Sharpe 44, 78, Clark 75	Matthews 10, 56
26	Sharpe 4	Lawther 25, Bloomfield 47
27	Atyeo 72	Saunders 63
28	—	Napier 60
29	Peters 51	Wagstaff 61, 82
30	Clark 78	Banks 69
31	—	Newman 26, 40
32	Clark 74, Bush 79	Davis 67p
33	Clark 5, Ford 58p, Atyeo 77	Stark 46, 79
34	Peters 14, 89, Bush 61	—

Line-ups (City player / opponent player)

No	1	2	3	4	5	6	7	8	9	10	11
24	Gibson / Reeves	Ford / Harper	Briggs / Hemstead	Bush / Lindsay	Connor / Neale	Low / Horstead	Savino / Hutton	Clark / Bramley	Atyeo / Thomas	Sharpe / Kirkman	Peters / Wilson
25	Gibson / Carling	Ford / Gregg	Briggs / Sissons	Bush / Meath	Connor / Smith T	Low / Atthey	Savino / Meek	Clark / Matthews	Atyeo / Clarke	Sharpe / McMorran	Peters / Taylor
26	Gibson / Bradie	Ford / Hawley	Briggs / Thomson	Bush / Scott	Connor / Gelson	Low / Higginson	Savino / Lazarus	Clark / Bloomfield	Atyeo / Lawther	Sharpe / Cobb	Peters / Fielding
27	Gibson / Goy	Ford / Furphy	Briggs / Williams	Bush / Welbourne	Connor / Chung	Low / Houghton	Savino / Owen	Clark / McAnearney	Atyeo / Saunders	Sharpe / Anderson	Peters / Harris
28	Gibson / Ower	Ford / Ogilvie	Thresher / Lumsden	Bush / Butler	Connor / Brown	Low / Burkinshaw	Savino / Lowes	Clark / Carr	Clark / Watson	Williams / Moran	Peters / Napier
29	Gibson / Williams	Ford / Davidson	Briggs / Butler D	Bush / Collinson	Connor / Milner	Low / Summers	Savino / McSeveney	Derrick / Wagstaff	Atyeo / Chilton	Clark / Houghton	Peters / Butler I
30	Gibson / Shearing	Ford / Smyth	Briggs / Patrick	Bush / Mitchell	Connor / Harvey	Low / Anderson	Savino / Welsh	Derrick / Banks	Atyeo / Curtis	Clark / Hancock	Peters / Thorne
31	Gibson / Simpson	Ford / Weston	Briggs / Hudson	Drury / Arnott	Connor / Burgess	Low / Farrall	Derrick / Newman	Clark / Rackstraw	Bush / Green	Williams / Gibbs	Peters / Meredith
32	Gibson / Hall	Ford / Stone	Briggs / Jones G	Drury / Oldfield	Connor / Davis	Low / Mabbutt	Derrick / Jarman	Atyeo / Brown	Bush / Jones R	Clark / Hamilton	Peters / Haverty
33	Gibson / Ames	Ford / Forbes	Briggs / Fowler	Drury / Jones	Connor / Loughton	Low / Docherty	Derrick / Grice	Atyeo / Stark	Bush / Langley	Clark / Trevis	Peters / Aitchison
34	Gibson / O'Neill	Ford / Andrew	Briggs / Sproson	Drury / Poole	Connor / Nicholson	Low / Bouton	Derrick / Rowland	Atyeo / Mudie	Bush / Trafford	Steele / Steele	Peters / Smith

Match reports

24 — SCUNTHORPE: With only nine fit men (Barry Horstead and Andrew Wilson limping from the 15th and 38th minutes respectively), Scunthorpe produce a fine battling performance at the Gate. Atyeo's perfectly judged shot and Bush's header are matched by a Barrie Thomas header and his later tap-in.

25 — WALSALL: Gibson lets a Graham Matthews drive slip into the net, but Bush levels with a narrow-angled pile-driver. Sharpe's simple nod-in from a Peters centre puts City in front, but an 18-yard cracker brings Walsall a deserved leveller. Headers from Clark and Sharpe clinch a hard-earned win.

26 — BRENTFORD: Sharpe keeps up his remarkable away scoring run when shooting City into the lead after hitting the keeper with his first attempt. Unfortunately, City fade after this, and Ian Lawther is left unmarked when firing the Bees level and Jimmy Bloomfield is able to pick his spot for the winner.

27 — WATFORD: This dull encounter is eventually enlivened when Ron Saunders moves past three defenders to fire past Gibson. City respond and have the Hornets under considerable pressure before an almost kneeling Atyeo heads in a centre after Peters had sped his way past Ken Furphy.

28 — WORKINGTON: City pay dearly for missing their chances when, after a clearance strikes Williams, Kit Napier, with the ball at his feet in front of an open goal, finds scoring a formality. Connor is deprived of his 75th-minute header, as the referee rules that his shout had put off the home defenders.

29 — HULL: Controversy changes the course of the game after Peters taps in Atyeo's knock-down to put dominant City in front. The referee is dealing with City's wall when a free-kick is chipped in for Ken Wagstaff's headed equaliser. Hull's No 8 neatly step-steps Gibson to tie up a lucky win.

30 — EXETER: Clark's late strike at the Covered End secures a rather fortunate share of the spoils, after Alan Banks had burst past three defenders to drive in for the visitors. The heading ability of ex-City player Dermot Curtis proves a handful, whilst both Gibson and Savino finish with rib injuries.

31 — GILLINGHAM: The Gills register their 49th home game without defeat to beat the League record set by Sunderland 72 years ago. Ron Newman forces Brian Gibb's shot over the line and later is alert enough to plant the ball into the net when Charlie Rackstraw touches on John Meredith's centre.

32 — BRISTOL ROV: City up the tempo after the half-time break, but are shocked by Joe Davis's perfect spot-kick after Drury had brought down Ian Hamilton right on the edge of the area. City respond with a furious onslaught that produces Clark's diving header, before Bush rams in the close-range winner.

33 — COLCHESTER: U's boss Neil Franklin comments 'it is a treat to see a visiting side play attacking football'. Clark's shot on the turn goes in off the bar, but Bill Stark levels with a deflected effort. With Duncan Forbes fisting away Atyeo's header, Ford sends Percy Ames the wrong way from the spot.

34 — PORT VALE: Despite the scoreline, City's performance, against bottom of the table Vale (under caretaker boss Jackie Mudie), is uninspiring. Apart from netting with two superb right-footed drives and having a role in setting up Bush's jabbed in effort at the Open End, Peters does little of note.

Matches 35–46

No	Venue	Opponent	Date	Pos	OppPos	Pts	Res	Score	HT	Attendance	Receipts	Scorers	Referee
35	H	BRENTFORD	2/3	6	7	41	W	3-2	1-1	11,150	(£1,974.0.6)	Bush 13, 70, Ford 83p / *Cobb 37, Block 90p*	Ref: J Taylor
36	A	EXETER	6/3	4	18	43	W	1-0	0-0	7,369		Clark 56	Ref: G Davis
37	A	GRIMSBY	9/3	4	8	45	W	2-0	1-0	5,973		Bush 37, Drury 82	Ref: P Hackney
38	H	LUTON	13/3	3	23	47	W	1-0	0-0	11,001	(£1,974.1.0)	Ford 74p	Ref: H New
39	A	MANSFIELD	20/3	6	3	47	L	0-3	0-0	9,434		*Middleton 57, 68, Curry 60*	Ref: J Bullough
40	H	GRIMSBY	26/3	3	11	49	W	4-0	2-0	11,464	(£2,019.13.6)	Atyeo 6, 74, Clark 17, Peters 50	Ref: A Weller
41	A	PETERBOROUGH	3/4	5	9	51	W	1-0	1-0	8,156		Bush 38	Ref: J Osborne
42	H	BOURNEMOUTH	9/4	4	13	52	D	0-0	0-0	12,861	(£2,732.11.0)		Ref: D Corbett
43	A	CARLISLE	16/4	5	1	53	D	1-1	0-0	16,069		Bush 52 / *Harland 62*	Ref: C Duxworthy
44	A	SHREWSBURY	19/4	4	15	55	W	5-1	1-1	5,857		Clark 4, Atyeo 50, 66, 70, 83 / *Boardman 23*	Ref: K Walker
45	H	SHREWSBURY	20/4	2	16	57	W	3-0	3-0	16,423	(£3,050.1.6)	Clark 4, Bush 12, Atyeo 32	Ref: G Davis
46	H	OLDHAM	24/4	2	20	59	W	2-0	1-0	28,248		Clark 45, Atyeo 83	Ref: E Jennings (£5,558.16.6)

Home Average 12,198 Away 8,583

Line-ups (City / opponents)

No	1	2	3	4	5	6	7	8	9	10	11
35	Gibson	Ford	Briggs	Drury	Connor	Low	Savino	Atyeo	Bush	Clark	Peters
	Brodie	*Hawley*	*Jones*	*Scott*	*Gelson*	*Higginson*	*Lazarus*	*Ward*	*Lawther*	*Cobb*	*Block*
36	Gibson	Ford	Briggs	Drury	Connor	Low	Savino	Atyeo	Bush	Clark	Peters
	Shearing	*Smyth*	*Patrick*	*Mitchell*	*Harvey*	*Anderson*	*Welsh*	*Carter*	*Curtis*	*Hancock*	*Thorne*
37	Gibson	Ford	Briggs	Drury	Connor	Low	Savino	Atyeo	Bush	Clark	Peters
	Wright	*Thompson*	*Taylor*	*Cockerill*	*Jobling*	*Clifton*	*Pennington*	*Allen*	*McLean*	*Foster*	*Hill*
38	Gibson	Ford	Briggs	Parr	Connor	Low	Savino	Atyeo	Bush	Clark	Hooper
	Tinsley	*Barton*	*Jardine*	*Gibson*	*Fincham*	*Reid*	*Pleat*	*McKechnie*	*O'Rouke*	*Phillips*	*Riach*
39	Gibson	Ford	Briggs	Drury	Connor	Low	Savino	Atyeo	Bush	Clark	Peters
	Treharne	*Jones*	*Humble*	*Hall*	*Gill*	*Morris*	*Gregson*	*Macready*	*Curry*	*Middleton*	*Scanlon*
40	Gibson	Ford	Briggs	Drury	Connor	Low	Savino	Atyeo	Bush	Clark	Peters
	Wright	*Thompson*	*Taylor*	*Cockerill*	*Jobling*	*Clifton*	*Haydock*	*Allen*	*McLean*	*Foster*	*Hill*
41	Gibson	Ford	Briggs	Drury	Connor	Low	Savino	Atyeo	Bush	Clark	Peters
	Duff	*Cooper*	*Crawford*	*Orr*	*Wright*	*Bennett*	*Conmy*	*Mouldon*	*Shields*	*Deakin*	*McNamee*
42	Gibson	Ford	Briggs	Drury	Connor	Low	Savino	Atyeo	Bush	Clark	Peters
	Best	*Keith*	*Coxon*	*Groves*	*Gater*	*Naylor*	*Bumstead*	*Hodgson*	*Coughlin*	*Archer*	*Crickmore*
43	Gibson	Ford	Briggs	Drury	Connor	Low	Savino	Atyeo	Bush	Clark	Peters
	Dean	*Neil*	*Caldwell*	*McConnell*	*Passmoor*	*Harland*	*Blain*	*Carlin*	*Large*	*Evans*	*Simpson*
44	Gibson	Ford	Briggs	Drury	Connor	Low	Savino	Atyeo	Bush	Clark	Peters
	Boswell	*Wright*	*Turner*	*Hemsley*	*Dolby*	*Harris*	*Meredith*	*Rowley*	*Ross*	*Boardman*	*Scott*
45	Gibson	Ford	Briggs	Drury	Connor	Derrick	Savino	Atyeo	Bush	Clark	Peters
	Boswell	*Wright*	*Turner*	*Hemsley*	*Dolby*	*Brodie*	*Meredith*	*Regan*	*Ross*	*Boardman*	*Taylor*
46	Gibson	Ford	Briggs	Drury	Connor	Low	Sharpe	Atyeo	Bush	Clark	Peters
	Swan	*Branagan*	*Martin*	*Bowie*	*Williams*	*Lawther*	*Ledger*	*McCall*	*Harris*	*Frizzell*	*Colquhoun*

Match reports

35 – Postponed in December, this long-awaited clash of the promotion candidates lives up to its pre-match billing. City's victory margin does them but scant justice as the Bees are outpaced after the break. Ford sends Chic Brodie the wrong way from the spot after Mel Scott floors Clark.

36 – Once City take the lead when Clark glides in Savino's corner, Exeter lose their earlier enthusiasm. Taking control, City should have added to their tally as Peters misses two easy chances and has an effort kicked off the line, whilst only a super save prevents Clark netting at the close.

37 – Terry Bush will never secure a luckier goal than the one he gets in this game. His attempted cross from near the corner-flag bounces onto the foot of a post before spinning just over the goal-line. Drury's firm shot makes sure of Grimsby surrendering their unbeaten home tag.

38 – Promotion jitters almost cost City this game. Struggling to get into their stride, City are saved by the fortunate award of a penalty when Gordon Fincham's header spins towards goal and strikes Ken Barton on the arm. Ford beats Colin Tinsley to maintain his perfect spot-kick record.

39 – City slide to defeat in the rain, snow and mud at Field Mill, but Fred Ford is of the opinion that his side still have a slight chance of promotion. An offside-looking Harry Middleton volleys in the opener, but no doubt over Bill Curry's close-range shot or Middleton's lashed in effort.

40 – Pay-night soccer pays off handsomely for City, for whom Atyeo's fine cross-drive completes an impressive display. Despite Graham Taylor, the Mariners full-back, deflecting a Peters cross into his own net, City boss Fred Ford asserts that the goal will be awarded to his left-winger.

41 – Bush's hammer-shot proves enough to win this incident-packed game for City. Both sides create many chances, but capable goalkeeping by Gibson and Willie Duff keeps the score down. Unfortunately, Hull, Gillingham and Mansfield all win to keep City out of the promotion frame.

42 – Despite the fact that the visitors are hardly ever in this game, City fail to turn their midfield superiority into goals. Unlucky when David Best parries Low's 25-yard drive onto a post, City are let down by poor wing supply and they are forced to play out their first goalless home game.

43 – With the loss of Savino suffering a broken leg just after they had taken the lead with Bush's well-taken goal, City do well to share the spoils in this important promotion clash. Gibson pulls off two stupendous saves to deny Carlisle after Stan Harland had stabbed in their messy equaliser.

44 – At half-time City are indebted to Gibson for keeping the scores level, but they are transformed after the break. Atyeo's side-foot flip sets up a goal-feast, but his third is the best of the night. Deftly flicking the ball over Peter Dolby on the edge of the area, he nips forward to volley in.

45 – Given the boost of Clark's soft opener, when his tame header finds the back of the net, City are brilliant in the first half. Bush's 12-yard power-packed drive and Atyeo firing in from Low's free-kick has the fans singing, but after the half-time interval Shrewsbury are able to take control.

46 – Much relief as Clark and Atyeo clinch City's promotion on goal-average from Mansfield. Clark glides home a Peters half-hit effort in first-half injury-time, but it takes Atyeo's shot into the Covered End net from the edge of the area, to calm the nerves prior to post-match celebrations.

CUP-TIES

Manager: Fred Ford

SEASON 1964-65

League Cup

		1	2	3	4	5	6	7	8	9	10	11	Scorers, Times, and Referees
2 A CARLISLE 23/9	10,055 10	Gibson	Ford	Briggs	Parr	Connor	Low	Derrick	Clark	Bush	Williams	Hooper	Hooper 37 /Brayton 24/ McIlmoyle 13, 34, Evans 17,
L 4 1-4 1-4		*Ross*	*Neil*	*Caldwell*	*McConnell*	*Passmoor*	*Harland*	*Brayton*	*Evans*	*McIlmoyle*	*Murray*	*Johnstone*	Ref: C Cooke

Quick-fire shooting brings lively Carlisle a well-deserved success. Connor, returning to his local roots, finds Hugh McIlmoyle a hot handful, though he looked offside when sweeping in the opener. A typical left-footed Hooper effort is City's only reply in this remarkably clean game.

FA Cup

		1	2	3	4	5	6	7	8	9	10	11	Scorers, Times, and Referees
1 H BRIGHTON 14/11	12,618 4:4 (£2,786)	Gibson	Ford	Briggs	Bush	Connor	Low	Savino	Clark	Atyeo	Sharpe	Peters	Savino 56
6 W 1-0 0-0		*Powney*	*Hopkins*	*Baxter*	*Bertolini*	*Gall*	*Turner*	*Gould*	*Collins*	*Smith R*	*Smith J*	*Goodchild*	Ref: D Lyden

Former England goal-grabbers Atyeo and Bobby Smith are so well marked that they only have one chance between them – Smith's twelfth-minute shot parried by Gibson - in this disappointing game. City just about deserved their success, courtesy of Savino's Open End screamer.

		1	2	3	4	5	6	7	8	9	10	11	Scorers, Times, and Referees
2 A BOURNEMOUTH 5/12	10,592 11 (£2,274)	Gibson	Ford	Briggs	Bush	Connor	Low	Savino	Clark	Atyeo	Sharpe	Peters	Clark 27, Sharpe 36, 42
4 W 3-0 3-0		*Best*	*Farmer*	*Keith*	*Standley*	*Gater*	*Bolton*	*Bumstead*	*O'Neil*	*Hodgson*	*Archer*	*Crickmore*	Ref: R Paine

Atyeo is the inspiration in what must be the result of the round as City win at Dean Court for the second successive week. On a wet, miserable afternoon, three great goals (Clark's drive, followed by Sharpe's unstoppable shot and a great header) has City in cruise mode after the break.

		1	2	3	4	5	6	7	8	9	10	11	Scorers, Times, and Referees
3 H SHEFFIELD UTD 9/1	20,091 1:14 (£4,599)	Gibson	Ford	Briggs	Bush	Connor	Low	Savino	Clark	Atyeo	Sharpe	Peters	Ford 76p
7 D 1-1 0-1		*Hodgkinson*	*Badger*	*Shaw G*	*Richardson*	*Shaw J*	*Matthewson*	*Woodward*	*Kettleborough*	*Jones*	*Birchenall*	*Hartle*	Jones 18 Ref: J Pickles

The Blades are lucky to survive after Mick Jones hooked them in front. City played them off the park after the break. Both sides are surprised when the referee rules out Savino's 84th-minute hammered in-off the bar effort. Poetic justice perhaps as United disputed City's penalty award.

		1	2	3	4	5	6	7	8	9	10	11	Scorers, Times, and Referees
3R A SHEFFIELD UTD 11/1	27,688 1:14 (£5,599)	Gibson	Ford	Briggs	Bush	Connor	Low	Savino	Clark	Atyeo	Williams	Hooper	Woodward 24, Jones 44, 75
7 L 0-3 0-2		*Hodgkinson*	*Badger*	*Shaw G*	*Richardson*	*Shaw J*	*Matthewson*	*Woodward*	*Kettleborough*	*Jones*	*Birchenall*	*Hartle*	Ref: J Pickles

Despite the scoreline this was a close match at Bramall Lane, where City spurn many easy chances. United's keeper is in top form with four great saves. Following Brian Woodward's left-footed opener, Mick Jones nets with a magnificent 30-yarder before finishing with a header.

Gloucestershire Cup

		1	2	3	4	5	6	7	8	9	10	11	Scorers, Times, and Referees
F A BRISTOL ROV 26/4	8,907 6	Gibson	Ford	Briggs	Parr	Connor	Low	Peters	Clark	Bush	Sharpe	Bartley	Bush 2, Clark 71
2 L 2-3 1-1		*Hall*	*Hilliard*	*Jones G*	*Oldfield*	*Davis*	*Mabbutt*	*Jarman*	*Brown*	*Jones R*	*Hamilton*	*Munro*	Parr 34 (og), Jones R 73, Hamilton 83 Ref: W Mardon

The Rovers, who had led the Third Division for more than half the season, gain small compensation for missing out on promotion by winning this closely fought encounter. Ian Hamilton, making a comeback after a cartilage operation, nips in smartly to slide the winner past Gibson.

League table

Pos	Team	P	Home W	D	L	F	A	Away W	D	L	F	A	Pts
1	Carlisle	46	14	5	4	46	24	11	5	7	30	29	60
2	BRISTOL C	46	14	6	3	53	18	10	5	8	39	37	59
3	Mansfield	46	17	4	2	61	23	7	7	9	34	38	59
4	Hull	46	14	6	3	51	25	9	6	8	40	32	58
5	Brentford	46	18	4	1	55	18	6	5	12	28	37	57
6	Bristol Rov	46	14	7	2	52	21	6	8	9	30	37	55
7	Gillingham	46	16	5	2	45	13	5	8	10	25	37	55
8	Peterborough	46	16	3	4	61	33	6	4	13	26	43	51
9	Watford	46	11	10	2	45	21	5	8	10	31	46	50
10	Grimsby	46	11	10	2	37	21	6	5	12	32	39	49
11	Bournemouth	46	12	4	7	40	24	5	9	9	30	47	47
12	Southend	46	14	4	5	48	24	4	6	13	25	44	46
13	Reading	46	14	4	5	45	26	4	6	13	24	57	46
14	QP Rangers	46	15	5	3	48	23	2	7	14	28	47	46
15	Workington	46	11	7	5	30	22	6	5	12	34	46	46
16	Shrewsbury	46	10	6	7	42	38	5	6	12	18	25	42
17	Exeter	46	8	7	8	33	27	5	8	10	23	45	41
18	Scunthorpe	46	9	8	6	42	27	4	6	13	21	44	40
19	Walsall	46	9	4	10	34	36	6	3	14	21	44	37
20	Oldham	46	10	5	8	40	39	3	5	15	21	44	36
21	Luton	46	6	8	9	32	36	5	3	15	19	58	33
22	Port Vale	46	7	6	10	27	33	4	4	15	14	43	32
23	Colchester	46	7	6	10	30	34	3	4	16	20	55	30
24	Barnsley	46	8	5	10	33	31	1	6	16	21	59	29
		1104	285	139	128	1030	637	128	139	285	637	1030	1104

Odds & ends

Double wins: (7) Barnsley, Walsall, Southend, Port Vale, Peterborough, Grimsby, Shrewsbury.
Double losses: (2) Hull, Gillingham.

Won from behind: (4) Port Vale (a), Barnsley (a), Walsall (a), Bristol Rov (h).
Lost from in front: (5) Scunthorpe (a), Hull (a), Brentford (a), Hull (h), Bristol Rov (a) (GC).

High spots: The win over Bristol Rovers on 13 February.
End of season run (one defeat in 15 games) that launched promotion.
The early season goal-glut with high-scoring wins over Barnsley, Walsall, Southend (twice) and Workington.
Winning at Bournemouth in League and Cup on successive Saturdays.
Beating Oldham at Ashton Gate to clinch promotion.

Low spots: The mid-season slump that included a 3-7 defeat at Oldham.
The 0-3 defeat at Mansfield on 20 March, ending seven straights wins.

AGM (Brecknell, Dolman & Rogers, Pennywell Road, 2 June 1966):
Profit £13,917.0s.0d. Season Ticket Sales £7,613.0s.0d.

Player of the year: John Atyeo & Brian Clark.
Ever-presents: (4) Brian Clark, Tony Ford, Mike Gibson, Gordon Low.
Hat-tricks: (5) John Atyeo (3), Brian Clark (2).
Leading scorer: Overall: Brian Clark (28). League: Brian Clark (24).

Appearances and Goals

Player	Appearances Lge	Cup	Goals Lge	Cup	Tot
Atyeo, John	38	4	23		23
Bartley, Danny		1			
Briggs, Alec	39	6			
Bush, Terry	37	6	16	1	17
Clark, Brian	46	6	24	2	26
Connor, Jack	43	6	3		3
Derrick, Jantzen	11	1			
Drury, Charles	16				
Ford, Tony	46	6	1		1
Gibson, Mike	46	6			
Hooper, Peter	7	2	5	1	6
Low, Gordon	46	6	1	1	2
Parr, Gordon	21	2	1		1
Peters, Roger	40	4	1		1
Savino, Ray	34	4	6		6
Sharpe, Gerry	13	4	1	1	2
Thresher, Mike	7				
Williams, Bobby	16	2	6	2	8
(own-goals)			4		4
18 players used	506	66	92	8	100

LEAGUE DIVISION 2 — Manager: Fred Ford — SEASON 1965-66

No	Date	V	Opponent	Att	Pos	Pt	F-A	H-T	1	2	3	4	5	6	7	8	9	10	11	12 sub used
1	21/8	H	ROTHERHAM	16,801 (£3,052.3.6)		W 2	2-1	1-1	Gibson	Ford	Briggs	Drury	Connor	Low	Peters	Atyeo	Bush	Clark	Hooper	Showell
			(opp)						Morritt	Wilcockson	Clish	Hardly	Madden	Tiler	Lyons	Chappell	Galley	Williams	Pring	
2	25/8	A	NORWICH	16,616		D 3	0-0	0-0	Gibson	Ford	Briggs	Drury	Connor	Low	Peters	Atyeo	Bush	Clark	Hooper	Showell
			(opp)						Keelan	Sharpe	Mullett	Lucas	Butler	Allcock	Anderson	Bolland	Davies	Bryceland	Punton	
3	28/8	A	MANCHESTER C	19,349	7	D 4	2-2	2-0	Gibson	Ford	Briggs	Drury	Connor	Low	Peters	Atyeo*	Bush	Clark	Hooper	Showell
			(opp)						Dowd	Bacuzzi	Connor	Doyle	Cheetham	Oakes	Summerbee	Crossan	Murray	Brand	Pardoe	
4	31/8	H	NORWICH	15,737 (£2,795.16.0)	12	D 5	0-0	0-0	Gibson	Ford	Briggs	Drury	Connor	Low	Peters	Sharpe	Bush	Clark	Hooper	Bolland
			(opp)						Keelan	Stringer	Mullett	Lucas	Butler	Allcock	Anderson*	Bryceland	Davies	Sutton	Punton	
5	4/9	H	HUDDERSFIELD	15,704 (£2,843.17.6)	2	W 7	2-1	1-1	Gibson	Ford*	Briggs	Drury	Connor	Low	Peters	Sharpe	Bush	Clark	Hooper	Showell
			(opp)						Oldfield	Atkins	McNab	Nicholson	Coddington	Meagan	McHale	Massie	Gilliver	Quigley	O'Grady	
6	7/9	A	BURY	6,331	19	W 9	2-1	0-0	Gibson	Showell	Briggs	Drury	Connor	Low	Peters	Sharpe	Bush	Clark	Hooper	Thomas
			(opp)						Harker	Bray	Eastham	Colquhoun	Clunie	Lindsay	Henderson	Maltby	Pointer	Bell	Parry*	
7	11/9	H	COVENTRY	19,887 (£3,881.5.0)	8	D 10	1-1	1-0	Gibson	Showell	Briggs	Drury	Connor	Low	Peters	Sharpe	Bush*	Clark	Hooper	Derrick
			(opp)						Wesson	Kearns	Harris	Bruck	Curtis	Hill	Rees	Hale	Hudson	Machin	Clements	
8	17/9	A	CARLISLE	10,694	7	L 10	0-5	0-1	Gibson	Ford	Briggs	Drury	Connor	Low	Peters	Sharpe	Atyeo	Clark	Hooper	Livingstone
			(opp)						Dean	Neil	Green	McConnell	Passmoor	Harland	Blain	Evans	Large*	Balderstone	Simpson	
9	25/9	H	CARDIFF	15,300 (£2,884.3.6)	16	D 11	1-1	0-0	Gibson	Ford	Briggs	Drury	Showell	Low	Derrick	Clark	Atyeo	Sharpe	Peters	Charles
			(opp)						John	Rodrigues	Baker	Coldrick	Murray	Hole	Johnston	King	Williams	Harkin*	Lewis	
10	2/10	A	DERBY	11,012	20	L 11	1-2	0-1	Gibson	Ford	Briggs	Parr	Low	Drury	Derrick	Clark	Atyeo	Sharpe	Peters	
			(opp)						Matthews	Richardson	Daniel	Webster	Saxton	Upton	Hughes	Thomas	Burton	Durban	Hodgson	

Scorers, Times, and Referees

1. Atyeo 28, Hooper 50; Williams 2; Ref: E Jennings
2. Ref: P Bye
3. Atyeo 22, Drury 42; Brand 46, Gibson 53 (og); Ref: W Handley
4. Ref: D Corbett
5. Bush 42, Peters 62; Nicholson 32; Ref: W Clements
6. Sharpe 62, 87; Bell 47; Ref: W Holian
7. Bush 16; Connor 63 (og); Ref: H Richards
8. [Livingstone 65, 67, Blain 76] Harland 13, Balderstone 52; Ref: D Pritchard
9. Atyeo 47; Lewis 70; Ref: J Pickles
10. Peters 64; Thomas 4, Hughes 60; Ref: K Seddon

Match reports

1. After Bobby Williams, playing only his third game for the Millers since his £9,500 move from City, opens the scoring with a 20-yarder, City make hard work pay against more skilful opponents. Atyeo blasts in an equaliser, before Hooper wins the game with his 30-yard thunderbolt.

2. Gibson is City's saviour at Carrow Road, where he pulls off two point-blank saves in the space of a minute after the break when Norwich are on the rampage. City are well worthy of a draw, however, as they should have scored in the first half when the Canaries were often outplayed.

3. Atyeo hammers spirited City ahead, and shortly before half-time Mike Doyle increases their advantage by inadvertently helping Drury's shot over the line. Ralph Brand's bullet header gets the Blues back in the game, before Gibson fists the ball into his own net to gift them a point.

4. In contrast to last week's thriller, this contest is a dreary affair, the only notable event being when Gordon Bolland becomes the first Ashton Gate substitute when Terry Anderson limps off. Despite the presence of £35,000 Ron Davies, the Canaries only manage one real shot on target.

5. City stage a stunning fight-back to topple the skilful leaders from their perch. Gibson is partially to blame for letting Jim Nicholson's softish shot bounce through his arms, but a thundering 30-yarder from Peters brings due reward for City's great team-work, energy and enthusiasm.

6. A couple of Denis Law-class goals from Sharpe – ten now in ten away games since his debut – brings City the points thanks to their quick counter-attacking. The sparsely built youngster might have claimed a hat-trick, but the referee strangely disallowed a first-half header.

7. After Bush puts City ahead with a brilliant 20-yard shot on the turn, it seems as though the Robins defence would be able to contain the Sky Blues attack, but star man Connor errs. Attempting to blast the ball away for corner, his full-blooded drive ends up in the corner of his own net.

8. City, for whom Clark has his first-half free-kick equaliser disallowed for offside, surrender their unbeaten tag. Joe Livingstone, replacing the injured Frank Large on 23 minutes, announces his arrival by hitting a post, before registering with a back-heel and a header after the break.

9. Coming on without permission as a 73rd-minute substitute, soccer great John Charles is lectured by the referee and City awarded a free-kick. The only thing missing from this superb City display is their finishing. Many chances are spurned and Sharpe twice fires against an upright.

10. With Edward Thomas firing wide from the spot, after Low had foolishly handled, City are fortunate to be trailing by only one goal at the break. After the interval, though, it is a different tale as, inspired by Derrick, who lays on the cross for Peters to head in, City should have drawn level.

Bristol City — Match records 11–21

11. 9/10 — A CRYSTAL PALACE — Pos 13 — **L 1-2** (HT 1-0) — Att 16,356 — (5 / 11 pts)
Scorers: Clark 1 — Lawson 60, Kevan 85. Ref: L Hamer
City: Gibson, Ford, Briggs, Drury, Connor, Low*, Derrick, Clark, Atyeo, Sharpe, Peters, Bush
Palace: Jackson, Long*, Howe, Payne, Stephenson, Bannister, Woods, Whitehouse, Lawson, Kevan, Kellard, Yard
No luck for City in this rough 96-minute affair. Atyeo is denied a penalty when John Jackson grabs his legs, whilst Derek Kevan's winner is allowed to stand despite him fouling Gibson. Worst of all is the disallowing of Clark's 92nd-minute effort after being originally awarded.

12. 16/10 — H PRESTON — Pos 10 — **W 1-0** (HT 0-0) — Att 15,583 — (8 / 13 pts) — (£2,834.15.6)
Scorers: Bush 84. Ref: L Callaghan
City: Gibson, Ford, Briggs, Drury, Connor, Low, Derrick, Clark, Atyeo, Sharpe, Peters, Bush
Preston: Kelly, Ross, Donnelly, Lawton, Cranston, Kendall, Wilson, Ashworth, Dawson, Godfrey, Watt, Peters
Superbly marshalled by centre-half Connor, City clearly demonstrate that they possess one of the Division's best defences. In attack Derrick is in good form, but it takes Bush's mis-hit effort, spinning into the Covered End net from the left-wing corner flag, to clinch a deserved victory.

13. 23/10 — A CHARLTON — Pos 8 — **W 4-1** (HT 0-0) — Att 11,315 — (15 / 15 pts)
Scorers: Atyeo 58, Clark 72, 83, Peters 89 — Campbell 81. Ref: K Dagnall
City: Gibson, Ford, Briggs, Drury, Connor, Low, Derrick, Clark, Atyeo, Sharpe, Peters, Bush
Charlton: Jones, Bonds, Hewie, Bailey, Haydock, Tocknell, Kenning, Campbell, Saunders, Peacock, Glover
With doubts over Gibson's fitness, City have young keeper Macey as substitute at the Valley. At last City get the goals that their play has deserved, but strange that it should happen against erstwhile hoodoo side Charlton. Atyeo's 300th League goal sets City on the victory path.

14. 30/10 — H PLYMOUTH — Pos 8 — **D 0-0** (HT 0-0) — Att 17,533 — (16 / 16 pts) — (£3,437.14.6)
Ref: D Lyden
City: Gibson, Ford, Briggs, Drury, Connor, Low, Derrick, Clark, Atyeo, Sharpe, Peters, Bush
Plymouth: Leiper, Book, Baird, Williams, Nelson, Hore, Jones, Newman, Lord, Trebilcock, Jennings
Argyle's skill and City's stamina produce one of the best goal-less draws for a long while. Bush misses City's best chance by shooting wide of an open goal on 23 minutes, but the enterprising display of the visitors, with three teenagers in their side, should have brought them full points.

15. 6/11 — A PORTSMOUTH — Pos 6 — **W 4-2** (HT 2-1) — Att 15,748 — (8 / 18 pts)
Scorers: Ford 4p, Bush 35, Atyeo 75, 77 — McClelland 8, McCann 49. Ref: T Dawes
City: Gibson, Ford, Briggs, Drury, Connor, Low, Derrick, Clark, Atyeo, Sharpe, Peters, Bush
Portsmouth: Armstrong, Wilson, Tindall, Gordon, Harris, Campbell, Barton, Lewis, Hiron, McCann, McClelland
City boss Ford perseveres with the forward line that was subjected to much criticism last week and they respond with this demolition of proud Pompey. Bush's cleverly clipped in effort gives City the half-time advantage and Atyeo's two beautifully taken goals clinch a deserved victory.

16. 13/11 — H BOLTON — Pos 7 — **D 2-2** (HT 1-1) — Att 19,912 — (11 / 19 pts) — (£3,792.19.6)
Scorers: Atyeo 37, Clark 65 — Ford 15 (og), Davies 58. Ref: H New
City: Gibson, Ford, Briggs, Drury*, Connor, Low, Derrick, Clark, Atyeo, Sharpe, Peters, Bush
Bolton: Hopkinson, Hartle, Farrimond, Rimmer, Napier, Hatton, Butler, Hill, Davies, Bromley, Taylor, Sharpe
City shrug off their Ashton Gate blues and show their fans the composed, relaxed football that has typified most of their away games this season. Unfortunately, they fail to win as their normally cast-iron defence twice falters to present the Trotters with a share of the spoils.

17. 20/11 — A IPSWICH — Pos 7 — **D 0-0** (HT 0-0) — Att 8,939 — (15 / 20 pts)
Ref: D Wells
City: Gibson, Ford, Briggs, Parr, Connor, Low, Derrick, Clark, Atyeo, Sharpe, Peters, Bush
Ipswich: Hancock, Smith, McNeil, Lea, Baxter, Thompson, Hegan, Walsh, Brogan, Baker, Spearitt
City pay Gibson something like £1,500 per year to stop sides scoring goals. At Portman Road he gives full value as City gain a point thanks to his stirring efforts. Briggs also deserves much praise for clearing the ball off the goal-line on the two occasions that his goalkeeper is beaten.

18. 27/11 — H BIRMINGHAM — Pos 7 — **W 2-0** (HT 0-0) — Att 13,727 — (21 / 22 pts) — (£2,446.1.6)
Scorers: Low 53, Peters 73. Ref: E Wallace
City: Gibson, Ford, Briggs, Parr, Connor, Low, Derrick, Clark, Atyeo, Sharpe, Peters, Bush
Birmingham: Herriot, Green, Martin, Wylie, Foster, Beard, Hockey, Jackson, Fenton, Vowden, Thwaites
The man the fans love to hate unleashes one of the season's best shots to wake City up against the relegation haunted Blues. Low's powerful shot, from Bush's short free-kick, travels 30 yards into the top corner of the net, and that, as far as Birmingham are concerned, is that.

19. 4/12 — A LEYTON ORIENT — Pos 5 — **W 4-0** (HT 2-0) — Att 5,549 — (22 / 24 pts)
Scorers: Atyeo 20, Clark 44, 80, 85. Ref: G Roper
City: Gibson, Ford, Briggs, Parr, Connor, Low, Derrick, Clark, Atyeo, Sharpe, Peters, Bush
Orient: Rouse, Webb, Worrell, Sorrell, Ferry, Allen, Musgrove, Shaw, Flatt, Smith, Elwood
In the quagmire conditions at Brisbane Road, City are in scintillating form against struggling Orient. Quite a day for Clark who, after his cross-shot is diverted in by Atyeo, notches a hat-trick with a stirring run into the penalty area, a climbing header and a ferocious left-footed drive.

20. 11/12 — H MIDDLESBROUGH — Pos 6 — **D 2-2** (HT 0-0) — Att 16,086 — (19 / 25 pts) — (£2,907.9.0)
Scorers: Clark 52, Low 83 — Irvine 66, Holliday 71. Ref: P Brandwood
City: Gibson, Ford, Briggs, Parr, Connor, Low, Derrick, Clark, Atyeo, Sharpe, Peters, Bush
Middlesbrough: McPartland, Gates, Jones, Anderson, Rooks, Davidson, Ratcliffe*, McMordie, Irvine, Gibson, Holliday, Townsend
City are denied by debutant keeper Des McPartland in the first half as they produce the finest display of attacking football at the Gate in many years. Following the break, Peters is denied by a questionable offside decision, but Clark soon hammers in City's valid opener.

21. 18/12 — A PRESTON — Pos 5 — **D 1-1** (HT 0-0) — Att 10,766 — (9 / 26 pts)
Scorers: Atyeo 53 — Kendall 83. Ref: H Hackney
City: Gibson, Ford, Briggs, Parr, Connor, Low, Derrick, Clark, Atyeo, Sharpe, Peters, Bush
Preston: Barton, Ross, Smith, Kendall, Singleton, Lapet, Singleton, Hannigan, Wilson, Greenhaigh, Spavin, Lee
Mild City protests follow Howard Kendall's scuffled equaliser, but City keeper Gibson admits after the game that the goal was perfectly valid. In this entertaining tussle in the Deepdale mud, Atyeo, unfortunate not to be awarded a penalty when hauled down, nudges in City's goal.

LEAGUE DIVISION 2

Manager: Fred Ford **SEASON 1965-66**

Match details (City line-up shown first, opponents in italics; *Pos* = City league position, opponent position in brackets; Res = result; Pt = cumulative points):

No	Date	V	Opponent	Att (Receipts)	Pos	Res	Pt	F-A	H-T	1	2	3	4	5	6	7	8	9	10	11	12 sub used
22	27/12	A	WOLVERHAMPTON	32,526	6 (4)	D	27	1-1	0-0	Gibson	Ford	Briggs	Parr	Connor	Low	Savino	Atyeo	Bush	Clark	Peters	Bartley
										Davies	*Wilson*	*Thomson*	*Woodruff*	*Woodfield*	*Holsgrove*	*Wharton*	*Hunt*	*McIlmoyle*	*Knowles*	*Buckley*	
23	28/12	H	WOLVERHAMPTON	36,184 (£7,302.15.0)	6 (4)	L	27	0-1	0-0	Gibson	Ford	Briggs	Parr*	Connor	Low	Sharpe	Atyeo	Bush	Clark	Peters	Bartley
										Davies	*Wilson*	*Thomson*	*Woodruff*	*Woodfield*	*Holsgrove*	*Wharton*	*Hunt*	*McIlmoyle*	*Knowles*	*Buckley*	
24	1/1	H	CRYSTAL PALACE	16,428 (£3,056.15.6)	6 (10)	D	28	1-1	1-1	Gibson	Showell	Briggs	Drury	Connor	Low	Derrick	Atyeo	Bush	Clark	Peters	*Burnside*
										Jackson	*Sewell*	*Woods*	*Long*	*Stephenson*	*Whitehouse*	*Kember*	*Smith*	*Cutler*	*Payne*	*Yard**	
25	8/1	A	BOLTON	10,405	5 (16)	W	30	2-1	0-0	Gibson	Ford	Briggs	Drury	Connor	Low	Derrick	Atyeo	Bush	Clark	Peters	
										Hopkinson	*Hartle*	*Farrimond*	*Rimmer*	*Napier*	*Hatton*	*Lee*	*Bromley*	*Davies*	*Hill*	*Taylor*	
26	29/1	A	ROTHERHAM	10,667	5 (8)	W	32	2-1	2-0	Gibson	Ford	Briggs	Drury	Connor*	Low	Savino	Atyeo	Derrick	Clark	Peters	
										Jones	*Wilcockson*	*Clish*	*Rabjohn*	*Haselden*	*Tiler*	*Lyons*	*Chappell*	*Galley*	*Casper*	*Pring*	
27	5/2	H	MANCHESTER C	25,723 (£5,153.7.0)	6 (1)	D	33	1-1	1-1	Gibson	Ford	Briggs	Drury	Connor*	Low	Savino	Atyeo	Derrick	Clark	Peters	Showell
										Dowd	*Kennedy*	*Sear*	*Doyle*	*Heslop*	*Oakes*	*Summerbee*	*Crossan*	*Pardoe*	*Young*	*Connor*	
28	11/2	H	BURY	18,363 (£3,439.13.0)	4 (19)	W	35	2-1	1-0	Gibson	Ford	Briggs	Drury	Showell	Low	Savino	Atyeo	Derrick	Clark	Peters	
										Ramsbottom	*Turner*	*Leech*	*Atherton*	*Colquhoun*	*Parry*	*Lowes*	*Bell*	*Maltby*	*Kerr*	*Claxton*	
29	19/2	A	HUDDERSFIELD	18,544	6 (2)	L	35	0-3	0-3	Gibson	Ford	Briggs	Drury	Showell	Low	Savino	Atyeo	Derrick	Clark	Peters	*Meagan*
										Oldfield	*Atkins*	*McNab*	*Nicholson*	*Coddington*	*Dinsdale*	*Smith*	*Massie*	*Weston*	*Quigley*	*McHale**	
30	26/2	A	COVENTRY	30,089	6 (3)	D	36	2-2	1-1	Gibson	Ford	Briggs	Drury	Showell	Low	Savino	Atyeo	Derrick*	Clark	Peters	Parr
										Wesson	*Kearns*	*Harris*	*Bruck*	*Curtis*	*Farmer*	*Rees*	*Pointer*	*Hudson*	*Machin*	*Clements*	
31	5/3	A	MIDDLESBROUGH	13,744	6 (17)	L	36	2-4	0-3	Gibson	Ford	Briggs	Drury	Showell	Parr	Savino	Atyeo	Derrick	Clark	Peters	*Braithwaite Smith*
										McPartland	*Chapman*	*Jones*	*Horner**	*Gates*	*Anderson*	*Downing*	*Smith*	*Gibson*	*Rooks*	*Irvine*	

Scorers, Times, and Referees

- **22** — Atyeo 78; *Buckley 60*. Ref: L Faulkner
- **23** — *Knowles 79*. Ref: J Finney
- **24** — Clark 30; *Long 22*. Ref: K Burns
- **25** — Peters 78, Atyeo 88; *Lee 77p*. Ref: V James
- **26** — Clark 11, Derrick 36; *Connor 56 (og)*. Ref: S Kayley
- **27** — Clark 26; *Young 8*. Ref: E Jennings
- **28** — Atyeo 36, Peters 67; *Maltby 81*. Ref: P Bye
- **29** — *Coddington 8p, Weston 24, 36*. Ref: J Parkinson
- **30** — Atyeo 21, 72; *Pointer 22, Hudson 75*. Ref: R Egan
- **31** — Atyeo 57, 61; *Irvine 12, 30, Gibson 29, Rooks 64*. Ref: J Bullough

Match reports

- **22** — City's full-blooded defenders risk all to keep out Wolves on the frost-covered pitch, but can do nothing when Pat Buckley steers in the opener when Gibson pushed out the winger's powerful five-yard header. Fortunately, Atyeo's gentle header brings City a well-deserved point.
- **23** — On the night the new floodlights are switched on, City look well capable of winning this game until the loss of Parr, with a broken nose on 35 minutes. Wolves take charge and Peter Knowles' cross-shot from the right, touched in by Ford, deprives City of their unbeaten home record.
- **24** — City, the shock team in the Division, badly needed a skilful midfielder in this match, especially as much of their normal endeavour is missing. Clark's stab-in equalises Terry Long's close-range goal, but City are somewhat lucky to hang onto a point as the Palace are the better side.
- **25** — Atyeo's winner, deftly turning to meet Drury's header on the half-volley and send the ball sweetly into the corner of the net, makes City the division's best away side. The award of a dubious penalty brings Bolton their score, but Peters immediately responds with a searing drive.
- **26** — Derrick is City's star in his deep-lying centre-forward role. Distributing passes like confetti, he climaxes a great performance with a superb solo run and searing drive for his first goal of the season. Unfortunately, it is his clearance that strikes Connor to zoom in for an own-goal.
- **27** — In front of the *Match of the Day* cameras, City's poor passing lets them down in this top of the table clash. Neil Young's cracking shot gives the visitors an early lead, but Clark soon heads in a fine equaliser from Savino's cross. Atyeo shoots wide when clean through after the interval.
- **28** — This match, postponed on 14th September because of City's new floodlights not being ready, is worth the wait. Bury play football with a flourish in midfield, but their long-range shooting rarely troubles City. In a game of many squandered chances, Atyeo turns in City's opener.
- **29** — City give one of their worst displays of the season after Low needlessly handles to gift Huddersfield their penalty opener. Whilst there is a suspicion of offside about the second goal after Low loses possession, Gibson should have cut out the centre which leads to the third.
- **30** — Despite injuries to three key players, forcing Fred Ford to play Low at inside-left, City seldom resemble even an average League Two side. Low's passes lead to both of Atyeo's goals. The blustery wind causes the keepers difficulties and both Coventry's equalisers follow corners.
- **31** — Against opponents still facing the threat of relegation, City's two goals in a four-minute spell raise hopes of a fight-back, but Dickie Rooks soon changes that. He rises to a fantastic height to head in the game's final goal.

No		Opponent	Date	Pos	Res	Score	HT		Pts	Attendance	Receipts	Scorers	Referee
32	H	CARLISLE	12/3	5	W	2-0	1-0	19	38	14,724	(£2,589.11.6)	Clark 25, Sharpe 58	H Davies
33	A	CARDIFF	18/3	6	L	1-2	0-2	16	38	13,405	(£1,938.5.0)	Clark 82 / King 15, Toshack 40	W Handley
34	H	DERBY	25/3	5	D	1-1	1-1	8	39	13,614	(£2,398.3.0)	Atyeo 15 / Thomas 33	A Weller
35	H	PORTSMOUTH	2/4	5	W	1-0	1-0	16	41	11,804	(£1,938.5.0)	Lewis 27 (og)	C Duxbury
36	H	SOUTHAMPTON	8/4	6	L	0-1	0-1	5	41	25,106	(£4,917.3.0)	Connor 13 (og)	W Clements
37	A	PLYMOUTH	9/4	5	W	2-0	1-0	13	43	15,435		Clark 30, Bush 55	R Pritchard
38	A	SOUTHAMPTON	11/4	5	D	2-2	1-1	6	44	23,120		Sharpe 37, Ford 61p / Channon 33, Paine 90	N Burtenshaw
39	A	BIRMINGHAM	22/4	6	W	3-1	2-0	11	46	11,732		Clark 21, Sharpe 42, 77 / Beard 61p	A Jones
40	H	LEYTON ORIENT	30/4	6	W	2-0	0-0	22	48	10,649	(£1,695.9.6)	Bush 61, 80	H Davey
41	H	CHARLTON	3/5	6	D	0-0	0-0	18	49	10,478	(£1,685.13.6)		G Gow
42	H	IPSWICH	10/5	5	W	4-1	1-1	15	51	13,893	(£2,452.0.0)	Bush 17, Parr 88, Atyeo 75, 84 / Crawford 10	K Burns

Home Average 17,297   Away 14,873

Line-ups (City / Opposition):

32 Carlisle — Gibson, Ford, Briggs, Drury, Connor, Low, Peters, Clark, Atyeo, Sharpe, Bartley / Dean, Neil, Caldwell, McConnell, Passmoor, Harland, Welsh, Wilson, Livingstone, Carlin, Balderstone

33 Cardiff — Gibson, Ford, Briggs, Drury, Connor, Low, Peters, Clark, Atyeo, Sharpe, Bartley / John, Carver, Ferguson, Williams, Coldrick, Hole, Farrell, Andrews, Toshack, Johnston, King

34 Derby — Gibson, Ford, Briggs, Drury, Connor, Low, Derrick, Clark, Atyeo, Sharpe, Peters / Matthews, Richardson, Daniel, Webster, Saxton, Upton, Hughes, Thomas, Burton, Durban, Bowers

35 Portsmouth — Gibson, Ford, Briggs, Parr, Connor, Low, Derrick, Clark, Atyeo, Sharpe, Bartley / Milkins, Wilson, Tindall, Gordon, Haydock, Lewis, McClelland, Portwood, Hiron, McCann, Kellard

36 Southampton — Gibson, Ford, Briggs, Drury, Connor, Low, Derrick, Clark, Atyeo, Sharpe, Peters / Forsyth, Webb, Hollywood, White, Knapp, Huxford, Paine, Chivers*, Spencer, Melia, Williams

37 Plymouth — Gibson, Ford, Briggs, Drury, Connor, Low, Derrick, Clark, Bush, Bartley, Sharpe / Leiper, Book, Baird, Williams, Nelson, Newman, Corbett, Jones, Bickle, Piper, Jennings

38 Southampton — Gibson, Ford, Briggs, Parr, Connor, Low, Derrick, Clark, Bush, Sharpe, Sydenham / Forsyth, Webb, Hollywood, White, Knapp, Huxford, Paine, Channon, Spencer*, Melia, Williams

39 Birmingham — Gibson, Ford, Briggs, Parr, Connor, Low, Derrick, Clark, Bush, Sharpe, Sydenham / Herriot, Fraser, Martin, Wyllie, Foster, Beard, Jackson, Vincent, Fenton, Vowden, Hockey*, Thomson

40 Leyton Orient — Gibson, Ford, Briggs, Parr, Connor, Low, Derrick, Clark, Bush, Sharpe, Jenkins / Rouse, Jones, Worrell, Allen, Ferry, Sorrell, Price, Carter, Smith, Metchick*, Went

41 Charlton — Gibson, Ford, Briggs, Parr, Connor, Low, Derrick, Clark, Bush, Sharpe, Bartley / Wright, Bonds, Whitehouse, Burridge, Holton, Snedden, Kenning, Myers, Matthews, Halom, Peacock

42 Ipswich — Gibson, Ford, Briggs, Parr, Connor, Low, Derrick, Clark, Atyeo, Clark, Bartley / Hancock, Mills, Bolton J, Harper, Baxter, Bolton R, Spearitt, Hegan, Crawford, Baker, Brogan

Match reports:

32 Bartley gives one of the most productive wing performances by a City player this season, but despite laying on many chances, home fans have to be satisfied with just two goals. Sharpe nets for the first time at Ashton, whilst Low wastes an indirect free-kick when shooting directly in.

33 City stage a terrific finale after Clark snaps up a rebound following Ford's drive. Unfortunately, the damage had been done in the first half with Peter King's magnificent shot (his first goal of the season) and John Toshack expertly stroking in Dave Carver's free-kick to double the deficit.

34 If Atyeo continues to play with such determination and score such superb goals as in this game, then his planned retirement at the end of the season is premature. After his brilliant header puts City in front, he is denied five minutes later by Reg Matthews brilliantly saving his volley.

35 On a cold and windy afternoon, the fans who decided to give this fixture a miss must have had a premonition. This was one of the dullest games in a long while, a scrappy, scratchy and often-shoddy exhibition settled by Brian Lewis slicing Derrick's low centre into his own net.

36 To City the honour and the glory, but, unfortunately, not the points in this thrill-a-second contest. A one-sided second half has So'ton clinging on nervously to Connor's diverted own-goal, but City are denied by many goal-line clearances as well as the dominant play of Tony Knapp.

37 Fortunate to survive when Nick Jennings fires against a post with a fine cross-shot, Clark hits home for City from ten yards not long after. Playing attractive football and captained by Low in Atyeo's absence, City make sure of victory when Bush heads in from Bartley's centre.

38 Terry Paine's 20-yarder in the third minute of injury-time prevents City recording a deserved win. Sharpe races clear to slot in yellow-shirted City's equaliser to debutant Mick Channon's opener. Dennis Hollywood's use of an arm to keep out Atyeo's header gives Ford his spot-kick.

39 This stirring exhibition in the St Andrew's mud confirms City as the best away side in the Second Division. A pity therefore that home form has cost them a promotion position. Clark seizes on James Herriot's poor goal-kick and rounds the advancing keeper to steer in City's opener.

40 A shocker of a game against an Orient side only playing out their fixtures before starting next season in the Third Division. Apart from the usual touches of genius from Derrick, there is little to enthuse over. Two goals from Bush allow City to record their fifth double of the season.

41 For those with an interest in the tactical methods and strategies, which have now infiltrated the game, Charlton's negative defensive policy is intriguing. Frustration for the fans as Charlton escape with a point from a one-sided contest which sees City having 90% or more of possession.

42 After all the pre-match hype about Atyeo's last game, the two goals he requires to raise his total in League and Cup to 350 take a long time in coming. His first is obtained with a faint touch of his forehead to an inswinging corner, whilst a firm shot makes the second more satisfactory.

CUP-TIES

Manager: Fred Ford

SEASON 1965-66

League Cup

				F-A	H-T	Scorers, Times, and Referees	1	2	3	4	5	6	7	8	9	10	11	12 sub used
2	A	SHREWSBURY	10 L	0-1	0-1	Clarke 8	Gibson	Ford	Briggs	Drury	Connor	Low	Derrick	Clark	Bush	Sharpe	Peters	
		7,158 3:10				Ref: L Faulkner	*Boswell*	*Wright*	*Fellows*	*Hemsley*	*Brodie*	*Harris*	*Meredith*	*Regan*	*Clarke*	*Boardman*	*Broadbent*	

Only the referee fails to spot Geoff Fellows acting as goalkeeper, making a magnificent somersaulting leap to fist out Clark's 73rd-minute header. Shrewsbury, therefore, progress through to the next round, thanks to Frank Clarke's gentle header from Eric Brodie's free-kick.

FA Cup

				F-A	H-T	Scorers, Times, and Referees	1	2	3	4	5	6	7	8	9	10	11	12 sub used
3	A	BIRMINGHAM	5 L	2-3	1-1	Bush 35, Low 54	Gibson	Ford	Briggs	Drury	Connor	Low	Derrick	Atyeo	Bush	Clark	Peters	
		24,340 12				*Vowden 23, 47, Thomson 73*	*Herriot*	*Fraser*	*Martin*	*Wyllie*	*Foster*	*Beard*	*Hockey*	*Jackson*	*Thomson*	*Vowden*	*Thwaites*	
						Ref: E Crawford												

A thrilling contest on an icy St Andrew's pitch, where mistakes bring Birmingham their three superbly taken goals. After first Bush, and then Low, equalise, City play brilliantly. They slice through the Blues defence with much verve, before Derrick fatally loses the ball in midfield.

Gloucestershire Cup

				F-A	H-T	Scorers, Times, and Referees	1	2	3	4	5	6	7	8	9	10	11	12 sub used
F	H	BRISTOL ROV	5 L	0-1	0-1	Jarman 17	Gibson	Ford	Briggs	Parr	Connor	Low	Derrick	Bush	Clark	Sharpe	Bartley	
		9,431 3:16				Ref: D Smith	*Hall*	*Hillard*	*Davis*	*Petts*	*Taylor*	*Mabbutt*	*Jarman*	*Frude*	*Biggs*	*Ronaldson*	*Jones R*	

Harold Jarman's savage long-range drive proves enough for Rovers to retain possession of the County trophy. City's attack is often laboured and unimaginative, though two good second-half chances are thwarted by goalkeeper Bernard Hall. Most of the play is confined to midfield.

		P	W	D	L	F	A	W	D	L	F	A	Pts
				Home						Away			
1	Manchester C	42	14	7	0	40	14	8	8	5	36	30	59
2	Southampton	42	13	4	4	51	25	8	6	6	34	31	54
3	Coventry	42	14	5	2	54	31	6	8	7	19	22	53
4	Huddersfield	42	12	7	2	35	12	7	6	8	27	24	51
5	BRISTOL C	42	9	10	2	27	15	8	7	6	36	33	51
6	Wolves	42	15	4	2	52	18	5	6	10	35	43	50
7	Rotherham	42	12	6	3	48	29	4	8	9	27	45	46
8	Derby	42	13	2	6	48	31	3	9	9	23	37	43
9	Bolton	42	12	2	7	43	25	4	7	10	19	34	41
10	Birmingham	42	10	6	5	41	29	6	3	12	29	46	41
11	Crys Palace	42	11	7	3	29	16	3	6	12	18	36	41
12	Portsmouth	42	13	4	4	47	26	3	4	14	27	52	40
13	Norwich	42	8	7	6	33	27	4	8	9	19	25	39
14	Carlisle	42	16	2	3	43	19	1	3	17	17	44	39
15	Ipswich	42	12	6	3	38	23	3	3	15	20	43	39
16	Charlton	42	10	6	5	39	29	4	5	12	22	41	38
17	Preston	42	7	10	4	37	23	4	5	11	25	47	37
18	Plymouth	42	7	8	6	37	26	5	5	11	17	37	37
19	Bury	42	12	5	4	45	25	2	2	17	17	51	35
20	Cardiff	42	10	3	8	37	35	2	7	12	34	56	34
21	Middlesboro	42	8	8	5	36	28	2	5	14	22	58	33
22	Leyton Orient	42	3	9	9	19	36	2	4	15	19	44	23
		924	241	128	93	879	542	93	128	241	542	879	924

Appearances / Goals

	Appearances				Goals		
	Lge	Sub	Cup	Sub	Lge	Cup	Tot
Atyeo, John	35				19		19
Bartley, Danny	8	1			1		
Briggs, Alec	40		3				
Bush, Terry	26	1	3		8	1	9
Clark, Brian	42		3		15		15
Connor, Jack	36		3				
Derrick, Jantzen	27	1	3		1		1
Drury, Charles	28		2		1		1
Ford, Tony	40		3		2		2
Gibson, Mike	42		3				
Hooper, Peter	9				1		1
Low, Gordon	42		3		2	1	3
Parr, Gordon	17	1	1		1		1
Peters, Roger	35		2		6		6
Savino, Ray	8						
Sharpe, Gerry	18	1	2		6		6
Showell, George	9	3					
(own-goals)					1		1
17 players used	462	8	33		63	2	65

Odds & ends

Double wins: (4) Rotherham, Bury, Portsmouth, Birmingham, Orient.

Double losses: (0).

Won from behind: (5) Rotherham (h), Huddersfield (h), Bury (a), Bolton (a), Ipswich (h).

Lost from in front: (1) Crystal Palace (a).

High spots: Drawing at Manchester City on 28 August.

Winning 4-2 at Portsmouth on 6 November.

Rampant City in the mud at Leyton Orient on 4 December.

The inspiring goalkeeping displays of Mike Gibson.

The home win over Ipswich that saw the end of John Atyeo's career.

Low spots: Defeat at Carlisle that ended City's unbeaten start.

The dropping of three points against Southampton that cost promotion

AGM (The 51 Club, Ashton Gate, 16 February 1967):

Profit £22,701.0s.0d. Season Ticket Sales £14,178.0s.0d. (1,571 No).

Player of the year: Mike Gibson.

Ever-presents: (3) Brian Clark, Mike Gibson, Gordon Low.

Hat-tricks: (0).

Leading scorer: Overall: John Atyeo (19). League: John Atyeo (19).

LEAGUE DIVISION 2 — Manager: Fred Ford — SEASON 1966-67

No		Date	Att	Pos	Pt	F-A	H-T	1	2	3	4	5	6	7	8	9	10	11	12 sub used
1	A HUDDERSFIELD	20/8	10,123 (£2,355.18.0)	— 0	L	0-2	0-2	Gibson / *Oldfield*	Ford / *Atkins*	Briggs / *Coddington*	Parr / *Meagan*	Connor / *McNab*	Low / *Quigley*	Derrick / *Weston*	Clark / *Dinsdale*	Bush / *McHale*	Sharpe / *Leighton*	Bartley / *Smith*	
2	H CRYSTAL PALACE	23/8	13,365	— 0	L	0-1	0-0	Gibson / *Jackson*	Ford / *Sewell*	Briggs / *Howe*	Parr / *Payne*	Connor / *Stephenson*	Low / *Bannister*	Derrick / *Kember*	Bush / *Burnside*	Sharpe / *White*	Clark / *Woodruff*	Bartley / *O'Connell*	
3	H CARDIFF	27/8	11,952 (£2,041.14.6)	22 / 13	L 0		1-2	1-1	Gibson / *John*	Ford / *Carver*	Briggs / *Ferguson*	Parr / *Williams*	Connor / *Murray*	Low / *Coldrick*	Derrick / *Farrell*	Clark / *Andrews*	Clark / *King*	Sharpe / *Toshack*	Bartley / *Lewis*	
4	A CRYSTAL PALACE	31/8	16,476	22 / 4	L 0		1-2	0-1	Gibson / *Jackson*	Ford / *Sewell*	Briggs / *Howe*	Parr / *Payne*	Connor / *Stephenson*	Low / *Bannister*	Derrick / *Kember*	Bush / *Burnside*	Sharpe / *White*	Clark / *Woodruff*	Bartley / *Imlach*	
5	A WOLVERHAMPTON	3/9	17,952	20 / 16	D 1		1-1	0-0	Gibson / *Davies*	Davies / *Wilson*	Briggs / *Thomson*	Parr / *Bailey*	Connor / *Woodfield*	Low / *Holsgrove*	Peters / *Wagstaff*	Bush / *Hunt*	Clark / *McIlmoyle*	Sharpe / *Knowles*	Bartley / *Buckley*	
6	H CHARLTON	6/9	11,182 (£1,910.5.6)	18 / 17	W 3		4-0	1-0	Gibson / *Rose*	Rose / *Bonds*	Briggs / *Kinsey*	Parr / *Burridge*	Connor / *King*	Low / *Keirs*	Peters / *Kenning*	Derrick / *Gregory*	Bush / *Saunders*	Sharpe / *Campbell*	Bartley / *Peacock*	
7	H IPSWICH	10/9	12,971 (£2,273.2.0)	18 / 2	D 4		1-1	0-1	Gibson / *Hancock*	Hancock / *Mills*	Briggs / *Houghton*	Parr / *Harper*	Connor / *Baxter*	Low / *Lee*	Peters / *Spearritt*	Derrick / *Hegan*	Bush / *Crawford*	Sharpe / *Baker**	Bartley / *Bolton*	*Mitchell*
8	A COVENTRY	17/9	21,140	20 / 5	L 4		0-1	0-0	Gibson / *Glazier*	Glazier / *Kearns*	Briggs / *Bruck*	Parr / *Farmer**	Connor / *Curtis*	Low / *Hill*	Peters / *Rees*	Clark / *Gibson*	Down / *Gould*	Sharpe / *Pointer*	Bartley / *Clements*	*Mitten*
9	A CARLISLE	24/9	9,948	22 / 13	L 4		1-2	0-1	Gibson / *Ross*	Ross / *Neil*	Briggs / *Gallacher*	Parr / *McConnell*	Connor / *Passmoor*	Low / *Marsland*	Savino / *McVitie*	Peters / *Carlin*	Clark / *Welsh*	Sharpe / *Balderstone*	Bartley / *Hartle**	*Wilson*
10	A CHARLTON	27/9	10,463	22 / 12	L 4		0-5	0-1	Gibson / *Wright*	Wright / *Bonds*	Briggs / *Kinsey*	Parr / *Appleton*	Connor / *King*	Low / *Burridge*	Savino / *Kenning*	Clark / *Gregory*	Bush / *Saunders*	Sharpe / *Campbell*	Peters / *Glover*	

Scorers, Times, and Referees

1. Derrick 5 (og), Weston 41 — Ref: D Pritchard
2. Burnside 47 — Ref: K Burns
3. Low 37 / Toshack 19p, Andrews 54 — Ref: R Paine
4. Clark 74 / Kember 36, Woodruff 65 — Ref: J Osborne
5. Peters 49 / Knowles 73 — Ref: K Walker
6. Ford 25, Burridge 53 (og), Bush 56, [Sharpe 85] — Ref: D Lyden
7. Low 66 / Baker 36 — Ref: J Clarke
8. Kearns 65p — Ref: H Richards
9. Sharpe 78 / Carlin 9, McVitie 63 — Ref: F Nicholson
10. [Saunders 75, 83, Gregory 80] Campbell 13, Bonds 70, — Ref: P Bye

Match notes

1. After conceding an early own goal - Briggs's intended pass to Gibson being deflected in off Derrick's heel - woeful misses do little to help City's cause. Increasingly forced on the defensive, there was no way back for them after Donald Weston's 20-yarder just before half-time.

2. Bobby Woodruff is the architect of Palace's victory with his renowned long throws. He sets up Dave Burnside, who gently places the ball beyond Gibson for the only goal of a game in which Atyeo-less City do little to demonstrate they have the players to replace the great man.

3. With both sides seeking their first League win and goals of the season it is Cardiff who look the more likely. An all-out attacking game from the outset, Ford keeps out George Andrew's header with his hands and 17-year-old John Toshack puts Cardiff ahead from the resulting penalty.

4. A much-improved City performance at Selhurst Park, but alas they still remain pointless. The Palace opener is a scrambled affair, but their second is well worked with Bobby Woodruff heading in Dave Burnside's accurate centre. Clark turns and shoots in City's solitary reply.

5. A deserved point at Molineux, where Peters's half-hit shot is deflected into the net by John Holsgrove. Mike Bailey's long throw sets up the Wolves equaliser, the ball landing deep in the City penalty area where Peter Knowles appears to knock it down with his hand before firing in.

6. Bristolian Gary Grant, the famous film star, is in attendance at this game to see the club he supported as a boy power their way to a masterly victory. In contrast to last season, Charlton are as committed to open attacking football as City. Ford's rasping 25-yard drive puts City in front.

7. The promise and potential of City's young attack fails to produce the victory that their play deserved. At last possessing a winger in Bartley who can centre the ball with accuracy, City have plenty of chances, but, apart from Low's headed equaliser, they are all criminally wasted.

8. City's continuing inability to put away their chances is proving worrying, though at Highfield Road the Sky Blues are almost as bad. City skipper Low handles to concede the match-winning penalty. Gibson almost saves it, but the ball bounces off his body into the roof of the net.

9. The same old story as City, with 20 goal-worthy chances compared to Carlisle's six, fail to make their opportunities pay. Carlisle are perhaps lucky with their opener as, at first, the referee appeared to disallow it for offside. Sharpe shoots in for City from just inside the penalty area.

10. Believe it or not, despite the score, City come close to winning. The hosts are reeling as City attempt to recover from a one-goal deficit, but luck is not with them. Numerous goalworthy attempts are diverted via posts and outstretched legs prior to Charlton's late goal-rush.

11 H BLACKBURN 1/10
21 D 10 · 2:2 · 1-1
12,824 (£2,240.16.0)
Ford 23p, Peters 67
McEvoy 44, 64
Ref: D Wells

Gibson	Ford	Briggs	Parr	Connor	Low	Derrick	Clark	Bush	Sharpe	Peters
Barton	Newton	Joyce	Clayton	Holt	Hole	Connelly	McEvoy	Gilliver	Douglas	Harrison

The spoils are well shared, but City badly need a quality striker. Derrick had a lot to do with City's classy first-half display, but the forwards repeat their failure to make up their minds when presented with chances. Andy McEvoy shows the way by helping himself to two for Rovers.

12 H NORWICH 8/10
19 W 22 · 1-0 · 1-0
11,008 7 (£1,849.9.6)
Sharpe 20
Ref: A Diamond

Gibson	Ford	Briggs	Parr	Connor	Low	Derrick	Clark	Bush	Sharpe	Peters
Keelan	Stringer	Black	Lucas*	Brown	Sharpe	Heath	Balland	Allcock	Curran	Anderson	Kelly

A scrambled, narrow victory in this poor match still leaves City with problems in attack. Clark, who has run the gauntlet of criticism from almost everyone this season, performs like a man carrying all City's burdens on his shoulders. Low is unfortunate when his shot hits a post.

13 A BIRMINGHAM 15/10
19 L 12 · 0-4 · 0-1
15,358 7
[Thwaites 72]
Vowden 10, Murray 65, Ford 69 (og).
Ref: G Kew

Gibson	Ford	Briggs	Parr	Connor	Low	Peters	Derrick	Bush	Sharpe	Bartley
Herriot	Martin	Green	Wylie	Foster	Beard	Bridges	Thomson	Fenton	Vowden*	Murray	Thwaites

City are unfortunate in having goals by Peters and Sharpe disallowed for offside in the opening thirteen minutes, but they still created enough chances to have been ahead at half-time. Unfortunately, confusion between Parr and Gibson, meant they trailed to Geoff Vowden's gifted goal.

14 H PORTSMOUTH 21/10
19 D 16 · 3:3 · 3-2
16,384 8 (£2,981.6.0)
Down 1, Giles 25, Bartley 42
McCann 5, 10, 85
Ref: W Gow

Gibson	Ford	Briggs	Parr	Connor	Low	Derrick	Giles	Down	Sharpe	Bartley
Milkins	Pack	Tindall	Gordon	Haydock	Harris	McClelland	McCann	Hiron	Lewis*	Kellard	Edwards

Ford's gamble of youth would have paid off, but for defensive slips in this hugely entertaining game in which the City forwards - average age 19 - sparkled. It was thrills all the way, from Down's final touch to Parr's 37-second shot right to Albert McCann's late match-saving header.

15 A HULL 29/10
19 W 3 · 2-0 · 2-0
26,630 10
Derrick 14, Down 44
Ref: M Fussey

Gibson	Ford	Briggs	Parr	Connor	Low	Derrick	Giles	Down	Sharpe	Bartley
McKechnie	Davidson	Butler D	Jarvis	Petitt	Collinson	Henderson	Wagstaff	Chilton	Houghton	Butler I

A coupon-busting win as City end the Tigers' 13-month unbeaten home record. Derrick takes a pass from Down to fire in the first goal, whilst the No 9 himself crashes in the second almost on the stroke of half-time. With others offside, Ken Houghton has his late shot struck off.

16 H PLYMOUTH 5/11
19 W 10 · 1-0 · 0-0
19,385 12
Down 88
Ref: D Corbett

Gibson	Ford	Briggs	Parr	Connor	Low	Derrick	Giles	Down	Sharpe	Bartley
Shearing	Rounsevell	Baird	Hore	Nelson	Newman	Jones	Bloomfield	Bickle	Reynolds	Piper

It is hard luck on Argyle when Peter Shearing drops Derrick's long high ball down the middle and Down chests City's late winner over the line. The Pilgrims' fine football deserved a much better fate, especially as Mike Bickle had an 80th-minute header disallowed for offside.

17 A NORTHAMPTON 12/11
20 L 21 · 1:2 · 0-1
10,004 12
Sharpe 88
Jones 34, Kurila 83
Ref: V James

Gibson	Ford	Briggs	Parr	Connor	Low	Derrick	Sharpe	Down	Quigley	Bartley
Brown	Mackin	Walker	Kurila	Branston	Kiernan	Best	Martin	Moore	Jones	Lines

A disappointing debut for Quigley in a City side that never looks like making much impression against the Cobblers on their narrow County Ground pitch. What makes it worse is that Northampton's goals are netted by ex-Rover Bobby Jones and former City player John Kurila.

18 H MILLWALL 19/11
19 D 11 · 1-1 · 1-1
11,792 13
Sharpe 10
Hunt 24
Ref: H New

Gibson	Ford	Briggs	Parr	Connor	Low	Derrick	Sharpe	Connor	Quigley	Bartley
Leslie	Gilchrist	Cripps	Jones	Snowdon	Wilson	Broadfoot	Hunt	Julians	Dunphy*	Neil	McCullough

Following Sharpe's headed opener and Bobby Hunt's great equalising drive, City fail to take their chances, though both sides had a goal disallowed after the break. No question that Sharpe is correctly ruled offside, but it is harsh for Joe Broadfoot in having to retake his free-kick.

19 A ROTHERHAM 26/11
20 D 15 · 3:3 · 0-3
8,978 14
Bartley 79, Low 83, Sharpe 90
Chappell 5, 35, Jacobs 22 (og)
Ref: J Cattlin

Gibson	Ford	Briggs	Parr	Connor	Low	Savino	Sharpe	Bush	Quigley	Bartley
Hill	Wilcockson	Clish	Rabjohn	Haselden	Tiler	Casper	Williams	Galley	Chappell	Pring

This type of spirit can save City as they stage an amazing comeback against opponents who played like Real Madrid for much of the game. Gibson kept the score down with many fine saves then, as United tired, City took control and, but for running out of time, could have won.

20 H PRESTON 3/12
17 W 10 · 2-0 · 1-0
10,804 16 (£1,829.3.0)
Quigley 32, Bush 78
Ref: C Nicholls

Gibson	Ford	Briggs	Drury	Connor	Low	Savino	Garland	Bush	Quigley	Bartley
Kelly	Ross	Smith	Lawton	Singleton	Kendall	Hannigan	Godfrey	Dawson	Spavin	Lee

Quigley's first goal for City is a particularly fine effort - a scorching shot past Alan Kelly from 15 yards - but this even strike is eclipsed by Bush's effort. City's No 9 unleashes an amazing acute-angled 40-yard drive that hums into the top corner of the net to make sure of the points.

21 A BURY 10/12
19 L 18 · 1:2 · 0-2
4,433 16
Low 57
Jones 20, Parry 42
Ref: R Harper

Gibson	Ford	Briggs	Parr	Connor	Low	Savino	Garland	Bush	Quigley	Bartley
Ramsbottom	Leech	Eastham	Turner	Waldron	Colquhoun	Claxton	Jones	Owen	Parry	Lindsay

This abject performance has the distress signals flying for City as the existing players demonstrate they are not good enough. Even Quigley is often caught in possession against mediocre opponents, who well deserve their success. The clear message is that Ford needs to buy quickly.

LEAGUE DIVISION 2   Manager: Fred Ford   SEASON 1966-67

Match summary

No	Date	Venue	Opponent	Att (Receipts)	Pos	Opp Pos	Pt	Res	F-A	H-T	Scorers, Times, and Referees
22	17/12	H	HUDDERSFIELD	11,387 (£1,960.18.6)	18	8	17	D	1:1	1-0	Meagan 27 (og); Nicholson 69. Ref: J Taylor
23	26/12	H	BOLTON	16,725 (£3,264.1.6)	18	12	18	D	1:1	0-1	Low 85; Lee 26. Ref: W Handley
24	31/12	A	CARDIFF	12,306	19	21	18	L	1:5	0:2	Sharpe 61; [Bird 47, 62] Brown 14, 72, Low 41 (og). Ref: M Sinclair
25	7/1	H	WOLVERHAMPTON	17,699 (£3,357.13.0)	18	2	20	W	1:0	0-0	Quigley 63. Ref: K Walker
26	14/1	A	IPSWICH	13,876	19	7	21	D	0:0	0-0	Ref: R Paine
27	21/1	H	COVENTRY	21,600 (£4,255.4.0)	18	1	22	D	2:2	2:2	Crowe 12, Bush 18; Curtis 14, Bruck 36. Ref: G Roper
28	4/2	H	CARLISLE	23,279 (£4,627.15.0)	17	6	24	W	3:0	1-0	Derrick 12, Bush 46, Crowe 57. Ref: J Yates
29	11/2	A	BLACKBURN	12,089	18	8	24	L	0:1	0:1	Connelly 35. Ref: K Stokes
30	25/2	A	NORWICH	28,147	18	19	24	L	0:1	0-0	Sheffield 67. Ref: H Davey
31	4/3	H	HULL	23,496 (£4,593.4.6)	17	6	26	W	2:1	2-0	Peters 25, McIlmoyle 36; Chilton 53. Ref: R Pritchard

Line-ups (1–11, 12 sub used; opponents in italics)

No	Team	1	2	3	4	5	6	7	8	9	10	11	12 sub used
22	City	Gibson	Ford	Briggs	Drury	Connor	Low	Savino	Sharpe	Bush	Quigley	Bartley	
22	*Huddersfield*	*Oldfield*	*Parkin*	*Cattlin*	*Nicholson*	*Coddington*	*Meagan*	*Hellawell*	*Clark*	*Leighton*	*Dobson*	*Hill*	
23	City	Gibson	Ford	Briggs	Drury	Connor	Low	Derrick	Sharpe	Bush	Quigley	Bartley	
23	*Bolton*	*Hopkinson*	*Farrimond*	*Cooper*	*Rimmer*	*Napier**	*Hatton D*	*Butler*	*Byrom*	*Lee*	*Lennard*	*Hulme*	
24	City	Gibson	Ford	Briggs	Drury	Connor	Low	Derrick	Sharpe	Bush	Quigley	Bartley	
24	*Cardiff*	*Wilson*	*Coldrick*	*Ferguson*	*Williams**	*Murray*	*Harris*	*Farrell*	*Johnston*	*Brown*	*King*	*Bird*	*Sumerhayes*
25	City	Gibson	Ford	Briggs	Parr	Connor	Low	Derrick	Crowe	Bush	Quigley	Peters	
25	*Wolverhampton*	*Davies*	*Taylor*	*Thomson*	*Bailey*	*Woodfield*	*Flowers*	*Wharton*	*Hunt*	*McIlmoyle*	*Hatton*	*Wagstaffe*	
26	City	Gibson	Ford	Briggs	Parr	Connor	Low	Derrick	Crowe	Bush	Quigley	Peters	
26	*Ipswich*	*Hancock*	*Mills*	*McNeil*	*Harper*	*Baxter*	*Lea*	*Spearritt*	*Hegan*	*Crawford*	*Baker*	*Brogan*	
27	City	Gibson	Ford	Briggs	Parr	Connor	Low	Derrick	Crowe	Bush	Quigley	Peters	
27	*Coventry*	*Glazier*	*Kearns*	*Bruck*	*Farmer*	*Curtis*	*Clements*	*Key*	*Machin*	*Gould*	*Gibson*	*Rees*	
28	City	Gibson	Ford	Briggs	Parr	Connor	Low	Derrick	Crowe	Bush	Quigley	Peters	
28	*Carlisle*	*Ross*	*Gallagher*	*Caldwell*	*McConnell*	*Passmoor*	*Garbutt*	*Welsh*	*Carlin*	*Wilson*	*Balderstone*	*Hartle**	*Neil*
29	City	Gibson	Ford	Briggs	Parr	Connor	Low	Derrick	Crowe	Bush	Quigley	Peters	
29	*Blackburn*	*Barton*	*Ferguson*	*Wilson*	*Sharples*	*Clayton*	*Hole*	*Douglas*	*Newton*	*Lord*	*Joyce*	*Connelly*	
30	City	Gibson	Ford	Briggs	Parr	Connor	Low	Derrick	Crowe	Bush	Quigley	Peters	
30	*Norwich*	*Keelan*	*Stringer*	*Mullett*	*Lucas*	*Brown*	*Allcock*	*Kenning*	*Bolland*	*Sheffield*	*Bryceland*	*Anderson*	
31	City	Gibson	Ford	Briggs	Parr	Connor	Low	Derrick	Crowe	McIlmoyle	Quigley	Peters	
31	*Hull*	*McKechnie*	*Davidson*	*Butler*	*Jarvis*	*Milner*	*Simpkin*	*Henderson*	*Wagstaff*	*Chilton*	*Wilkinson*	*Young*	

Match notes

22 — Huddersfield. A fair enough result, though both sides have the opportunities to have won outright. Mick Meagan turns Bartley's waist-high corner into his own net to give City the lead, but James Nicholson runs onto Tony Leighton's through ball to head in with Gibson stranded in no-man's land.

23 — Bolton. Despite only getting a late leveller, when Low's left-foot sends the ball crashing into the net from Bush's pass, City should have won this game. After Francis Lee drives in from Dennis Butler's pass, Bush (twice), Sharpe and Connor all miss first-half chances for unlucky City.

24 — Cardiff. At Ninian Park, City give their worst display so far this season as their defence is make to look more cumbersome than usual by Cardiff's nippy forwards. Controversy over Cardiff's third goal as many are of the opinion that Connor had prevented the ball crossing the goal-line.

25 — Wolverhampton. Superb defending, great keeping and some luck brings City a morale-boosting victory over the League leaders. The visitors always looked the better side, but Quigley's shot, which appears as though it might have been drifting wide before Gerry Taylor deflects it in, wins it for City.

26 — Ipswich. The referee errs in disallowing Crowe's tenth-minute shot when Ken Hancock drops the ball following Bush's challenge. Watching Newcastle pair Stan Seymour (director) and Joe Harvey (manager) see nothing untoward and it is now three successive goalless draws for Ipswich.

27 — Coventry. The Sky Blues survive intense second-half pressure to extend their record to ten successive unbeaten games. Crowe's eight-yard volley at the Open End is matched by a George Curtis header. Dietmar Bruck's drive brings a point-a-piece after Bush shoots into the net from close range.

28 — Carlisle. The best crowd of the season so far is lured to Ashton Gate by vouchers being issued for the So'ton cup game. Carlisle capitulate after Bush cracks in City's second with his left foot. Exhilarating City show the sort of form that should keep them well clear of the relegation zone.

29 — Blackburn. Connor puts in a faultless display at the heart of the defence, but overall City give a shoddy performance at Ewood Park. They only wake up for the last ten minutes when, as if realising that a point is there for the taking, they set up a series of raids that should have brought reward.

30 — Norwich. City demonstrate few attacking ideas at Carrow Road, though twice they are denied by the post. The only goal comes with the referee playing advantage as Gordon Bolland keeps going on being obstructed by Briggs and Low. He delivers a fine centre for Laurie Sheffield to head home.

31 — Hull. Record £27,500 signing Hugh McIlmoyle finds prodigious power to head in a Peters corner from the left at the Open End. Chris Chilton's first-time 18-yard volley gets the Tigers back into the game and following Chris Simpkin's handball, Ford has his 67th-minute spot-kick saved.

32 A PORTSMOUTH 15 D 1:1 1:1
18/3   14,649 13 27
Peters 34
Kellard 17
Ref: N Burtenshaw

City	Opponent
Gibson	*Armstrong*
Ford	*Pack*
Briggs	*Wilson*
Parr	*Gordon*
Connor	*Tindall*
Low	*Harris*
Derrick	*Portwood*
Crowe	*Hiron*
McIlmoyle	*Painter*
Quigley	*Kellard*
Peters	*Jennings*

City shrug off their away-day complex to put on a fine display at Fratton Park, that should have resulted in both points. McIlmoyle's headwork is prominent as he fits in well to City's pattern of play, but he adopts the inside-forward role, whilst Crowe operates as the spearhead.

---

33 H BIRMINGHAM 15 W 3:1 1:1
25/3   20,594 11 29
Crowe 3, Quigley 53, Peters 81
Vincent 30
(£3,976.7.6)
Ref: J Clarke

City	Opponent
Gibson	*Herriot*
Ford	*Murray*
Briggs	*Green*
Parr	*Thomson*
Connor	*Sharples*
Low	*Beard*
Derrick	*Hockey*
Crowe	*Wylie*
McIlmoyle	*Vowden*
Quigley	*Vincent*
Peters	*Bridges*
	Buxton

McIlmoyle's shot is disallowed because Crowe is given offside, but the City No 8 soon makes amends by lashing in the opener from Derrick's corner in the next attack. John Vincent's right-foot brings the Blues level, but a shot from Quigley and a Peters header secures City's victory.

---

34 A DERBY 16 L 0:2 0:2
27/3   15,491 15 29
Thomas 77, Low 82 (og)
Ref: J Cattlin

City	Opponent
Gibson	*Boulton*
Ford	*Daniel*
Briggs	*Richardson*
Parr	*Webster**
Connor	*Saxton*
Low	*Waller*
Derrick	*Hughes*
Crowe	*Hector*
McIlmoyle	*Thomas*
Quigley	*Durban*
Peters	*Hodgson*
	Buxton

In the swirling wind, missed chances and defensive errors are City's undoing. Two centres from the left do the damage. The first is deflected into the path of Ted Thomas to head home, whilst the second, headed into his own net by Low, is the result of a ghastly mix-up with Gibson.

---

35 H DERBY 14 W 4:1 2:0
28/3   20,150 15 31
Peters 1, Crowe 10, 74, Derrick 56
Derrick 10, 74
(£3,851.5.0)
Ref: B Homewood

City	Opponent
Gibson	*Boulton*
Ford	*Daniel*
Briggs	*Richardson*
Parr	*Thomas*
Connor	*Saxton*
Low	*Thomas*
Derrick	*Hughes*
Crowe	*Hector*
McIlmoyle	*Buxton*
Quigley	*Durban*
Peters	*Hodgson*

Peters gets City off to a great start, slipping in Parr's pull-back after just 37 seconds. Thereafter, playing with verve and panache, City never relax their grip and two drives by Crowe and a header from Derrick has the crowd in raptures as relegation fears are almost banished.

---

36 A PLYMOUTH 14 W 2:1 2:1
1/4   12,242 17 33
Quigley 7, Derrick 21
Davey 23
Ref: L Callaghan

City	Opponent
Gibson	*Dunne*
Ford	*Sillett*
Briggs	*Everitt*
Parr	*Piper*
Connor	*Nelson*
Low	*Newman*
Derrick	*Davey*
Crowe	*Reynolds*
McIlmoyle	*Bickle*
Quigley	*Bloomfield*
Peters	*Mitten*

A well-earned success at Home Park as City register their first away win in five months. Despite another tale of missed chances, a pair of comfortably taken goals prove good enough against a Plymouth side that, following Steve Davey's header, subjects City to much pressure.

---

37 H NORTHAMPTON 13 W 1:0 1:0
7/4   23,750 21 35
Peters 23
(£4,568.8.0)
Ref: L Jones

City	Opponent
Gibson	*Harvey*
Ford	*Foley*
Briggs	*Walker*
Parr	*Mackin*
Connor	*Branston*
Low	*Kurila*
Derrick	*Felton*
Crowe	*Moore*
McIlmoyle	*Large*
Quigley	*Hall*
Peters	*Walden*

Despite a septic knee McIlmoyle - defying medical advice to play - turns in his best display to date. A tense affair against a Cobblers side looking far better than their position suggests. Peters looked offside when driving in the only goal between the goalkeeper and the far post.

---

38 A MILLWALL 14 L 2:3 2:3
15/4   11,344 7 35
McIlmoyle 79, Quigley 83
Julians 9, Jacks 35, Cripps 63p
Ref: K Howley

City	Opponent
Gibson	*Leslie*
Ford	*Cripps*
Briggs	*Kitchener*
Parr	*Jones*
Connor	*Gilchrist*
Low	*Plume*
Derrick	*Dunphy*
Crowe	*Hunt*
McIlmoyle	*Neil*
Quigley	*Julians*
Peters	*Jacks*

Goals from McIlmoyle, who drives in a centre and Quigley who heads in from Derrick's corner, raises hopes of a late City comeback at Cold Blow Lane. Unfortunately, it is too little too late as, despite playing much good football, City are made to pay for failing to take their chances.

---

39 A BOLTON 13 D 0:0 0:0
19/4   8,647 10 36
Ref: P Partridge

City	Opponent
Gibson	*Hopkinson*
Ford	*Hatton D*
Briggs	*Farrimond*
Parr	*Rimmer*
Connor	*Hulme*
Low	*Lennard*
Derrick	*Lee*
Crowe	*Byrom*
McIlmoyle	*Hatton R*
Quigley	*Bromley*
Peters	*Taylor*

City's disciplined display, in which the forwards (with the exception of Crowe) chase back to reinforce their defence, earns a point to remove the fear of relegation. Bolton only threaten when John Hulme's header thuds against the bar and two chances are missed from the rebound.

---

40 H ROTHERHAM 14 L 1:2 0:1
22/4   16,888 18 36
Crowe 54
Rabjohn 22, Galley 77
Ref: D Lyden

City	Opponent
Gibson	*Hill*
Ford	*Wilcockson*
Briggs	*Clish*
Parr	*Rabjohn*
Connor	*Haselden*
Low	*Tiler*
Derrick*	*Shepherd*
Crowe	*Galley*
McIlmoyle	*Massey*
Quigley	*Chappell*
Peters	*Pring*
	Bush

The Millers shatter City's eight-month unbeaten home record with this deserved success. Chris Rabjohn heads the visitors in front, but Crowe levels from a retaken free-kick. John Galley runs in Rotherham's winner following Derrick's 65th-minute departure with a pulled thigh muscle.

---

41 A PRESTON 15 D 2:2 2:1
29/4   9,431 12 37
Peters 6, Sharpe 38
Briggs 5 (og), Forrest 82
Ref: J Clarke

City	Opponent
Gibson	*Kelly*
Ford	*Ross*
Briggs	*Ritchie*
Parr	*Spavin*
Connor	*Smith*
Low	*Cranston*
Savino	*Hannigan*
Crowe	*Greenhalgh*
McIlmoyle	*Forrest*
Sharpe	*Godfrey*
Peters	*Lee*

By their unnecessary defensive approach after Sharpe had put them ahead, City throw away the chance of their first ever win at Deepdale. Recovering well after unluckily conceding an early own-goal, City produce an easy flowing pattern of play that brings them a deserved lead.

---

42 H BURY 14 D 3:3 2:2
6/5   12,614 22 38
Ford 8p, Peters 19, Low 81
Dawson 33, 43, Farrell 63
Ref: M Sinclair
(£2,128.19.0)

City	Opponent
Gibson	*Ramsbottom*
Ford	*Leech*
Briggs	*Timney*
Parr	*Aimson*
Connor	*Turner*
Low	*Lindsay*
Sharpe	*Farrell*
Crowe	*Jones**
McIlmoyle	*Dawson*
Quigley	*Parry*
Peters	*Carter*
	Bain

Despite the encouragement of two goals in the first 19 minutes against a side doomed to relegation, City needed Low's controversial strike near the end to avert defeat. A fortunate draw as Low is clearly offside when he diverts McIlmoyle's pass into the net past Neil Ramsbottom.

Home Average 16,183   Away 13,797

CUP-TIES

Manager: Fred Ford

SEASON 1966-67

		1	2	3	4	5	6	7	8	9	10	11

League Cup

		F-A	H-T	Scorers, Times, and Referees												12 sub used

2 H SWANSEA 13/9 18 D 1-1 0-1
6,952 3:20 (£1,388.0.0)
Scorers: Ford 87 / McLaughlin 10
Ref: W Handley

Pos	1	2	3	4	5	6	7	8	9	10	11
City	Gibson	Ford	Briggs	Bush	Connor	Low	Peters	Derrick	Clark	Sharpe	Bartley
Swansea	*Heyes*	*Evans R*	*Gomersall*	*Jones*	*Purcell*	*Williams*	*Humphries*	*McLaughlin*		*Allchurch*	*Evans B*

City's interest in the League Cup has always been brief, and this time it takes a scrambled late equaliser to earn them a replay. Swansea's thrusting attack give City a rather difficult time, after James McLaughlin's right knee had put the ball over the line for their shock early goal.

2R A SWANSEA 19/9 20 L 1-2 1-0 aet
5,466 3:22
Scorers: Down 3 / Todd 75, Evans 99
Ref: K Burns

Pos	1	2	3	4	5	6	7	8	9	10	11
City	Gibson	Ford	Briggs	Parr	Connor	Low	Savino	Clark	Down	Sharpe	Bartley
Swansea	*Heyes*	*Evans R*	*Gomersall*	*Jones*	*Purcell*	*Hughes*	*Humphries*	*McLaughlin*	*Todd*	*Allchurch*	*Evans B*

Despite the encouragement of Down's early goal, City give a poor display. Had Roy Evans not stroked his 78th-minute penalty wide, shortly after Keith Todd had levelled matters, there would have been no need for extra-time. A low angled drive from Brian Evans wins the game.

FA Cup

3 A HALIFAX 28/1 18 D 1-1 0-0
15,591 4:15
Scorers: Peters 66 / Parks 55
Ref: K Stokes

Pos	1	2	3	4	5	6	7	8	9	10	11
City	Gibson	Ford	Briggs	Parr	Connor	Low	Derrick	Crowe	Down	Quigley	Peters
Halifax	*White*	*Russell*	*Bodell*	*Smith*	*Holt*	*Lee J*	*Taylor*	*Hutchinson*	*Parks*	*Atkins*	*McCarthy*

City waste their chances at the Shay, where they are shocked when Jack Parks puts Halifax in front with a scrambled effort. Crowe is the star forward on view, but twice City fail with open-goal opportunities. Peters, who notches City's equaliser, misses six other reasonable chances.

3R H HALIFAX 31/1 18 W 4-1 2-0
23,188 4:15
Scorers: Peters 13, Crowe 15, 64, Down 65 / Hutchinson 58
Ref: K Stokes

Pos	1	2	3	4	5	6	7	8	9	10	11
City	Gibson	Ford	Briggs	Parr	Connor	Low	Derrick	Crowe	Down	Quigley	Peters
Halifax	*White*	*Russell*	*Bodell*	*Smith*	*Holt*	*Lee J*	*Taylor*	*Hutchinson*	*Parks*	*Atkins*	*McCarthy*

A perfectly hit Peters half-volley and a well-placed shot by Crowe has City taking it easy much too soon. Halifax fight back well and Gibson does well to save Barry Hutchinson's 48th-minute penalty. The No 8 makes amends later by steering the ball in from Phil McCarthy's corner.

4 H SOUTHAMPTON 18/2 18 W 1-0 1-0
38,017 1:18 (£8,879)
Scorers: Bush 26
Ref: N Burtenshaw

Pos	1	2	3	4	5	6	7	8	9	10	11
City	Gibson	Ford	Briggs	Parr	Connor	Low	Derrick	Crowe	Down	Quigley	Peters
Southampton	*MacLaren*	*Webb*	*Hollywood*	*Walker*	*Knapp*	*Huxford*	*Paine*	*Chivers*	*Davies*	*Melia*	*Sydenham*

Connor is in outstanding form as, not for the first time in his career, he keeps a firm control over Ron Davies. The Saints hardly get a look in, but there is an element of luck about the strike that settles the game. Bush's innocuous shot is deflected in by Southampton's Cliff Huxford.

5 A TOTTENHAM 11/3 17 L 0-2 0-1
54,610 1:5
Scorers: Greaves 11, 89p
Ref: K Burns

Pos	1	2	3	4	5	6	7	8	9	10	11
City	Gibson	Ford	Briggs	Parr	Connor	Low	Derrick	Crowe	Down	Quigley	Peters
Tottenham	*Jennings*	*Kinnear*	*Knowles*	*Mullery*	*England*	*Mackay*	*Robertson*	*Greaves*	*Gilzean*	*Venables*	*Jones*

After Jimmy Greaves slips in a long pass from Terry Venables, inexcusable misses shatter City in the gripping cup-tie. A tale of spot-kicks, thereafter, as whilst Greaves has no trouble with his, 14 minutes earlier Ford has his effort saved and Crowe puts the re-take well wide.

Gloucestershire Cup

F A BRISTOL ROV 9/5 15 W 3-0 1-0
17,433 3:5
Scorers: Peters 27, Crowe 65, Ford 70p
Ref: W Summerhayes

Pos	1	2	3	4	5	6	7	8	9	10	11
City	Gibson	Ford	Briggs	Parr	Connor	Low	Savino	Crowe	McIlmoyle	Quigley	Peters
Bristol Rov	*Taylor L*	*Mabbutt*	*Parsons*	*Williams*	*Lloyd*	*Munro*	*Graydon*	*Frude*	*Biggs*	*Jones W*	*Jarman*

An easy success against a young Rovers side. Peters slams in the opener after McIlmoyle's shot is cleared from behind the line. Later Crowe is on hand to tap in when Larry Taylor drops the ball, whilst Ford takes advantage from the spot after Alex Munro punched out Quigley's jab.

	P	W	D	L	F	A	W	D	L	F	A	Pts
		Home					Away					
1 Coventry	42	17	3	1	46	16	6	10	5	28	27	59
2 Wolves	42	15	4	2	53	20	10	4	7	35	28	58
3 Carlisle	42	15	3	3	42	16	8	3	10	29	38	52
4 Blackburn	42	13	6	2	33	11	6	7	8	23	35	51
5 Ipswich	42	11	8	2	45	25	6	8	7	25	29	50
6 Huddersfield	42	14	3	4	36	17	6	6	9	22	29	49
7 Crys Palace	42	14	4	3	42	23	5	6	10	19	32	48
8 Millwall	42	14	5	2	33	17	4	4	13	16	41	45
9 Bolton	42	10	7	4	36	19	4	7	10	28	39	42
10 Birmingham	42	11	5	5	42	23	5	3	13	28	43	40
11 Norwich	42	10	7	4	31	21	3	7	11	18	34	40
12 Hull	42	11	5	5	46	25	3	2	14	31	47	39
13 Preston	42	14	4	3	44	23	2	4	15	21	44	39
14 Portsmouth	42	7	5	9	34	37	6	8	7	25	33	39
15 BRISTOL C	42	10	8	3	38	22	2	6	13	18	40	38
16 Plymouth	42	12	4	5	42	21	2	5	14	17	37	37
17 Derby	42	8	6	7	40	32	4	6	11	28	40	36
18 Rotherham	42	10	5	6	39	28	3	5	13	22	42	36
19 Charlton	42	11	4	6	34	16	2	5	14	15	37	35
20 Cardiff	42	9	7	5	43	28	3	2	16	18	59	33
21 Northampton	42	8	6	7	28	33	2	0	17	19	51	30
22 Bury	42	9	3	9	31	30	2	3	16	18	53	28
	924	253	111	98	858	503	98	111	253	503	858	924

Odds & ends

Double wins: (2) Plymouth, Hull.
Double losses: (2) Crystal Palace, Cardiff.

Won from behind: (0).
Lost from in front: (0).

High spots: The signings of Quigley, Crowe and McIlmoyle that brought about an almost euphoric second-half of the season.
Beating Charlton at Ashton Gate on 6 September.
Recovering from a three-goal deficit to share the spoils at Millmoor.
Beating Southampton in the FA Cup on 18 February.

Low spots: The campaign's poor start, only one point from five games.
The poor display at Northampton on 12 November.
The twice-missed penalty at White Hart Lane in the FA Cup.

AGM (The 51 Club, Ashton Gate, 13 November 1967):
Loss £26,890.0s.0d. Season Ticket Sales £13,000.0s.0d. (1,442 No).

Player of the year: Chris Crowe and John Quigley.
Ever-presents: (3) Alec Briggs, Jack Connor, Mike Gibson.
Hat-tricks: (0).
Leading scorer: Overall: Roger 'Lou' Peters (13). League: Peters (9).

	Appearances			Goals		
	Lge	Sub	Cup	Lge	Cup	Tot
Bartley, Danny	20		2	2		2
Briggs, Alec	42		7			
Bush, Terry	21	1	3	4	1	5
Clark, Brian	10		2	1		1
Connor, Jack	42		7			
Crowe, Chris	18		5	6	3	9
Derrick, Jantzen	33		5	4		4
Down, David	5		3	3	2	5
Drury, Charles	7					
Ford, Tony	40		7	3	2	5
Garland, Chris	1					
Gibson, Mike	42		7			
Giles, John	3			1		1
Jacobs, Trevor	2					
Low, Gordon	41		7	6		6
McIlmoyle, Hugh	12		1	2		2
Parr, Gordon	38		6			
Peters, Roger	28		6	9	3	12
Quigley, John	25		5	5		5
Savino, Ray	7		2			
Sharpe, Gerry	25		2	8		8
(own-goals)				2		2
21 players used	462	1	77	56	11	67

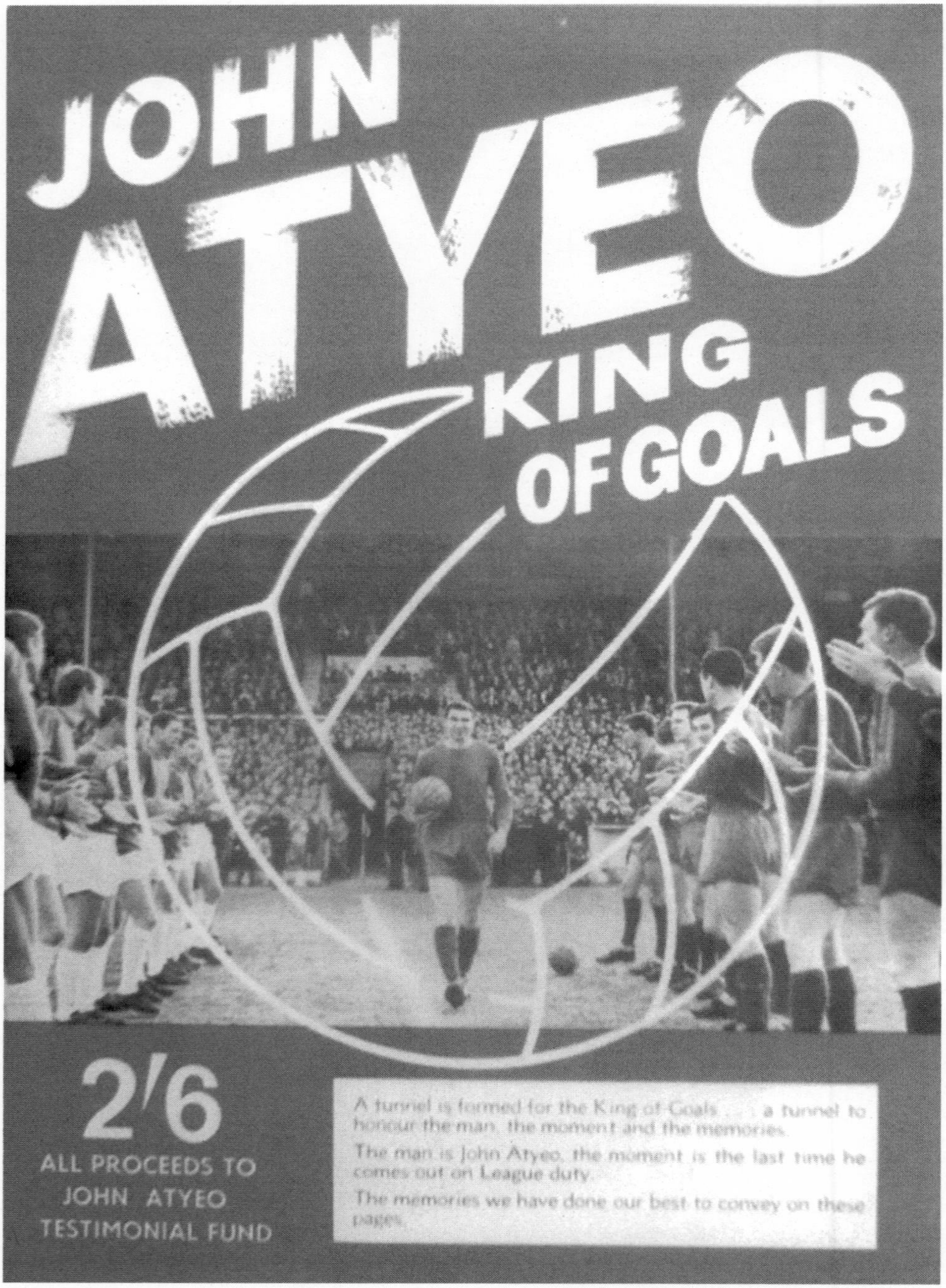
JOHN
ATYEO
KING
OF GOALS
2/6
ALL PROCEEDS TO
JOHN ATYEO
TESTIMONIAL FUND
A tunnel is formed for the King of Goals . . . a tunnel to honour the man, the moment and the memories.
The man is John Atyeo, the moment is the last time he comes out on League duty.
The memories we have done our best to convey on these pages.